NO LONGER PROP'
SEATTLE PUBLIC L

Praise for *Realizin*

D0517343

"Compelling, important, accessible, and erudite, this new and substantially expanded edition of *Realizing Freedom* brings together decades' worth of insight by Tom G. Palmer, one of the global liberty movement's leading advocates. Whether read cover-to-cover or sampled and savored, there's no mistaking Palmer's generosity of spirit, his gift for explaining profoundly important ideas, and the mixture of principle and practicality with which he approaches opportunities to free people from tyranny's most pervasive myths."

—Robert M. S. McDonald, associate professor of history,
United States Military Academy, West Point

"Tom Palmer has been one of liberty's most eloquent and learned spokespersons for many years. It is a joy to have so many of his lucid, readable, and trenchant essays, written over most of those years, between one set of covers. The essays are independent of each other, enough so that you can sit down and read one here, one there, without needing to know also the hundred or two hundred pages in between. Whatever sort of essay you pick, I guarantee you a good read."

—Jan Narveson, University of Waterloo; author, *You and the State:
A Short Introduction to Political Philosophy and The Libertarian Idea*

"The libertarian conception of individual autonomy is often attacked as fostering narrow and selfish individuals who take scant notice of the larger world around them. Tom Palmer's great contribution in this collection of essays is to lay those misconceptions to rest. He shows how autonomous individuals use their powers to promote exchange and cooperation, which enrich all facets of social life. He exposes the cultural imperialists whose high-falutin' rhetoric is all too often the prescription for economic protectionism and social stagnation. He reminds us yet again that individual liberty is our most precious social good."

—Richard A. Epstein, James Parker Hall Distinguished Service
Professor of Law, University of Chicago;
author, *Simple Rules for a Complex World*

"Much of this book is devoted to lively defenses of classical liberal and libertarian rights theory against critics and false friends of many sorts. Even more interesting than these sharp rejoinders, though, is Palmer's reframing and recharacterization of that rights theory. Drawing on his extraordinary interdisciplinary learning, Palmer offers a sociologically, institutionally, and historically informed libertarianism—one that is true to the rich legacy and tradition of classical liberalism."

—Jacob T. Levy, Tomlinson Professor of Political Theory, McGill University; author, *The Multiculturalism of Fear*

"Tom Palmer's *Realizing Freedom* is essential reading for libertarians and their critics alike. It offers clear and concise rejoinders to common and not so common objections to the case for a strictly limited government. In the process, it demonstrates not only the breadth and depth of libertarianism as a political tradition but also the brilliance and clarity of Palmer's thought."

—Mark Pennington, professor of political economy, King's College, University of London

"In *Realizing Freedom*, Tom Palmer explores the intellectual origins of libertarian ideas, defends them against critics from both the left and right, and makes vividly clear why they matter if we want to make the world a freer and more humane place to live. Nobody is more qualified to write about the combination of libertarian theory, history, and practice than Tom Palmer. And this book is Palmer at his best."

—Matt Zwolinski, associate professor of philosophy; codirector, Institute for Law and Philosophy, University of San Diego

REALIZING
FREEDOM

TOM G. PALMER

REALIZING FREEDOM

Libertarian Theory, History, and Practice

CATO INSTITUTE
WASHINGTON, D.C.

Copyright © 2009 by Cato Institute.
All rights reserved.

Paperback printing: 2014
ISBN 978-1-939709-25-7

Library of Congress Cataloging-in-Publication Data

Palmer, Tom G.
  Realizing freedom : libertarian theory, history, and practice / by Tom G. Palmer.
    p. cm.
  Includes bibliographical references and index.
  ISBN 978-1-935308-11-9 (cloth : alk. paper)   1. Liberty.   2. Libertarianism.
I. Title.

JC585.P29 2009
320.51'2—dc22   2009015372

Cover design by Jon Meyers.

Printed in the United States of America.

CATO INSTITUTE
1000 Massachusetts Ave., N.W.
Washington, D.C. 20001
www.cato.org

This book is dedicated to the memory of my parents,
Gordon F. Palmer and Martha A. Palmer

Acknowledgments

I wish I had the time and space to thank all of the people who assisted me in producing these essays. I don't, so I will start by thanking Jason Kuznicki, who helped me to collect the essays and get all of the rights in order, and who helped me decide which essays to eliminate. My colleagues Ed Crane and David Boaz at the Cato Institute both tolerated my interest in a wide array of topics and provided a great place to work while I wrote some of them. David offered helpful criticism of a number of the essays, forced me to think about hard problems, and pushed me to get this collection put together on time (sort of). Of all the others who helped, I wish to single out one who is no longer here to be thanked in person: Priscilla K. Slocum, known as PK Slocum to her book buyers decades ago. When I was a young teenager, PK helped me find and purchase out-of-print and sometimes obscure books on a wide range of topics, including libertarianism, a vision to which she was passionately committed. (I still own the collected works of Herbert Spencer in 15 volumes, which I bought from her when I was 15 or 16 for ten dollars a volume, paid out in installments over many months. Also still in my collection are Lenin, by Leon Trotzky; *My Autobiography*, by Benito Mussolini; and *Leninism*, by Joseph Stalin. PK helped to spark my interest not only in understanding liberty, but in knowing its enemies, as well.) Every time I give or lend a book to a younger person, I think of PK and my debt to her, which will never be fully repaid. To all the others who helped me at various times, I offer my gratitude.

Content

Preface to Expanded Edition

Is freedom valuable and important? Most people seem to think so, but they often disagree vehemently over just what it entails. The essays in this book explore the meaning, history, and promise of freedom. Some are strongly historical, others analytical. Some are journalistic and without scholarly apparatus, while others are heavily footnoted. (Those interested in the ideas of freedom will find a whole library in the references to explore the ideas further on their own.) There is method in the arrangement of the essays, but readers should feel quite free to read what they want, skip around, use the book as a reference work, and generally wrestle with the ideas presented in it. There's something, I hope, for everyone interested in the ideas of freedom, regardless of his or her "ideological" orientation.

Some of the essays present a straightforward libertarian vision, while others contrast libertarian views with other perspectives, both of the "left" and the "right," and subject those perspectives to rigorous scrutiny. (And I do so in the expectation that my own libertarian views should be scrutinized and criticized with similar vigor.)

This revised edition contains a lot of material that was written after the first edition was published, including scholarly research, essays on activism, contributions to political theory, and a few personal items, such as my recollections of decades of libertarian activism. Some are drawn from books that have appeared since the first edition, some from journals and magazines. They deal with such topics as the nature of wealth and poverty, the nature and origins of the recent global financial crisis, the origins and future of the welfare state, the relationship of law to the state, sustainable democracy, and why one ought to consider embracing liberty as one of one's life projects, even if it does not become one's primary life project, as it has for me.

A few of the essays appeared in books I edited that were widely distributed around the world in dozens of languages, including *The*

Morality of Capitalism, *After the Welfare State*, and *Why Liberty*. (*The Morality of Capitalism* has come out in several dozen languages.) If you'd like to read more on those topics, I recommend you find copies of those books, as they contain a lot of other material I did not write, but which I commissioned and edited. (A little hint: you can search for the titles online, and you may be able to download free PDF copies.)

I've learned some things since the first edition, too, some of which are reflected in the new essays. I'm happy to share those lessons here. I've also done a great deal of traveling, during which I've lectured, debated, run seminars, held meetings, and done a lot of listening. (In the last month, I've been with libertarians in Ethiopia, Kenya, Namibia, South Africa, Zambia, Georgia, Italy, San Marino, the United States, and Hungary, and tomorrow I travel to Romania, then the Netherlands, Belgium, and Colombia.) During those trips, I've come to better appreciate the importance of comradeship among libertarians worldwide. I have the honor and the privilege to work closely with dedicated champions of liberty in Afghanistan, Egypt, Kyrgyzstan, Malaysia, Russia, Nigeria, Kenya, Iran, Guatemala, China, and the United States, to list but a few. They struggle for liberty in quite varied circumstances, often under the worst conditions of tyranny, war, oppression, intimidation, and violence. And yet, because those champions believe that people have the right to live their own lives, their critics constantly accuse them of being "selfish" and uncaring. That accusation is the refuge of people who find themselves unable to criticize the arguments advanced by libertarians. It also shows a remarkable incoherence of thought: people who risk all to defend the rights of peaceful people to live their own lives, who stand up for the rights of others, are not being "selfish," as the term is normally understood. They are working for justice.

I work with libertarians who risk everything to stand up the rights of victims of violence, although they are not themselves likely to be victims; who stand up for the rights of gay people, although they are not gay; who stand up for the rights of women, although they are not female; who stand up for the rights of Christians, although they are not Christians, for the rights of Muslims, although they are not Muslims, for the rights of atheists, although they are not atheists; for the rights of everyone.

Sometimes I wish I could introduce the socialists who slander libertarians – from the comfort of their isolated academic posts – to people who work for freedom, not just for themselves, but for everyone. It's merely a fantasy, of course, because people who are reduced merely to assailing the motivations of others are not worth the effort; they have already abdicated the fight by acknowledging that they have no argument other than insult.

This book has, I hope, a positive message: liberty is inspiring; it is hopeful; it is worthy of a life's commitment. I hope that the rather substantial additions this revised edition contains may prove useful, interesting, perhaps inspiring, and even sometimes amusing to those seeking to understand the theory, the history, and the practice of liberty.

I'd like to thank too many people to list, but two are especially important because of their work to bring many of these essays to the public: Clark Ruper of Students for Liberty and David Lampo of the Cato Institute. Thank you, Clark and David, for your patience and for your hard work on behalf of the worthy cause of liberty.

Budapest, September 14, 2013

1. Introduction

On the 23rd of March, 1775, Patrick Henry mounted the pulpit of St. John's Church in Richmond, Virginia, to deliver his famous "Give Me Liberty" speech before the delegates to the Virginia Convention. His topic was the undecided question of war for independence and freedom. He understood that the issue was one that required thought, debate, and high seriousness—in a word, *theory*. As he stated:

> The question before the house is one of awful moment to this country. For my own part, I consider it as nothing less than a question of freedom or slavery; and in proportion to the magnitude of the subject ought to be the freedom of the debate. It is only in this way that we can hope to arrive at the truth, and fulfill the great responsibility which we hold to God and our country.

But he also knew that theoretical speculation alone was not sufficient; theory without history is blind. *History* is the key to understanding the affairs of mankind:

> I have but one lamp by which my feet are guided, and that is the lamp of experience. I know of no way of judging of the future but by the past.

Neither contemplation nor observation, however, is sufficient to secure justice and liberty. Ideas and policies do not implement themselves. For that, action—*practice*—is required:

> Why stand we here idle? What is it that gentlemen wish? What would they have? Is life so dear, or peace so sweet, as to be purchased at the price of chains and slavery? Forbid it, Almighty God! I know not what course others may take; but as for me, give me liberty or give me death!

This book is about the theory, the history, and the practice of liberty. It consists of a selection of the essays, long and short, that

1

I have published over the past few decades. As I reviewed my published works and culled out those that were too dated, or too esoteric, or too juvenile, I noted several themes that have matured in my thinking on the themes of freedom, justice, and social order and that recur in various forms in the essays in this volume.

Liberty, Rights, and the Rule of Law

The first theme regards the intimate connections between liberty, rights, and the rule of law. That sentence, concluding with "the rule of law," may sound stale and uninspiring to some, but the rule of law is the key to freedom. I recall watching, some years ago, a German film that had a doddering old man pronouncing gravely that "the Rechtsstaat [the law-governed state] is a great accomplishment." The point of the vignette in the film was to belittle the idea of the rule of law, but the elderly gentleman, who no doubt lived through the horrors of National Socialism, had good reason to be appreciative of the law-governed state. It should, in fact, be inspiring, and the more I have worked to advance liberty, the more I have come to appreciate the central importance of the rule of law and to be inspired by it. Its centrality has been made all the more evident in my work in post-totalitarian societies, in which the central issue is the development of the legal and political legal institutions of liberty. Without the rule of law, one is at the mercy of the arbitrary will of others, and that is to exist in a condition of nonfreedom. The rule of law is always at the center of the struggle for liberty, whether in the countries of central Asia, China, east Asia, Russia, Eastern Europe, Africa, Latin America, or North America.

When I first began to think seriously about the issue, after my exposure to the great theorists of the Rechtsstaat and the writings of James Madison, Bruno Leoni, F. A. Hayek, Lon Fuller, Harold Berman, and others, I saw how naïve are formulations of liberty that rest on merely "doing what you want," or on "enjoying one's rights," without attention to the legal/institutional framework within which equal freedom can only be realized. More specifically, stability of rules (and rights are rules that govern actions) is a necessary condition of freedom. I have quoted several times in this book, in several essays, Locke's statement that:

> [T]he end of law is not to abolish or restrain, but to preserve
> and enlarge Freedom: For in all the states of created beings

2

capable of Laws, *where there is no Law, there is no Freedom.*
For *Liberty* is to be free from restraint and violence from
others which cannot be, where there is no Law: But Freedom
is not, as we are told, *A Liberty for every Man to do what he
lists*: (For who could be free, when every other Man's Humour
might domineer over him?) But a *Liberty* to dispose, and
order, as he lists, his Person, Actions, Possessions, and his
whole Property, within the Allowance of those Laws under
which he is; and therein not to be subject to the arbitrary
Will of another, but freely follow his own. (John Locke, *Second
Treatise of Government*, Chap. VI, §57.)

Those who have the power to arbitrarily reassign, eradicate, or
create "rights" to achieve their ideas of fairness, efficiency, or community, put the rest of us at their mercy and eradicate our freedom.
Moreover, rights that are so mutable are not rights at all. James
Madison put it quite succinctly in *Federalist* No. 62, when he said of
a "mutable policy":

It poisons the blessings of liberty itself. It will be of little
avail to the people that the laws are made by men of their
own choice if the laws be so voluminous that they cannot
be read, or so incoherent that they cannot be understood; if
they be repealed or revised before they are promulgated, or
undergo such incessant changes that no man, who knows
what the law is today, can guess what it will be tomorrow.
Law is defined to be a rule of action, but how can that be a
rule, which is little known, and less fixed?

It was the great accomplishment of classical rights theory to connect
"subjective right" (it's her right to X) and "objective right" (it is right
to Y), meaning that the way in which justice is achieved is mutual
respect for rights. That achievement is in peril from theorists who
sever the relationship, such that rights must be systematically overridden in order to achieve "social justice," a process that—to the
extent that it is realized—weakens or even eliminates the rule of
law, rights, justice, and freedom.

I consider alternative, nonlibertarian accounts of freedom in the
first essay in this volume, "Freedom Properly Understood"; nonlibertarian accounts of rights in the essays "Saving Rights Theory from
Its Friends" and "What's *Not* Wrong with Libertarianism," in my

essay on John Rawls's theory of justice, "No Exit: Framing the Problem of Justice," and in several of the reviews included in the section on "Books and Ideas."

The topic of the relationship between freedom, rights, and the rule of law is one that deserves much more thought and study. I hope that my studies may help others to delve more deeply into the issues and may help us to understand the interconnection of dignity and rights, autonomy and freedom, and justice and the rule of law.

Abstract Rights Concretely Situated

The second theme regards the historical rootedness of abstractly formulated accounts of rights, and the importance of identifying narratives of liberty for each culture. I strongly disagree with those who identify libertarian principles with "Western culture," for several reasons. "Western culture" includes not only the ideas of freedom, justice, peaceful trade, respect for rights, and the rule of law, but also coercion, theft, slavery, genocide, war, and other decidedly nonlibertarian practices. As my Chinese friends have pointed out, communist totalitarianism is not really a "Chinese idea," unless you consider the German communist Karl Marx to have been "Chinese." *All* cultures and civilizations contain within themselves narratives of freedom and narratives of subjugation, and the task of libertarians is to identify within each cultural context the indigenous narratives of freedom and connect them with the present struggle for freedom. The task may be harder or easier to carry out in different contexts, but there is no culture that is purely libertarian, nor any that is purely anti-libertarian.

The rights claims of the classical liberal tradition are abstractly formulated; as the American Declaration of Independence put it:

> We hold these truths to be self-evident, that all men are created equal, that they are endowed by their Creator with certain unalienable Rights, that among these are Life, Liberty and the pursuit of Happiness.

The text does not say that "people like us" are so endowed, but that all human beings have such rights. Like the claims of law generally, it is abstractly formulated.

Notably, though, the text of the Declaration of Independence was written and deployed in a particular context; that text, in different

4

contexts, later provided powerful intellectual support and moral inspiration for more consistent application of the idea of equal rights, regardless of gender, race, and other accidental features of human beings. But its rootedness in a particular historical tradition (for example, drawing on item 39 of Magna Carta of 1215) gave it more of a grip, so to speak, than purely abstractly formulated claims not rooted in such identifiable narrative traditions. Its history gave it an appeal that a merely abstract statement would have lacked. Item 39 of the Magna Carta stated that:

> No freeman shall be captured or imprisoned or disseised [to have one's estate seized] or outlawed or exiled or in any way destroyed, nor will we [the King] go against him or send against him, except by the lawful judgment of his peers or by the law of the land.

That statement had a great impact on the subsequent development of the ideas of liberty and the rule of law, including key elements of the Constitution of the United States of America (trial by jury and due process of law, for example). But as Voltaire reminded us, the phrase "freeman" in that text does not refer—as it was later interpreted and deployed to mean—"everyone," for if so, why specify "freeman" at all? It tells us that at that time not everyone was a freeman; indeed the term freeman specified a narrowly defined class of people. But in later contexts, that text was deployed to achieve freedom for more people. That text, with its deep connection to English identity, provided strong roots for the more libertarian applications of it that came later. Magna Carta is largely forgotten among speakers of English today, but it was well known by those who penned the American Declaration of Independence and the U.S. Constitution. Today, the role of Magna Carta is played by those later documents in the consciousness of American advocates of liberty.

In a Chinese context, the writings of Lao Tzu and Meng Tzu (Mencius) play a similar role, and create a culturally Chinese context for basic libertarian insights that were expressed long before Magna Carta, the Declaration of Independence, or *The Wealth of Nations* were written. Similar statements and claims can be found in the writings of Lao Tzu and Meng Tzu, and in the writings of the Islamic tradition, in African legal culture, and in every culture and every civilization—for the desire for freedom has been present in all of them.

The great challenge for libertarians in all cultures and contexts is to identify the roots of liberty in their own culture and to connect our struggle with those roots. I have learned much—including reason for humility—from my libertarian friends and colleagues in Russia and Eastern Europe, in the Muslim world, in Africa, in China, in Central and South America, in south and central Asia, well . . . everywhere, about the dialectic of the universal and the particular that characterizes the struggle for liberty. The roots of freedom are there in each culture; they must be excavated and reconnected with the present for our cause to be successful. That effort will give liberty the deep roots that it needs in order to flourish and to resist the efforts of the enemies of freedom who try to eradicate it; and at the same time it will reveal the universal character of fundamental justice.

I have treated some of those themes in "Classical Liberalism and Civil Society" and "The Great Bequest," as well as in passing in some of the other essays. I hope that my friends in other contexts will be able to do a better job than I at identifying the roots of liberty in their own cultures and creating narratives of freedom that will change the world for the better.

Ideas as an Independent Variable

The third theme, which may seem obvious to some, is the independent role—for good or for ill—of ideas. The idea that the "superstructure" is determined by the "material base" has been substantially discredited, certainly in the primitive form posited by Marxists. (For the way in which Marx adopted from libertarian writers—and then completely muddled—the idea of group conflict, see "Classical Liberalism, Marxism, and the Conflict of Classes: The Classical Liberal Theory of Class Conflict.") Ideas have an ability to sway us, sometimes in very self-destructive ways. The challenges posed to libertarian ideas toward the end of the nineteenth century by nationalism, socialism, racism, and imperialism are examples of the independent power of ideas. There was no "material necessity" for European society to abandon the ideas of freedom; it was a failure of the liberals of the time to meet the challenges posed by their competitors that doomed so much of humanity to the violence, oppression, brutality, poverty, and suffering inflicted on them in the name of "the nation," "the state," "the race," "the universal class," or the other false gods to which flesh and blood humans were sacrificed. It was in the battle of ideas that liberalism was first defeated. As the libertarian editor of *The Nation* E. L. Godkin opined in 1900, "Only a remnant, old men for the most part, still uphold the Liberal doctrine, and when they are gone, it will have no champions." In one of the most chilling prophecies ever penned, he predicted that:

> We hear no more of natural rights, but of inferior races, whose part it is to submit to the government of those whom God has made their superiors. The old fallacy of divine right has once more asserted its ruinous power, and before it is again repudiated there must be international struggles on a terrific scale.

And so it turned out to be. Godkin identified as the enemy of liberty, not an irresistible force, but "the old fallacy," that is, an old and previously refuted idea.

The German novelist and philosopher Robert Musil portrayed the experience of that generation of liberals very well in his book *The Man Without Qualities*, in the form of the experience of a Jewish businessman in pre–World War I Vienna, who has to suffer the involvement of his daughter in the milieu of "Christian socialism," with its horrible promise of future anti-Semitic mass murder. Musil wrote:

> Director Leo Fischel of the Lloyds Bank enjoyed philosophizing, but only for ten minutes a day. He enjoyed thinking that human life had a solid rational basis and that it paid off intellectually; he imagined this on the pattern of the harmonious hierarchy of a great bank and noted with satisfaction the daily signs of progress he read about in the papers.

> The faith in the immutable guidelines of reason and progress had for a long time enabled him to dismiss his wife's carpings with a shrug or a cutting retort. But since misfortune had decreed that in the course of this marriage the mood of the times would shift away from the old guidelines of liberalism that had favored Leo Fischel—the great guiding ideals of tolerance, the dignity of man, and free trade—and reason and progress in the Western world would be displaced by racial theories and street slogans, he could not remain

untouched by it either. He started by flatly denying the existence of these changes, just as Count Leinsdorf was accustomed to deny the existence of certain "unpleasant political manifestations" and wait for them to disappear of their own accord. Such waiting is the first almost imperceptible degree of the torture of exasperation that life inflicts on men of principle. The second degree is usually called, and was therefore also called by Fischel, "poison." This poison is the appearance, drop by drop, of new views on morals, art, politics, the family, newspapers, books, and social life, already accompanied by the hopeless feeling that there is no turning back and no indignant denials, which cannot avoid a certain acknowledgement of the thing denied. Nor was Director Fischel spared the third and final degree, when the isolated showers and sprinklings of the New turn into a steady, drenching rain. In time this becomes one of the most horrible torments that a man who has only ten minutes a day to spare for philosophy can experience.

It was first in the realm of ideas that liberty suffered defeat, followed by truly horrifying forms of oppression, and it is in the realm of ideas that some of the greatest and most important battles will be fought in the future. Libertarians must never shrink from the battle of ideas, from confronting—in fair and open debate—the ideas of collectivism, violence, and statist oppression. We must not shrink from the debate, as liberals of the past did, and leave the field to the enemies of freedom. In the words of F. A. Hayek, "We must make the building of a free society once more an intellectual adventure, a deed of courage."

I have tried, in many of the essays in this volume, to engage the critics of libertarian ideas and institutions, and to offer a vigorous defense of libertarian principles. Whether I have succeeded is a matter to be left to others, but I hope, at least, that we will not repeat the disastrous experience of previous generations of libertarians, many of whom conceded too much, fled the field, or did not take seriously the challenge of socialism, racism, and other anti-libertarian ideologies.

The Challenge of Implementing Liberty

The fourth theme is the great task of understanding how to implement libertarian proposals for reform and improvement. When I

8

was working to spread libertarian ideas and practices in the Soviet Union and its satellite states, I heard for the first time the concern of Soviet/Russian libertarians, as expressed in a rather pithy statement by Boris Pinsker over coffee in Moscow: "It is easy to turn an aquarium into fish soup. But to turn fish soup into an aquarium is a more challenging task." How to actually implement libertarian principles is not a matter of merely enunciating them. We have a very good understanding of what works to produce freedom and prosperity (the rule of law, well defined and legally secure property, toleration, etc.), but how to generate the institutions of law, property, and toleration is not well understood. I wish I could offer more insight into those problems, but little will be found in this volume. I have organized a number of conferences and symposia to bring together people to share their ideas on those issues—in Tbilisi, in Beijing, and elsewhere—but the issue remains a great challenge for libertarians. I do offer some—admittedly inadequate—ideas in "Challenges of Democratization" and "The Role of Institutions and Law in Economic Development." Whoever can provide us general models of institutional change in the direction of liberty that can provide guidance to implementing social change will do a great service for the human race, and perhaps earn a Nobel Prize in the process.

Related to those issues is my treatment of public goods theory, in "Infrastructure: Public or Private?" and in several essays on intellectual property that are not included in this volume. The assumption that state coercion is "necessary" to produce public goods sterilizes the discussion by precluding from consideration forms of voluntary cooperation to produce collective goods. The theory of public goods, I am convinced, is at the heart of understanding the emergence of liberty, for liberty is the greatest public good of all, a theme I explore in "Myths of Individualism," which was written in response to the truly absurd—and self-refuting—claim that libertarians "actively oppose the notion of 'shared values' or the idea of 'the common good.'"

Making a Difference

The final theme I will discuss here is the importance of action, of taking responsibility for freedom, and not retreating in the face of challenges. Perhaps it was my interaction, many years ago, with

Murray Rothbard and his circle, which led me to understand that the goal of libertarian activism is not merely "to be radical," but to make a difference for freedom, for justice, for the rule of law, and for peace and toleration. Some self-styled libertarians think that the most important thing is, at all costs, to be radical, although what they identify as "radical" most people would identify as deliberate alienation of potential allies. I choose my comrades from among those who are willing to work to realize freedom, regardless of whether we would end up at the same point were all our goals to be realized, not from those who are content merely to fantasize about freedom and who seek to remain "big fish" (actually, more like goldfish) in small ponds. I would rather be a small fish in a great sea of liberty. If I can make even a small positive step toward realizing freedom, all of my efforts will have been worth it.

This book contains a few essays indicative of my views on the importance of active engagement to advance liberty, such as "The 'Crime' of Blogging in Egypt" and "Moscow's Pride and Prejudice." Most of my efforts on that front, however, are not evident in the written essays, but in my efforts to effect change for liberty. My work in years past—in student activism; with the anti-conscription movement; with various political campaigns; and as an activist for taxpayer rights, free trade, civil liberties, and so on—left, in general, less of a "paper trail" than my more academic work, but I hope that those efforts have had a positive impact. Time will tell. My current work with the Atlas Economic Research Foundation and the Atlas Global Initiative for Free Trade, Peace, and Prosperity is intended to take the ideas and policies of liberty to every corner of the globe, to connect the struggle for liberty to the roots of liberty in all the major cultures of the world (and some of the smaller ones, too), and to do so in over a dozen languages. The impact may not be felt in some cases for years, but it is a task well worth a lifetime.

I hope that you, dear reader, will benefit from reading these essays, for I know that I have benefited from writing them.

Almaty, Kazakhstan
February 15, 2009

PART I

THEORY

2. Why Be Libertarian?

As you go through life, chances are almost 100 percent that you act like a libertarian. You might ask what it means to "act like a libertarian." It's not that complicated. You don't hit other people when their behavior displeases you. You don't take their stuff. You don't lie to them to trick them into letting you take their stuff, or defraud them, or knowingly give them directions that cause them to drive off a bridge. You're just not that kind of person.

You respect other people.

You respect their rights. You might sometimes feel like smacking someone in the face for saying something really offensive, but your better judgment prevails and you walk away, or answer words with words. You're a civilized person.

Congratulations. You've internalized the basic principles of libertarianism. You live your life and exercise your own freedom with respect for the freedom and rights of others.

You behave as a libertarian.

Libertarians believe in the voluntary principle, rather than force. And more than likely, you do follow that principle in your everyday dealings with other people.

But hold on, isn't libertarianism a *political philosophy*, a set of ideas about government and policy? It is. So why isn't it rooted in what government should be doing, rather than in what individuals should be doing? Ah, here's the major difference between libertarianism and other ideas about politics. Libertarians don't believe that government is magical. It's made up of people. They're just like us. There's no special race of people—call them kings, emperors, wizards, Magi, presidents, legislators, or prime ministers—with super-normal intelligence, wisdom, or powers that elevate them above normal people. Rulers, even when democratically elected, are no more "public spirited," and sometimes far less, than average people. There's no evidence that they're any less selfish than other people or any more benevolent. And there's no evidence that they're more concerned with right or wrong than average people. They're like us.

But hold on again. Political rulers do exercise powers that other people don't have. They exercise the powers to arrest people, to start wars and kill people, to decree what other people may or may not read, whether and how they may worship God, whom they may marry, what they may or may not eat, drink, or smoke, what they may or may not do for a living, where they may live, where they must attend school, whether they may travel, what goods and services they may provide to others and what prices they may charge, and a lot more. They certainly exercise powers the rest of us don't have.

Precisely. They wield force, and they do it as a matter of course—it's what distinguishes government from other institutions. But they have powers of perception, insight, or foresight no greater than the rest of us, nor standards of right and wrong that are higher or more rigorous than the average person. Some may be smarter than average, others perhaps even less intelligent, but there's no evidence that they really exceed the rest of humanity in such a way that they should be considered elevated above us, as our natural masters.

Why do they exercise force, while the rest of us rely on voluntary persuasion when we deal with others? The holders of political power aren't angels or gods, so why do they claim the authority to exercise powers that none among us would claim the right to exercise? Why should we submit to their exercise of force? If I have no authority to burst into your home to tell you what you should eat, or what you should smoke, or when you should go to bed, or with whom, why should a politician, or a bureaucrat, or an army general, or a king, or a governor have that authority?

Did We Consent to Be Coerced?

But wait, we are the government, aren't we? At least, in a democracy, as some clever philosophers, such as Jean-Jacques Rousseau, have argued, we consent to whatever the government tells us to do or not to do. The government carries out the "general will" of the people, and that means that it's exercising our very own will. So when the government uses force against us, it's just forcing us to be free, by making us follow our own wills, and not what we happen to think we will. As Rousseau argued in his extraordinarily influential book *The Social Contract*, "the general will is always rightful and tends to the public good; but it does not follow that the deliberations of the people are always equally right. . . . There is often a great difference between the will of all [what all individuals want] and the general will."[1]

In his theory, Rousseau combined force with freedom, for, as he argued, "whoever refuses to obey the general will shall be constrained to do so by the whole body, which means nothing other than that he shall be forced to be free."[2] After all, you don't know what you really want until the state has decided what you want, so when you think you want to do something, but are stopped by the police and imprisoned, you're being made free. You were deluded into thinking you wanted to disobey the state, and the police are merely helping you to choose what you really wanted, but were too stupid, ignorant, foolish, or weak to know that you wanted.

Now that may be getting overly metaphysical, so let's dial back a bit and think about what is being argued by advocates of majority rule. Somehow, through elections or some other procedures, we generate the "will of the people," even though some of the people may not agree (at least the ones who lost the vote didn't agree with the majority). Those people will be coerced to go along with the majority, say, by not consuming alcohol or marijuana or by being made to give up their money to pay for things they oppose, such as foreign wars or subsidies to influential economic interests. A majority voted for the law banning X or requiring Y, or for candidates who pledged to ban X or require Y, and so now we know the "will of the people." And if someone still drinks a beer or smokes a joint or hides his or her income, that person is somehow not following the will of the people, to which he or she has consented. Let's unpack that a bit more.

Let's say a prohibitionist law was passed into effect and you had voted for the prohibitionist law or candidate. Some would say that you consented to be bound by the outcome. And if you voted against the prohibitionist law or for an antiprohibitionist candidate? Well, they would add, you participated in the procedure by which the decision was made, so you consented to be bound by the outcome. And if you didn't vote, or didn't even have an opinion? Well, they would add, you surely can't complain now, since you forfeited your chance to influence the outcome by not voting! As the English libertarian Herbert Spencer observed a long time ago of such arguments, "curiously enough, it seems that he gave his consent in whatever way he acted—whether he said yes, whether he said no, or whether he remained! A rather awkward doctrine this."[3] Awkward, indeed. If you always "consent," regardless of what you actually say or do, then the term "consent" means nothing, because it means "nonconsent," as well as "consent." When that is the case, a word has been emptied of meaning.

The fact is that a person who's arrested for smoking marijuana in his or her own house didn't in any meaningful sense "consent" to being arrested. That's why the police carry sticks and guns—to threaten people with violence.

But maybe those powers are delegated to the government by the people, so if the people could choose not to smoke marijuana, then they could choose to arrest themselves. But if you don't have the authority to break down your neighbor's door and go in with guns drawn to drag them out and put them in a cage, how can you delegate that power to someone else? So we're back with the magical claim that your pot-smoking neighbors authorized their own arrest, regardless of what opinion they expressed, or how they behaved. But maybe just being alive in a country means you've consented to everything the government demands of you. After all, if you come into my house, you certainly agree to be bound by my rules. But a "country" isn't quite like "my house." I own my house, but I don't "own" my country. It's made up of a lot of people who have their own ideas about how to live their lives. And they don't belong to me. That's really the most important realization of mature people: *other people don't belong to me.* They have their own lives to lead. You, as a mature person, understand that, and your actions reflect it. You don't burst into the homes of others to tell them how to live. You don't steal their stuff when you think you have a better use for it. You don't hit, punch, stab, or shoot people when they disagree with you, even about matters of the greatest importance.

So, if you already *act like* a libertarian, maybe you should *be* one.

What Does It Mean to Be a Libertarian?

It means not only refraining from harming the rights of other people, namely, respecting the rules of justice with regards to other people, but also equipping yourself mentally to understand what it means for people to have rights, how rights create the foundation for peaceful social cooperation, and how voluntary societies work.

It means standing up, not only for your own freedom, but for the freedom of other people. A great Brazilian thinker dedicated his life to the abolition of the greatest violation of liberty imaginable: slavery. His name was Joaquim Nabuco and he stated the libertarian creed that guided his own life:

> Educate your children, educate yourselves, in the love for the freedom of others, for only in this way will your own freedom not be a gratuitous gift from fate. You will be aware of its worth and will have the courage to defend it.[4]

Being a libertarian means caring about freedom for everyone. It means respecting the rights of other people, even when we find their actions or words disagreeable. It means refraining from the use of force and instead pursuing one's goals, whether personal happiness, or the improvement of the condition of humanity, or knowledge, or all of those, or something else, *exclusively* through voluntary and peaceful action, whether in the "capitalist" world of free enterprise and exchange, or in science, philanthropy, art, love, friendship, or any of the other human endeavors framed by the rules of voluntary cooperation.

Skepticism about Power and Authority

Being a libertarian means understanding that rights are secure only when power is limited. Rights require the rule of law. John Locke, the English radical philosopher and activist, helped to lay the foundations for the modern world. He argued against the advocates of "absolutism," those who believed that the rulers should exercise unlimited powers. Those who defended absolute power sneered that allowing people their "liberty" would mean everyone just doing whatever he or she "lists," that is, whatever he or she was inclined to do, as a matter of whim and without regard to consequences or the rights of others.

Locke responded that what the party of liberty sought was "a Liberty to dispose, and order, as he lists, his Person, Actions, Possessions, and his whole Property, within the Allowance of those Laws under which he is; and therein not to be subject to the arbitrary Will of another, but freely follow his own."[5] One has the right to do whatever one chooses with what is one's own—to freely follow one's own will, rather than the commands of another, so long as one respects the equal rights of others.

The philosopher Michael Huemer grounds libertarianism in what he calls "common sense morality," which is comprised of three elements: "A nonaggression principle" that forbids individuals from attacking, killing, stealing from, or defrauding one another; "A recognition of the coercive nature of government . . . which is supported by credible threats of physical force directed against those who would disobey the state"; and "A skepticism of political authority . . . that the state may not do what it would be wrong for any nongovernmental person or organization to do."[6] As he notes, "it is the notion of authority that forms the true locus of dispute between libertarianism and other political philosophies."[7]

Liberty, Prosperity, and Order

Being a libertarian means understanding how wealth is created; not by politicians giving commands, but by free people working together, inventing, creating, saving, investing, buying and selling, all based on respect for the property, that is, the rights, of others. "Property" isn't limited just to "my stuff," as one might use the term today, but encompasses the rights to "Life, Liberty, and Estate," to use Locke's famous phrase.[8] As James Madison, the principal author of the U.S. Constitution, argued, "[A]s a man is said to have a right to his property, he may be equally said to have a property in his rights."[9]

Love and affection may be enough for small groups to cooperate peacefully and efficiently, but libertarians understand that they aren't sufficient to create peace and cooperation among large groups of people who don't interact face-to-face. Libertarians believe in the rule of law, meaning rules that are applicable to everyone and not bent or stretched this way or that based on the preferences of people with power. The rules of free societies are not crafted to benefit this or that person or group; they respect the rights of every human being, regardless of gender, color, religion, language, family, or other accidental feature.

The rules of property are among the most important foundations for voluntary cooperation among strangers. Property isn't just what you can hold in your hands; it's the complex relationships of rights and obligations by which people who are unknown to each other can guide their actions and that allow them to live peacefully, to

18

cooperate in firms and associations, and to trade for mutual advantage, because they know the baseline—what's mine and what's yours—from which each may act to improve his or her condition. Well-defined, legally secure, and transferrable property rights form the foundation for voluntary cooperation, widespread prosperity, progress, and peace.[10] That includes not only the things you can hold in your hand or stand on, but shares of complicated business enterprises that produce any of the uncountable things that require the cooperation of thousands and thousands of people, whether medicines or aircraft or pineapples delivered to your table in winter.

The libertarian law professor Richard Epstein titled one of his best books *Simple Rules for a Complex World*.[11] The title brilliantly captures his theme, that you don't need complex rules to generate complex forms of order. Simple rules will do. In fact, simple, understandable, and stable rules tend to generate order, whereas complicated, incomprehensible, and fluctuating rules tend to generate chaos.

Well-defined property and the right to trade on mutually agreeable terms make possible large-scale cooperation without coercion. Free markets incorporate more, not less, order and foresight than coercively directed or commanded societies. The spontaneous order of markets is far more abstract, complex, and farsighted than all the five-year plans or economic interventions ever devised. Institutions such as prices, which emerge when people are free to exchange, help to guide resources to their most highly valued uses, without vesting coercive power in a bureaucracy.[12] Coercively imposed "planning" is, in fact, the opposite of planning; it is a disruption of the continuous process of plan coordination embodied in freely developed social institutions.

Order emerges spontaneously from the free interactions of people who are secure in the enjoyment of their rights. That applies not only to economic order, but also to language, social mores, customs, science, and even fields such as fashion and style. To use force in the attempt to subject any or all of those areas to the arbitrary will of a ruler, a dictator, a president, a committee, a legislature, or a bureaucracy is to replace order with chaos, freedom with force, and harmony with discord.

Libertarians believe in and work for a world at peace, in which the rights of each and every unique human being are recognized and respected, a world in which widely shared prosperity is generated by voluntary cooperation, based on a legal system that protects rights and facilitates mutually beneficial exchanges. Libertarians believe in and work for limits on power, for the subjection of heretofore arbitrary power to the rule of law, for the limitation and minimization of violence of all sorts. Libertarians believe in and stand up for the freedom to think, to work, to behave in any way one chooses, so long as one respects the equal freedom of others. Libertarians believe in and work for a world in which each person is free to pursue her or his own happiness, without requiring anyone else's permission to be, to act, to live.

So . . . Why Be Libertarian?

Why be libertarian? It may sound glib, but a reasonable response is, Why not? Just as the burden of proof is on the one who accuses another of a crime, not on the one accused, the burden of proof is on the one who would deny liberty to another person, not the one who would exercise liberty. Someone who wishes to sing a song or bake a cake should not have to begin by begging permission from all the others in the world to be allowed to sing or bake. Nor should she or he have to rebut all possible reasons against singing or baking. If she is to be forbidden from singing or baking, the one who seeks to forbid should offer a good reason why she should not be allowed to do so. The burden of proof is on the forbidder. And it may be a burden that could be met, if, for example, the singing were to be so loud it would make it impossible for others to sleep or the baking would generate so many sparks it would burn down the homes of the neighbors. Those would be good reasons for forbidding the singing or the baking. The presumption, however, is for liberty, and not for the exercise of power to restrict liberty.

A libertarian is someone who believes in the presumption of liberty. And with that simple presumption, when realized in practice, comes a world in which different people can realize their own forms of happiness in their own ways, in which people can trade freely to mutual advantage, and disagreements are resolved with words, and not with clubs. It would not be a perfect world, but it would be a world worth fighting for.

Notes

1. Jean-Jacques Rousseau, *The Social Contract*, trans. Alan Cranston (New York: Penguin Books, 1968), p. 72.

2. Ibid., p. 64.

3. The full text of Spencer's memorable passage, from his essay "The Right to Ignore the State," is: "Perhaps it will be said that this consent is not a specific, but a general one, and that the citizen is understood to have assented to everything his representative may do, when he voted for him. But suppose he did not vote for him; and on the contrary did all in his power to get elected someone holding opposite views—what then? The reply will probably be that, by taking part in such an election, he tacitly agreed to abide by the decision of the majority. And how if he did not vote at all? Why then he cannot justly complain of any tax, seeing that he made no protest against its imposition. So, curiously enough, it seems that he gave his consent in whatever way he acted—whether he said yes, whether he said no, or whether he remained neuter! A rather awkward doctrine this. Here stands an unfortunate citizen who is asked if he will pay money for a certain proffered advantage; and whether he employs the only means of expressing his refusal or does not employ it, we are told that he practically agrees; if only the number of others who agree is greater than the number of those who dissent. And thus we are introduced to the novel principle that A's consent to a thing is not determined by what A says, but by what B may happen to say!" Herbert Spencer, *Social Statics: or, The Conditions essential to Happiness specified, and the First of them Developed* (London: John Chapman, 1851), chapter xix: The Right to Ignore the State. Accessed from http://oll.libertyfund.org/title/273/6325 on 2013-03-23.

4. Joaquim Nabuco, *Abolitionism: The Brazilian Antislavery Struggle*, trans. and ed. Robert Conrad (Urbana: University of Illinois Press, 1977), p. 172. (In Conrad's translation, thus: "Let them educate their children—indeed, let them educate themselves—to enjoy the freedom of others without which their own liberty will be a chance gift of destiny. Let them acquire the knowledge that freedom is worth possessing, and let them attain the courage to defend it.")

5. John Locke, "The Second Treatise of Government," in *Two Treatises of Government*, ed. Peter Laslett (Cambridge: Cambridge University Press, 1988), p. 306.

6. Michael Huemer, *The Problem of Political Authority* (New York: Palgrave Macmillan, 2013), p. 177.

7. Ibid., p. 178.

8. Locke, p. 323. Locke located the root of property in general in each and every person's "Property in his own Person. This no Body has any Right to but himself." Ibid., p. 287.

9. James Madison, "Property," in *The Papers of James Madison*, vol. 14: April 6, 1791—March 16, 1793 (Charlottesville: University Press of Virginia, 1983), p. 266. The wider statement (available online at http://oll.libertyfund.org/title/875/63884) is: "This term in its particular application means 'that dominion which one man claims and exercises over the external 125 things of the world, in exclusion of every other individual.' In its larger and juster meaning, it embraces everything to which a man may attach a value and have a right; and *which leaves to every one else the like advantage*. In the former sense, a man's land, or merchandise, or money is called his property. In the latter sense, a man has a property in his opinions and the free communication of them. He has a property of particular value in his religious opinions, and in the profession and practice dictated by them. He has a property very dear to him in the safety and liberty of his person. He has an equal property in the free use of his faculties and free choice of the objects on which to employ them. In a word,

as a man is said to have a right to his property, he may be equally said to have a property in his rights."

10. The data assembled over decades by the researchers at the Fraser Institute of Canada in the annual *Economic Freedom of the World Report* and made publicly available at www.freetheworld.com show clearly that more freedom produces better results everywhere, whether Europe or Asia, Africa, or Latin America.

10. Richard Epstein, *Simple Rules for a Complex World* (Cambridge, Mass: Harvard University Press, 1995).

12. The science of economics emerged hundreds of years ago when people began to notice that countries that had freer markets tended to be more orderly and prosperous and that the king's ministers were not needed to coordinate supply and demand. As the historian Joyce Appleby noted, "Economic writers had discovered the underlying regularity in free market activity. Where moralists had long urged that necessity knows no law, the economic analysts who pursued price back to demand had discovered a lawfulness in necessity, and in doing so they had come upon a possibility and a reality. The reality was that individuals making decisions about their own persons and property were the determiners of price in the market. The possibility was that the economic rationalism of market participants could supply the order to the economy formerly secured through authority." Joyce Appleby, *Economic Thought and Ideology in Seventeenth-Century England* (Princeton, N.J.: Princeton University Press, 1978), pp. 187–88.

3. Freedom Properly Understood

> In people's day-to-day struggle to live, in the extreme efforts workers put forth to earn an extra ruble through moonlighting, in the collective farmers' battle for bread and potatoes as the one and only fruit of their labor, he could sense more than the desire to live better, to fill one's children's stomachs and to clothe them. In the battle for the right to make shoes, to knit sweaters, in the struggle to plant what one wished, was manifested the natural, indestructible striving toward freedom inherent in human nature.
>
> —Vasily Grossman, *Forever Flowing*

Ladies and gentlemen, it is an honor to be asked to come before such a distinguished group to address such a very serious issue. The theme of "Freedom Properly Understood" is certainly timely when our freedom is being chipped away by those who believe that no alleged threat to security, no matter how tiny, might ever be insufficient reason to override our liberties. That issue—whether we face a tradeoff between freedom and security, with more of one meaning less of the other, or the two tend to reinforce each other—deserves careful and systematic attention. As urgent as that question is, it is also a topic for another occasion, as I hope to focus our attention today, not on whether the small threats posed by terrorists warrant overriding freedom, but on the deeper issue of the proper understanding of freedom.

Freedom is notoriously one of those "essentially contested concepts" that so exercise political theorists (Gallie 1956). Or, as Ronald Dworkin put it in his discussion of "fairness," we can distinguish the "concept" of freedom from various specific "conceptions" of freedom (Dworkin 1972).

Competing conceptions of freedom have been with us since the dawn of philosophy in Greece. In *The Republic*, Plato has Socrates ask about the character of freedom in a democratic regime:

Paper presented at the 60th anniversary meeting of the Liberal International, Hamburg, Germany, November 17, 2007.

> "In the first place, then, aren't they free? And isn't the city full of freedom and free speech? And isn't there license in it to do whatever one wants?"
>
> "That is what is said, certainly," he said.
>
> "And where there's license, it's plain, that each man would organize his life in it privately just as it pleases him." (Plato, 235, 557b)

The natural outcome of such a regime, of course, is a litany of horrors, for, according to Socrates,

> "And the ultimate in the freedom of the multitude, my friend," I said, "occurs in such a city when the purchased slaves, male and female, are no less free than those who have bought them. And we almost forgot to mention the extent of the law of equality and of freedom in the relations of women with men and men with women."
>
> "Won't we," he said, "with Aeschylus, 'say whatever just came to our lips'?" (Plato, 241, 563b–c)

Such freedom, we are instructed, merely leads to the greatest slavery. True freedom is not merely to "say whatever just came to our lips." True freedom is to be unimpeded, not in our *pursuit* of the truth, or of happiness, or of virtue, but in its *attainment*. In Book III of *The Republic*, Socrates described the important role of the properly educated Guardians, which is to "give up all other crafts and very precisely be craftsmen of the city's freedom and practice nothing other than what tends to it" (Plato, 73–74, 395c). To be free is to stand in the presence of truth, and to be freed means to be freed from illusion and falsehood. True freedom is the freedom to do what is good and not merely "whatever one wants." Knowledge is freedom and as truth is one and knowledge must of necessity be of truth and of truth alone, the free are all in agreement. Disagreement is only a sign of unfreedom, as Socrates notes in his dismissal of the freedom of democracy, for under democratic freedom "all sorts of humans come to be" (Plato, 235, 537c).

The very existence of a plurality of "sorts of humans" denies to such a regime even the designation of "constitution," for it is not one regime, but "contains all species of regimes" (Plato, 235, 537d).

It is a common view that democracy and freedom emerged among Greek thinkers. It's more accurate to think that freedom emerged at various times among some Greek cities, but rarely was it popular among its intellectuals, and certainly not in the case of Plato, who offered in its place an allegedly higher or truer freedom that consisted in the knowledge of the good; as Winston Coleman summarized Plato's view, "real freedom is reduced to the rule of knowledge" (Coleman 1960, 42). A modern statement of that view was provided recently by Charles Taylor, who argued that to "exalt" freedom of choice means to exalt it "as a human capacity." And to do so means that,

> It carries with it the demand that we become beings capable of choice, that we rise to the level of self-consciousness and autonomy where we can exercise choice, that we not remain enmired through fear, sloth, ignorance, or superstition in some code imposed by tradition, society, or fate which tells us how we should dispose of what belongs to us. (Taylor 1982a, 197)[1]

This is all rather familiar territory. It was canvassed quite well by Isaiah Berlin in his famous essay "Two Concepts of Liberty." Berlin pointed out that Plato's conception of freedom, which posited removal of encumbrances on the "real," "true," or "higher" self, has led to very real enslavement. Rulers have merely to declare that those who resist their guidance

> . . . are actually aiming at what in their benighted state they consciously resist, because there exists within them an occult entity—their latent rational will, or their "true" purpose—and that this entity, although it is belied by all that they overtly feel and do and say, is their "real" self, of which the poor empirical self in space and time may know nothing or little, and that this inner spirit is the only self that deserves to have its wishes taken into account. Once I take this view, I am in a position to ignore the actual wishes of men or societies, to bully, oppress, torture them in the name, and on behalf, of their "real" selves, in the secure knowledge that whatever is the true goal of man (happiness, performance of duty, wisdom, a just society, self-fulfillment) must be identical with his freedom—the free choice of his "true," albeit often submerged and inarticulate, self. (Berlin 2002, 180)

Freedom Ancient and Modern, Collective and Individual

The freedom that Plato praises is frequently, as Berlin also notes, married to a conception of the bearer of freedom that is collectivist.

25

Real freedom is the freedom of a collective self. It is a view that keeps recurring among western intellectuals. Harvard philosopher Michael Sandel has argued, for example, that classical liberal individualism fails to deal adequately with the problem of personal identity, for, as he argues, "to be capable of a more thoroughgoing reflection, we cannot be wholly unencumbered subjects of possession, individuated in advance and given prior to our ends, but must be subjects constituted in part by our central aspirations and attachments, always open, indeed vulnerable, to growth and transformation in the light of revised self-understandings. And in so far as our constitutive self-understandings comprehend *a wider subject than the individual alone, whether a family or tribe or city or class or nation or people,* to this extent they define a community in a constitutive sense" (Sandel 1982, 172) (emphasis added).[2]

Participation in collective decisionmaking is, we are also told, a higher kind of freedom, for then we are not merely saying, in Plato's dismissive terms, "whatever just came to our lips," but truly "deliberating":

> Those issues, which can only be effectively decided by society as a whole and which often set the boundary and framework for our lives, can indeed be discussed freely by politically irresponsible individuals wherever they have license to do so. But they can only be truly *deliberated* about politically. A society in which such deliberation was public and involved everyone would realize a freedom not available anywhere else or in any other mode. (Taylor 1982a, 208)[3]

Benjamin Constant referred to such collective freedom as "ancient freedom" and contrasted it with "modern freedom."[4] The confusion between the two, Constant argued, was at least one major reason for the collapse of the French Revolution into an orgy of murder and terror. Ancient freedom was, he believed, incompatible with modern conditions and required terrible measures in the attempt to realize it. Ancient freedom was a response to the ever-present threat of war among ancient polities. The loss of a war in the ancient world typically meant the complete elimination or enslavement of the population; if the uniformity of opinion and action characteristic of ancient freedom was the price to be paid to avoid defeat and enslavement, one can certainly understand its attractions. But to confuse such collective freedom with the freedom characteristic of the modern world generated a catastrophe.

Modern freedom is the product of a distinctive set of political relationships that emerged in Europe that were quite unlike the polities of the ancient world. Commerce, rather than war, determined the character of the modern age, but the language of political science did not reflect that difference. Indeed, much of the hottest political-theoretical debate of the past few hundred years may be traced to the application of the concepts and terms of ancient political science—as recovered by western thinkers with the texts of Plato and Aristotle—to institutions and practices that were radically different in kind and character from those known by Plato and Aristotle. The nature of the relationship among persons in the modern world is primarily contractual, based on agreements and oaths of various sorts (e.g., *Eidgenossenschaften*) and accordingly voluntary.[5] In western European history the seedbed of modern liberty is the commune. Those communes were not merely hypothetical social contracts among purely rational entities—higher selves, as it were—but robustly empirical agreements. Harold Berman described the process in the English town of Ipswich as recorded in *Domesday Book of Ipswich*.

> On Thursday, June 29, 1200, the whole community of the town assembled in the churchyard of St. Mary at the Tower. They proceeded to elect, with one voice, two bailiffs, who were sworn to keep the office of provost, and four coroners, who were sworn to keep the pleas of the crown and to handle other matters affecting the crown in the town "and to see to it that the aforesaid bailiffs justly and lawfully treat the poor as well as the rich." . . . On Sunday, July 2, . . . all the townsmen stretched forth their hands toward the Book (the Gospels) and with one voice solemnly swore to obey and assist, with their bodies and their goods, the bailiffs, coroners, and every one of the capital portmen in safeguarding the borough, its new charter, its liberties and customs, in all places against all persons, the royal power excepted, "according to their ability, so far as they ought justly and rationally to do." (Berman 1983, 383–84)

The freedom that has characterized the legal and political experience of western society emerged, not from a rediscovery of the texts of the ancients, but from the experience of civic freedom in the communes of Europe, where Europeans had to sort out legal and political arrangements anew. The cities of Europe were islands of freely organized production and exchange protected by walls that were built to exclude the practitioners of violence and theft. As a fortified place—a *Burg*—a city made possible the freedom of the Bürger. The new cities of Europe were generally places of trade and commerce, rather than administrative centers of vast empires, centers of religious cults, or centers of exploitative rule over subject peasant populations. The communes represented something new; they were often founded by people with no place in the feudal order of the countryside, divided as it was between those who fought, those who prayed, and those who worked. The cities were typically founded and populated by wandering peddlers, by fleeing vassals, by mechanics and craftsmen and others without status in the legal order of feudalism. It was in the cities that they found freedom. The communes, notably those of northern Italy, of the Low Countries and the Rhineland, and of Germany east of the Elbe, were governed by written charters—or constitutions—that guaranteed the liberties of their inhabitants. The old German slogan about city air and freedom was a matter of law, recognized, for example, as a privilege of the City of Lübeck, fully acknowledged by the Emperor Frederick I in the year 1188. "Stadtluft macht frei nach Ablauf von Jahr und Tag" was since the twelfth century a legal principle of the majority of civitates, the distinguishing feature of their civil freedom (Planitz 1954, 117–118). Serfs or vassals who could make it to a city and live there for a year and a day were freed of feudal obligations and would be defended by the city. Freedom under the rule of law was what attracted people to the cities, which were surrounded by thick walls that effectively defended civil society from the barbarians, greedy nobles and knights, bandits, and plundering armies outside. Such communes were the seedbeds of modern civil society—of free-market capitalism, of freedom, of the security of person and property.

Henri Pirenne noted in his classic study *Medieval Cities: Their Origins and the Revival of Trade* that "just as agrarian civilization had made of the peasant a man whose normal state was servitude, trade made of the merchant a man whose normal condition was liberty" (Pirenne 1937, 50). The civil liberty of modern society is the product of civil society, that is, of the society that grew in the cities of Europe.

The liberty of the person was individual liberty, but it was acquired by being a member of a civil society, by enjoying a particular kind of legal relationship with others, through membership in a guild, company, or association. Antony Black notes, "The crucial point about both guilds and communes was that here individuation and association went hand in hand. One achieved liberty by belonging to this kind of group. Citizens, merchants, and artisans pursued their own individual goals by banding together under oath" (Black 1984, 65).[6]

Such freedom could only be freedom under the rule of law. Civil liberty is not "liberation" from all constraint of any sort, but mutual enjoyment of equal freedom. In John Locke's memorable critique of the vision of lawless "freedom" painted by the advocate of royal absolutism Sir Robert Filmer,

> [T]he end of Law is not to abolish or restrain, but *to preserve and enlarge Freedom*: For in all the states of created beings capable of Laws, *where there is no Law, there is no Freedom.* For *Liberty* is to be free from restraint and violence from others which cannot be, where there is no Law: But Freedom is not, as we are told, *A Liberty for every Man to do what he lists*: (For who could be free, when every other Man's Humour might domineer over him?) But a *Liberty* to dispose, and order, as he lists, his Person, Actions, Possessions, and his whole Property, within the Allowance of those Laws under which he is; and therein not to be subject to the arbitrary Will of another, but freely follow his own. (Locke 1988, 306)

The freedom of modern civil society, in Constant's words, is

> the right to be subjected only to the laws, and to be neither arrested, detained, put to death or maltreated in any way by the arbitrary will of one or more individuals. It is the right of everyone to express their opinion, choose a profession and practice it, to dispose of property, and even to abuse it; to come and go without permission, and without having to account for their motives or undertakings. It is everyone's right to associate with other individuals, either to discuss their interests, or to profess the religion which they and their associates prefer, or even simply to occupy their days or hours in a way which is most compatible with their inclinations or whims. Finally it is everyone's right to exercise some influence on the administration of the government, either by

> electing all or particular officials, or through representations, petitions, demands to which the authorities are more or less compelled to pay heed. (Constant 1988, 311)

The modern conception of freedom is compatible with plurality of religions, plurality of styles of life, plurality of opinions. Under modern liberty "all sorts of humans come to be." It's unpredictable. The rules of the process are known, but the outcome is not. Moreover, the complex outcome of the interaction of so many free persons is not a consciously chosen outcome; it can't be. Modern freedom and self-direction is individual, not collective.

Where does that bring us? Isn't modern liberty triumphant? Haven't we seen the retreat of all advocates of collectivist conceptions of liberty, the collapse of totalitarian projects to free man by abolishing false consciousness, the universal triumph of liberalism, even the end of history? Hardly. I won't address the hybrid of pre-modern and post-modern horror that is Islamist radicalism, with its confused mélange of twentieth-century European fascism and an imagined tradition of the golden age of Islam.[7] That, too, is a subject for another occasion. Rather, I will address the reemergence of theories of freedom that promise us "real," "true," "higher," "effective," or "substantive" freedom through the rather softer techniques of the modern welfare state.

"Real" and "Substantive" Freedom and the Presumptions of Power

The opponents of mere freedom modify their alternative as "true freedom," "higher freedom," "real freedom," or "substantive freedom." They tell us that the exercise of a choice is free only if it is justified, or part of the attainment of a life that we "have reason to value." Such intellectuals presuppose that the rest of us must justify ourselves to them. They propose a fundamental shift in the burden of proof. In place of the authentically liberal adage that "all that is not clearly forbidden is permitted," we are told that real freedom consists in following the adage that "what is not clearly justified may be forbidden." Only justified freedoms are enumerated, and only those that are enumerated are protected.

The idea was set forth very clearly by one of the authors of liberalism's collapse in the late nineteenth and early twentieth centuries, the English philosopher and follower of G. W. F. Hegel, Thomas

Hill Green. In his famous 1881 lecture against freedom of contract, Green stated,

> We shall probably all agree that freedom, rightly under-stood, is the greatest of blessings; that its attainment is the true end of all our effort as citizens. But when we thus speak of freedom, we should consider carefully what we mean by it. We do not mean merely freedom from restraint of compulsion. We do not mean merely freedom to do as we like irrespectively of what it is that we like. We do not mean a freedom that can be enjoyed by one man or one set of men at the cost of a loss of freedom to others. When we speak of freedom as something to be so highly prized, we mean a positive power or capacity of doing or enjoying something worth doing or enjoying, and that, too, something that we do or enjoy in common with others. We mean by it a power which each man exercises through the help or security given him by his fellow-men, and which he in turn helps to secure for them. (Green 1906, 370–71)

Thus, to understand freedom rightly (or properly) is to understand that "the mere removal of compulsion, the mere enabling a man to do as he likes, is in itself no contribution to true freedom" (Green 1906, 371). Indeed, we are made free precisely when we are subjected to compulsion in the name of forcing us to do what we ought to do, which is, after all, what we "really" want to do. In his argument for prohibition of alcohol (one of Green's pet causes), Green concluded,

> The citizens of England now make its law. We ask them by law to put a restraint on themselves in the matter of strong drink. We ask them further to limit, or even altogether to give up, the not very precious liberty of buying and selling alcohol, in order that they may become more free to exercise the faculties and improve the talents which God has given them. (Green 1906, 386)

Arguments offered in support of an obviously failed policy such as prohibition of alcohol may seem like a mere historical curiosity, were it not for the fact that Green's conception of freedom has become dominant among most intellectuals. In place of mere "freedom from restraint of compulsion," such intellectuals offer us a life of justifying our behavior to them. And when we finally realize our true desires and submit ourselves to the rule of the intellectuals, we will enjoy, not mere freedom, or merely empirical freedom, but "real" or "substantive" freedom.

In his wide-ranging book *Development as Freedom*, Nobel Laureate Amartya Sen repeats the language of Green, when he explains that to treat "the freedoms of individuals as the basic building blocks," one must be focused on "the expansion of the 'capabilities' of persons to lead *the kind of lives they value—and have reason to value*" (Sen 1999, 18, emphasis added). Not merely the kind of lives they actually value, but the kind of lives they have reason to value. Have reason to value means can offer reasons for being allowed to pursue them. "To whom" is never specified, of course. Green formulated the same principle as "a positive power or capacity of doing or enjoying something worth doing or enjoying." The focus is on the giving of reasons: It is something "worth doing" or something they "have reason to value." The fact that they value it is by itself of no significance. Attaining a value is an exercise of freedom if and only if it is a justified value. Otherwise, not.

Accordingly, freedoms must be enumerated. They must be enumerated because they require justification. The complement to enumerated freedoms, each requiring a justification, is a background of unenumerated powers of the state to compel, to prohibit, to forbid, to coerce. When the presumption of liberty is replaced with the presumption of power, liberalism is turned on its head.

The American Bill of Rights, written when liberalism was emerging into its own, added to the enumeration of rights a most important qualifier: the Ninth Amendment, which states that "The enumeration in the Constitution, of certain rights, shall not be construed to deny or disparage others retained by the people." With the exception of procedural legal rights (such as due process of law, a speedy and public trial, and trial by jury), all of the enumerated rights are rights to freedom from state power. The Ninth Amendment to the U.S. Constitution tells us that the listing of rights does not imply that if a right is not listed, it is no right.[8] The Tenth Amendment ("The powers not delegated to the United States by the Constitution, nor prohibited by it to the States, are reserved to the States respectively, or to the people.") tells us that the enumeration of powers means that if the power is not enumerated, the state authorities do not have that power.

Contrast that approach with the Universal Declaration of Human Rights, which offers twenty-one articles that are compatible with modern conceptions of freedom, and then with Article Twenty-Two, which initiates a list of entitlements to security, health, housing, periodic holidays with pay, and so on. The capstone to the list tells us that we have left the presumption of freedom far behind and entered into the realm of the presumption of power:

> Article 29.
> (1) Everyone has duties to the community in which alone the free and full development of his personality is possible.
>
> (2) In the exercise of his rights and freedoms, everyone shall be subject only to such limitations as are determined by law solely for the purpose of securing due recognition and respect for the rights and freedoms of others and of meeting the just requirements of morality, public order and the general welfare in a democratic society.
>
> (3) These rights and freedoms may in no case be exercised contrary to the purposes and principles of the United Nations.
>
> Article 30.
> Nothing in this Declaration may be interpreted as implying for any State, group or person any right to engage in any activity or to perform any act aimed at the destruction of any of the rights and freedoms set forth herein.

A Universal Declaration of Human Rights that concludes with a "right" to have duties "to the community," that is, duties to obey the state, is entirely different in kind from a declaration that concludes with an explicit statement of unenumerated rights ("The enumeration in the Constitution, of certain rights, shall not be construed to deny or disparage others retained by the people.") and enumerated powers ("The powers not delegated to the United States by the Constitution, nor prohibited by it to the States, are reserved to the States respectively, or to the people."). Moreover, nothing in the Universal Declaration, it insists, should be construed to recognize "any right to engage in any activity or to perform any act" that might be "aimed at the destruction of any of the rights and freedoms set forth herein," which means not merely that there are no rights to suggest that there are no rights, but far more importantly, that there is no right to challenge the presumption of the state to enjoy the obedience of its subjects.

Moreover, by including in such a declaration rights to "food, clothing, housing and medical care and necessary social services" along side the right to "freedom of thought, conscience and religion," the difference between such "positive entitlements" and rights to noninterference is elided. All rights are grants from the state. Indeed, that is another moment in the conception of freedom, not as "mere" freedom, but as "substantive" freedom, the freedom to do what we are directed to do by the state. As law professors Stephen Holmes and Cass Sunstein put it in their interesting work *The Cost of Rights: Why Liberty Depends on Taxes* "apparently nonwelfare rights are welfare rights too" and "all legal rights are, or aspire to be, welfare rights" (Holmes and Sunstein, 219 and 222).[9]

Discriminating among Stipulations

If there are different conceptions of freedom, are there any reasons to prefer one to another? One can always stipulate that by freedom, or justice, or equality one means this or that and, if the stipulation is clearly understood at the outset, others have little reason to complain. But are there reasons why one stipulation should be preferred to another? Yes, there are.

First, as the apostle of "positive freedom" Thomas Hill Green himself admitted, "As soon as the term 'freedom' comes to be applied to anything else than an established relation between a man and other men, its sense fluctuates much more" (Green 1960, 2). That fluctuation of sense means that some stipulations have disadvantages, at least if we hope to use language precisely. Why is the classical liberal conception of freedom—"mere" freedom, as it were—preferable to the vague and imprecise stipulation offered by advocates for "higher," "real," "true," "substantive" freedom? The "relation between a man and other men" is the historical core of the experience of freedom and the foundation of the concept.[10] Other uses are, at best, analogical, as when we say that one is "freed" from a bad habit or "freed" from ignorance or want. This intellectual territory is also quite well trod and was considered in considerable depth by F. A. Hayek in the opening chapters of *The Constitution of Liberty*:

> It so happens that the meaning of freedom that we have adopted seems to be the original meaning of the word. Man, or at least European man, enters history divided into free and unfree; and this distinction had a very definite meaning. The freedom of the free may have differed widely, but only in the degree of an independence which the slave did not possess at all. It meant always the possibility of a person's acting according to his own decisions and plans, in contrast to the position of one who was irrevocably subject to the will of another, who by arbitrary decision could coerce him to act or not to act in specific ways. The time-honored phrase by which this freedom has often been described is therefore "independence of the arbitrary will of another." (Hayek 1961, 12)

To that we could add a few other reasons, notably that to call wealth or health or intelligence or education or beauty "freedom" because it enables us to do more than those who lack it is to do violence to language; we already have quite good words to denote those concepts, namely, wealth, health, intelligence, education, and beauty. Sen simply confuses the discussion when he writes that "The usefulness of wealth lies in the things that it allows us to do—the substantive freedoms it helps us to achieve" (Sen 1999, 14). By that logic, all kinds of lack of goods "deny freedom." Indeed, according to Sen, "Very many people across the world suffer from varieties of unfreedom. Famines continue to occur in particular regions, denying to millions the basic freedom to survive" (Sen 1999, 15). Do HIV, shark attacks, and traffic accidents also "deny" to people "the basic freedom to survive"? Surviving is a good thing, to be sure, but does anything that gets in the way of surviving count as a denial of freedom? Is freedom just another word for ability?[11] It is hard to see what is added to discourse by such language, other than confusion.

Amartya Sen attempts to seize the high ground in the debate by accusing "the 'libertarian'" (in scare quotes) of "preoccupation with procedures for liberty (with deliberate neglect of consequences that derive from those procedures)," thus confusing the reason for a rule (the consequences) with the rules themselves. It's processes that can be directly addressed by policies, not outcomes.[12] All a policy can set in motion is a process that will result in an outcome. We don't live in a world of magic, in which we have but to say the magic words—"no hunger" or "universal health care"—and those things

35

come to be. What we can affect directly are institutions and incentives, but not outcomes. We create, form, or reform institutions. Institutions form incentives. Incentives form behavior. Behavior forms outcomes. We may evaluate the institutions by the outcomes they generate.[13] In contrast, we can directly impinge on the freedom of another by exercising coercion over her. If I use force to confiscate a person's wealth, I have directly violated his freedom and made him poorer. The loss of wealth is not equivalent to the denial of freedom; it is its consequence.

Those who favor plain, old, evidently uninspiring, merely empirical "freedom"—as distinguished from adjectivally modified "higher," "true," "real," "effective," or "substantive" freedom—have the advantage of using a term to denote something distinct from its consequences. Freedom may lead to more wealth and knowledge, but it does not follow that freedom is wealth or that wealth is freedom, nor that freedom is knowledge or knowledge is freedom. Indeed, scientific investigation of cause and effect relationships is greatly hindered by such confusion. If all good things are freedom, then freedom cannot be isolated as a cause of any of them, for they are all freedom. The best that those who consider all good things to be freedom can do is to distinguish between different "kinds" of freedom, but they fail to inform us of what distinguishes those kinds. Rather than asking whether freedom leads to more prosperity, they have to argue that one kind of freedom leads to another, but without acknowledging what might distinguish one of those "kinds" of freedom from the other.

The simple and unmodified use of the term avoids such political/ linguistic catastrophes as concluding that people living under a technologically more advanced despotism or dictatorship are "freer" because they can do things that people living in less technologically advanced societies cannot. To take the obvious case, very, very few Germans in 1913 could take antibiotics or use machines to peel potatoes or make telephone calls, but it does not follow that Germans in 1939 were "freer" because they could do so. To say that they were wealthier seems quite reasonable; to say that they were freer is absurd.

Finally, there are good epistemic reasons not to identify freedom with those "'capabilities' of persons to lead the kind of lives they value—and have reason to value" (Sen 1999, 18). To say that they "have reason to value" their lives means that they must be justified to others. In other words, in place of a presumption of freedom to live and act, there is a presumption that one must justify one's life and free action to others or be subject to permissible coercion by someone else. That is to say, there is a presumption of permissible prohibitions, rather than of permissible actions. That's why the view of freedom put forth by advocates of "truer," "higher," "real," or "substantive" freedom is typically instantiated in bills of enumerated rights. Things you have reason to value are put on lists of things to which you have rights. Those that you don't have reason to value are left off of lists of things to which you have rights. Thus, the list of enumerated "rights" in the Universal Declaration is concluded by a "duty" to the community, meaning that if something is not enumerated, there is a presumption that it is not a matter of right, but is subject to the power of state compulsion.

A presumption of liberty, the exercise of which needs no specific justification, puts the burden of proof on those who would impede the actions of others. Such a presumption of liberty has an overwhelming advantage. As "A Federal Farmer" noted in 1788, "we often find it easier to enumerate particularly the powers to be delegated to the federal head, than to enumerate particularly the individual rights to be reserved" (Federal Farmer 1981, 401). In the debate over the constitution and whether there should be included an enumeration of rights, James Wilson famously declaimed,

> Enumerate all the rights of men! I am sure, Sir, that no gentleman in the late convention would have attempted such a thing. . . . (Farrand 1911, 162)

Wilson had a good point. You cannot make an exhaustive list of all the things one might freely undertake. You have a right to set your alarm clock for 6:00 AM, or 6:05 AM, or 7:00 AM, or not at all, to wear a hat or not wear a hat, to listen to Brahms, Mozart, or New Sound Theory. As Anthony de Jasay has noted, "the list of feasible actions is indefinitely long" (de Jasay 1996, 24).[14] The presumption of liberty is justified for the same reason—the relative weight of the burden of proof—that justifies the presumption of innocence of the accused and the presumption of possession of property.[15] The burden of proof is on the one who would put one in jail, not on the one who would remain free. Of course, those who follow Rousseau and Thomas Hill Green would have to agree that when they are compelled by violence to do what they ought to do or to refrain from doing what they ought not, to do what they have reason to do and to refrain from what they do not have reason to do, they are not "really" being compelled, punished, or coerced, for they are experiencing "true" freedom.

For clarification, let me turn to the words of a man who understood what it means to be compelled in the name of "higher," "true," "real," "substantive," and "effective" freedom, and in being so liberated to lack simple and unmodified freedom. To live in a society without unmodified freedom is to live in a society in which violence and power can be visited upon one with no reason whatsoever, for no reason had to be given for the exercise of power.[16] In place of the presumption of liberty, he lived in a system based on the presumption of power. I will conclude with the words of Vasily Grossman, a writer for the Red Army paper *Red Star* who witnessed some of the greatest crimes of the twentieth century, all perpetrated in the name of one or another form of "higher" freedom.

In his novel *Forever Flowing*, a work never published in his lifetime, he described the punishment in the USSR of "parasites and nonworking elements," meaning people who created—at night after working for the state by day—sweaters, shoes, bags, food, and other goods. Grossman's character Ivan Grigoryevich concludes,

> I used to think freedom was freedom of speech, freedom of the press, freedom of conscience. But freedom is the whole life of everyone. Here is what it amounts to: You have to have the right to sow what you wish to, to make shoes or coats, to bake into bread the flour ground from the grain you have sown, and to sell it or not sell it as you wish; for the lathe operator, the steelworker, and the artist it's a matter of being able to live as you wish and work as you wish and not as they order you to. And in our country there is no freedom—not for those who write books nor for those who sow grain nor for those who make shoes. (Grossman 1986, 99)

Let us not, then, confuse freedom with ability, capability, knowledge, virtue, health, or wealth. Let us hold up a standard of freedom, expressed in clear and precise terms, not modified by misleading adjectives, and promote that standard to the public, in the knowledge that with freedom—because of freedom—we enjoy prosperity, peace, dignity, knowledge, health, and so many other benefits. But as we enjoy the blessings of freedom, let us not confuse those blessings with freedom itself, for on that path we are led to lose both freedom and its blessings.

References

Applebaum, Anne. 2003. *Gulag: A History*. New York: Doubleday.

Berlin, Isaiah. 2002. "Two Concepts of Liberty," in *Liberty*, ed. Henry Hardy. Oxford: Oxford University Press.

Berman, Harold. 1983. *Law and Revolution: The Formation of the Western Legal Tradition*. Cambridge: Harvard University Press.

Berman, Paul. 2003. "The Philosopher of Islamic Terror," *New York Times Magazine*, March 3.

Black, Antony. 1984. *Guilds and Civil Society in European Political Thought from the Twelfth Century to the Present*. Ithaca, N.Y.: Cornell University Press.

Coleman, Winston R. 1960. "Knowledge and Freedom in the Political Philosophy of Plato," *Ethics* 71(1), October, pp. 41–45.

Constant, Benjamin, 1988. *Political Writings*, ed. Biancamaria Fontana. Cambridge: Cambridge University Press.

Dworkin, Ronald. 1972. "The Jurisprudence of Richard Nixon," *The New York Review of Books* 18(8), May, pp. 27–35.

Farrand, Max, ed. 1911. *The Records of the Federal Convention of 1787, Vol. III*. New Haven, CT: Yale University Press.

Federal Farmer No. 16. 1981. In *The Complete Anti-Federalist, Vol. 5*, ed. Herbert J. Storing. Chicago: University of Chicago Press.

Fustel de Coulanges, Numa Denis. 1956. *The Ancient City*. New York: Doubleday Anchor.

Gallie, W. B. 1956. "Essentially Contested Concepts," *Proceedings of the Aristotelian Society* 56, pp. 167–98.

Godkin, E. L. 1900. "The Eclipse of Liberalism," *The Nation*, August 9, reprinted in *The Libertarian Reader*, ed. David Boaz. New York: The Free Press, 1998, pp. 324–26.

Green, Thomas Hill. 1906. "Lecture on Liberal Legislation and Freedom of Contract," in *Works of Thomas Hill Green*, ed. R. L. Nettleship. London: Longmans, Green, and Co., pp. 365–86.

Green, Thomas Hill. 1960. "On the Different Senses of 'Freedom' as Applied to Will and to the Moral Progress of Man," in *Lectures on the Principles of Political Obligation*. London: Longmans, Green, & Co.

Grossman, Vasily. 1986. *Forever Flowing*, trans. by Thomas P. Whitney. New York: Harper & Row.

Haldane, John J. 1985. "Individuals and the Theory of Justice," *Ratio* 27(2), December, pp. 189–96.

Hayek, F. A. 1961. *The Constitution of Liberty*. Chicago: University of Chicago Press.

Holmes, Stephen, and Sunstein, Cass R. 1999. *The Cost of Rights: Why Liberty Depends on Taxes*. New York: Norton.

de Jasay, Anthony. 1996. *Before Resorting to Politics*. Cheltenham: Edward Elgar.

de Jasay, Anthony. 2005. "Freedom from a Mainly Logical Perspective," *Philosophy* 80, 565–84.

Locke, John. 1988. *Two Treatises of Government*, ed. Peter Laslett. Cambridge: Cambridge University Press.

North, Douglass C. 1991. "Institutions," *Journal of Economic Perspectives* 5(1), Winter, 97–112.

Palmer, Tom G. 1999. "Review of *The Cost of Rights*," Cato Journal 19(2), Fall, 331–36.

Patterson, Orlando. 1991. *Freedom: Volume I, Freedom in the Making of Western Culture.* New York: Basic Books.

Pirenne, Henri. 1937. *Economic and Social History of Medieval Europe.* New York: Harcourt, Brace, Jovanovich.

Planitz, Hans. 1954. *Die Deutsche Stadt im Mittelalter: Von der Römerzeit bis zu den Zunftkämpfen.* Graz-Löln: Böhlau Verlag.

Plato. 1968. *The Republic*, trans. Alan Bloom. New York: Basic Books.

Sandel, Michael. 1982. *Liberalism and the Limits of Justice.* Cambridge: Cambridge University Press.

Sen, Amartya. 1999. *Development as Freedom.* New York: Anchor Books.

Siger of Brabant. 1969. "On the Intellective Soul," in *Medieval Philosophy: From St. Augustine to Nicholas of Cusa*, ed. John F. Wippel and Allan B. Wolter. London: Collier Macmillan Publishers.

Skinner, Quentin. 1978. *The Foundations of Modern Political Thought: Volume Two, The Age of Reformation.* Cambridge: Cambridge University Press.

Skinner, Quentin. 1998. *Liberty before Liberalism.* Cambridge: Cambridge University Press.

Spencer, Herbert. 1884. "The New Toryism," in *Political Essays*, ed. by John Offer (1994). Cambridge: Cambridge University Press.

Taylor, Charles. 1982a. "Atomism," in *Philosophy and the Human Sciences: Philosophical Papers* 2. Cambridge: Cambridge University Press, pp. 187–210.

Taylor, Charles. 1982b. "What's Wrong with Negative Liberty," in *Philosophy and the Human Sciences: Philosophical Papers* 2. Cambridge: Cambridge University Press, pp. 211–29.

Thomas Aquinas. 1968. *On the Unity of the Intellect Against the Averroists.* Milwaukee: Marquette University Press.

Van Parijs, Philippe. 1995. *Real Freedom for All.* Oxford: Oxford University Press.

Notes

1. "I must be actually exercising self-understanding in order to be truly or fully free" (Taylor 1982b, 229).

2. The move from shared understandings to the constitution of a "wider self" is unjustified. As John Haldane remarks, "even if this were granted it would not follow from it that subjects of these relationships are anything other than distinct persons. To suppose otherwise is to infer fallaciously that epistemological considerations enter into the constitution of the object known." That individuals share notions of justice, compassion, and self-understanding does not imply that the boundaries of those individuals melt into a vast fondue of communal understandings, for, as Haldane points out, "Features can only be shared if they attach to bearers which at base are numerically diverse" (Haldane 1985, 195). That is an old debate, and the outlines can be traced quite clearly in the debate between the "Latin Averroists," notably Siger of Brabant, and St. Thomas Aquinas over whether there is one "intellective soul" for all of mankind. The Averroists argued that, for two individuals to know the same

thing, they have to have the same form impressed by the agent intellect into the same material (or possible) intellect; to know the same form, they must share the same material intellect; and, as some sources reported, it was believed by some in the thirteenth century that that thesis had radical implications for the moral responsibilities of the individual. If Peter was saved, then I will be saved too, as we share the same intellective soul, so I am free to engage in whatever sinful behavior I wish, in the knowledge that I will be saved nonetheless. Thomas responded that the impressed intelligible species is not literally the very form of the thing raised to a higher level of intelligibility, but rather that by which we know the thing. (See Siger of Brabant and Thomas Aquinas.)

3. Quentin Skinner identifies a "neo-Roman theory of free states" that he presents as an alternative to liberalism, according to which "a state or nation will be deprived of its liberty if it is merely subject or liable to having its actions determined by the will of anyone other than the representatives of the body politic as a whole" (Skinner 1998, 49). The dichotomy that Skinner asserts between "republicanism" and "liberalism" discounts or ignores the substantial tradition of "liberal republicanism." The discussion on p. 84 ignores the element in the traditional understanding of Locke and others of liberty "a Liberty to dispose, and order, as he lists, his Persons, Actions, Possessions, and his whole Property, within the Allowance of those Laws under which he is; and therein not to be subject to the arbitrary Will of another, but freely follow his own" (Locke 1988, 306).

4. As Fustel de Coulanges found, "The ancients knew . . . neither liberty in private life, liberty in education, nor religious liberty. The human person counted for very little against that holy and almost divine authority which was called country or the state" (Fustel de Coulanges 1956, 222). Indeed, "They did not believe that there could exist any right as against the city and its gods" (Fustel de Coulanges 1956, 223).

5. "The idea that any legitimate polity must originate in an act of consent was of course a scholastic commonplace, one which the followers of Ockham no less than Aquinas had always emphasised" (Skinner 1978, 163).

6. Black notes also that "It is worth noticing how the idea of contract, which was later embodied in a political theory peculiarly suited to the values of civil society, was already acquiring a special status in the Middle Ages. Contractual relations were one thing the feudal world and the world of commerce had in common. Mutual trust that contracts will be honoured, bills paid and goods delivered was a prerequisite for the development of trade. The Roman law jurists were the first to introduce contract into political theory" (Black 1984, 37).

7. For a flavor, see Berman 2003.

8. For the right to travel, see *Kent v. Dulles*, 357 U.S. 116 (1958).

9. I display the logical incoherence of their thesis in my review of *The Cost of Rights*, in *Cato Journal* 19(2), Fall 1999, and also in "Saving Rights Theory from Its Friends," reprinted in this volume. Some even identify the receipt of benefits from the state as the experience of "real freedom," including the "freedom" to live one's life as a surfer who refuses to work to produce wealth and is instead supported entirely by the taxpayers. See Van Parijs 1995.

10. "[S]ome notion of freedom existed wherever slavery was found" (Patterson 1991, 41).

11. For example, "In the foregoing discussion, I have been concentrating on a very elementary freedom: the ability to survive rather than succumb to premature mortality" (Sen 1999, 24). Sen also refers to "basic capabilities and effective freedoms"

(19), suggesting that he equates "capability" with "effective freedom." It is not clear what work is being done by the word "effective."

12. "The gaining of a popular good, being the external conspicuous trait common to Liberal measures in earlier days (then in each case gained by a relaxation of restraints), it has happened that popular good has come to be sought by Liberals, not as an end to be indirectly gained by relaxation of restraints, but as the end to be gained directly. And seeking to gain it directly, they have used methods intrinsically opposed to those originally used" (Spencer 1884, 69). Compare E. L. Godkin, writing in *The Nation* in 1900, "To the principles and precepts of Liberalism the prodigious material progress of the age was largely due. Freed from the vexatious meddling of governments, men devoted themselves to their natural task, the bettering of their condition, with the wonderful results which surround us. But it now seems that its material comfort has blinded the eyes of the present generation to the cause which made it possible. In the politics of the world, Liberalism is a declining, almost a defunct force" (Godkin 1900, 105–06).

13. "Institutions provide the incentive structure of an economy; as that structure evolves, it shapes the direction of economic change towards growth, stagnation, or decline" (North 1991, 97).

14. "There are two rival presumptions: 'everything is admitted that is not specifically excluded,' and 'everything is excluded that is not specifically admitted.' Whichever hypothesis is adopted, either the list of excluded, or the list of admitted actions is sufficient for identifying any action as either admitted or not. Both are not needed for guidances in choosing actions. However, the list of feasible actions is indefinitely long. Compiling the full list of interdictions is, under ordinary circumstances, a less onerous task than compiling a full list of permissions; enumerating what we must not do, and monitoring that we not do it, are less exacting than listing what we have a right to do, and monitoring that we do not do what we have no right to do" (de Jasay 1996, 24).

15. "It takes no particular insight to realise that the presumptions of innocence and of property are special cases of the presumption of liberty. They are derived by the same source in the asymmetry between verification and falsification" (de Jasay 2005, 575).

16. "Starting in 1937, [Stalin] signed orders which were sent to the regional NKVD bosses, listing quotas of people to be arrested (no cause was given) in particular regions. Some were to be sentenced to the 'first category' of punishment—death—and others to be given the 'second category'—confinement in concentration camps for a term ranging from eight to ten years" (Applebaum 2003, 94).

4. Myths of Individualism

It has recently been asserted that libertarians, or classical liberals, actually think that "individual agents are fully formed and their value preferences are in place prior to and outside of any society." They "ignore robust social scientific evidence about the ill effects of isolation," and, yet more shocking, they "actively oppose the notion of 'shared values' or the idea of 'the common good.'" I am quoting from the 1995 presidential address of Professor Amitai Etzioni to the American Sociological Association (*American Sociological Review*, February 1996). As a frequent talk show guest and as editor of the journal *The Responsive Community*, Etzioni has come to some public prominence as a publicist for a political movement known as communitarianism.

Etzioni is hardly alone in making such charges. They come from both left and right. From the left, *Washington Post* columnist E. J. Dionne Jr. argued in his book *Why Americans Hate Politics* that "the growing popularity of the libertarian cause suggested that many Americans had even given up on the possibility of a 'common good,'" and in a recent essay in the *Washington Post Magazine*, that "the libertarian emphasis on the freewheeling individual seems to assume that individuals come into the world as fully formed adults who should be held responsible for their actions from the moment of birth." From the right, the late Russell Kirk, in a vitriolic article titled "Libertarians: The Chirping Sectaries," claimed that "the perennial libertarian, like Satan, can bear no authority, temporal or spiritual" and that "the libertarian does not venerate ancient beliefs and customs, or the natural world, or his country, or the immortal spark in his fellow men."

More politely, Sen. Dan Coats (R-Ind.) and David Brooks of the *Weekly Standard* have excoriated libertarians for allegedly ignoring the value of community. Defending his proposal for more federal

Originally published in *Cato Policy Report* 18, no. 5, September/October 1996.

programs to "rebuild" community, Coats wrote that his bill is "self-consciously conservative, not purely libertarian. It recognizes, not only individual rights, but the contribution of groups rebuilding the social and moral infrastructure of their neighborhoods." The implication is that individual rights are somehow incompatible with participation in groups or neighborhoods.

Such charges, which are coming with increasing frequency from those opposed to classical liberal ideals, are never substantiated by quotations from classical liberals; nor is any evidence offered that those who favor individual liberty and limited constitutional government actually think as charged by Etzioni and his echoes. Absurd charges often made and not rebutted can come to be accepted as truths, so it is imperative that Etzioni and other communitarian critics of individual liberty be called to account for their distortions.

Atomistic Individualism

Let us examine the straw man of "atomistic individualism" that Etzioni, Dionne, Kirk, and others have set up. The philosophical roots of the charge have been set forth by communitarian critics of classical liberal individualism, such as the philosopher Charles Taylor and the political scientist Michael Sandel. For example, Taylor claims that, because libertarians believe in individual rights and abstract principles of justice, they believe in "the self-sufficiency of man alone, or, if you prefer, of the individual." That is an updated version of an old attack on classical liberal individualism, according to which classical liberals posited "abstract individuals" as the basis for their views about justice.

Those claims are nonsense. No one believes that there are actually "abstract individuals," for all individuals are necessarily concrete. Nor are there any truly "self-sufficient" individuals, as any reader of *The Wealth of Nations* would realize. Rather, classical liberals and libertarians argue that the *system of justice* should abstract from the concrete characteristics of individuals. Thus, when an individual comes before a court, her height, color, wealth, social standing, and religion are normally irrelevant to questions of justice. That is what equality before the law means; it does not mean that no one actually *has* a particular height, skin color, or religious belief. Abstraction is a mental process we use when trying to discern what is essential or relevant to a problem; it does not require a belief in abstract entities.

It is precisely because neither individuals nor small groups can be fully self-sufficient that cooperation is necessary to human survival and flourishing. And because that cooperation takes place among countless individuals unknown to each other, the rules governing that interaction are abstract in nature. Abstract rules, which establish in advance what we may expect of one another, make cooperation possible on a wide scale.

No reasonable person could possibly believe that individuals are fully formed outside society—in isolation, if you will. That would mean that no one could have had any parents, cousins, friends, personal heroes, or even neighbors. Obviously, all of us have been influenced by those around us. What libertarians assert is simply that differences among normal adults do not imply different fundamental rights.

Sources and Limits of Obligations

Libertarianism is not at base a metaphysical theory about the primacy of the individual over the abstract, much less an absurd theory about "abstract individuals." Nor is it an anomic rejection of traditions, as Kirk and some conservatives have charged. Rather, it is a political theory that emerged in response to the growth of unlimited state power; libertarianism draws its strength from a powerful fusion of a normative theory about the moral and political sources and limits of obligations and a positive theory explaining the sources of order. Each person has the right to be free, and free persons can produce order spontaneously, without a commanding power over them.

What of Dionne's patently absurd characterization of libertarianism: "individuals come into the world as fully formed adults who should be held responsible for their actions from the moment of birth"? Libertarians recognize the difference between adults and children, as well as differences between normal adults and adults who are insane or mentally hindered or retarded. Guardians are necessary for children and abnormal adults, because they cannot make responsible choices for themselves. But there is no obvious reason for holding that some normal adults are entitled to make choices for other normal adults, as paternalists of both left and right believe. Libertarians argue that no normal adult has the right to

45

impose choices on other normal adults, except in abnormal circumstances, such as when one person finds another unconscious and administers medical assistance or calls an ambulance.

What distinguishes libertarianism from other views of political morality is principally its theory of *enforceable* obligations. Some obligations, such as the obligation to write a thank-you note to one's host after a dinner party, are not normally enforceable by force. Others, such as the obligation to not punch a disagreeable critic in the nose or to pay for a pair of shoes before walking out of the store in them, are. Obligations may be universal or particular. Individuals, whoever and wherever they may be (i.e., in abstraction from particular circumstances), have an enforceable obligation to all other persons: not to harm them in their lives, liberties, health, or possessions. In John Locke's terms, "Being all equal and independent, no one ought to harm another in his life, health, liberty, or possessions." All individuals have the right that others not harm them in their enjoyment of those goods. The rights and the obligations are correlative and, being both universal and "negative" in character, are capable under normal circumstances of being enjoyed by all simultaneously. It is the *universality* of the human right not to be killed, injured, or robbed that is at the base of the libertarian view, and one need not posit an "abstract individual" to assert the universality of that right. It is his veneration, not his contempt, for the "immortal spark in his fellow men" that leads the libertarian to defend individual rights.

Those obligations are universal, but what about "particular" obligations? As I write this, I am sitting in a coffee house and have just ordered another coffee. I have freely undertaken the particular obligation to pay for the coffee: I have transferred a property right to a certain amount of my money to the owner of the coffee shop, and she has transferred the property right to the cup of coffee to me. Libertarians typically argue that particular obligations, at least under normal circumstances, must be created by consent; they cannot be unilaterally imposed by others. Equality of rights means that some people cannot simply impose obligations on others, for the moral agency and rights of those others would then be violated. Communitarians, on the other hand, argue that we all are born with many particular obligations, such as to give to this body of persons— called a state or, more nebulously, a nation, community, or folk— so much money, so much obedience, or even one's life. And they argue that those particular obligations can be coercively enforced. In fact, according to communitarians such as Taylor and Sandel, I am actually *constituted as a person*, not only by the facts of my upbringing and my experiences, but also by a set of very particular unchosen obligations.

To repeat, communitarians maintain that we are constituted as persons by our particular obligations, and therefore those obligations cannot be a matter of choice. Yet that is a mere assertion and cannot substitute for an *argument* that one is obligated to others; it is no justification for coercion. One might well ask, if an individual is born with the obligation to obey, who is born with the right to command? If one wants a coherent theory of obligations, there must be someone, whether an individual or a group, with the right to the fulfillment of the obligation. If I am constituted as a person by my obligation to obey, who is constituted as a person by the right to obedience? Such a theory of obligation may have been coherent in an age of god-kings, but it seems rather out of place in the modern world. To sum up, no reasonable person believes in the existence of abstract individuals, and the true dispute between libertarians and communitarians is not about individualism as such but about the source of particular obligations, whether imposed or freely assumed.

Groups and Common Goods

A theory of obligation focusing on individuals does *not* mean that there is no such "thing" as society or that we cannot speak meaningfully of groups. The fact that there are trees does not mean that we cannot speak of forests, after all. Society is not merely a collection of individuals, nor is it some "bigger or better" thing separate from them. Just as a building is not a pile of bricks but the bricks *and* the relationships among them, society is not a person, with his own rights, but many individuals *and* the complex set of relationships among them.

A moment's reflection makes it clear that claims that libertarians reject "shared values" and the "common good" are incoherent. If libertarians share the value of liberty (at a minimum), then they cannot "actively oppose the notion of 'shared values,'" and if libertarians believe that we will all be better off if we enjoy freedom, then they have not "given up on the possibility of 'a common good,'" for a central part of their efforts is to assert what the common good is!

In response to Kirk's claim that libertarians reject tradition, let me point out that libertarians defend a tradition of liberty that is the fruit of thousands of years of human history. In addition, pure traditionalism is incoherent, for traditions may clash, and then one has no guide to right action. Generally, the statement that libertarians "reject tradition" is both tasteless and absurd. Libertarians follow religious traditions, family traditions, ethnic traditions, and social traditions such as courtesy and even respect for others, which is evidently not a tradition Kirk thought it necessary to maintain.

The libertarian case for individual liberty, which has been so distorted by communitarian critics, is simple and reasonable. It is obvious that different individuals require different things to live good, healthy, and virtuous lives. Despite their common nature, people are materially and numerically individuated, and we have needs that differ. So, how far does our common good extend?

Karl Marx, an early and especially brilliant and biting communitarian critic of libertarianism, asserted that civil society is based on a "decomposition of man" such that man's "essence is no longer in community but in difference"; under socialism, in contrast, man would realize his nature as a "species being." Accordingly, socialists believe that collective provision of everything is appropriate; in a truly socialized state, we would all enjoy the same common good, and conflict simply would not occur. Communitarians are typically much more cautious, but despite a lot of talk, they rarely tell us much about what our common good might be. The communitarian philosopher Alasdair MacIntyre, for instance, in his influential book *After Virtue*, insists for 219 pages that there is a "good life for man" that must be pursued in common and then rather lamely concludes that "the good life for man is the life spent in seeking for the good life for man."

A familiar claim is that providing retirement security through the state is an element of the common good, for it "brings all of us together." But who is included in "all of us"? Actuarial data show that African-American males who have paid the same taxes into the Social Security system as have Caucasian males over their working lives stand to get back about half as much. Further, more black than white males will die before they receive a single penny, meaning all of their money has gone to benefit others and none of their "investments" are available to their families. In other words, they are being robbed for the benefit of nonblack retirees. Are African-American males part of the "all of us" who are enjoying a common good, or are they victims of the "common good" of others? (As readers of *Cato Policy Report* should know, all would be better off under a privatized system, which leads libertarians to assert the common good of freedom to choose among retirement systems.) All too often, claims about the "common good" serve as covers for quite selfish attempts to secure private goods; as the classical liberal Austrian novelist Robert Musil noted in his great work *The Man without Qualities*, "Nowadays only criminals dare to harm others without philosophy."

Libertarians recognize the inevitable pluralism of the modern world and for that reason assert that individual liberty is at least part of the common good. They also understand the absolute necessity of cooperation for the attainment of one's ends; a solitary individual could never actually *be* "self-sufficient," which is precisely why we must have rules—governing property and contracts, for example— to make peaceful cooperation possible and why we institute government to enforce those rules. The common good is a system of justice that allows all to live together in harmony and peace; a common good more extensive than that tends to be not a common good for "all of us," but a common good for some of us at the expense of others of us. (There is another sense, understood by every parent, to the term "self-sufficiency." Parents normally desire that their children acquire the virtue of "pulling their own weight" and not subsisting as scroungers, layabouts, moochers, or parasites. That is a necessary condition of self-respect; Taylor and other critics of libertarianism often confuse the virtue of self-sufficiency with the impossible condition of never relying on or cooperating with others.)

The issue of the common good is related to the beliefs of communitarians regarding the personality or the separate existence of groups. Both are part and parcel of a fundamentally unscientific and irrational view of politics that tends to personalize institutions and groups, such as the state or nation or society. Instead of enriching political science and avoiding the alleged naiveté of libertarian individualism, as communitarians claim, however, the personification thesis obscures matters and prevents us from asking the interesting questions with which scientific inquiry begins. No one ever put the matter quite as well as the classical liberal historian Parker T. Moon

of Columbia University in his study of 19th-century European imperialism, *Imperialism and World Politics*:

> Language often obscures truth. More than is ordinarily
> realized, our eyes are blinded to the facts of international
> relations by tricks of the tongue. When one uses the simple
> monosyllable "France" one thinks of France as a unit, an
> entity. When to avoid awkward repetition we use a personal
> pronoun in referring to a country—when for example we
> say "France sent *her* troops to conquer Tunis"—we impute
> not only unity but personality to the country. The very words
> conceal the facts and make international relations a glamor-
> ous drama in which personalized nations are the actors, and
> all too easily we forget the flesh-and-blood men and women
> who are the true actors. How different it would be if we had
> no such word as "France," and had to say instead—thirty-
> eight million men, women and children of very diversified
> interests and beliefs, inhabiting 218,000 square miles of terri-
> tory! Then we should more accurately describe the Tunis
> expedition in some such way as this: "A few of these thirty-
> eight million persons sent thirty thousand others to conquer
> Tunis." This way of putting the fact immediately suggests a
> question, or rather a series of questions. Who are the "few"?
> Why did they send the thirty thousand to Tunis? And why
> did these obey?

Group personification obscures, rather than illuminates, important political questions. Those questions, centering mostly around
the explanation of complex political phenomena and moral responsibility, simply cannot be addressed within the confines of group
personification, which drapes a cloak of mysticism around the
actions of policymakers, thus allowing some to use "philosophy"—
and mystical philosophy, at that—to harm others.

Libertarians are separated from communitarians by differences on
important issues, notably whether coercion is necessary to maintain
community, solidarity, friendship, love, and the other things that
make life worth living and that can be enjoyed only in common
with others. Those differences cannot be swept away a priori; their
resolution is not furthered by shameless distortion, absurd characterizations, or petty name-calling.

5. Saving Rights Theory from Its Friends

Rights are an integral part of the American experiment. They enjoy pride of place in the founding document of American independence, which famously proclaims

> that all men are created equal, that they are endowed by their creator with certain unalienable rights, that among these are life, liberty, and the pursuit of happiness; that to secure these rights, governments are instituted among men, deriving their just powers from the consent of the governed.

Perhaps because securing the mere "pursuit" of happiness does not guarantee success, or perhaps because "pursuit" seems such an elastic term, some modern interpreters of this tradition of rights believe that new rights can be and are coined by the legislature. Some seem to believe that since rights are such good things, the more of them we have, the better off we are. Hence, whenever we determine that something is good—education, housing, or the general condition of well-being we refer to as "welfare"—then legislatures should recognize rights, not merely to pursue those things, but to have them. Others have perceived that rights can be "costly," precisely because they normally imply some restriction or obligation for others, and therefore that we should coin only those rights whose benefits (to whomever) are greater than their costs. The coining of "new rights" in recent years has led to such absurdities that some have proposed a moratorium on rights talk, or even dispensing with rights talk altogether.

It has long been recognized that the subject of rights is fraught with difficulty, partly because all talk of moral obligation is difficult (the is-ought problem always raises its head) and partly because of

---

Originally published in *Individual Rights Reconsidered: Are the Truths of the U.S. Declaration of Independence Lasting?* edited by Tibor Machan. Stanford, CA: Hoover Institution Press, 2001.

the wide variety of existing or possible rights regimes and the difficulty of settling on just what does or does not qualify as a right. Recently to these age-old problems of moral and political philosophy have been added far more serious problems of logical coherence. As a result, it would not be too strong a statement to say that there is a crisis in rights theory.

How to straighten out the tangled knot that rights talk has become? I propose a conceptual clarification of what we mean by rights, undertaken first by means of a critique of some prominent critics of traditional rights theory and then by means of a brief excursus through the history of the concept of rights that informed the American founding. Like all concepts, discourse about rights must be guided by logic, and the use of logic may help us to arrive at a coherent and useful conception of rights. Also, like all concepts, the concept of rights has a history, and that history may help us to get straight on what rights are.

Incoherent Rights Talk

I'll begin with a look at a work on rights by two leading legal philosophers. I do so not only because of the prominence of the work's authors but also because the problems revealed in their work are symptomatic of the current crisis in rights theory. Stephen Holmes and Cass R. Sunstein, in *The Cost of Rights: Why Liberty Depends on Taxes*, propose to achieve "enhanced clarity of focus" by considering "exclusively rights that are enforceable by politically organized communities."[1] They declare, "Under American law, rights are powers granted by the political community."[2] It's not at all clear from the text what Holmes and Sunstein mean by "American law," for all of their claims are purely conceptual and have no connection with distinctly American jurisprudence or history. In addition, of course, it flies in the face of the explicit declarations of the Declaration of Independence and the Constitution of the United States of America. But let's set that aside and turn to their philosophical arguments on behalf of the idea that rights are purely creatures of the state.

Holmes and Sunstein seek in their work to eliminate even the possibility of a conceptual distinction between "negative" rights to noninterference (the right not to be murdered, for example, or the right to free exercise of religion) and "positive" or "welfare" rights (such as the right to a subsidized education or to a house built by another person). They argue that "apparently nonwelfare rights are welfare rights too" and that "all legal rights are, or aspire to be, welfare rights."[3] Thus, they see no difference between the right to the "pursuit" of happiness and the right to happiness itself (or to a house, an education, or some other benefit); all rights are "powers granted by the political community."[4]

Holmes and Sunstein identify the traditional view of rights with "opposition to government," which would be a confusion, for, as they note, "individual rights and freedoms depend fundamentally on vigorous state action."[5] More radically, "Statelessness spells rightslessness."[6] But what they intend by the term "depend fundamentally" is not

> that to secure these rights, governments are instituted among men, deriving their just powers from the consent of the governed; that whenever any form of government becomes destructive of these ends, it is the right of the people to alter or to abolish it, and to institute new government, laying its foundation on such principles, and organizing its powers in such form, as to them shall seem most likely to effect their safety and happiness.

Nor do they seem to mean that

> We the people of the United States, in order to form a more perfect union, establish justice, insure domestic tranquility, provide for the common defense, promote the general welfare, and secure the blessings of liberty to ourselves and our posterity, do ordain and establish this Constitution for the United States of America.

Under the traditional conception, the people are endowed with rights, some of which (the execution of their natural rights) they give up in order to enter civil society and which they then transfer to a government in order to defend those rights they have "retained." But, apparently finding this approach incompatible with their own philosophical orientation or agenda, Holmes and Sunstein assert as a truism that government creates rights *ex nihilo* and that this is a matter of "American law." These authors brush aside discussion of moral rights and consider only legal rights—those rights that a state will actually enforce—on the ground that "When they are not backed by legal force, by contrast, moral rights are toothless by definition. Unenforced moral rights are aspirations binding on conscience, not powers binding on officials."[7]

A careful look at the theory advanced by Holmes and Sunstein will go far in showing the profound conceptual and logical problems inherent in attempts to replace the traditional approach to rights articulated by and embodied in the Declaration of Independence and the United States Constitution.

Holmes and Sunstein ground their attempt to erase the distinction between negative and positive rights on a commonsense observation: All choices have costs. That is a conceptual or analytical claim, for to choose X over Y is to give up Y, which (if it is the most highly valued alternative forgone) is defined as the cost of choosing X. This is unobjectionable, thus far. They proceed to note that the act of choosing to enforce a right, like all choices, has a cost—namely, the most highly valued opportunity forgone. Combining that insight with the claim that the only rights that are meaningful are those that are actually enforced, they conclude that since the enforcement of rights has costs, rights themselves have costs. Thus the subtitle to the book: *Why Liberty Depends on Taxes*. All acts of enforcement have costs and require the mobilization of resources—police, judges, jailers, executioners, and so on—and are therefore positive claims on the expenditure of taxes (or other forms of compulsion; conscription would fill the bill as well as taxation) to secure those resources. The right not to be killed is thereby converted into the right to police protection, which entails the expenditure of resources and therefore choices among alternative uses of those resources. Thus, the allegedly "negative" right not to be killed is indistinguishable from the "positive" right to the expenditure of resources to hire or conscript police.

According to Holmes and Sunstein,

> Rights are costly because remedies are costly. Enforcement is expensive, especially uniform and fair enforcement; and legal rights are hollow to the extent that they remain unenforced. Formulated differently, almost every right implies a correlative duty, and duties are taken seriously only when dereliction is punished by the public power drawing on the public purse.[8]

Even "the right against being tortured by police officers and prison guards" is, contrary to traditional thinking, not a negative right against interference but a positive right to have monitors hired by the state to supervise the police officers and prison guards:

> A state that cannot arrange prompt visits to jails and prisons by taxpayer-salaried doctors, prepared to submit credible evidence at trial, cannot effectively protect the incarcerated against torture and beatings. All rights are costly because all rights presuppose taxpayer-funding of effective supervisory machinery for monitoring and enforcement.[9]

Here their theory begins to run into very serious logical difficulties, for the account of rights and obligations on which they base that theory generates an infinite regress.

Holmes and Sunstein argue that I cannot have a right not to be tortured by the police unless the police have an obligation not to torture me, and the police can only have an obligation not to torture me if there are some taxpayer-funded persons (monitors) above the police who can punish them (since "duties are taken seriously only when dereliction is punished by the public power drawing on the public purse"). So to have a right not to be tortured by the police, I would have to have a right that the monitors exercise their power to punish the police in the event that the police torture me. But do I have a right that the monitors exercise their power to punish the police for torturing me? According to Holmes and Sunstein, I would have such a right only if the monitors had a duty to punish the police, and the monitors would have a duty to punish the police only if there were some taxpayer-funded persons above the monitors who could (and would) punish the monitors for failing to punish the police, and so on, ad infinitum. For there ever to be a right of any sort, by their own reasoning, there would have to be an infinite hierarchy of people threatening to punish those lower in the hierarchy. Since there is no infinite hierarchy, we are forced to conclude that Holmes and Sunstein have actually offered an impossibility theorem of rights in the logical form of *modus tollens*: If there are rights, then there must be an infinite hierarchy of power; there is not an infinite hierarchy of power, therefore there are no rights.

In working out their theory, Holmes and Sunstein generate not "clarity of focus" but logical chaos and incoherence.

The theory of liberty that Holmes and Sunstein advance also leads to strange conclusions. Holmes and Sunstein use the terms "rights" and "liberty" interchangeably, not only in the title of the book but also in the text.[10] Taking their definition of a right as an interest that "qualifies as a right when an effective legal system treats it as such by using collective resources to defend it,"[11] and treating "rights" and "liberty" as interchangeable terms, we are justified in deducing the following:

- If I have an interest in not taking habit-forming drugs, and
- If the state uses collective resources to stop me from taking drugs, then
- I have a right that the state use collective resources to stop me from taking drugs.

Let us stipulate that the state places me in prison in order to keep me from taking drugs (and let's set aside the fact that real states have failed to keep drugs out of prison). Since to have my rights enforced is to enjoy the protection of my liberty, by putting me in prison the state is making me free. Indeed, if the state were somehow to fail to imprison me, they would be violating my rights. (But then, if the right were not actually enforced by the state, it would be no right. Trying to follow the implications of their theory is like thinking out the implications of the elevation of evil to good by the members of "The Addams Family." Ultimately, the attempt collapses into incoherence.)

Finally, the theory Holmes and Sunstein advance collapses into circularity by page 203 of the book, which contains the first consideration of "moral ideas" since the introduction, where moral rights were dismissed in order to achieve "an enhanced clarity of focus." After maintaining for over 200 pages that rights are dependent upon power, which they defined as the power to impose punishment (again, "duties are taken seriously only when dereliction is punished by the public power drawing on the public purse"), they make the following startling admission: "The dependency of rights on power does not spell cynicism because power itself has various sources. It arises not from money or office or social status alone. It also comes from moral ideas capable of rallying organized social support."[12]

The example they give is the civil rights movement, which brought the state into protecting the civil rights of African Americans. But if moral ideas count as a form of "power," then what is the justification for the dismissal of moral rights at the outset? Could we not say that a police officer should abstain from torturing me firstly because it is a wicked and immoral thing to do—because it is a violation of my right not to be tortured—and not merely because the officer fears being punished by his superiors, who, in turn, must fear being punished by their superiors? Their theory becomes circular when they incorporate "moral ideas" into their definition of power, which was offered as an alternative to moral ideas in the first place.

The point of the foregoing is not merely to pummel two harmless law professors, no matter how much they may deserve it,[13] but also to illustrate the conceptual problems inherent in recent attempts to formulate theories of rights. The problem with much contemporary rights theorizing goes deeper than the logical chaos generated by Holmes and Sunstein in their attempt to jettison traditional rights thinking. It afflicts the background understandings of rights with which Holmes and Sunstein combine their claim that all rights are "powers granted by the political community." To understand those deeper problems, I turn to the work of two other distinguished contemporary theorists of rights, Joseph Raz and Ronald Dworkin.

In his book *The Morality of Freedom*, Raz defines a right as follows, "'X has a right' if and only if X can have rights, and, other things being equal, an aspect of X's well-being (his interest) is a sufficient reason for holding some other person(s) to be under a duty."[14] Raz rejects one of the mainstays of traditional rights theory, the thesis that rights and duties are (at least normally) correlative: "A right of one person is not a duty on another. It is the ground of a duty, ground which, if not counteracted by conflicting considerations, justifies holding that other person to have a duty."[15]

Thus, for Raz, to assert a right is not necessarily to assert any duty on the part of another person, whether that duty has a negative or a positive character. Rather, asserting a right merely offers a *reason* to hold another person under a duty, but that reason may be overridden by some greater reason, and it is the balance of reasons that determines whether that person is held under a duty or not.

Similarly, the rights theorist Ronald Dworkin has defined rights as "trumps," but these "trumps" seem simply to serve as weights rather than as trumps as understood by players of card games:

> Individual rights are political trumps held by individuals. Individuals have rights when, for some reason, a collective goal is not a sufficient justification for denying them what

they wish, as individuals, to have or to do, or not a sufficient justification for imposing some loss or injury upon them.[16]

Further,

No one has a political right (on my account) unless the reasons for giving him what he asks are stronger than some collective justification that normally provides a full political justification for a decision.[17]

When rights are grounded in this or a similar manner, they have, as Raz notes, "a dynamical character," that is to say, they change in often quite unpredictable ways; in particular, they change in ways unpredictable to the citizenry generally.[18] Thus, some citizens may have thought that they had the right "peaceably to assemble, and to petition the government for a redress of grievances" (First Amendment) or the right to "be secure in their persons, houses, papers, and effects, against unreasonable searches and seizures" (Fourth Amendment), but, without their knowledge, something had changed such that those rights articulated in the First and Fourth Amendments no longer generated any duties on the government or on their fellow citizens to allow (or refrain from prohibiting) them to assemble peaceably and petition the government for a redress of grievances or to allow them to be secure in their persons, houses, papers, and effects. Let us say that some other citizens had been discovered (perhaps by the legislature) to have some new interest in overriding those rights, possibly because they were offended by the speeches given at the peaceable assemblies of their fellow citizens or because they wanted to have the persons, papers, or effects of their fellow citizens. Then, the existence of such interests might easily be construed to generate some reason(s) to hold the first group of citizens under a duty. If so, then the second group of citizens would have a right to override the rights of the first group. But even that is not a sufficient reason for the state to override the rights secured by the First and Fourth Amendments, for the balance of rights would have to be such that the rights of the second group would outweigh the first, thus generating a duty on the part of the first to submit to the second. Just as surely as interests conflict, rights will conflict, when construed in the manner of Raz, Dworkin, and their followers.

58

Put in more concrete terms, if I have an interest in taking your farm or in stopping you from making remarks that I consider demeaning, there is a case to be made that I have a right to take your farm or to suppress your speech. If either the balance of reasons (Raz) or the "collective goal" (Dworkin) is weightier than your claim to your farm or to your speech, then you have a duty to submit to the confiscation of your farm or the suppression of your speech.

This might be made more clear if we consider a product of this general approach to rights, the Universal Declaration of Human Rights adopted by the United Nations in 1948. According to Article 24,

> Everyone has the right to rest and leisure, including reasonable limitation of working hours and periodic holidays with pay.

And according to Article 25,

> Everyone has the right to a standard of living adequate for the health and well-being of himself and of his family, including food, clothing, housing and medical care and necessary social services, and the right to security in the event of unemployment, sickness, disability, widowhood, old age or other lack of livelihood in circumstances beyond his control.

Let us say that Bill needs medical care and necessary social services and that Janet is a doctor. If Bill has the right to Janet's services (Article 25), but Janet has the right to rest, leisure, reasonable working hours, and periodic holidays with pay (Article 24), and those conflict (as they surely do on occasions), whose rights will be realized?[19]

One of the defenders of the "interest theory" propounded by Raz, Jeremy Waldron, rather cheerfully admits that rights construed in this manner will not only be "dynamic" but will also generate conflicts as a matter of course:

> I shall argue as follows: first, that if rights are understood along the lines of the Interest Theory propounded by Joseph Raz, then conflicts of rights must be regarded as more or less inevitable; second, that rights on this conception should be thought of, not as correlative to single duties, but as generating a multiplicity of duties; and third, that this multiplicity stands in the way of any tidy or single-minded account of

the way in which the resolution of rights conflicts should be approached.[20]

Waldron takes up the challenge to such interests-as-rights (or rights-as-interests) theories, laid down by Maurice Cranston, a defender of a more traditional liberal rights conception. According to Cranston,

> If it is impossible for a thing to be done, it is absurd to claim it as a right. At present it is utterly impossible, and will be for a long time yet, to provide "holidays with pay" [per Article 24, Universal Declaration of Human Rights] for everybody in the world.[21]

Cranston offered the criterion of possibility as part of a critique of those who argue that leisure, income, health care, housing, and so on are "human rights"; he does not deny that we have interests in such goods, but merely notes that "ought" implies "can" and asks how something that is impossible can be considered a right. Waldron's response to Cranston's critique of such claims trades on an equivocal use of terms rather than grappling with the very real problem that Cranston raises:

> But for each of the inhabitants of these regions, it is not the case that his government is unable to secure holidays with pay, or medical care, or education, or other aspects of welfare, *for him*. Indeed, it can probably do so (and does!) for a fair number of its citizens, leaving it an open question who these lucky individuals are to be. For any inhabitant of these regions, a claim might sensibly be made that his interest in basic welfare is sufficiently important to justify holding the government to be under a duty to provide it, and it would be a duty that the government is capable of performing.
>
> So, in each case, the putative right does satisfy the test of practicability. The problems posed by scarcity and underdevelopment only arise when we take all the claims of right together. It is not the duties in each individual case which demand the impossible . . . rather it is the combination of all the duties taken together which cannot be fulfilled.
>
> But one of the important features of rights discourse is that rights are attributed to individuals one by one, not collectively or in the aggregate.[22]

In other words, if one person could be provided with all of these goods, then every person has a right to have all of them. The error in the response is to take the idea that rights inhere in individuals and interpret it to mean that rights claims must be examined one at a time, in isolation from all other rights claims, rather than altogether. But there is nothing in the idea of individual rights that requires such an approach. The upshot of Waldron's response is that for each person whose right is respected, another must see his or her right denied, creating a "zero-sum game" of rights. But it is precisely a feature of rights that they are supposed to make social life possible, not impossible.

In John Locke's words,

> The duties of life are not at variance with one another, nor do they arm men against one another—a result which, secondly, follows of necessity from the preceding assumption, for upon it men were, as they say, by the law of nature in a state of war; so all society is abolished and all trust, which is the bond of society.[23]

Compounding the strange and unwarranted interpretation of individualism to mean claims-taken-in-isolation-and-without-regard-to-any-other-claims is the naïveté Waldron exhibits when considering as a mere detail "the open question of who these lucky individuals are to be." Does Waldron expect a lottery to be held in poor countries in which governments have the power to determine who these "lucky individuals are to be," or does he think some sort of favoritism (familial, ethnic, bribe-induced, tribal, religious, or the like) might be more likely? (The question virtually answers itself.)

Raz's and Waldron's approaches to rights effectively dispense with rights, for a conception of rights that entails that "conflicts of rights must be regarded as more or less inevitable" still leaves us with the problem of how to decide among conflicting claims. And since each of the parties to a conflict of rights is already stipulated to have the right, then the conflict cannot be decided on the basis of rights. Some principle other than right must be invoked to resolve the conflict. In Raz's and Waldron's formulations of rights, rights become otiose, a useless ornament decorating a system of jurisprudence that seeks to order society on some other, unspecified basis.[24]

Matthew H. Kramer glosses the problems of conflict generated by such theories as follows:

> Unlike a duty to do φ and a liberty to abstain from doing
> φ, a duty to do φ and a duty to abstain from doing φ are
> not starkly contradictory. They are in conflict rather than in
> contradiction. Though the fulfillment of either one must rule
> out the fulfillment of the other, the existence of either one
> does not in any way preclude the existence of the other.[25]

That is to say, the two statements are not logically contradictory; only the fulfillment of the duties they enjoin is impossible. (Some) logicians may be comforted by such remarks, but the parties to social conflict probably will not be. Experience shows that political power and influence, not to mention brute force and violence, come readily to mind as likely resolutions to such conflicts, which—by stipulation—cannot be resolved on the basis of rights.

Even further along the spectrum of illiberal rights theorists is Attracta Ingram, who presents us with a "rights" theory in which rights are not merely made otiose but are also effectively annulled altogether. In *A Political Theory of Rights*, she attempts to ground "rights" on a specific theory of autonomy and criticizes traditional liberal theory on the grounds that "it neglects to specify an ideal of the person under which a scheme of constraints is derived."[26] She appeals to the autonomy-based theory of Immanuel Kant but radically collectivizes the concept of autonomy, such that the principles that result

> are not the maxims of private acts of moral law-making, but
> principles that command the assent of a plurality of agents.
> In the absence of empirical conditions favouring impartiality
> we must envisage the relevant assent as hypothetical. It is
> the assent we would give were our motives and rationality
> unwarped by all those traits of personal and social character
> that we ordinarily regard as prejudicing the pursuit of good-
> ness or justice.[27]

What is especially noteworthy is the radical indeterminacy of the resulting principles: They are the principles that a "plurality of moral agents" who were sufficiently "unwarped" would assent to. The radical intolerance resulting from this approach is suggested in an ominous passage of the book regarding competing substantive ideals of goodness:

> There are many conceptions of happiness. Their relative
> merits are disputed. From the point of view of autonomy

> they function as so many resources from which we can choose
> our conception of the good, *provided only that they fall within
> the range of autonomy-regarding moralities.*[28] (emphasis added)

Thus, conceptions of the good that are not "autonomy-regarding" are not allowed. Ingram is perhaps too embarrassed by the implications of her chilling statement to address the obvious question of whether Orthodox Judaism, Roman Catholicism, Islam, or other religious (or nonreligious) belief systems provide sufficiently "autonomy-regarding" conceptions of the good for us to be allowed to choose among them. In the name of autonomy, all personal ideals are to be regulated by the collectivity. "Since the exercise of autonomy leads to incompatible personal ideals there is no option but to regulate their claims collectively in politics."[29]

Thus, we arrive at a theory of "rights" that justifies the authoritarian or totalitarian state. Alternatives to traditional liberal conceptions of rights, as we have seen, generate contradiction and incoherence; some even explicitly aim at authoritarian or even totalitarian political structures, thus not merely discombobulating rights theory but destroying it altogether.

Logic and Functionality

The internal logic of the theories of rights offered by advocates of welfare statism such as Raz, Waldron, Holmes, and Sunstein generates contradiction, circularity, incoherence, and, as a consequence, uncertainty and irreconcilable social conflict.

What such thinkers fail to appreciate is that rights have a social function. For one thing, they have made possible the complex civilization we see around us today. Without individual rights, such complex institutions and the extended order of modern civilization would not have been possible. Social order has its requirements, and those will have their analog in the structure and the theory of rights that accompany a social order. Just as the architectural and engineering plans for a building must not contradict mathematical and physical principles if the building is to serve its function (assuming that its function is not to collapse on its inhabitants), so the rules of social order, including rights, must not contain contradictions or violate basic principles of inference if the social order is to serve its function—indeed, if social *order* is to exist at all.[30]

Contrary to the assertions of extreme social constructivists who believe that all institutions and practices are "social constructions," by which they mean pure assertions of will, human nature is not infinitely plastic.[31] Objective reality, including the nature of the human being, imposes on human institutions certain constraints. Histories of institutions and of concepts can be formulated and understood precisely because reality is capable of being grasped by the mind.

To say that humans are constrained in various ways or that there are coherent patterns in human history is not the same as to make claims on behalf of a grand scheme of history, in the style of G. W. F. Hegel. Even if we reject Hegel's grandiose philosophy of history (as I do), we can still acknowledge a kind of logic that shapes human responses to problems, a logic that the philosopher Karl Popper called the "logic of the situation."[32] Without the possibility of tracing out the logic of situations, there would be little reason, if any, to listen to the explanations of political scientists, historians, military strategists, economists, or other students of human interaction; there would be no narrative to follow, no reason why, given that X was done, Y was the consequence.

If social order and cooperation are correlative to some system or systems of rights, then a conceptual formulation of such a system or systems of rights should not entail logical chaos, for that logical chaos will show up in the world of human action as social conflict and warfare rather than as social order and cooperation.

The conflicts of rights that Waldron admits are an inevitable feature of interest theories, and the infinite regress, circularity, and incoherence that are necessary features of the theory of Holmes and Sunstein, indicate that such theories do not correspond to and are not compatible with plan coordination and peaceful cooperation.

Liberal civilization requires mutual coordination and peaceful cooperation, as F. A. Hayek explains:

> What is required if the separate actions of the individuals are to result in an overall order is that they not only do not unnecessarily interfere with one another, but also that in those respects in which the success of the action of the individuals depends on some matching action by others, there will be at least a good chance that this correspondence will actually occur.[33]

Such correspondence will not occur if rights and duties are unpredictably "dynamic," nor if they generate conflicts, nor if they rest on infinite regresses or circular reasoning.

Such an order and such coordination require a system of rights over the things of the world, as Thomas Aquinas noted in offering three reasons why property "is necessary to human life":

> First because every man is more careful to procure what is for himself alone than that which is common to many or to all: since each would shirk the labor and leave to another that which concerns the community, as happens where there is a great number of servants. Secondly, because human affairs are conducted in more orderly fashion if each man is charged with taking care of some particular thing himself, whereas there would be confusion if everyone had to look after any one thing indeterminately. Thirdly, because a more peaceful state is ensured to man if each one is contented with his own. Hence it is to be observed that quarrels arise more frequently where there is no division of the things possessed.[34]

The "more peaceful state" ensured to man is a function of the system of rights that accompanies it. A peaceful state requires a fundamental stability of property; it requires that rights not have Raz's "dynamic character" or generate Waldron's inevitable conflicts. As James Madison noted in *Federalist* Number 62, the effect of a "mutable policy" (for "mutable" read "dynamic") "poisons the blessings of liberty itself."

> It will be of little avail to the people that the laws are made by men of their own choice if the laws be so voluminous that they cannot be read, or so incoherent that they cannot be understood; if they be repealed or revised before they are promulgated, or undergo such incessant changes that no man, who knows what the law is today, can guess what it will be tomorrow. Law is defined to be a rule of action; but how can that be a rule, which is little known, and less fixed?
>
> Another effect of public instability is the unreasonable advantage it gives to the sagacious, the enterprising, and the moneyed few over the industrious and uninformed mass of the people. Every new regulation concerning commerce or revenue, or in any manner affecting the value of the different species of property, presents a new harvest to those who watch the change, and can trace its consequences; a harvest,

> reared not by themselves, but by the toils and cares of the great body of their fellow-citizens. This is a state of things in which it may be said with some truth that laws are made for the *few*, not for the *many*.[35]

What I propose is to look at the history of the development of the traditional theories of rights that Raz, Waldron, Ingram, and Holmes and Sunstein seek to replace and to see how it reveals a convergence of rights theory with institutions of social cooperation and coordination. By showing how liberal rights theories correspond to and support liberal civilization, we may see why and how they are superior to the proposed replacements offered by philosophical advocates of dynamic and conflicting rights.[36]

Objective Right, Subjective Right, and Law

It is beyond the scope of this essay to offer a detailed historical account of the development of rights, of their roots in Greek philosophy, Roman law, and medieval theology and philosophy, so I will offer instead a sketchy presentation of the outlines of that history, for the purpose of demonstrating the coherence of the concepts of justice and rights that emerged.

Objective right, or the right ordering of society, is intimately related to subjective right, or the rights of the individuals who make up a social order. Objective right is what we could call the right arrangement of things. It refers to how things ought to be: thus, it is right that X and Y should obtain. Subjective right refers to the rights of the acting subjects who constitute asocial order: thus, it is A's right that B happen (or not happen).[37] As Brian Tierney notes about the connection of objective right with subjective rights,

> to affirm a right ordering of human relationships is to imply a structure of rights and duties. In propounding a system of jurisprudence one can emphasize either the objective pattern of relationships or the implied rights and duties of persons to one another—and then again one can focus on either the rights or the duties.[38]

Objective right and subjective right are not only logically compatible, but in a well-ordered theory of justice they should also be complementary.

Whereas the approaches of Raz, Waldron, Ingram, and Holmes and Sunstein would set the right ordering society (objective right) and the rights of individuals (subjective right) at odds, the classical tradition of rights thinking was premised on their unity, complementarity, or mutual implication.

One of the most significant occurrences in the history of rights theory was the fusion of Aristotelian ethical philosophy with the legal categories of the Roman law, as James Gordley has brilliantly shown in his book *The Philosophical Origins of Modern Contract Doctrine*.[39]

For Aristotle, justice is understood as "that disposition which renders men apt to do just things, and which causes them to act justly and to wish what is just."[40] Justice or right is oriented to the object of action, that is, to the thing done. In contrast, the Roman law tradition emphasized not so much the thing done as the recipient's claim, as one might expect of the law of a great commercial civilization. The Roman law was transmitted to the civilizations that succeeded Rome through the *Digest of Justinian*, a codification of centuries of Roman law that was drawn up in the sixth century C.E. under the direction of the jurist Tribonian and rediscovered in the Latin west in the eleventh century.

The definition of justice offered by the Roman jurist Ulpian was prominently offered as authoritative in the *Digest*:

> Justice is a steady and enduring will to render unto everyone his right. 1. The basic principles of right are: to live honorably, not to harm another person, to render to each his own. 2. Practical wisdom in matters of right is an awareness of God's and men's affairs, knowledge of justice and injustice.[41]

In the thirteenth century C.E., Thomas Aquinas, the great synthesizer, undertook to synthesize those approaches in his *Summa Theologica;* Ulpian's definition, he stated, is compatible with Aristotle's

> if understood aright. For since every virtue is a habit that is the principle of a good act, a virtue must needs be defined by means of the good act bearing on the matter proper to that virtue. Now the proper matter of justice consists of those things that belong to our intercourse with other men. . . . Hence the act of justice in relation to its proper matter and object is indicated in the words, *Rendering to each one his right,*

> since, as Isidore says (Etym. x), *a man is said to be just because he respects the rights* (jus) *of others.*[42]

Thus, right is something due to another person, something that belongs to that person and to which he or she can make a just claim.

As Annabel Brett notes, however, although Thomas attempts to reconcile the definitions of justice offered by Aristotle and by Ulpian, "the primary and theoretically important sense of iustum in Aquinas . . . remains that of 'just action.'"[43] A theoretical formulation of subjective right remained for the Spanish Scholastics to formulate and transmit to later generations of legal theorists and practitioners.

Here it is important to stress the significance of the work of philosophers in rationalizing legal practices, for the abstract formulation of those principles helped to create the abstract order that characterizes modern society. Such abstract formulation is inherently well suited or oriented toward a normative order of universality and equality, for abstract formulations do not take account of the concrete characteristics (race, birth, color, wealth, and so on) of the persons who fit particular legal categories (buyer, seller, parent, child, and so on).

For that reason, philosophy is particularly well suited to the formulation of the principles of liberalism. The absurdities to which collectivist/communitarian philosophy has been led in recent decades shows that it is at least remarkably difficult to formulate abstractly principles that divide human beings into separated "incommensurable" communities, classes, nations, or races, as communitarian critics of liberalism seek to do.[44]

By attempting to substitute for individual responsibility a concept of collective responsibility, collectivists and coercive communitarians undermine the very thing they often seek to support, which is deliberative and democratic decisionmaking, for by erasing the distinction among persons, they eliminate at the same time the very point of deliberation, which is for numerically individuated persons to decide on a common course. Thomas pointed out the problem in concluding from the observed fact of common ideas and attachments that those who share the same ideas and attachments make up one self:

> If . . . the intellect does not belong to this man in such a way that it is truly one with him, but is united to him only through phantasms or as a mover, the will will not be in this

man, but in the separate intellect. And so this man will not
be the master of his act, nor will any act of his be praiseworthy
or blameworthy. That is to destroy the principles of moral
philosophy. Since this is absurd and contrary to human life
(for it would not be necessary to take counsel or to make
laws), it follows that the intellect is united to us in such a
way that it and we constitute what is truly one being.[45]

Democratic deliberation requires individualism and the abstract
formulation of claims of justice; to deny the latter is to deny the
former.

Dominium, Responsibility, and Property

The concepts of individualism and of responsibility have a history,
and an examination of that history is likely to lead to greater understanding of the concepts themselves. The debates over property that
divided the papal and imperial parties provided great opportunities
for the philosophers who enlisted on one side or the other to clarify
the concept of rights. The key issue was what was meant by *dominium*
("mastery" or "ownership"), a term that was to prove of great significance to the development of rights talk.

The issue of dominium figured prominently in the debates concerning the relations between the church as a corporate body and
the empire, notably in the debate over "apostolic poverty"—over
whether priests, and therefore the church, were required to abjure
claims to property. The advocates of the imperial power were eager
to argue that the church should not own lands and other wealth,
and naturally the German emperors were quite happy to relieve the
church of their burdens. John XXII had responded in 1322 C.E. in
the bull *Ad conditorem canonum* against the arguments for apostolic
poverty by pointing out the inseparability of the right of use in
consumable goods (which priests, as human beings, surely enjoyed)
from the right of ownership; to exercise the right to consume is
necessarily to exclude, and therefore to exercise a claim of a right
to exclude.[46] Marsilius of Padua responded in 1324 C.E. and in the
process clarified the meaning of property or ownership (dominium):
"In its strict sense, this term means the principal power to lay claim
to something rightfully acquired. . . ; that is, the power of a person
who . . . wants to allow no one else to handle that thing without
his, the owner's, express consent, while he owns it."[47] Most notably,

69

Marsilius grounded the entire edifice of jurisdiction over resources in the world on one's dominium over oneself:

> Again, this term "ownership" [dominium] is used to refer to the human will or freedom in itself with its organic executive or motive power unimpeded. For it is through these that we are capable of certain acts and their opposites. It is for this reason too that man alone among the animals is said to have ownership or control of his acts; this control belongs to him by nature, it is not acquired through an act of will or choice.[48]

The issue received perhaps its most clear and powerful formulation in the famous debates over the treatment of the American Indians by the Spanish empire. The proto-liberal thinkers of the School of Salamanca, from whom so much liberal thinking was to emerge (including the morality of private property, the justice of the market price and of the charging of interest, the role of contracts in regulating production and exchange, and the contractual nature of political society),[49] initiated a debate over the proper status and treatment of the American Indians, in the process articulating a theory of universal individual rights.[50] Much of the dispute drew on the earlier debates concerning the Crusades and whether it was just to dispossess "infidels" from their lands, wealth, and political systems. A seminal text in this context was a statement of Pope Innocent IV (issued c. 1250 C.E.) on the rights of non-Christians, in which the pope drew inspiration from the Sermon on the Mount.

> I maintain ... that lordship, possession and jurisdiction can belong to infidels licitly and without sin, for these things were made not only for the faithful but for every rational creature as has been said. For he makes his sun to rise on the just and the wicked and he feeds the birds of the air, Matthew c.5, c.6. Accordingly we say that it is not licit for the pope or the faithful to take away from infidels their belongings or their lordships or jurisdictions because they possess them without sin.[51]

Francisco de Vitoria, in his famous essay *De Indis*, argued that the American Indian "barbarians" were "true masters" and therefore "may not be dispossessed without due cause."[52] For "if the barbarians were not true masters before the arrival of the Spaniards, it can only have been on four possible grounds," which he lists as "that they were either sinners (*peccatores*), unbelievers (*infideles*), madmen (*amentes*), or insensate (*insensati*)."[53] The first two grounds are dismissed as not sufficient to deny rights, for it was recognized that even sinners and unbelievers can have rights; the third, although a sufficient ground for denying rights (dominion), is inapplicable to the American Indians, for "they are not in point of fact madmen, but have judgment like other men."[54] (Whether the fourth is sufficient to deny "civil rights of ownership" Vitoria leaves to "the experts on Roman law," but he denies that the American Indians are mad or irrational, as shown by their cities, their laws, marriages, religion, and so on.[55])

What are most noteworthy in this context are the criteria that Vitoria sets out for being "true masters," that is, masters—or owners—of themselves and their properties.

> *Irrational creatures cannot have any dominion,* for dominion is a legal right (*dominium est ius*), as Conrad Summenhart himself admits. Irrational creatures cannot have legal rights; therefore they cannot have any dominion. The minor premise is proved by the fact that irrational creatures cannot be victims of an injustice (*inuria*), and therefore cannot have legal rights: this assumption is proved in turn by considering the fact that to deprive a wolf or a lion of its prey is no injustice against the beast in question, any more than to shut out the sun's light by drawing the blinds is an injustice against the sun. And this is confirmed by the absurdity of the following argument: that if brutes had dominion, then any person who fenced off grass from deer would be committing a theft, since he would be stealing food without its owner's permission.
>
> And again, wild animals have no rights over their own bodies (*dominium sui*); still less, then, can they have rights over other things ... only rational creatures have mastery over their own actions (*dominium sui actus*), as Aquinas shows ... [a person is master of his own actions insofar as he is able to make choices between one course and another; hence, as Aquinas says in the same passage, we are not masters as regards our appetite or our own destiny, for example]. If, then, brutes have no dominion over their own actions, they can have no dominion over other things.[56]

To have mastery over one's own actions, that is, *dominium*,[57] is to "be able to make a choice between one course and another," and this ability to choose is, in effect, what allows us to "own" our actions, that is, to have them truly attributed to us.[58] To be a "true master" is to be an agent who can "own" his or her actions, that is, one to whom the actions can be attributed and who therefore can be said to be responsible for those actions and therefore entitled as a matter of justice or right to take those actions necessary to fulfill his or her moral obligations, both to others and to self (minimally, that entails self-preservation). According to Vitoria: "Every Indian is a man and thus is capable of attaining salvation or damnation"; "Every man is a person and is the master of his body and possessions"; "Inasmuch as he is a person, every Indian has free will, and, consequently, is the master of his actions"; "By natural law, every man has the right to his own life and to physical and mental integrity."[59]

The core of the arguments of Innocent IV, Vitoria, John Locke, and other pioneers of the theory of rights of self-propriety, as of their followers up to the present time, is a recognition that other humans are not simply mobile machines, automata, or insensate brutes, but acting agents to whom choice and responsibility may be attributed. The debate between Bartolomé de Las Casas and Juan Ginés de Sepúlveda in 1550 on the status of the Indians revolved largely around the intellectual and moral capacities of the Indians. As Las Casas argued,

> Now if we shall have shown that among our Indians of the western and southern shores (granting that we call them barbarians and that they are barbarians) there are important kingdoms, large numbers of people who live settled lives in a society, great cities, kings, judges and laws, persons who engage in commerce, buying, selling, lending, and the other contracts of the law of nations, will it not stand proved that the Reverend Doctor Sepúlveda has spoken wrongly and viciously against peoples like these, either out of malice or ignorance of Aristotle's teaching, and, therefore, has falsely and perhaps irreparably slandered them before the entire world?[60]

The issue was of more than academic interest, for had it been proven that the Indians were the "natural slaves" described by Aristotle in the *Politics*,[61] then the Spaniards would have been justified in applying to them the direction that they were incapable of providing themselves. By arguing that the Indians were indeed fully human and were capable of, and indeed were actively exercising, self-direction, Las Casas, following Vitoria before him, sought to refute the claims of the Spanish slaveholders and affirm the rights of the Indians to their lives, liberties, and properties. The *proper* relationship between the Spaniards and the Indians, Vitoria and Las Casas insisted, was persuasion in religion and consent-based free trade in material affairs.[62]

The common humanity of Indians and Spaniards, and therefore of any and all who might meet on a basis of unequal technological, military, or other power, provided a ground for recognition of a common set of rights. But why should a common nature entail common rights? Lobsters share a common nature, but there is no justice among lobsters, still less rights. Even if a lobster can "recognize" another creature as a lobster, there is no mutual recognition of moral agents, no sense that "this is an agent capable of choice, as am I," nor that "this is an agent deserving of some kind of respect." The recognition of humans as choosers, as agents who can "own" their actions and be responsible for them, and who have purposes and goals of their own, which may or may not coincide with yours, involves a special kind of recognition and comportment altogether different from that appropriate to inanimate or nonrational entities.

Identity, Knowledge, Rights, and Justice

The idea of dominium, of personal responsibility, of an ability to "own" our acts, is central to the development of the idea of rights, and to the extension of the concept of rights to ever-wider categories of human beings.

That idea of responsibility is ultimately founded on the idea of the dominium one has over one's body. Bodies are scarce; there is only one per person. If one person were to get more than one body, that would necessarily leave at least one person without a body. That is why referring to one's *own* body is redundant; "one's own body" denotes nothing more than "one's body" and differs from the former in connotation only by emphasis.[63]

The scarcity of bodies entails that if they are to be used or, eschewing instrumentalist language, if their spatio-temporal dispositions are to be determined, choices must be made. The law of contradiction, "the most certain of all principles,"[64] creates a problem of decision: "It is impossible for the same attribute at once to belong and

73

not to belong to the same thing and in the same relation."[65] A body cannot be reading in the Bodleian Library at the same time that it is drinking in the King's Arms or picking corn on an Iowa farm. Scarcity arises from the transposition of the law of contradiction into the context of choice. Rights arise from the transposition of scarcity into the context of justice. Rights are the moral and legal instruments by which scarcity problems are addressed, that is, by which agents are informed as to who is entitled to the use of a scarce resource under what conditions.

The centrality of dominium to personal identity, and thus to identifying who has jurisdiction over what body, was clearly stated during the English Civil War by the Levellers, a group that exerted a great influence on later English and American political thought. One of their more eloquent leaders, Richard Overton, appealed to rights to defend religious liberty in a pamphlet of 1646:

> To every individual in nature is given an individual property by nature not to be invaded or usurped by any. For every one, as he is himself, so he has a self-propriety, *else could he not be himself*; on this no second may presume to deprive any of without manifest violation and affront to the very principles of nature and of the rules of equity and justice between man and man. Mine and thine cannot be, except this be. No man has power over my rights and liberties, and I over no man's. I may be but an individual, enjoy myself and my self-propriety and may right myself no more than my self, or presume any further; if I do, I am an encroacher and an invader upon another man's right—to which I have no right. For by natural birth all men are equally and alike born to like propriety, liberty and freedom; and as we are delivered of God by the hand of nature into this world, every one with a natural, innate freedom and propriety—as it were writ in the table of every man's heart, never to be obliterated—even so are we to live, everyone equally and alike to enjoy his birthright and privilege; even all whereof God by nature has made him free.[66] (emphasis added)

Such "self-propriety" was based on the recognition of the choice and freedom that individuals exercise over their own bodies. Notably, it served as the philosophical justification for the still current resister's strategy of "going limp" when arrested by state agents, as Overton argued in refusing to walk to prison when ordered to do so:

> My *Leggs* were borne as free as the rest of my *Body*, and
> therefore I scorne that *Leggs, or Armes, or hands of mine* should
> do them any *villeine-Service*, for as I am a *Freeman by birth*,
> so I am resolved to live and dye, both in heart word and
> deed, in substance and in shew.[67]

Overton was quite cruelly dragged to prison as a consequence. His
remarks on this experience remind us of the clear relationship of
self-propriety and moral agency:

> But in case you object, that I knew well enough, that if I
> would not go, they would carrie me, therefore it had been
> better for me to have gone, then to have exposed my selfe
> to their cruelty, I answer, 1. If I had known they would have
> hanged me, must I therefore have hanged my selfe? 2. A
> good conscience had rather run the hazard of cruelty then to
> abate an hairesbreadth of contestation and opposition against
> illegality, injustice, and tyranny. 3. If they had had any legall
> jurisdiction over my leggs, then at their Commands my leggs
> were bound to obey: And then, (in that case) I confesse it
> had been better to obey, then to have exposed my person to
> the cruelty of threatening mercilesse Gaolers: But being free
> from their Jurisdiction *from the Crowne of my head to the Soale
> of my foote*, I know no reason, why I should foote it for them,
> or in any the least dance any attendance to their *Arbitrary
> Warrants*; their Lordships may put up their pipes, except
> they will play to the *good old tune of the Law of the Land*,
> otherwise their Orders and Warrants are never like to have
> the service of my leggs or feet, for they were never bred to
> tread in their *Arbitrary Steps*, but I shall leave *their Orders*
> and *their execution to themselves*. And therefore, Sir, concern-
> ing that action of mine, I shall continue in the said esteeme
> thereof, till my defense be made voide, and it be legally
> proved, that by the Law of the Land, *I* was bound to set one
> legge before another in attendance to that Order.[68]

Regardless of the consequences, Overton retained the control over
his own legs. His actions remained his own.

The rather better-known philosopher of rights, John Locke, considered the relation between "person" and "self" in his *Essay Concerning
Human Understanding*:

> Any substance vitally united to the present thinking Being,
> is a part of that very *same self* which now is: Any thing united

> to it by a consciousness of former Actions makes also a part
> of the *same self*, which is the same both then and now.
>
> *Person*, as I take it, is the name for this self. Where-ever a
> Man finds, what he calls *himself*, there I think another may
> say is the same *Person*. It is a Forensick Term appropriating
> Actions and their Merit; and so only belongs to intelligent
> Agents capable of a Law, and Happiness and Misery. This
> personality extends it *self* beyond present Existence to what
> is past, only by consciousness, whereby it becomes concerned
> and accountable, owns and imputes to it self past Actions,
> just upon the same ground, and for the same reason, that it
> does the present.[69]

It is clear from his remarks in *The Second Treatise* that Locke identified the person with an animated body. After claiming that "every
Man has a *Property* in his own *Person*," he immediately clarifies this
by explaining that "This no Body has any Right to but himself. The
Labour of his Body, and the *Work* of his Hands, we may say, are
properly his."[70] Each person is an individual and the owner of his
or her acts, which are the acts of an animated body. The body is the
seat of one's personhood, one's personhood is achieved by the acts
that one owns, and the responsibility for those acts is the foundation
for one's rights, for the reason that hindering another from fulfilling
his or her obligations is precisely to hinder that person from doing
what is right, and therefore to act contrary to right.

Given that human beings are embodied persons, ascribing personal responsibility for one's acts means ascribing them to some*body*.
One need not embrace any particular theory of the relationship of
mind and body to know that, certainly under normal circumstances,
each person is associated with, or embodied in, one body and one
body only. Aristotle makes mention of this principle when he
describes "slaves who merit being such by nature," surely a kind of
person whose acquaintance he had never made:

> For the same thing is advantageous for the part and the
> whole and for body and soul, and the slave is a sort of part
> of the master—a part of his body, as it were, animate yet
> separate. There is thus a certain advantage—and even
> affection of slave and master for one another—for those
> [slaves] who merit being such by nature; but for those who
> do not merit it in this way but [who are slaves] according
> to law and by force, the opposite is the case.[71]

Surely Aristotle was aware that the actual slaves he knew were "according to law and by force," and, as he suggests, such slaves do not usually exhibit affection for their masters. Slaves by force are not a part of the master's body but have their own bodies, desires, wishes, and, in general, their own principles of motion. The core of what is one's own is one's body; it is the kernel around which we build our self-identity and extend our personality into the wider world of experience, through acquisition of attachments to other persons and to corporeal things, to causes, and so on. This basic core of what is "one's own" is central to the rights theory of the legal theorist Hugo Grotius; it encompasses one's life, limbs, and liberty, the last being "the power, that we have over ourselves."[72]

One's body is centrally, inescapably connected to one's identity. As *Economist* editor and political theorist Thomas Hodgskin noted,

> Mr. Locke says, that every man has a property in his own person; in fact, individuality—which is signified by the word *own*—cannot be disjoined from the person. Each individual learns his own shape and form, and even the existence of his limbs and body, from seeing and feeling them. These constitute his notion of *personal* identity, both for himself and others; and it is impossible to conceive—it is in fact a contradiction to say—that a man's limbs and body do not belong to himself: for the words him, self, and his body, signify the same material thing.
>
> As we learn the existence of our own bodies from seeing and feeling them, and as we see and feel the bodies of others, we have precisely similar grounds for believing in the individuality or identity of other persons, as for believing in our own identity. The ideas expressed by the words mine and thine, as applied to the produce of labour, are simply then an extended form of the ideas of personal identity and individuality.[73]

Recognition of that fact was central to the liberal tradition, both in Europe and in America. Thus, as Destutt de Tracy noted in a work edited by Thomas Jefferson (and endorsed by Jefferson with his "hearty prayers, that while the Review of Montesquieu, by the same author, is made with us the elementary book of instruction in the principles of civil government, so the present work may be in the particular branch of Political Economy"), as soon as this individual knows accurately itself, or its moral person, and its capacity to enjoy and to suffer, and to act necessarily, it sees clearly also that this self is the exclusive proprietor of the body which it animates, of the organs which it moves, of all their passions and their actions: for all this finishes and commences with this *self*, exists but by it, is not moved but by its acts, and no other moral person can employ the same instruments nor be affected in the same manner by their effects. The idea of property and of exclusive property arises then necessarily in a sensible being from this alone, that it is susceptible of passion and action, and it arises in such a being because nature has endowed it with an inevitable and inalienable property, that of its individuality.[74]

Certainly there are other theories of personal identity that do not rely on an individual's perception of his limbs and body in order, in Hodgskin's words, to "constitute his notion of personal identity, both for himself and others."[75] But not all theories of personal identity are or need be relevant to the formulation of a theory of rights. Theories based on strange hypotheticals and counterfactuals and on nonstandard cases, such as multiple personalities, Siamese twins, or amnesiacs, are unlikely to meet the criteria of publicity and generality necessary for a functional rights theory. "Bodily self-ascription" (to use Gareth Evans's phrase for the principle advanced here), on the other hand, has the marked advantage of "immunity to error through misidentification."[76] As Evans notes,

we have what might be described as a general capacity to perceive our own bodies, although this can be broken down into several distinguishable capacities. . . . Each of these modes of perception appears to give rise to judgments which are immune to error through misidentification. None of the following utterances appears to make sense when the first component expresses knowledge gained in the appropriate way: "Someone's legs are crossed, but is it my legs that are crossed?"; "Someone is hot and sticky, but is it I who am hot and sticky?"; "Someone is being pushed, but is it I who am being pushed?" There just does not appear to be a gap between the subject's having information (or appearing to have information), in the appropriate way, that the property of being F is instantiated, and his having information (or appearing to have information) that he is F; for him to have,

> or to appear to have, the information that the property is instantiated just is for it to appear to him that *he* is F.[77]

Each person is identified with one and only one body, spatiotemporally distinct from all others. Each person is a source or principle of motion for one body.[78] Each body provides demarcation of a sphere of "ownness." The values that one acts to attain or preserve are the values of materially individuated agents; they are "agent relative." Each person is responsible for those acts in cases in which he or she "could have done otherwise." Each person is responsible for the acts of his or her own body, but not (excepting special cases, such as guardianship of minors and the mentally deficient) for the acts of the bodies of others, for these are the responsibility of other agents—those whose spheres of "ownness" are defined by those bodies.[79]

Recognizing that each person bears responsibility for his or her acts entails that each person is also obliged to act in accordance with deontic constraints on behavior. Moving from "normative solipsism" to "normative pluralism"—from the view that one is the only agent acting to achieve values in the world to a recognition that one is one among a multitude of acting agents—need not entail a move from the agent-relativity of values to the agent-neutrality of values, as some have asserted,[80] but provides the groundwork for recognition of a deontic constraint on the pursuit of agent-relative values—that the spheres of ownness of others are not to be invaded or usurped in pursuit of one's own agent-relative values.[81] In recognizing that persons bear responsibility for their acts, we are not compelled by the structure of practical reason to adopt a special perspective that ranks all values and lives equally from a maximizing perspective, such that an aggregate of equally valid lives or values is what is to be conserved or advanced from some agent-neutral perspective,[82] but we are moved toward a constraint on behavior that affects others.[83] Some have suggested that it would be a failure of deliberative or practical rationality to fail to recognize the equal claims of others or to integrate their values into one's own, but while this is attractive, I see little warrant for it. A far stronger ground for recognizing deontic constraints on behavior is that the realm of responsibility of each individual maps precisely on to a realm of legitimate claims; the fact that each has a life to lead is coextensive in moral significance with the fact that each bears responsibility for acts in a well-delineated sphere of ownness. Each governs in his or her own body; each body has its own principle of motion; each is held by others to be responsible for what he or she does with that body; the body demarcates that person as an identity, as the same with himself or herself and as different from others; and that body is the seat of the claim to pursue one's *own* values—those with which one identifies as an agent, which give coherence to one's life and integrate one as one person, rather than as simply a random and unintegrated conglomeration of desires.[84]

Precisely because each person has one and only one body, rights over bodies—a "property in one's person"—offer a secure foundation for the entire structure of rights, one that does not necessarily generate conflicts. The starting point is secure. It provides a foundation for a system of "compossible" rights, that is, rights that are capable of being jointly realized.[85]

If a theory of rights generates *in*compossible claims to act legitimately, as do the theories criticized earlier in this essay, that theory generates contradictions as fatal to it as are logical contradictions to a system of mathematics.[86] It is in the nature of "right" that two mutually incompatible actions cannot both be "right"; they may be understandable, or virtuous, or even noble, but both cannot be right and just at the same time and in the same respect. Recall Socrates' warning when discussing justice: "The argument is not about just any question, but about the way one should live."[87] Justice is about which acts are permissible or obligatory and which are not, and rights are the signposts that tell individuals how they may and may not act. Incompossible rights give contradictory information; they are like signposts for "north" that point in opposite direction.

A theory that recognizes the responsibilities and duties of each entails recognition of a set of corresponding rights. As Hillel Steiner notes, "A duty-holder who lacks any rights is one whose liberties are all naked and whose duties may thus be incompossible either with one another or with those of others or both."[88] In order to fulfill our duties, rights are necessary, and if our duties are equal, then those rights are equal rights. The rights to our own spheres of ownness—over that for which we are responsible—is the natural correlative to the obligations associated with the sphere of ownness.[89] And that sphere of ownness defines both rights and duties: It is the right of all persons to themselves, to their own bodies. The obligations derive from the engagement in moral discourse, from the equality involved in the giving of reasons among agents all of whom bear responsibility for their own acts and who have their own lives and purposes, rights derived both from the necessity of avoiding incompossibility of obligations and duties, extensionally defined, and from the claims of all to live their lives.[90] What defines and makes possible the discharge of obligations and the enjoyment of rights is self-proprietorship, or a "property in one's person."[91]

Property in one's person provides a foundation for a system of compossible rights, which themselves are the juridical structure of a society of freedom and justice. As Kant noted, "Right is ... the sum total of those conditions within which the will of one person can be reconciled with the will of another in accordance with a universal law of freedom."[92]

Kant recognized quite clearly that what distinguishes the just from the unjust system is the ability of all of the legitimate claims to be exercised at the same time, to be compossible. Objective right has to do with the "sum total" of the acts of persons, not merely "the duties in each individual case," in Waldron's terms; in order for justice and rights (or objective and subjective right) to be complementary, the duties in each individual case can be duties only if the sum total of them yields justice or right. Kant concludes that,

> Every action which by itself or by its maxim enables the freedom of each individual's will to co-exist with the freedom of everyone else in accordance with a universal law is right.[93]

I have a right to those actions that are compatible with the equal freedom of all others; the sum total of those actions yields justice.[94]

Conclusion

Formulating theories of rights that generate logical chaos and social conflict does not advance rights or justice. Such theories tear asunder rights and justice, eliminating both and substituting for them "human wish," arbitrary power, and violence. In so doing, they undermine the very civilization that justice, law, and rights have made possible.

It is no accident that the traditional view of rights that I have sketched out (quite incompletely, to be sure) motivated the American founding and the formulation of the sets of rights articulated in the Constitution of the United States. The incompatibilities and failures (most strikingly in the case of the injustices and rights violations suffered by African slaves), although clear to some at the time of the founding, took time for their elimination. Practice did not correspond to theory but, partly through the Thirteenth, Fourteenth, and Fifteenth Amendments to the Constitution, were brought into closer correspondence. To this day they remain incompletely correspondent; it is in the nature of morality and justice that they are not always observed, for the simple reason of human choice, which makes possible both virtue and vice, both justice and injustice. Injustices and rights violations will never be completely eliminated, however much we are called to eliminate them. But, unlike the rights theories criticized earlier, a compossible set of rights has the advantage that it can be realized in the most part, that it does not necessarily lead to conflicts and to the abandonment of rights as criteria for deciding conflicts of interest. It is in this way that the project initiated by the American founders—which was in fact a continuation of a wider tradition of European civilization, constitutionalism, and law—reveals its greatest wisdom. That is why the American experiment, even with all its flaws, remains an attractive model for the world.

Recall the wisdom of Aristotle: "It is better if all these things are done in accordance with law rather than in accordance with human wish, as the latter is not a safe standard."[95] The statement is no less true in the twentieth century C.E., a century washed in blood by the arbitrary power of rulers unlimited by secure principles of justice and attached instead to "dynamic," unpredictable, irreconcilable "rights."

Notes

1. Stephen Holmes and Cass R. Sunstein, *The Cost of Rights: Why Liberty Depends on Taxes* (New York: W. W. Norton, 1999), p. 21. To be more precise, what Holmes and Sunstein consider are not rights that are enforceable, but rights that actually are enforced. They combine a strong attachment to legal positivism, i.e., to the doctrine that rights are posited, with an "interest" theory of rights: "an interest qualifies as a right when an effective legal system treats it as such by using collective resources to defend it" (p. 17). For a comparison of "interest" theories and "choice" theories of rights, see Matthew H. Kramer, Nigel Simmonds, and Hillel Steiner, *A Debate over Rights: Philosophical Enquiries* (Oxford: Clarendon Press, 1998). For the working out of the different approaches in courts of law, see John Hasnas, "From Cannibalism

to Caesareans: Two Conceptions of Fundamental Rights," *Northwestern University Law Review* 89(3), Spring 1995: pp. 900–941.

2. Holmes and Sunstein, p. 17.

3. Holmes and Sunstein, pp. 219, 222.

4. Nowhere do Holmes and Sunstein justify this remarkable claim about the character of rights under "American law." Indeed, it would be a very difficult task to reconcile such a claim with the Ninth Amendment to the Constitution: "The enumeration in the Constitution of certain rights shall not be construed to deny or disparage others retained by the people." The language is quite clear: Just because some rights are enumerated does not mean that those are all there are. Indeed, the unenumerated rights are "retained" by the people, which means that they must preexist the establishment of government; otherwise, they could not be "retained."

5. Ibid., pp. 13, 14.

6. Ibid., p. 19.

7. Ibid., p. 17.

8. Ibid., p. 43. Thus, Holmes and Sunstein incorporate a principle of positive social theory into their normative account of rights, namely, that order obtains *only* when a sovereign power threatens punishment. This is hardly a self-evident claim, but it is clearly an important element of their assault on the traditional view of rights. Traditional rights theory is normally complemented by a theory of "spontaneous order," according to which order need not be the result of an ordering authority with power to punish deviations from its imposed order. That does not mean that punishment is never needed, but that the ever-present threat of punishment is not the only or even the primary force in creating social order.

9. Ibid., p. 44.

10. Ibid., e.g., pp. 39, 46, 83, 93.

11. Ibid., p. 17.

12. Ibid., p. 203.

13. It should not go unremarked that *The Cost of Rights* is extraordinarily polemical, unscholarly, and nasty in its criticisms of those with differing views. For example, immediately after gallantly conceding that "many critics of the regulatory-welfare state are in perfectly good faith" (p. 216), they turn around to tar all critics of the welfare state with the charge of racism: "But their claim that 'positive rights' are somehow un-American and should be replaced by a policy of nonintervention is so implausible on its face that we may well wonder why it persists. What explains the survival of such a grievously inadequate way of thinking? There are many possible answers, but inherited biases—including racial prejudice, conscious and unconscious—probably play a role. Indeed, the claim that the only real liberties are the rights of property and contract can sometimes verge on a form of white separatism: prison-building should supplant Head Start. Withdrawal into gated communities should replace a politics of inclusion" (p. 216). Their slithery charge is not only unsubstantiated, it is beneath contempt.

14. Joseph Raz, *The Morality of Freedom* (Oxford: Oxford University Press, 1986), p. 166.

15. Ibid., p. 171.

16. Ronald Dworkin, *Taking Rights Seriously* (Cambridge, Mass.: Harvard University Press, 1978), p. xi.

17. Ronald Dworkin, *Taking Rights Seriously*, p. 365. As Anthony de Jasay remarks of this theory, "In brief, it all depends on which reason weighs more. But what is

the good of enunciating that the heavier weight outweighs the lighter one and it all depends on which is which? Manifestly, 'rights are trumps' when the balance of benefit does not outweigh them; they are not trumps when it does. But this is saying nothing more than that a card may be stronger than some other card yet weaker than a third one. It is not saying that the card is a trump." Anthony de Jasay, *Choice, Contract, Consent: A Restatement of Liberalism* (London: Institute of Economic Affairs, 1991), pp. 39–40. Contrast Dworkinian "rights," a mere juridical residue or after-thought capable of justifying claims only when "a collective good is not a sufficient justification for denying them what they wish," with Joel Feinberg's description of rights, "whose characteristic use and that for which they are distinctively well suited, is to be claimed, demanded, affirmed, insisted upon. They are especially sturdy objects to 'stand upon,' a most useful sort of moral furniture. Having rights, of course, makes claiming possible; but it is claiming that gives rights their special moral significance. This feature of rights is connected in a way with the customary rhetoric about what it is to be a human being. Having rights enables us to 'stand up like men,' to look others in the eye, and to feel in some fundamental way the equal of anyone." Joel Feinberg, "The Nature and Value of Rights," in *Rights, Justice, and the Bounds of Liberty: Essays in Social Philosophy* (Princeton, N.J.: Princeton University Press, 1980), p. 151.

18. Joseph Raz, *The Morality of Freedom*, p. 185. As Raz explains, "They are not merely the grounds of existing duties. With changing circumstances they can generate new duties" (p. 186).

19. It seems no accident that the penultimate article in this entire declaration of "human rights" is a statement of an obligation: "Everyone has duties to the community in which alone the free and full development of his personality is possible." That is to say, everyone has the right to have "duties to the community," a phrase normally interpreted to mean a duty to obey the state. Under this conception, one's rights evaporate into a duty to obey the state, which is the institution charged with determining which of many and varied conflicting interests will be fulfilled.

20. Jeremy Waldron, "Rights in Conflict," in *Liberal Rights: Collected Papers 1981–1991* (Cambridge: Cambridge University Press, 1993), p. 203.

21. Maurice Cranston, "Human Rights: Real and Supposed," in *Political Theory and the Rights of Man*, ed. D. D. Raphael (Bloomington: Indiana University Press, 1967), p. 50.

22. Waldron, p. 207.

23. John Locke, "Essays on the Law of Nature," in *Political Essays*, ed. Mark Goldie (Cambridge: Cambridge University Press, 1997), p. 132.

24. "Law" and "right" are related concepts, with a complex historical connection. To reject "right" is, in effect, to reject law in favor of arbitrary will. But, as Aristotle wryly noted in *Politics*, "it is better if all these things are done in accordance with law rather than in accordance with human wish, as the latter is not a safe standard" (1272b5–8). Aristotle, *Politics*, trans. Carnes Lord (Chicago: University of Chicago Press, 1984), p. 80.

25. Matthew H. Kramer, "Rights Without Trimmings," in *A Debate over Rights: Philosophical Enquiries*, ed. Matthew H. Kramer, Nigel Simmonds, and Hillel Steiner (New York: Oxford University Press, 2000), p. 19.

26. Attracta Ingram, *A Political Theory of Rights* (Oxford: Clarendon Press, 1994), p. 117.

27. Ibid., p. 153.

28. Ibid., p. 164.

29. Ibid., p. 166.

30. The analogy of social rules to architectural principles is explored at greater length by Randy Barnett in *The Structure of Liberty: Justice and the Rule of Law* (Oxford: Clarendon Press, 1998), esp. pp. 1–24. The function of laws and rules in securing social order was central to the influential approach of the seventeenth-century legal philosopher Samuel Pufendorf. As he noted, "Men are not all moved by one simple uniform desire, but by a multiplicity of desires variously combined. For these reasons careful regulation and control are needed to keep them from coming into conflict with each other. . . . The conclusion is: in order to be safe, it is necessary for him to be sociable; that is to join forces with men like himself and so conduct himself towards them that they are not given even a plausible excuse for harming him, but rather become willing to preserve and promote his advantages [*commoda*]. The laws of this sociality [*socialitas*], laws which teach one how to conduct oneself to become a useful [*commodum*] member of human society, are called natural laws." Samuel Pufendorf, *On the Duty of Man and Citizen According to Natural Law*, trans. Michael Silverthorne, ed. James Tully (Cambridge: Cambridge University Press, 1991), p. 35.

31. I criticize only "extreme" social constructivists because it is undeniable that institutions are products of human action, and sometimes even of conscious human design. The error of the extremists is to believe that because social institutions are products of human action, they can be any way we choose or want them to be.

32. Karl Popper, *The Poverty of Historicism* (Boston: Beacon Press, 1957), pp. 149–52.

33. F. A. Hayek, *Law, Legislation, and Liberty, vol. I, Rules and Order* (Chicago: University of Chicago Press, 1973), pp. 98–99.

34. St. Thomas Aquinas, *Summa Theologica*, IIa, IIae, Q. 66, trans. Fathers of the English Dominican Province (Westminster, Md.: Christian Classics, 1981), vol. III, p. 1471. Thomas represents in this regard, as in many others, a great advance over Aristotle's account of property in the *Politics*, esp. bk. 2, chaps. 3–5, 7.

35. James Madison, "Concerning the Constitution of the Senate with Regard to the Qualifications of the Members, the Manner of Appointing Them, the Equality of Representation, the Number of the Senators, and the Duration of their Appointments," No. 62, in James Madison, Alexander Hamilton, and John Jay, *The Federalist Papers* (New York: Penguin Books, 1987), p. 368.

36. It should be remembered that recognizing that some system of rights is integral to a social order is not the same as claiming that those rights are always respected and never violated. That even broadly liberal societies still suffer from criminal aggression—both from states and from freelance criminals—is not necessarily an indictment of the liberal system of rights that seeks to outlaw such violations of rights. Some rights schemes may be unstable and self-destructive when attempts are made to put them into practice (the catastrophe of classical socialism is a good example of an unstable social order), but in general, liberal rights have shown themselves to be stable, even in the face of violations by state officials and other criminals.

37. These categories are related, but not reducible, to Aristotle's categories of universal and particular justice. See the discussion in Fred Miller Jr., *Nature, Justice, and Rights in Aristotle's* Politics (Oxford: Clarendon Press, 1995), esp. pp. 68–74.

38. Brian Tierney, *The Idea of Natural Rights* (Atlanta: Scholars Press, 1997), p. 33.

39. James Gordley, *The Philosophical Origins of Modern Contract Doctrine* (Oxford: Clarendon Press, 1991). Gordley focuses most of his attention on the late scholastics of the Spanish natural law school, but the movement is already perceptible in the

work of Thomas Aquinas, as Annabel S. Brett notes in *Liberty, Right, and Nature: Individual Rights in Later Scholastic Thought* (Cambridge: Cambridge University Press, 1997), pp. 89–97.

40. Aristotle, *Nichomachean Ethics*, V, i., 1129a8–9, trans. H. Rackham (Cambridge, Mass.: Harvard University Press, 1934), p. 253.

41. *The Digest of Justinian*, trans. and ed. Alan Watson (Philadelphia: University of Pennsylvania Press, 1998), pp. I, i, 10.

42. Thomas Aquinas, IIa, IIae, Q. 58, p. 1429.

43. Annabel S. Brett, *Liberty, Right, and Nature*, p. 92.

44. One noted critic of traditional liberal principles, Michael Sandel, has argued in his *Liberalism and the Limits of Justice* (Cambridge: Cambridge University Press, 1982) that selves need not be "individuated in advance," but should "comprehend a wider subject than the individual alone, whether a family or tribe or city or class or nation or people," and "to this extent they define a community in a constitutive sense" (p. 172). In other words, rather than speaking merely of Mary and William and Tadd and Sylvia, we would speak of the "self" composed of Mary, William, Tadd, and Sylvia. What Sandel is arguing is that an epistemological principle can be transformed into an ontological principle: "this notion of community [the constitutive conception] describes a framework of self-understandings that is distinguishable from and in some sense prior to the sentiments and dispositions of individuals within the framework" (p. 174). Because shared understandings are necessary for our self-understanding, i.e., because they are asserted to be an epistemic criterion for self-knowledge, it is asserted that these shared understandings are constitutive of our identity and that therefore "the bounds of the self are no longer fixed, individuated in advance and given prior to experience" (p. 183). This move is unjustified. As John Haldane remarks, "even if this were granted it would not follow from it that subjects of these relationships are anything other than distinct persons. To suppose otherwise is to infer fallaciously that epistemological considerations enter into the constitution of the object known." ("Individuals and the Theory of Justice," *Ratio* 27[2], December 1985: pp. 189–96). This is an old debate, and the outlines can be traced quite clearly in the debate between the "Latin Averroists," notably Siger of Brabant, and St. Thomas Aquinas over whether there is one "intellective soul" for all of mankind. The Averroists argued that for two individuals to know the same thing, they have to have the same form impressed by the agent intellect into the same material (or possible) intellect; to know the same form, they must share the same material intellect. See Siger of Brabant, "On the Intellective Soul," in *Medieval Philosophy: From St. Augustine to Nicholas of Cusa*, ed. John F. Wippel and Allan B. Wolter, O.F.M. (London: Collier Macmillan Publishers, 1969), pp. 358–65. As some sources note, it was reported in the thirteenth century that this thesis had radical implications for the moral responsibilities of the individual: If Peter was saved, then I will be saved too, as we share the same intellective soul. So I am free to engage in whatever sinful behavior I wish, in the knowledge that I will be saved nonetheless. Thomas responded that the impressed intelligible species is not literally the very form of the thing raised to a higher level of intelligibility but rather that by which we know the thing: "It is . . . one thing which is understood both by me and by you. But it is understood by me in one way and by you in another, that is, by another intelligible species. And my understanding is one thing, and yours, another; and my intellect is one thing, and yours another." Thomas Aquinas, *On the Unity of the Intellect against the Averroists* (Milwaukee: Marquette University Press, 1968), chap. V, par. 112, p. 70. The issue is

canvassed in Herbert Davidson, *Alfarabi, Avicenna, and Averroes on Intellect* (Oxford: Oxford University Press, 1994).

45. Thomas Aquinas, *On the Unity of the Intellect against the Averroists*, chap. II, par. 82, p. 57.

46. See the discussion in Brian Tierney, "Marsilius on Rights," *Journal of the History of Ideas* 52(1), Jan.–March, 1991: pp. 3–17, and Brian Tierney, *The Idea of Natural Rights*, pp. 93–130. Compare the modern economist of property rights Yoram Barzel: "The ability to consume commodities, including those necessary to sustain life, implies the possession of rights over them." *Economic Analysis of Property Rights* (Cambridge: Cambridge University Press, 1989), p. 62.

47. Marsilius of Padua, *The Defender of the Peace: The Defensor Pacis*, trans. Alan Gewirth (New York: Harper and Row, 1956), discourse II, chap. XII, 13, p. 192. I have omitted from the quotation material relating to Marsilius's claim that priests have voluntarily taken vows of poverty, which was a central part of the claim of the imperial party on this matter.

48. Marsilius of Padua, discourse II, chap. XII, 16, p. 193.

49. See, for example, Joseph Schumpeter, *History of Economic Analysis* (Oxford: Oxford University Press, 1954), who highlights the significance of Luis de Molina's views on the importance of free prices, since "we are not as a rule in the habit of looking to the scholastics for the origin of the theories that are associated with nineteenth-century laissez-faire liberalism" (p. 99); Alejandro Chafuen, *Christians for Freedom: Late-Scholastic Economics* (San Francisco: Ignatius Press, 1986); and Quentin Skinner, *The Foundations of Modern Political Thought, vol. II, The Age of Reformation* (Cambridge: Cambridge University Press, 1978), pp. 135–73.

50. As Blandine Kriegel notes, "In his *De Indis* of 1539, Vitoria maintained that Indians had the same right to liberty and property as all other human beings and that a number of rights can be deduced logically from human nature itself." Blandine Kriegel, "Rights and Natural Law," in *New French Thought: Political Philosophy*, ed. Mark Lilla (Princeton, N.J.: Princeton University Press, 1994), p. 155. Brian Tierney has suggested that Francisco de Vitoria may have been directly influenced by Marsilius, for "the *Defensor Pacis* was certainly well known at Paris in the years Vitoria studied there. One difficulty is that Catholic authors usually referred to Marsilius by name only when they intended to disagree with him. When they wanted to borrow his ideas they preferred not to mention such a questionable source." Tierney, "Marsilius on Rights," p. 5.

51. Innocent IV, "On *Decretales*, 3.34.8, *Quod Super, Commentaria* (c. 1250), fol. 429–30," in *The Crisis of Church and State, 1050–1300*, ed. Brian Tierney (Toronto: University of Toronto Press, 1988), p. 153. The primary passage cited by Innocent bears greater mention: "You have heard that it was said, 'You shall love your neighbor and hate your enemy.' But I say to you, Love your enemies and pray for those who persecute you, so that you may be sons of your Father who is in heaven; for he makes his sun rise on the evil and on the good, and sends rain on the just and on the unjust. For if you love those who love you, what reward have you? Do not even the tax collectors do the same?" (Matthew 5:43–46, Revised Standard Version).

52. Francisco de Vitoria, "On the American Indians," in *Political Writings*, ed. Anthony Pagden and Jeremy Lawrence (Cambridge: Cambridge University Press, 1991), p. 240.

53. Ibid., p. 240.

54. Ibid., p. 250.

55. Ibid., pp. 249–50. Vitoria also notes that, even were it to be conceded, *arguendo*, that the Indians suffered from "mental incapacity," any power the Spaniards might exercise over them would apply only "if everything is done for the benefit and good of the barbarians, and not merely for the profit of the Spaniards" (p. 291).

56. Ibid., pp. 247–48. (The passage in brackets does not appear in some editions of Vitoria's works.)

57. For the complex relationship between power, right, law, and property, as expressed in the terms *dominium*, *lex*, and *ius*, see Richard Tuck, *Natural Rights Theories: Their Origins and Development* (Cambridge: Cambridge University Press, 1979), but see also the criticism in Brian Tierney, "Tuck on Rights: Some Medieval Problems," *History of Political Thought* 4(3), Winter 1983: pp. 429–39. Tierney claims that the use of *dominium* is more complex in the medieval context than Tuck believes, although this is less significant in the context of the later thinkers dealt with here. Tierney also suggests an alternative route to that sketched by Tuck for a medieval development of "a possessive theory of rights," starting with "Innocent IV's defence of the rights of infidels to property and jurisdiction, and the assertion attributed to Alexander of Hales that natural law actually dictated the institution of private property among fallen men" (p. 440). Tierney suggests a direct route to a "possessive theory of rights," starting from the declaration of Innocent IV and leading to "the Indies debates of Las Casas and Sepúlveda."

58. It is noteworthy that the idea of personal responsibility intrudes even in cases in which the self-proprietorship of the actor is denied. Consider the Roman law of noxal actions: "Noxal actions lie when slaves commit delicts—theft, robbery, loss, or contempt. The actions give the condemned owner an option to pay the damages as assessed in money or to make noxal surrender of the slave." *Justinian's Institutes*, trans. and intro. by Peter Birks and Grant McLeod (London: Duckworth, 1987), 4.8, p. 137. Ulpian noted the central role of moral responsibility for misdeeds on the part of either the master or the slave: "If a slave has killed with his owner's knowledge, the owner is liable in full; for he himself is deemed to have done the killing, but if he did not know, the action is noxal; for he should not be held liable for his slave's misdeed beyond handing him over noxally." The *Digest of Justinian*, op. cit., IX, 4, 2. The Roman law scholar Barry Nichols argues that "The liability was that of the wrongdoer, and the injured person could take vengeance on him. . . . The true character of this noxal liability is plain from the rule that it followed the wrongdoer (*noxa caput sequitur*). This meant that if the slave was, for example, manumitted before the action was brought, he himself was liable to an ordinary action; or if he were sold, the noxal action lay against his new owner." Nichols, *An Introduction to Roman Law* (Oxford: Clarendon Press, 1991), p. 223.

59. These statements are drawn from a variety of Vitoria's writings and are collected in Luciano Pereña Vicente, ed., *The Rights and Obligations of Indians and Spaniards in the New World, According to Francisco de Vitoria* (Salamanca, Spain: Universidad Pontificia de Salamanca, 1992); they are to be found on p. 17 of Vicente's work.

60. Bartolomé de Las Casas, *In Defense of the Indians*, trans. Stafford Poole (Dekalb, Ill.: Northern Illinois University Press, 1992), p. 42. Las Casas concluded his work with a moving plea: "The Indians are our brothers, and Christ has given his life for them. Why, then, do we persecute them with such inhuman savagery when they do not deserve such treatment? The past, because it cannot be undone, must be attributed to our weakness, provided that what has been taken unjustly is restored" (p. 362).

61. See the discussion in Aristotle, *Politics*, bk. I, chaps. 4–7.

62. In his *De Unico Vocationis Modo*, las Casas praised mutual advantage over exploitation: "Worldly, ambitious men who sought wealth and pleasure placed their hope in obtaining gold and silver by the labor and sweat, even through very harsh slavery, oppression, and death, of not only innumerable people but of the greater part of humanity. . . . And the insolence and madness of these men became so great that they did not hesitate to allege that the Indians were beasts or almost beasts, and publicly defamed them. Then they claimed that it was just to subject them to our rule by war, or to hunt them like beasts and then reduce them to slavery. Thus they could make use of the Indians at their pleasure. But the truth is that very many of the Indians were able to govern themselves in monastic, economic, and political life. They could teach us and civilize us, however, and even more, would dominate us by natural reason as the Philosopher said speaking of Greeks and barbarians." Cited in Lewis Hanke, *All Mankind Is One: A Study of the Disputation between Bartolomé de las Casas and Juan Ginés de Sepúlveda on the Religious and Intellectual Capacity of the American Indians* (Dekalb, Ill.: Northern Illinois University Press, 1974), p. 157.

63. In the course of this chapter, I articulate and defend a theory of personal identity that, although perhaps not superior in every respect to every other theory, provides a superior foundation for a political theory of justice. Various other thinkers have articulated theories of personal identity that are not dependent upon the identity or continuity of bodies. Notable among them is Derek Parfit, who, in his *Reasons and Persons* (Oxford: Oxford University Press, 1986), argues that "personal identity is not what matters" and that "what matters" is "psychological connectedness and/or continuity with the right kind of cause . . . [that] could be any kind of cause" (p. 215). My reasons for preferring a corporeal criterion of personal identity, and why such corporeal identity matters, are set forth in the course of this chapter.

64. Aristotle, *The Metaphysics*, trans. Hugh Tredennick (Cambridge, Mass.: Harvard University Press, 1933), IV, iii, 9, 1005b19, p. 161.

65. Ibid., IV, iii, 9, l005b20–23. The law of contradiction and the law of the excluded middle are, in the current context, equivalent.

66. Richard Overton, "An Arrow against All Tyrants and Tyranny," in *The English Levellers*, ed. Andrew Sharp (Cambridge: Cambridge University Press, 1998), p. 55. Sharp has modernized spelling, punctuation, and grammar. Interestingly, the phrase "right myself no more than my self" is "write my self no more than my self" in the excerpted version of the essay in G. E. Aylmer, ed., *The Levellers in the English Revolution* (Ithaca, N.Y.: Cornell University Press, 1975), p. 68, which has a more poetic ring to it and may be more true to Overton's style. It is worth noting that Overton is not endorsing unrestricted "egotism," or the right of each to whatever he or she can get. Rather, it is a right to equality: "No man has power over my rights and liberties, and I over no man's." On the relationship between self-proprietorship and freedom of conscience, see the discussion of Overton and other Levelers, as well as of John Locke and James Madison, in George H. Smith, "Philosophies of Toleration," in *Atheism, Ayn Rand, and Other Heresies* (Buffalo: Prometheus Press, 1991), pp. 97–129. Madison expressed the basis of property in conscience when he wrote, of every individual, that "He has a property of peculiar value in his religious opinions and the free communication of them." James Madison, "Property," *National Gazette*, March 27, 1792, in *The Papers of James Madison*, ed. R. A. Rutland and others (Charlottesville: University Press of Virginia, 1983), pp. 266–68, quotation from p. 266.

67. Richard Overton, "The Commoner's Complaint," in *Tracts on Liberty in the Puritan Revolution, 1638–1647, vol. III*, ed. W. Haller (New York: Columbia University Press, 1943), pp. 371–95, material quoted is on p. 381.

68. Ibid., p. 382.

69. John Locke, *An Essay Concerning Human Understanding*, ed. Peter H. Nidditch (1684; Oxford: Clarendon Press, 1975), bk. II, chap. XXVII, sec. 26, p. 346.

70. John Locke, *Two Treatises of Government*, ed. Peter Laslett (Cambridge: Cambridge University Press, 1988), II, sec. 27, pp. 287–88.

71. Aristotle, *Politics*, 1255b10–15, p. 43.

72. Hugo Grotius, *The Rights of War and Peace*, trans. A. C. Campbell (London: M. Walter Dunne, 1901), bk. I, chap. 11, 4, p. 19. Grotius's concept of the "suum"—Latin for "one's own"—is elucidated in Stephen Buckle, *Natural Law and the Theory of Property, Grotius to Hume* (Oxford: Clarendon Press, 1991), pp. 29–52.

73. Thomas Hodgskin, *The Natural and Artificial Right of Property Contrasted* (1832; Clifton, N.J.: Augustus M. Kelley, 1973), pp. 28–29.

74. The Count Destutt de Tracy, *A Treatise on Political Economy*, trans. Thomas Jefferson (1817; New York: Augustus M. Kelley, 1970), p. 47. Destutt relates the institution of several property, or of mine and thine, to the distinction between me and thee: "[T]he thine and the mine were never invented. They were acknowledged the day on which we could say *thee* and *me*; and the idea of *me* and *thee* or rather of *me* and something *other than me*, has arisen, if not the very day on which a feeling being has experienced impressions, at least the one on which, in consequence of these impressions, he has experienced the sentiment of willing, the possibility of acting, which is a consequence thereof, and a resistance to this sentiment and to this act. When afterwards among these resisting beings, consequently other than himself, the feeling and willing being has known that there were some feeling like himself, it has been forced to accord to them a *personality* other than his own, a *self* other than his own and different from his own. And it always has been impossible, as it always will be, that that which is *his* should not for him be different from that which is *theirs*" (p. 49). The "Review of Montesquieu" mentioned by Jefferson is *A Commentary and Review of Montesquieu's Spirit of Laws*, by Antoine Louis Claude Destutt de Tracy, trans. Thomas Jefferson (1811; New York: Burt Franklin, 1969).

75. See, for example, the arguments offered on behalf of psychological continuity as criterion of personal identity in Derek Parfit, *Reasons and Persons* (Oxford: Oxford University Press, 1986), and those offered by Thomas Nagel in *The View from Nowhere* (Oxford: Oxford University Press, 1986) on behalf of "the hypothesis that I am my brain" (p. 40). The "closest continuer" view of identity and the added concept of the reflexive self-referring of the "self-synthesizing self," advanced by Robert Nozick in his *Philosophical Explanations* (Cambridge, Mass.: Harvard University Press, 1981), are compatible with the view I expound in this essay, insofar as the "weighted metric" to which I appeal is one suitable to a "social matrix." As Nozick notes, "[P]roblems of overlap [in applying notions of identity to people] can arise at one time, given the different possibilities of carving up the world. If you can clump yourself along any (artificial) relations around reflexive self-referring, can your demarcation of yourself include my arms, or my whole body? Or even my capacity to reflexively self-refer? Some uniformity of delimitation is achieved in a social matrix. Rewards and punishments will lead to a boundary in a particular location along given innate salient features or dimensions. Recalcitrant individuals who act on their deviant classifications wherein part of their own body includes someone else's arms, will be punished, institutionalized, or killed. Usually, the mutual compatibility of self-definitions occurs with less hardship" (pp. 107–8). See also the consideration of the role of personal identity in assigning responsibility and in the attribution of benefits and obligations

in Eddy M. Zemach, "Love Thy Neighbor as Thyself, or Egoism and Altruism," in *Studies in Ethical Theory*, ed. Peter A. French, Theodore E. Uehling Jr., and Howard K. Wettstein, *Midwest Studies in Philosophy, vol. III* (Minneapolis: University of Minnesota Press, 1980), pp. 148–58. Zemach's approach suffers, however, from an excessively nominalist orientation, which, while allowing him to admit that "although everything in nature is, under some classification or other, a part of the agent of any given action x, there must be some parts of nature which are closer to x than others" (p. 154), keeps him from admitting substances or natural entities that are materially and numerically individuated; were he to admit such entities, individual personal responsibility would be a natural consequence of his analysis.

76. See Gareth Evans, "Self-Identification," in *Self-Knowledge*, ed. Quassim Cassam (Oxford: Oxford University Press, 1994), pp. 184–209. As Evans puts it, the judgment "*a* is F" is immune to error through misidentification if "it is based upon a way of knowing about objects such that it does not make sense for the subject to utter 'Something is F, but is it *a* that is F?' when the first component expresses knowledge which the subject does not think he has, or may have, gained in any other way" [than the normal way]. See Gareth Evans, *The Varieties of Reference*, ed. John McDowell (Oxford: Oxford University Press, 1982), pp. 189–90, quoted in a footnote in Gareth Evans, "Self-Identification," p. 194. The Stoic philosopher Epictetus considered such self-ascription the most certain kind of knowledge. In his response to the skepticism of the Pyrrhonists and the Academic philosophers, Epictetus argued, "But that you and I are not the same persons, I know very certainly. Whence do I get this knowledge? When I want to swallow something, I never take the morsel to that place, but to this." Epictetus, *The Discourses as Reported by Arrian*, vol. I, bk. I–II, trans. W. A. Oldfather (Cambridge, Mass.: Harvard University Press, 1998), I.27, 18–19, p. 173.

77. Gareth Evans, "Self-Identification," p. 198. Evans also allows certain forms of mental self-ascription to be immune from errors of misidentification, for perceptual states "must occur in the context of certain kinds of knowledge and understanding on the part of the subject" (p. 208) that will entail knowledge of a persisting self: "No judgment will have the content of a psychological self-ascription, unless the judger can be regarded as ascribing to himself a property which he can conceive as being satisfied by a being not necessarily himself—a state of affairs which he will have to conceive as involving a persisting subject of experience. He can know that a state of affairs of the relevant type obtains simply by being aware of a tree, but he must conceive the state of affairs that he then knows to obtain as a state of affairs of precisely that type. And this means that he must conceive of himself, the subject to whom the property is ascribed, as a being of the kind which he envisages when he simply envisages someone seeing a tree—that is to say, a persisting subject to experience, located in space and time" (p. 208).

78. As Adam Smith notes of "the man of system," "apt to be very wise in his own conceit . . . [and] . . . so enamoured with the supposed beauty of his own ideal plan of government, that he cannot suffer the smallest deviation from any part of it": "He seems to imagine that he can arrange the different members of a great society with as much ease as the hand arranges the different pieces upon a chess-board. He does not consider that the pieces upon the chess-board have no other principle of motion besides that which the hand impresses upon them; but that, in the great chessboard of human society, every single piece has a principle of motion of its own, altogether different from that which the legislature might chuse to impress upon it." *The Theory of Moral Sentiments* (Oxford: Oxford University Press, 1976), pp. 233–34.

79. As Hugo Grotius notes, "It is the *civil* law . . . which makes an owner answerable for the mischief or damage done by his slave, or by his cattle. For in the eye of natural justice he is not to blame." *The Rights of War and Peace*, bk. II, chap. XVII, par. XXI, p. 201.

80. That is the claim of Thomas Nagel, regarding at least pleasure and pain, in *The View from Nowhere*, pp. 156–62. Nagel claims that the idea that "pleasure is a good thing and pain is a bad thing" (p. 159) is "self-evident" and that to deny it and to assert the agent-relativity of all values "is a very peculiar attitude to take toward the primitive comforts and discomforts of life" (p. 160). I do not find Nagel's claims convincing, although "something like it" seems to be true. That "something like it" is to be found in the principle of sympathy (most normal people are concerned about the welfare, including the pleasures and pains, of others) and in the deontic side constraints to be discussed in a moment. For a defense of the agent-relativity of all values, see Eric Mack, "Agent-Relativity of Value, Deontic Restraints, and Self-Ownership," in *Value, Welfare, and Morality*, ed. R. G. Prey and Christopher W. Morris (Cambridge: Cambridge University Press, 1993), pp. 209–32.

81. See Eric Mack, "Personal Integrity, Practical Recognition, and Rights," *The Monist* 76(1), January 1993: pp. 101–18.

82. See the discussion of the issues related to such an agent-neutral consequential-ism in Samuel Scheffler, *The Rejection of Consequentialism: A Philosophical Investigation of the Considerations Underlying Rival Moral Conceptions* (Oxford: Clarendon Press, 1982). Scheffler attempts to integrate into an agent-neutral consequentialist approach an "agent-centered prerogative" that would allow individuals to avoid pursuing agent-neutral values in certain cases where they might violate the integrity of the agent.

83. Eric Mack, "Personal Integrity, Practical Recognition, and Rights," p. 102: "in general, in such [favorable social and material] circumstances the constraining deontic reason prevails in the sense that, although the value of the ends which the agent seeks is not denigrated, the agent is precluded from obtaining them through the contemplated course of action."

84. On the role of value and project pursuit in the attainment of personal identity and coherence, see Loren Lomasky, *Persons, Rights, and the Moral Community* (Oxford: Oxford University Press, 1987). As Lomasky notes, "[R]egard for someone as a rights holder is grounded in the recognizability of that being as a distinct individual. It is not *personhood* which calls for respect but rather distinct persons. Between these two conceptions there is a sharp divide, one separating an ethic in which individualism is valued from an ethic subscribing entirely to an impersonal standard of value" (p. 167). Cf. Thomas Nagel ("Equality," in Thomas Nagel, *Mortal Questions* [Cambridge: Cambridge University Press, 1979]): "The concern with what one is doing to whom, as opposed to the concern with what happens, is an important primary source of ethics that is poorly understood" (p. 115).

85. For a fuller explanation of compossibility, see Hillel Steiner, "The Structure of a Theory of Compossible Rights," *Journal of Philosophy* 74, 1977: pp. 767–75.

86. Cf. Hillel Steiner, *An Essay on Rights* (Oxford: Blackwell, 1994), p. 3: "Any justice principle that delivers a set of rights yielding contradictory judgements about the permissibility of a particular action either is unrealizable or (what comes to the same thing) must be modified to be realizable."

87. Plato, *The Republic*, trans. Allan Bloom (New York: Basic Books, 1968), 352d, p. 31.

88. Hillel Steiner, *An Essay on Rights*, p. 88. In justification of this claim, Steiner notes immediately before it (pp. 87–88) that "[S]ince (i) a right is entailed by a correlative duty, and (ii) a set of categorically compossible rights is entailed by a set of categorically compossible correlative duties, and (iii) such duties are ones involving the duty-holder's exercise of only his vested liberties, and (iv) vested liberties imply duties of forbearance in others, it follows that *a set of categorically compossible rights implies the presence of rights in duty-holders*: namely, rights correlative to those forbearance duties that conjunctively form the perimeter surrounding any dutyholder's vested liberties."

89. See the discussion of the relationship between duties and rights in John Locke's theory in A. John Simmons, *The Lockean Theory of Rights* (Princeton, N.J.: Princeton University Press, 1992), pp. 72–75.

90. Not all rights are directly derivable from obligations, for there are many cases in which one may assert a claim that does not prejudice others, which is neither a necessary condition for fulfilling an obligation nor a forbearance from failing to fulfill an obligation. As Locke notes, every person has from birth "*A Right of Freedom to his Person*, which no other Man has a Power over, but the free Disposal of it lies in himself." John Locke, *Two Treatises of Government*, II, sec. 190, pp. 393–94. Locke asserts that "Wherever others are not 'prejudiced,' 'every man' may consider what suits his own convenience, and follow what course he likes best." As cited in A. John Simmons, *The Lockean Theory of Rights*, p. 77. For a careful exposition and use of the distinction between intensionally described and extensionally described actions, see Hillel Steiner, *An Essay on Rights*.

91. See Steiner, *An Essay on Rights*: "The rights constituting a person's domain are ... easily conceived as property rights; they are (time-indexed) rights to physical things. A set of categorically compossible domains, constituted by a set of property rights, is one in which each person's rights are demarcated in such a way as to be mutually exclusive of every other person's rights" (p. 91).

92. Immanuel Kant, "The Metaphysics of Morals," in *Political Writings*, ed. Hans Reiss (Cambridge: Cambridge University Press, 1992), p. 133.

93. Ibid., p. 133.

94. The one basic right, then, is the right to freedom: "Freedom (independence from the constraint of another's will), insofar as it is compatible with the freedom of everyone else in accordance with a universal law, is the one sole and original right that belongs to every human being by virtue of his humanity." Immanuel Kant, *The Metaphysical Elements of Justice*, trans. John Ladd (New York: Macmillan Publishing Co., 1985), pp. 43–44.

95. Aristotle, *Politics* (1272b5–8), p. 80.

6. No Exit: Framing the Problem of Justice

Recent years have seen a marked retreat from cosmopolitan liberalism in moral and political theory. What is remarkable is that that retreat has been carried out under the banner of liberalism. Many modern "liberals" (in contrast to "classical" liberals) have taken as their touchstone adherence to the redistributive welfare state. The obligations and benefits allocated by welfare states are normally limited to particular groups of subjects or citizens; they are not universal.[1]

John Rawls has prepared the field for much of that retreat. In his books and various articles Rawls has combined powerful sources of legitimacy for institutions and practices—mutual advantage, fairness, and agreement—into one account: justice as fairness. When he stipulates that the principles of a just society "are those a person would choose for the design of a society in which his enemy is to assign him his place," Rawls builds in a highly illiberal premise into his theory of justice by foreclosing the exit option.[2] What was implicit in *A Theory of Justice* is made explicit in *Political Liberalism*: in setting out "the context of a social contract," Rawls insists that "membership in our society is given, that we would not know what we would have been like had we not belonged to it. . . . Since membership in their society is given, there is no question of the parties comparing the attractions of other societies."[3] Rawls finds that for his construction to work it must be restricted to "a structure of basic institutions we enter only by birth and exit only by death";[4] strikingly, "the question of our entering another society does not arise."[5] Rawls has attempted to generate allegedly liberal outcomes from a choice situation that

Originally published in *Ordered Anarchy: Jasay and His Surroundings*, edited by Hardy Bouillon and Hartmut Kliemt. Aldershot, UK: Ashgate Publishing Limited, 2007.

is highly illiberal. Cosmopolitanism, universalism, and internationalism—defining characteristics of traditional liberalism—disappear in the Rawlsian enterprise. That disappearance represents a general trend in contemporary political theory. Communitarians, socialists, welfare statists, nationalists (and the various combinations among those) have been drawn away from cosmopolitanism for many of the very same reasons that Rawls posits "a structure of basic institutions we enter only by birth and exit only by death." The case for preferring coercion over free association rests on an assumption that is both hardly self-evident and incompatible with core elements of the liberal tradition. "Fairness" is a solution to a problem that was slipped into the specification of the choice situation by fiat, by arbitrarily excluding well-established, well-understood, and widely employed principles of free association from the options available to choosers.

The sleight-of-hand involved is remarkably similar to that typically involved in specification of the choice situation governing the provision of public goods. Once a decision has been made to produce a good on a non-exclusive basis, it is then asserted that the good cannot be produced through voluntary, uncoerced cooperation. Or the demonstration begins by assuming the existence of a good from which consumers cannot be excluded (or can only be excluded at some cost), when the problem is to produce such goods in the first place. Assuming that the good exists is hardly a solution to the problem of how to produce it. Similarly, by excluding exit or choice among options *as* an option, the problem of distribution of rights and obligations is converted into a pure bargaining game, which sets the stage for Rawls's voluminous writings and the many jots and tittles added by his followers. By eliminating such options, Rawls does not solve a problem of justice or fair division; he creates it.

What follows is a brief excursion through the Rawlsian choice situation, setting out several unresolved problems and showing the significance of a quite problematic assumption that has received too little attention.

Mutual Advantage and Distributive Justice

In order to elicit agreement to the basic structure of society, Rawls argues, all groups, including the worst off, must benefit from the scheme of cooperation that governs a society: "since everyone's well-being depends upon a scheme of cooperation without which no one could have a satisfactory life, the division of advantages should be such as to draw forth the willing cooperation of everyone taking part in it, including those less well situated."[6] Rawls stands firmly in the tradition of social contract theory in seeking to ground the social contract on mutual advantage. All must expect to benefit, in order for all to be obligated.

Rawls believes that people seeking their mutual advantage behind a veil of ignorance would insist on a benchmark of equality in the distribution of resources, departures from which would require justification. As Rawls states, "from the standpoint of one person selected arbitrarily":

> Since it is not reasonable for him to expect more than an equal share in the division of social goods, and since it is not rational for him to agree to less, the sensible thing for him to do is to acknowledge as the first principle of justice one requiring an equal distribution. Indeed, this principle is so obvious that we would expect it to occur to anyone immediately.
>
> Thus, the parties start with a principle establishing equal liberty for all, including equality of opportunity, as well as an equal distribution of income and wealth. But there is no reason why this acknowledgment should be final. If there are inequalities in the basic structure that work to make everyone better off in comparison with the benchmark of initial equality, why not permit them?[7]

The reason that inequalities may be to the advantage of those who end up with less is that if "these inequalities set up various incentives which succeed in eliciting more productive efforts, a person in the original position may look upon them as necessary to cover the costs of training and to encourage effective performance."[8] That leads Rawls to the formulation of his "difference principle," according to which "social and economic inequalities are to be arranged so that they are both: (a) to the greatest benefit of the least advantaged, consistent with the just savings principle, and (b) attached to offices and positions open to all under conditions of fair equality of opportunity."[9]

How Much Inequality Does the Difference Principle License?

In an early review of *A Theory of Justice*, Thomas C. Grey raised a serious objection to the justification of the difference principle, suggesting that it suffers from "a psychological or moral if not a logical inconsistency."[10] The inconsistency concerns the combination of the insistence on a baseline of equality in the distribution of wealth, arising from the alleged "moral irrelevance" of natural or inherited talents or capabilities, and the admission of incentives in the justification of divergence from equality and the establishment of a regime of inequality in the distribution of wealth.

Grey argues that that justification suffers from a "failure to establish any limits of justice on the bargaining power of those with more than average productive abilities. The standard is in principle indeterminate between complete equality of income, on the one hand, and income wholly determined by productivity, on the other."[11] As Grey notes, "The principle apparently contemplates some extra payment to those with scarce or special skills . . . [in the belief that] paying differential incomes to those with extra skills will bring forth extra production from them."[12]

> How can I justly bargain for more than an equal share by threatening to withhold my scarce talent? It must be because I have some special claim on these talents and their fruits. But if they are considered a social asset—as Rawls apparently regards them—I can have no such special claim. On the other hand, if my talents and the fruits of the use I choose to make of them belong to me, then there can be no justified coercion of me if I do not choose to share them with others. The inequalities which Rawls would permit suggest some acquiescence in this view. But those who press this view to its limits will reject the notion that greater equality of income is a legitimate aim of public policy.[13]

Let us press that view to its limits: the difference principle either results in no deviation from voluntary market outcomes, as the allowance of incentives entails the recognition of claims by possessors of natural assets and consequently of bargaining rights, *or*, if the difference principle *is* to realize a redistributive aim, it requires both premises and outcomes that are highly objectionable and counterintuitive, and certainly highly *illiberal*.[14] Rawls's attempt to justify a redistributive state can only succeed by rejecting such fundamental liberal precepts as the right of exit and the universality of principles of justice.

A problem ancillary to the problem that Grey identifies as the indeterminacy of the difference principle "between complete equality of income, on the one hand, and income wholly determined by productivity, on the other," is, what is the baseline of equality in the distribution of wealth from which inequality is to be measured? Given that there is some wealth in existence at any given time, are we to say that inequalities are to be measured from the base currently existing at time t_1 (Wt_1), with Wt_1 to be shared out precisely equally? Setting aside the perhaps insuperable difficulties in determining how much inequality (not too much and not too little) is necessary to satisfy the difference principle from any base, we can ask why the total wealth later on, say at t_2, should not be shared out equally. How are we to determine the baseline of equal distribution of wealth from which inequality is to be justified?

Why use Wt_1 rather than Wt_2 as the baseline of equal wealth distribution? Given that production is a process that takes place over time, why should any one of the periods $Wt_1 \ldots \infty$ be subject to strict equalization, but not others? There seems little in the specification of the original position to lend us guidance; certainly the discussion in *A Theory of Justice* of "intergenerational justice"[15] is no guide.

Besides those problems of determining the baseline and the allowable divergences therefrom, there is the far more serious problem of determining just why some are allowed to demand more than are others. Under a principle of strictly equal distribution of total product, one who produces more would be expected to produce for the benefit of others, as well as for herself, since out of a population of k, she would receive only $1/k$ of the increase in productivity due to her additional efforts. But Rawls specifically insists that we cannot expect individuals to serve one another in that way:

> One might think that ideally individuals should want to serve one another. But since the parties are assumed not to take an interest in one another's interests, their acceptance of these inequalities is only the acceptance of the relations in which men stand in the circumstances of justice. They have no grounds for complaining of one another's motives. A person in the original position would, therefore, concede the justice of these inequalities.[16]

What is being asserted, then, is that those who insist on being paid more to produce more are allowed to demand a larger share of the total product than others receive. What they are allowed to say, in effect, is that they will not produce anything, or they will deliberately produce less, unless they are allowed to demand (and to receive) a special incentive in the form of an unequal share, that is, unless they are allowed to make an "unreasonable" claim.[17]

The very idea of incentives for greater production (as opposed to covering the costs of training and production, which is fully consistent with equal distribution of consumer goods, so long as no residual remains over the costs of production)[18] is an admission of a *right* of the better endowed, or of those who are simply better at bargaining (which need not entail any absolute advantage in productive capacity), to demand a larger share of the product. If a person must be *allowed* to "hold out" for more, it can only be because she has a right to do so. Having a right *not* to work entails a right to bargain for a larger share of the product in exchange for working; if she has a right to employ or to withhold her time, labor, and endowments, then she has a liberty right to them (to employ them) and a claim right (to exclude others from employing them against her will). Rawls, however, has committed himself to the position that such factors as intelligence, strength, cleverness, and even motivation (and *certainly* bargaining ability) are "undeserved" and that they are therefore morally irrelevant in the decision of a fundamentally moral problem—the distribution of goods in society.[19] Yet by introducing incentives for greater production, he tacitly allows those "morally irrelevant" factors to play a role in the distribution of goods. The difference principle seems to allow either voluntary market distribution or completely equal distribution; nothing in between complete equality and completely voluntary arrangements (which may, of course, also be equal, depending on the voluntary choices of the cooperating agents) seems to be derivable from Rawls's arguments. There is a fundamental contradiction in Rawls's enterprise.

Exile to the Production Frontier

Rawlsian justice faces a problem: either it amounts to classical liberal voluntarism, with no fairness-based coercive redistribution of income, or it demands complete equality in the distribution of wealth. The latter route leads Rawls away from traditional liberalism and universalism, for if the difference principle were taken seriously as a redistributive principle, it would entail an enforceable obligation to produce at one's production frontier, that means, work could be made compulsory on the principle of conscript labor. As Alan Donagan notes, the difference principle "is a principle of servitude: not only does it expropriate to a common pool everything above the minimum to the social product, returning only what is necessary to ensure that the difference will continue to be produced, but it also requires a social structure that takes away the option of idleness when one's own needs and the demands of beneficence have been met."[20] Rawls's scheme, to be made operational, would entail a duty to work up to the point where the worst off have been made as well off as possible, as "social and economic inequalities are to be arranged . . . *to the greatest benefit* of the least advantaged"[21] (emphasis added).

Rawls is not saved by his first principle of justice (equal liberties) from the unpleasant conclusion that forced labor may be justified to enforce the universal obligation to produce one's maximum product so as to enable redistribution to the greatest benefit of the worst off group, because the only liberties he includes in the "basic liberties" are "political" and, in Donagan's words, "*these* basic liberties would not directly exclude the conscription of labor in time of peace."[22] What *could* save the principle, according to Brian Barry, is the second half of Rawls's second principle, which Rawls states as follows:

> Social and economic inequalities are to be arranged so that they are both (a) to the greatest benefit of the least advantaged and (b) attached to offices and positions open to all under conditions of fair equality of opportunity.[23]

Part (b) of the second principle above, Barry claims, "looks like a pretty strong statement of the importance of occupational choice, and I think that, even if Rawls does not list it among the 'basic liberties,' the best interpretation of his theory is that he regards it as having priority over the difference principle."[24] So construed, the constraints placed upon the difference principle by the second half of the second principle make the limitation on inequality of wealth (or income) otiose, because one can always claim that one wants (or "needs") a larger than equal share of the product and back up the claim by a threat not to produce if one does not receive a larger share. That threat would be justified by Barry's construal of part (b) of the second principle. There is a further problem: Even if conscripted labor services *were* ruled out by the principle of open offices and fair opportunity (something that is *not* entirely clear from the priorities of principles that Rawls lays out, but which seems a fair enough move to make in defense of the Rawlsian approach), the principle of fair equality of opportunity would *not* be *in*consistent with taxation of labor at its highest assessed use, as land and other assets are taxed.

To understand how such a capacity tax would work, consider the case of taxation of the productive asset of land. Land is typically taxed on the basis of an assessment of its most highly remunerative employment (measured in money), regardless of whether it is actually being employed in that way. In the same way, a capacity tax could be assessed based on what one "could earn" even if one were not in fact earning that at the moment because one placed a high value on leisure or simply because one does not like the occupation that would produce the highest income.[25] That would not run afoul of the "principle of fair opportunity," even under its most generously liberal construal of it, although the effects of such a capacity tax would be difficult to differentiate from chattel slavery.[26] If such a capacity tax were deemed to maximize the position of the least advantaged, then it would seem to be demanded by the difference principle. There must surely be some wealth producers (or even classes of them) who are producing less wealth than they *could* produce; were they to produce more of those goods, there would be a larger surplus available for distribution to the least well off. Hence, by not producing what they *could* produce, such "slackers" are diminishing the prospects of the least well off, relative to what the least well off could enjoy were the "slackers" to produce more.

Who Is Everyone?

The considerations above go to the question of whether Rawls has developed an authentically *liberal* theory of justice. If forced labor were the outcome, it would be hard to see how that could be squared with the tradition of liberalism, which has, after all, the concept of liberty in its very name.

One could attempt to make a system of illiberal coercion universal, but Rawls does not take that approach. In the process, he abandons cosmopolitanism, as well. The reason is embedded in the difference principle itself, for when Rawls in *A Theory of Justice* refers to "inequalities in the basic structure that work to make everyone better off in comparison with the benchmark of equality" (p. 151) he leaves ambiguous the question of whom he is designating by the term "everyone." Does it mean every party to a transaction, or every party to the social contract, or does it mean literally every human being, or even every rational creature? Who is covered? Presumably, Rawls intends every member of the basic cooperating group governed by the contract and that is invariably cashed out to mean the subjects of a particular nation state. Allan Gibbard, in his review of Brian Barry's *Theories of Justice*,[27] addresses the issue of the membership of the group over which the difference principle is to extend. In response to Brian Barry's challenge, on grounds of "impartiality," to extend the principle to the entirety of humanity, Gibbard draws out of Rawls's work an approach that does not "hover uneasily . . . between impartiality and mutual advantage," as Barry claims, but that is "intrinsically reciprocal."[28] Gibbard imagines a "well-off person" putting to Rawls the following question: "Why limit myself in pursuit of my own advantage?"[29] Gibbard answers for Rawls as follows:

> Rawls, in effect, gives this answer: "You have what you have only because others constrain themselves, in ways that make for a fair cooperative venture for mutual advantage. Constrain yourself by those rules in return, and you give them fair return for what they give you."[30]

Gibbard offers a thought experiment to clarify the notion of reciprocity: imagine that "each person sprang into existence on a separate island, adult and able, and each was protected by the water from threats and takings" and that the islands differ in fertility.[31] Gibbard concludes that

> from the bare assumption that fertility is morally arbitrary, no obligation to share follows. The lucky ones could still admit that their luck is morally arbitrary, and still ask "Why share?" One answer that they could not be given is that sharing pays others back for their cooperation or their restraint. No one has cooperated and no one has restrained

himself, and so there is nothing to pay back. Motives of fair reciprocity, then, would not lead the lucky ones to share, even though they freely admitted that their luck was morally arbitrary.[32]

Rawls takes up that theme in *Political Liberalism*, endorsing Gibbard's approach and maintaining that "the idea of reciprocity is not the idea of mutual advantage."[33] Gibbard's attempted solution comes at a high cost, however, in the form of contradicting openly another basic Rawlsian tenet. Among the "formal constraints of the concept or right" in *A Theory of Justice* are the requirements that conceptions of justice must be general, universal, public, capable of imposing a transitive ordering on conflicting claims, and final.[34] In his elaboration of the penultimate item on his list of formal constraints, the requirement that a concept of right create a transitive ordering of competing claims, Rawls notes that "it is to avoid the appeal to force and cunning that the principles of right and justice are accepted. Thus I assume that to each according to his threat advantage is not a conception of justice."[35] But a consequence of the very definition of an "intrinsically reciprocating group," to which Gibbard and Rawls limit the range of the principles of justice, is that they rest the entire theory of justice on threat advantage, on the possibility of the employment of force and cunning. Those who can make credible threats of harm are accorded membership in intrinsically reciprocating groups and are entitled to be treated "fairly," while those who cannot make credible threats do not deserve to be treated justly.

Gibbard sets up his thought experiment by specifying that among the islanders "each was protected by the water from threats and takings." In his scenario there is no *reciprocity* of restraint, because the islanders have no intercourse whatsoever; the islanders need not even know of each other's existence. There is neither mutual advantage nor reciprocity. But if the parties *are* capable of harming each other it might reasonably be said that they *do* reciprocate simply by *abstaining* from aggressive "threats and takings"; if not killing or stealing qualifies as "cooperation," then, Gibbard's argument maintains, the difference principle *does* extend over all of the islanders—lucky and unlucky—as a group, and inequalities among them must be specially justified (if, that is, such inequalities can be justified at all, given the problems with "incentives" noted above). Gibbard and Rawls define "intrinsically reciprocal" groups by determining whether the members of the groups have the capacity to harm one another, which seems more congenial to starting with a Hobbesian threat advantage (which Rawls dismisses from his construction) than with the idea of people joined voluntarily together in an ongoing project of social cooperation.

There is an ancillary problem: if "everyone" (however defined) must be made better off, what does "better off" mean? Jan Narveson distinguishes two possible meanings of the phrase:

> D1. "Everyone is better off" = "No one is worse off" (persons outside the transaction may be unaffected, compatibly with the requirement)
>
> D2. "Everyone is better off" = "Each person's situation is improved by comparison with what it was before the transaction" (persons outside the transaction must be favorably affected, to meet the requirement)[36]

As Narveson notes, interpreting the phrase in the first way would make the difference principle otiose, and interpreting it in the second way makes it indeterminate, for the reasons that Thomas Grey offered. What "make everyone better off" must mean, if the difference principle is not to be rendered otiose (as Narveson's interpretation "D1" would do), is that some people are to be given a veto power over the mutually advantageous interactions of others. Thus, even though C is *not hurt* by A's and B's voluntary cooperation, C is able to insist forcibly that A and B not be allowed to cooperate unless C receive a payment for not exercising her veto; the payment would come in the form of some share (in principle indeterminate) of the results of A's and B's cooperation. That means that C has a kind of ownership claim over A and B; she would determine how A and B shall use their resources and demand a payment from them for the privilege of being allowed to cooperate together.[37]

If it were to be responded that Rawls only intends for the difference principle to be embedded in the "basic structure" and not to be applied to individual transactions, one can point out that *all* the transactions to which it might be applied necessarily *are* individual transactions (there being no abstract or universal transactions) and that the principle must be applied over some temporal horizon, whether transaction-by-transaction (regardless of the duration of the transaction), or on a daily, monthly, yearly, or some other basis. The difference principle may be *articulated* at the stage of determining the basic structure in the original position, but it is *exercised* upon the transactions that take place after the basic structure has been determined. Which time horizon is chosen, from minute-by-minute to every hundred years, is not relevant to the general point I am making. One group (C) is given a right of veto over the voluntary transactions of others (A and B) unless it gets a cut, and that amounts to holding a claim right or a power against the members of A and B by being able to stop them by force from transacting.[38] If mutual advantage defines socially cooperative groups, and therefore the membership of the social contract, one can legitimately ask why a group cannot separate out if it believes that *its* mutual advantage would lie in a contract governing distribution of a joint product produced *without* the cooperation of others who might produce a smaller share and then demand and enforce a share of the product disproportionate to its contribution.[39] Allowing such withdrawal would undercut the difference principle by allowing the exit of those who believe that they could do better without having their product redistributed to others.

It is for that reason—to salvage the difference principle—that Rawls must "close the door" of exit by insisting that entry into society "is only by birth and exit from it is only by death." If individuals were to be able to withdraw and form other groups at will, the core problems of fair distribution with which Rawls is concerned would effectively disappear. The closure move does not so much solve a problem of justice and fair division, as create it.

Joint Products and the Problem of Distribution

The Rawlsian enterprise rests on the idea of the "fair distribution" of a joint product. Before discussing "fair distribution," an examination of the idea of a "joint product" is in order. Social cooperation may be valuable for a number of reasons, but surely prominent (if not foremost) among them is because cooperation results in a product greater than would be possible in its absence. The problem of justice is (at least principally) a problem of how that joint product is shared, allocated, or distributed, or of how the rewards of cooperative activity are imputed to those who have contributed to such activity. As Russell Hardin poses the problem, "If the bulk of what we enjoy is the result of collective endeavors in our society, then the bulk of what we have is up for redistribution."[40]

Economic science has something to say about the distribution of joint products among cooperators. In general, when markets exist (meaning, in this context, alternative uses of goods and free choice of factor owners among alternative employments of their factors) and factors of production are complementary and non-specific, meaning that they can be combined in various ways and put to a range of productive uses (for example, land for farming, recreation, or housing), then the proportion of the anticipated final value of the joint product imputed to the factors, that is, the *prices* paid for the factors, will tend to reflect their marginal value product (MVP). (To be more precise, what is imputed to the factors of production is the *discounted* marginal value product (DMVP), with the discount reflecting preference accorded to the time between the payment of the factor and the realized value or sale price of the final product.) When two or more factors of production are complementary but purely product-specific, then no market (in the sense of alternative uses of the factors, which entails the existence of opportunity costs) exists, meaning that a determinate marginal value product cannot be imputed to the factors in the form of a price or dividend paid; all that can be determined is a joint MVP, namely the MVP of the combination of the two factors. (When the factors can only be combined in fixed ratios, then there is no way to determine marginal value product at all.) That is to say, the MVP to be imputed to the two factors together is equal to the total product (TP) minus the sum of the MVPs of all other factors. The proportion of the residual joint MVP of the specific factors to be shared by the factor owners will be purely a result of bargaining and cannot be determined by reference to marginal product. It is precisely the lack of an alternative employment or allocation of the factor that results in an indeterminate distribution of imputed value over which the factor owners must bargain or arrive at some salient or "reasonable" distributive outcome or principle.[41]

One way to *create* a situation of bargaining over the distribution of a joint product is to eliminate all alternative uses of the factor inputs by not allowing factor possessors to withdraw some or all of the factors and employ them elsewhere or not at all. If alternative uses disappear—perhaps due to radical changes in technology—or are cut off by fiat, the result is an indeterminate range of distributions (or imputation) of the value of the joint product to the factors in the form of the prices that they can command.

In effect, what Rawls and his followers are arguing is that "society" is a joint product the distribution of the value of which cannot be allowed to result from market principles of voluntary choice among alternatives, principles which normally result in a tendency for factor owners to receive their marginal value products.[42] The reason is that no alternative allocation of the factors, including our labor power, can be considered that will generate reservation prices capable of establishing at least a set of highest and lowest exchange ratios (or set of baselines) within which the value product is to be determined. It then follows that, as Hardin notes, "the bulk of what we have is up for redistribution."[43] This notion of a joint product attributable to factors of production that are *specific* (that is, for which there is no market or range of uses among or within which they may be allocated) is crucial to the enterprise of generating fair principles of distribution. It is the *closing off* of alternative uses by fiat that results in a pure bargaining or agreement problem.

One could argue that I am guilty here of the fallacy of affirming the consequent:

> (A) If two or more factors of production have no alternative employments, then there is a bargaining (or rational agreement) problem.
> (B) There is a bargaining (or rational agreement) problem.
> (C) Therefore, there are two or more factors of production that have no alternative employments.

This would be a fallacious argument. Rawls has, however, saved me from falling into fallacy by specifically noting that, in order to avoid admitting market principles of voluntary agreement into "the political," entry and exit options (that is alternative employments of our resources, most notably of our persons) are to be shut off.

In *Political Liberalism*, Rawls straightforwardly acknowledges that freedom of entry and exit do generate "measures of worth" and therefore "a basis for contractual calculations" (other than bargaining, salience, or some other form of agreement). But he claims that that applies only to "particular agreements" and not to "the political." In the case of association, one simply notes how the venture or association would fare without that person's joining, and the difference measures their worth to the venture or association. The attractiveness of joining to the individuals is ascertained by a comparison with their opportunities. Thus particular agreements are reached in the context of existing and foreseeable configurations of relationships within the basic structure; and it is these configurations that provide a basis for contractual calculations.

The context of a social contract is strikingly different, and must allow for three facts, among others: namely, that membership in our society is given, that we cannot know what we would have been like had we not belonged to it (perhaps the thought itself lacks sense), and that society as a whole has no ends or ordering of ends in the way that associations and individuals do. The bearing of these facts is clear once we try to regard the social contract as an ordinary agreement and ask how deliberations leading up to it would proceed. Since membership in their society is given, there is no question of the parties comparing the attractions of other societies. Moreover, there is no way to identify someone's potential contribution to society who is not yet a member of it; for this potentiality cannot be known and is, in any case, irrelevant to their present situation.[44]

Rawls acknowledges that free allocation of resources among alternative employments generates "measures of worth" but states that "there is no way to identify someone's potential contribution to society who is not yet a member of it." That is patently false; many people *do* make decisions to emigrate from one society to another, sometimes more than once, and they do so on the basis of the kinds of estimations that Rawls asserts are not possible.

In order to avoid market solutions to the problems he intends to treat, Rawls must stipulate that "membership in society" is "given," that is, unalterable. It is a stipulation that is contradicted by the experience of millions of persons. In addition to being an unhelpful characterization of the problem of political choice, the stipulation that parties cannot choose "membership in our society" does not help us to *solve* problems of "distributive justice," for it *generates* them instead.

Fairness and Inescapable Public Goods

Rawls places great weight in the generation of obligations on what he calls "the principle of fairness." According to Rawls,

> The main idea is that when a number of persons engage in a mutually advantageous cooperative venture according to rules, and thus restrict their liberty in ways necessary to yield advantages for all, those who have submitted to these restrictions have a right to a similar acquiescence on the part of those who have benefited from their submission. We are not to gain from the cooperative labors of others without doing our fair share.[45]

Rawls even claims, quite implausibly, that "All obligations arise in this way."[46]

The cooperative venture with which Rawls is concerned in setting out his theory of justice as fairness is "the basic structure of society, or more exactly, the way in which major social institutions distribute fundamental rights and duties and determine the division of advantages from social cooperation."[47] It is significant that he refers to the basic structure of society as "the arrangement of major social institutions into *one* scheme of cooperation"[48] (emphasis added). Rawls is a very careful writer, and I believe that in *A Theory of Justice* he had, even if not in a fully articulated way, the idea that the option of comparing alternative "arrangement[s] of social institutions" would not be allowed to play any role in agreement on the principles of social cooperation. In effect, by insisting on that restriction, he conjured up the very problem that his work was written to solve.

The social cooperation made possible by the basic structure is to the advantage of all members of society, and that advantage is demonstrated through their agreement to the basic structure governing the division of the advantages: "the guiding idea is that the principles of justice for the basic structure of society are the object of the original agreement."[49] The choice situation, as well as the agreement itself, are understood "as a purely hypothetical situation characterized so as to lead to a certain conception of justice."[50] Robert Nozick has responded to that assertion of the principle of fairness with a counterargument and a counterassertion. The counterargument concerns the coherence of Hart's general argument about the generation of special obligations,[51] and the counterassertion is as follows:

> On the face of it, enforcing the principle of fairness is objectionable. You may not decide to give me something, for

example a book, and then grab money from me to pay for
it, even if I have nothing better to spend the money on.[52]

On its face, Nozick's counterassertion seems quite plausible, at
least for most situations, especially considering the experience so
many have had in airports with disciples of messianic religious or
political leaders thrusting books or flowers into their hands and
then insisting on "contributions." We cannot admit a theory of obligations that allows people gratuitously and unilaterally to impose
benefits on others and thereby to create obligations with corollary
"rights to force" on the part of the unilateral benefit-imposers.[53]

But perhaps Rawls and others in the tradition of "hypothetical"
social contract have only a certain class of benefits in mind: those
from which one "cannot" escape. They may readily admit that the
pressing of a flower into the hand of a traveling passenger does not
generate an enforceable obligation on the part of the recipient to
pay her "fair share" of the costs of producing and distributing the
flowers. These goods are private goods, the enjoyment of which is
best left to the voluntary choices of producers and consumers; that
is so because such benefits are easy to "escape."[54]

A significant literature has emerged defending the fairness principle on the grounds of the inescapability or presumptive benefits of
public goods. Richard Arneson, for example, admits the force of
Nozick's objections to the principle of fairness but argues that it can
be "revised" such that obligations and corollary rights to force only
arise in the case of "particular types of benefits"[55] that satisfy certain
carefully specified criteria: The benefits must derive from the provision of "pure public goods," characterized by jointness of consumption, non-excludability, and equal consumption by all members of
the group.[56] In such cases, to allow "free riders to enjoy the benefit
of the scheme without helping defray its cost . . . [is] often morally
repugnant."[57]

Arneson carefully specifies the cases in which free riders are to
be distinguished or selected out from the class of potential beneficiaries, to wit, with respect to a group of beneficiaries "G" of a good
"B," it is specified: (a) that B is genuinely collective with respect to
G; (b) that the benefits to each member of G are greater than her
"fair share" of the costs of supplying them;[58] (c) that "no beneficiary
who has a disinterested motive for not contributing . . . is required

111

to contribute";[59] (d) that it is unfeasible to provide B through the supply of private benefits to "each beneficiary" sufficient to induce her contribution;[60] (e) that each person finds her "fair share of the costs" to entail a disutility;[61] (f) that "no member's choice is made under the expectation that it will influence any other member's choice";[62] and (g) that "No single member of G . . . [nor] any coalition of a few members of G find it possible to divide the costs of B among the members of the coalition so that each member of the coalition will find the benefits of B to him outweigh the cost to him of contributing toward the supply of B according to the terms of the coalition. A large number of persons must contribute toward the supply of B if the benefits each receives are to overbalance the cost of each one's contribution."[63]

Under those conditions, according to Arneson, "each person who benefits from the cooperative scheme supplying B can correctly reason as follows: either other persons will contribute sufficient amounts to assure continued provision of B, or they will not. In either case, the individual is better off if he does not contribute. . . . If this reasoning induces an individual not to contribute, he counts as a free rider."[64] Free riding is, according to Arneson, unfair and therefore activates the "rights to force" entailed by the fairness principle.

Not only has the range of applicability of the principle been limited to a very small set (perhaps the null set) of goods, leaving obligations to do our "fair share" for all of the rest unjustified (at least by that principle), but perhaps more importantly, he has made it very difficult to know precisely whether any good actually meets those criteria. That is so not only because it requires asking questions about motivations and "reasoning," which are notoriously difficult to ascertain, but also because if the good *is already produced* by the state and funded coercively on the basis of the principle of fairness, we cannot know whether it *could* have been produced through discriminatory pricing, tie-ins, altruism, conditionally binding assurance contracts (for example, "matching pledges"), or "straddle pay-off" strategies.[65] Especially considering that such factors as technology, motivation, and expectations figure in Arneson's criteria, it is difficult to imagine how we would determine whether a good should be provided collectively or privately, in the absence of the competition made possible by voluntary choice,[66] and, if collectively, whether it satisfies the criteria set out by Arneson and that we should there-fore conclude that the burdens of its production should be shared on the basis of the principle of fairness.[67]

We should remember, further, that the difference between a collec-tive good and a private good is not an inherent quality of the good as such, at least for most conceivable goods, namely those for which the publicness is not definitionally a part of the good (as publicness would be, for example, for the good of "republicanism").[68] As Ken-neth Goldin has argued:

> The evidence suggests that we are not faced with a set of goods and services which have the inherent characteristics of public goods. Rather, we are faced with an unavoidable choice regarding every good or service: shall everyone have equal access to that service (in which case the service will be similar to a public good) or shall the service be available selectively: to some, but not to others? In practice, public goods theory is often used in such a way that one overlooks this important choice problem.[69]

Thus, collective or private provision may be a matter of choice and not of the inherent characteristics of the good as such. The choice may indeed be a response to high costs of exclusion or of contractual mechanisms in some cases, but it is *no less a choice* for that.[70] To say that the publicness of the good entails an obligation is to say that *the choice to produce it publicly* is what determines the obligation, which simply means that the *choice* of the majority can obligate the minority (or vice versa), thus undermining the claim that it is a problem of fairness *simpliciter* that generates obligations and rights to force non-contributors.[71] To take the constantly raised "hardest" case, the current political system of nation states, for example, con-jures up "units" of "national" defense when it is not at all clear that citizens of, say, Hawaii and New Hampshire are naturally "enjoying the same good of defense," such that citizens of one may be coerced on the basis of the principle of fairness into paying for the defense of the other.[72] Arneson attempts to meet Nozick's objection to the fairness principle by arguing that "a principle that Nozick cannot disavow without disavowing central commitments of his political philosophy requires acceptance of a revised principle of fairness."[73] Arneson's argument is that, if appropriation of property is to be justified, not on the basis of universal consent, but on the basis of the benefits generated even for those who face diminished opportunities of common use, then the principle of benefit can certainly be used to generate obligations without voluntary consent. While it is not clear that Nozick would agree with this argument, there is some evidence in the text of Locke to support a Lockean "fairness principle."[74] It is true that there is an implicit appeal to fairness at work as a part of Locke's account of political obligation,[75] but it is less clear that his argument for rights of appropriators to protect their justly appropriated property and exclude others from its enjoyment must rest solely or even partially on the *benefits* to the excluded; Locke argues strenuously that they are not *harmed* by this appropriation, but that they are equally *benefited* is not necessary, since Locke is seeking to avoid entirely the problem of "Consent of all the Commoners": "And the taking of this or that part, does not depend on the express consent of all the Commoners."[76] Indeed, one can argue not only that the Lockean enterprise is not about demonstrating the benefits of appropriation to all the non-appropriators, but also that it is the benefit to *appropriators* that is the central issue; Locke shows that "commoners" should *become* appropriators both in their own interest and, of great if not equal importance, in order to secure freedom:

> [Y]et being given for the use of Men, there must of necessity be a means *to appropriate* them some way or other before they can be of any use, or at all beneficial to any particular Man. The Fruit, or Venison, which nourishes the wild *Indian*, who knows no Inclosure, and is still a Tenant in common, must be his, and so his, *i.e.*, a part of him, that another can no longer have any right to it, before it can do him any good for the support of his Life.[77]

The key phrase is "a part of him," for "Though the Earth, and all inferior Creatures be common to all Men, yet every Man has a Property in his own Person. This no Body has any Right to but himself."[78] Pace Rawls, our fundamental rights are to our bodies, and those are rights that are in no way held in common with others (that is, each person owns her own body and only her body, rather than a share in common rights to the use of all bodies). Without property in corporeal objects there is no way to delineate for embodied persons the spheres of action that constitute individual liberty, within which it would be unjust to initiate violence.[79]

The generation of benefits for others need not figure prominently in a Lockean justification of rights of appropriators, and therefore endorsing a Lockean defense of property need not entail endorsement of the principle of benefit-based obligations. Arneson's appeal to the text of Locke fails to provide support for his revised principle of fairness.

To deal with the problem of "honest holdouts," George Klosko has sought to ground fairness-based obligations by identifying "presumptively beneficial" goods, which "must be desired by rational individuals regardless of whatever else they desire, though even this account presupposes a background of generally accepted values and beliefs."[80] Identifying such goods, Klosko argues, negates the validity of claims on the part of non-contributors to be "honest holdouts" or "genuinely conscientious objectors." According to Klosko:

> There can be little doubt that the citizens of many modern states enjoy nonexcludable presumptive goods that depend upon the cooperative efforts of their fellows. Among such goods are . . . national defense, protection from environmental hazards, and public health assurances. I think it is clear that individuals are obligated to contribute to the provision of these goods . . . the principle of fairness presents an attractive account of the nature of their obligation.[81]

Klosko *asserts* that the principle of fairness provides an "attractive account" of the obligation he claims, but he gives no *argument* for it. The closest that he comes is a citation of a series of studies, mainly of American subjects, purporting to show that "people's feelings that they are obligated to bear various burdens are significantly affected by their assessment of the burdens that other individuals are bearing or willing to bear."[82] This may show that some—or even most—Americans believe in the principle of fairness and "doing one's share" in paying taxes, but it is hardly an *argument* for "doing one's fair share" being obligatory or coercively enforceable. It may simply reflect the fact of decades of state control of education and not of some universally (or even widely) intuited truth.

The dependence of "publicness" on choice, rather than on inherent characteristics of goods, leads us to the conclusion that the principle of fairness does not apply to goods from which we *cannot* escape, but to goods from which we will not be *allowed* to escape. In Arneson's terms, "once a public good is supplied," that means, after a decision has been made by some group with the power to make such decisions, then "One cannot voluntarily accept a good one cannot voluntarily reject."[83] The "principle of fairness" depends on closure of exit options, on a *choice* by some not to allow others to evade alleged benefits.

A Hypothetical Contract with People You Cannot Escape

It is central to the Rawlsian social contractarian enterprise that parties to the contract not be allowed to escape from either its benefits or its burdens and that the terms of the social contract must reflect that inescapability. The consequences of that inescapability are significant. If, for example, you cannot escape from your enemies in order to associate only with your friends, or at least with those who bear you no ill will, then it makes sense to establish rules of a rather different cast from those you would establish if you *could* escape those who are liable to make various coercive demands on you. Rawls raises that very scenario in *A Theory of Justice*,

> [T]he two principles are those a person would choose for the design of a society in which his enemy is to assign him his place.[84]

Perhaps a better way to "protect themselves against such a contingency" would be to have exit rights from the start so that parties could escape from situations in which their enemies might assign them their places. What is remarkable about Rawls's formulation is that the supposition that our enemies will assign us our places in society, even if only an "as if" constraint in the choice situation, implies a concern for the strategic interaction of rationally maximizing parties with conflicting interests and no preexisting moral restraint, something that is denied in Rawls's work. Since we know that the constraints on the original position entail complete symmetry of interests, knowledge, and the like, we "can view the choice in the original position from the standpoint of one person selected at random."[85] The consequence of that symmetry and of reduction to the situation of a single individual choosing among principles is that "the parties have no basis for bargaining in the usual sense."[86] The ignorance of the parties makes possible a unanimous choice of a particular conception of justice. Without these limitations on knowledge the bargaining problem of the original position would be hopelessly complicated. Even if theoretically a solution were to exist, we would not, at present anyway, be able to determine it.[87]

Yet Rawls supposes that a party should adopt a conservative strategy, "reasoning as if" the party were coping with a situation in which "his enemy is to assign him his place." The allegedly "hopelessly complicated bargaining problem," contrary to Rawls's assertion, is amenable to solution by specifying a suitable set of initial endowments (along the lines of Lockean self proprietorship) and allowing free exit rights in accordance with principles of voluntary association. (That would be to take the proposal of David Gauthier in *Morals by Agreement*[88] a step further, not only establishing a non-agreement point to serve as a baseline for distribution of the cooperative surplus over non-agreement, but introducing as well the very realistic option of choosing from among a variety of contracting groups.)

In his later work, Rawls spells out in detail why in the choice situation one can not be *allowed* to escape and how one should reason to principles accordingly. In *Political Liberalism*, Rawls takes great pains to differentiate "a well-ordered democratic society" from a "community" and from an "association."[89] The form of cooperative endeavor about which Rawls is writing "is closed . . . in that entry into it is only by birth and exit from it is only by death."[90] Further, "we are not seen as joining society at the age of reason, as we might join an association, but as being born into society where we will lead a complete life."[91]

Justice and Exit Rights

Rawls rejects the exit option in the specification of the choice situation for two primary reasons. First, exit rights cannot be cited to warrant the justice of an arrangement. Thus, "While the principles adopted will no doubt allow for emigration (subject to suitable qualifications), they will not permit arrangements that would be just only if emigration were allowed."[92] Rawls writes: "Political society is closed: we come to be within it and we do not, and indeed cannot,

117

enter or leave it voluntarily."[93] The reason is that "the right of emigration does not make the acceptance of political authority voluntary in the way that freedom of thought and liberty of conscience make the acceptance of ecclesiastical authority voluntary."[94] Thus, "The political is distinct from the associational, which is voluntary in ways that the political is not."[95]

Rawls may have in his crosshairs the theory of John Locke, who offered as an argument for an obligation to submit to certain commands of government the claim that continued residence on a territory attached to a political society and governed by a government to which the members of that political society had entrusted their executive powers, and from which exit was not blocked by force, constituted tacit consent to submit. David Hume accused Locke and his followers of building "a tory consequence of passive obedience, on a whig foundation of the original contract."[96] But it is a mistake to assume that advancing a Lockean or Lockean-type argument entails asserting that exit rights *guarantee* the justice of a political arrangement; other conditions may also be necessary. If, for example, you were deliberately to create a dependency of some sort in another party through coercive means (for example by injecting a poison to which only you have the antidote), and only after that had been accomplished were you to unlock the door and offer to allow her to leave, the resulting dependent relationship would not be warranted as just merely because of the now available exit option. Exit options alone do not guarantee justice, but they do, in a Lockean-type argument, satisfy three desirable purposes:

> 1. they are just in themselves, as recognitions of a fundamental human right;
> 2. they are an engine of further liberalization and extension of human freedom and prosperity, by constraining political associations and authorities to recognize the rights of subjects or risk losing their human capital to other states and systems that offer more attractive arrangements; and
> 3. they can warrant the justice of political arrangements that *are* entered into voluntarily and in accordance with just procedures (i.e., they serve, in effect, as a background requirement for "justice preserving transformations" in matters of political order).[97]

To avoid the "tory consequences" of which Hume warned, it is only necessary to specify further conditions relating to how one enters into a political society and what is necessary to exit it.[98] Eliminating entry and exit options from the choice situation is unwarranted, adds a needless element of *ir*reality, and contradicts a fundamental liberal principle.

The right to leave does not, of course, entail any correspondingly symmetrical right to enter. My right to quit my membership in a chess club need not entail a right to be accepted by any other chess club. In a world governed by cosmopolitan principles, it is possible (but quite unlikely) that no one would be willing to associate with or accept some particular emigrant. In the world of national states, such as largely exists today and as almost all other theorists posit, exit rights actually are restricted in some places and entrance rights are tightly controlled everywhere. For example, to keep out potential cooperators (or recipients of taxpayer funded benefits) the U.S. government apprehends (and sometimes kills) would-be immigrants along the U.S.–Mexico border, despite the willingness of other American citizens (and land owners) to receive them. Although it is logically possible that no current U.S. citizen would accept immigrants onto their land, it does not seem likely, and certainly far, far, far less likely than the stark certainty of encountering the barbed wire, guard dogs, and armed guards currently deployed by nation states.

Natural Assets and Desert

The second motivation for Rawls's making closure move explicit seems to be to meet David Gauthier's objection to Rawls's formulation of the redistributive difference principle on the grounds that it does not meet the criterion of mutual advantage. Gauthier challenges Rawls's assertion that natural assets are "not deserved," noting that although "they are not undeserved, they are not contrary to desert."[99] Gauthier asks why, if mutual advantage and contractual agreement are to be the bases of the principles of justice, parties would not adopt a difference principle that would guarantee each an improvement over their non-agreement points. Writes Gauthier,

> Behind the veil of ignorance, no one knows her natural abilities and talents, and hence no one knows what she would get in the absence of agreement. Yet each knows that she has certain natural abilities and talents, and that people differ in this endowment, so that in the absence of agreement people would secure different levels of well being. It is therefore possible for everyone to take account of the "no agreement

119

point" in their reasoning, even though no particular person knows how it will affect her.[100]

In response, Rawls rejects his earlier insistence on mutual benefit by jettisoning entirely the options of no agreement and of comparison of alternative agreements and, therefore, of bargaining. For the "rational," Rawls substitutes the "reasonable," which is certainly a less exacting and less rigorous concept. In a defense of that move, Samuel Freeman, in a paper cited approvingly by Rawls in *Political Liberalism*, combines the highly questionable assertion of the inescapability of one's "given" society with an explanation of reasonableness:

> What is inescapable . . . is one's being a member of a social group, recognizing the group's system of norms, and understanding how the norms function as reasons in public argument. Though that requirement does not involve endorsing all the norms of the group, whatever they may be, it does mean that one who is unwilling to cooperate with others on *any* terms except those most conducive to achieving his own particular ends is being *unreasonable*.[101]

Further, "For Rawls there is no place for comparing the benefits and burdens of cooperation with cooperation-free interaction . . . noncooperation is not a viable option for us."[102]

Rawls associates the political exclusively with territorial monopoly, which is not a timeless feature of political association, whether past or present, and conflates state, nation, and society. As Rawls notes in contrasting the associational and the political, "the government's authority cannot be evaded except by leaving the territory over which it governs, and not always then."[103] (The claim is clearly false. Every day hundreds of millions of people—possibly billions—evade governmental authority without ever leaving home.[104]) Rawls concludes from that patently false claim that,

> The government's authority cannot, then, be freely accepted in the sense that the bonds of society and culture, of history and social place of origin, begin so early to shape our life and are normally so strong that the right of emigration (suitably qualified) does not suffice to make accepting its authority free, politically speaking, in the way that liberty of conscience suffices to make accepting ecclesiastical authority free, politically speaking.[105]

The social contract is *hypothetical*, rather than actual, because it takes as *already preexisting and unquestionable* an inescapable political unit—the nation state, with its all embracing claim over the full life of the individual—and offers a purely hypothetical justification for its power. No alternative is or can even be considered.

Kantian Constructivism and Inescapable Groups

Immanuel Kant explains the nature of the hypothetical contract as follows:

> we need by no means assume that this contract (*contractus originarius* or *pactum sociale*), based on a coalition of the wills of all private individuals in a nation to form a common, public will for the purposes of rightful legislation, actually exists as a *fact*, for it cannot possibly be so.[106]

Despite his explicit criticisms of Hobbes, Kant posits a hypothetical social contract establishing an absolute state with an absolute sovereign. He is moved to do so by the specter of anarchy: "universal violence and the distress it produces must eventually make a people decide to submit to the coercion which reason itself prescribes (i.e., the coercion of public law), and to enter into a *civil* constitution."[107] In the *Metaphysics of Morals*, he claims that

> Experience teaches us the maxim that human beings act in a violent and malevolent manner, and that they tend to fight among themselves until an external coercive legislation supervenes. But it is not experience or any kind of factual knowledge which makes public legal coercion necessary. On the contrary, even if we imagine men to be as benevolent and law-abiding as we please, the *a priori* rational idea of a non-lawful state will still tell us that before a public and legal state is established, individual men, peoples and states can never be secure against acts of violence against one another, since each will have his own right to do *what seems right and good to him*, independent of the opinion of others.[108]

Kant and Rawls are engaged in moral and political constructivism, an exercise in pure "autonomy." As Rawls remarks,

> The parties in the original position do not recognize any principles of justice as true or correct and so as antecedently given; their aim is simply to select the conception most rational for them, given their circumstances. This conception is

not regarded as a workable approximation to the moral facts: there are no such moral facts to which the principles adopted could approximate.[109]

Kant insists, as Rawls does after him, that the social contract presupposes people who cannot escape one another, that is with whom one "cannot avoid having intercourse":

> [T]he first decision the individual is obliged to make, if he does not wish to renounce all concepts of right, will be to adopt the principle that one must abandon the state of nature in which everyone follows his own desires, and unite with everyone else (with whom he cannot avoid having intercourse) in order to submit to external, public and lawful coercion.[110]

Thus, the account of social contract for Kant, as for his follower Rawls, presupposes the unavoidability of a natural or inevitable political unit—the nation state—made up of people "with whom one cannot avoid having intercourse." The logic of the Rawlsian hypothetical social contract dictates that that is, and must be, a closed group.

The choice to close off exit options in the specification of the choice situation of the social contract is supposed to produce fundamentally liberal conclusions, but it violates at the outset a fundamental liberal principle, the principle of exit rights and freedom of movement, and important elements of the liberal tradition, that is cosmopolitanism and internationalism. It is also starkly at odds with Rawls's statement that people do have the right to emigrate, a statement offered *en passant* and without justification.[111] (Is Rawls claiming that when people do decide to emigrate, they should not "consider the attractions of other societies?" But, if so, on what basis would they decide whether to emigrate, and to where?)

But why must persons acquiesce in any "given" political arrangement? Why should they not be free to choose those arrangements most conducive to their needs or desires, in voluntary association with others equally free, and to reject those that they find oppressive or unbearable? According to those following the logic of the Rawlsian project, "a coalition that withdraws from society renounces any claim to justice from those who remain."[112] In other words, outside of the nation state, justice is simply unthinkable. Presumably that means that before there were nation states, there was no justice.

"Given" a justified, inevitable, inescapable collectivity (invariably a nation state) within which one comes to be and without which one would be nothing at all, that collectivity has complete ownership of all assets "within" it, none of which may be withdrawn. The problem of allocating the benefits of social cooperation is thereby reduced to a pure bargaining problem. No person and no assets get out; no person and no assets get in (because they would have had to leave another collectivity, which is not allowed).[113] But in order to institute the "fair" distribution, with all "social and economic inequalities . . . arranged so that they are both (a) to the greatest benefit of the least advantaged,"[114] recourse must be had to withdrawal of assets on the margin, which is excluded from the principles on the basis of which calculations are to be made in the first place.

Slamming shut the exit door creates the problem to which fairness is alleged to be the answer, but it also makes it impossible to put the solution into practice. Not only is the game rigged; it is not even possible to play it by the rules stipulated.

References

Arneson, Richard, "The Principle of Fairness and Free-Rider Problems," *Ethics* 92, July 1982, pp. 616–33.

———, "Lockean Self-Ownership: Towards a Demolition," *Political Studies* 39, 1991, pp. 36–54.

———, "Property Rights in Persons," *Social Philosophy and Policy* 9, no. 1, 1992, pp. 201–30.

Atiyah, P. S., *The Rise and Fall of Freedom of Contract* (Oxford: Oxford University Press, 1979).

Azarya, Victor, and Chazan, Naomi, "Disengagement from the State in Africa: Reflections on the Experience of Ghana and Guinea," *Comparative Studies in Society and History* 29, no. 1, January 1987, pp. 106–31.

Barnett, Randy, "A Consent Theory of Contract," *Columbia Law Review* 86, no. 2, March 1986.

———, "Contract Remedies and Inalienable Rights," *Social Philosophy and Policy* 4, no. 1, Autumn 1986.

———, *The Structure of Liberty: Justice and the Rule of Law* (Oxford: Clarendon Press, 1998).

Barry, Brian, *Theories of Justice* (London: Harvester-Wheatsheaf, 1989).

Bittlingmayer, George, "Property Rights, Progress, and the Aircraft Patent Agreement," *Journal of Law and Economics* 76, 1986, pp. 227–48.

Brubaker, Earl R., "Free Ride, Free Revelation, or Golden Rule?" *Journal of Law and Economics* 18, April 1975, pp. 147–61, reprinted in Tyler Cowen (ed.), *The Theory of Market Failure* (Fairfax, Va.: George Mason University Press, 1988).

Coase, Ronald, "The Lighthouse in Economics," *Journal of Law and Economics* 17, October 1974, pp. 357–76.

Cohen, G. A., "Incentives, Inequality, and Community," in Grethe B. Peterson, ed., *The Tanner Lectures on Human Values, Volume Thirteen* (Salt Lake City: University of Utah Press, 1992).

Donagan, Alan, *Morality, Property, and Slavery* (The Lindley Lecture, 1980 [Lawrence, Kan.: Philosophy Department of the University of Kansas, 1981]).

Fichte, Johann Gottlieb, *Beitrag zur Berichtigung der Urteile des Publikums über die Französische Revolution*, Reinhard Strecker, ed. (1793; Leipzig, Germany: Verlag von Felix Meiner, 1922).

Freeman, Samuel, "Reason and Agreement in Social Contract Views," *Philosophy and Public Affairs* 19, Spring 1990, pp. 122–57.

Gauthier, David, *Morals by Agreement* (Oxford: Oxford University Press, 1986).

———, "Justice and Natural Endowment: Toward a Critique of Rawls's Ideological Framework," in *Moral Dealing: Contract, Ethics, and Reason* (Ithaca, N.Y.: Cornell University Press, 1990).

Gibbard, Allan, "Constructing Justice," *Philosophy and Public Affairs* 20, Summer 1991, pp. 264–79.

Goldin, Kenneth D., "Equal Access vs. Selective Access: A Critique of Public Goods Theory," *Public Choice* 29, Spring 1977, pp. 53–71.

Grey, Thomas C., "The First Virtue," *Stanford Law Review* 25, 1973, pp. 286–327.

Griffin, James, "Some Problems of Fairness," *Ethics* 96, October 1985, pp. 100–118.

Hampton, Jean, *Hobbes and the Social Contract Tradition* (Cambridge: Cambridge University Press, 1986).

———, "Two Faces of Contractarian Thought," in Peter Vallentyne (ed.), *Contractarianism and Rational Choice* (Cambridge: Cambridge University Press, 1991).

Hardin, Russell, *Morality within the Limits of Reason* (Chicago: University of Chicago Press, 1988).

Hart, H. L. A., "Are There Any Natural Rights?" *Philosophical Review* 64, 1955, pp. 175–91, reprinted in Jeremy Waldron (ed.), *Theories of Rights* (Oxford: Oxford University Press, 1984).

Hayek, F. A., "Competition as a Discovery Procedure," in *New Studies in Philosophy, Politics, Economics and the History of Ideas* (Chicago: University of Chicago Press, 1978).

Hirschleifer, Jack, "The Private and Social Value of Information and the Reward to Inventive Activity," *American Economic Review* 61, 1971, pp. 561–73.

Hirschman, Albert, *Exit, Voice, and Loyalty* (Cambridge, Mass.: Harvard University Press, 1970).

Hume, David, "Of the Original Contract," in *Essays, Moral, Political, and Literary* (1777; Indianapolis: Liberty Classics, 1987).

de Jasay, Anthony, *Social Contract, Free Ride: A Study of the Public Goods Problem* (Oxford: Oxford University Press, 1989).

———, *Justice and Its Surroundings* (Indianapolis: Liberty Fund, 2002).

Kant, Immanuel, *Political Writings*, Hans Reiss (ed.), H. B. Nisbet (trans.) (Cambridge: Cambridge University Press, 1992).

Klein, Daniel, "Tie-Ins and the Market Provision of Public Goods," *Harvard Journal of Law and Public Policy* 10, 1987, pp. 451–74.

Klosko, George, "The Principle of Fairness and Political Obligation," *Ethics* 97, January 1987, pp. 353–62.

Locke, John, *Two Treatises of Government*, Peter Laslett (ed.) (Cambridge: Cambridge University Press, 1988).

Mises, Ludwig von, *Socialism: An Economic and Sociological Analysis* (1922; first English ed., 1936; London: Jonathan Cape, 1972).

Moon, Parker T., *Imperialism and World Politics* (New York: The MacMillan Company, 1926).

Musgrave, Richard A., and Peacock, Alan T., eds., *Classics in the Theory of Public Finance* (2nd ed., New York: St. Martin's Press, 1994).

Narveson, Jan, "A Puzzle about Economic Justice in Rawls's Theory," *Social Theory and Practice* 4, 1976, pp. 1–27.

———, "Rawls on Equal Distribution of Wealth," *Philosophia* 17, 1977, pp. 281–92.

Nozick, Robert, *Anarchy, State, and Utopia* (New York: Basic Books, 1974).

Palmer, Tom G., "Intellectual Property: A Non-Posnerian Law and Economics Approach," *Hamline Law Review* 12, Spring 1989, pp. 261–304.

———, "G. A. Cohen on Self-Ownership, Property, and Equality," *Critical Review* 12, no. 3, Summer 1998, pp. 225–51.

Posner, Richard, *Economic Analysis of Law* (Boston: Little, Brown and Company, 1972).

Pufendorf, Samuel, *The Political Writings of Samuel Pufendorf*, Craig L. Carr (ed.), Michael J. Seidler (trans.) (Oxford: Oxford University Press, 1994).

Rawls, John, *A Theory of Justice* (Cambridge, Mass.: The Belknap Press of Harvard University, 1971).

———, "Kantian Constructivism in Moral Theory: The Dewey Lectures," *Journal of Philosophy* 77, 1980, pp. 515–72.

———, *Political Liberalism* (New York: Columbia University Press, 1993).

———, "The Law of Peoples," in Susan Shute and Susan Hurley (eds.), *On Human Rights: The Oxford Amnesty Lectures 1993* (New York: Basic Books, 1993).

Rose, Carol, "The Comedy of the Commons: Custom, Commerce, and Inherently Public Property," *University of Chicago Law Review* 53, no. 3, Summer 1986, pp. 711–81.

Scanlon, T. M., "Contractualism and Utilitarianism," in Amartya Sen and Bernard Williams (eds.), *Utilitarianism and Beyond* (Cambridge: Cambridge University Press, 1982).

Schmidtz, David, *The Limits of Government: An Essay on the Public Goods Argument* (Oxford: Westview Press, 1991).

Simmons, A. John, *The Lockean Theory of Rights* (Princeton, N.J.: Princeton University Press, 1992).

———, *On the Edge of Anarchy: Locke, Consent, and the Limits of Society* (Princeton, N.J.: Princeton University Press, 1993).

Spencer, Herbert, *Social Statics* (1850; New York: The Robert Schalkenbach Foundation, 1970).

Sterba, James, "From Liberty to Welfare," *Ethics* 105, no. 1, October 1994, pp. 64–98.

Vallentyne, Peter, ed., *Contractarianism and Rational Choice* (Cambridge: Cambridge University Press, 1991)

Wheeler, Samuel C. III, "Natural Property Rights as Body Rights," *Noûs* 14, no. 2, 1980, pp. 171–94.

Wicksell, Knut, "A New Principle of Justice Taxation," in Richard A. Musgrave and Alan T. Peacock (eds.), *Classics in the Theory of Public Finance* (2nd ed.; New York: St. Martin's Press, 1994).

Notes

1. Rights theorists traditionally distinguished "connate" and "adventitious" obligations: The former are universal and are justified on grounds of universal features of human life or sociality, whereas the latter are particular and accordingly require particular justifications, albeit according to universal principles. See Samuel Pufendorf, *The Political Writings of Samuel Pufendorf*, Craig L. Carr (ed.), Michael J. Seidler (trans.) (Oxford, 1994), esp. p. 51.

2. John Rawls, *A Theory of Justice* (Cambridge, Mass., 1971), p. 152.

3. Rawls, *Political Liberalism* (New York: Columbia University Press, 1993), p. 276.

4. Ibid., pp. 135–6.

5. Ibid., p. 277.

6. Rawls, *A Theory of Justice*, p. 15.

7. Ibid., pp. 150–51. Note that Rawls uses the term "reasonable" to restrict claims for more than an equal share and the term "rational" to preclude acquiescence to less than an equal share. In *A Theory of Justice*, Rawls claims, in effect, that the "reasonable" can be deduced from the "rational," understood in terms of maximization of interest satisfaction: "The theory of justice is a part, perhaps the most significant part, of the theory of rational choice" (p. 16). That claim is retracted in his later book, *Political Liberalism*, in which he argues that his earlier statement was mistaken, that it did not accurately express his intentions: "There is no thought of deriving those principles from the concept of rationality as the sole normative concept" (p. 53). Rawls cites approvingly T. M. Scanlon's essay, "Contractualism and Utilitarianism" (T. M. Scanlon, "Contractualism and Utilitarianism," in Amartya Sen and Bernard Williams, eds., *Utilitarianism and Beyond* (Cambridge, 1982), pp. 103–28, in which Scanlon argues that the contractualist enterprise is properly understood as driven by "the desire to find and agree on principles which no one who had this desire could reasonably reject" (p. 111) and that that "moral argument" (p. 111) is to be distinguished from the rational calculation of advantage. Scanlon concludes his distinction between contractualist views driven by the "rational" and those driven by the "reasonable" as follows: "On one view, concern with protection is fundamental, and general agreement becomes relevant as a means or a necessary condition for securing this protection. On the other, contractualist view, the desire for protection is an important factor determining the content of morality because it determines what can reasonably be agreed to. But the idea of general agreement does not arise as a means of securing protection. It is, in a more fundamental sense, what morality is all about" (p. 128). After rejecting his earlier formulation of the theory of justice as a part of the theory of rational choice, Rawls claims, in *Political Liberalism*: "I believe that the text of *Theory* as a whole supports this interpretation" (p. 53). The distinction in the text cited Rawls, *A Theory of Justice*, pp. 150–51, in which "reasonable" limits claims for more and "rational" limits acquiescence in less, supports this interpretation, but it still leaves problems in the justification for inequality in Rawls's theory, as we shall see later, and may leave unjustified certain central Rawlsian principles.

8. Rawls, *A Theory of Justice*, p. 151.

9. Ibid., p. 302.

10. Thomas C. Grey, "The First Virtue," *Stanford Law Review* 25 (1973), pp. 286–327, p. 325.

11. Ibid., p. 322.

12. Ibid., p. 322.

13. Ibid., p. 325.

14. The fundamental issues I will deal with were first raised by Grey, "The First Virtue"; others who have trod this ground, in one way or another, are the following: Robert Nozick, *Anarchy, State, and Utopia* (New York, 1974), esp. pp. 183–97; Jan Narveson, "A Puzzle about Economic Justice in Rawls's Theory," *Social Theory and Practice* 4 (1976), pp. 1–27 and, by the same author, "Rawls on Equal Distribution of Wealth," *Philosophia* 17 (1977), pp. 281–92. Also see on these issues Alan Donagan, *Morality, Property, and Slavery. The Lindley Lecture 1980* (Lawrence, Kan., 1981); Brian Barry, *Theories of Justice* (London, 1989); and G. A. Cohen, "Incentives, Inequality, and Community," in Grethe B. Peterson (ed.), *The Tanner Lectures on Human Values, Volume Thirteen* (Salt Lake City, 1992), pp. 263–329.

I intend to draw on some of their arguments, but also to extend the critique further and to connect these problems with the problem of the membership of the contracting group, that is with Rawls's "closure" move discussed above. Barry notes that "Rawls has never, it seems to me, addressed himself to this line of attack" (p. 234). I believe that, although he does not address those criticisms directly, Rawls's move to close entry and exit options to the contracting parties can be understood as his response to problems of this sort.

15. Rawls, *A Theory of Justice*, pp. 284–93.

16. Ibid., p. 151.

17. Recall that Rawls writes that "it is not reasonable for him to expect more than an equal share in the division of social goods" (Rawls, *A Theory of Justice* p. 150). Narveson responds to the claim that those who receive less "have no grounds for complaining of one another's motives" as follows: "they do have a ground for 'complaining of one another's motives.' The ground is that they are likely to end up with less, with a smaller than equal share, if people are permitted to be motivated by self-interest (say) instead of by equality. Indeed, Rawls's argument here really seems to concede my basic point, which is that on this showing, the motive of justice would always direct one to sharing equally with one's fellows" (p. 287). Cohen claims that "when true to itself, Rawlsian justice condemns such incentives, and . . . no society whose members are themselves unambiguously committed to the difference principle need use special incentives to motivate talented producers" (Cohen, "Incentives, Inequality, and Community," p. 310).

18. See Narveson, "Rawls on Equal Distribution of Wealth," pp. 285–86.

19. Rawls, *A Theory of Justice*, p. 102: "No one deserves his greater natural capacity nor merits a more favorable starting place in society."

20. Donagan, p. 21. Rawls in a *A Theory of Justice* characterizes the Kantian principle of treating persons as ends in themselves as follows: "To regard persons as ends in themselves in the basic design of society is to agree to forgo those gains which do not contribute to their representative expectations. By contrast, to regard persons as means is to be prepared to impose upon them lower prospects for the sake of the higher expectations of others" (p. 180). Donagan does not directly raise the following point in his critique, but his approach suggests the further specification that, if leisure (or even simple idleness) is a good, and the attainment of an additional increment of it a gain, which seem plausible enough assumptions, then parties to the contract must forgo leisure or idleness that does "not contribute" to the representative expectations of others less well situated than they are. That would imply a duty to produce until, at least, the well being of the least well situated is maximized.

21. Rawls, *A Theory of Justice*, p. 302; Rawls adds "consistent with the just savings principle."

22. Donagan, p. 19. Nor, it might be added, in time of war.

23. Rawls, *A Theory of Justice*, p. 83.

24. Barry, p. 399. Donagan considers and rejects this interpretation of the significance of fair conditions of equality of opportunity, noting *en passant* that "the word 'opportunity' is less than felicitous when the inequalities are burdens rather than rewards" (p. 19). It is also a bit difficult to understand how an inequality of liberty or of opportunity would enhance the liberty or opportunity of those with the lesser liberty or opportunity; if liberty is precisely the sort of thing that can be distributed precisely equally, how can diminishing the liberty of one increase the liberty of another? Rawls notes this problem obliquely when he distinguishes between "liberty" and the "value of liberty." As Rawls notes (*A Theory of Justice*, p. 204), "liberty and the worth of liberty are distinguished as follows: liberty is represented by the complete system of the liberties of equal citizenship, while the worth of liberty to persons and groups is proportional to their capacity to advance their ends within the framework the system defines. Freedom as equal liberty is the same for all; the question of compensating for a lesser than equal liberty does not arise. But the worth of liberty is not the same for everyone." On the other hand, if opportunities are differentiated from simple liberty (for instance, as in the sense in which we say, "A had more opportunities than B," even though they were equally free to take advantage of what opportunities they did face), then we could arrange *in*equalities in opportunities so that "an inequality of opportunity . . . [will] enhance the opportunities of those with the lesser opportunity" (ibid., p. 303). Why would such an allowable inequality of opportunity not extend to limiting one's access to choice of occupation? ("Affirmative action" requirements and mandatory hiring quotas, by limiting the opportunities of some groups in competition with others, limit the opportunities of those who are excluded or who are not included in the quotas; the excluded certainly no longer enjoy "equality of opportunity.") And if the principle is admitted that choice can be limited in this way, then could it be limited to one option—and one only? If so, that would be equivalent to a mandate to pursue the one remaining option, which result would lead us from the principle of fair equality of opportunity, construed as differentiated from equality of liberty, *not* to a defense of labor market freedom against coercion, but to a justification of inequalities in choice options in labor markets, with the choice set reduced to one, all in pursuit of advancing the opportunities (or perhaps the value of the opportunities) of the least advantaged.

25. For proposals along these lines, see Richard Arneson, "Lockean Self-Ownership: Towards a Demolition," *Political Studies* 39 (1991), pp. 36–54 and "Property Rights in Persons," *Social Philosophy and Policy* 9, no. 1 (1992), pp. 201–30. Also confer James Sterba, "From Liberty to Welfare," *Ethics* 105, no. 1 (October 1994), pp. 64–98.

26. This lesson was learned by the indigenous inhabitants of Africa and South America, among other places, when European states colonized them and, perhaps in line with the principle that taxes must be paid for benefits received, imposed taxes that could be paid, of course, only in European money. The only way for most of the indigenous inhabitants to get this European money was to work in plantations and mines owned by Europeans. See Parker T. Moon, *Imperialism and World Politics* (New York, 1926) for a graphic and detailed description of colonial taxing policies in Africa.

27. Allan Gibbard, "Constructing Justice," *Philosophy and Public Affairs* 20 (Summer 1991), pp. 264–79.

28. Ibid., p. 266.

29. Ibid., p. 269.

30. Ibid., p. 269.

31. Ibid., p. 269.

32. Ibid., p. 269.

33. John Rawls, *Political Liberalism*, p. 17.

34. Rawls, *A Theory of Justice*, pp. 130–36.

35. Ibid., p. 134.

36. Narveson, p. 9.

37. If my analysis of Gibbard's formulation of the principle of reciprocity is correct, and the group over which the principles of justice are to apply is apparently defined by whether they can hurt each other through "threats or takings," then this begins to sound more like a classic "protection racket," in which parties must pay third parties to be able to cooperate in peace, than like a cooperative venture. Gibbard, "Constructing Justice," indicates that something of the sort must be the case when he notes, "It is not only cooperation that is at stake in questions of justice, but mutual restraint: nonaggression and respect for a system of property rights. Just people forgo chances to seize advantage, and the idea of Justice as Fair Reciprocity is that they forgo these chances in return for others' voluntary support of just arrangements. Now a coalition that withdraws from society renounces any claim to justice from those who remain" (p. 272). If those who attempt to withdraw have *no claim to justice*, then those who remain are indeed free to attempt to enslave the withdrawing members, as Gibbard notes. Perhaps a more truly liberal approach would be to construe "cooperation" such that withdrawal from it need not mean dropping all restraint from aggression against persons and property; withdrawal would be simply an attempt to get away from other aspects of a cooperative scheme that are not to the interest or liking of the withdrawing parties. The proper reciprocal response to mere non-aggression, it seems, is simply non-aggression, rather than equalization of assets subject to the difference principle; if that is so—if withdrawal from a group need not entail complete withdrawal from all considerations of morality and justice, as it does for Gibbard—then why cannot any group of cooperators withdraw from the reciprocal scheme governed by the difference principle, but remain in the more limited "cooperative" relationship of not aggressing against one another? This would make the difference principle a truly voluntary principle among full cooperators, defined by those who actually consent to remain within the "fully cooperative" group. Just as the members of a club of equals might arrive at a principle of equal distribution, but are not constrained to do so if they agree to another principle, those who agree to cooperate in Rawls's favored sense would be bound to his principles of distributive justice, while others would not.

38. Rawls, *A Theory of Justice*, p. 282: "Because they start from equal shares, those who benefit least (taking equal division as the benchmark) have, so to speak, a veto. And thus the parties arrive at the difference principle."

39. Compare Barry, p. 243: "It is fairly clear that allowing the withdrawal of whole blocs from the society to define alternative nonagreement points would pose severe dangers to the claim that the difference principle is better for (almost) everyone than they could do in the absence of cooperation."

40. Russell Hardin, *Morality within the Limits of Reason* (Chicago, 1988), p. 134. Rawls is even more strenuous in setting the non-agreement point and therefore the inclusiveness of what is up for distribution: "The difference principle represents, in effect, an agreement to regard the distribution of natural talents as a common asset and to share in the benefits of this distribution whatever it turns out to be" (Rawls, *A Theory of Justice*, p. 101). It seems that *everything*, and not merely "the bulk of what we enjoy," viz. what we enjoy in excess of what we could have in total isolation from others, is up for distribution. See also David Gauthier, *Morals by Agreement* (Oxford, 1986), p. 254: "In seeking to treat persons as pure beings, freed from the arbitrariness of their individuating characteristics, Rawls succeeds in treating persons only as social instruments. In denying to each person a right to his individual assets, Rawls succeeds in treating persons only as social assets. In denying to each person a right to his individual persons, Rawls is led to collectivize those assets." Thus, Rawls's own account suffers from the same defect on the basis of which he rejects utilitarianism, namely that it "does not respect the distinction between persons" (Rawls, *A Theory of Justice*, p. 27).

41. Note that a similar problem exists in the case of bilateral monopoly, in which there is both only one seller ("monopoly") and only one buyer ("monopsony"), meaning that only a range of prices could be theoretically established, namely between the lowest price that would be accepted by the seller and the highest price that would be paid by the buyer. Precisely where the actual price would fall between these two boundaries is purely a matter of bargaining. As Richard Posner notes, "When a monopolistic supplier of labor confronts a monopsonistic buyer of labor, the exact price and quantity that will be set depend upon the parties' relative skills at bargaining, ability to use intimidation or bring political pressures to bear, and perhaps other factors" (Richard Posner, *Economic Analysis of Law* [Boston, 1972], p. 136).

42. If the idea of the margin is rejected as entirely inappropriate to the analysis of justice, perhaps because individual contributions to the "joint product" in question (the products of social cooperation) cannot in any way be identified, then the basis of the difference principle itself is altogether obliterated. As Robert Nozick notes, "When it is necessary to provide incentives to some to perform their productive activities, there is no talk of a joint social product from which no individual's contribution can be disentangled. If the product was all that inextricably joint, it couldn't be known that the extra incentives were going to the crucial persons; and it couldn't be known that the additional product produced by these now motivated people is greater than the expenditure to them in incentives" (Robert Nozick, *Anarchy, State, and Utopia*, p. 189). Knut Wicksell, in his "A New Principle of Just Taxation," similarly argued against Mill's principles of distributive justice, for even when considering activities of the state (rather than all social activities, as Rawls does), "the discussion is almost always concerned with this or that change in the scope of the State's operations, this or that extension or (much more rarely) contraction of the separate branches of public activity" (Knut Wicksell, "A New Principle of Just Taxation" in Richard A. Musgrave and Alan T. Peacock (eds.), *Classics in the Theory of Public Finance* [2nd ed., New York, 1994], p. 78). Wicksell defends the marginal principle against Mill's claim that "Government must be regarded as so pre-eminently a concern of all, that to determine who are most interested in it is of no real importance," which means that allocation of burdens on the basis of benefits is beside the point (quoted by Wicksell, p. 78).

43. Note that Hardin does not write "distribution," but "*re*distribution," implying that assets have already been allocated and must now be *re*allocated. If the initial

distribution occurred in compliance with the rules of justice, and then the results were judged to merit redistribution, then the rules of justice that resulted in the initial distribution are not action-guiding, in the sense of ensuring that when they are followed the parties need not fear coercive sanctions; the redistribution principle is incompatible with the rule of law. Rawls asserts otherwise, but his characterization of redistributive taxation could just as easily be applied to rape, muggings, or lynchings: "Taxes and restrictions are all in principle foreseeable, and holdings are acquired on the known condition that certain transfers and redistributions will be made" (Rawls, *Political Liberalism*, p. 283).

44. Rawls, *Political Liberalism*, pp. 275–76.

45. Rawls, *A Theory of Justice*, pp. 111–12. Rawls acknowledges a debt to H. L. A. Hart's essay, "Are There Any Natural Rights?" (H. L. A. Hart, "Are There Any Natural Rights?" *Philosophical Review* 64 (1955), pp. 175–91, reprinted in Jeremy Waldron [ed.], *Theories of Rights* [Oxford, 1984], pp. 77–109).

46. Rawls, *A Theory of Justice*, p. 112. Rawls distinguishes "obligations" from "natural duties"; the former "arise as a result of our voluntary acts" and are "normally owed to definite individuals, namely, those who are cooperating together to maintain the arrangement in question" (p. 113), while the latter "apply to us without regard to our voluntary acts" (p. 114) and "are owed not only to definite individuals, say to those cooperating together in a particular social arrangement, but to persons generally" (p. 115).

47. Ibid., p. 7.

48. Ibid., p. 54.

49. Ibid., p. 11.

50. Ibid., p. 12.

51. The counterargument is that, in Hart's argument, what Nozick refers to as "the point" of special rights to force others to behave as they are obligated can only be illustrated against a background of a general right not to be forced; this would, argues Nozick, entail that "only against a background of *permitted* forcing can we understand the point of *general* rights," which would undercut Hart's claim (Hart, "Are There Any Natural Rights?" p. 90) that "in the case of special rights as well as of general rights recognition of them implies the recognition of the equal right of all men to be free" (Nozick, p. 92). The general force of Nozick's response is that "rights of forcing" are not strictly deducible as corollaries from obligations, even of the strong sort (distinguished from moral duties) that Hart is describing. An alternative account of special obligations that entails no corollary "right of forcing" is to be found in Randy Barnett ("A Consent Theory of Contract" and "Contract Remedies and Inalienable Rights"). In this "consent theory of contract" such obligations are to respect property titles that have been transferred by contractual means, rather than to perform certain actions; in the case of non-feasance, the remedy is not specific performance, entailing a "right to force," but transference of a property claim, for example, a non-performance bond.

52. Nozick, *Anarchy, State, and Utopia*, p. 95.

53. It may be worth noting that benefit-based obligations are infiltrating contract law itself, and not just political theory, as P. S. Atiyah, *The Rise and Fall of Freedom of Contract* (Oxford, 1979), pp. 764–70 shows.

54. The language of "escaping" is borrowed from Albert Hirschman's treatment of public goods: "The distinguishing characteristic of these goods is not only that they *can* be consumed by anyone, but that there is *no escape* from consuming them

unless one were to leave the community by which they were provided" (Albert Hirschman, *Exit, Voice, and Loyalty* [Cambridge, Mass., 1970], p. 101).

55. Richard Arneson, "The Principle of Fairness and Free-Rider Problems," *Ethics* 92 (July 1982), pp. 616–33, p. 618.

56. Ibid., p. 618. Limiting the class of benefits to "pure public goods" obviates the necessity for voluntary acceptance, asserts Arneson, for, "once a pure public good is supplied to a group of persons, there cannot really be any voluntary acceptance or enjoyment of the benefit by individual consumers. One cannot voluntarily accept a good one cannot voluntarily reject" (p. 619). Attention should be paid to the emphasized terms: "*once* a pure public good is supplied"; and "a good one *cannot voluntarily reject*." The assumptions that the good has already been supplied and that one cannot escape it are crucial—and highly problematic—moves in the argument, for they foreclose the option of precontract excludability; they assume away the problem of *producing* goods by assuming that they already exist; and they may limit the applicability of the principle to a very tiny class of "inherited" goods that are found (assuming no investment in the finding) and not produced.

57. Ibid., p. 621.

58. Note that application of this criteria to providers of collective goods could create havoc for, among others, the airline, cinema, and hotel industries, which engage in "discriminatory pricing" as part of a profit-maximizing strategy, charging often widely different rates for physically identical benefits, such as a hotel room or a seat in an airplane or a cinema. (The losers in such schemes are often professional business travelers, who must book in advance and spend a Saturday night away from family, in the case of the travel industry, and young to middle-aged movie goers, who are charged more than children, students, and senior citizens.) The existence of the hotel facilities (corridors, elevators, security, and so on) and the fact of the plane's flight and the movie's showing, regardless of whether it is empty, half-full, or full, are clearly collective goods with respect to those staying in rooms or sitting in seats; however, discriminatory pricing, that is, a clear case of "unfair shares," are among the most effective means of providing such collective goods by charging the most to those who receive the most benefit from the non-rivalrous good, as measured by willingness to pay.

59. Arneson explains in a footnote that that criterion is "intended to ensure that the principle of fairness will not lay obligations upon those who are genuinely conscientious objectors to the scheme for supplying public goods. My understanding of the requirement is that, in order to have a disinterested motive, the beliefs which give rise to the motive cannot be acquired or sustained in a culpably irrational fashion." How one would determine "the beliefs that give rise to the motive" is left quite unclear, except for his explanation (Arneson, "The Principle of Fairness and Free-Rider Problems," p. 632) that "If Jones has a deeply entrenched belief grossly at variance with the facts, and this counts as negligent or culpable ignorance, his obligation stands. Just having bizarre beliefs about the origins of the collective benefits one enjoys does not relieve one of the obligation to pay one's fair share." Thus, it might seem that the Amish belief that the Social Security System in the United States is a retirement plan (given current actuarial facts, this certainly may qualify as a "bizarre belief" by itself) and their view that divine providence requires their abstention from commercial insurance and retirement plans because participation evidences a lack of faith in providence, "does not relieve [them] of the obligation to pay [their] fair share." That entails, then, a right on behalf of admitted beneficiaries to override

stated preferences of others in pursuit of their own benefit. As David Schmidtz remarks of what he calls "honest holdouts" and Arneson refers to as "genuinely conscientious objectors," after discussing the difficulties of distinguishing free riders who are strategically passing themselves off as honest holdouts: "The prospect of justifying institutionalized coercion as a solution to public goods problems depends upon whether there is a prior justification for engaging in actions that can be expected to force some people (perhaps a minority, but not necessarily so) to help pay for other people's projects. Without this prior justification, the argument begs a most important question: Coercion may be necessary to force honest holdouts to pay for other people's projects, but what exactly is it that makes pursuing this goal permissible in the first place? Merely pointing out that coercing people is the most efficient way for others to get what they want does not even begin to discharge the burden of proof" (David Schmidtz, *The Limits of Government: An Essay on the Public Goods Argument* [Oxford, 1991], p. 84).

60. That would eliminate the enormous category of public goods that can be provided through "tie-ins" with private goods. See for instance, Daniel Klein, "Tie-Ins and the Market Provision of Public Goods," *Harvard Journal of Law and Public Policy* 10 (1987), pp. 451–74, and for a classic case study Ronald Coase, "The Lighthouse in Economics," *Journal of Law and Economics* 17 (October 1974), pp. 357–76.

61. That seems to exclude cases where altruists might derive pleasure from the sheer knowledge that they were helping to bring about a pure public good. How we would know what the motivations of contributors are is not explained and may render this criterion non-operational.

62. That criterion is a bit puzzling. Arneson (in Arneson, "The Principle of Fairness and Free-Rider Problems") offers in a footnote the explanation that "No single individual's decision is expected to influence the decisions of others, but note that this is compatible with individuals basing their choices on expectations about what the aggregate of others will decide." If the aggregate of others is intended to mean unanimity-minus-yourself, it would mean that expectation of unanimous contribution would be an acceptable motivation to contribute, but the knowledge that another has agreed to contribute on the condition that you do would not be an acceptable motivation, presumably because, unless it is a two person game, there might still be free riders who are outside of the agreement. Such a requirement would eliminate those solutions to collective goods problems set forth in Earl R. Brubaker: "it seems worth proposing an additional rival to the free-rider hypothesis, and for convenience it might be called the golden rule of revelation. It asserts that under pre-contract group excludability the dominant tendency will be for each individual to reveal accurately his preference for a collective good provided that he has some assurance that others will match his offer in amounts he perceives as appropriate" (Earl R. Brubaker, "Free Ride, Free Revelation, or Golden Rule?" *Journal of Law and Economics* 18 [April 1975], pp. 147–61, reprinted in Tyler Cowen [ed.], *The Theory of Market Failure* [Fairfax, Va., 1988], pp. 99–100). That thesis has been expanded and provided additional evidence from experimental economics by Schmidtz, *The Limits of Government: An Essay on the Public Goods Argument*; see especially chapters 4 and 5 on "conditionally binding assurance contracts." Such contracts would only meet Arneson's criterion "f" if the group of contractors included each and every beneficiary of the pure public good and the decision were made simultaneously and with no stepwise movement toward unanimity. That strikes me as a strange and unreasonable limitation on the provision of public goods.

63. That seems to rule out voluntary solutions to public goods problems that exhibit the "straddle payoff" considered by de Jasay (in Anthony de Jasay, *Social Contract, Free Ride: A Study of the Public Goods Problem* [Oxford, 1989]), under which "under certain conditions being a 'sucker' is superior to having the exchange regime" (p. 144), a condition found more commonly than one would expect were one looking through lenses ground to Paul Samuelson's specifications. See, for example, the study of voluntary and non-patent protected industrial and technological innovation in Tom G. Palmer, "Intellectual Property: A Non-Posnerian Law and Economics Approach," *Hamline Law Review* 12 (Spring 1989), pp 261–304, reprinted in Adam Moore (ed.), *Intellectual Property: Moral, Legal, and International Dilemmas* (New York, 1998), pp. 179–224; Jack Hirschleifer, "The Private and Social Value of Information and the Reward to Inventive Activity," *American Economic Review* 61 (1971), pp. 561–73; and George Bittlingmayer, "Property Rights, Progress, and the Aircraft Patent Agreement," *Journal of Law and Economics* 76 (1986), pp. 227–48.

64. Arneson, "The Principle of Fairness and Free-Rider Problems," p. 622.

65. Actually, the last would, apparently, be considered "unfair" and hence unjust to those who produce the good. Contrast with Arneson's conclusion of injustice the interesting discussion in de Jasay, *Social Contract, Free Ride: A Study of the Public Goods Problem*, chapters 9 and 10. De Jasay reaches rather different conclusions from Arneson. "Straddle payoff" games have structures similar to "battle-of-the-sexes" coordination games; for a description of the latter, see Jean Hampton, *Hobbes and the Social Contract Tradition* (Cambridge, 1986), pp. 151–61.

66. See F. A. Hayek, "Competition as a Discovery Procedure," in *New Studies in Philosophy, Politics, Economics and the History of Ideas* (Chicago, 1978), pp. 179–90.

67. The criteria might even limit the class of goods subject to the principle to those *already* produced (or in a sense inherited), and since the good is already *produced*, there is no problem of allocating the burdens of its production. What might arise, however, would be problems of equal or universal access to such already-produced collective goods. An example might be the so-called Royal Roads of England, so-called not because the crown produced them but because the crown seized them (they were produced centuries before by the Romans). Issues of access to collective goods are discussed in Carol Rose, "The Comedy of the Commons: Custom, Commerce, and Inherently Public Property," *University of Chicago Law Review* 53, no. 3 (Summer 1986), pp 711–81. I disagree, however, with the range of goods to which Rose's reasoning might apply: I do not see how her arguments apply to goods that must be produced, rather than merely found without any opportunity cost incurred in the finding.

68. To define the good as including state (or "public") action is to rig the game; goods such as community, which people may actually desire, should not be defined in terms of how they are produced, as doing so renders the conclusion that they can only be produced in that way merely trivially true.

69. Kenneth D. Goldin, "Equal Access vs. Selective Access: A Critique of Public Goods Theory," *Public Choice* 29 (Spring 1977), pp. 53–71, p. 68.

70. If there are good reasons for collective provision, then there are benefits to the parties that can be offered to induce holdouts to become participants. If the response is that the beneficiaries of public provision don't *want* to forgo some of their benefits in order to induce others to cooperate, then one response may be that they have no right to force others to "cooperate" merely in order to gratify *their own* desires at the lowest cost.

134

71. De Jasay notes that it is not "logistics" but "social choice" that determines which goods will be provided publicly: "Instead of being public because it was non-excludable, a good became non-excluded because the 'public' wanted it so" (de Jasay, *Social Contract, Free Ride: A Study of the Public Goods Problem*, p. 156). See also the treatment in Anthony de Jasay, *Justice and Its Surroundings* (Indianapolis, 2002).

72. Of course, it should also be noted that one person's benefit may be another person's bane. As Albert Hirschman notes, "[H]e who says public goods says public evils. The latter result not only from universally sensed inadequacies in the supply of public goods, but from the fact that what is a public good for some—say, a plentiful supply of police dogs and atomic bombs—may well be judged a public evil by others in the same community" (Hirshman, *Exit, Voice, and Loyalty*, p. 101).

73. Arneson, "The Principle of Fairness and Free-Rider Problems," p. 617.

74. As Locke argues in the *Second Treatise* of the transfer of rights of enforcement of the law of nature from the individual to the political society: "For being now in a new State, wherein he is to enjoy many Conveniences from the labour, assistance, and society of others in the same Community, as well as protection from its whole strength; he is to part with as much of his natural liberty in providing for himself, as the good, prosperity, and safety of the society shall require: which is not only necessary, but just; since the other Members of the Society do the like" (John Locke, *Two Treatises of Government*, Peter Laslett [ed.] [Cambridge, 1988] II, §130, p. 353).

75. See the treatment of this issue generally from a Lockean perspective in Simmons, *On the Edge of Anarchy: Locke, Consent, and the Limits of Society* (1993), pp. 248–60.

76. Locke (1988), II, §28, p. 289. Locke's contractarian argument is limited to political institutions and not to moral institutions or practices generally. He is a "state contractarian" and not a "moral contractarian," to use Jean Hampton's terminology in her essay "Two Faces of Contractarian Thought" (in Peter Vallentyne [ed.], *Contractarianism and Rational Choice* [Cambridge, 1991], pp. 31–55). Locke, in fact, explicitly *rejects* "moral contractarianism" by insisting that the principle of property in one's person and subsequent appropriation of unowned resources "do not depend on the express consent of all the Commoners." Contractual agreement is used only to justify—and limit—political institutions. The realms of justice, morality, and the state for Locke are not, as they seem to be for Rawls, virtually co-extensive. As Hampton remarks, "Interestingly, Rawls does not even question the state's legitimacy in *A Theory of Justice*" (p. 32).

77. Locke, II, §26, p. 287.

78. Ibid., II, §27, p. 287.

79. For one Lockean grounding of natural property rights in property in one's person, see Samuel C. Wheeler III, "Natural Property Rights as Body Rights," *Noûs* 14, no. 2 (1980), pp. 171–94.

80. George Klosko, "The Principle of Fairness and Political Obligation," *Ethics* 97 (January 1987), pp. 353–62, esp. p. 353.

81. Ibid., p. 356.

82. Ibid., p. 357.

83. Arneson, "The Principle of Fairness and Free-Rider Problems," p. 619. There may be some externalities from which we cannot, in fact, escape that may pose fairness problems; they are negative externalities—such as air or noise pollution—for which there are threshold effects, for example, two people enjoying wood fires or two people playing rock music is not a negative externality, but three people doing so is. A property rights approach can solve the problem of such externalities

by enforcing rights against coercive interference with our property rights (for instance, tort law) and by allowing contractual internalization of the externalities, but those activities below the threshold necessary to produce a rights-violating externality could be considered allocatable on the basis of fair access (for example by taking turns or auctioning off the rights), since strong Kantian-like solutions ("nobody may enjoy log fires, because if everybody did it would be disastrous") are clearly suboptimal, for *some* log-burning or rock-music playing below the rights-violating-externality-producing threshold produces goods for some without harming others. Griffin (in James Griffin, "Some Problems of Fairness," *Ethics* 96 (October 1985), pp. 100–118) suggests fairness-based solutions to such cases.

84. Rawls, *A Theory of Justice*, p. 152. Rawls goes on (p. 153) to assert that the parties "should not reason from false premises," but that the parties are still to reason as if they "were forced to protect themselves against such a contingency."

85. Ibid., p. 139.

86. Ibid., p. 139.

87. Ibid., p. 140.

88. David Gauthier, *Morals by Agreement* (Oxford, 1986).

89. Rawls, *Political Liberalism*, p. 40.

90. Ibid., pp. 40–41.

91. Ibid., p. 41.

92. Ibid., p. 277. Rawls does not tell us why the principles adopted would "no doubt" allow for emigration, nor why any "suitable qualifications" would be necessary, unless all of the justificatory work is being done by the term "suitable," in which case "*no* qualifications" might be consistent with "allowing" emigration.

93. Ibid., p. 136.

94. Ibid., p. 136.

95. Ibid., p. 137.

96. David Hume, "Of the Original Contract," in *Essays, Moral, Political, and Literary* (1777; Indianapolis: Liberty Classics, 1987), p. 487.

97. On the idea of justice preserving transformations, see Nozick, *Anarchy, State, and Utopia*, pp. 150–53.

98. For example, territorial monopoly combined with inalienability of land, at least with respect to the political society to which it is attached, may be inconsistent with a properly Lockean or Lockean-type liberalism that seeks to avoid "tory consequences." One could, for example, exit from the state without having to leave the territory or piece of land on which one currently lives. For such proposals, see Johann Gottlieb Fichte, *Beitrag zur Berichtigung der Urteile des Publikums über die Französische Revolution*, Reinhard Strecker (ed.) (1793; Leipzig, 1922); Herbert Spencer, *Social Statics* (1850; New York, 1970), pp. 185–93, and Randy Barnett, *The Structure of Liberty: Justice and the Rule of Law* (Oxford, 1998).

99. David Gauthier, "Justice and Natural Endowment: Toward a Critique of Rawls's Ideological Framework," in *Moral Dealing: Contract, Ethics, and Reason* (Ithaca, N.Y., 1990), p. 161. Robert Nozick makes an objection similar to that of Gauthier, but it is not followed up in such detail and Rawls seems nowhere ever to address it. Nozick questions whether the fruits of cooperation to be distributed on the basis of the difference principle are to include the total product, or the total product minus "what each individual gets acting separately." If the "noncooperative shares" are to be considered, "we should note that this certainly is not how people entering into

cooperation with one another would agree to conceive the problem of dividing up cooperation's benefits" (Nozick, *Anarchy, State, and Utopia*, pp. 184–85).

100. Ibid., p. 154. It is worth asking why "no agreement," rather than a range of alternative agreements, is the appropriate alternative to "agreement." Rawls sees the point in his response to Gauthier and not only insists that we *must* agree, but that we must come to *one* agreement, and one only, without being allowed to consider the possibility of entering into alternative contractual groups with different principles of association.

101. Samuel Freeman, "Reason and Agreement in Social Contract Views," *Philosophy and Public Affairs* 19 (Spring 1990), pp. 122–57, p. 132.

102. Ibid., p. 136.

103. Rawls, *Political Liberalism*, p. 222.

104. In extreme cases, they withdraw from the state entirely. See Victor Azarya and Naomi Chazan, "Disengagement from the State in Africa: Reflections on the Experience of Ghana and Guinea," *Comparative Studies in Society and History* 29, no. 1 (January 1987), pp. 106–31.

105. Rawls, *Political Liberalism*, p. 222. I have already dealt with the concern expressed here that exit rights do not by themselves guarantee or warrant the justice of a political arrangement. What is notable here is Rawls's explicit identification of political order with a territorial monopoly and with a particular nation.

106. Immanuel Kant, *Political Writings*, Hans Reiss (ed.), H. B. Nisbet (trans.) (Cambridge, 1992), p. 79.

107. Ibid., p. 90.

108. Ibid., p. 137.

109. John Rawls, "Kantian Constructivism in Moral Theory: The Dewey Lectures," *Journal of Philosophy* 77 (1980), pp. 515–72, p. 564.

110. Kant, *Political Writings* (1992), p. 137.

111. Rawls, *Political Liberalism*, p. 68.

112. Gibbard, "Constructing Justice," p. 272. In pressing the logic of the difference principle toward an extreme enforced egalitarianism, Cohen dismisses trans-communal moral principles applicable between individuals of different "justificatory communities." He argues that the existence of a "justificatory community" entails "a set of people among whom there prevails a norm (which need not always be satisfied) of comprehensive justification" (Cohen, "Incentives, Inequality, and Community," p. 282). Further, "an argument for a policy satisfies the requirement of justificatory community, with respect to the people it mentions, only if it passes the interpersonal test. And if all arguments for the policy fail that test, then the policy itself evinces lack of justificatory community, whatever else might nevertheless be said in its favor" (ibid.). The "interpersonal test" "asks whether the argument could serve as a justification of a mooted policy when uttered by any member of society to any other member" (ibid., p. 280). Some arguments, Cohen asserts (but does not demonstrate) fail to meet this test: "The incentive argument does not serve as a justification of inequality on the lips of the talented rich" (ibid.). Cohen concludes from this that those who could not justify their behavior in this way fail the interpersonal test and that if they "do not think that they *need* to provide a justification, then they are forswearing community with the rest of us in respect of the policy issue in question. They are asking us to treat them like a set of Martians in the light of whose predictable aggressive, or even benign, behavior it is wise for us to take certain steps, but whom we should not expect to engage in justificatory dialogue" (ibid., p. 282). Cohen makes

a significant unjustified move in attempting to press the extreme egalitarian case: he moves from the idea of failure of "comprehensive justificatory community," defined by the interpersonal test, to failure of *all* "justificatory dialogue," for which move he offers no argument, although one is clearly needed, as his notion of "comprehensive justification" does not encompass all forms of justification or of justificatory dialogue. Further, his "test" of whether justification fails is not as rigorous as it at first appears, for clearly "could not justify" does not mean "could not utter a claim with meaning," but rather, something like "would feel queasy or uncomfortable or guilty making the claim if she were to make the claim." That, however, is a matter of psychology, and intuitions and feelings could differ. Imagine a Cohenite untalented person making the following claim to a talented person (I specify "talented person" and not "talented rich person," because there would be no rich people, only talented and untalented, in Cohen's ideal world): "You must work longer and harder at no additional benefit to yourself, entirely so that I may benefit." At least some untalented people would feel uncomfortable, queasy, or guilty in making such a claim. For an examination of the myriad errors and confusions in Cohen's argument for radical egalitarian redistribution, see Tom G. Palmer, "G. A. Cohen on Self-Ownership, Property, and Equality," reprinted in this volume.

113. As I argued in section three, "Exile to the Production Frontier," all assets must be employed to their fullest. But then, without prices, no one could know what the "fullest" use of any resource would be. Prices require exchange, which requires property and the liberty to add or withdraw units at the margin, which is precluded by fiat. The enterprise rests for its fulfillment on the very principle—free withdrawal or addition of assets—that is precluded at the outset. See Ludwig von Mises, *Socialism: An Economic and Sociological Analysis* (1922; first English ed., 1936; London, 1972).

114. Rawls, *A Theory of Justice*, p. 83.

7. G. A. Cohen on Self-Ownership, Property, and Equality

In a number of articles, G. A. Cohen has set out an intricate set of arguments rebutting attempts to derive property claims in alienable objects ("world ownership") and nonpatterned distributions of income ("capitalist inequality") from property claims in one's person ("self-ownership").[1] As Cohen (1995b, 14) describes his enterprise in *Self-Ownership, Freedom, and Equality*, "I entertained an alternative to Nozick's 'up for grabs' hypothesis about the external world, to wit, that it is jointly owned by everyone, with each having a veto over its prospective use. And I showed that final equality of condition is assured when that egalitarian hypothesis about ownership of external resources is conjoined with the thesis of self-ownership." Cohen concludes that "equality had indeed been derived with no breach of the rules of self-ownership" (ibid.), a result that, when conjoined with additional arguments, "succeeded in exploding the libertarian position" (ibid., 15).

The argument—once one gets past Cohen's strange assumptions—is ingenious and has been extraordinarily influential. Will Kymlicka (1990, 118), for example, asks, in his *Contemporary Political Philosophy: An Introduction*, "What would happen if the world was [sic] jointly owned, and hence not subject to unilateral privatization? There are a variety of possible outcomes, but in general they will negate the inegalitarian implications of self-ownership."[2] Kymlicka cites, without rehearsing his argument, Cohen's authority in support of this strong claim. More recently, Justin Weinberg (1997, 324) has reproduced parts of Cohen's argument in an article in *Critical Review*, concluding that "Cohen shows that libertarianism cannot be defended in the way that most libertarian philosophers want to defend it."[3]

Originally published in *Critical Review* 12, no. 3, Summer 1998, pp. 225–51.

The conclusion that Cohen reaches and that has been so influential is, however, based on errors in Cohen's reasoning. There are numerous steps in the argument that may be open to objection, but even granting all of his assumptions, the logic of the argument fails.

I shall first outline Cohen's aims and general procedure. Second, I shall identify two crucial moves in his influential argument. Third, I shall show that the first move is insupportable. Fourth, I shall show that the second move is based on a confusion. I examine only two steps of Cohen's argument, but they are vitally important to his conclusions and, if they are wrong, his polemic against property in one's person, and against attempts to ground several property on this foundation, is severely weakened.

Finally, I will conclude with some general remarks about where this leaves Cohen and the issue of property rights. Cohen asserts that libertarianism is unjustified if we grant his assumption—offered without any argument whatsoever—that communism *is* justified. I conclude by rebutting this strange position.

Before turning directly to Cohen's case, I should offer a justification for plunging the reader into an often complicated and technical argument, so much so that few readers have bothered to read it carefully. Cohen's mistakes, although fatal to his enterprise of undermining libertarianism, are instructive. Cohen does not succeed in "exploding the libertarian position" (1995b, 15), but his failed effort does draw our attention profitably to such matters as the role of expectations in determining bargaining outcomes, the limitations of purely hypothetical models for moral and political theory, and the importance of the history of legal and political institutions and of the history of moral, legal, and political thought. In his attack on property, Cohen conjoins the unjustified and untenable assumption of initial communism with faulty reasoning and an argument so convoluted that he becomes entangled in his own scenarios and confuses them—to the destruction of his enterprise.

Joint Ownership

Cohen's principal concern is to defend a thoroughgoing egalitarian distribution of *income*, which he considers to be incompatible with an inegalitarian pattern of *ownership*. He asserts that "a union of self-ownership and unequal distribution of worldly resources leads to indefinitely great inequality of private property in external goods and, hence, to inequality of condition, on any view of what equality of condition is" (1995b, 69). His concern is to delegitimize the appropriation of external resources by individuals or groups, by which they might come to have a property in such resources that would exclude the rival claims of others. Cohen takes as his sole target Robert Nozick's remarks on property in *Anarchy, State, and Utopia* and attempts to unravel the relationship Nozick asserts between private (or several) property and individual liberty. In doing so, Cohen affirms the plausibility of (without indicating ultimate agreement with) Nozick's insistence on each person's property in her person.[4] Cohen then reduces Nozick's entire theory of appropriation to Nozick's version of the "Lockean proviso," which holds that "a process normally giving rise to a permanent bequeathable property right in a previously unowned thing will not do so if the position of others no longer at liberty to use the thing is thereby worsened" (Nozick 1974, 178). Cohen (1995b, 76) considers the proviso, not as a proviso *to* a theory of appropriation, but simply to *be* Nozick's theory of appropriation; thus, the proviso just quoted, "with Nozick's elaboration of it, is Nozick's doctrine of appropriation; or, speaking more cautiously, if Nozick presents any doctrine of appropriation, then the quoted statement is the controversial element in his doctrine, and therefore the element which requires close scrutiny." I shall set to the side questions about whether Cohen has fairly characterized Nozick's proviso as constituting his principle of appropriation,[5] and will merely reproduce the conclusion of his treatment, as prolegomenon to his central argument that "self-ownership" can be so construed or integrated with other arrangements as to necessitate completely equal distribution of wealth and income.

Cohen (1995b, 90) insists that any appropriation will make someone worse off, for no other reason than that someone will no longer be able to appropriate the now-appropriated item: "It is clear beyond doubt that an appropriation of private property can contradict an individual's will just as much as levying a tax on him can." If contradicting one's will is the criterion for a theory that is supposed to be based on liberty, then, according to Cohen, no private appropriation could meet the requirements of a suitably formulated Nozickian proviso, for, even if a latecomer finding no unappropriated resources left to appropriate were to be compensated by greater material wealth, this compensation could not undo the fact that the latecomer's will has been overruled. As Cohen (ibid., 89) argues, "Nozick disallows objectively paternalist use of people's private property. But he permits objectively paternalist treatment of people in other ways. For, since he permits appropriations that satisfy nothing but his proviso, he allows A to appropriate against B's will when B benefits as a result, or, rather, as long as B does not lose." If someone were to chop off my arm, even if he later made me better off, we would still say that my rights had been violated.

In the process of making this move, allegedly showing that Nozick's approach cannot justify appropriation by individuals (or groups) from an unowned commons, Cohen suggests that Nozick's baseline of comparison—what one could get in a condition of no appropriation or ownership at all—is arbitrary, and that a variety of collective ownership arrangements should be considered as candidates for the baseline, as well.[6] There are, according to Cohen (1995b, 78), "other intuitively relevant counterfactuals, and ... they show that Nozick's proviso is too lax, that he has arbitrarily narrowed the class of alternatives with which we are to compare what happens when an appropriation occurs with a view to determining whether anyone is harmed by it." The alternative that he singles out as "intuitively relevant" is that of joint ownership, according to which a resource

> is owned, by all together, and what each may do with it is subject to collective decision. The appropriate procedure for reaching that decision may be hard to define, but it will certainly not be open to any one of the joint owners to privatize all or part of the asset unilaterally, no matter what compensation he offers to the rest. . . . So if joint ownership rather than no ownership is, morally speaking, the initial position, then B has the right to forbid A to appropriate, even if B would benefit by what he thereby forbids. (Ibid., 83)

In setting up the problem, Cohen (1995b, 92) strives to "reconcile self-ownership with equality (or not too much inequality) of condition, by constructing an economic constitution which combines self-ownership with an egalitarian approach to raw worldly resources." (Cohen never makes clear what "not too much inequality" can or should mean, or how one might know how much was too much.) The principle of joint ownership, according to Cohen, when combined with strict "self-ownership," would 1) preclude individual or subgroup property rights (or property in severalty through subdivision) through free agreement and 2) generate completely equal distributions of income (or, if any inequalities were to be allowed, they would not reflect differences in control over productive powers, i.e., they would not be due to one's property in one's person). Cohen tries to base both of those conclusions on the rationality of the parties. The point of Cohen's exertions is to attempt to show that self-ownership would not entail rights to several property, or world-ownership, under conditions of initial joint ownership of resources other than labor. Cohen claims that no individual or subgroup appropriation can meet a properly formulated Nozickian proviso against harm, so there can be no legitimate individual or subgroup appropriation from a condition of no-ownership. His next two steps are to argue that rationality would preclude mutually agreeable individual or subgroup division of the jointly owned assets, and that it would be irrational for joint owners to agree to unequal distribution of their joint product. Those are the steps I will now contest.

Is Unequal Division of Jointly Owned Resources Irrational?

The first of Cohen's two rationality-based arguments concerns the division of assets ("appropriation"). He rejects individual or subgroup division or appropriation of jointly owned assets on the grounds that "*B* might have good reason to exercise his right to forbid an appropriation by *A* from which *B* himself would benefit. For, if he forbids *A* to appropriate, he can then bargain with *A* about the share of output he will get if he relents and allows *A* to appropriate. *B* is then likely to improve his take by an amount greater than what *A* would otherwise have offered him" (Cohen 1995b, 84). According to Cohen, *B* does not seek a more equal distribution of assets, but the improvement of his "share of output" of the jointly owned asset.

It is not at all clear from the text how *B*'s veto threat would "improve his take" unless *B* might later relent and allow *A* to appropriate, in which case the output would no longer be jointly owned and subject to distribution. The argument that *B* might forbid *A*'s appropriation in order to hold out for a larger share of output is thus incoherent, for if *A* were to be allowed to appropriate, there would be no joint product to share.

Setting aside the above confusion, it bears noting that Cohen is careful to indicate that an agent "might" have good reason to refuse an appropriation, for the agent *also* might very well have good reasons to agree to such an appropriation. There are many observable cases, after all, in which jointly owned resources (e.g., in business partnerships and in marriage partnerships) are divided on the basis of free agreement. These occasions happen when one or more of the following situations obtain:

a) The parties no longer wish to cooperate, because of differences unrelated to the physical productivity of cooperation. (They may, for example, mutually prefer not to be subject to the veto powers of joint owners over the disposition of jointly owned assets.)

b) The size or composition of the group of joint owners entails transaction costs, in coming to agreement over the disposition of the jointly owned asset, that are greater than the sum of the losses that would be suffered by even the worst off under a loss of the right to an aliquot portion of the income stream generated by a jointly owned asset. This would entail that those who would fare worst under division could still be compensated for their losses from the resources freed up by the elimination of the high transaction costs attributable to joint ownership. Under such conditions, and assuming that the transaction costs of a one-time negotiation and arrangement of a division were not prohibitively high, then it would be rational for the joint owners to agree to division of their jointly owned assets.

c) One or more of the parties believe that she or they could manage a subdivided portion of the currently jointly owned resource better than the collectivity could, thereby generating a surplus. From this surplus she or they could offer the other joint owners compensation for the lost aliquot portion of the income stream they would have received from the asset were it to remain jointly owned.

d) The joint owners differ in their discounting of future income streams, and have correspondingly different preferences for savings versus consumption, such that a division into several property would allow them to allocate income between investment and consumption differently. For example, if *A* prefers a policy of "eat, drink, and be merry, for tomorrow we may die," whereas *B* prefers a policy of "a penny saved is a penny earned" (or if *A* simply has a shorter time horizon than *B*, due to advanced age or impending death, for example), then they may find it impossible to agree on whether to sacrifice current consumption for future satisfaction or what would be the best tradeoff; whereas with division, each would be able to satisfy her own preference, even if it were to come at the cost of a lower aggregate physical product.

Cohen's arguments attempt to show that, under conditions of joint ownership, division (appropriation) resulting in some inequality of assets would be irrational, but his arguments fail to justify that conclusion. Cohen is not clear on whether it is appropriation per se or appropriation that would result in unequal distribution of "output" that matters to him. Whichever it is, though, the argument fails.[7]

Cohen does allow for the possibility, at least under conditions of unanimity, of a precisely equal division of initial assets, in the manner favored by Hillel Steiner.[8] Joint ownership, unlike equal division, "forbids a Nozickian formation of unequal private property by placing all resources under collective control" (Cohen 1995b, 102). Cohen (ibid., 105) admits that, under conditions of unanimity, joint ownership and equal division "may readily be converted into the other." But arrangements other than strict equality, and not including the entirety of the human race, or of all rational agents, seem to be ruled out *tout court*.[9]

Of course, if property in resources were to be divided and several property established, joint ownership could be voluntarily reestablished by the several owners agreeing jointly to recombine their assets into jointly owned assets.[10] But Cohen's insistence that joint owners would not—or would be irrational to—agree to division is unsupported.

Before proceeding to the next serious error in Cohen's argument, a short digression about Cohen's misunderstanding of Nozick is in order, although this correction is not necessary to show the errors in Cohen's reasoning. Cohen (1995b, 84) claims that "Nozick must suppose that the world's resources are, morally speaking, nothing like jointly owned, but very much up for grabs, yet, far from establishing that premiss, he does not even bother to state it, or show any awareness that he needs it." This is untrue; Nozick (1974, 178) clearly states that he believes that any ownership claim must be justified, whether collective or individual or mixed: "It is not only persons favoring *private* property who need a theory of how property rights legitimately originate. Those believing in collective property, for example those believing that a group of persons living in an area jointly own the territory, or its mineral resources, also must provide a theory of how such property rights arise; they must show why the persons living there have rights to determine what is done with the land and resources there that persons living elsewhere don't have (with regard to the same land and resources)." Rather than Nozick being guilty of "not even bothering to state . . . or show any awareness that he needs" such a theory, it is Cohen who fails to provide a theory of how or why joint ownership might be, or might have been, justified, beyond asserting that it is "intuitively relevant."

Again, however, this clarification is not essential to showing the error in Cohen's argument. Even granting Cohen's assumption of initial joint ownership, he has failed to show that it would be irrational to agree to divide ownership of assets.

Is Unequal Division of Jointly Produced Output Irrational?

Cohen's second and more complex argument is an attempt to show that, assuming inescapably joint ownership (i.e., insisting that, contrary to historical experience and the considerations listed above, it would be irrational to agree to division), unequal contributions to a jointly produced product (i.e., a product to which all factor inputs save one—labor—are jointly owned) will result in precisely equal distribution of the joint product ("final equality of condition"). (This conclusion further assumes equal preference for leisure over labor; what Cohen is concerned to show is that unequal marginal productivity, under such conditions, will not result in an unequal distribution of the joint product.) Cohen assumes, like Rawls, that all income is jointly produced and that the distribution of the joint product is to be the result of some sort of agreement among the joint owners. Where Cohen differs from Rawls is in granting, for the sake of his attempted refutation of Nozick, that the parties to the agreement know what their productive abilities are and have property in those natural talents. Joint ownership of external resources means that each owner has a full veto right over any proposed distribution of the joint product, because each has a veto right over the disposition of the factor inputs, other than labor, that contribute to the production of the joint product. Thus, Cohen writes that "I entertained an alternative to Nozick's 'up for grabs' hypothesis about the external world, to wit, that it is jointly owned by everyone, with each having a veto over its prospective use. And I showed that final equality of condition is assured when that egalitarian hypothesis about ownership of external resources is conjoined with the thesis of self-ownership" (14). Careful examination demonstrates, however, that Cohen's arguments do not show that "final equality of condition is assured."

Cohen (1995b, 94) proposes that we consider a two-person world, populated by "Able" and "Infirm," in which there is an asymmetry in the productive capabilities of the two parties, who are jointly owners of all available external resources. In this situation, "Each owns himself and both jointly own everything else." Cohen (ibid., 95) then describes three cases in which bargaining between the two parties is impossible:

a) Able cannot produce per day what is needed for one person for a day, so Able and Infirm both die.
b) Able can produce enough or more than enough for one person, but not enough for two. Infirm lets Able produce what he can, since only spite or envy would lead him not to. Able lives and Infirm dies.
c) Able can produce just enough to sustain both himself and Infirm. So Infirm forbids him to produce unless he produces that much. Able consequently does, and both live at subsistence.

In these three cases, there is no surplus over which to bargain. The two cases in which bargaining over a surplus might take place are described as follows:

d) If Able produces at all, then the amount he produces is determined independently of his choice, and it exceeds what is needed to sustain both Able and Infirm. They therefore bargain over the distribution of a fixed surplus. The price of failure to agree (the "threat point") is no production, and, therefore, death for both.

147

e) Again, Able can produce a surplus, but now, more realistically, he can vary its size, so that Able and Infirm will bargain not only, as in (d), over who gets how much, but also over how much will be produced (Cohen 1995b, 95).

Cohen (1995b, 96) acknowledges that Able and Infirm may differ in their preferences for leisure or labor (which he rather oddly characterizes as "the disutility of labour for Able and the disutility of infirmity for Infirm"),[11] and that this asymmetry may be a factor in the bargaining process, presumably allowing divergences from complete equality of product. Such differences in preferences, Cohen asserts, are unrelated to abilities. Thus, "the crucial point is that Able's talent will not, just as such, affect how much he gets. If the exercise of his talent is irksome to him, then he will indeed get additional compensation, but only because he is irked, not because it is his labour which irks him" (ibid.).

Cohen thus tries to establish that under conditions of joint ownership of assets, the more productive would never receive a share of output proportional to productivity or otherwise unequal to purely egalitarian division, i.e., simple division of the total product by the number of joint owners. If Able works 10 hours and picks 100 bushels of apples and Infirm works 3 hours and picks 10 bushels of apples, their mutual rationality demands that at the end of the day Able will receive 55 bushels and Infirm will receive 55 bushels. Perhaps because this is so wildly implausible, Cohen tries to suggest a reason why Able might get more than 55 bushels after all, to wit, that picking apples is unpleasant (it "irks" her). This may be the strangest part of Cohen's exposition and simply heaps confusion on confusion, as he tries to make a distinction without a difference. Cohen conjures up the distinction between one's abilities and one's preferences in order to justify, on the basis of pure rationality, divergences from strict egalitarianism. In effect, he argues that if joint owners were to agree to unequal division, it could only be because of different preferences for leisure (the irksomeness of labor) and never because of unequal talents or abilities.

Thus, Cohen (1995b, 96) states that "if the exercise of [Able's] talent is irksome to him, then he will indeed get additional compensation, but only because he is irked, not because it is his labour which irks him." But there is no meaningful sense to the term "additional" here, since the questions are what amount of product will be produced and the ratio at which it will be shared between Able and Infirm. Infirm may be able to demand a price for her consent to the use of the jointly owned assets, but whether she will be successful in doing so and how much she will get depend on her bargaining abilities. Given that in Cohen's model leisure and labor are directly convertible, at least above the mutual subsistence baseline, an irksome *decrease* of leisure is precisely convertible into an irksome *increase* of labor, so if Able is irked, it *must* be because of the irksomeness of labor.[12] Cohen's distinction between labor and the irksomeness of labor is both confusing and confused. It fails to make his argument any more plausible.

Cohen also assumes that the outcome will be in the form of a percentage share and argues that a 50/50 split is the only rational outcome. A percentage split in the case of Able and Infirm would be unlikely in scenario (e), in any case, since, for any percentage split (40/60, 50/50, or whatever) of output and any quantity of labor input, a lump-sum distribution to Infirm would be preferable from both Infirm's and Able's perspectives. Consider the case of Cohen's preferred 50/50 split at the expenditure of Able's labor that produces 100 units of product. Infirm and Able will each receive 50 units, meaning that Able faces a 50 percent average tax rate and a 50 percent marginal tax rate. By accepting a lump-sum payment of 50 units plus 1, Infirm is made better off and Able's marginal tax rate over 51 units is reduced to zero, which, if he has a normally shaped supply curve for labor, will generate a larger expenditure of labor. Thus, both Able and Infirm would be better off by substituting a lump-sum payment to Infirm for her agreement to allow Able to labor on the jointly owned resources; hence, Cohen's insistence on a 50/50 split of output, regardless of the amount of output, is not to the advantage of either party. Cohen's argument for a strictly egalitarian (50/50) distribution of income fails even at the level of insisting that a percentage of final product is rationally preferable to a lump-sum payment.

I now turn to the most serious confusion in Cohen's convoluted argument. The fact that Infirm has a full veto power over Able's efforts entails, according to Cohen, that the distribution of the product will not be influenced by Able's greater ability. Able

> gets nothing extra just because it is he, and not Infirm, who
> does the producing. Infirm controls one necessary condition

of production (relaxing his veto over use of the land), and Able controls two, but that gives Able no bargaining advantage. If a good costs $101, and you have one hundred of the dollars and I only have one of them, then, if we are both rational and self-interested, you will not get a greater share of the good if we buy it jointly just because you supply so much more of what is required to obtain it. (Cohen 1995b, 96)

This claim is based on a confusion, however, as it assumes that "*a* good costs $101" (my italics), i.e., that there is no variability in the ratio of inputs and outputs. (For $101 you get the minimal amount of the good, but for $100 you get none, and for $102 you get no more.) Cohen is here confusing cases (c) and (d) with case (e), which is the more normal and certainly the most interesting case. Cohen has stipulated in cases (c) and (d) that Able cannot decide to produce more or less, so the total product to be divided is rigidly fixed.

Both of these scenarios are radically different from the situation described by case (e), for in this (most realistic) case the input of labor is variable, so there is not "*a* good" costing a fixed amount, as there is in cases (c) (where the maximum possible product is the minimum necessary to sustain both Able and Infirm) or (d) (where the only possible output is greater than the minimum necessary to sustain both Able and Infirm, but variation of neither input nor output is possible). In case (e), both factor input and product are variable. Able has the option of varying her expenditure of labor in return for varying product; if the $100 were to represent the amount of labor necessary to sustain both Able and Infirm, and the $1 were the relaxing of Infirm's veto over Able's activities, then the interesting question is what would happen to the increased production made possible by Able's additional investments of $5, $30, $68.43, etc., since Infirm has nothing other than the magical $1 (necessary to make production possible) to contribute. All that we can say with certainty is that, given Cohen's assumptions, Infirm will receive at least the minimum necessary to sustain her, as she would not, under any circumstances, agree to less; above that it is a matter of bargaining. *Pace* Cohen, there is no reason to insist that *any* increased production over the input of Able's $100 and Infirm's $1 would be shared equally. The distribution depends not only on Able's preferences for leisure over labor, but also on the expectations of the parties,

and this involvement of expectations by itself entails a radical indeterminacy of result, for, as Thomas Schelling (1960, 21) points out,
such situations "ultimately involve an element of pure bargaining—
bargaining in which each party is guided mainly by his expectations
of what the other will accept. But with each guided by expectations
and knowing that the other is too, expectations become com-
pounded."

In a case of the sort that Cohen describes, in bargaining over a
surplus, the bargainer who can precommit credibly will get the
share she prefers, so long as the other party has not precommitted
simultaneously.[13] What Cohen's remarks tell us is that G. A. Cohen
has committed himself, through the vehicle of his published writings, to a certain strategy (fully equal division) in the sorts of cases
that he describes (as it would, presumably, entail a loss of face or
of academic reputation if he were to practice other than he preaches).
Anyone who finds herself in a pure bargaining situation with G. A.
Cohen may expect that the only viable move will be to demand one-
half of whatever is at stake—no more and no less—which is the
complementary equilibrium strategy to an irrevocably committed
strategy of demanding one-half.[14] But that strategy may not work
with bargainers other than G. A. Cohen. Strict egalitarianism is not
the uniquely rational bargaining strategy that Cohen claims it is.

Cohen believes that his example of the $100 and the $1 necessary
jointly to purchase a good proves that "there will be no . . . inequality,
or its source will not be Able's ownership of his own powers, but
the influence of the parties' utility functions on the outcome of
the bargaining process." This conclusion has not, however, been
supported by Cohen's arguments.

Cohen proceeds to consider what he calls "a relatively minor
objection to the argument," which is, however, fatal to Cohen's claim
that "self-ownership" conjoined with joint ownership of everything
else will necessarily result in equal income.

The objection is that an owner of a factor of production could
threaten to destroy the factor or, what amounts to the same thing
(all relevant effects being relative here), to allow it to decay in value
or to fail to augment its productivity. Able, in the cases considered
above (d and e), "has it in his power to let (part of) his talent decay"
(Cohen 1995b, 97). However, according to Cohen (ibid., 97), "What
is unclear, because of difficulties in the concept of rationality, is

whether such a Schellingian threat would be credible, and, therefore, effective, *under the assumption that everyone is rational*. If it would be, then those with greater power to produce could get more in a jointly owned world for reasons which go beyond the consideration that their labour might be irksome to them" (emphasis original). (In an earlier published version of the essay Cohen [1986, 82] had written, "What I do not know how to assess, because of my uncertain grasp of bargaining theory, is whether such a Schellingian threat would be credible. . . .")

Cohen (1995b, 97) dismisses this objection as "minor" because "it achieves purchase only in the rather peculiar case in which Able can indeed diminish his own productive power." Cohen implies that Able would threaten to diminish her own present powers, perhaps by cutting off her feet or blinding herself; Cohen seems to believe that such a strategy may be less than credible. But let us look at the cases Cohen describes in which such a threat might be made. Such a strategy would be pointless in cases (a) and (b), and would not be credible in case (c), since the maximum product is stipulated to be only enough to sustain Able and Infirm, with no surplus available for bargaining, so that the outcome is clear: Infirm will insist that Able work and produce the maximum possible, which is precisely enough to sustain them both (regardless of whether it is distributed equally), but no surplus is available for distribution above survival level. Such a strategy may or may not be credible in case (d), in which labor inputs cannot vary but there is a surplus available for distribution; the credibility is entirely a matter of Able's ability to commit herself and to convince Infirm that she will abide by the threat, which may be difficult to do in the absence of a third party with whom to contract for enforcement, or some other way to limit Able's post-agreement options. (It bears noting that Infirm could also precommit to demanding one-half, or a greater-than-one-half share, as well; nothing in case (d) stops Infirm from precommitting to exercise her veto in order to extract a greater-than-equal share of the surplus potentially available for bargaining.) But Cohen cannot conclude from the unavailability of such a strategy in case (c), and the questionable credibility of such a strategy in case (d), that it is not credible in the much-more-realistic scenario of case (e), in which labor inputs can vary over the amount necessary to ensure that both Able and Infirm are sustained and that a correspondingly variable surplus can be generated by Able's labor. All that Able has to do in case (e) is exercise her claim rights and liberty rights *not to work*, i.e., to withdraw her labor from the productive process.

Given the disutility of labor that Cohen presupposes, i.e., that each unit of disvalued labor can be converted into a unit of valued leisure, and the fact that only Able has the power and the right to decline to work, Able's threatened refusal to work is a highly credible strategy, indeed. Thus, it is *not* incredible that Able would refuse to work beyond the labor necessary for both Able and Infirm to subsist without being compensated in accordance with, say, her marginal product.

To clarify matters further, we can distinguish two cases. In the first, one allows one's ability to decay by eliminating one's own options. (Burning one's bridges can increase one's bargaining power, and such moves are neither irrational nor otherwise objectionable; they are quite common to bargaining situations.) In the second case, on which I have focused, one simply withdraws one's labor, but without diminishing one's productive capacity or otherwise limiting one's options. Either is a credible strategy, although the latter is certainly more commonly observed. It is precisely the strategy of "going on strike" that Cohen (1995b, 250) condemns—consistently for a socialist "saddened" by what looked, at the time Cohen wrote one of the essays in the book, "to be the impending final abandonment of the Bolshevik experiment." Strikes, after all, were not allowed in the Soviet Union. In response to the libertarian challenge, Cohen seeks to root out of socialist theory the idea that one has a right to property in one's person, in one's labor, or in one's product.

The Reality of Socialist Practice

Cohen writes as if his experiment has never in fact been carried out in practice and that we have only his a priori speculation as the basis for thinking rationally about the joint-ownership scenario that he describes. But there is ample experience of joint ownership being imposed on people, and it does not bear out Cohen's conclusions in any way. The English colony at Jamestown offers a clear example of what happens when joint ownership is imposed on those living on land that was "good and fruitfull." As one eyewitness wrote:

> So great was our famine, that a Savage we slew and buried, the poorer sorte tooke him up againe and eat him; and so

did divers one another boyled and stewed with roots and herbs. It were too vile to say, and scarce to be beleeved, what we endured: but the occasion was our own, for want of providence, industrie and government, and not the barrennesse and defect of the Country, as is generally supposed. (Bethell 1998, 34)

Sir Thomas Dale, upon his arrival in Virginia in May of 1611, noted that the colonists were bowling in the streets rather than working. It was the introduction of several property that put an end to the "starving time" that resulted from joint ownership of assets and egalitarian distribution of the joint product.

Cohen's experiment was also tried at Plymouth Colony a few years later. As Governor William Bradford noted:

The experience that was had in this common course and condition, tried sundry years and that among godly and sober men, may well evince the vanity of that conceit of Plato's and other ancients applauded by some of later times: that the taking away of property and bringing in community into a commonwealth would make them happy and flourishing; as if they were wiser than God. For this community (so far as it was) was found to breed much confusion and discontent and retard much employment that would have been to their benefit and comfort. For the young men, that were most fit and able for labour and service, did repine that they should spend their time and strength to work for other men's wives and children without any recompense. The strong, or man of parts, had no more in division of victuals and clothes than he that was weak and not able to do a quarter the other could; this was thought injustice. The aged and graver men to be ranked and equalized in labours and victuals, clothes, etc., with the meaner and younger sort, thought it some indignity and disrespect unto them. And for men's wives to be commanded to do service for other men, as dressing their meat, washing their clothes, etc., they deemed it a kind of slavery, neither could many husbands well brook it. Upon the point all being to have alike, and all to do alike, they thought themselves in the like condition, and one as good as another; and so, if it did not cut off those relations that God hath set among men, yet it did at least much diminish and take off the mutual respects that should have been preserved amongst them. And would have been worse if they had been men of another condition. Let none

object this is men's corruption, and nothing to the course
itself. I answer, seeing all men have this corruption in them,
God in His wisdom saw another course fitter for them. (Bethell 1998, 41)

When Cohen's thought experiment has been run in reality, it turns
out that Able ("the strong, or man of parts") does *not* agree to work
hard and then share equally with Infirm ("he that was weak and
not able to do a quarter the other could"), but simply refuses to
work, resulting in starvation for all.

The extreme egalitarian typically blames the moral failings of the
parties involved, rather than the abolition or attenuation of several
property for the failures of such collectivist schemes. Thus, Cohen
(1995a, 396) has criticized the reliance on incentives, in the form of
the possibility of unequal holdings or unequal division, with which
Rawls amends purely equal division of assets and income, on the
grounds that it effectively institutionalizes immorality:

> My principal contention about Rawls is that (potential)
> high fliers would forgo incentives properly so-called in a full
> compliance society governed by the difference principle and
> characterized by fraternity and universal dignity. I have not
> rejected the difference principle in its lax reading as a princi-
> ple of public policy: I do not doubt that there are contexts
> where it is right to apply it. What I have questioned is its
> description as a principle of (basic) justice, and I have
> deplored Rawls's willingness to describe those at the top end
> of a society governed by it as undergoing the fullest possible
> realization of their moral natures.

Recall, however, Governor Bradford's observation that joint ownership and enforced equal division failed miserably "amongst godly
and sober men" and "would have been worse if they had been men
of another condition." To what, then, are we to attribute the fact
that such schemes result, not in harmony and prosperity, but in
famine and cannibalism? Who or what bears the blame? The question
was never put more directly than by Vasily Grossman (1986, 164),
a witness to the imposition of joint ownership on the peasant farmers
in Ukraine:

> Some went insane. They never did become completely still.
> One could tell from their eyes—because their eyes shone.
> These were the people who cut up and cooked corpses, who

killed their own children and ate them. In them the beast rose to the top as the human being died. I saw one. She had been brought to the district center under convoy. Her face was human, but her eyes were those of a wolf. These are cannibals, they said, and must all be shot. But they themselves, who drove the mother to the madness of eating her own children, are evidently not guilty at all! For that matter, can you really find anyone who is guilty? Just go and ask, and they will all tell you that they did it for the sake of virtue, for everybody's good. That's why they drove mothers to cannibalism!

It would require too long a digression to offer a full critique of what is wrong with blaming the victims of communism for failing to live up to its "high" moral standards. I will merely suggest a hypothesis that seems simpler and more straightforward than the claim that human beings have not yet proven good enough for socialism: socialism is not good enough for human beings.

Cohen errs in thinking that rational parties would never refuse to work or bargain or allow their abilities to decay if they were not compensated unequally. He simply dismisses the possibility: "No libertarian would want to defeat the Able/Infirm argument (for the consistency of equality and self-ownership) on so adventitious a basis" (Cohen 1995b, 97). According to Cohen (ibid., 97–98), the libertarian "would want, instead, to overcome it by pressing . . . [a] more fundamental objection . . . that to affirm joint ownership of the world is, as the story of Able and Infirm might be thought to show, inconsistent with achieving the purpose and expected effect of self-ownership." But Cohen's hypothetical opponent need not choose on which basis to refute Cohen's arguments, for the Able/Infirm story does not show what Cohen claims that it shows. Cohen has not demonstrated that joint owners would not or should not agree to division of their assets; nor that the distribution of a surplus over what is necessary to sustain both Able and Infirm must be evenly divided; nor that Able could not bargain for a greater share on the basis of a threat to diminish her productivity or her productive effort. Finally, real-world experience with joint ownership contradicts Cohen's rosy egalitarian description and raises the issue of why joint ownership should ever be seriously considered in the first place.

Positive vs. Negative Community

Cohen's conclusions are frequently repeated, but his arguments are rarely read. Those arguments fail to show that property in one's person is irrelevant to the distribution of wealth and income, even accepting their underlying assumptions.

Cohen does direct our attention, perhaps contrary to his intentions, to the question of why joint ownership should be assumed in the first place. No argument is given as to why such assets should be assumed, even for the sake of argument, to be jointly owned; they may be, but why must or should they be? Classical liberals and libertarians are open on the question of whether particular bits of land or other resources should be considered jointly or individually owned.[15] What is unargued for by Cohen (aside from asserting that it is "intuitively relevant"), but is of dubious plausibility, is the idea that every resource other than our own persons should be considered the joint property of all human beings, or perhaps of all rational agents. If rational agents were to be discovered on Mars, would the joint owners of Earth be required to obtain the permission of every rational Martian before any terrestrial resource might be used, and would the agreement have to be unanimous across species? This would be a strange basis on which to build a theory of jurisdiction over scarce resources. As almost all previous writers on property have emphasized, requiring the permission of everyone before anyone could pick an apple would result in the extinction of humanity. Joint ownership requiring unanimous approval to every act of transformation of resources is ultimately rejected by Cohen, on the ground that it interferes with any reasonable sense of autonomy, but it is not clear why it should even be entertained in the first place.

There may be good reasons to believe that very early in its actual history, property took one of various forms of positive community, principally familial, as Fustel de Coulanges (1864), Maine (1888), and other anthropologists and historians of property have shown; but that is not Cohen's argument. Nor are the forms of positive community described by legal historians consistent with the egalitarian ownership described by Cohen as "joint ownership," for they did not encompass all humans or all rational agents, but were always forms of community that established rights against all nonmembers of the owning communities. As Locke noted of common property, "And though it be common, in respect of some Men, it is not so to all Mankind, but is the joint property of this Country, or this Parish" (*Two Treatises*, II.35). In this respect, "negative community," i.e., the idea that all have a right to appropriate unowned objects, is a far more egalitarian starting point than any form of "positive community," which in every form ever observed was a nonuniversal, group-limited right. This issue was carefully considered by the modern natural-law writers on property, who distinguished between negative community and positive community, the latter corresponding to the joint ownership that Cohen proposes as the proper baseline.[16]

It is remarkable that figures such as Cohen persistently overlook the distinction between negative and positive community when considering claims, by Locke and other writers on several property, that, prior to appropriation, the world was open to mankind in common. As Pufendorf (1994, 178) noted quite explicitly,

> It is plain that before all human agreements there was a communion of all things. Not a positive communion, of course, but a negative one; that is, all things were available to all and belonged no more to one person than to another. But since things are not useful to men unless at least their fruits are laid hold of, and indeed, since this is done in vain if others are in turn allowed to seize what we have already actively intended for our own use, the first agreement among mortals concerning things is understood to have been this: Whatever anyone had taken for himself from the common stock or its fruits, with the intention of using it for himself, would not be seized from him by another.

Cohen reproduces the argument against liberal property put forth by Sir Robert Filmer (1991, 234), an apologist for royal absolutism:

> Certainly it is a rare felicity that all the men in the world at one instant of time should agree together in one mind to change the natural community of things into private dominion. For without such an unanimous consent it was not possible for community to be altered. For if but one man in the world had dissented, the alteration had been unjust, because that man by the law of nature had a right to the common use of all things in the world, so that to have given a property of any one thing to any other had been to have robbed him of his right to the common use of all things.

Locke, who was replying to Filmer, rejected joint ownership of this sort (in which each joint owner has a veto right, requiring unanimity for anything to be appropriated and consumed) as a baseline: "If such a consent as that was necessary, Mankind had starved, notwithstanding the Plenty God had given him" (*Two Treatises*, II.28). By asserting property in one's person, Locke managed to avoid the trap set by Filmer, for

> Though the Earth, and all inferior Creatures be common to all Men, yet every Man has a *Property* in his own *Person*. This no Body has any Right to but himself. The *Labour* of his Body, and the *Work* of his Hands, we may say, are properly his. Whatsoever then he removes out of the State that Nature hath provided, and left it in, he hath mixed his *Labour* with, and joyned to it something that is his own, and thereby makes it his *Property*. (Ibid., II.27)[17]

It is property in one's person that justifies the appropriation of that to which everyone earlier had a right. Cohen's attempted rebuttal does not shake this connection; Cohen's case against libertarianism rests on basic errors of reasoning and fails on its own terms.

There are certainly many observable scenarios in which one or another form of joint ownership is highly desirable, such as partnerships, co-ops, various sorts of clubs and religious institutions, and marriages, but there is no reason to posit that joint ownership is the only rational or desirable arrangement, nor that property in severalty is irrational or immoral. Nor does Cohen even offer any good reason as to why joint ownership should be seriously entertained at all; the *only* justification that Cohen offers for attempting to work through the logic of joint ownership is that joint ownership is "intuitively plausible." To say that one's intuition tells one that a claim is reasonable or probable is hardly to offer an *argument* on its behalf; and, in any case, "joint ownership" or "positive community" has certainly been considered by defenders of several property and decisively rejected for very good *reasons*, as opposed to mere intuition. Finally, Cohen has failed to demonstrate that the unequal division of joint products is irrational (much less that it is immoral).

The central pillars of Cohen's polemic against conjoining property in one's person with several property rest on errors of reasoning; his argument against the conjunction of property in one's person with several property will have to proceed without his often-cited but erroneous claims about the bargaining situation of self-owners who own the world jointly. His bare assertion of the "plausibility" of positive community is not an argument for a policy that has been rejected for clear and compelling reasons by many other writers on the topic.

It may be that libertarian claims about the conjunction of property in one's person and property in the world are false, but, if it is so, it is not for the reasons that Cohen has advanced.

References

Barry, Brian. 1996. "You Have to Be Crazy to Believe It." *Times Literary Supplement*, October 25.

Bethell, Tom. 1998. *The Noblest Triumph: Property and Prosperity through the Ages*. New York: St. Martin's Press.

Buckle, Stephen. 1991. *Natural Law and the Theory of Property*. Oxford: Clarendon Press.

Christman, John. 1994a. "Distributive Justice and the Complex Structure of Ownership." *Philosophy and Public Affairs* 23, pp. 225–50.

Christman, John. 1994b. *The Myth of Property: Toward an Egalitarian Theory of Ownership*. Oxford: Oxford University Press.

Cohen, G. A. 1985. "Nozick on Appropriation." *New Left Review* 150, pp. 89–105.

Cohen, G. A. 1986a. "Self-Ownership, World-Ownership, and Equality." In *Justice and Equality Here and Now*, edited by Frank S. Lucash. Ithaca: Cornell University Press.

Cohen, G. A. 1986b. "Self-Ownership, World Ownership, and Equality: Part II." *Social Philosophy & Policy* 3, no. 2, pp. 77–96.

Cohen, G. A. 1989. "Are Freedom and Equality Compatible?" In *Alternatives to Capitalism*, edited by Jon Elster and Karl Ove Moene. Cambridge: Cambridge University Press.

Cohen, G. A. 1995a. "Incentives, Inequality, and Community." In *Equal Freedom: Selected Tanner Lectures on Human Values*, edited by Stephen Darwall. Ann Arbor: University of Michigan Press.

Cohen, G. A. 1995b. *Self-Ownership, Freedom, and Equality*. Cambridge: Cambridge University Press.

Cohen, G. A. 1996. "Self-Ownership and the Libertarian Challenge." *Times Literary Supplement*, November 8.

de Coulanges, Numa Denis Fustel. [1864] 1956. *The Ancient City: A Study on the Religion, Laws, and Institutions of Greece and Rome*. Garden City, N.Y.: Doubleday Anchor.

Ellickson, Robert C. 1993. "Property in Land." *Yale Law Journal* 102, pp. 1315–1440.

Filmer, Robert. 1991. "Observations Concerning the Original of Government, upon Mr. Hobs 'Leviathan,' Mr. Milton against Salmasius, H. Grotius 'De Jure Belli.'" In idem, *Patriarcha and Other Writings*, edited by Johann P. Sommerville. Cambridge: Cambridge University Press.

Friedman, Jeffrey. 1997. "What's Wrong with Libertarianism." *Critical Review* 11, no. 3, pp. 407–67.

Gordon, David. 1990. *Resurrecting Marx: The Analytical Marxists on Freedom, Exploitation, and Justice*. New Brunswick, N.J.: Transaction Books.

Grossman, Vassily. 1986. *Forever Flowing*. New York: Harper & Row.

Haworth, Alan. 1994. *Anti-Libertarianism: Markets, Philosophy and Myth*. London: Routledge.

Hayek, F. A. 1988. *The Fatal Conceit: The Errors of Socialism*, edited by W. W. Bartley, III. London: Routledge.

Ingram, Attracta. 1994. *A Political Theory of Rights*. Oxford: Oxford University Press.

Kymlicka, Will. 1990. *Contemporary Political Philosophy: An Introduction*. Oxford: Clarendon Press.

Libecap, Gary D. 1989. "Distributional Issues in Contracting for Property Rights." *Journal of Institutional and Theoretical Economics* 145, pp. 6–24.

Lueck, Dean. 1993. "Contracting into the Commons." In *The Political Economy of Customs and Culture: Informal Solutions to the Commons Problem*, edited by Terry L. Anderson and Randy T. Simmons. Lanham, Md.: Rowman & Littlefield.

Madison, James. 1983. "Property." In *The Papers of James Madison*, vol. 14: April 6, 1791–March 16, 1793. Charlottesville: University Press of Virginia.

Maine, Henry Sumner. 1888. *Lectures on the Early History of Institutions*. New York: Henry Holt.

Munzer, Stephen R. 1990. *A Theory of Property*. Cambridge: Cambridge University Press.

Narveson, Jan. 1990. *The Libertarian Idea*. Philadelphia: Temple University Press.

Norberg, Kathryn. 1988. "Dividing Up the Commons: Institutional Change in Rural France, 1789–1799." *Politics and Society* 16, pp. 265–86.

Nozick, Robert. 1974. *Anarchy, State, and Utopia*. New York: Basic Books.

Pufendorf, Samuel. 1994. *The Political Writings of Samuel Pufendorf*, edited by Craig L. Carr. Oxford: Oxford University Press.

Rosenberg, Alexander. 1988. "The Political Philosophy of Biological Endowments." *Social Philosophy and Policy* 5, no. 1, pp. 1–31.

Ryan, Alan. 1994. "Self-Ownership, Autonomy, and Property Rights." In *Property Rights*, edited by Ellen Frankel Paul, Fred D. Miller, and Jeffrey Paul. Cambridge: Cambridge University Press.

Schelling, Thomas, 1960. *The Strategy of Conflict*. Cambridge, Mass.: Harvard University Press.

Simmons, A. John. 1994. "Original-Acquisition Justifications of Property." In *Property Rights*, edited by Ellen Frankel Paul, Fred D. Miller, and Jeffrey Paul. Cambridge: Cambridge University Press.

Sreenivasan, Gopal. 1995. *The Limits of Lockean Rights in Property*. Oxford: Oxford University Press.

Steiner, Hillel. 1994. *An Essay on Rights*. Oxford: Blackwell.

Sugden, Robert. 1986. *The Economics of Rights, Co-operation and Welfare*. Oxford: Basil Blackwell.

Waldron, Jeremy. 1988. *The Right to Private Property*. Oxford: Oxford University Press.

Weinberg, Justin. 1997. "Freedom, Self-Ownership, and Libertarian Philosophical Diaspora." *Critical Review* 11, no. 3, pp. 323–44.

Young, H. Peyton. 1996. "Dividing the Indivisible." In *Wise Choices: Decisions, Games, and Negotiations*, edited by Richard J. Zeckhauser, Ralph L. Keeney, and James K. Sebenius. Boston: Harvard Business School Press.

Notes

1. Cohen's criticisms have appeared in numerous forms and publications, notably Cohen 1985, Cohen 1986a, Cohen 1986b, and Cohen 1989, and have been revised and collected together in Cohen 1995b.

2. Other recent works that have cited without criticism or have incorporated at least some of Cohen's basic claims into their critique of several property include Waldron 1988, Munzer 1990, Ingram 1994, Haworth 1994, Christman 1994a and 1994b, and Sreenivasan 1995. Cohen's approach has been criticized by David Gordon (1990) and by Jan Narveson (1990), although without raising the problems I point out in this critique. Unlike the criticisms of Gordon and Narveson, my refutation of Cohen's central arguments is immanent.

3. Part of Weinberg's claim is that Cohen's critique of libertarian views on liberty is a decisive refutation of libertarians' claims to be defenders of freedom. I dealt with that issue in my separate reply to Friedman in *Critical Review* 12, no. 3 (Summer 1998), reprinted in this volume ("What's *Not* Wrong with Libertarianism"), in response to his claim that "one stipulative definition is as good as another" (Friedman 1997, 432), so I will instead focus my criticism here on Cohen's critique of "self-ownership," which Weinberg (1997, 324) considers to be, if anything, "too sympathetic an analysis of libertarian concepts." Weinberg cites in support of this claim a particularly outlandish attack on Cohen by Brian Barry for even bothering to address classical liberalism at all. (See Barry 1996 and Cohen's response [1996].)

4. Cohen quite oddly proceeds to define each person's property in herself in terms of its very negation, viz., "According to the thesis of self-ownership, each person possesses over himself, as a matter of moral right, all those rights that a slaveholder has over a complete chattel slave as a matter of legal right, and he is entitled, morally speaking, to dispose over himself in the way that a slaveholder is entitled, legally speaking, to dispose over his slave" (68). This is a strange way of understanding "self-ownership," one that would not generally be endorsed by defenders of property in one's person, but which has been taken up as paradigmatic by many who have recently followed in Cohen's footsteps. The possibility of the inalienability of certain rights is a clear case in which the (illegitimate) property claimed by a slaveholder in her slaves is misleading, rather than illuminating, as a paradigm of property in one's person. Although misleading in other respects, the definition need not be disputed to show that Cohen's conclusions do not follow from his premises.

5. See for a correction, Gordon 1990, 78–80. Gordon (1990, 83) also takes Cohen to task for "seizing on the exact words while ignoring their sense" in misunderstanding Nozick's point concerning redistribution of wealth gained under a determinate system of rights—namely, that "things come into the world already attached to people having entitlements over them" (Nozick 1974, 160)—as a claim about *initial* appropriation.

6. Cohen is demanding, in effect, that it be shown not merely that appropriation may be *permissible*, but that it must be *optimal* as well. See the discussion of the two kinds of justification in Simmons 1994.

7. It is worth noting that even "indivisible" goods can be divided on the basis of agreement, and quite commonly are. H. Peyton Young describes "eight fairly universal techniques for defining ex ante property rights in an indivisible good" (Young 1996, 373).

8. See, for example, Steiner 1994, especially the epilogue on just redistributions.

9. It is worth pointing out that, in many actual cases, joint-ownership arrangements have generated voluntary divisions of land (as also of other resources), and Cohen offers no evidence that the joint owners who have agreed to division were suffering from irrational delusions. For some of the relevant literature and case studies, see Ellickson 1993, especially 1388-92, and Libecap 1989. For a historical study of voluntary division of jointly held common property, see Norberg 1988. Norberg (1988, 268)

notes, of popular votes on division of common lands in revolutionary France, that "whether the peasants voted for or against partition, they generally did so by very large margins, often unanimously." Of communities with commons, 71.95 percent voted for partition in the 1793 referenda (ibid., 271).

10. The conditions under which such arrangements prove mutually beneficial are set out and used to illuminate case studies in Lueck 1993.

11. It is not clear how Infirm's infirmity can be a source of disutility for her in the way that Able's labor is a source of disutility for her, as Infirm cannot, by hypothesis, vary her infirmity in the way that Able can vary her labor effort. Whether it was Cohen's intention or not, such remarks color the situation he describes by engaging natural feelings of sympathy for the unfortunate, thereby introducing elements that are not explicitly acknowledged in the description of the bargaining situation. Such feelings of sympathy are also brought to the fore by the specification of the bargaining situation as one of two persons dealing with one another face to face, and therefore probably on an intimate, and not on an anonymous, basis, rather than the situation of anonymous interaction among strangers who do not meet each other face to face. Thus, although Cohen (1995, 95) stipulates that Able and Infirm are "rational, self-interested, and mutually disinterested," the situation he describes is not the sort in which such motivations are common, and his description evokes sentiments that are common to small-group, face-to-face, and intimate settings. The importance of distinguishing between the two kinds of settings has been highlighted by F. A. Hayek (1988, 18), who points out that "the structures of the extended order are made up not only of individuals but also of many, often overlapping, sub-orders within which old instinctual responses, such as solidarity and altruism, continue to retain some importance by assisting voluntary collaboration, even though they are incapable, by themselves, of creating a basis for the extended order. Part of our present difficulty is that we must constantly adjust our lives, our thoughts and our emotions, in order to live simultaneously within different kinds of orders according to different rules. . . . So we must learn to live in two sorts of worlds at once."

12. A nail is driven into the "preference vs. productivity" coffin by Alexander Rosenberg (1988, 15), who notes that "the economic effects of a talent or a disability may be exactly the same as those of a preference or taste," using the example of acrophobia or acrophilia and the talent for tree climbing among coconut harvesters; the preference for high places would generate an economic "rent" (or profit) indistinguishable from the "rent" or profit generated by a talent for climbing, and thus preferences and talents are difficult, if not impossible, to distinguish.

13. The party who can make an "irrevocable commitment" will be able to "squeeze the range of indeterminacy down to the point most favorable to him" (Schelling 1960, 24).

14. For a treatment of complementary strategies, see Sugden 1986, 67–69.

15. For an informed discussion of the variety of land regimes possible and consistent with classical liberal views, see Ellickson 1993.

16. The issue is usefully canvassed in Buckle 1991, especially 36, 93, 104–5, 164–67, and 183–87. See also the careful discussion of the issue in Pufendorf 1994, especially 176–85.

17. Alan Ryan (1994) criticizes the notion of "property in one's person," but he does not consider the advantages to the concept of "property in" objects. Contemporary imprecise English usage identifies property and object; thus, I might say that "this land [watch, book, etc.] *is* my property." The older usage of speaking of having "a

property in a thing" is far more precise and reflects the complex multiplicity of property arrangements that are possible and that are fully compatible with the libertarian defense of several property. Thus, it may be that each of many different persons has "a property" in a piece of land; one has the right to live on it, another has the right to walk across it, yet another has the right to the rental income from it, and so on. As the Roman lawyers and the modern law-and-economics scholars realize, "ownership" normally represents a bundle of such rights. Presenting the rights that one has over oneself (not to be raped, not to be killed, not to be beaten, to express one's opinions, to consent to one's marriage, and other bourgeois indulgences) as property in one's person allows the legal system to rest on a coherent and integrated foundation. The transition from the classical formulation ("person X has a property in object Y") to the modern and less precise formulation ("object Y is X's property") has made legal discussion less clear and has led—in the attempt to focus attention on the right rather than the object—to the formation of such concepts as "property rights," which means "right rights." James Madison (1983, 266) made a valiant attempt to retain the precision of the classical formulation, and to relate the rights to freedom of speech and religion to the rights to dominion over land and other objects, in his essay "Property":

> This term in its particular application means "that dominion which one man claims and exercises over the external things of the world, in exclusion of every other individual." In its larger and juster meaning, it embraces every thing to which a man may attach a value and have a right; and *which leaves to every one else the like advantage*. In the former sense, a man's land, or merchandise, or money is called his property. In the latter sense, a man has a property in his opinions and the free communication of them. He has a property of particular value in his religious opinions, and in the profession and practice dictated by them. He has a property very dear to him in the safety and liberty of his person. He has an equal property in the free use of his faculties and free choice of the objects on which to employ them. In a word, as a man is said to have a right to his property, he may be equally said to have a property in his rights.

8. Twenty Myths about Markets

When thinking about the merits and the limitations of solving problems of social coordination through market mechanisms, it's useful to clear away some common myths. By myths I mean those statements that simply pass for obviously true, without any need for argument or evidence. They're the kind of thing you hear on the radio, from friends, from politicians—they just seem to be in the air. They are repeated as if they're a kind of deeper wisdom. The danger is that, because they are so widespread, they are not subjected to critical examination. That's what I propose to do here.

Most, but not all, such myths are spread by those who are hostile to free markets. A few are spread in much smaller circles by people who are perhaps too enthusiastic about free markets.

What follows are twenty such myths, grouped into four categories:

- Ethical Criticisms;
- Economic Criticisms;
- Hybrid Ethical-Economic Criticisms; and
- Overly Enthusiastic Defenses.

Ethical Criticisms

1. Markets Are Immoral or Amoral

Markets make people think only about the calculation of advantage, pure and simple. There's no morality in market exchange, no commitment to what makes us distinct as humans: our ability to think not only about what's advantageous to us, but about what is right and what is wrong, what is moral and what is immoral.

A more false claim would be hard to imagine. For there to be exchange there has to be respect for justice. People who exchange differ from people who merely take; exchangers show respect for the

---

Paper presented at the Regional Meeting of the Mont Pelerin Society, Nairobi, Kenya, February 2007.

rightful claims of other people. The reason that people engage in exchange in the first place is that they want what others have but are constrained by morality and law from simply taking it. An exchange is a change from one allocation of resources to another; that means that any exchange is measured against a baseline, such that if no exchange takes place, the parties keep what they already have. The framework for exchange requires a sound foundation in justice. Without such moral and legal foundations, there can be no exchange.

Markets are not merely founded on respect for justice, however. They are also founded on the ability of humans to take into account not only their own desires, but the desires of others, to put themselves in the places of others. A restaurateur who didn't care what his diners wanted would not be in business long. If the guests are made sick by the food, they won't come back. If the food fails to please them, they won't come back. He will be out of business. Markets provide incentives for participants to put themselves in the position of others, to consider what their desires are, and to try to see things as they see them.

Markets are the alternative to violence. Markets make us social. Markets remind us that other people matter, too.

2. Markets Promote Greed and Selfishness

People in markets are just trying to find the lowest prices or make the highest profits. As such, they're motivated only by greed and selfishness, not by concern for others.

Markets neither promote nor dampen selfishness or greed. They make it possible for the most altruistic, as well as the most selfish, to advance their purposes in peace. Those who dedicate their lives to helping others use markets to advance their purposes, no less than those whose goal is to increase their store of wealth. Some of the latter even accumulate wealth for the purpose of increasing their ability to help others. George Soros and Bill Gates are examples of the latter; they earn huge amounts of money, at least partly in order to increase their ability to help others through their vast charitable activities.

A Mother Teresa wants to use the wealth available to her to feed, clothe, and comfort the greatest number of people. Markets allow her to find the lowest prices for blankets, for food, and for medicines to care for those who need her assistance. Markets allow the creation of wealth that can be used to help the unfortunate and facilitate the charitable to maximize their ability to help others. Markets make possible the charity of the charitable.

A common mistake is to identify the purposes of people with their "self-interest," which is then in turn confused with "selfishness." The purposes of people in the market are indeed purposes of selves, but as selves with purposes we are also concerned about the interests and well-being of others—our family members, our friends, our neighbors, and even total strangers whom we will never meet. And as noted above, markets help to condition people to consider the needs of others, including total strangers.

As has often been pointed out, the deepest foundation of human society is not love or even friendship. Love and friendship are the fruits of mutual benefit through cooperation, whether in small or in large groups. Without such mutual benefit, society would simply be impossible. Without the possibility of mutual benefit, Tom's good would be June's bad, and vice versa, and they could never be cooperators, never be colleagues, never be friends. Cooperation is tremendously enhanced by markets, which allow cooperation even among those who are not personally known to each other, who don't share the same religion or language, and who may never meet. The existence of potential gains from trade and the facilitation of trade by well-defined and legally secure property rights make possible charity among strangers and love and friendship across borders.

Economic Criticisms

3. Reliance on Markets Leads to Monopoly

Without government intervention, reliance on free markets would lead to a few big firms selling everything. Markets naturally create monopolies, as marginal producers are squeezed out by firms that seek nothing but their own profits, whereas governments are motivated to seek the public interest and will act to restrain monopolies.

Governments can—and all too often do—give monopolies to favored individuals or groups; that is, they prohibit others from entering the market and competing for the custom of customers. That's what a monopoly means. The monopoly may be granted to a government agency itself (as in the monopolized postal services in many countries) or it may be granted to a favored firm, family, or person.

Do free markets promote monopolization? There's little or no good reason to think so and many reasons to think not. Free markets rest on the freedom of persons to enter the market, to exit the market, and to buy from or sell to whomever they please. If firms in markets with freedom of entry make above-average profits, those profits attract rivals to compete those profits away. Some of the literature of economics offers descriptions of hypothetical situations in which certain market conditions *could* lead to persistent "rents," that is, income in excess of opportunity cost, defined as what the resources could earn in other uses. But concrete examples are extremely hard to find, other than relatively uninteresting cases such as ownership of unique resources (for example, a painting by Rembrandt). In contrast, the historical record is simply full of examples of governments granting special privileges to their supporters.

Freedom to enter the market and freedom to choose from whom to buy promote consumer interests by eroding those temporary rents that the first to offer a good or service may enjoy. In contrast, endowing governments with power to determine who may or may not provide goods and services creates the monopolies—the actual, historically observed monopolies—that are harmful to consumers and that restrain the productive forces of mankind on which human betterment rests. If markets routinely led to monopolies, we would not expect to see so many people going to government to grant them monopolies at the expense of their less powerful competitors and customers. They could get their monopolies through the market, instead.

It's always worth remembering that government itself seeks to exercise a monopoly; it's a classic defining characteristic of a government that it exercises a monopoly on the exercise of force in a given geographic area. Why should we expect such a monopoly to be more friendly to competition than the market itself, which is defined by the freedom to compete?

4. Markets Depend on Perfect Information, Requiring Government Regulation to Make Information Available

For markets to be efficient, all market participants have to be fully informed of the costs of their actions. If some have more information than others, such asymmetries will lead to inefficient and unjust outcomes. Government has to intervene to provide the information that markets lack and to create outcomes that are both efficient and just.

Information, like every other thing we want, is always costly, that is, we have to give something up to get more of it. Information is itself a product that is exchanged on markets; for example, we buy books that contain information because we value the information in the book more than we value what we give up for it. Markets do not require for their operation perfect information, any more than democracies do. The assumption that information is costly to market participants but costless to political participants is unrealistic in extremely destructive ways. Neither politicians nor voters have perfect information. Significantly, politicians and voters have less incentive to acquire the right amount of information than do market participants, because they aren't spending their own money. For example, when spending money from the public purse, politicians don't have the incentive to be as careful or to acquire as much information as people do when they are spending their own money.

A common argument for state intervention rests on the informational asymmetries between consumers and providers of specialized services. Doctors are almost always more knowledgeable about medical matters than are patients, for example; that's why we go to doctors, rather than just curing ourselves. Because of that, it is alleged that consumers have no way of knowing which doctors are more competent, or whether they are getting the right treatment, or whether they are paying too much. Licensing by the state may then be proposed as the answer; by issuing a license, it is sometimes said, people are assured that the doctor will be qualified, competent, and upright. The evidence from studies of licensure, of medicine and of other professions, however, shows quite the opposite. Whereas markets tend to generate gradations of certification, licensing is binary; you are licensed, or you are not. Moreover, it's common in licensed professions that the license is revoked if the licensed professional engages in "unprofessional conduct," which is usually defined as including advertising! But advertising is one of the means that markets have evolved to provide information—about the availability of products and services, about relative qualities, and about prices. Licensure is not the solution to cases of informational asymmetry; it is a cause.

5. Markets Only Work When an Infinite Number of People with Perfect Information Trade Undifferentiated Commodities

Market efficiency, in which output is maximized and profits are minimized, requires that no one is a price setter, that is, that no buyer or seller, by entering or exiting the market, will affect the price. In a perfectly competitive market, no individual buyer or seller can have any impact on prices. Products are all homogenous, and information about products and prices is costless. But real markets are not perfectly competitive, which is why government is required to step in and correct things.

Abstract models of economic interaction can be useful, but when normatively loaded terms such as "perfect" are added to theoretical abstractions, a great deal of harm can be done. If a certain condition of the market is defined as "perfect" competition, then anything else is "imperfect" and needs to be improved, presumably by some agency outside of the market. In fact, "perfect" competition is simply a mental model, from which we can deduce certain interesting facts, such as the role of profits in directing resources (when they're higher than average, competitors will shift resources to increase supply, undercut prices, and reduce profits) and the role of uncertainty in determining the demand to hold cash (since if information were costless, everyone would invest all their money and arrange it to be cashed out just at the moment that they needed to make purchases, from which we can conclude that the existence of cash is a feature of a lack of information). "Perfect" competition is no guide to how to improve markets; it's a poorly chosen term for a mental model of market processes that abstracts from real world conditions of competition.

For the state to be the agency that would move markets to such "perfection," we would expect that it, too, would be the product of "perfect" democratic policies, in which infinite numbers of voters and candidates have no individual impact on policies, all policies are homogenous, and information about the costs and benefits of policies is costless. That is manifestly never the case.

The scientific method of choosing among policy options requires that choices be made from among actually available options. Both political choice and market choice are "imperfect" in all the ways specified above, so choice should be made on the basis of a comparison of real—not "perfect"—market processes and political processes.

Real markets generate a plethora of ways of providing information and generating mutually beneficial cooperation among market participants. Markets provide the framework for people to discover information, including forms of cooperation. Advertising, credit bureaus, reputation, commodity exchanges, stock exchanges, certification boards, and many other institutions arise within markets to serve the goal of facilitating mutually beneficial cooperation. Rather than discarding markets because they aren't perfect, we should look for more ways to use the market to improve the imperfect state of human welfare.

Finally, competition is better understood, not as a state of the market, but as a process of rivalrous behavior. When entrepreneurs are free to enter the market to compete with others and customers are free to choose from among producers, the rivalry among producers for the custom of customers leads to behavior favorable to those customers.

6. Markets Cannot Possibly Produce Public (Collective) Goods

If I eat an apple, you can't; consumption of an apple is purely rivalrous. If I show a movie and don't want other people to see it, I have to spend money to build walls to keep out non-payers. Some goods, those for which consumption is non-rival and exclusion is costly, cannot be produced on markets, as everyone has an incentive to wait for others to produce them. If you produce a unit, I can just consume it, so I have no incentive to produce it. The same goes for you. The publicness of such goods requires state provision, as the only means to provide them. Such goods include not only defense and provision of a legal system, but also education, transportation, health care, and many other such goods. Markets can never be relied on to produce such goods, because non-payers would free-ride off of those who pay, and since everyone would want to be a free-rider, nobody would pay. Thus, only government can produce such goods.

The public goods justification for the state is one of the most commonly misapplied of economic arguments. Whether goods are rivalrous in consumption or not is often not an inherent feature of the good, but a feature of the size of the consuming group: a swimming pool may be non-rivalrous for two people, but quite rivalrous for two hundred people. And costs of exclusion are applicable to all goods, public or private: If I want to keep you from eating my apples, I may have to take some action to protect them, such as building a fence. Many goods that are non-rivalrous in consumption, such as a professional football game (if you see it, it doesn't mean that I can't see it, too), are produced only because entrepreneurs invest in means to exclude non-payers.

Besides not being an inherent feature of the goods per se, the alleged publicness of many goods is a feature of the political decision to make the goods available on a non-exclusive and even non-priced basis. If the state produces "freeways," it's hard to see how private enterprise could produce "freeways," that is, zero-priced transportation, that could compete. But notice that the "freeway" isn't really free, since it's financed through taxes (which have a particularly harsh form of exclusion from enjoyment, known as jail), and also that the lack of pricing is the primary reason for inefficient use patterns, such as traffic jams, which reflect a lack of any mechanism to allocate scarce resources (space in traffic) to their most highly valued uses. Indeed, the trend around the world has been toward pricing of roads, which deeply undercuts the public goods argument for state provision of roads.

Many goods that are allegedly impossible to provide on markets have been, or are at present, provided through market mechanisms—from lighthouses to education to policing to transportation—which suggests that the common invocation of alleged publicness is unjustified, or at least overstated.

A common form of the argument that certain goods are allegedly only producible through state action is that there are "externalities" that are not contracted for through the price mechanism. Thus, widespread education generates public benefits beyond the benefits to the persons who are educated, allegedly justifying state provision and financing through general tax revenues. But despite the benefits to others, which may be great or small, the benefits to the persons educated are so great for them that they induce sufficient investment in education. Public benefits don't always generate the defection of free-riders. In fact, as a wealth of research is demonstrating today, when states monopolize education they often fail to produce it for the poorest of the poor, who nonetheless perceive the benefits to them of education and invest substantial percentages of their meager incomes to educate their children. Whatever externalities may be generated by their children's education does not stop them from paying their own money to procure education for their children.

Finally, it should be remembered that virtually every argument alleging the impossibility of efficient production of public goods through the market applies at least equally strongly—and in many cases much more strongly—to the likelihood that the state will produce public goods. The existence and operation of a just and law-governed state is itself a public good, that is, the consumption of its benefits is non-rivalrous (at least among the citizenry), and it would be costly to exclude non-contributors to its maintenance (such as informed voters) from the enjoyment of its benefits. The incentives for politicians and voters to produce just and efficient government are not very impressive, certainly when placed next to the incentives that entrepreneurs and consumers have to procure public goods through cooperation in the marketplace. That does not mean that the state should never have any role in producing public goods, but it should make citizens less willing to cede to the state additional responsibilities for providing goods and services. In fact, the more responsibilities are given to the state, the less likely it is to be able to produce those public goods, such as defense of the rights of its citizens from aggression, at which it might enjoy special advantages.

7. Markets Don't Work (or Are Inefficient) When There Are Negative or Positive Externalities

Markets only work when all of the effects of action are borne by those who make the decisions. If people receive benefits without contributing to their production, markets will fail to produce the right amount. Similarly, if people receive "negative benefits," that is, if they are harmed and those costs are not taken into account in the decision to produce the goods, markets will benefit some at the expense of others, as the benefits of the action go to one set of parties and the costs are borne by another.

The mere existence of an externality is no argument for having the state take over some activity or displace private choices. Fashionable clothes and good grooming generate plenty of positive externalities, as others admire those who are well clothed or groomed, but that's no reason to turn choice of or provision of clothing and grooming over to the state. Gardening, architecture, and many other activities generate positive externalities on others, but people undertake to beautify their gardens and their buildings just the same. In all those cases, the benefits to the producers alone—including the approbation of those on whom the positive externalities are showered—are sufficient to induce them to produce the goods. In other cases, such as the provision of television and radio broadcasts, the public good is "tied" to the provision of other goods, such as advertising for firms; the variety of mechanisms to produce public goods is as great as the ingenuity of the entrepreneurs who produce them.

More commonly, however, it's the existence of *negative* externalities that leads people to question the efficacy or justice of market mechanisms. Pollution is the most commonly cited example. If a producer can produce products profitably because he imposes the costs of production on others who have not consented to be a part of the production process, say, by throwing huge amounts of smoke into the air or chemicals into a river, he will probably do so. Those who breathe the polluted air or drink the toxic water will bear the costs of producing the product, while the producer will get the benefits from the sale of the product. The problem in such cases, however, is not that markets have failed, but that they are absent. Markets rest on property and cannot function when property rights are not defined or enforced. Cases of pollution are precisely cases, not of market failure, but of government failure to define and defend the property rights of others, such as those who breathe polluted air or drink polluted water. When people downwind or downstream have the right to defend their rights, they can assert their rights and stop the polluters from polluting. The producer can install at his own expense equipment or technology to eliminate the pollution (or reduce it to tolerable and non-harmful levels), or offer to pay the people downwind or downstream for the rights to use their resources (perhaps offering them a better place to live), or stop producing the product, because he is harming the rights of others who will not accept his offers, showing that the total costs exceed the benefits. It's property rights that make such calculations possible and that induce people to take into account the effects of their actions on others. And it's markets, that is, the opportunity to engage in free exchange of rights, that allow all of the various parties to calculate the costs of actions.

Negative externalities such as air and water pollution are not a sign of market failure, but of government's failure to define and defend the property rights on which markets rest.

8. The More Complex a Social Order Is, the Less It Can Rely on Markets and the More It Needs Government Direction

Reliance on markets worked fine when society was less complicated, but with the tremendous growth of economic and social connections, government is necessary to direct and coordinate the actions of so many people.

If anything, the opposite is true. A simple social order, such as a band of hunters or gatherers, might be coordinated effectively by a leader with the power to compel obedience. But as social relations become more complex, reliance on voluntary market exchange becomes more—not less—important. A complex social order requires the coordination of more information than any mind or group of minds could master. Markets have evolved mechanisms to transmit information in a relatively low-cost manner; prices encapsulate information about supply and demand in the form of units that are comparable among different goods and services, in ways that voluminous reports by government bureaucracies cannot. Moreover, prices translate across languages, social mores, and ethnic and religious divides and allow people to take advantage of the knowledge possessed by unknown persons thousands of miles away, with whom they will never have any other kind of relationship. The more complex an economy and society, the more important reliance on market mechanisms becomes.

9. Markets Don't Work in Developing Countries

Markets work well in countries with well-developed infrastructures and legal systems, but in their absence developing countries simply cannot afford recourse to markets. In such cases, state direction is necessary, at least until a highly developed infrastructure and legal system is developed that could allow room for markets to function.

In general, infrastructure development is a feature of the wealth accumulated through markets, not a condition for markets to exist, and the failure of a legal system is a reason why markets are underdeveloped, but that failure is a powerful reason to reform the legal system so it could provide the foundation for the development of markets, not to postpone legal reform and market development. The only way to achieve the wealth of developed countries is to create the legal and institutional foundations for markets so that entrepreneurs, consumers, investors, and workers can freely cooperate to create wealth.

All currently wealthy countries were once very poor, some within living memory. What needs explanation is not poverty, which is the natural state of mankind, but wealth. Wealth has to be created, and the best way to ensure that wealth is created is to generate the incentives for people to do so. No system better than the free market, based on well-defined and legally secure property rights and legal institutions to facilitate exchange, has ever been discovered for generating incentives for wealth creation. There is one path out of poverty, and that is the path of wealth creation through the free market.

The term "developing nation" is frequently misapplied when it is applied to nations whose governments have rejected markets in favor of central planning, state ownership, mercantilism, protectionism, and special privileges. Such nations are not, in fact, developing at all. The nations that are developing, whether starting from relatively wealthy or relatively impoverished positions, are those that have created legal institutions of property and contract, freed markets, and limited the powers, the budget, and the reach of the state power.

10. Markets Lead to Disastrous Economic Cycles, Such as the Great Depression

Reliance on market forces leads to cycles of "boom and bust," as investor overconfidence feeds on itself, leading to massive booms in investment that are inevitably followed by contractions of production, unemployment, and a generally worsening economic condition.

Economic cycles of "boom and bust" are sometimes blamed on reliance on markets. The evidence, however, is that generalized overproduction is not a feature of markets; when more goods and services are produced, prices adjust and the result is general affluence, not a "bust." When this or that industry expands beyond the ability of the market to sustain profitability, a process of self-correction sets in and profit signals lead resources to be redirected to other fields of activity. There is no reason inherent in markets for such correction to apply to all industries; indeed, it is self-contradictory (for if investment is being taken away from all and redirected to all, then it's not being taken away from all in the first place).

Nonetheless, prolonged periods of general unemployment are possible when governments distort price systems through foolish manipulation of monetary systems, a policy error that is often combined with subsidies to industries that should be contracting and wage and price controls that keep the market from adjusting, thus prolonging the unemployment. Such was the case of the Great Depression that lasted from 1929 to the end of World War II, which economists (such as Nobel Prize winner Milton Friedman) showed was caused by a massive and sudden contraction in the money supply by the U.S. Federal Reserve system, which was pursuing politically set goals. The general contraction was then deepened by the rise in protectionism, which extended the suffering worldwide, and prolonged greatly by such programs as the National Recovery Act, programs to keep farm prices high (by destroying huge quantities of agricultural products and restricting supply), and other "New Deal" programs that were aimed at keeping market forces from correcting the disastrous effects of the government's policy errors. More recent crashes, such as the Asian financial crisis of 1997, have been caused by imprudent monetary and exchange rate policies that distorted the signals to investors. Market forces corrected the policy failures of governments, but the process was not without hardship; the cause of the hardship was not the medicine that cured the disease, but the bad monetary and exchange rate policies of governments that caused it in the first place.

With the adoption of more prudent monetary policies by governmental monetary authorities, such cycles have tended to even out. When combined with greater reliance on market adjustment processes, the result has been a reduction in the frequency and severity of economic cycles and long-term and sustained improvement in those countries that have followed policies of freedom of trade, budgetary restraint, and the rule of law.

11. Too Much Reliance on Markets Is as Silly as Too Much Reliance on Socialism: The Best Is the Mixed Economy

Most people understand that it's unwise to put all your eggs in one basket. Prudent investors diversify their portfolios, and it's just as reasonable to have a diversified "policy portfolio," as well, meaning a mix of socialism and markets.

Prudent investors who don't have inside information do indeed diversify their portfolios against risk. If one stock goes down, another may go up, thus evening out the loss with a gain. Over the long run, a properly diversified portfolio will grow. But policies aren't like that. Some have been demonstrated time and time again to fail, while others have been demonstrated to succeed. It would make no sense to have a "diversified investment portfolio" made up of stocks in firms that are known to be failing and stocks in firms that are known to be succeeding; the reason for diversification is that one doesn't have any special knowledge of which firms are more likely to be profitable or unprofitable.

Studies of decades of economic data carried out annually by the Fraser Institute of Canada and a worldwide network of research institutes have shown consistently that greater reliance on market forces leads to higher per capita incomes; faster economic growth; lower unemployment; longer life spans; lower infant mortality; falling rates of child labor; greater access to clean water, health care, and other amenities of modern life, including cleaner environments; and improved governance, such as lower rates of official corruption and more democratic accountability. Free markets generate good results.

Moreover, there is no "well-balanced" middle of the road. State interventions into the market typically lead to distortions and even crises, which then are used as excuses for yet more interventions, thus driving policy one direction or another. For example, a "policy portfolio" that included imprudent monetary policy, which increases the supply of money faster than the economy is growing, will lead to rising prices. History has shown repeatedly that politicians tend to respond, not by blaming their own imprudent policies, but by blaming an "overheated economy" or "unpatriotic speculators" and imposing controls on prices. When prices are not allowed to be corrected by supply and demand (in this case, the increased supply of money, which tends to cause the price of money, as expressed in terms of commodities, to fall), the result is shortages of goods and services, as more people seek to buy limited supplies of goods at the below-market price than producers are willing to supply at that price. In addition, the lack of free markets leads people to shift to black markets, under-the-table bribes of officials, and other departures from the rule of law. The resulting mixture of shortage and corruption then typically induces yet greater tendencies toward authoritarian assertions of power. The effect of creating a "policy portfolio" that includes such proven bad policies is to undermine the economy, to create corruption, and even to undermine constitutional democracy.

Hybrid Ethical-Economic Criticisms

12. Markets Lead to More Inequality Than Non-Market Processes

By definition, markets reward ability to satisfy consumer preferences, and as abilities differ, so incomes will differ. Moreover, by definition, socialism is a state of equality, so every step toward socialism is a step toward equality.

If we want to understand the relationships between policies and outcomes, it should be kept in mind that property is a legal concept;

wealth is an economic concept. The two are often confused, but they should be kept distinct. Market processes regularly redistribute wealth on a massive scale. In contrast, unwilling redistribution of property (when undertaken by individual citizens, it's known as "theft") is prohibited under the rules that govern free markets, which require that property be well defined and legally secure. Markets can redistribute wealth, even when property titles remain in the same hands. Every time the value of an asset (in which an owner has a property right) changes, the wealth of the asset owner changes. An asset that was worth 600 euros yesterday may today be worth only 400 euros. That's a redistribution of 200 euros of wealth through the market, although there has been no redistribution of property. So markets regularly redistribute wealth and in the process give owners of assets incentives to maximize their value or to shift their assets to those who will. That regular redistribution, based on incentives to maximize total value, represents transfers of wealth on a scale unthinkable for most politicians. In contrast, while market processes redistribute wealth, political processes redistribute property by taking it from some and giving it to others; in the process, by making property less secure, such redistribution tends to make property in general less valuable, that is, to destroy wealth. The more unpredictable the redistribution, the greater the loss of wealth caused by the threat of redistribution of property.

Equality is a characteristic that can be realized along a number of different dimensions, but generally not across all. For example, people can all be equal before the law, but if that is the case, it is unlikely that they will have exactly equal influence over politics, for some who exercise their equal rights to freedom of speech will be more eloquent or energetic than others, and thus more influential. Similarly, equal rights to offer goods and services on free markets may not lead to exactly equal incomes, for some may work harder or longer (because they prefer income to leisure) than others or have special skills for which others will pay extra. On the flip side, the attempt to achieve through coercion equality of influence or equality of incomes will entail that some exercise more authority or political power than others, that is, the power necessary to bring about such outcomes. In order to bring about a particular pattern of outcomes, someone or some group must have the "God's Eye" view of outcomes necessary to redistribute, to see a lack here and a surplus there and

179

thus to take from here and move to there. As powers to create equal outcomes are concentrated in the hands of those entrusted with them, as was the case in the officially egalitarian Soviet Union, those with unequal political and legal powers find themselves tempted to use those powers to attain unequal incomes or access to resources. Both logic and experience show that conscious attempts to attain equal or "fair" incomes, or some other pattern other than what the spontaneous order of the market generates, are generally self-defeating, for the simple reason that those who hold the power to redistribute property use it to benefit themselves, thus converting inequality of political power into other sorts of inequality, whether honors, wealth, or something else. Such was certainly the experience of the officially communist nations and such is the path currently being taken by other nations, such as Venezuela, in which total power is being accumulated in the hands of one man, Hugo Chavez, who demands such massively unequal power, ostensibly in order to create equality of wealth among citizens.

According to the data in the 2006 *Economic Freedom of the World Report*, reliance on free markets is weakly correlated to income inequality (from the least free to the most free economies the world over, divided into quartiles, the percentage of income received by the poorest 10% varies from an average of 2.2% to an average of 2.5%), but it is very strongly correlated to the levels of income of the poorest 10% (from the least free to the most free economies the world over, divided into quartiles, the average levels of income received by the poorest 10% are $826, $1,186, $2,322, and $6,519). Greater reliance on markets seems to have little impact on income distributions, but it does substantially raise the incomes of the poor and it is likely that many of the poor would certainly consider that a good thing.

13. Markets Cannot Meet Human Needs, Such as Health, Housing, Education, and Food

Goods should be distributed according to principles appropriate to their nature. Markets distribute goods according to ability to pay, but health, housing, education, food, and other basic human needs, precisely because they are needs, should be distributed according to need, not ability to pay.

If markets do a better job of meeting human needs than other principles, that is, if more people enjoy higher standards of living

180

under markets than under socialism, it seems that the allocation mechanism under markets does a better job of meeting the criterion of need, as well. As noted above, the incomes of the poorest tend to rise rapidly with the degree of market freedom, meaning that the poor have more resources with which to satisfy their needs. (Naturally, not all needs are directly related to income; true friendship and love certainly are not. But there is no reason to think that those are more "equitably" distributed by coercive mechanisms, either, or even that they can be distributed by such mechanisms.)

Moreover, while assertions of "need" tend to be rather rubbery claims, as are assertions of "ability," willingness to pay is easier to measure. When people bid with their own money for goods and services, they are telling us how much they value those goods and services relative to other goods and services. Food, certainly a more basic need than education or health care, is provided quite effectively through markets. In fact, in those countries where private property was abolished and state allocation substituted for market allocation, the results were famine and even cannibalism. Markets meet human needs for most goods, including those that respond to basic human needs, better than do other mechanisms.

Satisfaction of needs requires the use of scarce resources, meaning that choices have to be made about their allocation. Where markets are not allowed to operate, other systems and criteria for rationing scarce resources are used, such as bureaucratic allocation, political pull, membership in a ruling party, relationship to the president or the main holders of power, or bribery and other forms of corruption. It is hardly obvious that such criteria are better than the criteria evolved by markets, nor that they generate more equality; the experience is rather the opposite.

14. Markets Rest on the Principle of the Survival of the Fittest

Just like the law of the jungle, red in tooth and claw, the law of the market means survival of the fittest. Those who cannot produce to market standards fall by the wayside and are trampled underfoot.

Invocations of evolutionary principles such as "survival of the fittest" in the study of living systems and in the study of human social interaction lead to confusion unless they identify what it is in each case that survives. In the case of biology, it is the individual animal and its ability to reproduce itself. A rabbit that is eaten by a cat because it's too slow to escape isn't going to have any more offspring. The fastest rabbits will be the ones to reproduce. When applied to social evolution, however, the unit of survival is quite different; it's not the individual human being, but the form of social interaction, such as a custom, an institution, or a firm, that is "selected" in the evolutionary struggle. When a business firm goes out of business, it "dies," that is to say, that particular form of social cooperation "dies," but that certainly doesn't mean that the human beings who made up the firm—as investors, owners, managers, employees, and so on—die as well. A less efficient form of cooperation is replaced by a more efficient form. Market competition is decidedly unlike the competition of the jungle. In the jungle animals compete to eat each other or to displace each other. In the market, entrepreneurs and firms compete with each other for the right to cooperate with consumers and with other entrepreneurs and firms. Market competition is not competition for the opportunity to live; it is competition for the opportunity to cooperate.

15. Markets Debase Culture and Art

Art and culture are responses to the higher elements of the human soul and, as such, cannot be bought and sold like tomatoes or shirt buttons. Leaving art to the market is like leaving religion to the market, a betrayal of the inherent dignity of art, as of religion. Moreover, as art and culture are opened more and more to competition on international markets, the result is their debasement, as traditional forms are abandoned in the pursuit of the almighty dollar or euro.

Most art has been and is produced for the market. Indeed, the history of art is largely the history of innovation through the market in response to new technologies, new philosophies, new tastes, and new forms of spirituality. Art, culture, and the market have been intimately connected for many centuries. Musicians charge fees for people to attend their concerts, just as vegetable mongers charge for tomatoes or tailors charge to replace buttons on suits. In fact, the formation of wider markets for music, film, and other forms of art by the creation of records, cassettes, CDs, DVDs, and now iTunes and mp3 files allows more and more people to be exposed to more and more varied art and for artists to create more artistic experiences, to create more hybrid forms of art, and to earn more income. Unsurprisingly, most of the art produced in any given year won't stand the test of time; that creates a false perspective on the part of those who condemn contemporary art as "trashy," in comparison to the great works of the past; what they are comparing are the best works winnowed out from hundreds of years of production to the mass of works produced in the past year. Had they included all of the works that did not stand the test of time and were not remembered, the comparison would probably look quite different. What accounts for the survival of the best is precisely the competitive process of markets for art.

Comparing the entirety of contemporary artistic production with the very best of the best from past centuries is not the only error people make when evaluating markets for art. Another error common to observers from wealthy societies who visit poor societies is the confusion of the poverty of poor societies with their cultures. When wealthy visitors see people in countries that are poor-but-growing-economically using cell phones and flipping open laptops, they complain that their visit is not as "authentic" as the last one. As people become richer through market interactions made possible by increasing liberalization or globalization, such as the introduction of cell telephony, anti-globalization activists from rich countries complain that the poor are being "robbed" of their culture. But why equate culture with poverty? The Japanese went from poverty to wealth, and it would be hard to argue that they are any less Japanese as a result. In fact, their greater wealth has made possible the spread of awareness of Japanese culture around the world. In India, as incomes are rising, the fashion industry is responding by turning to traditional forms of attire, such as the sari, and adapting, updating, and applying to them aesthetic criteria of beauty and form. The people of the very small country of Iceland have managed to maintain a high literary culture and their own theater and movie industry because per capita incomes are quite high, allowing them to dedicate their wealth to perpetuating and developing their culture.

Finally, although religious belief is not "for sale," free societies do leave religion to the same principles—equal rights and freedom of choice—as those at the foundation of the free market. Churches, mosques, synagogues, and temples compete with each other for adherents and for support. Unsurprisingly, those European countries that provide official state support of churches tend to have very low church participation, whereas countries without state support of religion tend to have higher levels of church participation. The reason is not so hard to understand: Churches that have to compete for membership and support have to provide services—sacramental, spiritual, and communal—to members, and that greater attention to the needs of the membership tends to create more religiosity and participation. Indeed, that's why the official established state church of Sweden lobbied to be disestablished in the year 2000; as an unresponsive part of the state bureaucracy, the church was losing connection with its members and potential members and was, in effect, dying.

There is no contradiction between the market and art and culture. Market exchange is not the same as artistic experience or cultural enrichment, but it is a helpful vehicle for advancing both.

16. Markets Only Benefit the Rich and Talented

The rich get richer and the poor get poorer. If you want to make a lot of money, you have to start out with a lot. In the race of the market for profits, those who start out ahead reach the finish line first.

Market processes aren't races, which have winners and losers. When two parties voluntarily agree to exchange, they do so because they both expect to benefit, not because they hope they will win and the other will lose. Unlike in a race, in an exchange, if one person wins, it doesn't mean that the other has to lose. Both parties gain. The point is not to "beat" the other, but to gain through voluntary cooperative exchange; in order to induce the other person to exchange, you have to offer a benefit to him or her, as well.

Being born to wealth may be a good thing, something the citizens of wealthy countries probably do not appreciate as much as do those who seek to emigrate from poor countries to rich countries; the latter usually understand the benefits of living in a wealthy society better than those who are born to it. But within a free market, with freedom of entry and equal rights for all buyers and sellers, those who were good at meeting market demands yesterday may not be the same as those who will be good at meeting market demand tomorrow. Sociologists refer to the "circulation of elites" that characterizes free societies; rather than static elites that rest on military power, caste membership, or tribal or family connection, the elites of free societies—including artistic elites, cultural elites, scientific elites, and economic elites—are open to new members and rarely pass on membership to the children of members, many of whom move from the upper classes to the middle classes.

184

Wealthy societies are full of successful people who left behind countries where markets are severely restricted or hampered by special favors for the powerful, by protectionism, and by mercantilistic monopolies and controls, where opportunities for advancement in the market are limited. They left those societies with little or nothing and found success in more open and market-oriented societies, such as the United States, the United Kingdom, and Canada. What was the difference between the societies they left and those they joined? Freedom to compete in the market. How sad for poor countries it is that the mercantilism and restrictions in their home countries drive them abroad, so they can not stay at home and enrich their neighbors and friends by putting their entrepreneurial drive to work.

Generally, in countries with freer markets, the greatest fortunes are made, not by satisfying the desires of the rich, but by satisfying the desires of the more modest classes. From Ford Motors to Sony to Wal-Mart, great companies that generate great fortunes tend to be those that cater, not to the tastes of the richest, but to the lower and middle classes.

Free markets tend to be characterized by a "circulation of elites," with no one guaranteed a place or kept from entering by accident of birth. The phrase "the rich get richer and the poor get poorer" applies, not to free markets, but to mercantilism and political cronyism, that is, to systems in which proximity to power determines wealth. Under markets, the more common experience is that the rich do well (but may not stay "rich" by the standards of their society) and the poor get a lot richer, with many moving into the middle and upper classes. At any given moment, by definition, 20% of the population will be in the lowest quintile of income and 20% will be in the highest quintile. But it does not follow either that those quintiles will measure the same amount of income (as incomes of all income groups rise in expanding economies) or that the income categories will be filled by the same people. The categories are rather like rooms in a hotel or seats on a bus; they are filled by someone, but not always by the same people. When income distributions in market-oriented societies are studied over time, a great deal of income mobility is revealed, with remarkable numbers of people moving up and down in the income distributions. What is most important, however, is that prosperous market economies see all incomes rise, from the lowest to the highest.

17. When Prices Are Liberalized and Subject to Market Forces, They Just Go Up

The fact is that when prices are left to market forces, without government controls, they just go up, meaning that people can afford less and less. Free-market pricing is just another name for high prices.

Prices that are controlled at below market levels do tend to rise, at least over the short time, when they are freed. But there is much more to the story than that. For one thing, some controlled prices are kept above the market level, so that when they are freed, they tend to fall. Moreover, when looking at money prices that are controlled by state power, it's important to remember that the money that changes hands over the table is not usually the only price paid by those who successfully purchase the goods. If the goods are rationed by queuing, then the time spent waiting in line is a part of what people have to spend to get the goods. (Notably, however, that waiting time represents pure waste, since it's not time that is somehow transferred to producers to induce them to make more of the goods to satisfy the unmet demand.) If corrupt officials have their hands open, there are also the payments under the table that have to be added to the payment that is made over the table. The sum of the legal payment, the illegal bribes, and the time spent waiting in lines when maximum prices are imposed by the state on goods and services is quite often higher than the price that people would agree on through the market. Moreover, the money spent on bribes and the time spent on waiting are wasted—they are spent by consumers but not received by producers, so they provide no incentive for producers to produce more and thereby alleviate the shortage caused by price controls.

While money prices may go up in the short time when prices are freed, the result is to increase production and diminish wasteful rationing and corruption, with the result that total real prices—expressed in terms of a basic commodity, human labor time—goes down. The amount of time that a person had to spend laboring to earn a loaf of bread in 1800 was a serious fraction of his or her laboring day; as wages have gone up and up and up and up, the amount of working time necessary to buy a loaf of bread has fallen to just a few minutes in wealthy countries. Measured in terms of labor, the prices of all other goods have fallen dramatically, with one exception: labor itself. As labor productivity and wages rise, hiring human labor becomes more expensive, which is why modestly well off people in poor countries commonly have servants, whereas even wealthy people in rich countries find it much cheaper to buy machines to wash their clothes and dishes. The result of free markets is a fall in the price of everything else in terms of labor and a rise in the price of labor in terms of everything else.

18. Privatization and Marketization in Post-Communist Societies Were Corrupt, Which Shows That Markets Are Corrupting

Privatization campaigns are almost always rigged. It's a game that just awards the best state assets to the most ruthless and corrupt opportunists. The whole game of privatization and marketization is dirty and represents nothing more than theft from the people.

A variety of formerly socialist states that have created privatization campaigns have had quite varied outcomes. Some have generated very successful market orders. Others have slipped back toward authoritarianism and have seen the "privatization" processes result in new elites gaining control of both the state and private businesses, as in the emerging "Siloviki" system of Russia. The dirtiness of the dirty hands that profited from rigged privatization schemes was a result of the preexisting lack of market institutions, notably the rule of law that is the foundation for the market. Creating those institutions is no easy task, and there is no well-known generally applicable technique that works in all cases. But the failure in some cases to fully realize the institutions of the rule of law is no reason not to try; even in the case of Russia, the deeply flawed privatization schemes that were instituted were an improvement over the one-party tyranny that preceded them and that collapsed from its own injustice and inefficiency.

Mere "privatization" in the absence of a functioning legal system is not the same as creating a market. Markets rest on a foundation of law; failed privatizations are not failures of the market, but failures of the state to create the legal foundations for markets.

Overly Enthusiastic Defenses

19. All Relations among Humans Can Be Reduced to Market Relations

All actions are taken because the actors are maximizing their own utility. Even helping other people is getting a benefit for yourself, or you wouldn't do it. Friendship and love represent exchanges of services for mutual benefit, no less than exchanges involving sacks of potatoes. Moreover, all forms of human interaction can be understood in terms of markets, including politics, in which votes are exchanged for promises of benefits, and even crime, in which criminals and victims exchange, in the well-known example, "your money or your life."

Attempting to reduce all actions to a single motivation falsifies human experience. Parents don't think about the benefits to themselves when they sacrifice for their children or rush to their rescue when they're in danger. When people pray for salvation or spiritual enlightenment, their motivations are not quite the same as when they are shopping for clothes. What they do have in common is that their actions are purposeful, that they are undertaken to achieve their purposes. But it does not follow logically from that that the purposes they are striving to achieve are all reducible to commensurable units of the same substance. Our purposes and motivations may be varied; when we go to the market to buy a hammer, when we enter an art museum, and when we cradle a newborn baby, we are realizing very different purposes, not all of which are well expressed in terms of buying and selling in markets.

It is true that intellectual constructs and tools can be used to understand and illuminate a variety of different kinds of interaction. The concepts of economics, for example, which are used to understand exchanges on markets, can also be used to understand political science and even religion. Political choices may have calculable costs and benefits, just like business choices; political parties or mafia cartels may be compared to firms in the market. But it does not follow from such applications of concepts that the two choice situations are morally or legally equivalent. A criminal who offers you a choice between keeping your money and keeping your life is not relevantly like an entrepreneur who offers you a choice between keeping your money and using it to buy a commodity, for the simple reason that the criminal forces you to choose between two things to both of which you have a moral and legal entitlement, whereas the entrepreneur offers you a choice between two things, to one of which he has an entitlement and to one of which you have an entitlement. In both cases you make a choice and act purposively, but in the former case the criminal has forced you to choose, whereas in the latter case the entrepreneur has offered you a choice; the former lessens your entitlements, and the latter offers to increase them by offering you something you don't have but may value more for something you do have but may value less. Not all human relationships are reducible to the same terms as markets; at the very least, those that involve involuntary "exchanges" are radically different, because they represent losses of opportunity and value, rather than opportunities to gain value.

20. Markets Can Solve All Problems without Government at All

Government is so incompetent that it can't do anything right. The main lesson of the market is that we should always weaken government, because government is simply the opposite of the market. The less government you have, the more market you have.

Those who recognize the benefits of markets should recognize that in much of the world, perhaps all of it, the basic problem is not only that governments do too much, but also that they do too little. The former category—things that governments should not do— includes A) activities that should not be done by anyone at all, such as "ethnic cleansing," theft of land, and creating special legal privileges for elites, and B) things that could and should be done through the voluntary interaction of firms and entrepreneurs in markets, such as manufacturing automobiles, publishing newspapers, and running restaurants. Governments should stop doing all of those things. But as they cease doing what they ought not to do, governments should start doing some of the things that would in fact increase justice and create the foundation for voluntary interaction to solve problems. In fact, there is a relation between the two: governments that spend their resources running car factories or publishing newspapers, or worse—confiscating property and creating legal privileges for the few—both undercut and diminish their abilities to provide truly valuable services that governments are able to provide. For example, governments in poorer nations rarely do a good job of providing clear legal title, not to mention securing property from takings. Legal systems are frequently inefficient, cumbersome, and lack the independence and impartiality that are necessary to facilitate voluntary transactions.

For markets to be able to provide the framework for social coordination, property and contract must be well established in law. Governments that fail to provide those public benefits keep markets from emerging. Government can serve the public interest by exercising authority to create law and justice, not by being weak, but by being legally authoritative and at the same time limited in its powers. A weak government is not the same as a limited government. Weak unlimited governments can be tremendously dangerous because they do things that ought not to be done but do not have the authority to enforce the rules of just conduct and provide the security of life, liberty, and estate that are necessary for freedom and free market exchanges. Free markets are not the same as the sheer absence of government. Not all anarchies are attractive, after all. Free markets are made possible by efficiently administered limited governments that clearly define and impartially enforce rules of just conduct.

It is also important to remember that there are plenty of problems that have to be solved through conscious action; it's not enough to insist that impersonal market processes will solve all problems. In fact, as Nobel Prize winning economist Ronald Coase explained in his important work on the market and the firm, firms typically rely on conscious planning and coordination to achieve common aims, rather than on constant recourse to market exchanges, because going to the market is costly. Each contract arranged is costly to negotiate, for example, so long-term contracts are used instead to reduce contracting costs. In firms, long-term contracts substitute for spot-exchanges and include labor relations involving teamwork and conscious direction, rather than constant bidding for particular services. Firms—little islands of teamwork and planning—are able to succeed because they navigate within a wider ocean of spontaneous order through market exchanges. (The great error of the socialists was to try to manage the entire economy like one great firm; it would be a similar error not to recognize the limited role of conscious direction and teamwork within the wider spontaneous order of the market.) To the extent that markets can provide the framework of creation and enforcement of rules of just conduct, advocates of free markets should promote just that. Private security firms are often better than state police (and less violent, if for no other reason than that the costs of violence are not easily shifted to third parties, except by the state); voluntary arbitration often works far better than state courts. But recognizing that entails recognizing the central role of rules in creating markets and, thus, favoring efficient and just rules, whether provided by government or by the market, rather than merely being "anti-government."

190

Finally, it should be remembered that property and market exchange may not, by themselves, solve all problems. For example, if global warming is in fact a threat to the entire planet's ability to sustain life, or if the ozone layer is being degraded in ways that will be harmful to life, coordinated government solutions may be the best, or perhaps the only, way to avoid disaster. Naturally, that does not mean that markets would play no role at all; markets for rights to carbon dioxide emissions might, for example, help to smooth adjustments, but those markets would first have to be established by coordination among governments. What is important to remember, however, is that deciding that a tool is not adequate and appropriate for *all* conceivable problems does not entail that it is not adequate and appropriate for *any* problems. The tool may work very well for some or even most problems. Property and markets solve many problems and should be relied on to do so; if they do not solve all, that is no reason to reject them for problems for which they do offer efficient and just solutions.

Free markets may not solve every conceivable problem humanity might face, but they can and do produce freedom and prosperity, and there is something to be said for that.

9. What's *Not* Wrong with Libertarianism

There are many problems in Jeffrey Friedman's "What's Wrong with Libertarianism" (*Critical Review* 11, no. 1), but one is so important to his entire critique that I wish to get right to it.

Friedman insists that there is an inconsistency between believing that individuals have rights, on the one hand, and evaluating policies on the grounds of their good or bad consequences generally (setting aside the trivial consequence that the policies may be compatible or incompatible with the asserted rights themselves). Friedman calls the attempt to get around this inconsistency "libertarian straddling," which "tries to marry instrumentalist and intrinsic defenses of libertarianism while giving primacy to the latter"; he expresses amazement that this straddling allows "the armchair philosopher," "the economist," "the sociologist," "and the political scientist" all to reach "the same conclusion—libertarianism" (Friedman 1997, 435). "Divine intervention might seem to be the only thing that could make sense of this libertarian straddle," he writes, suggesting that perhaps the reconciliation of rights and consequences is delusory.

Friedman writes:

> The effect of libertarian straddling on libertarian scholarship is suggested by a passage in the scholarly appendix to Boaz's collection of libertarian essays, *The Libertarian Reader*. There, Tom G. Palmer (also of the Cato Institute) writes that in libertarian scholarship "the moral imperatives of peace and voluntary cooperation are *brought together* with a rich understanding of the spontaneous order made possible by such voluntary cooperation, and of the ways in which coercive intervention can disorder the world and set in motion complex trains of unintended consequences" (Boaz 1997b, 416, emphasis added). Palmer's ambiguous "brought together" suggests (without coming right out and saying) that even if there were no rich understanding of spontaneous

Originally published in *Critical Review* 12, no. 3, Summer 1998, pp. 337–58.

order, libertarianism would be sustained by "moral imperatives." But in that case, why develop the rich understanding
of spontaneous order in the first place, and why emphasize
its importance now that it has been developed? Spontaneous
order is, on Palmer's own terms, *irrelevant*, since even if a
rich understanding of it yielded the conclusion that markets
are *less* orderly or less spontaneous than states, or that the
quality of the order they produce is *inferior* to that produced
by states, we would still be compelled to be libertarians by
moral imperatives. The premise of the philosophical
approach is that nothing can possibly trump freedom-cum-
private property. (Friedman 1997, 436, emphasis in original)

The best that I can make of this is that Friedman assumes that by
"moral imperative" I meant "categorical imperative," for that is the
only reading that would make sense of his claim. If an imperative
were truly categorical, then it would indeed trump all other considerations. For example, no concern with the consequences of an act
could override a categorical imperative to perform the act. Friedman's description could easily lead one to think that I was being
very, very sneaky, in "suggest[ing] (without coming right out and
saying)" that consequences are irrelevant, but the truth is far less
interesting. I did not write "categorical imperative," not because I
hoped to slip something past the unsophisticated reader, but merely
because I did not *mean* categorical imperative. Friedman's language
implies that I am secretly in agreement with him but won't "come
right out and say so" and suggests the existence among libertarian
philosophers of the kind of conspiracy attributed to the Pythagore-
ans, who are reputed to have killed cult members who disclosed
the existence of incommensurable quantities, such as the sides of a
right triangle, thereby revealing the error of asserting that the universe could be expressed in terms of whole numbers, which was
the central tenet of the Pythagorean cult. That would, admittedly, be
more interesting than merely discovering that I and other libertarians
disagree with Jeffrey Friedman.

Allow me to set the record straight. Not all imperatives are categorical. Some imperatives, for example, are hypothetical. Thus, "If you
wish to be strong, you must exercise and eat well" is a hypothetical
imperative. Implicit in Friedman's entire essay is the view that all
moral claims are *necessarily* categorical claims, and thus, it would
seem, that the only (or at least the first) moral philosopher was

Immanuel Kant. That may be right, but it is hardly self-evident or a widely accepted claim. Kant (1964, 82) himself distinguished between kinds of imperatives:

> All *imperatives* command either *hypothetically* or *categorically*. Hypothetical imperatives declare a possible action to be practically necessary as a means to the attainment of something else that one wills (or that one may will). A categorical imperative would be one which represented an action as objectively necessary in itself apart from its relation to a further end.

Kant limited claims of morality to "the relation of actions to the autonomy of the will—that is, to a possible making of universal law by means of its maxims" (ibid., 107). Only if morality is limited in this or some similar way is it true that consequences are irrelevant to moral or legal evaluation. If spontaneous order is irrelevant, it is not on "Palmer's own terms," but on *Friedman's* terms.

The reason that I did not "come right out and say" that consequences are irrelevant to evaluating claims of morality or justice is that I don't believe that they are irrelevant.[1] Nor do I think that "the effects of libertarianism could not conceivably outweigh the putative intrinsic value of private property" (Friedman 1997, 436). And I am in pretty good company here: Aristotle, Aquinas, Grotius, Locke, Pufendorf, Hume, Smith, and a few hundred others who fancied themselves moral philosophers would agree. Indeed, some philosophers explicitly ground morality on hypothetical imperatives: Given the facts of reality, if you want to achieve X, then you must do Y (e.g., Foot 1972 and Barnett 1998). The empirical investigation of reality is at the foundation of the rights claims of the modern natural-rights tradition (as also of the classical tradition). That is why it should *not* seem an amazing coincidence that a sociologist, a philosopher, a political scientist, and an economist might come to convergent, compatible, or even identical conclusions.[2] They are all trying to study the same topic: humanity. Is it merely an amazing coincidence that biologists find that the investigations of mathematicians regarding the relationship between the cubic volume and the surface of a sphere explain why unicellular algae are not the size of basketballs (see Thompson 1966)? Or that the chemist and the physicist collaborate and reinforce each other's research into the nature of chemical reactions? These are not surprising because there is one reality that is being studied in different ways by different disciplines.

The principle of Ockham's Razor suggests that the singular nature (or unicity) of the topic of study is a more likely explanation of convergent conclusions than a conspiracy among social scientists.

It is only because Friedman assumes (without ever stating explicitly) that moral claims—most strongly claims of right—are necessarily categorical claims that he can set up his opposition between rights claims and consequentialism.[3] But not everyone understands claims of right as categorical. If claims of right are understood in other ways, the alleged conflict between rights claims and consideration of consequences disappears.

The modern natural-rights theorists based their claims on behalf of rights precisely on the relationship between rules and good consequences, and they advocated regimes of imprescriptible rights rather than regimes of arbitrary power for the very epistemic reasons Friedman invokes in his critique of what he mistakes to be David Boaz's understanding of individual rights (Friedman 1997, 437–38).[4] As Friedman (1997, 437) states, Boaz makes claims "about the empirical consequences of libertarianism. As such, its validity cannot be known in advance." This is true and important. It is precisely because we cannot know in advance the consequences of each and every action, and thus judge the goodness or badness (hence permissibility or impermissibility) of each and every act, that we need rules to guide us. It tells moral agents nothing to say "always do what is best" or "always do what yields the best consequences," for such knowledge is normally not available to us. Rights and the rules of justice provide the standard of action, but not the goal. The goal or justification of a system of rights is its good consequences (life, prosperity, peace, cooperation, knowledge, social harmony, etc.), but we find that we cannot aim at those goals directly. Much as economic planning cannot work in the absence of a system of markets and prices, peaceful cooperation cannot come about except by means of a system of rules and claims of justice that we refer to as rights. Attempts to achieve good consequences directly may be self-defeating (see Parfit 1986). Requiring agents to act so as always to attempt to generate the best consequences may very well generate consequences inferior to the consequences generated by requiring agents to follow a set of rules.

In the modern natural-rights tradition, the invocation of the good or bad consequences of rules and institutions plays a role in justifications of the claim that individuals have rights; the question is, at what level do we invoke this justification? Do we ask about the consequences of each and every act, taken singly, or do we ask about the consequences of adhering to *systems of rules*? Surely, only the latter course is open to us, given our epistemic limitations. As F. A. Hayek noted,

> rules are a device for coping with our constitutional igno-rance. There would be no need for rules among omniscient people who were in agreement on the relative importance of all the different ends. Any examination of the moral or legal order which leaves this fact out of account misses the central problem. (Hayek 1976, 8)

Friedman is quite impressed by the critique of socialism offered by Mises and Hayek, but he seems not to understand that the very same considerations are at the base of the modern natural-rights tradition.

As David Hume (1978, III.II.ii, 496–97) noted,

> if men pursu'd the publick interest naturally, and with a hearty affection, they wou'd never have dream'd of restrain-ing each other by these rules; and if they pursu'd their own interest, without any precaution, they wou'd run head-long into every kind of injustice and violence. These rules, there-fore, are artificial, and seek their end in an oblique and indi-rect manner; nor is the interest, which gives rise to them, of a kind that cou'd be pursu'd by the natural and inartificial passions of men.

Hume—along with others in the modern natural-rights tradi-tion—realized that certain good consequences can only be attained indirectly, by establishing or fostering a system of rights that are action-guiding, i.e., that let agents know what they may do and what they may not do. Hume (1978, III.II.i, 484) was merely stating what was widely understood among writers on natural right:[5]

> To avoid giving offence, I must here observe, that when I deny justice to be a natural virtue, I make use of the word, natural, only as oppos'd to artificial. In another sense of the word; as no principle of the human mind is more natural than a sense of virtue; so no virtue is more natural than justice. Mankind is an inventive species; and where an inven-tion is obvious and absolutely necessary, it may as properly be said to be natural as any thing that proceeds immediately

> from original principles, without the intervention of thought
> or reflexion. Tho' the rules of justice be artificial, they are
> not arbitrary. Nor is the expression improper to call them
> Laws of Nature; if by natural we understand what is common
> to any species, or even if we confine it to mean what is
> inseparable from the species.

So evaluation of consequences *does* matter, but it matters at the level of justifying a general system of rights. Precisely because of the limitations of human knowledge that Friedman acknowledges were the downfall of socialism, we cannot normally invoke consequentialism on a case-by-case basis. That is, after all, as Hume (and more recently, Hayek) so strongly emphasized, the justification for rules. It is for this reason that Friedman's stipulated test of the validity of libertarian conclusions sets an impossible standard and misunderstands the nature of the libertarian argument: "Libertarian conclusions require not only extensive evidence of government failure, but an empirically substantiated reason to think that such failure is *always* more likely than the failure of civil society" (Friedman 1997, 412, emphasis in original).

It seems at first that Friedman is demanding a proof that voluntarism (understood as libertarians understand it) is *always* better than coercion. Such a proof would be impossible. But another look indicates that in this sentence all that he demands is to be shown that "such failure is always *more likely*" (emphasis added). If I understand this rather imprecise formulation, I think that such a standard could be met, if one were to compare real civil societies with real states, rather than real (and therefore imperfect) civil societies with ideal (and therefore perfect) states. On the next page, Friedman, however, explicitly sets the standard higher: "the utilitarian libertarian" must show that "*all* government intervention with [property rights] is bound to fail" (emphasis added). Now, what would a proof of that form be like? Well, it would certainly be very different from a proof that "such failure is always more likely." Friedman goes from demanding a proof that freedom is always *more likely* to work to demanding a proof that freedom *is always better*. As Aristotle noted in the *Nicomachean Ethics* regarding standards of proof in political thinking, "it is the mark of an educated mind to expect that amount of exactness in each kind which the nature of the particular object admits. It is equally unreasonable to accept merely probable conclusions from a mathematician and to demand strict demonstration from an orator" (1094b25–30). It is unreasonable to demand that libertarians prove that respect for rights is superior in every respect and in all possible circumstances to coercion, but not to make the same demand of advocates of statism. No political theory could meet Friedman's test.

To sum up: there need not be any contradiction between assertions of right and justice and scientifically validated claims about the consequences of different kinds of political and legal regimes. As Boaz (1997b, xv) asked in the introduction to *The Libertarian Reader*:

> Do libertarians believe in free markets because of a belief in individual rights or an empirical observation that markets produce prosperity and social harmony? The question ultimately makes no sense. As Hume said, the circumstances confronting humans are our self-interestedness, our necessarily limited generosity toward others, and the scarcity of resources available to fulfill our needs. Because of these circumstances, it is necessary for us to cooperate with others and to have rules of justice—especially regarding property and exchange—to define how we can do so. If individuals using their own knowledge for their own purposes didn't generate a spontaneous order of peace and prosperity, it would make little sense to advocate either natural rights or free markets.[6]

It would take an essay as long as Friedman's to answer all of his charges. (It would even take an essay just to note his demeaning and personal attacks on libertarian writers, e.g., the frequent questioning of the motives of libertarian writers, the slighting reference to "the untroubled sleep and closed minds of libertarians," the characterization of social scientific research by libertarians as "propaganda," the suggestion of a conspiracy among libertarian social scientists, and so on.) I will merely consider a few logical and factual errors.

Can We Define Freedom Any Way We Want?

In defense of his preferred understanding of "freedom," Friedman (1997, 432) writes that "one stipulative definition is as good as another." Logicians would find this a surprising claim. As Irving Copi (1982, 149–50) noted in his treatment of definitions,

It is not the case that any stipulative definition is as "good" as any other, but the grounds for their comparison must clearly be other than truth or falsehood, for these terms simply do not apply. Stipulative definitions are arbitrary only in the sense specified. ("A symbol defined by a stipulative definition did not have that meaning prior to being given it by the definition.") Whether they are clear or unclear, advantageous or disadvantageous, or the like, are factual questions.

A stipulated definition that fails to distinguish a thing in terms of exclusive categories, for example, would be disadvantageous and inferior to an alternative definition that does use categories properly. Thus, the stipulated definition of a human being as a "featherless biped" fails as a definition of "human being." It is not false, but it is *not* "as good" as any number of other definitions. Simply defining freedom as ability, which is the route taken by some of the figures whom Friedman cites approvingly, is an exercise in bad definition, because we already *have* a good word to denote ability. It's "ability."

Definitions are tools of the mind. They are more or less useful depending on how well they help us to understand, organize, and affect the world.[7] Friedman's rejection of libertarian conceptions of freedom and his rather confusing defense of a (never clearly articulated) alternative definition suffer from the central flaw that they don't help us to understand the world of human action or to distinguish between different kinds of actions. For example, consider his claim that libertarian-compatible property systems are just as coercive and restrictive of freedom as systems that are *not* compatible with libertarianism. If that were true, then using force to prevent another person from having sexual congress with yourself (conventionally termed "rape" by those beset with "bourgeois complacency," as Friedman [1997, 419] characterizes Charles Murray) would be just as much a use of force as is using force to have sexual congress with another person who does not desire it. Therefore there must be no difference between the two, at least with respect to whether one approach is more or less coercive or free than the other. "Raping" is no more coercive than "resisting rape." Freedom is slavery, after all!

According to Friedman (1997, 428),

Inasmuch as there is just as much of the world to be parcelled out under each system's set of property rules, and the rights

> governing all of this property are just as coercively enforced
> in all systems, there is no difference in the "amount" of
> coercion—or conversely, the amount of (negative) freedom—
> under different legal systems, including libertarianism. . . .
> So, strictly in terms of negative liberty—freedom from physi-
> cal coercion—libertarianism has no edge over any other
> system.

For example, Canada in 1944 and Germany in 1944 were equally free
and had equal "amounts" of coercion. Friedman cites the venerable
authority of G. A. Cohen in support of this remarkable and counterintuitive claim.[8] But is it in fact true that the system of several property
that is found in "capitalist" societies and is largely respected on the
basis of custom, morality, and reciprocal respect is indistinguishable
in terms of coercion and freedom from the communism that G. A.
Cohen spent his life defending, which rests on the constant exercise
of terror against a subject population?[9] Friedman and Cohen argue
that it is. It is on the basis of this claim that Friedman concludes
that "negative" freedom cannot be the freedom in which we should
be interested (the "true" freedom?), and that we should instead
plump for "positive" freedom, apparently understood as doing
whatever I want to do.

Three hundred years ago Locke labeled such a condition "licence"
and distinguished it from "liberty." As Locke argued in his *Second
Treatise of Government* (sec. 6), "*The State of Nature* has a Law of
Nature to govern it, which obliges every one: And Reason, which
is that Law, teaches all Mankind, who will but consult it, that being
all equal and independent, no one ought to harm another in his
Life, Health, Liberty, or Possessions."[10] Writers in the Whig/classical
liberal tradition did not generally consider the freedom or liberty
that they sought as mere lack of constraint, but as freedom from
subjection to the arbitrary and lawless will of another. In Algernon
Sidney's words, "liberty solely consists in an independency upon
the will of another, and by the name of slave we understand a man,
who can neither dispose of his person nor goods, but enjoys all at
the will of his master" (Sidney 1990, 17). That is why libertarians
have always placed so much stress on the rule of law: again, Locke
(sec. 57) notes,

> *The end of Law* is not to abolish or restrain, *but to preserve and
> enlarge Freedom*: For in all the states of created beings capable

> of Laws, *where there is no Law, there is no Freedom*. For *Liberty* is to be free from restraint and violence from others which cannot be, where there is no Law: But Freedom is not, as we are told, *A Liberty for every Man to do what he lists*: (For who could be free, when every other Man's Humour might domineer over him?) But a *Liberty* to dispose, and order, as he lists, his Person, Actions, Possessions, and his whole Property, within the Allowance of those Laws under which he is; and therein not to be subject to the arbitrary Will of another, but freely follow his own.

(Cf. Barnett 1998, Introduction.)

Libertarianism: Both the Status Quo and Outside of the Mainstream?

Friedman (1997) claims on one page to have shown "libertarianism's extreme cultural marginality" (440) and *also* claims in footnote 7 (463) that libertarian philosophers "portray status-quo property relationships, reconceived as 'Lockean,' as natural ones." On p. 433 Friedman suggests that the libertarian "worldview rests on unexamined presuppositions absorbed unconsciously from the culture of capitalism." So libertarians are guilty of "willful isolation from the mainstream" (441) at the same time that they are carriers of "unexamined presuppositions absorbed unconsciously" from the dominant culture and hostage to "status-quo property relationships" i.e., shills for existing (and perhaps sinister) interests. If "the mainstream" is exemplified by the Harvard faculty lounge, Friedman may be right that libertarianism is isolated from the mainstream, but if he has a wider notion of the mainstream, it is hard to see how libertarianism is both marginal *and* the philosophy of the status quo. That would be quite a trick. (It may be that many property relationships in largely liberal societies are just—in the sense that no better titles can be shown than the existing ones—but that is at least partly the result of the efforts of libertarians over the centuries to defend and extend freedom and justice. The idea that libertarian ideas are a defense of the "status quo" is an insult to the uncounted martyrs who have sacrificed so much to achieve justice in those societies that approximate free societies, to the libertarians who failed because they were murdered by communist, monarchist, fascist, national socialist, and other collectivist states, and to the billions of people who today live in regimes that are decidedly *un*just.)

Logic and the "Right to Do Wrong"

Friedman (1997) evinces amazement that libertarians might believe that one could have "a right to do wrong." His treatment, in footnote 11 (465), is written as if no moral philosopher had ever thought about the problem. He admits that "many consequentialist reasons for such a right are conceivable," such as the negative effects of civil wars, but argues that it is a "prima facie logical contradiction" to "contend that it is intrinsically valuable to be able to do what is bad—intrinsically valuable, that is, to be able to do what is intrinsically valueless." Friedman exhibits an unusual and unorthodox understanding of the nature of logical contradiction.

A logical contradiction has the form of "p and (not p)" (or "p • ~p") (Copi 1982, 314). Thus, for Friedman to make the claim that the conjunction of "I have a right to do X" and "it is wrong to do X" is a logical contradiction, he must argue that "it is wrong to do X" is the same statement as "it is not the case that I have a right to do X," but he claims that as his conclusion, so to make it a premise of the proof is hardly a valid demonstration! There would be a contradiction only if we were to assume as a premise what Friedman presents as a conclusion. It would indeed be a contradiction to affirm simultaneously

> "It is good to do X"
> and
> "It is not good to do X,"

but that is *not* what advocates of a "right to do wrong" affirm. What they affirm simultaneously is

> "It is good *to be allowed* to do X"
> and
> "It is not good to do X."

The all-important phrase "to be allowed," present in the first statement and absent in the second, is what distinguishes "the right to do wrong" from a logical contradiction. Under no understanding of the term "logical contradiction" could "the right to do wrong" qualify as a logical contradiction.

There is no logical contradiction in asserting that the free exercise of moral agency is intrinsically valuable. It may not be true, but it is not a logical contradiction. The achievement of a good life on the basis of one's own choices, rather than on the basis of having been beaten into making the outward motions consistent with doing the "right thing," may be the only way actually to achieve a good life, for self-direction may be one of the necessary ingredients of a good life. As Aristotle noted in the *Nicomachean Ethics* (1199b20–21), "it is better to be happy as a result of one's own exertions than by the gift of fortune," and it could surely be argued that it is better to be happy as a result of one's own choices than as a result of the violent interventions of others—indeed, that such "coerced happiness" would not be happiness at all, for "happiness is an activity in accordance with virtue" (ibid., 1098b30). Happiness is not a passive state, but an active one, for "just as at the Olympic games the wreaths of victory are not bestowed upon the handsomest and strongest persons present, but on men who enter for the competitions—since it is among those that the winners will be found,—so it is those who act rightly who carry off the prizes and good things of life" (ibid., 1099a4–10).[11]

Aristotle may be wrong about this, but if he is, it is not because of a "prima facie logical contradiction."[12] Nor was it a logical contradiction for Tertullian to argue against forced conversion to what he considered the highest truth—the Christian faith—when he argued:

> It is a fundamental human right, a privilege of nature, that every man should worship according to his own convictions: one man's religion neither harms nor helps another man. It is assuredly no part of religion to compel religion—to which free will and not force should lead us. (Quoted in Smith 1991, 97)

For Tertullian, true Christian faith simply could not be acquired through compulsion, but was a gift from God that could only be accepted freely.

There is a long tradition of inquiry into justice and freedom that focuses attention on the faculty of human choice.[13] In his funeral oration, Pericles praised Athens for its freedom and connected this with the condition that each citizen was "the rightful lord and owner of his own person":

> Taking everything together then, I declare that our city is an education to Greece, and I declare that in my opinion, each single one of our citizens, in all the manifold aspects of life, is able to show himself the rightful lord and owner of his

own person, and do this, moreover, with exceptional grace and exceptional versatility. (Thucydides 1986, 147–48)[14]

This concern with the ability of choice, or "freedom of the will," as it is sometimes termed, is at the foundation of the entire libertarian tradition. Human beings are sources of changes in the world; they have the faculty of choice and can be held accountable for their acts. As Marsilius of Padua (1956, II.xii, 193) noted in 1324,

> this term "ownership" (dominium) is used to refer to the human will or freedom in itself with its organic executive or motive power unimpeded. For it is through these that we are capable of certain acts and their opposites. It is for this reason too that man alone among the animals is said to have ownership or control of his acts; this control belongs to him by nature, it is not acquired through an act of will or choice.

Dominium, or self-mastery, was the central feature of the debate over the rights of the American Indians (see de Vitoria 1991a and 1991b and de las Casas 1992). The advocates of enslaving the Indians argued that they were the "natural slaves" of whom Aristotle had written in his *Politics*, incapable of self-mastery and thus requiring the guiding hand of their Spanish overlords. This was hotly disputed by the protolibertarians of the school of Salamanca. In de Vitoria's words,

> Every Indian is a man and thus is capable of attaining salvation or damnation. Every man is a person and is the master of his body and possessions. Inasmuch as he is a person, every Indian has free will and, consequently, is the master of his actions. (1991b, 17)

De Vitoria (1991a, 250–51) concluded in his famous lectures of 1539 that the Indians had the same rights as the Christian Europeans:

> The conclusion of all that has been said is that the barbarians possessed as true dominion, both public and private, as any Christians. That is to say, they could not be robbed of their property, either as private citizens or as princes, on the grounds that they were not true masters (*ueri domini*). It would be harsh to deny to them, who have never done us any wrong, the rights we concede to Saracens and Jews, who have been continual enemies of the Christian religion. Yet we do not deny the right of ownership (*dominium reum*) of

the latter, unless it be in the case of Christian lands which they have conquered.

The theme of personal dominium was central to the arguments of the first libertarians, the Levellers. (See, for example, Walwyn 1989 and Overton 1943, esp. 381–82 and 1997.) Locke, too, focused attention on choice and responsibility in the very conception of the human person:

> *Person*, as I take it, is the name for this *self*. Where-ever a Man finds, what he calls *himself*, there I think another may say is the same *Person*. It is a Forensick Term appropriating Actions and their Merit; and so belongs only to intelligent Agents capable of a Law, and Happiness and Misery. This personality extends it *self* beyond present Existence to what is past, only by consciousness, whereby it becomes concerned and accountable, owns and imputes to it *self* past Actions, just upon the same ground, and for the same reason, that it does the present. (1979, II.xxvii, 26)

We own our actions. We can be held accountable by our fellows (see Strawson 1993). As human beings we are rational creatures capable of choice and therefore capable of being held responsible and accountable for our actions. The exercise and development of this faculty is intrinsically valuable. To be able to *choose* the good means that one is also able to choose the bad. Friedman may be baffled by this, but if so, he is simply baffled by reality. Indeed, to attempt to deny the possibility of choice, i.e., to choose to deny it, is to engage in a contradiction, viz. a performative contradiction: examples of performative contradiction are the written statement "Me always write grammatical," the spoken utterance "I am now silent," and the choice to deny that choice is possible. It is not libertarians who contradict themselves by asserting a "right to do wrong," but those who deny the possibility of human choice.[15]

With Lack of Charity toward Some

Friedman is remarkably uncharitable in his interpretations of those whom he criticizes. Friedman contends that Charles Murray is guilty of "bourgeois complacency" (Friedman 1997, 419); he calls his argument "facile" (ibid., 421); and he dismisses Murray's discussion of the role of achievement as "ruminations" (ibid., 421). In addition,

Murray the eudaimonist is labeled "a utilitarian" (ibid., 418) because he is concerned about consequences, which obscures the difference between a consequentialist and a utilitarian (I would say that they are related as genus is to species, but that might make me a "Scholastic," evidently a term of abuse to Friedman [ibid., 431]), and he ignores Murray's well-articulated views on the significance of human achievement, which have, after all, been stated in his much longer book *In Pursuit: Of Happiness and Good Government*. (Human achievement is also the subject of Murray's current research and writing.)

In Friedman's dismissal of another distinguished libertarian scholar, he writes, "it was Milton Friedman who, after all, most famously equated capitalism with freedom" (Friedman 1997, 436). Milton Friedman (1962, 8) did not *equate* capitalism with freedom; he argued something very different, viz. that "On the one hand, freedom in economic arrangements is itself a component of freedom broadly understood, so economic freedom is an end in itself. In the second place, economic freedom is also an indispensable means toward the achievement of political freedom." An important part of Milton Friedman's case was the concession that "history suggests only that capitalism is a necessary condition for political freedom. Clearly it is not a sufficient condition" (ibid., 10). To say that X is part of Y, or that X is a necessary but not sufficient condition of Y, is not to equate X and Y.

These are by no means the only faults in Jeffrey Friedman's rebuttal of libertarianism. I leave the others to the reader to find. I will merely conclude by thanking him for allowing me the opportunity to rethink and rediscover just why I find libertarianism as a political theory superior to its competitors and to offer my criticisms of his arguments in the journal he edits.

References

Barnett, Randy. 1998. *The Structure of Liberty: Justice and the Rule of Law*. Oxford: Clarendon Press.

Boaz, David. 1997a. *Libertarianism: A Primer*. New York: Free Press.

Boaz, David. 1997b. *The Libertarian Reader: Classic and Contemporary Writings from Lao-tzu to Milton Friedman*. New York: Free Press.

Brett, Annabel S. 1997. *Liberty, Right and Nature: Individual Rights in Later Scholastic Thought*. Cambridge: Cambridge University Press.

Buckle, Stephen. 1991. *Natural Law and the Theory of Property: Grotius to Hume*. Oxford: Clarendon Press de las Casas, Bartolomé. 1992. *In Defense of the Indians*, trans. Stafford Poole. DeKalb: Northern Illinois University Press.

Cicero. 1991. *On Duties*, ed. M. T. Griffin and E. M. Atkins. Cambridge: Cambridge University Press.

Cohen, G. A. 1995. *Self-Ownership, Freedom, and Equality*. Cambridge: Cambridge University Press.

Constant, Benjamin. 1988. "The Liberty of the Ancients Compared to That of the Moderns." In idem, *Political Writings*, ed. Biancamaria Fontana. Cambridge: Cambridge University Press.

Copi, Irving M. 1982. *Introduction to Logic*. New York: Macmillan.

Davidson, Donald. 1982. *Essays on Actions and Events*. Oxford: Clarendon Press.

Foot, Philippa. 1972. "Morality as a System of Hypothetical Imperatives." *The Philosophical Review* 81, pp. 305–16.

Friedman, Jeffrey. 1997. "What's Wrong with Libertarianism." *Critical Review* 11, no. 3, pp. 407–67.

Friedman, Milton. 1962. *Capitalism and Freedom*. Chicago: University of Chicago Press.

Hayek, F. A. 1976. *Law, Legislation and Liberty*, vol. II: *The Mirage of Social Justice*. Chicago: University of Chicago Press.

von Humboldt, Wilhelm. 1993. *The Limits of State Action*, ed. J. W. Burrow. Indianapolis: Liberty Fund.

Hume, David. 1978. *A Treatise of Human Nature*, ed. L. A. Selby-Bigge, rev. P. H. Nidditch. Oxford: Clarendon Press.

Kant, Immanuel. 1964. *Groundwork of the Metaphysics of Morals*, trans. H. J. Paton. New York: Harper & Row.

Kelley, David. 1998. *A Life of One's Own: Individual Rights and the Welfare State*. Washington, D.C.: Cato Institute.

Locke, John. 1979. *An Essay Concerning Human Understanding*. Oxford: Clarendon Press.

Locke, John. 1997. *Political Essays*, ed. Mark Goldie. Cambridge: Cambridge University Press.

Marsilius of Padua. 1956. *Defensor Pacis: The Defender of the Peace*, trans. Alan Gewirth. New York: Harper & Row.

Overton, Richard. 1943. "The Commoner's Complaint." In *Tracts on Liberty in the Puritan Revolution*, ed. W. Haller. New York: Columbia University Press.

Overton, Richard. 1997. "An Arrow against All Tyrants." In Boaz 1997b.

Palmer, Tom. 1998. "G. A. Cohen on Self-Ownership, Property, and Equality." *Critical Review* 12, no. 3, pp. 225–52.

Parfit, Derek. 1986. *Reasons and Persons*. Oxford: Oxford University Press.

Rasmussen, Douglas B., and Douglas J. Den Uyl. 1991. *Liberty and Nature: An Aristotelian Defense of Liberal Order*. La Salle, Ill.: Open Court.

Ridley, Matt. 1996. *The Origins of Virtue: Human Instincts and the Evolution of Cooperation*. New York: Viking.

Sandel, Michael. 1982. *Liberalism and the Limits of Justice*. Cambridge: Cambridge University Press.

Schmidtz, David, and Robert E. Goodin. 1998. *Social Welfare and Individual Responsibility*. Cambridge: Cambridge University Press.

Sidney, Algernon. 1990. *Discourses Concerning Government*, ed. Thomas G. West. Indianapolis: Liberty Fund.

Smith, George H. 1991. "Philosophies of Toleration." In idem, *Atheism, Ayn Rand, and Other Heresies*. Buffalo: Prometheus Press.

Strawson, P. F. 1993. "Freedom and Resentment." In *Perspectives on Moral Responsibility*, ed. John Martin Fischer and Mark Ravizza. Ithaca, N.Y.: Cornell University Press.

Thompson, D'arcy Wentworth. 1966. *On Growth and Form*, abridged ed. Cambridge: Cambridge University Press.

Thucydides. 1986. *History of the Peloponnesian War*, trans. Rex Warner. New York: Penguin Books.

Tierney, Brian. 1983. "Tuck on Rights: Some Medieval Problems." *History of Political Thought* 4, no. 3, pp. 429–41.

Tierney, Brian. 1988. "Conciliarism, Corporatism, and Individualism: The Doctrine of Individual Rights in Gerson." *Cristianesimo Nella Storia* 9, pp. 81–111.

Tierney, Brian. 1989. "Origins of Natural Rights Language: Texts and Contexts, 1150–1250." *History of Political Thought* 10, no. 4, pp. 616–46.

Tierney, Brian. 1991. "Marsilius on Rights." *Journal of the History of Ideas* 52 (January–March), pp. 3–17.

Tierney, Brian. 1998. *The Idea of Natural Rights*. Atlanta: Scholars Press.

de Vitoria, Francisco. 1991a. "On the American Indians." In idem, *Political Writings*, ed. Anthony Pagden and Jeremy Lawrance. Cambridge: Cambridge University Press.

de Vitoria, Francisco. 1991b. *The Rights and Obligations of Indians and Spaniards in the New World*, recon. Luciano Pereña Vicente. Salamanca, Spain: Universidad Pontifica de Salamanca.

Walwyn, William. 1989. *The Writings of William Walwyn*, ed. Jack R. Michael and Barbara Taft. Athens: University of Georgia Press.

Notes

1. Despite my deep admiration for Immanuel Kant's achievements, I do not accept his bifurcation between the phenomenal world of appearance and the noumenal world of intelligibility, which is central to his grounding of the categorical imperative, and thus I do not accept his claim that

> *the intelligible world contains the ground of the sensible world and therefore also of its laws*; and so in respect of my will, for which (as belonging entirely to the intelligible world) it gives laws immediately, it must also be conceived as containing such a ground. Hence, in spite of regarding myself from one point of view as a being that belongs to the sensible world, I shall have to recognize that, *qua* intelligence, I am subject to the law of the intelligible world—that is, to the reason which contains this law in the Idea of freedom, and so to the autonomy of the will—and therefore I must look on the laws of the intelligible world as imperatives for me and on the actions which conform to this principle as duties. (Kant 1964, 121, emphasis in original)

2. One could easily add others. See, for example, the work of the zoologist and libertarian Matt Ridley, *The Origins of Virtue: Human Instincts and the Evolution of Cooperation* (1996).

3. It should be noted that "consequentialism" by itself is not a political theory, nor even a theory of the good. What counts as a good or a bad consequence cannot by itself be determined by invoking consequentialism; there must be some deeper reflection (or "rumination," to use the term that Friedman uses to dismiss Charles

Murray's considered views on the matter) about what consequences we should seek to achieve or avoid. Friedman's position, although presented as clearly superior to "philosophical libertarianism," is naive and unreflective.

4. Friedman subjects Boaz's defense of individualism to a series of misinterpretations, missing Boaz's main point, viz., that when we speak of groups deliberating or acting, the group that deliberates or acts is made up of the numerically individuated humans and the various relations among them; the group does not constitute another person that is essentially like the numerically individuated persons who make up the group. A forest is made up of individual trees and all of their complex relations; without the particular trees, we would not have a forest, and the forest is not another tree. So, too, for group behavior involving humans. The group formed by Mary, Bill, and Deirdre is not another person like Mary, Bill, or Deirdre. A number of forms of collectivism explicitly deny this, and not merely the extreme forms that might come to mind, but the tamer forms that abound in American universities. For example, the coercive communitarian political theorist Michael Sandel criticizes liberal individualism for relying on an "antecedent individuation of the subject" and proposes instead that "in so far as our constitutive self-understandings comprehend a wider subject than the individual alone, whether a family or tribe or city or class or nation or people, to this extent they define a community in a constitutive sense" (Sandel 1982, 172). Thus, "the bounds of the self are no longer fixed, individuated in advance and given prior to experience" (ibid., 183). A community, nation, class, or state could then be a "self." Boaz simply tries to bring some common sense to the discussion, for the "self" that is constituted by Bill and Mary would not be the same kind of self that Bill is or that Mary is. Using the same terms (self and person, for example) to describe these "wider subjects" is a category error with significant consequences for political theory.

5. As Stephen Buckle (1991, 90) notes, "rather than, as is sometimes held, being a decisive break from the tradition of natural law, Hume's account depends crucially on distinctions already established by Pufendorf."

6. John Locke also considered the issue of the relationship of utility (generally considered) and right in his writings on natural law: "utility is not the basis of the law or the ground of obligation, but the consequence of obedience to it. . . . And thus the rightness of an action does not depend on its utility; on the contrary, its utility is a result of its rightness" (Locke 1997, 133). Both Locke (at least in this text) and Pufendorf argued that the natural law had the sanction of God, through the prospect of reward or punishment in the next life. Thus, Pufendorf (1991, 36) noted that "though these precepts [of the natural law] have a clear utility, they get the force of law only upon the presupposition that God exists and rules all things by His providence, and that He has enjoined the human race to observe as laws those dictates of reason which He has Himself promulgated by the force of the innate light." Friedman might fasten upon the theological element of Locke's and Pufendorf's formulations and argue that, if we don't agree with their theology, we must reject all of what they said about natural law. But the theological claim is by no means a necessary part of their argument, as Hume realized, nor is it relevant to the question at hand, viz., whether claims of right can be grounded on predictions of consequences and the evaluation thereof. Rights claims, for Locke, Pufendorf, Hume, and indeed for all investigators of the natural law, are necessarily justified by the consequences that follow from their general observance. Justice is necessarily contextual: under the normal circumstances of justice, the rules of justice and property yield overall good

210

consequences, but when those circumstances are radically altered, say, in a natural disaster, then those rules of justice and property either do not apply or are modified appropriately. (See the discussion of "the limits of social and political life" in Rasmussen and Den Uyl 1991, 144–51.)

7. See the neat discussion of this issue in Kelley 1998, especially 65–77.

8. Cohen is a noted critic of libertarianism. I address directly his ingenious and intricate but erroneous and confused arguments about the relationship between property in one's person and property in external objects in Palmer 1998, reprinted in this volume.

9. Cohen (1995, 250) shared (in an essay written "substantially" in 1989 and published in 1995) his thoughts about one of the most murderous, cruel, and vicious regimes in the history of humanity, the USSR. He notes that he had developed over some years "a pretty adverse assessment of the Soviet Union's claim to be a socialist society. Some people have therefore found it surprising that I should be saddened by what I perceive to be the impending final abandonment of the Bolshevik experiment. . . . It is true that I was heavily critical of the Soviet Union, but the angry little boy who pummels his father's chest will not be glad if the old man collapses." In the footnote to the last sentence, he writes,

> Those of us on the left who were stern critics of the Soviet Union long before it collapsed needed it to be there to receive our blows. The Soviet Union needed to be there as a defective model so that, with one eye on it, we could construct a better one. It created a non-capitalist mental space in which to think about socialism.

How many tens of millions of innocent people had to die, and how many hundreds of millions had to live lives of daily oppression, so that G. A. Cohen and his comrades could have "a non-capitalist mental space in which to think about socialism"?

10. The insight is of ancient provenance. Compare with Cicero's observation in *De Officiis*:

> All men should have this one object, that the benefit of each individual and the benefit of all together should be the same. If anyone arrogates it to himself, all human intercourse will be dissolved. Furthermore, if nature prescribes that one man should want to consider the interests of another, whoever he may be, for the very reason that he is a man, it is necessary, according to the same nature, that what is beneficial to all is something common. If that is so, then we are all constrained by one and the same law of nature; and if that also is true, then we are certainly forbidden by the law of nature from acting violently against another person. The first claim is indeed true; therefore the last is true. (Cicero 1991, 109–10)

11. Friedman seems to have a very primitive understanding of human action. Two motions of a human body may be described identically in purely physical or corporeal terms, but be very different actions, nonetheless. Holding a door for a person in a wheelchair may be either an act of politeness, in the case of a freely chosen act, or, if done only under threat of coercion from the "politeness police," an act of simple submission motivated by fear. A purely physicalist understanding of action, which ignores the intentional dimension of human action, misses these distinctions. Friedman's mistaken claim that it is a logical contradiction to affirm a "right to do wrong" indicates that he does not grasp the important difference between freely chosen and

coerced acts. Although two such acts may be comprehended under the same physical-ist description, they are not the same acts. (See Davidson 1982, especially the essays on "Actions, Reasons, and Causes," "Agency," and "Intending.") P. F. Strawson (1993) neatly explained the related difference between what he called the "participant" attitude and the "objective" attitude and the inability to sustain the "objective" attitude. The "objective" attitude, as Strawson understands it, is incompatible with the very enterprise of moral investigation or action.

12. The importance of self-directedness is neatly considered in Rasmussen and Den Uyl 1991, especially 73–75 and 93–96. It is also the foundation of the liberalism of Wilhelm von Humboldt (1993), who began his influential defense of liberty (which included a withering attack on what we now identify as the welfare state) as follows:

> The true end of Man, or that which is prescribed by the eternal and immutable dictates of reason, and not suggested by vague and transient desires, is the highest and most harmonious development of his powers to a complete and consistent whole. Freedom is the first and indispensable condition which the possibility of such a development presupposes; but there is besides another essential—intimately connected with freedom, it is true—a variety of situa-tions. (Ibid., 10)

As Humboldt argued, a system of several property is a necessary condition for both freedom and a variety of situations.

13. A great many influential writings on individual rights have focused on what the medieval writers termed "dominium," or self-mastery; to have dominium means that one can be held responsible for one's choices, and hence that one has a faculty of moral agency that should command respect. Especially good historical treatments of this tradition can be found in the work of Brian Tierney; see, for example, Tierney 1983, 1988, 1989, 1991, and 1998. For the relationship between the concepts of "objective right" (e.g., "the right thing to do") and "subjective right" (e.g., "my right to do it") in later scholastic thinking, see also Brett 1997.

14. Compare also the arguments of Benjamin Constant (1988), who considered the exceptional personal freedom (what Constant terms "modern freedom") of the Athenians an anomaly in the ancient world and attributed this freedom to commerce and several property.

15. Friedman (1997, 421) asserts, *ex cathedra*, that Charles Murray's "libertarianism is just as vulnerable as Victorianism was to the discovery that people are not, in fact, solely or even largely responsible for their good or ill fortune." To what momentous "discovery" is Friedman alluding? More to the point, is he asserting that choice is irrelevant to happiness, or that people are not "even largely responsible" for their own well-being or happiness? Surely no reasonable person would deny that one bears no responsibility for one's birth, nor that good things can happen to bad people and bad things to good; this was hardly a surprise to "the Victorians," but has been known for some time. In "the words of the Preacher, the son of David, king in Jerusalem,"

> Again I saw that under the sun the race is not to the swift, nor the battle to the strong, nor bread to the wise, nor riches to the intelligent, nor favor to the men of skill; but time and chance happeneth to them all. For man does not know his time. Like fish which are taken in an evil net, and like birds which are caught in a snare, so the sons of men are snared at an evil time, when it suddenly falls upon them. (Ecclesiastes 9:11)

Given that everyone (including Charles Murray) acknowledges this, what are we to make of it? Should we deny the very possibility of choice, or use violence to ensure that people do not bear the good or bad consequences of their own actions, or subsidize any foolish choice that one might make? Or should we recognize the cause and effect relationships of the world of facts and "internalize externalities" by means of institutions such as property? For an excellent contrast between a libertarian understanding of these issues and a socialist (or social-democratic) understanding, see Schmidtz and Goodin 1998. It is hard to imagine a reasonable reader reading both sections of that little book and finding Goodin's arguments more convincing than Schmidtz's. But then, some people believe in astrology, witchcraft, and the goodness of the "Bolshevik experiment," and I find that hard to imagine, too.

10. The Role of Institutions and Law in Economic Development

Thanks substantially to the pioneering work of a number of scholars, the attention of scholars, policy makers, and the public has been focused on the role of law in shaping institutions and the role of institutions in shaping economic development.[1] Liberalism has contributed to human well being primarily by its focus on simultaneously authorizing and limiting a set of institutions that find, create, and enforce law. To understand the relationship of liberalism to those institutions, it helps to make a rather simple distinction. That is the distinction between being "anti-government" and being in favor of "limited government." The two are frequently confused, especially by avowed enemies of liberalism who favor unlimited government, but they could not in fact be more different. Criminals and terrorists, for example, who seek to destroy life, liberty, and property, are "anti-government." They seek to weaken government. In contrast, liberals, who seek to limit government, are not seeking to destroy it, but to strengthen it so that it can effectively perform a limited set of valuable functions.

What liberals seek is not weakened government, but effective, lawful, legitimate, limited government—government that can carry out certain functions effectively and efficiently, but which is limited to those and only those functions. What is needed is a government of law, rather than of simple force or violence.

Most governments around the world currently do both too much and too little. They do too much when they carry out functions that either should not be carried out at all, such as imposing monopolies or restraints on voluntary trade, or that could and should be carried

Prepared for "A Liberal Agenda for the New Century: A Global Perspective," a conference cosponsored by the Cato Institute, the Institute of Economic Analysis, and the Russian Union of Industrialists and Entrepreneurs, April 8–9, 2004, Moscow, Russian Federation.

out by the organizations of civil society, whether providing telephone services or running child care centers. They do too little when they fail to define rights to the use of scarce resources and when they fail to provide the service of defending life, liberty, and property. One way to free up resources to allow government to carry out its valuable functions well is to stop it from doing all those things that it shouldn't be doing, either because they are unjust by themselves or because they could be done better by the free and voluntary coordination of citizens. Not only would government do its job better, but when government does a better job of defining and defending rights, markets and voluntary organizations do a better job of creating wealth and progress.

Why Do Institutions Matter?

Institutions matter because incentives matter. Incentives induce individuals and groups to behave in some ways and not in others. Good incentives induce individuals and groups to cooperate to produce value by production and exchange and to eschew and avoid violence. Good incentives induce individuals and groups to transfer responsibility to those who are best capable of producing value. Incentives are given particular form by institutions, which include not only formal organizations and procedures, such as legislative and executive governmental bodies, courts of law, written legal rules, and police agencies, but also informal and non-governmental bodies and procedures, such as moral and ethical norms, reputation, mutual behavioral expectations, and much more. Enforcement of rules and procedures can be internal, i.e., by the parties affected by a transaction, or external, i.e., by third-party arbitration or the organs of the judiciary system.[2] When someone anticipates shame, a loss of valuable reputation, a missed opportunity for gain, or a punishment or a reward imposed by others, whether organized in a governmental body or not, he or she is facing an incentive.[3]

Getting the institutions right matters. Many people simply don't understand that issue. They don't understand it because they still believe in magic. Few people believe that the chanting of magic words or incantations exercises power over the world. Most of us believe in cause and effect—in tracing out the effects to their causes. The scientific approach has been triumphant in such fields of inquiry as physics, chemistry, biology, and geology. Unfortunately, when it comes to the science of human behavior, many people—possibly most—still believe in magic, because they believe that a special class of wizards and magicians actually can change the world just by the power of words. Those wizards and magicians are called legislators, rulers, governors, and presidents, and so most people believe, when they say such words as "It shall be the law that all shall have the right to good health care, or a good education, or a higher living standard," that those words carry the power to bring about the intentions behind them.

Those who believe in the principles of cause and effect are not content to inquire into the intention announced in a law. They inquire not only about the intention of the legislators, but also into the mechanism of causation. How will that intention be realized? What is the likely effect of the law announced by the legislators? To ask about the likely effects is to ask about the incentives individuals and groups will face. Will the law create incentives that will induce people to create better health care, better education, or higher living standards? To ask about incentives is to ask about the institutions that give particular form to incentives.

The difference between North Korea and South Korea is clear from nighttime satellite pictures. The North is completely dark, while the South is ablaze with light. What accounts for that? The incentives people have to create light. And the incentives are shaped by the institutions.

Institutions and Technology

It has been well demonstrated that the long-term determinant of economic growth is not simple capital investment—the addition of more machines or buildings—but the growth and application of knowledge. As Joel Mokyr points out, "Differences in institutions are better at explaining differences in income *levels* in cross section at a given moment. Knowledge can and does flow across national boundaries, if not always with the frictionless ease that some economists imagine. If the only reason why Germany is richer than Zimbabwe today were that Germany possesses more useful knowledge, the difference might be eliminated in a relatively short time. If we were to ask, however, why Germany is richer today than it was in 1815, the importance of technology becomes unassailable—though better institutions might still be of importance as well."[4]

Nonetheless, as Mokyr shows, the growth of technology is itself deeply dependent on the maintenance of the right institutions. Some institutions are more propitious to the growth of knowledge and technology than others, and even when technology is available in books or other forms, the lack of protected property rights may make it virtually useless.[5] The good news is that a change to new institutions may allow very poor countries to increase income and human welfare through economic growth with remarkable rapidity by adapting "off-the-shelf" technology from other countries and putting it to good use. As Johan Norberg points out, "History shows that economies can grow faster by riding on the prosperity and technology of other countries. From 1780, it took England 58 years to double its wealth. A hundred years later, Japan did it in only 34 years, and another century later it took South Korea only 11 years."[6] The rapid rise in living standards in previously deeply impoverished countries such as South Korea is strong evidence of the ability of workable institutions to allow poor people to skip the hundreds of years of slow upward development that other countries experienced and to arrive in a relatively short time at extraordinary prosperity.

On a smaller scale, the recent leapfrogging of many countries into mobile telephony when state monopolies were removed shows that technology can be rapidly imported when the right institutions are created, thus allowing rapid advances in economic growth and well-being. That's the good news. But first the institutions have to be sorted out properly.

Cargo Cults vs. Scientific Inference

A scientific approach can't, however, stop at merely invoking the magic word of "institutions." One must go further and ask, what institutions account for the difference and how? Would it be enough simply to copy all the institutions of the rich societies and recreate them in poor societies?

The effort to do so is reminiscent of the "cargo cults" of the South Pacific. The famous physicist Richard Feynman described what he called "cargo cult science" in a commencement address at the California Institute of Technology:

> In the South Seas there is a cargo cult of people. During the war they saw airplanes land with lots of good materials, and they want the same thing to happen now. So they've arranged

> to imitate things like runways, to put fires along the sides of the runways, to make a wooden hut for a man to sit in, with two wooden pieces on his head like headphones and bars of bamboo sticking out like antennas—he's the controller—and they wait for the airplanes to land. They're doing everything right. The form is perfect. It looks exactly the way it looked before. But it doesn't work. No airplanes land. So I call these things cargo cult science, because they follow all the apparent precepts and forms of scientific investigation, but they're missing something essential, because the planes don't land.
>
> Now it behooves me, of course, to tell you what they're missing. But it would be just about as difficult to explain to the South Sea Islanders how they have to arrange things so that they get some wealth in their system. It is not something simple like telling them how to improve the shapes of the earphones.[7]

Too often policy makers in underdeveloped countries—and, more importantly, policy makers in developed countries and in international aid organizations—simply tell people in underdeveloped countries to improve the shape of their earphones. They conclude that if the poor only had the institutions enjoyed today by the rich, they, too, would be rich. I recall working in the USSR and running into American government officials who were busy setting up a copy of the Securities and Exchange Commission of the United States, since that was clearly a necessary prerequisite to the existence of a functioning capital market. Although there was virtually no private property yet, they applied a simple—but fallacious—logic:

(A) the United States has an SEC;
(B) the United States has a highly developed capital market;
therefore (C) the United States has a highly developed capital market because it has an SEC;
therefore, (D) if Russia is to have a highly developed capital market, it first needs its own SEC.

In Romania, soon after the fall of the Ceaușescus, a great effort was made to install computerized trading systems for a stock market that didn't yet exist. Similar stories could be told about the attempt to copy the outward forms—the shape of the earphones—of banking and financial systems, competition law, and other institutions. Those are examples of "cargo cult policy making." If you create a Securities and Exchange Commission or a system of computerized trading stations, the stock traders, the entrepreneurs, and the capitalists will see them as they fly overhead, and they will decide to land, lured by the cleverly designed decoys set up by policy makers.

The cargo cult approach to economic development is hardly a new one. Indeed, one of the most disastrous examples of that mentality was given by Vladimir I. Lenin at the very foundation of the socialist experiment. As Lenin pointed out, managing factories is easy: "*All* citizens become employees and workers of a *single* nation-wide state 'syndicate.' All that is required is that they should work equally, do their proper share of work, and get equally paid. The accounting and control necessary for this have been *simplified* by capitalism to the extreme and reduced to the extraordinarily simple operations—which any literate person can perform—of supervising and recording, knowledge of the four rules of arithmetic, and issuing appropriate receipts."[8] What could be simpler? Lenin and his colleagues had observed capitalist enterprises as carefully as any stone-age Melanesian had observed airstrips and control towers. They knew what had to be done and did it. And with much the same result.

If one is going to make such comparisons, in any case, it would be better to look, not at what wealthy countries have today, but at what they developed during the period when they were changing from underdeveloped to developed nations—not what institutions rich countries have today, when they are rich and can afford inefficient policies, but what they had that accounted for their development.[9]

In 1992, Milton Friedman warned an audience at a conference in Mexico City, "The United States is not the model for Mexico or any of these countries. . . . Take as your model the U.S. in its first hundred and fifty years." In recent years, as Friedman pointed out, a number of highly inefficient institutions had been created in the United States that had diminished economic growth below what it could have been, but which were nonetheless affordable to a very wealthy nation. "We can afford our nonsense because we had so long a period during which to build a base, so we can afford the waste."[10] Let's apply Friedman's reasoning by looking at the current edicts of the regulatory state in the United States. In 2002, those edicts filled 75,606 pages of the Federal Register and cost Americans $860 billion in lost wealth opportunities and $25 billion in administrative expenses, for a combined cost of $885 billion. In comparison, all combined U.S. corporate pretax profits in that year came to $699 billion, or $186 billion less than the cost of regulations.[11] A poorer nation—especially one at a subsistence level of existence—would more directly feel the cost of such complex regulatory structures. Such regulatory institutions, although they coexist with substantial wealth, would be disastrous in poor countries that could not afford such enormous compliance costs. The World Bank recently reported, "For regulatory systems in developing countries to have a realistic chance of success, they need to be simpler, often less information-intensive, and less burdensome on the courts."[12] They could have added that such criteria would be welcome in wealthy countries, as well.[13]

Mere Copying Won't Do

Another example of cargo cult policy making is the attempt to copy American capital structures as the foundation for industrial organization in developing countries. America has a system of widely held stock ownership, with some 50 percent of American households holding shares in publicly traded firms. But as former World Bank official Robert Anderson points out, widely held stock ownership is not a necessary condition for economic growth: "Of the large public companies, the proportion that is widely held is not high except in the United States, the United Kingdom, and Japan. In these three countries, the proportion is 80 to 100 percent. In other countries, the proportion is smaller, for example, 60 percent in Canada, Switzerland, and France; 50 percent in Germany; and 10 percent or less in Hong Kong, Austria, Belgium, and Greece."[14] Belgium is hardly a third world nation, despite the fact that its economy has a capital structure that differs dramatically from that of the United States. In countries that lack American-style legal systems and supervisory institutions, American-style capital structures merely invite conflict between managers and shareholders and between different classes of shareholders. (It should also be pointed out that such conflicts exist in the United States, as well, and are typically exacerbated by dysfunctional "anti-takeover rules" and complex tax rules that make it harder for investors to monitor the behavior of managers.[15])

What matters is not whether the shape of the earphones is the same as the shape in the United States, but whether they actually produce wealth and freedom. And that requires attention to patterns of cause and effect and to the constraints surrounding the implementation of procedures and rules. We cannot escape the problem of delineating cause and effect.[16]

Complex Orders Require Simple Rules

One causal relationship that has been well established is that simplicity of rules and institutions tends to promote complexity of orders. For example, when it is simple to gain legal title to land, people can create complex systems of economic and social order. Hernando de Soto has documented how complex the rules are that must be followed to gain legal title to land in many countries: in the Philippines it is a process taking "168 steps, involving fifty-three public and private agencies and taking thirteen to twenty-five years," and in Egypt, the process involves "at least 75 bureaucratic procedures at thirty-one public and private agencies," taking "anywhere from five to fourteen years."[17] The contrast with wealthy nations such as Canada, Germany, or Japan could not be clearer. Technological innovations, such as internet registration, may help, but they are no substitute for eliminating excessive bureaucratic complexity.[18] Complex and costly procedures are typically induced (or at least maintained) by the opportunity to create or sustain government employment or to generate extra legal income for government officials.[19]

Titling property acquired through occupation and conveying property through sale are not the only property systems that are made needlessly complex by institutions that are poorly designed from the perspective of the majority of the population, but well designed from the perspective of small groups who are endowed with monopoly privileges. In some countries, the transfer of title through inheritance is enormously complex, while in others it's relatively simple. The difference is institutional. For example, I learned during a trip to Guatemala that the legal profession has a monopoly in that country on the making of wills; a lawyer must be engaged to draw up a legally valid will. The result is that only a small percentage of the population—the wealthy elite—enjoy the protection of legally enforceable testaments. In contrast, in anticipation of a trip to Baghdad, I recently revised my will using a commercially available computer program called "Willmaker." Had I not had a computer available, I could have purchased a simple form at a stationery store for less than a dollar. I filled out the forms, signed them before three witnesses who also signed, and the result was a valid will. The consequence of that difference is that where inheritance procedures are made complex by such monopolies, family members expend a much higher percentage of inherited wealth fighting over its distribution than is the case in countries where inheritance procedures are simple and available to all.

There is also a strong connection between the scourge of governmental corruption and the extent of governmental intervention into the market. The more obstacles the state places in the way of willing buyers and sellers, for example, the more opportunities for bureaucrats to exact a toll.[20]

The lesson of such experiences is fairly clear: the rules and procedures governing transactions need to be simple to be effective. Governments can assist in simplifying rules by focusing on setting basic rules of procedure, not on guaranteeing outcomes. Rules governing conveyances that insist on fairness in outcomes, rather than simplicity of procedure, are likely to guarantee neither fairness nor simplicity.

Markets Need Regulation, Not Intervention

The extended order of the free society rests on what F. A. Hayek terms "an order of actions." As Hayek noted, "What is required if the separate actions of the individuals are to result in an overall order is that they not only do not unnecessarily interfere with one another, but also that in those respects in which the success of the action of the individuals depends on some matching action by others, there will be at least a good chance that this correspondence will actually occur."[21] What is needed is a system that can make transactions regular through reliance on simple and straightforward rules and procedures.[22]

What is currently called "regulation" is typically not regulation at all, but rather a system of arbitrary, capricious, and unpredictable intervention, with legislators or bureaucrats empowered to change the rules when and as they please and to impose on market participants enormously complex, burdensome, and unpredictable edicts and commands. "Rules" is not a very useful term to describe something so unpredictable and so changeable. James Madison, the principal author of the U.S. Constitution, described the perils of allowing legislators or bureaucrats to exercise such arbitrary power as is currently exercised in the name of "regulation."

> The internal effects of a mutable policy are still more calamitous. It poisons the blessings of liberty itself. It will be of little avail to the people that the laws are made by men of their own choice if the laws be so voluminous that they cannot be read, or so incoherent that they cannot be understood; if they be repealed or revised before they are promulgated, or undergo such incessant changes that no man, who knows what the law is today, can guess what it will be tomorrow. Law is defined to be a rule of action, but how can that be a rule, which is little known, and less fixed?

> Another effect of public instability is the unreasonable advantage it gives to the sagacious, the enterprising, and the moneyed few over the industrious and uninformed mass of the people. Every new regulation concerning commerce or revenue, or in any manner affecting the value of the different species of property, presents a new harvest to those who watch the change, and can trace its consequences: a harvest, reared not by themselves, but by the toils and cares of the great body of their fellow-citizens. This is a state of things in which it may be said with some truth that laws are made for the *few*, not for the *many*.[23]

Not only is the modern so-called regulatory state not productive of actual regulation, but regulation can be provided effectively by voluntary institutions, such as credit bureaus, quality certification, financial ratings, performance standards, and the like.[24] Such nonstate regulatory systems provide a high degree of predictability, but, because they are competitive and cannot command a coercive monopoly on setting regulations, they can nonetheless evolve in response to changes in technology and the needs of the market.[25]

Conclusion

Liberals, more than people of any another political perspective, are concerned with institutions. They emphasize the application of scientific principles to social relations, rather than magical thinking, and therefore liberals focus on incentives, which means that they are deeply interested in the design and evolution of institutions.[26] More is required than the *post hoc, ergo propter hoc* reasoning behind much of the attempt to copy institutions existing in wealthy societies, without asking whether the wealth of those societies is caused by the institutions, or the institutions—no matter how inefficient—are affordable because of the preexisting wealth of those societies, wealth that was caused by other institutions altogether. Free and wealthy societies need simple, predictable rules. Limited government can provide the basic framework of rules that makes social complexity possible. Regulation, understood as rules and principles that make transactions regular, should be contrasted with the empowerment of legislators or bureaucrats with the powers to change rules arbitrarily and to impose their will on others through edicts and commands. Such authentic regulation can be provided by the formal legal institutions of government, including legislatures and courts of law, or by voluntary institutions of civil society, such as credit bureaus and standard-setting associations.

Liberalism is the philosophy of freedom, law, and prosperity. It is the institutions of law—that is, of limited government—that create the framework within which we exercise freedom, and it is through freedom that people create wealth and general prosperity.

Notes

1. See the pioneering papers on property rights in Arnold Plant, *Selected Economic Essays and Addresses* (London: Routledge and Kegan Paul, 1974) and in R. H. Coase, *The Firm, the Market, and the Law* (Chicago: University of Chicago Press, 1988).

2. See Douglass C. North, *Structure and Change in Economic History* (New York: W. W. Norton & Co., 1981), esp. chap. 15: "Institutions are a set of rules, compliance procedures, and moral and ethical behavioral norms designed to constrain the behavior of individuals in the interests of maximizing the wealth or utility of principles" (pp. 201–2). See also World Bank, *Building Institutions: World Development Report 2002* (New York: Oxford University Press, 2002), esp. chap. 1, "Building Institutions: Complement, Innovate, Connect, and Compete."

3. "Institutions provide the incentive structure of an economy; as that structure evolves, it shapes the direction of economic change towards growth, stagnation, or decline." Douglass C. North, "Institutions," *Journal of Economic Perspectives* 5, no. 1 (Winter 1991), p. 97.

4. Joel Mokyr, *The Gifts of Athena: Historical Origins of the Knowledge Economy* (Princeton, N.J.: Princeton University Press, 2002), p. 286.

5. See the treatment in chapter three of William Easterly, *The Elusive Quest for Growth: Economists' Adventures and Misadventures in the Tropics* (Cambridge, Mass.: The MIT Press, 2002), pp. 47–69.

6. Johan Norberg, *In Defense of Global Capitalism* (Washington, D.C.: Cato Institute, 2003), p. 134.

7. Adapted from the commencement address given in 1974 at the California Institute of Technology (Caltech), www.physics.brocku.ca/etc/cargo_cult_science.html.

8. Vladimir I. Lenin, *The State and Revolution* (Beijing: Foreign Languages Press, 1973), pp. 120–21.

9. A good place to start would be Nathan Rosenberg and L. E. Birdzell, Jr., *How the West Grew Rich: The Economic Transformation of the Industrial World* (New York: Basic Books, 1987).

10. Milton Friedman, Keynote Address, Liberty in the Americas: Free Trade and Beyond, Cato Institute conference in Mexico City, May 19, 1992.

11. Clyde Wayne Crews, *Ten Thousand Commandments* (Washington, D.C.: Cato Institute, 2003); Crews bases his analysis of the costs of regulatory compliance on the work of W. Mark Crain and Thomas D. Hopkins, "The Impact of Regulatory Costs on Small Firms," report prepared for Small Business Administration, Office of Advocacy, RFP no. SBAHQA-00-R-0027, October 2001, www.sba.gov/advo/research/rs207tot.pdf.

12. World Bank, *Building Institutions: World Development Report 2002*, p. 12.

13. See Richard Epstein, *Simple Rules for a Complex World* (Cambridge, Mass.: Harvard University Press, 1995), p. 21: "The proper response to more complex societies should be an ever greater reliance on simple legal rules, including older rules too often and too easily dismissed as curious relics of some bygone horse-and-buggy age."

14. Robert E. Anderson, *Just Get Out of the Way: How Government Can Help Business in Poor Countries* (Washington, D.C.: Cato Institute, 2004), p. 43.

15. See, for example, Christopher L. Culp and William A. Niskanen, eds., *Corporate Aftershock: The Public Policy Lessons from the Collapse of Enron and Other Major Corporations* (New York: John Wiley & Sons, 2003).

16. A good example of such a causal account is given in Daron Acemoglu, Simon Johnson, and James A. Robinson, "An African Success Story: Botswana," July 11, 2001, http://econ-www.mit.edu/faculty/acemoglu/files/papers/Botswanafinal.pdf. As the authors point out, in Botswana, "the basic system of law and contract worked reasonably well. State and private predation have been quite limited. Despite the large revenues from diamonds, this has not induced domestic political instability or conflict for control of this resource. . . . We argue that Botswana's good economic policies, and therefore its economic success, reflect its institutions, or what we call institutions of private property [which] protect the property rights of actual and potential investors, provide political stability, and ensure that the political elites are constrained by the political system and the participation of a broad cross-section of the society."

17. Hernando de Soto, *The Mystery of Capital: Why Capitalism Triumphs in the West and Fails Everywhere Else* (New York: Basic Books, 2000), p. 20.

18. In some cases technology can improve the procedure, as in the case of Andhra Pradesh in India, where computerization cut the time to register a change of land title from 10 days to 1 hour, but in most cases it's far more valuable simply to eliminate the number of agencies involved and the number of permissions required. See the case study of Andhra Pradesh prepared by Subhash Chandra Bhatnagar at www1.worldbank.org/publicsector/egov/cardcs.htm.

19. World Bank, *Building Institutions: World Development Report 2002*, p. 13.

20. See the information from the *International Credit Risk Guide* in William Easterly, *The Elusive Quest for Growth*, pp. 248–52.

21. F. A. Hayek, *Law, Legislation, and Liberty: Volume I, Rules and Order* (Chicago: University of Chicago Press, 1973), pp. 98–99.

22. See the treatment of the meaning of regulation in Randy Barnett, *Restoring the Lost Constitution: The Presumption of Liberty* (Princeton, N.J.: Princeton University Press, 2004), esp. pp. 302–13.

23. James Madison ("Publius"), *Federalist* Number 62, February 27, 1788, in James Madison, *Writings*, ed. Jack N. Rakove (New York: The Library of America, 1999), p. 343.

24. See, for example, Yesim Yilmaz, "Private Regulation: A Real Alternative for Regulatory Reform," Cato Policy Analysis no. 303, April 20, 1998, www.cato.org/pubs/pas/pa-303es.html, and the studies in Daniel B. Klein, ed., *Reputation: Studies in the Voluntary Elicitation of Good Conduct* (Ann Arbor: University of Michigan Press, 1997).

25. See the treatment of the relationship between regulation and technology in Fred E. Foldvary and Daniel B. Klein, eds., *The Half-Life of Policy Rationales: How New Technology Affects Old Policy Issues* (New York: New York University Press, 2003).

26. For a theoretical framework for the study of institutions, with some case studies, see the papers in Martti Vihanto, *Discovering a Good Society through Evolution and Design* (Turku, Finland: Turku School of Economics and Business Administration, 1994).

11. The Case for Ordered Liberty without States

Thank you for opportunity to talk about such an interesting topic. I spend most of my time abroad, and when in China or Russia or Brazil or Afghanistan or Tajikistan or Kenya, I usually make the case for limited government, which I consider to be a great advance over unlimited government. But here we can discuss not only the immediate questions of the day, but also our ideals.

Let's start with a clear definition of the issue. "Anarchy" comes from the privative of the Greek term "Archon," a ruler, perhaps originally the first in a war party (the term is related to "arche," or first, origin, or principle), suggesting the origins of rulership in war. So to be anarchia means to be "without a ruler." It does not mean to be disordered; it's a topic for investigation whether that's a consequence of being without a ruler. That's the issue at stake here. Does being without a ruler mean forgoing order, law, and the security of life, liberty, and estate that we hold dear? The answer is, it depends. It depends on the presence or absence of other institutions that are not generally themselves dependent on the existence of a ruler.

For the dominant form of rulership that has almost completely displaced the others over the whole planet, I'll use Max Weber's canonical definition of the state as

> "that human community which (successfully) lays claim to the monopoly of legitimate physical violence within a certain territory, this 'territory' being another of the defining characteristics of the state."

These remarks were delivered during a debate on whether liberty can be enjoyed without a (limited) state. The debate featured John Mackey, Douglas Casey, Mark Skousen, and Tom G. Palmer, and occurred at Freedom Fest in Las Vegas, Nevada, on July 8, 2010. Opening cases were limited to five minutes.

In the United States, the term government is almost always used as a synonym for the state, unlike other English-speaking countries, where government refers to the prime minister and cabinet.

I prefer limited states to unlimited states, and, all things being equal, I prefer stateless liberty, stateless rule of law, and stateless order. No doubt John and Mark and some of you are saying, "But that's not possible! You can't have liberty, law, and order without a state." I disagree.

My argument has four parts.

First: Law and order without a state are possible. In fact, you don't have to turn to obscure cases in medieval Iceland or Ireland or 19th-century Nevada mining camps. Most of the law and order we observe around us comes from non-state initiative. There is a massive non-state system for generating laws in this country. Indeed, commercial law is overwhelmingly the product, not of state legislatures, but of private parties ordering their affairs. Debts are overwhelmingly collected by private collection agencies, not by the state. The common estimate is that there are at least twice as many private police, security guards, as police employed and empowered by the state, and the overwhelming majority of fugitives from the legal system who are returned are caught by private citizens, bounty hunters who are employed by bail bondsmen, also private citizens. And that happens with a tiny fraction of the violence—even brutality—routinely employed by state-empowered agents.

Second: John and Mark will say that they oppose violence and brutality. They want their state to be limited. Their intentions are noble. But my interest is institutions and incentives. What incentives does a monopoly have to produce good products? Think about it. Monopoly car companies, dairies, and phone companies have little incentive to cut costs, lower prices, increase quality, and so on. Why should the producers of law and order be any different?

Third: States systematically create crimes without victims. Indeed, the definition of a crime is an act against the state. If I were to strike John, the aggrieved party in any resulting criminal case would be the state, not John. States systematically expand their powers to punish behavior for which there is no complaining victim. No one turns himself or herself in for smoking pot or having consensual sex or engaging in thought crime. So the state employs vast armies of spies, snitches, and surveillance teams to uncover that behavior and punish it. And they get away with it by making the victims pay the bill. The costs of their own victimization are called "taxes." When you eliminate states you make it harder to prosecute or punish so-called crimes without victims. That's a big plus for a friend of liberty.

Fourth: States systematically create the conditions to legitimize their existence. Crises, wars, and the like are exploited by states to legitimate the expansions of their own powers. As Thomas Paine noted in *The Rights of Man*, vol. I, "In reviewing the history of the English government, its wars and its taxes, a by-stander, not blinded by prejudice, nor warped by interest, would declare, that taxes were not raised to carry on wars, but that wars were raised to carry on taxes." I prefer a world without wars, without taxes, without the systematic injustice that comes from any body of persons insisting that they are sovereign, that is, that they are above the laws. I prefer a world of ordered liberty, the rule of law, and peace. And in that world, there are no states.

Postscript: In the rebuttals and discussions, I raised the question of how many people are killed by privately employed security guards compared to state-empowered police. The incentives facing the different categories of parties are fairly clear, but data on that and related questions are very, very hard to come by. In the 2001 report of the Bureau of Justice Statistics of the Office of Justice Programs of the U.S. Department of Justice, "Policing and Homicide, 1976–98: Justifiable Homicide by Police, Police Officers Murdered by Felons" (Jodi M. Brown and Patrick A. Langan, March 2001, NCJ 180987), it is stated that "Police justifiably kill on average nearly 400 felons each year." The definitions used by the authors of the Department of Justice Study are noteworthy:

> "In this report, killings by police are referred to as 'justifiable homicides' and the persons that police kill are referred to as 'felons.' These terms reflect the view of the police agencies that provide the data used in this report."

The significance of defining all those killed by police as felons and all killings by police as justifiable homicides was not lost on the audience.

12. Poverty, Morality, and Liberty

"Classical liberalism" and "libertarianism" refer to that tradition of ethical, political, legal, and economic thought that places the freedom of the individual at the center of political concern and that sees that freedom as, in John Locke's language, each person's enjoyment of a "*Liberty* to dispose, and order, as he lists, his Person, Actions, Possessions, and his whole Property, within the Allowance of those Laws under which he is; and therein not to be subject to the arbitrary Will of another, but freely follows his own."[1]

Classical liberals, despite often vigorous disagreement among themselves over both the foundations of liberty and the proper limits on state power, have generally agreed on the thesis of the presumption of liberty; that is, that it is interference with the freedom of others that must be justified, and not their free action itself. The exercise of power requires justification; the exercise of liberty does not.[2]

Three commonly accepted core elements of classical liberal thought are:

> 1. A conviction, expressed in many different ways, that "individuals have rights and that there are things no person or group may do to them (without violating their rights)"[3];
> 2. An appreciation for the capacity for social order and harmony to emerge spontaneously, without the conscious direction of any mind or the imposition of any plan, as an unintended consequence of people interacting freely on the basis of rights (property) that are well defined, defendable, and structured by legal rules facilitating contract;
> 3. A commitment to constitutionally limited government that is authorized to enforce the rules of just conduct but is strictly limited in its powers.

A longer version of this essay was first published in the book *Poverty and Morality: Religious and Secular Perspectives*, edited by Peter Hoffenberg and William A. Galston. Cambridge: Cambridge University Press, 2010.

Thus, the tradition of classical liberal thinking draws primarily from three disciplines—moral philosophy, social science, and political (or juridical) science, supplemented by ancillary disciplines such as psychology, history, and sociology. Each of the three elements reinforces the others to produce a coherent theory of the relationship of freedom, rights, government, and order.

Adam Smith, a doyen of the classical liberal tradition and a contributor to all three of those primary disciplines—moral philosophy (*The Theory of Moral Sentiments*), social science (*An Inquiry into the Nature and Causes of the Wealth of Nations*), and political or juridical science (*The Lectures on Jurisprudence*)—connected all three pillars in a famous statement:

> Little else is requisite to carry a state to the highest degree of opulence from the lowest barbarism, but peace, easy taxes, and a tolerable administration of justice; all the rest being brought about by the natural course of things. All governments which thwart this natural course, which force things into another channel, or which endeavour to arrest the progress of society at a particular point, are unnatural, and to support themselves are obliged to be oppressive and tyrannical.[4]

Definitions

Classical liberalism has had a long engagement with the issue of poverty, partly because of its intimate association with economic science in particular and the study of spontaneous forms of social order and improvement in general. Classical liberals have insisted that the question of the "wealth of nations" comes logically before "the poverty of nations." Poverty is meaningful only in comparison to wealth, and wealth must be produced. Poverty is the natural base line against which wealth is measured; poverty is what you have if wealth is not produced. The classical liberal economist Peter Bauer of the London School of Economics famously retorted to John Kenneth Galbraith's discussion of the "causes of poverty": "Poverty has no causes. Wealth has causes." As the historians Nathan Rosenberg and L. E. Birdzell Jr. put the matter, "If we take the long view of human history and judge the economic lives of our ancestors by modern standards, it is a story of almost unrelieved wretchedness."[5] Widespread poverty is the historical norm; the wealth explosion of the past two centuries is the aberration that requires explanation.

Prosperity, as it is understood today, is a uniquely modern phenomenon. The experience of the great bulk of the human race for most of its existence, up until quite recently, has been the experience of early death, sickness, ignorance, almost unrelieved physical toil, and uncertain access to sufficient food to sustain life. The picture of the past commonly carried by so many intellectuals is deeply misleading, as it is derived almost entirely from the writings of other intellectuals, that is, from that tiny minority fortunate enough to enjoy the leisure to write about their lives. Such accounts are hardly representative of the lives of the great bulk of the human race. The difference between the material conditions of existence that characterized most of the human past and now is substantial. In the words of classical liberal economic historian Deirdre McCloskey,

> The heart of the matter is twelve. Twelve is the factor by which real income per head nowadays exceeds that around 1780, in Britain and in other countries that have experienced modern economic growth.
>
> . . . Most conservatively measured, the average person has about twelve times more bread, books, transport and innocent amusement than the average person had two centuries ago. No previous episode of enrichment approaches modern economic growth—not China or Egypt in their primes, not the glory of Greece or the grandeur of Rome.[6]

It is only the past few hundred years that have witnessed the explosion of productive energy, as shown by the enormous changes in per capita income from 1500 to 1998 (Table 1). The data are more striking when looked at graphically from the year 1 to the present (Figure 1).

The sudden and sustained rise in income from the takeoff period around the middle of the 18th century (for Western Europe and North America; a century or more later for others) is unprecedented in all of human history. It is the sudden shift from a nearly horizontal line to a nearly vertical line that demands explanation.

The conditions of most previous generations of humans—as judged by the standards of the present—are no less than horrifying. The focus on classical liberal historical, economic, and legal research has been on explaining the causes of that great change, and the general consensus has been that the key change was the growth of institutions conducive to the production of wealth.

235

Table 1

Levels of GDP Per Capita in European Colonial Powers and Former Colonies, 1500–1998 (1990 international dollars)

	1500	1700	1820	1913	1950	1998
Britian	762	1,405	2,121	5,150	6,907	18,714
France	727	986	1,230	3,485	5,270	19,556
Italy	1,100	1,100	1,117	2,564	3,502	17,759
Netherlands	754	2,110	1,821	4,049	5,996	20,224
Portugal	632	854	963	1,244	2,069	12,929
Spain	698	900	1,063	2,255	2,397	14,227
China	600	600	600	552	439	3,117
India	550	550	533	673	619	1,746
Indonesia	565	580	612	904	840	3,070
Brazil	400	460	646	811	1,672	5,459
Mexico	425	568	759	1,732	2,365	6,655
United States	400	527	1,257	5,301	9,561	27,331
Ireland	526	715	880	2,736	3,446	18,183

Source: A. Maddison, *The World Economy*, vol. 1: *A Millennial Perspective*, and vol. 2: *Historical Statistics* (Paris: OECD, 2006), p. 92.

Figure 1

Source: Indur M. Goklany, *The Improving State of the World* (Washington, DC: Cato Institute, 2007), p. 43.

Classical liberals insist that the explanation of wealth production—of what made possible the sudden trend upward in Figure 1—is primary not merely because of the suddenness of the change but also for reasons of conceptual clarity. Poverty is what results if wealth production does not take place, whereas wealth is not what results if poverty production does not take place.

The suddenness of the wealth explosion shown in Figure 1 is the reason that the dominant narrative in the classical liberal tradition has been one of prosperity defined against a norm of widespread poverty, not in terms of relative well-being.

Classical liberals have sought to explain the *presence of wealth* rather than taking as the fundamental puzzle its absence. The idea of a "vicious circle of poverty" as an explanation for the absence of wealth was criticized by the development economist P. T. Bauer:

> To have money is the result of economic achievement, not its precondition. That this is so is plain from the very existence of developed countries, all of which originally must have been underdeveloped and yet progressed without external donations. The world was not created in two parts, one with ready-made infrastructure and stock of capital, and the other without such facilities. Moreover, many poor countries progressed rapidly in the hundred years or so before the emergence of modern development economics and the canvassing of the vicious circle. Indeed, if the notion of the vicious circle of poverty were valid, mankind would still be living in the Old Stone Age.[7]

Almost all humans have escaped the Stone Age. In those countries that saw increases in per capita income, the effect was especially significant for the poor, whose status and even definition changed dramatically. As Carlo Cipolla noted of the impact of the "Industrial Revolution," it is undeniable that one of the main characteristics of preindustrial Europe, as of all traditional agricultural societies, was a striking contrast between the abject misery of the masses and the affluence and magnificence of a limited number of the very rich.[8] "The poor" referred to people on the verge of starvation:

> Most people lived at subsistence level. They had no savings and no social security to help them in case of distress. If they remained without work, their only hope of survival was charity. We look in vain in the language of the time for the

term *unemployed*. The unemployed were confused with the poor, the poor person was identified with the beggar, and the confusion of the terms reflected the grim reality of the times. In a year of bad harvest or of economic stagnation, the number of destitute people grew conspicuously . . . The people of preindustrial times were inured to drastic fluctuations in the number of beggars. Especially in the cities the number of the poor soared in years of famine because starving peasants fled the depleted countryside and swarmed to the urban centers, where charity was more easily available and hopefully the houses of the wealthy had food in storage. Dr. Tadino reported that in Milan (Italy) during the famine of 1629 in a few months the number of beggars grew from 3,554 to 9,715. Gascon found that in Lyon (France) "in normal years the poor represented 6 to 8 percent of the population; in years of famine their number rose to 15 or 20 percent."

The fundamental characteristic of the poor was that they had no independent income. If they managed to survive, it was because income was voluntarily transferred to them through charity.[9]

The great growth of industry made the poor—in the form of large numbers of urban workers—visible to literate urban dwellers in a way that they had not been before. But no longer were they swarming masses of starving peasants hoping for alms. Their status was decidedly different. The increases in population made possible by industrialism did not arise from an increase in birth rates but from a drop in death rates, notably premature death. "If we ask," F. A. Hayek wrote, "what men most owe to the moral practices of those called capitalists the answer is: their very lives. Socialist accounts that ascribe the existence of the proletariat to an exploitation of groups formerly able to maintain themselves are entirely fictional. Most individuals who now make up the proletariat could not have existed before others provided them with means to exist."[10]

Classical liberals have persistently worked to debunk the false image of the past—common to socialists and conservatives alike, in which happy peasants gamboled on the village green, life was tranquil and unstressed, and each peasant family enjoyed a snug little cottage.[11] The common yearning for a past "golden age," a yearning that is still with us ("Ah, for the 1950s, when everyone . . ."), was described and dismissed by the classical liberal historian Thomas Babington Macaulay in the mid-19th century:

> It is now the fashion to place the golden Age of England in
> times when noblemen were destitute of comforts the wants
> of which would be intolerable to a modern footman, when
> farmers and shopkeepers breakfasted on loaves the sight of
> which would raise a riot in a modern workhouse, when to
> have a clean shirt once a week was a privilege for the higher
> class of gentry.

The way of life of Macaulay's generation would today be considered unbearable by even the poorest among us, as Macaulay pre-
sciently recognized:

> We too shall, in our turn, be outstripped, and in our turn be
> envied. It may well be, in the twentieth century, that . . .
> numerous comforts and luxuries which are now unknown,
> or confined to a few, may be within the reach of every diligent
> and thrifty workingman. And yet it may then be the mode
> to assert that the increase of wealth and progress of science
> have benefited the few at the expense of many.[12]

As Macaulay understood, there is no naturally discernible dividing line between "poverty" and "wealth." The poor of today enjoy
amenities unavailable to the wealthy of the past, even the relatively
recent past. (If anyone doubts that, he or she should compare the
experience of dentistry among the super wealthy 50 years ago with
that of the poor in advanced countries today; who could doubt that
the wealthy of the past would have given their eye teeth, so to speak,
to enjoy the anesthesia and modern dental techniques available to
even the poorest in industrial countries today.)

Comparative approaches have not been lacking in the classical
liberal tradition. The Abbé de Condillac, in an influential work published in the same year as Adam Smith's *The Wealth of Nations*,
distinguished between mere lack of wealth and poverty, for "there
is only poverty where essential needs are not met, and it is not being
poor to lack a type of wealth of which one has not acquired a need,
and which one does not even know."[13] The progress of the arts and
sciences and the creation of ever-greater wealth generates new needs,
the satisfaction of which entails new forms of consumption.

Adam Smith added an additional element. Poverty consists not
only in the consciousness of unmet need but also in the comparison
of one's status with that of others in a way that causes shame. Shame

239

is a defining feature of what is a "necessity," that is, something without which one would be accounted poor:

> By necessities I understand, not only the commodities which are indispensably necessary for the support of life, but whatever the custom of the country renders it indecent for creditable people, even of the lowest order, to be without. A linen shirt, for example, is, strictly speaking, not a necessary of life. The Greeks and Romans lived, I suppose, very comfortably, though they had no linen. But in the present times, through the greater part of Europe, a creditable day-labourer would be ashamed to appear in public without a linen shirt, the want of which would be supposed to denote that disgraceful degree of poverty, which, it is presumed, no body can well fall into without extreme bad conduct. . . . Under necessaries therefore, I comprehend, not only those things which nature, but those things which the established rules of decency have rendered necessary to the lowest ranks of people. All other things, I call luxuries; . . . Nature does not render them necessary for the support of life; and custom no where renders it indecent to live without them.[14]

Under both absolute and comparative conceptions, wealth and poverty are moving standards. An accumulation of assets that may qualify one as wealthy in one year may, in a wealthier succeeding year, qualify one as poor, and a wealthy person in one society may be poor in another.

Consistent with their focus on wealth as the phenomenon to be explained, then, classical liberals addressed themselves assiduously to the analysis of why some fare better or worse than others. Smith's book was famously called *An Inquiry into the Nature and Causes of the Wealth of Nations*. Most prior writers had identified the wealth of a nation (its nature) with the wealth of the ruling elite. In contrast, Smith began his work by identifying the nature of a nation's wealth, not with its military power or the gold and silver in the king's treasury, but with the annual produce of the combined labor power of the nation, divided by the number of consumers, a conception that persists in the modern notion of per capita gross domestic product.[15]

The wealth of a nation is to be measured, then, not by the power of its rulers or the bullion in the state treasury, but by the access to wealth on the part of any randomly chosen member of it: "That state is properly opulent in which opulence is easily come at, or in which a little labour, properly and judiciously employed, is capable of procuring any man a great abundance of all the necessaries and conveniencies of life."[16] The primary causes or determinants of wealth are the institutions that create incentives for wealth production. Poverty, then, as measured against a background of wealth, represents a failure to create (or hold on to) wealth, and the causes of such failure are those institutions or practices that create *dis*incentives for wealth production and/or incentives for predatory transfers that directly impoverish some for the benefit of others.

If opportunities, understood as freedoms to engage in voluntary activities to create wealth, are unequally distributed, it is likely that that will entail an unequal distribution of wealth, not because a sum of "socially created" wealth has been divided unfairly, but because the opportunities to produce wealth have been withheld from some, who as a consequence are able to produce less. Classical liberals have emphasized that every act of production is itself an act of distribution. If freedom to produce is unequal, holdings of wealth will also be unequal. For example, recipients of state grants of monopoly can charge higher prices in the absence of competition and reap monopoly rents as a consequence, a process (now known as rent-seeking) that both transfers wealth from one party to another and, in the process, diminishes the aggregate of wealth produced, as resources are diverted to rent-seeking itself and away from production of value, thus making the society as a whole less wealthy than it would have been in the absence of rent-seeking behavior.[17]

If some have the power to force others to produce not for their own benefit but for the benefit of the powerful, they will transfer wealth from the coerced to those who coerce, sometimes at a great net loss in productivity. Slavery, serfdom, conscription, and other forms of forced labor transfer wealth from some to others. Theft and other forms of involuntary transfers confiscate from some what they have produced, generally to the benefit of the confiscators.[18] Restrictions on some from competing with others generate rents to those with monopolistic powers, at the expense of their customers and potential competitors. A society in which some are forbidden by force of law from owning land, entering certain trades, or purchasing commodities at freely negotiated prices would likely see a difference in per capita income between those groups that suffered from legal disabilities and those that did not. Examples from history abound.[19]

241

Vulnerability to Poverty

Vulnerability to poverty is seen by classical liberals as substantially dependent on institutional settings. When there are rewards to violence or procurement of political power and force, the violent and the politically ambitious will benefit by snatching from the industrious the wealth they have produced, impoverishing the industrious and diminishing incentives for further production of wealth, to the relative impoverishment of all. The history of civilization is a history of limitations on power and violence, achieved by a variety of means.[20]

In legal orders characterized by well-defined, legally secure, and transferable property rights, with strong limitations on predatory behavior, poverty tends to be transformed from the dividing line between survival and starvation and becomes a matter of relative affluence, with the lesser affluence of the poor largely a matter of inability or unwillingness to produce wealth or to save, rather than to squander, what one has acquired. Thus, "character" (also known as possession of the virtues)[21] is a factor, as the industrious and the thrifty are in such legal orders unlikely to experience poverty, reckoned in either absolute or relative terms.

In relatively free and prosperous societies, the best predictors of relative poverty tend to be the degree to which one is a recipient of state assistance, which, they have argued, tends to foster the vices of indolence and irresponsibility. The classic example was the working of the "Poor Laws" in relatively prosperous England, and especially the "Speenhamland System" of "outdoor relief" that subsidized the working poor.[22] As Alexis de Tocqueville argued in his *Memoir on Pauperism*, written after a tour of England, the availability of "legal charity" in wealthy countries such as Britain, before the reform of the "Poor Laws," was itself a cause of poverty, for it had, he argued, created a permanent class of paupers. His investigation was aimed at resolving an apparent paradox: "The countries appearing to be most impoverished are those which in reality account for the fewest indigents, and among the people most admired for their opulence, one part of the population is obliged to live on the gifts of the other in order to live."[23]

As Tocqueville concluded from his investigation, "Any measure that establishes legal charity on a permanent basis and gives it an administrative form thereby creates an idle and lazy class, living at the expense of the industrial and working class."[24] In addition to creating incentives for some to become dependent on others, the Poor Laws created incentives for the industrious to attempt to control the movement of the recipients of "outdoor relief," lest newcomers become burdens to ratepayers. According to Tocqueville,

> Legal charity affects the pauper's freedom as much as his morality. This is easily proved. When local governments are rigorously obligated to aid the indigent, they necessarily owe relief only to the poor who reside in their jurisdiction. This is the only fair way of equalizing the public burden which results from the law, and of proportioning it to the means of those who must bear it. Since individual charity is almost unknown in a country of organized public charity, anyone whose misfortunes or vices have made him incapable of earning a living is condemned, under pain of death, to remain in the place of his birth. If he leaves, he moves through enemy territory. The private interest within the parish, infinitely more active and powerful than the best organized national police could be, notes his arrival, dogs his every step, and, if he wants to establish a new residence, informs the public authority who takes him to the boundary line. Through their Poor Laws, the English have immobilized a sixth of their population. They have bound it to the earth like the medieval peasantry. Then, man was forced against his will to stay on the land where he was born. Legal charity keeps him from even wishing to move.[25]

A similar dynamic of control set in motion by welfare statism explains profoundly illiberal policies of restrictions on freedom of movement across international borders, as immigrants are often seen by the inhabitants of welfare states as parasites who threaten to consume the wealth of the locals, rather than as potential producers of wealth who come for mutual benefit.[26]

Institutionalization of the Political and Economic Means to Wealth Acquisition

A major—indeed, the most important—factor of production is the institutional framework that facilitates voluntary cooperation for mutual benefit. Wealth production is a result of institutional changes that create incentives for productivity and mutual gains resulting from trade. As Benjamin Friedman notes, "This bold new concept had strong moral content. For the first time people saw the possibility of acquiring wealth in a way that need not be inherently exploitive. At the individual level, the idea of voluntary exchange was that in any transaction both parties expected to come out ahead. But the same point applied even more strikingly at the level of the entire society. The route to national wealth was commerce, not conquest."[27] Following on that insight, classical liberals have distinguished two means of acquiring wealth: the "economic means" of production and exchange and the "political means" of deploying force.[28] Herbert Spencer distinguished between two ideal types of society, the "militant" and the "industrial": the former characterized by command and hierarchy and the latter by cooperation and contract.[29]

As special privileges in law will generate differences in wealth and income, classical liberals strove to identify and eliminate those special privileges that harmed some to the benefit of others.[30] Thus, classical liberals have campaigned vigorously against guild privileges that restricted entrance to trades; racial, ethnic, religious, and gender barriers to ownership of property or entry to trades; protectionist barriers to cheap imports, which raise prices to consumers to benefit small minorities of domestic producers; and a wide array of obstacles to the efforts of people to improve their situations. Legal equality, freedom of trade, and careers open to talent were watchwords of classical liberal theorists of social progress.[31]

Classical liberals prided themselves on the results of their efforts. As the classical liberal journalist E. L. Godkin noted in the pages of the *Nation* in 1900, "To the principle and precepts of Liberalism the prodigious material progress of the age was largely due. Freed from the vexatious meddling of governments, men devoted themselves to their natural task, the bettering of their condition, with the wonderful results which surround us."[32]

Wealth and Inequality

Just as classical liberals do not see poverty as "the cause" of poverty (in the "vicious circle of poverty" argument criticized by P. T. Bauer), they do not see the existence of wealth as the cause of poverty, as it is by some socialists, who argue that not giving a poor person goods and services is the "cause" of that person's poverty.[33] Voluntarily acquired wealth is, in fact, a cause of the wealth of others, not of their poverty. "Say's Law," according to which "it is production which opens a demand for products," postulated that the wealth of one person, group, or nation was to the benefit of those who traded with them.[34]

> What could an active manufacturer, or an intelligent merchant, do in a small, deserted and semi-barbarous town in a remote corner of Poland or Westphalia? Though in no fear of a competitor, he could sell but little, because little was produced; whilst at Paris, Amsterdam, or London, in spite of the competition of a hundred dealers in his own line, he might do business on the largest scale. The reason is obvious: he is surrounded with people who produce largely in an infinity of ways, and who make purchases, each with his respective products, that is to say, with the money arising from the sale of what he may have produced.[35]

Institutions create incentives and incentives shape behavior. As Douglass North puts it, "Institutions provide the incentive structure of an economy; as that structure evolves, it shapes the direction of economic change towards growth, stagnation, or decline."[36]

Outcomes are not in general subject to choice; at best, one can choose one process over another, not one outcome over another. What may seem like the choice of an outcome (e.g., higher wages) is, in fact, the choice of a process (prohibiting the creation of fulfillment of labor contracts below a certain wage). Processes do not always generate the outcomes that the choosers may have hoped for. Daniel Shapiro notes that "institutions cannot be adequately characterized by their aims."[37] Thus, classical liberals have criticized a great deal of intervention into voluntary exchange on the grounds that it does not generate the outcomes promised. Minimum wage laws, for example, do not raise wages—increasing the marginal product of labor raises wages, and that is not subject to control by legislative fiat, but such laws do increase unemployment and force people out of free markets into black markets, by forbidding those with low marginal value products (typically the low-skilled, the uneducated, and the young) from offering their services at prices that would command buyers.[38]

Societies characterized by fully equal rights and freedoms will still display income inequalities, just as do unfree societies. (No social order eliminates differences of income; they usually merely disguise the inequalities, as Mancur Olson argued in his essay "The

245

Theory of Soviet-Type Autocracies.")[39] What distinguishes free societies is a general circulation of elites—artistic, cultural, political, and
economic. In his general study of the "circulation of elites" among
different types of social orders, Vilfredo Pareto noted that, like militant societies, liberal, industrial societies are also characterized by the
circulation of elites, but on the basis of entirely different processes. In
a militaristic ("bellicose") society, war provides the impetus for "the
ordinary soldier to become a general," but in "commercial and industrial societies," for the poorest to attain wealth requires both freedom
and "commercial and industrial development of sufficient scale to
make this a real possibility for an appreciable number of citizens."[40]
Commercial relations based on production and voluntary exchange
tend to produce systems of dynamic inequalities, rather than rigidly
maintained systems of inequality; that is, persons and families rise
and fall in the relative scale of wealth, as the aggregate wealth of
the whole society is increasing.[41]

The key distinction that classical liberal sociologists and economists have drawn on in analyzing the ever-changing "distribution
of wealth" in free society is that between "ownership," a legal concept, and "wealth," an economic concept. Voluntary exchange entails
reallocation not only of ownership rights but of wealth as well, and
not only among those who are contractual parties to the exchange.
When Henry Ford bought steel, rubber, and glass from vendors
and employed workers to make automobiles, he not only caused
property to change hands among those involved directly in the
exchange but also bid up the value of those resources, caused the
value of the resources employed in making horse saddles to go
down, and increased the wages of labor by increasing its marginal
value product. The transfers of wealth involved were far greater
than the value of the property that changed hands in the transactions.
Changes in valuation determine what an asset is worth, that is, what
wealth it represents for the owner, and values change regularly, as
new production processes are introduced, tastes change, and so on,
causing the wealth of some to rise and that of others to fall.

> The market economy is thus seen to be a leveling process.
> In a market economy a process of redistribution of wealth
> is taking place all the time before which those outwardly
> similar processes which modern politicians are in the habit
> of instituting, pale into comparative insignificance, if for no

> other reason than that the market gives wealth to those who
> can hold it, while politicians give it to their constituents,
> who, as a rule, cannot.[42]

Classical liberals have rejected the "natural resource" theory of wealth in favor of an industrial approach. Wealth is not so much what we find, as what we produce. Thus, the influential classical liberal economist Jean-Baptiste Say distinguished "existing materials" (what would today be called "natural resources") from "wealth": "All that man can do is, to re-produce existing materials under another form, which may give them a utility they did not before possess, or merely enlarge one they may have before presented. So that, in fact, there is a creation, not of matter, but of utility; and this I call production of wealth."[43]

There are many societies surrounded by abundant natural resources whose populations are far, far poorer than societies with far fewer resources but governed by institutions that facilitate the creation of wealth. It has been commonly understood in development economics, dating back hundreds of years, that abundant resources are not a significant determinant of wealth.[44] Classical liberalism is characterized by the belief that the production of wealth is fostered, and absolute poverty eliminated, by the legal institutions of well-defined and legally secure rights that can be freely exchanged on the basis of a system of contract and law, or Adam Smith's "peace, easy taxes, and a tolerable administration of justice."[45] Moreover, freedom of production and exchange undermined hierarchies, castes, and other rigid forms of inequality.

But wealth production through free markets was never the only classical liberal response to poverty. Such exchanges are but one element in a wider array of cooperative activities to combat poverty.

Self-Help, Mutual Aid, Charity, and Public Assistance

Legal equality is a defining element of the classical liberal tradition, and classical liberals were pioneers in the extension of ideas of equality to both genders, and all races, nations, and social groups. Advocacy of equal rights for women to participate in the workplace, without gender-based job exclusion laws, and to acquire, own, and dispose of property independently has been promoted not only for reasons of moral consistency but to improve the lot of women and eliminate their involuntary dependence on men. As the 19th-century classical liberal abolitionist and feminist Sarah Grimké noted, "There are few things which present greater obstacles to the improvement and elevation of woman to her appropriate sphere of usefulness and duty, than the laws which have been enacted to destroy her independence, and crush her individuality; laws which, although they are framed for her government, she has had no voice in establishing, and which rob her of some of her *essential rights*."[46]

The freedom to exercise one's talents led to the improvement of the lot of the oppressed, of the have-nots, of the disadvantaged, of the poor. Self-help was promoted by the elimination of obstacles to self-help and the active assertion of personal responsibility.

But other means were also available. The first, which is widely associated with classical liberalism, is the advocacy of charity as a means to the improvement of the lot of the poor. Charity assists those who have fallen on hard luck or who need assistance from others, which is best provided by voluntary associations. The key for classical liberals was to avoid conditions of permanent dependence. Thus, Bernard Bosanquet, a stalwart of the Charity Organisation Society in Great Britain, was deeply critical of the institutionalization of poverty, of seeing "the institution of 'the poor' as a class, representing, as an ethical idea in the modern mind, a permanent object of compassion and self-sacrifice. 'Poverty,' it has been said, 'has become a status.' The 'déclassés' have become a social class, with the passive social function of stimulating the goodness of others."[47] The purpose of charity was not to further dependency but to foster the ability of the recipients of charity to take care of themselves and their families. Bosanquet argued that economic socialism, based on commands and central planning, would produce selfishness, while voluntary cooperation would produce respect for others and fellow feeling. The experience of life under real existing socialism would seem to have borne out that prediction.[48] And even in the case of modern welfare states, as Norman Barry notes, "Contemporary experience indicates that, far from encouraging a communitarian and socially concerned 'self,' the institutions of the welfare state have simply reproduced the traditional *homo economicus* in a different context."[49]

After self-help, which was promoted primarily by removing obstacles to the free exercise of one's faculties, classical liberals actively promoted and took part in a variety of "friendly societies," "fraternal societies," and "mutual-aid societies" that pooled both the efforts and the risks faced by persons of limited means. At their height, friendly societies actively involved millions of people in social movements that dwarfed the now much-better-known trade-union movements of the time. Although some of them had roots dating back even to the burial societies of ancient Rome, they flourished as never before in the 18th, 19th, and early to mid-20th centuries. As Otto von Gierke observed in 1868 of the "laws of fellowship": "In our century, initiative and creative power have passed back to the people: the free personal fellowship, never entirely extinguished, has been developed into a great number of different branches, and given a form capable of fitting the most varied purposes."[50]

Such fellowships not only provided insurance against illness, accident, death, and other catastrophes but also promoted good character and such virtues as civility, respect for women (male members who beat their wives were normally expelled from societies), sobriety, and charity. Through voluntary association, they went beyond the personal responsibility often associated with classical liberalism and voluntarily embraced various forms of collective responsibility, forms of interaction that are generally underappreciated parts of the classical liberal understanding of liberty and social order. David Schmidtz has argued that "it is internalized responsibility (rather than individual responsibility *per se*) that makes people better off. Institutions that lead people to take responsibility for themselves as a group also help to internalize responsibility, albeit in a collective form. They too can make people better off."[51] Mutual aid was historically a key element in the classical liberal approach to social order and improvement. Like marriage, such associations are seen by classical liberals not as restrictions on liberty, but as exercises of them.

The friendly societies represent perhaps the most poorly documented great social movements ever. They flourished in many countries as the obstacles to civil association were lowered or eliminated, and they faded away as for-profit firms competed with them by offering actuarially sound insurance policies (in fact, some friendly societies transformed themselves into insurance firms, such as the Modern Woodmen of America, Prudential Insurance, and Metropolitan Life)[52] and as the welfare state displaced them.[53]

Working-class people themselves drew distinctions between the deserving poor and the undeserving poor. Rather than acknowledging any unconditional right to assistance, groups of the poor who pooled their resources for mutual aid distinguished between those who deserved assistance and those who did not, either because of their own unwillingness to assist others when they could or because their situation was of their own voluntary making.

Classical liberal thinkers, as well as the leaders of voluntary organizations, focused on fostering the traits of character suitable for success in civil society. In Green's words, the members of friendly societies "were united not by their physical proximity but by their attachment to shared ideals. Central to the purpose of the societies was the promotion of good character, a consideration of great importance for classical-liberal thought, some of whose advocates tend to take good conduct and a desire for a better life for granted."[54] Assistance from a friendly society was, indeed, a matter of right, but not an unearned or unconditional right.

Mutual aid allowed the poor to escape the paternal condescension that accompanied charity, which was normally associated with cases of extreme desperation. Being needy was a state that one should seek to avoid, not to embrace.

Charity remains closely connected with classical liberal thought, but it was normally third in the list of methods of helping the poor, after self-help and mutual aid. Transfer payments from taxpayers were considered the least desirable means, to be employed only when other forms of improvement in the lot of the poor were unavailable or inadequate. As John Stuart Mill, in his essay on "The Claims of Labour," noted:

> To give money in alms has never been, either in this country or in most others, a rare virtue. Charitable institutions, and subscriptions for relief of the destitute, already abounded; and if new forms of suffering, or classes of sufferers previously overlooked, were brought to notice, nothing was more natural than to do for them what had already been done for others.[55]

The giving of alms was long associated with shared obligations and, unsurprisingly, often organized by religious institutions. The giving of alms to the needy has generally been understood in the classical liberal tradition as an exercise of the virtues of generosity and compassion.[56] Thus, classical liberals typically recognized a moral obligation to assist those in need as a result of misfortune and promoted a wide variety of voluntary arrangements to provide such assistance. While voluntary assistance was laudatory and virtuous, compulsion was not. A representative view can be found in Adam Smith's *The Theory of Moral Sentiments*. Although the sentiment of beneficence was a necessary element in virtuous activity ("No action can properly be called virtuous which is not accompanied with the sentiment of self-approbation"),[57] beneficence and charity were trumped by considerations of justice: he noted that "we feel ourselves to be under a stricter obligation to act according to justice, than agreeably to friendship, charity, or generosity: that the practice of these last mentioned virtues seems to be left in some measure of our own choice, but that somehow or other, we feel ourselves to be in a peculiar manner tied, bound and obliged to the observation of justice."[58] According to Smith, in a passage that represented one of the central moral commitments of most later classical liberals, "We must always, however, carefully distinguish what is only blamable, or the proper object of disapprobation, from what force may be employed either to punish or to prevent."[59]

The later utilitarian argument that a redistribution of wealth from the richer to the poorer would merely take what was of little value to the former to give what was of greater value to the latter was solidly rejected by classical liberals, who saw in the idea a threat to the general rules on which free and prosperous societies rest.[60] Thus, in Smith's words, "One individual must never prefer himself so much even to any other individual, as to hurt or injure that other, in order to benefit himself, though the benefit to the one should be much greater than the hurt or injury to the other. The poor man must neither defraud nor steal from the rich, though the acquisition might be much more beneficial to the one than the loss could be hurtful to the other." To do so would violate "one of those sacred rules, upon the tolerable observation of which depend the whole security and peace of human society."[61]

Bertrand de Jouvenel addressed directly the utilitarian arguments for redistribution: a leveling of income or wealth to maximize welfare (small reductions in the welfare of the rich being much more than offset by large improvements in the welfare of the poor) would effectively eliminate the expenditures on higher culture associated with wealth, which the advocates of redistribution invariably address by calling for taxation to redirect resources toward support of cultural establishments. As de Jouvenel noted, "All advocates of extreme redistribution couple it with most generous measures of state support for the whole superstructure of cultural activities."[62] He accused them of inconsistency, for the utilitarian welfare-maximization argument for income redistribution was undercut by the redirection of wealth by the state to favored cultural institutions: "It is then an inconsistency, and a very blatant one, to intervene with state support for such cultural activities as do not find a market. Those who spontaneously correct their schemes of redistribution by schemes for such support are in fact denying that the ideal allocation of resources and activities is that which maximizes the sum of satisfactions."[63]

J. S. Mill noted that the imposition of a "moral or a legal obligation, upon the higher classes, that they shall be answerable for the well-doing and well-being of the lower," was characteristic not of liberal societies but of illiberal societies. As he argued, "the ideal state of society which the new philanthropists [advocates of compulsory assistance] are contending for" was that of "The Russian boors." He continued, "There are other labourers, not merely tillers of the soil, but workers in great establishments partaking of the nature of manufactories, for whom the laws of our own country, even in our own time, compelled their employers to find wholesome food, and sufficient lodging and clothing. Who are these? The slaves on a West Indian estate."[64]

Compulsory assistance was associated in the minds of classical liberals not only with condescension but with systems of paternalistic control and loss of independence and liberty. The experience of the Poor Laws and the associated controls of behavior were still vivid memories for the liberals of the 19th and 20th centuries. As Mill noted, "There are governments in Europe who look upon it as part of their duty to take care of the physical well-being and comfort of the people. . . . But with paternal care is connected paternal authority. In these states we find severe restrictions on marriage. No one is permitted to marry, unless he satisfies the authorities that he has a rational prospect of being able to support a family."[65]

The fear of such controls has motivated much classical liberal opposition to, or at least uneasiness with, "welfare reform" schemes that require labor for the state as a condition for receipt of assistance.

A major concern about compulsory redistribution that was central to the critique of the Poor Laws and continues to this day in debates on welfare policy and "foreign aid" is whether such state measures actually improve the well-being of the poor, or merely make those who advocate them feel good about themselves, as if they had discharged a moral obligation, not by helping others but by advocating policies. For most classical liberals, consequences, and not merely stated intentions, matter in the evaluation of policies.[66] Thus, the question of whether state aid resting on compulsion in fact represents an improvement for the poor has always been a central concern of classical liberals when addressing plans of redistribution.

In listing the order of preferences among classical liberals, Wilhelm Röpke stated that "our rule and norm and our cheerfully accepted ideal should be security through individual effort and responsibility, supplemented by mutual aid."[67] Röpke differed from some classical liberals in accepting state provision of a minimum of assistance:

> We cannot, nowadays, do without a certain minimum of compulsory state institutions for social security. Public old-age pensions, health insurance, accident insurance, widows' benefits, unemployment relief—there must naturally be room for all these in our concept of a sound social security system in a free society, however little enthusiasm we may feel for them. It is not their principle which is in question, but their extent, organization, and spirit.[68]

Many classical liberals have thus accepted some state provision, but only with some reluctance and as the least preferred method of assistance to the poor. Milton Friedman, for example, offered two reasons to support a limited degree of state compulsion for purposes of assisting the poor. The first was the exercise of legal compulsion to force people to purchase annuities for their own old age because "the improvident will not suffer the consequences of their own action but will impose costs on others. We shall not, it is said, be willing to see the indigent aged suffer in dire poverty. We shall assist them by private and public charity. Hence the man who does not provide for his old age will become a public charge. Compelling him to buy an annuity is justified not for his own good but for the good of the rest of us."[69] (As he quickly noted, "The weight of this argument clearly depends on fact.") The second was the exercise of legal compulsion to force taxpayers as a class to support those who are in need, on the grounds that state coercion to provide a collective (or public) good is acceptable on liberal grounds: "It can be argued that private charity is insufficient because the benefits from it accrue to people other than those who make the gifts. . . . I am distressed by the sight of poverty; I am benefited by its alleviation; but I am benefited equally whether I or someone else pays for its alleviation; the benefits of other people's charity therefore partly accrue to me." Such concerns would, according to Friedman, set "a floor under the standard of life of every person in the community."[70]

F. A. Hayek also, although not an enthusiast for the welfare state, argued, on the grounds of provision of public goods, that some limited state provision of welfare was compatible with classical liberal principles: "All modern governments have made provision for the indigent, unfortunate, and disabled and have concerned themselves with questions of health and the dissemination of knowledge. There is no reason why the volume of these pure service activities should not increase with the general growth of wealth. There are common needs that can be satisfied only by collective action and which can be thus provided for without restricting individual liberty."[71]

Friedman's and Hayek's public goods argument was rejected by Robert Nozick, who offered a more consistently antistatist interpretation of classical liberalism. After a discussion of the economics and the ethics of public goods, Nozick concluded, "Since it would violate moral constraints to compel people who are entitled to their holdings to contribute against their will, proponents of such compulsion should attempt to persuade people to ignore the relatively few who don't go along with the scheme of voluntary contributions. Or, is it relatively *many* who are to be compelled to contribute, though they would not so choose, by those who don't want to feel they are 'suckers'?"[72]

The debates among classical liberals on those issues have been vigorous and have focused on a number of questions, such as how competent and trustworthy state institutions—even subject to democratic supervision—may be, whether any compulsion at all is consistent with the principles of liberalism, and whether state provision of even a "safety net" would set in motion a process of fostering dependence and displacing the network of mutual-aid associations that was closely associated with classical liberalism.

The legal theorist A. V. Dicey expressed the fear of state provision that was general among classical liberals:

> The beneficial effect of State intervention, especially in the form of legislation, is direct, immediate, and, so to speak, visible, whilst its evil effects are gradual and indirect, and lie out of sight . . . few are those who realize the undeniable truth that State help kills self-help. Hence the majority of mankind must almost of necessity look with undue favour upon governmental intervention. This natural bias can be counteracted only by the existence, in a given society, as in England between 1830 and 1860, of a presumption or prejudice in favour of individual liberty—that is, of *laissez faire*. The mere decline, therefore, of faith in self-help—and that such a decline has taken place is certain—is of itself sufficient to account for the growth of legislation tending towards socialism.[73]

Herbert Spencer, toward the end of his life, saw the growth of the state provision of services and of measures to substitute coercion for voluntary action as "the New Toryism" and "the Coming Slavery."[74] Like other classical liberals toward the end of the 19th century, he connected the rise of nationalism, imperialism, racism, socialism, and the welfare state as outgrowths from the shared root of collectivism.[75]

The fear of state provision was not limited to Anglo-Saxons but was—and remains—a common feature of classical liberal thought. As Francois Guizot noted, "Nothing is more evident or sacred than the duty of the government to come to the assistance of the classes less favoured by fate, to ease their wretchedness and to assist them in their endeavour to rise toward the blessings of civilization. But to maintain that it is through the defects in the social organisation that all the misery of so many human beings originates, and to impose on the government the task of guaranteeing and distributing equally the good things of life, is to ignore absolutely the human condition, abolish the responsibility inherent in human liberty and excite bad passions through false hopes."[76] Wilhelm von Humboldt despised the Poor Laws for killing charity and hardening hearts: "Does anything tend so effectually to deaden and destroy all true sympathy—all hopeful yet modest entreaty—all trust in man by man? Does not everyone despise the beggar, who finds it more convenient to be cared for in an almshouse than, after struggling with want, to find, not a mere hand flinging him a pittance, but a sympathizing heart?"[77]

There remain questions of the extent of moral obligations to the poor. Those are not easily answered from within the classical liberal tradition, for the simple reason that classical liberal thought distinguishes—as many other traditions do not—between those duties and obligations that are enforceable and those that are not. A classical liberal may embrace the obligation of tithing or of *zakat* but will insist that that obligation may not be made compulsory; it is an expression of one's religious and moral—not legal—obligations. The universalist tendencies of classical liberalism have generally promoted concerns with persons *per se* rather than with co-religionists or co-nationals. The responsibility of not harming others is applicable to all, regardless of whether they are close members of one's own community or complete strangers living in a far-distant nation. As Adam Smith noted, "Mere justice is, upon most occasions, but a negative virtue, and only hinders us from hurting our neighbour. The man who barely abstains from violating either the person, or the estate, or the reputation of his neighbours, has surely very little positive merit. He fulfils, however, all the rules of what is peculiarly called justice, and does every thing which his equals can with propriety force him to do, or which they can punish him for not doing. We may often fulfil all the rules of justice by sitting still and doing nothing."[78] Positive obligations, in the classical liberal view, are normally acquired on the basis of one's acts (they are adventitious rather than connate);[79] as such, one is not born with or assigned particular enforceable obligations to particular people on the basis of the relative poverty of those persons. Because of their focus on eliminating injustice, in the form of the harms visited by some on others, classical liberals led the international movements to abolish forced labor[80] and slavery, which movements promoted the freedom and well-being of the worst-off and most abused members of humanity. Similarly, the moral urgency of the classical liberal case for freedom of trade has focused a substantial amount of attention on the denial of opportunities for improved welfare among the people of poor nations, who are sacrificed by protectionist policies to the well-being of those much wealthier than they. Freeing the poor from coercive controls over their behavior benefits the poor, as well as all who engage in trade; classical liberals see the gains from trade as mutual. It is not a concession to others to remove restrictions on one's own ability to purchase freely. As the 19th-century German classical liberal economist and parliamentarian John Prince Smith argued, "The removal of import tariffs is an economic concession which we grant primarily to ourselves and not merely to foreign countries."[81]

The same logic has been applied to immigration, as classical liberals have generally promoted freedom of movement as much as they have freedom of trade.[82] As such, classical liberals have been active proponents of "globalization" through freedom of speech, trade, and travel.[83] It is ironic that socialists and welfare statists often pose as champions of the poor at the same time that they vigorously defend restrictions on migration that use barbed wire, armed patrols, and other forms of force to keep desperately poor people away from wealthy countries where they would have opportunities to improve their lot. Classical liberals have traditionally opposed such restrictions and favor freedom of trade, travel, and migration, which they consider a superior alternative to state redistributive programs that, they generally argue, are unsuccessful at lifting people from poverty to wealth.

Classical liberal thinkers, despite often robust disagreement among themselves, have agreed that the creation of more wealth is the solution to the alleviation of poverty and that, because outcomes are not themselves generally subject to choice, just and efficient institutions are the key to increasing wealth and diminishing poverty. Moreover, although many make room for state provision of assistance to the poor and indigent, all agree that there is a hierarchy of means for the alleviation of poverty, cascading from personal responsibility and self-help, to mutual aid, to charity, to the least preferred option, state compulsion.

Notes

1. John Locke, *Two Treatises of Government*, ed. Peter Laslett (Cambridge: Cambridge University Press, 1988), *Second Treatise*, VI, pp. 57, 306. Note that for Locke, the term "property" covers far more than the term does in contemporary English, in which it is limited to what Locke termed "estate." Locke, in contrast, refers to "Lives, Liberties, and Estates, which I call by the general name, *Property*." Ibid., *Second Treatise*, IX, pp. 123, 350. Compare also James Madison, in his essay "On Property." "This term in its particular application means 'that dominion which one man claims and exercises over the external things of the world, in exclusion of every other individual.' In its larger and juster meaning, it embraces every thing to which a man may attach a value and have a right, and which leaves to every one else the like advantage." *National Gazette*, March 29, 1792, http://press-pubs.uchicago.edu/founders/docu ments/VIchI6823.html.

2. See Anthony de Jasay, "Liberalism, Loose or Strict," *Independent Review* 9, no. 3 (Winter 2005), pp. 427–32.

3. Robert Nozick, *Anarchy, State, and Utopia* (New York: Basic Books, 1974), p. ix.

4. Quoted by Dugald Stewart from a now lost manuscript in Stewart's "Account of the Life and Writings of Adam Smith, LLD," in Adam Smith, *Essays on Philosophical Subject*, ed. W. P. D. Wightman and J. C. Bryce, vol. 3 of the *Glasgow Edition of the Works and Correspondence of Adam Smith* (Indianapolis: Liberty Fund, 1982), p. 322.

5. Nathan Rosenberg and L. E. Birdzell Jr., *How the West Grew Rich: The Economic Transformation of the Industrial World* (New York: Basic Books, 1986), p. 3.

6. Deirdre McCloskey, "1780–1860: A Survey," in *The Economic History of Britain 1700, vol. I: 1700–1860*, ed. Roderick Floud and Deirdre McCloskey (Cambridge: Cambridge University Press, 2000), p. 242.

7. Peter Bauer, *From Subsistence to Exchange* (Princeton, NJ: Princeton University Press, 2000), p. 6.

8. Carlo Cipolla, *Before the Industrial Revolution: European Society and Economy, 1000–1700* (New York: W. W. Norton, 1980), pp. 9–10.

9. Ibid., pp. 18–19. Economic historian Robert William Fogel has placed great stress on the role of access to nutrition in eliminating beggary:

> The relatively generous poverty program developed in Britain during the second half of the eighteenth century, and the bitter attacks on that program by Malthus and others, have given the unwarranted impression that government transfers played a major role in the secular decline in beggary and homelessness. Despite the relative generosity of English poor relief between 1750 and 1834, beggary and homelessness fluctuated between 10 and 20 percent. Despite the substantial reduction in the proportion of national income transferred to the poor as a result of the poor laws of 1834 and later years, homelessness declined sharply during the late nineteenth century and early twentieth centuries.
>
> The fact is that government transfers were incapable of solving the problems of beggary and homelessness during the eighteenth and much of the nineteenth centuries, because the root cause of the problems was chronic malnutrition. Even during the most generous phase of the relief program, the bottom fifth of the English population was so severely malnourished that it lacked the energy for adequate levels of work.
>
> At the end of the eighteenth century British agriculture, even when supplemented by imports, was simply not productive enough to provide more than 80 percent of the potential labor force with enough calories to sustain regular manual labor. It was huge increases in English productivity during the later part of the nineteenth and the early twentieth centuries that made it possible to feed even the poor at relatively high caloric levels. Begging and homelessness were reduced to exceedingly low levels, by nineteenth century standards, only when the bottom fifth of the population acquired enough calories to permit regular work.

Robert William Fogel, *The Escape from Hunger and Premature Death, 1700–2100: Europe, America, and the Third World* (Cambridge: Cambridge University Press, 2004), pp. 41–42.

10. F. A. Hayek, *The Fatal Conceit: The Errors of Socialism* (Chicago: University of Chicago Press, 1988), pp. 130–31.

11. The classic refutation can be found in Thomas Babington Macaulay's January 1830 review of Robert Southey's 1829 Tory attack on industrialism, *Sir Thomas More;*

or, *Colloquies on the Progress and Prospects of Society*, in "Southey's Colloquies," in Macaulay, *Critical and Historical Essays*, vol. 2 (New York: Dutton, 1967), pp. 187–224. See also for a summary T. S. Ashton, *The Industrial Revolution: 1760–1830* (Oxford: Oxford University Press, 1997).

12. Thomas Babingtom Macaulay, *The History of England from the Accession of James II* (Philadelphia: E. H. Butler, 1849), pp. 291–92. As Macaulay noted in his "Southey's Colloquies," "If we were to prophesy that in the year 1930 a population of fifty millions, better fed, clad, and lodged than the English of our time, will cover these islands, that Sussex and Huntingdonshire will be wealthier than the wealthiest parts of the West Riding of Yorkshire now are, that cultivation, rich as that of a flower-garden, will be carried up to the very tops of Ben Nevis and Helvellyn, that machines constructed on principles yet undiscovered will be in every house, that there will be no highways but railroads, no traveling but by steam, that our debt, vast as it seems to us, will appear to our great-grandchildren a trifling encumbrance, which might easily be paid off in a year or two, many people would think us insane." (p. 223)

13. Étienne Bonnot, Abbé de Condillac, *Commerce and Government Considered in Their Mutual Relationship*, trans. Shelagh Eltis (Cheltenham: Edward Elgar, 1997), p. 103.

14. Adam Smith, *An Inquiry into the Nature and Causes of the Wealth of Nations*, vol. 2, ed. R. H. Campbell and A. S. Skinner (Indianapolis: Liberty Fund, 1981), pp. 869–70.

15. "According therefore, as this produce, or what is purchased with it, bears a greater or smaller proportion to the number of those who are to consume it, the nation will be better or worse supplied with all the necessaries and conveniences for which it has occasion." Adam Smith, *An Inquiry into the Nature and Causes of the Wealth of Nations*, vol. I, ed. R. H. Campbell and A. S. Skinner (Indianapolis: Liberty Fund, 1981), p. 10.

16. Adam Smith, *Lectures On Jurisprudence*, ed. R. L. Meek, D. D. Raphael, and P. G. Stein (Indianapolis: Liberty Fund, 1982), p. 567.

17. See Gordon Tullock, "The Welfare Costs of Tariffs, Monopolies, and Theft," *Western Economic Journal* 5, no. 3 (June 1967), pp. 224–32, and Anne Krueger, "The Political Economy of the Rent-Seeking Society," *American Economic Review 64*, no. 3 (June 1974), pp. 291–303.

18. For a detailed description of the most egregious example of the 20th century, see Götz Aly, *Hitler's Beneficiaries: Plunder, Racial War, and the Nazi Welfare State* (New York: Henry Holt & Co., 2006).

19. The origins and functioning of the apartheid system as such an example is explained by the classical liberal economist W. H. Hutt, *The Economics of the Colour Bar* (London: Andre Deutsch, 1964). White-dominated trade unions succeeded in imposing restrictions on the abilities of blacks to create wealth, thus eliminating them as competitors and reaping special rents (pp. 58–81). See also Ralph Horwitz, *The Political Economy of South Africa* (New York: Frederick A. Praeger Publishers, 1967).

20. Taming violence as a means to create incentives for savings, investment, and productivity is the theme of Robert H. Bates's *Prosperity and Violence: The Political Economy of Development* (New York: W.H. Norton, 2001).

21. For a treatment of the virtues of liberalism, see Deirdre N. McCloskey, *The Bourgeois Virtues: Ethics for an Age of Commerce* (Chicago: University of Chicago Press, 2006). See also Thomas L. Haskell, "Capitalism and the Origins of the Humanitarian Sensibility," parts I and II, *American Historical Review* 90, no. 2 (April 1985), pp. 339–61 and no. 3 (June 1985), pp. 547–66.

22. "After 1795 many parishes in the South, following the policy of the magistrates of Speenhamland, began to give outdoor relief according to a scale based on the price of bread and the size of the family. There was nothing to object to in this: it was only sensible and humane to see that the income of the poor did not fall below the minimum of subsistence. But many of the authorities, confusing the problem of the wage-earner with that of the pauper, undertook to make up from the rates the amount by which the wages of the labourer fell short of their standard. A grant of relief that varies inversely with earnings is the worst form of subsidy, wince it destroys the incentive for the worker to demand, or employer to offer, higher wages." T. S. Ashton, *The Industrial Revolution*, p. 89.

23. Alexis de Tocqueville, *Memoir on Pauperism* (Chicago: Ivan R. Dec. 1997), p. 37.

24. Ibid., p. 58. Tocqueville clearly distinguished "voluntary charity" from "legal charity" and endorsed the former as establishing a "moral tie" "between those two classes whose interests and passions so often conspire to separate them from each other, and although divided by circumstances they are willingly reconciled. This is not the case with legal charity. The latter allows the alms to persist but removes its morality. The law strips the man of wealth of a part of his surplus without consulting him, and he sees the poor man only as a greedy stranger invited by the legislator to share his wealth." (p. 60)

25. Ibid., pp. 62–63.

26. See, for example, the treatment in Jason L. Riley, *Let Them In: The Case for Open Borders*, esp. pp. 91–125. As Riley concludes, "If conservatives are worried about too many snouts at the trough—and if they're remotely interested in any sort of ideological consistency—they should be working to restrict welfare payments, not immigrants." (p. 125)

27. Benjamin M. Friedman, *The Moral Consequences of Economic Growth* (New York: Alfred A. Knopf, 2005), p. 39.

28. See, for example, Franz Oppenheimer, *The State* (Indianapolis: Bobbs-Merrill, 1914). "There are two fundamentally opposed means whereby man, requiring sustenance, is impelled to obtain the necessary means for satisfying his desires. These are work and robbery, ones own labor and the forcible appropriation of the labor of others." (p. 24) Oppenheimer labeled the former the "economic means" and the latter the "political means." See also Vilfredo Pareto, *Sociological Writings*, especially the discussions of "spoliation."

29. See, for example, Herbert Spencer, *Structure, Function and Evolution*, ed. Stanislav Andreski (New York: Charles Scribner's Sons, 1971), pp. 153–65.

30. See, in the context of state-imposed disadvantages on the basis of race, Walter Williams, *The State against Blacks* (New York: McGraw Hill, 1982).

31. Henry Summer Maine described "the movement of the progressive societies" from inherited relations, based on family membership, to personal liberty and civil society as "a movement from Status to contract." Henry Summer Maine, *Ancient Law* (New Brunswick, NJ: Transaction, 2003), p. 170.

32. E. L. Godkin, "The Eclipse of Liberalism," *The Nation*, August 9, 1900. He continued in a very pessimistic vein, "But it now seems that its material comfort has blinded the eyes of the present generation to the cause which made it possible. In the politics of the world, Liberalism is a declining, almost a defunct force."

33. See G. A. Cohen, "Incentives, Inequality, and Community," in *The Tanner Lectures on Human Values*, vol. 13, ed. B. Peterson (Salt Lake City: University of Utah

Press, 1992), pp. 263–329, and Phillip Green, *The Pursuit of Inequality* (New York: Pantheon Books, 1981).

34. Jean-Baptiste Say, *A Treatise on Political Economy* (New York: Augustus M. Kelley, 1971), p. 133.

35. Ibid., 137. See also Jean-Baptiste Say, *Letters to Mr. Malthus* (London: Sherwood, Neely, and Jones, 1821), pp. 3–4: "Let us only look back two hundred years, and suppose that a trader had carried a rich cargo to the places where New York and Philadelphia now stand; could he have sold it? Let us suppose even, that he had succeeded in founding there an agricultural or manufacturing establishment; could he have there sold a single article of his produce? No, undoubtedly. He must have consumed them himself. Why do we now see the contrary? Why is the merchandize carried to, or made at Philadelphia or New York, sure to be sold at the current price? It seems to me evident that is because the cultivators, the traders, and now even the manufacturers of New York, Philadelphia, and the adjacent provinces, create, or send there, some productions, by means of which they purchase what is brought to them from two other quarters." The implications for the classical liberal theory of international relations are obvious and seriously undercut the arguments of advocates of protectionism, as also of imperialist mercantilism.

36. Douglass C. North, "Institutions," *Journal of Economic Perspectives 5, no. I* (Winter 1991), p. 97. See also Douglass C. North, *Structure and Change in Economic History* (New York: W. W. Norton, 1981), pp. 201–2: "Institutions are a set of rules, compliance procedures, and moral and ethical behavioral norms designed to constrain the behavior of individuals in the interests of maximizing the wealth or utility of principles."

37. Daniel Shapiro, *Is the Welfare State Justified?* (Cambridge: Cambridge University Press, 2007), p. 5.

38. "The state can legislate a minimum wage rate. It can hardly require employers to hire at that minimum wage all those who were formerly employed at wages below the minimum." Milton Friedman, *Capitalism and Freedom* (Chicago: University of Chicago, 2002), p. 180.

39. Mancur Olson, *Power and Prosperity* (New York: Basic Books, 2000), pp. 111–34.

40. Vilfredo Pareto, *Sociological Writings*, ed. S. E. Finer (Totowa, NJ: Rowman and Littlefield, 1976), p. 162.

41. For contemporary evidence, see W. Michael Cox and Richard Alm, *Myths of Rich and Poor* (New York: Basic Books, 1999), especially the discussion of upward mobility in incomes (pp. 69–78).

42. Ludwig Lachmann, "The Market Economy and the Distribution of Wealth," in Lachmann, *Capital, Expectations, and the Market Process* (Kansas City: Sheed Andrews and McMeel, 1977), p. 313.

43. Jean-Baptiste Say, *A Treatise on Political Economy*, p. 62.

44. Joyce Appleby notes, in her chapter on "The Dutch as a Source of Evidence," why the relatively "resource-poor" Dutch achieved enormous levels of per capita wealth: "The Dutch have been willing to nurture this complex social organization of the market by protecting the individual initiative on which it throve." *Economic Thought and Ideology in Seventeenth-Century England* (Princeton, NJ: Princeton University Press, 1978), p. 96.

45. Adam Smith, *Essays on Philosophical Subjects*, p. 322.

46. Sarah Grimké, "Legal Disabilities of Women," in *Freedom, Feminism, and the State*, ed. Wendy McElroy (Oakland: Independent Institute, 1991), p. 107.

47. Bernard Bosanquet, "Institutions as Ethical Ideas," in *The Philosophical Theory of the State and Related Essays*, ed. Gerald F. Gaus and William Sweet (South Bend, IN: St. Augustine's Press, 2001), p. 280.

48. As the classical liberal Soviet dissident Vladimir Bukovsky pointed out in his memoirs, "Khrushchev wasn't very far from the truth when he said in one of his speeches: 'If people in our country would cease stealing for even a single day, communism could have been built long ago.' But the thing he failed to understand was that, without this stealing, the Soviet system wouldn't work at all. Without these rigged figures and manipulations hardly a single target would be met, and without this private, hence illegal, initiative, nothing at all would be produced in our country. All these collective and State farms that have become showplaces, without turnovers in the millions, wouldn't have survived for one minute if they hadn't been managed by swindlers." Vladimir Bukovsky, *To Build a Castle: My Life as a Dissenter* (London: Andre Deutsch, 1978), pp. 150–51.

49. Norman Barry, *Welfare* (Buckingham: Open University Press, 1990), p. 120.

50. Otto von Gierke, *Community in Historical Perspective*, ed. Antony Black (Cambridge: Cambridge University Press, 1990), p. 205. See also Antony Black, *Guild and State* (New Brunswick, NJ: Transaction, 2003), esp. pp. 167–83.

51. David Schmidtz, "Taking Responsibility," in David Schmidtz and Robert E. Goodin, *Social Welfare and Individual Responsibility* (Cambridge: Cambridge University Press, 1998), p. 95.

52. David Beito, *From Mutual Aid to the Welfare State: Fraternal Societies and Social Services, 1890–1967* (Chapel Hill: The University of North Carolina Press, 2000), p. 24.

53. David Green makes much of the involvement of the medical profession in promoting the National Insurance Act of 1911, which substituted a monopsony controlled by doctors and their political allies for the competitive market created by multiple friendly societies of working people. See David Green, *Working Class Patients and the Medical Establishment* (New York: St. Martins Press, 1985); the result of substituting involuntary taxes for voluntary dues as a source of payment was, as Green dryly notes, that "pay increases were far more easy to obtain than in the market." (p. 115). The other result was the waning of the friendly societies, as working people found themselves paying twice for the same access to medical services—once to a friendly society or affiliated medical institute, and again to the state.

54. David G. Green, *Reinventing Civil Society: The Rediscovery of Welfare Without Politics* (London: Institute of Economic Affairs, 2000), p. 46.

55. John Stuart Mill, "The Claims of Labour," in *The Collected Works of John Stuart Mill*, vol. 4: *Essays on Economics and Society*, part I, ed. John Robson (Toronto: University of Toronto Press, 1967), p. 372.

56. In Bernard Bosanquet's words, "Morality . . . consists in the social purpose working by its own force on the individual will. Economic Socialism is an arrangement for getting the social purpose carried out just not by its own force, but by the force of those compulsory motives or sanctions which are at the command of the public power." Bernard Bosanquet, "The Antithesis between Individualism and Socialism" (1890), in Bosanquet, *The Philosophical Theory of the State and Related Essays*, p. 329. See also Tibor R. Machan, *Generosity: Virtue in Civil Society* (Washington, D.C.: Cato Institute, 1998).

57. Adam Smith, *The Theory of Moral Sentiments* (Indianapolis: Liberty Fund, 1982), p. 178.

58. Ibid., p. 80.

59. Ibid.

60. See ibid, p. 163: "Without this sacred regard to general rules, there is no man whose conduct can be much depended upon."

61. Ibid., p. 138.

62. Bertrand De Jouvenel, *The Ethics of Redistribution* (Indianapolis: Liberty Fund, 1990), p. 42.

63. Ibid., p. 44.

64. John Stuart Mill, "The Claims of Labour," p. 374.

65. Ibid. Bernard Bosanquet noted the unpromising history of state provision of welfare: "It is often alleged that the time of the factory development a hundred years ago was a time of unmixed Economic Individualism. But this is not so; perhaps the worst evils of that time arose directly from the intentionally lax or 'socialistic' Poor Law. It was the public institutions that for the most part supplied the children who were ill-treated." Bosanquet, "The Antithesis between Individualism and Socialism," p. 330.

66. See David Schmidtz's essay in Schmidtz and Goodin, *Social Welfare and Individual Responsibility*, especially the section on "Consequences Matter," pp. 86–88.

67. Wilhelm Röpke, *A Humane Economy: The Social Framework of the Free Market* (Indianapolis: Liberty Fund, 1971), p. 177.

68. Ibid., p. 175.

69. Milton Friedman, *Capitalism and Freedom*, p. 188.

70. Ibid., p. 191.

71. F. A. Hayek, *The Constitution of Liberty* (Chicago: University of Chicago Press, 1960), p. 257.

72. Nozick, *Anarchy, State, and Utopia*, p. 268.

73. A. V. Dicey, *Lectures on the Relation between Law and Public Opinion in England during the Nineteenth Century* (Indianapolis: Liberty Fund, 2008), p. 182.

74. Herbert Spencer, *The Man vs. the State*, in *Political Writings*, ed. John Offer (Cambridge: Cambridge University Press, 1994).

75. See Sheri Berman, *The Primacy of Politics: Social Democracy and the Making of Europe's Twentieth Century* (Cambridge: Cambridge University Press, 2006), on the common intellectual roots of Marxism, fascism, national socialism, and social democracy.

76. Francois Guizot, "Mémoires pour server à l'histoire de mon temps," in *Western Liberalism: A History in Documents from Locke to Croce*, ed. E. K. Bramstead and K. J. Melhuish (London: Longman Group, 1978), pp. 335–36.

77. Wilhelm von Humboldt, *The Limits of State Action* (Cambridge: Cambridge University Press, 1969), p. 40. See also the description of the opposition of German liberals to Bismarck's modern welfare state in Ralph Raico, "Der Aufstieg des modernen Wohlfartsstaates und die liberale Antwort," in Raico, *Die Partei der Freiheit: Studien zur Geschichte des deutschen Liberalismus* (Stuggart: Lucius & Lucius, 1999), pp. 153–79.

78. Adam Smith, *The Theory of Moral Sentiments*, p. 82.

79. Compare Samuel Pufendorf on "connate" and "adventitious" obligations: "Now obligation can, by reason of its origin, be divided into connate and adventitious. The former belongs to all men immediately upon birth by virtue of the fact that they are such, fully exerting itself as soon as they have begun to be able, on account of their age, to understand its force and to regulate their action through reason.... Adventitious obligations are those voluntarily assumed by those who have already been born, or those enjoined by the command of a superior or by law." *The Political*

Writings of Samuel Pufendorf, ed. Craig L. Carr, trans. Michael J. Seidler (Oxford: Oxford University Press, 1994), p. 50.

80. See, for example, the efforts by Anne Robert Jacques Turgot to eliminate forced peasant labor (the corvée) in France, described in *The Life and Writings of Turgot*, ed. W. Walker Stephens (New York: Burt Franklin, 1971), esp. pp. 124–49.

81. John Prince Smith, "On the Significance of Freedom of Trade in World Politics," in Bramstead and Melhuish, *Western Liberalism*, p. 357. The insistence on the value of unilateral free trade by classical liberals has received greater emphasis in recent years; see Razeen Sally, *Trade Policy, New Century: The WTO, FTAs, and Asia Rising* (London: Institute of Economic Affairs, 2008).

82. For recent works, see Philippe Legrain, *Immigrants: Your Country Needs Them* (London: Little, Brown, 2006), and Jason L. Riley, *Let Them In: The Case for Open Borders* (New York: Gotham Books, 2008).

83. The term "globalization" has many meanings. The project of the Soviet Union, for example, entailed worldwide imposition of one-party Communist rule; that is one kind of "globalization." Even nationalist and anticosmopolitan forces promote a kind of "globalization," in the form of a global movement of competing nationalisms, an idea that contains the seeds of endless conflict. Classical liberals have promoted certain universal standards of peaceful interaction through voluntary trade, tourism, travel, migration, and exchange of ideas. The result is compatible with a wide variety of different cultural forms, although hostile to any that are imposed by force on nonconsenting parties. For classical liberal treatments of such topics, see Tom G. Palmer, *Globalization and Culture: Homogeneity, Diversity, Identity, Liberty* (Berlin: Liberales Institut, 2004), http://tomgpalmer.com/wp-content/uploads/papers/liberales2.pdf, and "Globalization, Cosmopolitanism, and Personal Identity," *Etica & Politica*, no. 2 (2003), http://tomgpalmer.com/wp-content/uploads/papers/palmer-globcosmoidentity.pdf. Classical liberals have been disparaged by socialist critics as "neoliberals," a term that virtually no classical liberal has accepted, partly because the term is used to refer not only to freer trade, travel, and migration but to often very illiberal statist development programs promoted by state-backed organizations, such as the World Bank, the International Monetary Fund, and the USAID, which classical liberals have traditionally opposed.

13. The Morality of Capitalism

A few words about the title—*The Morality of Capitalism*—are in order. The term "capitalism" refers not just to markets for the exchange of goods and services, which have existed since time immemorial, but to the system of innovation, wealth creation, and social change that has brought to billions of people prosperity that was unimaginable to earlier generations of human beings.

This essay is about the moral justification of what philosopher Robert Nozick called "capitalist acts among consenting adults."[1] It's about the system of cooperative production and free exchange characterized by the predominance of such acts.

Capitalism refers to a legal, social, economic, and cultural system that embraces equality of rights and "careers open to talent" and that energizes decentralized innovation and processes of trial and error—what the economist Joseph Schumpeter called "creative destruction"—through the voluntary processes of market exchange. Capitalist culture celebrates the entrepreneur, the scientist, the risk-taker, the innovator, the creator. Although derided as materialistic by philosophers (notably Marxists) who are themselves adherents of materialism, capitalism is at its core a spiritual and cultural enterprise. As the historian Joyce Appleby noted in her recent study *The Relentless Revolution: A History of Capitalism*, "Because capitalism is a cultural system and not simply an economic one, it cannot be explained by material factors alone."[2]

Capitalism is a system of cultural, spiritual, and ethical values. As the economists David Schwab and Elinor Ostrom noted in a seminal game-theoretic study of the role of norms and rules in maintaining open economies, free markets rest firmly on the norms that constrain us from stealing and that are "trust enhancing."[3] Far from being an amoral arena for the clash of interests, as capitalism is often portrayed by those who seek to undermine or destroy it,

---

Originally published as the introduction to *The Morality of Capitalism*, edited by Tom G. Palmer. Ottawa, IL: Jameson Books, 2011.

capitalist interaction is highly structured by ethical norms and rules. Indeed, capitalism rests on a rejection of the ethics of loot and grab, the means by which most wealth enjoyed by the wealthy has been acquired in other economic and political systems. (In fact, in many countries today, and for much of human history, it has been widely understood that those who are rich are rich because they took from others, and especially because they have access to organized force—in today's terms, the state. Such predatory elites use this force to gain monopolies and to confiscate the produce of others through taxes. They feed at the state treasury and they benefit from state-imposed monopolies and restrictions on competition. It's only under conditions of capitalism that people commonly become wealthy without being criminals.)

Consider what the economist and historian Deirdre McCloskey calls *"The Great Fact"*: "Real income per head nowadays exceeds that around 1700 or 1800 in, say, Britain and other countries that have experienced modern economic growth by such a large factor as sixteen, at least."[4] That is unprecedented in all of human history. McCloskey's estimate is, in fact, quite conservative. It doesn't—it can't—take fully into account the amazing advances in science and technology that have put the cultures of the world at our fingertips.

Capitalism puts human creativity to the service of humanity by respecting and encouraging entrepreneurial innovation, that elusive factor that explains the difference between the way we live now and how generation after generation after generation of our ancestors lived prior to the 19th century. The innovations that have transformed human life for the better are not merely scientific and technological, but institutional, as well. New business firms of all kinds voluntarily coordinate the work efforts of enormous numbers of people. New financial markets and instruments connect the savings and investment decisions of billions of people 24 hours a day. New telecommunications networks bring together people from the corners of the world. (Today I had conversations with friends in Finland, China, Morocco, the United States, and Russia, and Facebook comments and communications from friends and acquaintances in the United States, Canada, Pakistan, Denmark, France, and Kyrgyzstan.) New products offer us opportunities for comfort, delight, and education unimaginable to previous generations. (I am writing this on my Apple MacBook Pro.) Those changes have made our societies in countless ways dramatically unlike all human societies that have preceded them.

Capitalism is not just about building stuff, in the way that socialist dictators used to exhort their slaves to "Build the Future!" Capitalism is about creating value, not merely working hard or making sacrifices or being busy. Those who fail to understand capitalism are quick to support "job creation" programs to create work. They have misunderstood the point of work, much less the point of capitalism. In a much-quoted story, the economist Milton Friedman was shown the construction on a massive new canal in Asia. When he noted that it was odd that the workers were moving huge amounts of earth and rock with small shovels, rather than earth moving equipment, he was told "You don't understand; this is a jobs program." His response: "Oh, I thought you were trying to build a canal. If you're seeking to create jobs, why didn't you issue them spoons, rather than shovels?"

The mercantilist and cronyist H. Ross Perot, when running for president of the United States in 1992, lamented during the presidential debates that Americans were buying computer chips from Taiwan and selling the Taiwanese potato chips. It seemed that Perot was ashamed that Americans were selling mere potato chips; he had bought into Lenin's view that value is added only by industrial production in factories. Economist Michael Boskin of Stanford University correctly noted that if you're talking about a dollar's worth of computer chips, or a dollar's worth of potato chips, you're talking about a dollar's worth. Adding value by growing potatoes in Idaho or by etching silicon in Taipei is adding value. Comparative advantage[4] is a key to specialization and trade; there is nothing degrading about producing value, as a farmer, as a furniture mover (I worked with three movers today to move much of my library and I have a very solid sense of how much value they added to my life), as a financier, and so on. The market—not arrogant mercantilist politicians—shows us when we are adding value, and without free markets, we cannot know.

Capitalism is not just about people trading butter for eggs in local markets, which has gone on for millennia. It's about adding value through the mobilization of human energy and ingenuity on a scale never seen before in human history, to create wealth for common people that would have dazzled and astonished the richest and most powerful kings, sultans, and emperors of the past. It's about the erosion of long-entrenched systems of power, domination, and privilege, and the opening of "careers to talent." It's about the replacement of force by persuasion.[5] It's about the replacement of envy by accomplishment.[6] It's about what has made my life possible, and yours.

(The only thing that the kings and sultans and emperors had that ordinary people today don't have was power over other people and the ability to command them. They had vast palaces built by slaves or financed by taxes, but no indoor heating or cooling; slaves and servants but no washing machines or dishwashers; armies of couriers but no cell phones or Wi-Fi; court doctors and magi, but no anesthetic to ease their agony or antibiotics to cure infections; they were powerful, but they were miserably poor by our standards.)

The History of a Word

Free markets, understood as systems of free exchange among persons with well-defined, legally secure, and transferable rights in scarce resources, are a necessary condition for the wealth of the modern world. But as economic historians, most notably Deirdre McCloskey, have convincingly shown, they are not sufficient. Something else is needed: an ethics of free exchange and of wealth production through innovation.

A few words about the use of the term "capitalism" are in order. The social historian Fernand Braudel traced the term "capital" to the period spanning the 12th and 13th centuries, when it referred to "funds, stock of merchandise, sum of money, or money carrying interest."[8] Of the many uses of the term "capitalist" that Braudel catalogued, he noted dryly, "The word is never . . . used in a friendly sense."[9] The word "Capitalism" emerged as a term, generally of abuse, in the 19th century, e.g., when the French socialist Louis Blanc defined the term as "the appropriation of capital by some to the exclusion of others."[10] Karl Marx used the term "capitalist mode of production," and it was his ardent follower Werner Sombart who popularized the term "capitalism" in his influential 1912 book *Der Moderne Kapitalismus*. (Marx's collaborator, Friedrich Engels, considered Sombart the only thinker in Germany who really understood Marx; Sombart later became a cheerleader for another form of anticapitalism, National Socialism, i.e., Nazism.)

In their attack on the "capitalists" and the "capitalist mode of production," Marx and Engels noted that "the bourgeoisie" (his term for the "class" who owned "the means of production") had radically changed the world:

> The bourgeoisie, during its rule of scarcely one hundred years, has created more massive and more colossal productive forces than have all preceding generations together. Subjection of Nature's forces to man, machinery, application of chemistry to industry and agriculture, steam-navigation, railways, electric telegraphs, clearing of whole continents for cultivation, canalisation of rivers, whole populations conjured out of the ground—what earlier century had even a presentiment that such productive forces slumbered in the lap of social labour?[11]

Marx and Engels marveled at not only technological innovation, but at "whole populations conjured out of the ground," which is a striking way to describe falling death rates, rising living standards, and increasing life spans. Despite such accomplishments, of course, Marx and Engels called for the destruction of the "capitalist mode of production," or, to be more precise, they thought that it would destroy itself and usher in a new system that would be so wonderful that it was not necessary—indeed, it was even offensively unscientific—to offer even the slightest hint as to how it might work.[12]

More importantly, Marx and Engels grounded their critique of capitalism (a critique that, despite the failure of all communist orders to fulfill their promises, remains extraordinarily influential among intellectuals around the world) on a mass of confusion over what they meant by the term "bourgeoisie," which they connected to the "capitalist mode of production." On the one hand, they use the term to mean owners of "capital" who organize productive enterprises, but on the other they use it to refer to those who live off of the state and its power, as Marx did in one of his most interesting essays on politics:

> [T]he material interest of the French bourgeoisie is most intimately imbricated [Note: a term for "overlapping"] precisely with the maintenance of that extensive and highly ramified state machine. It is that machine which provides its surplus population with jobs, and makes up through state salaries for what it cannot pocket in the form of profits,

interest, rents, and fees. Its political interest equally compelled it daily to increase the repression, and therefore to
increase the resources and the personnel of the state power.[13]

So on the one hand, Marx identified the "bourgeoisie" with the
entrepreneurs who gave "a cosmopolitan character to production
and consumption in every country," who made "national one-sided-
ness and narrow-mindedness" "more and more impossible," who
created "a world literature," who brought about "the rapid improvement of all instruments of production" and "immensely facilitated
the means of communication," and who overcame "the barbarians'
obstinate hatred of foreigners" by the "cheap prices of commodities"
they offered.[14] On the other, he used "bourgeoisie" to refer to those
who live off of "public credit" (i.e., government debt):

> The whole of the modern money market, the whole of the
> banking business, is most intimately interwoven with public
> credit. A part of their business capital is necessarily put out
> at interest in short-term public funds. Their deposits, the
> capital put at their disposal by merchants and industrialists
> and distributed by them among the same people, flow in
> part from the dividends of holders of government bonds.[15]

Marx saw the "bourgeoisie" as intimately involved in and benefit-
ing from the struggle to control the machinery of the state:

> All political upheavals perfected this machine instead of
> smashing it. The parties that strove in turn for mastery
> regarded possession of this immense state edifice as the main
> booty for the victory.[16]

In the words of the historian Shirley Gruner, "Marx felt he had
got a grip on reality when he found the 'bourgeoisie' but in fact he
had merely got hold of a very slippery term."[17] In some texts, Marx
used the term to refer to those innovative entrepreneurs who organize productive enterprises and invest in wealth creation, and in
others he used it to refer to those who cluster around the state, who
live off of taxation, who lobby to prohibit competition and restrict
the freedom to trade; in brief, to those who invest, not in creating
wealth, but in securing the power to redistribute or destroy the
wealth of others, and to keep markets closed, the poor in their place,
and society under their thumbs.

Because of the influence of Marx and his follower Sombart, the term "capitalism" came into general use. It's worth remembering that the term was popularized by people who not only confused productive entrepreneurship and market exchange with living off of taxes taken from others, but who advocated the abolition of property, markets, money, prices, the division of labor, and the entire edifice of liberalism: individual rights, religious freedom, freedom of speech, equality before the law, and constitutionally limited democratic government.

Not uncommonly, like many terms of abuse, "capitalism" was taken up by some of those intellectual advocates of free markets against whom the term was wielded. As a result of its history, those who adopted the term "capitalism" for what they advocated, or even simply as a neutral term for social scientific discussion, were disadvantaged by the facts that (1) the term was used equivocally (to refer to both free market entrepreneurship and to living off taxes and government power and patronage), and (2) that it was almost always used in a distinctly negative manner.

Some suggest abandoning the term altogether, because it is so fraught with conflicting meanings and ideological overtones.[18] That's tempting, but there remains a problem. Merely allowing people to trade freely and to be guided by profits and losses, while certainly necessary for economic progress, is not sufficient for the creation of the modern world. Modern markets both emerged from and fuel a whirlwind of institutional, technological, cultural, artistic, and social innovation that transcends the model of people exchanging eggs for butter. Modern free-market capitalism innovates, not at a glacial pace over millennia, but faster and faster—precisely what both the socialists (notably Marx) and their allies, the anti-market conservatives, found so terrifying about the modern world. In his *Capitalism, Socialism, and Democracy*, Joseph Schumpeter criticized those for whom "the problem that is usually being visualized is how capitalism administers existing structures, whereas the relevant problem is how it creates and destroys them."[19]

Modern free markets are not merely places of exchange, as were the market fairs of old. They are characterized by waves of "creative destruction"; what was new ten years ago is already old, superseded by improved versions, by new devices, institutional arrangements, technologies, and ways of interacting that were unimagined by any-one. That is what distinguishes modern free markets from the markets of old. The best available term to distinguish the free market relations that have made the modern world from those markets that preceded it, in my opinion, is "capitalism."

Capitalism isn't a form of disorder, though. It's a form of spontane-ous order, which emerges from a process. (Some writers refer to such orders as "emergent orders.") The predictable constancy of the rule of law and security of rights make possible such innovation. As David Boaz noted in *The Futurist*,

> People have always had trouble seeing the order in an appar-ently chaotic market. Even as the price system constantly moves resources toward their best use, on the surface the market seems the very opposite of order—businesses failing, jobs being lost, people prospering at an uneven pace, invest-ments revealed to have been wasted. The fast-paced Innova-tion Age will seem even more chaotic, with huge businesses rising and falling more rapidly than ever, and fewer people having long-term jobs. But the increased efficiency of trans-portation, communications, and capital markets will in fact mean even more order than the market could achieve in the industrial age. The point is to avoid using coercive govern-ment to "smooth out the excesses" or "channel" the market toward someone's desired result.[20]

Free-Market Capitalism vs. Crony Capitalism

In order to avoid the confusion caused by equivocal use of the term "capitalism" by socialist intellectuals, "free-market capitalism" should be clearly distinguished from "crony capitalism," from the system that has mired so many nations in corruption and backward-ness. In many countries, if someone is rich, there is a very good chance that he (rarely she) holds political power or is a close relative, friend, or supporter—in a word, a "crony"—of those who do hold power, and that that person's wealth came, not from being a pro-ducer of valued goods, but from enjoying the privileges that the state can confer on some at the expense of others. Sadly, "crony capitalism" is a term that can with increasing accuracy also be applied to the economy of the United States, a country in which failed firms are routinely "bailed out" with money taken from taxpayers, in which the national capital is little more than a gigantic pulsating hive of "rent-seeking" lobbyists, bureaucrats, politicians, consultants, and hacks, and in which appointed officials of the Treasury Department and the central bank (the Federal Reserve System) take it on themselves to reward some firms and harm others. Such corrupt cronyism shouldn't be confused with "free-market capitalism," which refers to a system of production and exchange that is based on the rule of law, on equality of rights for all, on the freedom to choose, on the freedom to trade, on the freedom to innovate, on the guiding discipline of profits and losses, and on the right to enjoy the fruits of one's labors, of one's savings, of one's investments, without fearing confiscation or restriction from those who have invested, not in production of wealth, but in political power.

The waves of change that free-market capitalism creates are often resented by entrenched elites. As they see the world, minorities become uppity and the lower classes no longer know their place. More shocking, from their perspective, is that under free-market capitalism women assert their own worth. Status is undermined. People create relationships based on choice and consent, rather than birth or status.[21] The conservative hatred of free-market capitalism, which was very neatly summarized and incorporated by Marx into his writings, reflects anger at such change and often anger at the loss of privilege. Leo Melamed (the Chairman Emeritus of the CME Group [formerly the Chicago Mercantile Exchange] whose own life story of escaping from the Gestapo and the KGB and going on to revolutionize world finance is a story of courage and vision), drew on his experience when he said that "in Chicago's financial markets it is not what you are—your personal pedigree, your family origin, your physical infirmities, your gender—but your ability to determine what the customer wants and where the market is headed. Little else matters."[22] Embracing free-market capitalism means embracing the freedom to change, to innovate, to invent. It means accommodating change and respecting the freedom of others to do as they please with what is theirs. It means making place for new technologies, new scientific theories, new forms of art, and new identities and new relationships. It means embracing the freedom to create wealth, which is the only means to the elimination of poverty. (Wealth has causes, but poverty does not; poverty is what results if wealth production does not take place, whereas wealth is not what results if poverty production does not take place.)[23] It means celebrating human liberation and realizing human potential.

Understanding Both Sides

In the course of my own career, I have read hundreds of books that attacked free-market capitalism; I've thought about the arguments and wrestled with them. In contrast, it is unusual to find critics of free-market capitalism who have read more than one author who dared to offer a defense of free-market capitalism. The one author who is most commonly cited, at least in the modern Anglo-Saxon intellectual world, is Robert Nozick, and even then it becomes clear that only one chapter of one book was read, the one in which he offered a challenging hypothetical thought experiment to test enemies of free-market capitalism. Most socialists think it sufficient to read one essay and rebut one thought experiment.[24] After reading and rebutting one argument, if those who condemn free-market capitalism even think it worthwhile to continue the critique, they usually rely on one or another misstatement or garbled version of what Milton Friedman or Ayn Rand or F. A. Hayek or Adam Smith believed, offered without citation.

To take one recent prominent example, Harvard professor Michael Sandel offered a rebuttal to the case for free-market capitalism in his recent book *Justice: What's the Right Thing to Do?*; besides Nozick, he cited Friedman and Hayek, but made it clear that he had not read them. He quoted Friedman asking, "Are we entitled to use coercion to prevent him [someone who won't save for retirement] from doing what he chooses to do?"[25] But he failed to note that in the very next paragraph Friedman actually offered reasons for such coercion[26] and stated that "The weight of this argument clearly depends on fact."[27] (Friedman was invoking the classical liberal principle of the "presumption of liberty,"[28] not making a categorical statement about rights, as Sandel incorrectly claims.) Sandel also states that "In *The Constitution of Liberty* (1960), the Austrian-born economist-philosopher Friedrich A. Hayek (1899–1992) argued that any attempt to bring about greater economic equality was bound to be coercive and destructive of a free society"—a claim that Hayek does not, in fact, make; he does argue that "progressive income taxation" (in which the rates of tax increase with income) is incompatible with the rule of law, for "unlike proportionality, progression provides no principle which tells us what the relative burden of different persons ought to be,"[29] but that is not the same as arguing that any attempt to bring about greater economic equality (say, by eliminating special subsidies and privileges for the rich) was bound to be coercive. (Both Sandel's erroneous claim and his description show that Sandel didn't even bother to consult Hayek's book; one wonders whether he would have described Adam Smith's *An Inquiry into the Nature and Causes of the Wealth of Nations* as a book about how pins are manufactured.)

Serious people should do better. I strongly encourage you, the reader of this essay, to do better. Read the best criticisms of free-market capitalism. Read Marx. Read Sombart. Read Rawls. Read Sandel. Understand them. Be open to being convinced by them. Think about them. I've read more arguments against free-market capitalism than most enemies of free-market capitalism have read, and I think I could usually make their case better than they can, because I know it better. What's typically missing is the other side of the debate, the side that is rarely even acknowledged to exist.

It's worth taking a chance. Wrestle with the arguments offered on both sides of the debate over free markets. Think about them. Then make up your own mind.

Notes

1. Robert Nozick, *Anarchy, State, and Utopia* (New York: Basic Books, 1974), p. 163.

2. Joyce Appleby, *The Relentless Revolution: A History of Capitalism* (New York: W. W. Norton and Co., 2010), pp. 25–26.

3. David Schwab and Elinor Ostrom, "The Vital Role of Norms and Rules in Maintaining Open Public and Private Economies," in *Moral Markets: The Critical Role of Values in the Economy*, ed. Paul J. Zak (Princeton: Princeton University Press, 2008), pp. 204–27.

4. Deirdre McCloskey, *Bourgeois Dignity: Why Economics Can't Explain the Modern World* (Chicago: University of Chicago Press, 2010), p. 48.

5. For a simple arithmetic explanation of the principle of comparative advantage, see http://tinyurl.com/p3vaztc.

6. For a remarkable account of the general decline of the experience of force in human affairs, see James L. Payne, *A History of Force* (Sandpoint, Idaho: Lytton Publishing, 2004).

7. Envy as an impulse harmful to social cooperation and inimical to free-market capitalism has been studied by many thinkers. A recent and interesting approach that draws on the Indian classic epic The Mahabharata can be found in Gurcharan Das, *The Difficulty of Being Good: On the Subtle Art of Dharma* (New York: Oxford University Press, 2009), esp. pp. 1–32.

8. Fernand Braudel, *Civilization and Capitalism, 15th–18th Century: The Wheels of Commerce* (New York: Harper & Row, 1982), p. 232.

9. Ibid., p. 236.

10. Louis Blanc, *Organisation du Travail* (Paris: Bureau de la Societé de l'Industrie Fraternelle, 1847), cited in Braudel, *Civilization and Capitalism, 15th–18th Century: The Wheels of Commerce*, op. cit., p. 237.

11. Karl Marx and Frederick Engels, *Manifesto of the Communist Party*, in Karl Marx and Frederick Engels, *Collected Works, Volume 6* (1976: Progress Publishers, Moscow), p. 489.

12. For a devastating seminal critique of Marx's economic theories, see Eugen von Böhm-Bawerk, *Karl Marx and the Close of His System* (1896; New York: Augustus M. Kelley, 1949). A better translation of Böhm-Bawerk's title would be, "On the Conclusion of the Marxian System." Böhm-Bawerk refers in his title to the publication of the third volume of *Capital*, which "concluded" the Marxian system. It should be noted that Böhm-Bawerk's criticism is altogether an internal critique, and does not rest in any way on the results of the "marginal revolution" in economic science that took place in 1870. See also the essay by Ludwig von Mises, "Economic Calculation in the Socialist Commonwealth," in *Collectivist Economic Planning*, ed. F. A. Hayek (London: George Routledge & Sons, 1935) on the inability of collectivism to solve the problem of economic calculation.

13. Karl Marx, "The Eighteenth Brumaire of Louis Bonaparte," in *Karl Marx: Surveys from Exile: Political Writings, Volume II*, ed. David Fernbach (New York: Vintage Books, 1974), p. 186. I describe the contradictions and confusions of Marxian economic and social analysis in "Classical Liberalism, Marxism, and the Conflict of Classes: The Classical Liberal Theory of Class Conflict," in *Realizing Freedom: Libertarian Theory, History, and Practice* (Washington, D.C.: Cato Institute, 2009), pp. 255–75.

14. Karl Marx and Friedrich Engels, *Manifesto of the Communist Party*, p. 488.

15. Karl Marx, "The Eighteenth Brumaire of Louis Bonaparte," p. 222.

16. Karl Marx, "The Eighteenth Brumaire of Louis Bonaparte," p. 238.

17. Shirley M. Gruner, *Economic Materialism and Social Moralism* (The Hague: Mouton, 1973), pp. 189–190.

18. See, for example, Sheldon Richman, "Is Capitalism Something Good?" www.thefreemanonline.org/columns/tgif/is-capitalism-something-good/.

19. Joseph Schumpeter, *Capitalism, Socialism, and Democracy* (London: Routledge, 2006), p. 84.

20. David Boaz, "Creating a Framework for Utopia," *The Futurist*, December 24, 1996, www.cato.org/pub_display.php?pub_id = 5976.

21. The legal historian Henry Sumner Maine famously described "the movement of the progressive societies" from inherited relations, based on family membership to personal liberty and civil society as "a movement from Status to Contract." Henry Sumner Maine, *Ancient Law* (Brunswick, NJ: Transaction Publishers, 2003), p. 170.

22. Leo Melamed, "Reminiscences of a Refugee," in *For Crying Out Loud: From Open Outcry to the Electronic Screen* (Hoboken, NJ: John Wiley & Sons, 2009), p. 136.

23. I address the issue of poverty and free-market capitalism more systematically in "Classical Liberalism, Poverty, and Morality," in *Poverty and Morality: Religious and Secular Perspectives*, ed. William A. Galston and Peter H. Hoffenberg (New York: Cambridge University Press, 2010), pp. 83–114.

24. This is an especially common attitude among philosophers, perhaps the saddest of whom was the late G. A. Cohen, who devoted much of his intellectual career to

attempting, but failing, to refute Nozick's one thought experiment. Citations to Cohen's articles and a demonstration of the failure of his critique can be found in "G. A. Cohen on Self-Ownership, Property, and Equality," in *Realizing Freedom*, pp. 139–54.

25. Quoted in Michael Sandel, *Justice: What's the Right Thing to Do?* (New York: Farrar, Straus, and Giroux, 2009), p. 61.

26. Milton Friedman, Capitalism and Freedom (Chicago: University of Chicago Press, 1962), p. 188: "A possible justification on liberal principles for compulsory purchase of annuities is that the improvident will not suffer the consequences of their own action but will impose costs on others. We shall not, it is said, be willing to see the indigent aged suffer in dire poverty. We shall assist them by private and public charity. Hence the man who does not provide for his old age will become a public charge. Compelling him to buy an annuity is justified not for his own good but for the good of the rest of us."

27. Milton Friedman, *Capitalism and Freedom* (Chicago: University of Chicago Press, 1962), p. 188.

28. For an explanation, see Anthony de Jasay, "Liberalism, Loose or Strict," *Independent Review*, vol. IX, no. 3, Winter 2005, pp. 427–32.

29. F. A. Hayek, *The Constitution of Liberty* (Chicago: University of Chicago Press, 1960), p. 313.

14. Adam Smith and the Myth of Greed

One frequently hears it said that Adam Smith believed that if people were only to act selfishly, all would go well in the world, that "Greed makes the world go round." Smith, of course, did not believe that relying exclusively on selfish motivations would make the world a better place, nor did he promote or encourage selfish behavior. His extensive discussion in *The Theory of Moral Sentiments* of the role of the "impartial spectator" should put such misinterpretations to rest. Smith was not an advocate of selfishness, but he was also not naive enough to think that selfless devotion to the welfare of others (or professing such devotion) would make the world better, either. As Steven Holmes noted in his corrective essay "The Secret History of Self-Interest,"[1] Smith knew very well the destructive effects of many "disinterested" passions, such as envy, malice, revenge, zealotry, and the like. The selfless zealots of the Spanish Inquisition did what they did in the hope that in the last moment of agony the dying heretics might repent and receive God's grace. That was known as the doctrine of salvific justification. Humbert de Romans, in his instruction to inquisitors, insisted that they justify to the congregation the punishments to be imposed on heretics, for "We beg God, and we beg you, that you should beg him together with me, that from the gift of his grace he should make it that those to be punished bear so patiently the punishments that we propose to impose upon them (in the demand of justice, nevertheless with grief), that it might redound to their salvation. Because of this we impose such a punishment."[2] In Smith's view, such selfless devotion to the welfare of others was not obviously morally superior to the allegedly selfish merchants seeking to enrich themselves by selling ale and salted fish to thirsty and hungry customers.

Originally published in *After the Welfare State*, edited by Tom G. Palmer. Ottawa, IL: Jameson Books, 2012.

Smith is hardly a general endorser of selfish behavior, for whether such motivations lead "as if by an invisible hand" to the promotion of the general good depends very much on the context of the actions, and particularly on the institutional setting. Sometimes the self-centered desire to be liked by others can lead one to adopt a moral perspective, by thinking about how we appear to others. In the kind of small-scale interpersonal settings typically described in *The Theory of Moral Sentiments*, such motivation may redound to the general benefit, for the "desire to become ourselves the objects of the like agreeable sentiments, and to be as amiable and as admirable as those whom we love and as admirable as those whom we love and admire the most" requires us to "become the impartial spectators of our own character and conduct."[3] Even in cases of apparently excessive self-interest, in the right institutional setting, it can be to the benefit of others, such as in the story Smith tells of the poor man's son whose ambition causes him to work tirelessly to accumulate wealth, only to find after a lifetime of hard work that he is no happier than the simple beggar sunning himself on the side of the road; the ambitiously excessive pursuit of self-interest on the part of the poor man's son benefited the rest of humanity by accumulating the wealth that made the very existence of many others possible, for "the earth by these labours of mankind has been obliged to redouble her natural fertility, and to maintain a greater multitude of inhabitants."[4]

In the larger context of political economy described in many passages of *An Inquiry into the Nature and Causes of the Wealth of Nations*, specifically those involving interaction with the institutions of the state, the pursuit of self-interest is not so likely to have positive effects. The self-interest of merchants, for example, leads them to lobby the state to create cartels, protectionism, and even war: "to expect, indeed, that the freedom of trade should ever be entirely restored in Great Britain, is as absurd as to expect that an Oceana or Utopia should ever be established in it. Not only are the prejudices of the public, but what is much more unconquerable, the private interests of many individuals, irresistibly oppose it."[5] The trifling gains of merchants of monopolies are purchased at the expense of horrific burdens to the public in the case of empires and wars:

> [I]n the system of laws which has been established for the management of our American and West Indian colonies, the interest of the home-consumer has been sacrificed to that of

the producer with a more extravagant profusion than in all our other commercial regulations. A great empire has been established for the sole purpose of raising up a nation of customers who should be obliged to buy from the shops of our different producers, all the goods with which these could supply them. For the sake of that little enhancement of price which this monopoly might afford our producers, the home-consumers have been burdened with the whole expense of maintaining and defending that empire. For this purpose, and for this purpose only, in the two last wars, more than two hundred millions have been spent, and a new debt of more than a hundred and seventy millions has been contracted over and above all that had been expended for the same purpose in former wars. The interest of this debt alone is not only greater than the whole extraordinary profit, which, it ever could be pretended, was made by the monopoly of the colony trade, but than the whole value of that trade or than that whole value of the goods, which at an average have been annually exported to the colonies.[6]

So Smith's views on whether, in the words of Gordon Gecko, the fictional character from Oliver Stone's film *Wall Street*, "Greed is good" is decidedly "sometimes yes, and sometimes no" (as if all self-interested behavior was "greed"). The difference is in the institutional setting.

What about the common view that markets promote selfish behavior, that the psychological attitude engendered by exchange encourages selfishness? I know of no good reason to think that markets promote selfishness or greed, in the sense that market interaction increases the quantum of greediness or the propensity of people to be selfish, over what is observed in societies governed by states that suppress or discourage or interfere in or disrupt markets. In fact, markets make it possible for the most altruistic, as well as the most selfish, to advance their purposes in peace. Those who dedicate their lives to helping others, use markets to advance their purposes, no less than those whose goal is to increase their store of wealth. Some of the latter even accumulate wealth for the purpose of increasing their ability to help others. George Soros and Bill Gates are examples of the latter; they earn huge amounts of money, at least partly in order to increase their ability to help others through their vast charitable activities. The creation of wealth in the pursuit of profits enables them to be generous.

A philanthropist or saint wants to use the wealth available to her to feed, clothe, and comfort the greatest number of people. Markets allow her to find the lowest prices for blankets, for food, and for medicines to care for those who need her assistance. Markets allow the creation of wealth that can be used to help the unfortunate and facilitate the charitable to maximize their ability to help others. Markets make possible the charity of the charitable.

A common mistake is to identify the purposes of people exclusively with their "self-interest," which is then in turn confused with "selfishness." The purposes of people in the market are indeed purposes of selves, but as selves with purposes we are also concerned about the interests and well being of others: our family members, our friends, our neighbors, and even total strangers whom we will never meet. Indeed, markets help to condition people to consider the needs of others, including total strangers.

Philip Wicksteed offered a nuanced treatment of motivations in market exchanges. Rather than using "selfishness" to describe the motivations for engaging in market exchanges (one might go to the market to buy food for the poor, for example), he coined the term "non-tuism."[7] We might sell our products to gain money to be able to help out our friends, or even distant strangers, but when we haggle for the lowest or highest price, we rarely do so out of a concern for the well being of the party with whom we're bargaining. If we do, we are making an exchange and a gift, which somewhat complicates the nature of the exchange. Those who deliberately pay more than they need to are rarely good businesspeople and, as H.B. Acton noted in his book *The Morals of the Markets*,[8] running a business at a loss is in general a very foolish, even stupid, way to be philanthropic.

To those who praise involvement in politics over involvement in industry and commerce, it is worth remembering that the former can do a great deal of harm and rarely does much good. Voltaire, writing before Smith, saw the difference clearly. In his essay "On Trade" from his *Letters Concerning the English Nation* (written by Voltaire in English, in which he was quite fluent, and then rewritten by him in French and published as *Lettres Philosophiques*) he noted that,

> In *France* the Title of Marquis is given gratis to any one who will accept of it; and whosoever arrives at Paris from the

midst of the most remote Provinces with Money in his Purse, and a Name terminating in *ac* or *ille*, may strut about, and cry, Such a Man as I! A Man of my Rank and Figure! And may look down upon a Trader with sovereign Contempt; whilst the Trader on the other Side, by thus often hearing his Profession treated so disdainfully, is Fool enough to blush at it. However, I cannot say which is most useful to a Nation; a Lord, powder'd in the tip of the Mode, who knows exactly at what a Clock the King rises and goes to bed; and who gives himself Airs of Grandeur and State, at the same Time that he is acting the Slave in the Anti-chamber of a prime Minister; or a Merchant, who enriches his Country, dispatches Orders from his Compting-House to *Surat* and *Grand Cairo*, and contributes to the felicity of the world.[9]

Merchants and capitalists need not blush when our contemporary politicians and intellectuals look down their noses at them, and strut about declaiming this and decrying that, all the while demanding that the merchants, capitalists, workers, investors, craftsmen, farmers, inventors, and other productive producers create the wealth that the politicians confiscate and the anti-capitalistic intellectuals resent but greedily consume.

Markets do not depend on or presuppose people being selfish, any more than politics does. Nor do market exchanges encourage more selfish behavior or motivation. But unlike politics, free exchange among willing participants does generate wealth and peace, which are conditions under which generosity, friendship, and love flourish. There is something to be said for that, as Adam Smith well understood.

Notes

1. "The Secret History of Self-Interest," in *Passions and Constraints: On the Theory of Liberal Democracy*, Stephen Holmes (Chicago: University of Chicago Press, 1995).

2. Quoted in Christine Caldwell Ames, *Righteous Persecution: Inquisition, Dominicans, and Christianity in the Middle Ages* (Philadelphia: University of Pennsylvania Press, 2008), p. 44.

3. Adam Smith, *The Theory of Moral Sentiments*, ed. D. D. Raphael and A. L. Macfie, vol. I of the *Glasgow Edition of the Works and Correspondence of Adam Smith* (Indianapolis: Liberty Fund, 1982). Chapter: a chap ii: Of the love of Praise, and of that of Praise–worthiness; and of the dread of Blame, and of that of Blame–worthiness; Accessed from http://oll.libertyfund.org/title/192/200125 on 2011-05-30.

4. Ibid. (Fund, 1982). Chapter: b chap. i b: Of the beauty which the appearance of Utility bestows upon all the productions of art, and of the extensive influence of

this species of Beauty; Accessed from http://oll.libertyfund.org/title/192/200137 on 2011-05-30.

5. Adam Smith, *An Inquiry Into the Nature and Causes of the Wealth of Nations*, vol. I, ed. R. H. Campbell and A. S. Skinner, vol. II of the *Glasgow Edition of the Works and Correspondence of Adam Smith* (Indianapolis: Liberty Fund: 1981). Chapter: [iv.ii] chapter ii: Of Restraints upon the Importation from Foreign Countries of such Goods as can be Produced at Home. Accessed from http://oll.libertyfund.org/title/220/217458/2313890 on 2010-08-23.

6. Ibid., Chapter: [IV.viii] chapter viii: Conclusion of the Mercantile System. Accessed from http://oll.libertyfund.org/title/200/217484/2316261 on 2010-08-23.

7. "The specific characteristic of an economic relation is not its "egoism," but its "non-tuism." Philip H. Wicksteed, *The Commonsense of Political Economy, Including a Study of the Human Basis of Economic Law* (London: Macmillan, 1910). Chapter 5, Accessed from http://oll.libertyfund.org/title/1415/38938/104356 on 2010-08-23.

8. H. B. Acton, *The Morals of Markets and Related Essays*, ed. David Gordon and Jeremy Shearmur (Indianapolis: Liberty Fund, 1993).

9. Voltaire, *Letters Concerning the English Nation*, ed. Nicholas Cronk (Oxford: Oxford University Press, 1999), p. 43.

PART II

HISTORY

15. Classical Liberalism and Civil Society

Classical liberalism has been so successful in so many ways that it is often taken for granted. Indeed as Fareed Zakaria has pointed out,

> Classical liberalism, we are told, has passed from the scene. If so, its epitaph will read as does Sir Christopher Wren's, engraved on his monument at St. Paul's Cathedral: "Si monumentum requiris, circumspice." If you are searching for a monument, look around. Consider the world we live in—secular, scientific, democratic, middle class. Whether you like it or not, it is a world made by liberalism. Over the last two hundred years, liberalism (with its powerful ally, capitalism) has destroyed an order that had dominated human society for two millennia—that of authority, religion, custom, land, and kings. From its birthplace in Europe, liberalism spread to the United States and is now busily remaking most of Asia.[1]

Naturally, the consequence is that the greatest disputes about policy take place at the margins. But debates about principles often go toward the core, rather than remaining on the margins. Differing conceptions of rights and justice, for example, are often at great variance, and if consistently carried out would lead to dramatically different policy outcomes. So while critics of classical liberalism—whether communitarians, welfare-state liberals, socialists, nationalists, or other collectivists—may offer what seem marginal changes from classical liberal policies, their core principles, if consistently carried through, could lead effectively to the elimination of liberal principles, policies, and practices.

In this essay I offer a defense of the classical liberal conception of civil society, followed by several suggestions for alternative classical liberal approaches to such central problems as distributive justice,

---

Originally published in *Civil Society and Government*, edited by Nancy Rosenblum and Robert Post. Princeton, N.J.: Princeton University Press, 2002.

corporate (or group) rights, and the relationship between liberalism, democracy, and popular consent.

Definitions of Civil Society

Definitions matter, for a number of reasons. The definition of civil society is one of the more important problems in moral, social, and political thought. One answer is simply to stipulate how one will use the term, but, as logicians insist, whether stipulative definitions "are clear or unclear, advantageous or disadvantageous, or the like, are factual questions."[2] Steven Scalet and David Schmidtz deal straightforwardly with this very thorny problem, by stipulating that

> [c]ivil society is that community . . . [that] delegates authority to government, and is the body within which ultimate authority resides. Civil society retains the right to dismiss those whom it hires to provide it with governance. In this sense, classical liberals typically use the term "civil society" to refer to anything *but* government; businesses, schools, clubs, unions, media, churches, charities, libraries, and any other nongovernmental forms of organization through which a community's members relate to each other. Civil society is in this sense a cluster concept. It refers to a cluster of things that bear a family resemblance to each other but share no common essence, apart from being nongovernmental forms of association.[3]

Scalet and Schmidtz did not have the space to defend their definition of civil society, to show why it is clear and advantageous, so the task falls to me. Their definition is superior to most common contemporary competing definitions because it is both consistent with a very long tradition, and therefore with most usage of the term, and because it satisfies the criteria of a good definition in ways that other proposed definitions do not.

Will Kymlicka, in his contribution to the same volume,[4] stipulates that by civil society he intends "Associational Life," which he distinguishes from "The State" and from "The Economy." The state can at least be understood as an organization, but seeing "The Economy" in this way reveals a socialist understanding of human interaction. It excludes from civil society all of the many forms of association (partnerships, cooperatives, stock markets, unions, joint-stock companies, etc.) organized for purposes of mutual benefit, all of which are lumped together and reified, converted into an entity known as "The Economy." This is a particularly striking example of an increasingly common trend of defining civil society as a "third sector" of society. For example, the social democratic theorist Benjamin Barber in his recent book on civil society defines civil society as "a 'third sector' (the other two are the state and the market) that mediates between our specific individuality as economic producers and consumers and our abstract collectivity as members of a sovereign people."[5] Barber recognizes his divergence from historical usage but defends his ahistorical and purely stipulative account on the grounds that the term *civil society*'s "lively history no more determines or limits the ideal of civil society in political discussion today than Smith's eighteenth-century account of laissez-faire liberalism determines or limits modern debates about global market economics. We all depend on intellectual history, but this does not mean that we must constantly engage in it."[6] The last point is fair enough, but it hardly licenses us simply to make up new meanings for a term or to make spurious appeals to grammar, as in "less inclusive groups certainly qualify as generically social, but if they are to count as part of a rigorously defined democratic *civil* society they need to be more than that. Otherwise, the modifier 'civil' loses its meaning."[7] The "civil" in civil society does not distinguish the civil parts of a society from the uncivil parts, but civil societies from uncivil societies—for example, from states of nature or from societies ruled by totalitarian states or based on rigid caste distinctions. Words and concepts have histories, and simply stipulating that one will use a term in a way entirely different from—indeed incompatible with—previous uses, in order to legitimate certain ideological goals, is misleading and unacceptable. In contrast, the use of the term by Scalet and Schmidtz comports well with historical usage, has the advantage of distinguishing institutions and practices in useful ways and in terms of appropriate categories, and serves as a foundation for the pursuit of ideas about justice, rather than as part of a conclusion.

Origins of Civil Society

The notion of civil society arose from the cities of Europe and was historically used to describe the new kind of life emerging there from about the eleventh century onward. It was the way of life of a particular order of society. As the church asserted its independence from the secular powers, the burghers of the cities asserted their independence from both.[8] The knightly order and the orders of the church had their peculiar characteristics, and so did the order of the burghers that began to take definite form in the eleventh century. The foundation of the way of life of the burghers was commerce, in the forms of both trade and manufacturing. In contrast with the hierarchical and coercive orders of the feudality and the hierarchical and mystical orders of the church, commercial orders tended to equality, liberty, and rationality. As Henri Pirenne noted, of the needs of the order of civil society, "the most indispensable was personal liberty. Without liberty, that is to say, without the power to come and go, to do business, to sell goods, a power not enjoyed by serfdom, trade was impossible."[9]

Max Weber saw the conception of the burgher as a member of an association endowed with rights and privileges as characteristic of occidental city life. In contrasting the cities of western Europe with other urban conglomerations on the Eurasian landmass, he observed,

> Most importantly, the associational character of the city and the concept of a *burgher* (as contrasted to the man from the countryside) never developed at all or existed only in rudiments. The Chinese townsman was legally a member of his sib and hence of his native village, where the temple of his ancestor-cult stood and with which he carefully upheld his association. Similarly, the Russian member of a village community who earned his living in the city remained a "peasant" in the eyes of the law. The Indian townsman was, in addition, a member of his caste.[10]

The citizens of the towns built strong walls to protect themselves from the various armed bands—including the princes and knights of the feudal orders, as well as their less-settled cousins, the Viking raiders and pirates. Within the walls they created social and legal bonds through the publicly sworn ritual oaths of the burghers. John of Viterbo (ca. 1250) even went so far as to invent an etymology of the term *civitas*:

> A city is called the liberty of citizens or the immunity of inhabitants. . . . [F]or that reason walls were built to provide help for the inhabitants. . . . "City" means "you dwell safe from violence" (*Civitas, id est "Ci(tra) vi(m)(habi)tas"*). For residence is without violence, because the ruler of the city will

protect the lowliest men lest they suffer injury from the more powerful, since "we cannot be equal with those more powerful" (*Digest* 4.7.3). Again, "no one must be unjustly treated on account of the power of his adversary . . ." (*Digest* 1.1.19). Again, since the home (*domus*) is for each person a most secure refuge and shelter, no one should be taken therefrom against their will; nor is it reasonable that anyone in a town should be compelled by violent fear and so on (*Digest* 2.4.18 and 2.4.1). Again [the city] is truly called a place of immunity, because its inhabitants are guarded by its walls and towers and protected in it from their enemies and foes.[11]

In very many cases the cities of Europe were built on historically well-documented (not merely hypothetical) social contracts. Harold Berman, drawing on the account in the *Domesday Book of Ipswich*, describes the act of oath taking in the town of Ipswich, England:

[O]n Thursday, June 29, 1200, the whole community of the town assembled in the churchyard of St. Mary at the Tower. They proceeded to elect, with one voice, two bailiffs, who were sworn to keep the office of provost, and four coroners, who were sworn to keep the pleas of the crown and to handle other matters affecting the crown in the town "and to see to it that the aforesaid bailiffs justly and lawfully treat the poor as well as the rich." . . . On Sunday, July 2, the bailiffs and the coroners, with the assent of the community, appointed four men of each parish of the borough, and they elected the twelve capital portmen. (Understandably, the two bailiffs and four coroners were among those elected.) After they were sworn faithfully to govern the borough and maintain its liberties, and justly to render the judgments of the courts "without respect to any person," all the townsmen stretched forth their hands toward the "Book" (the Gospels) and with one voice solemnly swore to obey and assist, with their bodies and their goods, the bailiffs, coroners, and every one of the capital portmen in safeguarding the borough, its new charter, its liberties and customs, in all places against all persons, the royal power excepted, "according to their ability, so far as they ought justly and rationally to do."[12]

The legal relations among the inhabitants of such places were normally governed by contract, rather than status; they were the quintessential "social order in which all these relations arise from the free agreement of individuals" described by Henry Sumner

Maine.[13] This was clear and obvious to all in the many cases in which the cities and towns were founded, rather than simply there from time immemorial. As contractually formed legal associations, cities had a juridical existence.[14] The principle that "city air makes one free after the lapse of a year and a day," a recognized privilege of Bremen from 1186 and of Lübeck from 1188,[15] was quite widely recognized throughout Europe. In the "Customs of Newcastle-Upon-Tyne in the Time of Henry I, 1068–1135" we find stated, "If a villein come to reside in the borough, and shall remain as a burgess in the borough for a year and a day, he shall thereafter remain there, unless there was a previous agreement between him and lord for him to remain there for a certain time."[16]

These associations were known by many different terms, but two came into wide usage to describe the legal status of such associations: the Germanic *burgenses* and the Latin *civitas*.[17] As Hans Planitz notes, "The expression burgenses was at first used only if the city was not a civitas, and civitas was at first only the old episcopal seat (*'Bischofsstadt'*)."[18] Both terms and their derivatives—*bürgerlich*/bourgeois and civil—have come down to the present age and are used interchangeably. The advantage of the former is its obvious connection with city life—with the burgh (retained in English as borough and in such names as Canterbury and Pittsburgh)—and the advantage of the latter is its obvious connection with a way of comporting oneself—with civility. Civil society is the society of those who live in a certain kind of relation. From its origins as a particular order of the wider world of human relationships, civil society has so grown that it has displaced the feudal and ecclesiastical orders as claimant to the status of all-encompassing or universal order or, as we might say today, as the default or background order. The growth of commerce and of the associated commercial and scientific mentality had brought in its wake pluralism, which had undermined the claims of the church to universality in practice, and equality, which had made both pointless and odious the privileges of "noble" birth.[19]

The unique characteristics of the order of civil society include individual liberty, peace, and equality before the law. Individuality and personal liberty developed along with civil society. In Antony Black's words,

> Civil society . . . was the beneficiary of the enhanced value
> now ascribed to the individual: the sacred was becoming

identified with the human, personality was beginning to be seen as the only human entity with absolute value. . . . The crucial point about both guilds and communes was that here individuation and association went hand in hand. One achieved liberty by belonging to this kind of group. Citizens, merchants, and artisans pursued their own individual goals by banding together under oath.[20]

Peace and personal security were central values. As Pirenne remarks, in the midst of widespread violence and predation, the medieval commune was a peace association: "The burghers were essentially a group of *homines pacis*—men of peace. The peace of the city (*pax villae*) was at the same time the law of the city (*lex villae*)."[21]

Legal equality and the rule of law developed in civil society. Antony Black describes the basic values of civil society as follows:

[F]irst, personal security in the sense of freedom from the arbitrary passions of others, and freedom from domination in general. This involves freedom (or security) of the person from violence, and of private property from arbitrary seizure. But these, it would appear, can only be maintained if legal process is credibly and successfully enforced as an alternative to physical force, in settlement of disagreements, and in redressing wrongs committed by violence. This leads to the notion of legal rights (whether or not so called), both in the sense of the right to sue in court on equal terms with everyone else—legal equality—and in the sense of claims, for example to property, recognized and upheld by law.[22]

A central part of the growth of equal legal rights was toleration of nonviolent beliefs and behaviors. Benedict de Spinoza observed of the civil society of his native city,

The city of Amsterdam reaps the fruit of this freedom in its own great prosperity and in the admiration of all other people. For in this most flourishing state, and most splendid city, men of every nation and religion live together in the greatest harmony, and ask no questions before trusting their goods to a fellow-citizen, save whether he be rich or poor, and whether he generally acts honestly, or the reverse. His religion and sect are considered of no importance; for it has no effect before the judges in gaining or losing a cause, and there is no sect so despised that its followers, provided that they harm no one, pay every man his due, and live uprightly, are deprived of the protection of the magisterial authority.[23]

Civil society rests on a foundation of fundamental equality and liberty, a legal foundation. This explains the use of the term to refer to both the various "private" contractual associations often associated with civil society—corporations, associations, unions, partnerships, clubs, churches, and so on—and the common use of the term to refer to the entire complex set of arrangements governed by a legal order. James Harrington used the term *civil society* to refer to the people governed by a common set of laws, or government, rather than by the arbitrary will of rulers: "Government (to define it *de jure* or according to ancient prudence) is an art whereby a civil society of men is instituted and preserved upon the foundation of common right or interest, or (to follow Aristotle and Livy) it is the empire of laws and not of men."[24]

The better-known John Locke uses "civil society" interchangeably with "political society" to refer to the relationship among those who form one body politic, which has the power to choose one government.[25] Thus,

> [t]he only way whereby any one divests himself of his Natu-ral Liberty, and *puts on the bonds of Civil Society* is by agreeing with other Men to joyn and unite into a Community, for their comfortable, safe, and peaceable living one amongst another, in a secure Enjoyment of their Properties, and a greater Security against any that are not of it. This any num-ber of Men may do, because it injures not the Freedom of the rest; they are left as they were in the Liberty of the State of Nature. When any number of Men have *so consented to make one Community* or Government, they are thereby presently incorporated, and make *one Body Politick*, wherein the *Major-ity* have a Right to act and conclude the rest.[26]

As such, a civil society or a body politic is distinguished from its government, from the body of people to whom the civil society may delegate its powers of enforcing and executing the laws. Unlike many later writers, Locke does not make the mistake of confusing the group to whom the members of civil society delegate certain powers with civil society as a whole.[27] The appropriate relationship between civil society and government is that of principal and agent, as understood in most normal contractual relationships. Although civil society might be referred to as an institution, as the term is used to refer to the "institutions" of property and marriage, it is not an organization. Government is both an institution in the sense that civil society and marriage are institutions *and* it is an organization to which the members of the civil society may entrust certain powers. The difference is important and helpful to delineate the rightful authority of government and its rightful limits.

Thus, civil society refers first and foremost to a kind of legal relationship among persons.[28] Above all, it is a relationship in which each is in possession of what is properly her own, of her property, or right. Fundamental rights—clustered around property in one's person—are equal for all. The concept of subjective right emerged and developed along with civil society.[29] Immanuel Kant identifies as a condition of civil society a well-defined understanding of *mine* and *thine*, which in turn requires that all are equally subject to the same known law:

> Now, with respect to an external and contingent posses-sion, a unilateral Will cannot serve as a coercive law for everyone, since that would be a violation of freedom in accor-dance with universal laws. Therefore, only a Will binding everyone else—that is, a collective, universal (common), and powerful Will—is the kind of Will that can provide the guar-antee required. The condition of being subject to general external (that is, public) legislation that is backed by power is the civil society. Accordingly, a thing can be externally yours or mine only in a civil society.[30]

Civil society is a kind of social order based on a particular kind of legal foundation. This legal foundation is not the civil society itself, but civil society can hardly be conceived, much less realized, in its absence. The social order made possible by a legal foundation of equal and compossible individual rights[31] protected by limited government admits of complexity far exceeding the power of the human intellect to design or control; what is important for the enter-prise of defining civil society is not what particular forms it may happen to take, what organizations or associations its members form, or what religion they profess, but that the infinite complexity and variability of which civil society is capable rests on a set of fairly simple rules.[32] Religious associations, business enterprises, self-help and mutual-aid societies, intellectual and scientific unions, and many other forms of association must conform to the rule of law, but within the rather wide parameters set by Kant's conditions, an infinite variety is possible. The satisfactions of life in society rest on a foundation of well-defined legal rights protected by government, but the satisfactions of human life in society are provided by the peaceful interactions of free citizens.[33] As the influential classical liberal Benjamin Constant noted in his 1819 speech "On the Liberty of the Ancients Compared with That of the Moderns,"

> The holders of authority ... are so ready to spare us all sort of troubles, except those of obeying and paying! They will say to us: what, in the end, is the aim of your efforts, the motive of your labours, the object of all your hopes? Is it not happiness? Well, leave this happiness to us and we shall give it to you. No, Sirs, we must not leave it to them. No matter how touching such a tender commitment may be, let us ask the authorities to keep within their limits. Let them confine themselves to being just. We shall assume the responsibility of being happy for ourselves.[34]

Civil Society and Motivation

Some philosophers, however, came to identify the social order of civil society principally with a particular kind of activity or motivation, rather than with the legal order that Locke, Kant, and others agreed was its foundation. Thus, G. W. F. Hegel asserted that "individuals in their capacity as burghers are private persons whose end is their own interest" and characterized civil society (*bürgerliche Gesellschaft*) as "the battleground where everyone's individual private interest meets everyone else's."[35] Hegel thus identified civil society not merely with a legal order, but also with a kind of partial and selfish motivation. Karl Marx followed Hegel in identifying this legal relationship with a particular motivation when he argued in "On the Jewish Question" that "the so-called *rights of man*, as distinct from the *rights of the citizen*, are simply the rights of a *member of civil society*, that is, of egoistic man, of man separated from other men and from the community."[36] Further, "the right of property is ... the right to enjoy one's fortune and to dispose of it as one will; without regard for other men and independently of society. It is the right of self-interest. This individual liberty, and its application, form the basis of civil society. It leads every man to see in other men, not the *realization*, but rather the *limitation* of his own liberty."[37]

Benjamin Barber and others share this view of a rights-based society as one of solitariness and selfishness. In Barber's words, "Rights secure our negative liberty, but since they are often claimed against others, they entail being left alone."[38] Barber decries "the atmosphere of solitariness and greed that surrounds markets."[39] Most recent attempts in the United States (at least) to come to grips with civil society have taken the same tack of focusing on motivation, but remarkably they have simply flipped Hegel and Marx on their heads by identifying civil society exclusively with *non*profit enterprises and activities. Thus, civil society is typically identified as that sector of society "between state and market," as Barber did in a passage quoted earlier. The conservative thinker Don Eberly has written of

> a departure from our current obsession with either the state or the market as instruments for social progress. Civil society is a different sphere. It is an intermediary sector, where private individuals join voluntarily in associations that operate neither on the principle of coercion, nor entirely on the principle of rational self-interest. In fact, the modus operandi of life in civil society gives expression to the pursuit of the common good, where actions are animated by a spirit of trust and collaboration.[40]

Definitions of civil society as "between state and market" or as a "third sector" have at least two serious defects: first, they represent a break from the long tradition of understanding civil society, generating confusion rather than illumination; second, to the extent that they identify the state with coercive power and the market with self-interest, they divide up the various possible forms of interaction in terms of nonexclusive categories. Coercion is a way of treating others, while self-interest is a motivation. One can coerce others for self-interested motives (robbers and politicians do this quite regularly) or for altruistic motives (the theory of righteous persecution behind the Spanish Inquisition, for example, ostensibly justified breaking people on the wheel for their own good, not for the good of the inquisitors). One can interact voluntarily with others for self-interested reasons (as merchants typically do when selling us products) or for altruistic reasons (as pious missionaries do). Motivations and behavior can be mixed in a wide variety of ways. Attempts to define civil society as self-interested (in contrast to government?) or as neither state nor market fails to do what good definitions ought to do: to mark out a part of reality in a way that helps us to increase our understanding.

Thus, we return to the problem of definition: civil society is that kind of human interaction made possible by equality of rights that are protected by institutions/organizations that exercise delegated, enumerated, and thus limited powers, such that those members of civil society not tied to one another by kinship, friendship, love, faith, or even geographical proximity can nonetheless interact in a "civil" manner. Civil society includes religious orders (monasteries, convents, mosques, synagogues, temples, church hierarchies, and circles of believers), business enterprises (including individual proprietorships, family enterprises, partnerships, joint-stock corporations, cooperatives, and other forms of enterprise), labor associations (including unions and a wide range of associations now less commonly found as compulsory unionism and welfare statism have narrowed the range available to employees), and the clubs, associations, neighborhood groups, bowling leagues, kaffeeklatsches, and the like that have been the topic of so much discussion lately. No one of those associations, and certainly not the state, need exhaust the personalities of the members of civil society. One may simultaneously be a Muslim and a businessperson who does business with nonbelievers as well as believers, a member of the Parent-Teacher Association and a member of a jazz group that meets every Wednesday at a local club. By resigning from any one of those associations one does not become a traitor to the entire civil society, an outcast, a pariah. That was recognized clearly by Otto von Gierke in his classic study of the law of association: "Our present system of association, which resembles a great number of infinitely intersecting circles, rests on the possibility of belonging with one part, one aspect of one's individuality, perhaps with only one closely defined part of one's range of ability, to one organization, and with others to others."[41]

Ernest Gellner, in his book *Conditions of Liberty: Civil Society and Its Rivals*, termed this feature of civil society modularity, in contrast to atomism:

> There are firms which produce, advertise, and market modular furniture. The point about such furniture is that it comes in bits which are agglutinative: you can buy one bit which

will function on its own, but when your needs, income or space available augment, you can buy another bit. It will fit in with the one acquired previously, and the whole thing will still have a coherence, aesthetically and technically. You can combine and recombine the bits at will. . . . What genuine Civil Society really requires is not modular furniture, but modular man.[42]

Gellner's point is that in civil society one can form attachments of one's own choosing; one can recombine them in new ways; and one can withdraw from them without thereby withdrawing from the civil society as an order of relations, as would be the case in a little gatherer/hunter band or perhaps a primitive society, at least, as they are conceived by organicists.

What makes this dazzling complexity and wide range of voluntary human association possible is liberty in the enjoyment of one's "civil rights," a term that has been degraded in meaning in recent years. From a term for the wide range of rights enjoyed by those in civil societies, "civil rights" has come in the United States to be used almost solely to refer to immunity from discrimination, while "civil liberties" has come to refer to a narrow—albeit important—set of rights, typically those of greatest importance to intellectuals. In a gathering of intellectuals there is often wide agreement to extend freedom primarily (or even only) to what intellectuals do—speak and write—just as in a gathering of farmers a consensus might be found to limit freedom to what farmers do. Limiting civil rights to those involved in speaking or writing is a dangerous and selfish conceit. It is only rarely criticized, but then, criticism is almost by definition the exclusive product of intellectuals.[43]

So much in defense of Scalet and Schmidtz's definition of civil society, which they do not arbitrarily restrict to the churches, bowling leagues, and kaffeeklatsches that have been the subject of so much attention lately.

Distributive Justice

Scalet and Schmidtz assert that "classical liberals deny that justice requires any particular distribution of economic goods."[44] The truth of the statement depends on what they mean by "economic goods," but the ambiguity in the term could lead readers to think that distributive justice plays no role in classical liberal theories of justice. In fact, there is in most classical liberal approaches a very robust theory of distributive justice at their foundation—namely, the right of each individual (under normal circumstances, at least) to have jurisdiction over one and only one body—her own. Most liberals have seen legitimate property in estate as in some way derived from or related to property in one's person.[45] This is a theme not only in the familiar works of Locke, but in the works of many other protoliberal and liberal thinkers, who considered property in one's person as the moral and legal implication of a recognition of human moral agency. Marsilius of Padua noted in 1324,

> This term "ownership" [*dominium*] is used to refer to the human will or freedom in itself with its organic executive or motive power unimpeded. For it is through these that we are capable of certain acts and their opposites. It is for this reason too that man alone among the animals is said to have ownership or control of his acts; this control belongs to him by nature, it is not acquired through an act of will or choice.[46]

This is not the place to set out an entire theory of distributive justice in holdings, but a short sketch of the relationship between property in one's person and property in estate may prove suggestive. Locke uses the metaphor of labor-mixing to refer both to "whatsoever then he removes out of the State that Nature hath provided, and left it in" and to "the first gathering";[47] what both of these have in common is that they involve taking possession. And, as Tony Honoré points out, "The right to possess, namely to have exclusive physical control of a thing, or to have such control as the nature of the thing admits, is the foundation on which the whole superstructure of ownership rests."[48] In order for naturally occurring resources to be useful at all, to provide even nourishment, as Locke notes, "there must of necessity be a means to appropriate them some way or other before they can be of any use, or at all beneficial to any particular Man."[49] They must be capable of being possessed, and they must actually be possessed before they can yield any benefit to anyone.

If persons have property in their persons and the right to appropriate naturally occurring objects through the right of first possession (which right is compatible with a wide variety of forms of property holding), then they have those rights normally considered under the rubric of the right to exchange, that is, the right mutually to abandon their property in objects (conditional on the abandonment by the other party of property in the goods title to which will be exchanged) and then to acquire property in new objects. If that is so, then they have the right to benefit from such exchanges and to enjoy the increased value that motivated the exchange and that would not be called into existence in the first place without the anticipation of enjoying such increased value. Although considered diachronically there is no "distribution" of property—for there is no consciously directed distributive power—at any moment we can account for holdings according to the following abstractly formulated principle of "distributive justice": "From each according to what he chooses to do, to each according to what he makes for himself (perhaps with the contracted aid of others) and what others choose to do for him and choose to give him of what they've been given previously (under this maxim) and haven't yet expended or transferred."[50]

The question is not, then, whether there is a classical liberal theory of distributive justice, but at what point it is invoked and what relationship it has to commutative justice. (Many contemporary theories of distributive justice in effect swallow up commutative justice into distributive justice, which has led some classical liberals to deny distributive justice entirely, rather than to see distributive justice and corrective justice in their proper relationship to each other.)

Thus, the overall "distribution" is not the result of the carrying out of any particular plan. Patterned theories, in contrast, face serious problems of implementation, for even if some set of distributions were to be preferred, it may very well be that attempts to secure them directly by legal means are self-defeating.[51] There has been much controversy over the actual effects of welfare states on their populations, for example, whether they encourage the dependence and growth of an underclass or rescue the poorest of the poor from even worse circumstances.[52] What seems clear is that the growth of coerced transfer payments is inversely related to the propensity of people to transfer wealth voluntarily on grounds of need.[53] In addition, political manipulation of welfare-state benefits may very well accentuate inequalities, rather than diminish them.[54] Attempts to generate equality of wealth by means of legal coercion may, in fact, merely generate greater inequality, as the experience of the socialist countries demonstrated so clearly. After all, as F. A. Hayek warned us in *The Road to Serfdom* in 1944, in order to diminish inequalities in wealth, we must endow some with the legal power to bring this about, and they will therefore no longer be equal in power to the rest of us. And, given the normal motivations of most people, it does not take long for that inequality in legal power to be translated into inequality of wealth. As Snowball discovered in George Orwell's story *Animal Farm*, all animals are equal, but some are more equal than others.

Boundaries

Scalet and Schmidtz quite correctly identify the classical liberal contribution to political theory as its focus on limited government, rather than (as classical liberals are often accused of preferring) "weak" government. The size of government is not the primary concern of classical liberals; its limits are. Limited governments tend to be small relative to unlimited governments. They also note that "classical liberals have been champions of democracy."[55] The two issues—limited government and democracy—have traditionally been linked together in classical liberal thought by the theory of constitutionalism, which limits the powers of majorities no less than of minorities.

The principal difference between the institutions of civil society and the institutions of government is that the latter are inherently endowed with coercive powers. As Scalet and Schmidtz note, "One can say 'No, thanks' to the church (when it does not have the power of the state behind it), but when government bureaucrats think up more forms for small businesspeople to fill out, there is nothing to do but either hire another lawyer or give up and shut up."[56] Precisely, but it should be made clear just why one can say "No, thanks," to the church but not to the state: the state has guns and the power to kill people. State actors claim legitimacy for their acts when they do use violence against people. They aspire to a monopoly over violence. As Benjamin Barber notes, after insisting for many pages that the term *civil society* be limited to his "third sector," between state and market, "Democratic central government is, in other words, civil society organized for common action. It is civil society when it picks up its law code and straps on its pistol and, legitimized and authorized by its popular mandate, becomes the sovereign."[57] Constitutional limits on power—on people with pistols—are among the greatest accomplishments of the classical liberal tradition.

Constitutionalism is one of classical liberalism's principal inheritances from the Whig tradition. As Thomas Jefferson noted in the Kentucky Resolutions of 1798, "Free government is founded in jealousy, not in confidence; it is jealousy and not confidence which prescribes limited constitutions, to bind down those whom we are obliged to trust with power."[58] Here it seems that I disagree with Scalet and Schmidtz when they write that "believing government is fundamentally evil may be one of those attitudes [whose inculcation damages those who internalize them]."[59] Deep distrust of those with the power to imprison and kill their fellow citizens seems quite appropriate to me and is certainly a central element of the Whiggish cultures that have been the most fertile soil for individual liberty.

The American attempt to impose limits on government included

- explicit constitutional limitations on power (in the forms of an enumeration in the Constitution of the United States of those powers delegated to government, thus reserving all others to the people; explicit prohibitions on exercises of power; and in the Ninth and Tenth Amendments, which state that "[t]he enumeration in the Constitution of certain rights shall not be construed to deny or disparage others retained by the people" and that "[t]he powers not delegated to the United States by the Constitution, nor prohibited by it to the States, are reserved to the States respectively, or to the people"); and
- a citizenship distrustful of power, jealous of its rights, and willing to exercise those rights to restrain power.

The reading of the American Constitution as one of enumerated powers and unenumerated rights is both a plausible reading of the text and of its history and is consistent with the traditional understanding of civil society that Scalet and Schmidtz advance. Civil society may delegate certain powers to government, but only those powers that individuals have may be so delegated. As the Declaration of Independence asserts:

> That to secure these Rights, Governments are instituted among Men, deriving their Just Powers from the Consent of the Governed, that whenever any Form of Government becomes destructive of these Ends, it is the Right of the People to alter or to abolish it, and to institute new Government, laying its Foundation on such Principles, and organizing its Powers in such Form, as to them shall seem most likely to effect their Safety and Happiness.

303

Only *just* powers may be delegated to government. Since individuals do not have the right to expropriate the possessions of others, enslave others, or threaten others with bodily harm for their peaceful religious practices, romantic attachments, or pharmacological preferences, then government cannot have a right to nationalize property, conscript soldiers or hospital orderlies, or enforce victimless crime laws. Government's legitimate powers are necessarily limited to those powers and only those powers that the people can and do delegate to it. I know of no clearer or more concise statement of the classical liberal theory of the relationship between civil society and the state than the Declaration of Independence of the American colonies.

Groups

Classical liberals are, in general, moral and political individualists.[60] Historically, they have insisted that the state recognize and respect individuals as such. Classical liberals have been very suspicious of group rights and have tended to view them as, at best, mere compromises that may be necessary to ensure greater stability of liberal political structures and thereby respect for individual rights. Examples would be federalism, in which political rights are often highly unequal (electors in Nebraska and in California have differently weighted electoral influences on the U.S. Senate and on the selection of presidents), and transitional regimes, in which corporate bodies are given veto powers over policies that might be harmful to them (examples would be the compromise of 1867 that created the dual monarchy in Austria and the recent transition to greater democracy in South Africa). These are, however, practical political matters of achieving stability in the face of often greatly conflicting interests; they are practical remedies intended to avoid far worse dangers, rather than statements of what is in principle desirable. In general, classical liberals believe that only individuals have moral rights and that justifiable legal and moral rights should be traceable back to individual moral agents.[61]

Classical liberals have typically emphasized the distinction between private and public realms. But making such distinctions does not necessarily determine the limits to legitimate legal intervention. For example, some feminists have criticized the treatment of the family as a private sphere within which the magistrates have little or no authority to intervene; such private spheres may in fact harbor gross violations of the rights of women, and these violations of rights may merit intervention by legal authorities. Insofar as their concern is with the rights of women as individual persons, these concerns are perfectly consonant with those of classical liberalism.[62]

More generally, however, a variety of political theorists have insisted, sometimes in the name of defending individual autonomy and dignity, that the appropriate bearers of rights may not be individuals, but groups.[63] Or they may argue that although the bearers of rights are in every case individuals, the individual members of different groups should be accorded different rights.[64] Those groups—typically ascriptive, rather than voluntary, associations—may have rights over the individuals that make them up, or rights to special treatment by the wider community (as contrasted to other groups), or some combination of these. This approach represents a direct reversal of the classical liberal movement to replace the Law of Persons with the Law of Contract as the primary law governing human interactions.[65]

Will Kymlicka has defended a version of group rights on the grounds that such group rights may be necessary to undergird the cultural infrastructure that alone can make individual autonomy possible.[66] Others have advanced additional arguments for group rights, often on grounds of collective responsibilities or political "realism."[67] Group rights may take the form of entitlements as against other groups in the wider society or rights of the group as against members of the same group, or both.[68] Both approaches are recipes for social conflict.[69]

Such approaches do not clearly distinguish between *interests* and *rights*.[70] Both individuals and groups, whether voluntary or ascriptive, may have well-defined interests, but classical liberals do not generally equate interests directly with rights, and for very good reasons.

Modern welfare-state liberals have tended more and more toward endorsing an "interest theory" of rights, in which the interests of persons are held to be the grounds for holding others under duties.[71] One of the interest theory's most noted exponents cheerfully admits that, so construed, rights have "a dynamical character."[72] They change in ways that are unknown and even unknowable to the holders of rights and obligations. Further, as another welfare-state liberal also cheerfully admits, "if rights are understood along the lines of the Interest Theory propounded by Joseph Raz, then conflicts of rights should be regarded as more or less inevitable."[73] Since interests conflict, rights will conflict under the increasingly dominant modern "liberal" approach. That is a very serious problem, for if Sam and Cathy both have "rights" that clash, then the determination of which of them should be allowed to exercise the right must be made on the ground of something other than right. Further, such theories also generate conflicting duties. Matthew H. Kramer, another defender of the interest theory of rights, glosses the problems of conflict generated by such theories as follows:

> Unlike a duty to do φ and a liberty to abstain from doing φ, a duty to do φ and a duty to abstain from doing φ are not starkly contradictory. They are in conflict rather than in contradiction. Though the fulfillment of either one must rule out the fulfillment of the other, the existence of either one does not in any way preclude the existence of the other. This non-contradictoriness is one main feature of jural logic (with its categories of "permissibility," "impermissibility," and "obligatoriness") that prevents it from being collapsed into modal logic (with its categories of "possibility," "impossibility," and "necessity").[74]

That is to say, the two statements are not logically contradictory; only the fulfillment of the duties they enjoin is impossible. (Some) logicians may be comforted by such remarks, but those with conflicting legally enforceable duties or rights probably will not be. Experience shows that political power and influence, not to mention simple force and violence, come readily to mind as likely solutions to such conflicts, which—by stipulation—cannot be resolved on the basis of right. The interest theory of rights actually tends to undermine rights and the rule of law as the characteristic feature of the legal order.[75] James Madison seemed to have had the theories of Raz, Waldron, and Kramer in mind—with their "dynamical" rights and obligations and conflicts of rights and duties—when he stated in *Federalist* number 62,

> It poisons the blessings of liberty itself. It will be of little avail to the people that the laws are made by men of their own choice if the laws be so voluminous that they cannot be read, or so incoherent that they cannot be understood; if

they be repealed or revised before they are promulgated, or undergo such incessant changes that no man, who knows what the law is today, can guess what it will be tomorrow. Law is defined to be a rule of action; but how can that be a rule, which is little known, and less fixed?[76]

Positing "dynamical" group rights makes matters even worse, for as group interests conflict, so will group rights, and there will be no means to resolve such conflicts on the basis of right (for the rights are already in conflict), meaning that groups will resort to other means to pursue their conflicting interests/rights. The prospect is decidedly unsettling for the stability of a liberal constitutional order. It is a recipe for tearing civil society asunder through intergroup warfare. Attention to the common good becomes more difficult, if not impossible, for by stipulation there no longer is any good that is actually common to all groups. Not surprisingly, the history of systems of group rights has been one of conflict—often very violent—rather than of peaceful cooperation. Indeed, something remarkably like the system of differential rights that Kymlicka endorses has already been tried in Europe and was criticized by the influential Hungarian classical liberal Josef Eötvös, who was a major participant in the revolution of 1848 and subsequent political developments in central Europe, as well as a learned writer on the problems of nationality. With apologies for the difficulties of translating a German text that was translated from Hungarian, I offer his very telling criticism of Kymlicka's proposals, published in 1865:

> The particular nationality may demand a separate territory to rule in order to secure its freedom. It may further demand the codification in law of its sphere of rights in a way that grants the rights of each single person regarding the use of his national language, not as something to which he is entitled as an individual, but rather as a member of a specific nationality. Moreover, it may be demanded that the offices of the country be divided up according to nationality, and that in particular areas only members of a certain nationality should be eligible for office. In short, there may be a movement that started in the name of freedom and equality, and afterwards everyone demands only privileges and endeavors that those privileges be as plentiful as possible. All those things described are truly not new, and everyone who knows history knows how in times past the various religious confessions stepped forth

under the same pretext and with the same demands against the others. The protection of one confession from oppression by the others and the abolition of the occasions for friction through the determination of the spheres of the rights of all the particular confessions: those were the reasons that then motivated the demands of the particular confessions, just as now they motivate the demands of the particular nations. In Catholic countries, Protestants were assigned to their own territories and particular fortresses were equipped, which served as weapons depots for the religion. Moreover, it was determined what number of individuals of every confession were allowed to run for a particular office, and what part of the city council should consist of members of one or of another confession. And what was the result of all these rules and measures in those places where the solution of the religious question was sought in this way? What else, besides never-ending frictions between different confessions, the suppression of those who were a minority in a particular territory, and unbounded intolerance on the side with the opportunity to express it. And, as a consequence of all this, it led to a bloody war lasting centuries, which shattered the most powerful states, brought about a not-yet-healed cleavage in one of the greatest nations of Europe and everywhere hindered the advance of civilization! In some states the conflict was bloodier, in others it resulted in complete suppression of one confession. In all states where complete suppression did not occur reconciliation among the confessions was sought by creating laws that determined the spheres of rights and the privileges of each confession. The consequence was the same, namely, the citizens of each such country, segregated according to confessions, stood in hostility against one another. The more numerous and the more detailed the laws intended to protect the confessions were, the less peace and harmony were achieved.

The newer age has followed different paths in this regard. Instead of special spheres of rights and privileges for each confession, the principle of freedom of belief was established, according to which confessional diversity is without any influence on the rights of individual citizens. It was recognized that, about the question of to which confession each individual is to belong, only his own conscience is to be decisive; that the maintenance and dissemination of every religion is to be left to the zeal of the individuals; that no other responsibility falls to the law, than to protect everyone

in the enjoyment of his freedom—and to the extent that this
principle was consistently applied, the religious question has
been solved.[77]

Individuals have many interests that are best served by being
members of groups. Groups, too, may have interests. But neither
consideration justifies eliminating the principle that all are equal
before the law and substituting for this one principle—one of the
greatest accomplishments of civilization—a variety of regimes of
differential rights. The pursuit of both individual and group interests
should be undertaken solely through voluntary associations within
the confines of a system of equal fundamental individual rights.

Some may ask, what guarantees that individual rights will be
respected by the groups within which individuals associate? That
is a misguided question, for life simply contains no guarantees. What
can be meaningfully discussed is likelihood or probability, and what
makes it more likely than not that the rights and dignity of members
will be respected is the right of exit. Most modern states recognize
a right of exit from the territory of the state, which is better than
restricting exit, but such territorial exit rights still set the cost of exit
from the state extremely high, for one must then also exit from *all*
of one's other associations in civil society. In contrast, exit from any
particular association of civil society does not normally mean exit
from all associations. A particularly promising approach offered by
some classical liberals has been what we might call the right of
"internal exit." Wilhelm von Humboldt pointed out the danger of
giving projects to an institution that exercises deadly force, and
then added,

> Nothing would be left to the unconsenting but to withdraw
> from the community in order to escape jurisdiction, and
> prevent the further application of a majority suffrage to their
> individual cases. And yet this is almost impossible when we
> reflect that to withdraw from the social body means the same
> as withdrawing from the State. Furthermore, it is better to
> enter into separate unions in specific associations, than to
> contract them generally for unspecified future contingencies.[78]

Along the same lines, Herbert Spencer proposed a "right to ignore
the state" in his influential work *Social Statics*.[79] A more concrete set
of proposals for "personal autonomy" was developed in central

Europe to deal with the severe problems of national conflicts. Eötvös proposed that conflicts over nationality could be diminished by limiting state authority and collective choice and leaving as much of social life to voluntary association as possible.[80] Others who followed in his footsteps proposed that nationality be made a matter of personal choice, to be registered by government. This idea of "personal autonomy" was proposed in the late years of the Austro-Hungarian monarchy and in the Austrian republic by the "Austro-Marxists" Otto Bauer and Karl Renner, who recognized that over matters of religion, language, and culture, collective choice could only generate conflict. Their Marxism led them to believe that "economic relations" would be harmonious after such affairs were made matters of collective choice (they might be forgiven for thinking that before socialism was actually tried), but their knowledge of religious, linguistic, and cultural conflicts convinced them, as it had Eötvös, that personal choice was the key to peace and harmony.[81]

Unfortunately, the trend among welfare-state liberals in recent years has instead been to restrict even exit from and entry into the territory of a state. Yael Tamir, in her recent work *Liberal Nationalism*, invokes the classical liberal prescription of freedom of trade and travel as a *reductio ad absurdum*, a theory so bizarre that no serious person could entertain it.[82]

Will Kymlicka notes that citizenship itself is "an inherently group-differentiated notion" and states that "[u]nless one is willing to accept either a single world-government or completely open borders between states—and very few liberal theorists have endorsed either of these—then distributing rights and benefits on the basis of citizenship is to treat people differentially on the basis of their group membership."[83] Freedom of travel and freedom of trade were once characteristic liberal positions, and it is profoundly sad that protectionism, guard dogs, and barbed wire are now endorsed by self-described "liberals." Brian Barry, apparently unaware that his proposal for restriction of the interstate mobility of African Americans had already been put into practice under Jim Crow, characteristically asserted without either evidence or argument that

> [a] counterfactual America combining state-level controls over immigration and strong federal policies to bring economic development to the South while ensuring legal and political rights to the Blacks would surely be a better one

than that which actually exists. And that is, in broad terms,
the formula that I advocate for the world as a whole.[84]

Barry seems unaware that such restrictions existed, that they were a major part of the state-enforced Jim Crow system, and that they were justified on the grounds of the well-being of African Americans themselves, for without them, "a wicked and corrupt agent" could "come into a community and at the dead hour of midnight, by promises and persuasions, induce an ignorant and wholly irresponsible (financially speaking) population to leave their peaceful homes and thereby disrupt the labor conditions."[85] In pursuit of social justice Barry would have suspended the rights of African Americans to move from state to state in search of better work and higher pay (he makes no mention of Caucasian statist British professors who emigrate from London to New York in search of better work and higher pay), and currently he seeks to implement such a system of restrictions on movement on a global scale. (Again, Brian Barry is himself presumably exempted from such restrictions; after all, all animals are equal, but some are more equal than others.)

The issue of freedom of movement is made all the more acute by the fact that upon entering the territory of a welfare state, one typically acquires a wide range of positive entitlements. The consequence of this is that emigrants are likely to be viewed as parasites or freeloaders by the citizens of the welfare state they have entered. (The existence of differential rights for citizens/insiders and for foreigners/outsiders is a particular case of differential group-based rights. It is objectionable on liberal grounds and has shown itself to be a powerful source of hatred, envy, resentment, racism, xenophobia, and brutal violence.) Accordingly, all welfare states have restrictions on immigration and effectively generate antiforeigner movements. If restrictions on freedom of movement are the logical conclusion of welfare-state liberalism (and a number of welfare-state liberals have followed the implications of adherence to the welfare state in precisely that direction), then there are good reasons for modern liberals to reject both group rights and the interest theory of rights behind them and to return to the classical liberal conception of rights and of the proper relation of individuals to groups.

In general, what should determine the appropriate relations among individuals, groups, and the state is consent. Individuals consent to form voluntary associations, on the basis of common interests; those voluntary associations interact with other associations and with individuals on the basis of mutual consent; and governments derive "their just powers from the Consent of the Governed," in the words of the American Declaration of Independence.

Individuals may consent to form voluntary groups through which to advance their common interests. In consenting to pool their assets, they may also create fictive persons (e.g., corporations), which may have legal relations with individuals, other corporations, and states. They may even be bearers of legal responsibility and may assume collective responsibility on behalf of their members. But for classical liberals such fictive persons should be founded on the consent of the materially and numerically individuated persons who are their members, rather than ascription.

Classical liberals insist that, under normal circumstances, at least, the liberty of the individual human being is the highest political end. It is not the end or goal of life itself, but the condition that makes the ends of life most likely to be attained.

Notes

1. Fareed Zakaria, "The 20 Percent Philosophy," *Public Interest* 129 (Fall 1997), pp. 96–101, esp. 101.

2. Irving Copi, *Introduction to Logic*, 6th ed. (New York: Macmillan Publishing, 1982), p. 150.

3. Steven Scalet and David Schmidtz, "State, Civil Society, and Classical Liberalism," in *Civil Society and Government*, ed. Nancy L. Rosenblum and Robert C. Post (Princeton, N.J.: Princeton University Press, 2002), p. 27. (This essay originally appeared in the same volume.) Compare Reinhard Bendix, *Kings or People: Power and the Mandate to Rule* (Berkeley and Los Angeles: University of California Press, 1978), p. 523: "civil society refers to all institutions in which individuals can pursue common interests without detailed direction or interference from the government." Bendix continues, "Western European regimes and Japan possessed civil societies because they had inherited a tradition of local privileges or liberties; Russia did not enjoy a comparable inheritance."

4. Will Kymlicka, "Civil Society and Government: A Liberal-Egalitarian Perspective," in *Civil Society and Government*, ed. Nancy L. Rosenblum and Robert C. Post, op cit., pp. 81–82.

5. Benjamin Barber, *A Place for Us: How to Make Society Civil and Democracy Strong* (New York: Hill and Wang, 1998), p. 4.

6. Ibid., p. 13.

7. Ibid., p. 53.

8. The great distinction between Latin Christendom and the inheritors of the Byzantine tradition is undoubtedly the relative independence of the church from the state. For the developments in Latin Christendom, see Harold Berman's account of the

Gregorian Reformation, which proceeded on the basis of the slogan of the "freedom of the church." See *Law and Revolution: The Formation of the Western Legal Tradition* (Cambridge, Mass.: Harvard University Press, 1983), esp. chap. 2, "The Origin of the Western Legal Tradition in the Papal Revolution," pp. 85–119. For a collection of the relevant historical documents, see Brian Tierney, *The Crisis of Church and State, 1050–1300* (Toronto: University of Toronto Press, 1988). For a learned description of Byzantine theories of church-state relations and their impact on later Eastern European politics, see Francis Dvornik, "Byzantine Political Ideas in Kievan Russia," *Dumbarton Oaks Papers*, nos. 9 and 10 (Cambridge, Mass.: Harvard University Press, 1956), pp. 73–121; and *The Slavs in European History and Civilization* (New Brunswick, N.J.: Rutgers University Press, 1962), pp. 369–76.

9. Henri Pirenne, *Economic and Social History of Medieval Europe* (New York: Harcourt Brace Jovanovich, 1937), p. 50. This association of civil society with city life has been known for a long time. See Adam Smith, *An Inquiry into the Nature and Causes of the Wealth of Nations* (Indianapolis, Ind.: Liberty Fund, 1981), esp. vol. 1, bk. 3, chap. 3, "Of the Rise and Progress of Cities and Towns, after the Fall of the Roman Empire," pp. 397–410.

10. Max Weber, *Economy and Society: An Outline of Interpretive Sociology*, ed. Guenther Roth and Claus Wittich (Berkeley and Los Angeles: University of California Press, 1978), vol. 2, p 1227.

11. Quoted in Antony Black, *Guilds and Civil Society in European Political Thought from the Twelfth Century to the Present* (Ithaca, N.Y.: Cornell University Press, 1984), p. 38. (The references in the text are to the codification of Roman law known as the Digest of Justinian.) Brunetto Lanni (ca. 1260) described how cities grew: "it came in the end to the point where those who wanted to live by their own law and escape the force of evildoers grouped themselves together in one place and under one government. Thence they began to build houses and establish towns (*viles*) and fortresses, and enclose them with walls and ditches. Thence they began to establish customs and law and rights (*drois*) which should be common to all the burghers (*borgois*) of the town" (ibid., p. 39). An illuminating account of the slow growth of a city, as defined by its fortifications, can be found in Paul Strait, *Cologne in the Twelfth Century* (Gainesville: University Presses of Florida, 1974), pp. 30–36. Cologne's status as an old Roman city and an episcopal seat distinguishes it in various ways from the new cities of Europe, but the identification of the city walls with the freedom of the city and the security of the citizens was a common factor.

12. Berman, *Law and Revolution*, pp. 383–84.

13. Henry Sumner Maine, *Ancient Law* (1861; reprint, Gloucester, Mass.: Peter Smith, 1970), p. 163.

14. As Berman observed, "The new European cities and towns of the eleventh and twelfth centuries were also legal associations, in the sense that each was held together by a common urban legal consciousness and by distinctive urban legal institutions. In fact, it was by a legal act, usually the granting of a charter, that most of the European cities and towns came into being; they did not simply emerge but were founded. Moreover, the charter would almost invariably establish the basic 'liberties' of citizens, usually including substantial rights of self-government" (*Law and Revolution*, p. 362).

15. Hans Planitz, *Die Deutsche Stadt im Mittelalter: Von der Römerzeit bis zu den Zünftkämpfen* (Graz, Austria, and Köln, Germany: Böhlau, 1954), p. 117.

16. In John H. Mundy and Peter Riesenberg, *The Medieval Town* (Princeton, N.J.: D. Van Nostrand, 1958), p. 138.

17. Antony Black lists the following names used to designate "the early town community": "*civitas, commune, communitas, universitas civium/burgensium, urbani, burgensis populus, universi cives,* and the vernacular *commune* (French and Italian), *Gemeinde, burgh.*" Black, *Guilds and Civil Society,* p. 49.

18. Planitz, *Die Deutsche Stadt im Mittelater,* p. 100.

19. As Thomas Paine noted, "The patriots in France have discovered in good time that rank and dignity in society must take a new ground. The old one has fallen through. It must now take the substantial ground of character instead of the chimerical ground of titles." *In The Rights of Man,* pt. 1, in *Thomas Paine: Political Writings,* ed. Bruce Kuklick (1791; reprint, Cambridge: Cambridge University Press, 1989), p. 90.

20. Black, *Guilds and Civil Society,* p. 65.

21. Henri Pirenne, *Medieval Cities: Their Origins and the Revival of Trade* (Princeton, N.J.: Princeton University Press, 1974), p. 200.

22. Black, *Guilds and Civil Society,* p. 32.

23. Benedict de Spinoza, *A Theologico-Political Treatise,* trans. R. H. M. Elwes (New York: Dover Publications, 1951), p. 264. The burghers of the Netherlands were pioneers of religious toleration, as Geoffrey Parker noted regarding the attempts by the king of Spain to reorganize the bishoprics of the Netherlands and, in the process, to appoint resident inquisitors: "There was violent opposition to this measure from the magistrates of Antwerp (Antwerp was to be one of the new sees) on the grounds that the inquisition was contrary to the privileges of Brabant and that, more specifically, so many heretics came to Antwerp to trade that its prosperity would be ruined if a resident inquisition were introduced." *The Dutch Revolt* (New York: Penguin Books, 1988), p. 47. Compare also the observations on the London Stock Exchange by Voltaire: "Go into the Exchange in London, that place more venerable than many a court, and you will see representatives of all the nations assembled there for the profit of mankind, There the Jew, the Mahometan, and the Christian deal with one another as if they were of the same religion, and reserve the name of infidel for those who go bankrupt." Voltaire, "On the Presbyterians," in *"Candide" and Philosophical Letters* (New York: Modern Library, 1992), p. 141.

24. James Harrington, *The Commonwealth of Oceana* (1656), in *The Commonwealth of Oceana and A System of Politics,* ed. J. G. A. Pocock (Cambridge: Cambridge University Press, 1992), p. 8. Further, "[a] commonwealth is but a civil society of men" (p. 23).

25. Locke does not maintain, however, that civil society or political society is the source of all obligation: "The Promises and Bargains for Truck, &c. between the two Men in the Desert Island, mentioned by *Garcilasso De la Vega,* in his History of *Peru,* between a *Swiss* and an *Indian,* in the Woods of *America,* are binding to them, though they are perfectly in a state of nature, in reference to one another. For Truth and keeping of Faith belongs to Men, as Men, and not as Members of Society." John Locke, *Two Treatises of Government,* ed. Peter Laslett (Cambridge: Cambridge University Press, 1988), bk. 2, sec. 14, p. 277.

26. Ibid., bk. 2, sec. 95, p. 330–31. Algernon Sidney, at about the same time, criticized the patriarchal theory of political power, noting that "for politick signifying no more in Greek, than civil in Latin, 'tis evident there could be no civil power, where there was no civil society; and there could be none between him [Adam] and his children, because a civil society is composed of equals, and fortified by mutual compacts, which could not be between him and his children." *Discourses Concerning Government,*

ed. Thomas G. West (Indianapolis, Ind.: Liberty Fund, 1990), p. 88. In a Boston election sermon of 1762, Abraham Williams pointed out to his listeners that "[t]he End and Design of civil Society and Government, from this view of it's Origin, must be to secure the Rights and Properties of it's Members, and promote their Welfare; or, in the Apostle's words, that Men may lead quiet and peaceable Lives in Godliness and Honesty." "An Election Sermon," in *American Political Writing during the Founding Era, 1760–1805*, vol. 1, ed. Charles S. Hyneman and Donald S. Lutz (Indianapolis, Ind.: Liberty Press, 1983), p. 6.

27. One particularly confused commentator writes as follows of the United States of America: "The United States, which, in contrast to both Eastern and Western Europe, has always lacked a coherent concept of the state, has traditionally been presented as a model of civil society. Yet in the closing decades of the twentieth century the adequacy of this model is increasingly being questioned." Adam B. Seligman, *The Idea of Civil Society* (Princeton, N.J.: Princeton University Press, 1992), p. 9. The author seems to think that a constitutional republic grounded on a written constitution that specifies enumerated powers and provides explicit limits on state power "lacks a coherent concept of the state."

28. This seems to be the general approach of Adam Ferguson in his rich and complex *Essay on the History of Civil Society* (1767; reprint, Cambridge: Cambridge University Press, 1995), in which he connects the rise of civil society with the emergence of property, and therefore of improvement and of civility.

29. See the historical treatment of these interconnected developments in Brian Tierney, *The Idea of Natural Rights* (Atlanta, Ga.: Scholars Press, 1998).

30. Immanuel Kant, *The Metaphysical Elements of Justice*, trans. J. Ladd (New York: Macmillan, 1985), p. 65. Kant defined "external proprietary rights" explicitly in terms of equal rights: "A thing is externally mine if it is something outside me which is such that any interference with my using it as I please would constitute an injury to me (a violation of my freedom, a freedom that can coexist with the freedom of everyone in accordance with a universal law)" (p. 55). The latter condition is equivalent to the condition of "compossibility" described in Hillel Steiner, *An Essay on Rights* (Oxford: Blackwell, 1994).

31. In Kant's words, "Every action is just [right] that in itself or in its maxim is such that the freedom of the will of each can coexist together with the freedom of everyone in accordance with a universal law." *The Metaphysical Elements of Justice*, p. 35. Or as John Locke noted in the seventh of his *Essays on the Laws of Nature*, in *Political Essays*, ed. Mark Goldie (Cambridge: Cambridge University Press, 1997), "The duties of life are not at variance with one another, nor do they arm men against one another—a result which, secondly, follows of necessity from the preceding assumption, for upon it men were, as they say, by the law of nature in a state of war; so all society is abolished and all trust, which is the bond of society" (p. 132).

32. See Richard Epstein, *Simple Rules for a Complex World* (Cambridge, Mass.: Harvard University Press, 1995), for an updated restatement of this thesis.

33. This theme is developed in classical liberal terms in Wilhelm von Humboldt's treatment of civil society, *The Limits of State Action* (Indianapolis, Ind.: Liberty Fund, 1993), esp. chap. 3, "On the Solicitude of the State for the Positive Welfare of the Citizen." Humboldt's views are well described in George G. Iggers, "The Political Theory of Voluntary Association in Early–Nineteenth Century German Thought," in *Voluntary Associations: A Study of Groups in Free Societies*, ed. D. B. Robertson (Richmond, Va.: John Knox Press, 1966).

315

34. Benjamin Constant, *Political Writings*, ed. Biancamaria Fontana (Cambridge: Cambridge University Press, 1988), p. 326. As Wilhelm von Humboldt noted, it is "the free cooperation of the members of the nation which secures all those benefits for which men longed when they formed themselves into society." *The Limits of State Action*, p. 137.

35. G. W. F. Hegel, *The Philosophy of Right*, trans. T. M. Knox (Oxford: Oxford University Press, 1977), pp. 124, 189.

36. In *Karl Marx: Early Writings*, trans. and ed. T. B. Bottomore (New York: McGraw-Hill Books, 1964), p. 24.

37. Ibid., p. 25.

38. Benjamin Barber, *A Place for Us*, p. 121.

39. Ibid., p. 65. Here Barber follows many in identifying classical liberalism with greed and selfishness, grossly distorting the simple insight of Adam Smith and others that self-interest rightly understood can be generally beneficial when, but only when, institutions are properly ordered. Smith and other liberal economists did not argue that all motivations are selfish, nor that societies that enjoy free markets are selfish societies, nor that self-interest is only present in free societies. For a correction, see Stephen Holmes, "The Secret History of Self-Interest," in *Passions and Constraint: On the Theory of Liberal Democracy* (Chicago: University of Chicago Press, 1995).

40. Don Eberly, "The New Demands of Citizenship," *Policy Review* (January–February 1996), pp. 30–31.

41. Otto von Gierke, *Community in Historical Perspective*, trans. Mary Fischer, ed. Antony Black (Cambridge: Cambridge University Press, 1990), p. 23.

42. Ernest Gellner, *Conditions of Liberty: Civil Society and Its Rivals* (New York: Penguin Books, 1994), p. 97. Clearly, only an academic would describe the furniture sold in Ikea stores as "agglutinative."

43. As Vasily Grossman wrote, based on his experiences as a subject of a state that attempted to eradicate civil society entirely and to integrate all human interactions into the organization of the state, freedom must mean freedom for all kinds of endeavor: "I used to think that freedom was freedom of speech, freedom of the press, freedom of conscience. But freedom is the whole life of everyone. Here is what it amounts to: you have to have the right to sow what you wish to, to make shoes or coats, to bake into bread the flour ground from the grain you have sown, and to sell it or not sell it as you wish; for the lathe operator, the steelworker, and the artist it's a matter of being able to live as you wish and work as you wish and not as they order you to. And in our country there is no freedom—not for those who write books nor for those who sow grain nor for those who make shoes." *Forever Flowing* (New York: Harper and Row, 1986), p. 99.

44. Scalet and Schmidtz, "State, Civil Society, and Classical Liberalism," p. 32.

45. For a denial of the relationship, see G. A. Cohen, *Self-Ownership, Freedom, and Equality* (Cambridge: Cambridge University Press, 1995). Cohen's account is fraught with confusion; see my "G. A. Cohen on Freedom and Equality," *Critical Review* (Summer 1998), reprinted in this volume, for a catalog of these errors and a response to his claims.

46. Marsilius of Padua, *The Defender of the Peace: The Defensor Pacis*, trans. Alan Gewirth (New York: Harper and Row, 1956), discourse 2, chaps. 12 and 13, p. 192. Francisco de Vitoria, who studied in Paris and was probably influenced by Marsilian thought, noted in his defense of the rights of the American Indians, "If . . . brutes have no dominion over their own actions, they can have no dominion over other

things." In "On the American Indians [De Indis]," in *Francisco de Vitoria: Political Writings*, ed. Anthony Pagden and Jeremy Lawrance (Cambridge: Cambridge University Press, 1991), p. 248.

47. Locke, *Two Treatises of Government*, bk. 2, sec. 27, p. 288, and sec. 28, p. 288.

48. Tony Honoré, "Ownership," in *Making Law Bind: Essays Legal and Philosophical* (Oxford: Oxford University Press, 1987), p. 166. That is the basic claim of John XXII in his bull of 1323, *Ad Conditorem*. See Tierney, *The Idea of Natural Rights*, esp. pp. 93–97.

49. Locke, *Two Treatises of Government*, bk. 2, sec. 26, pp. 286–87.

50. Robert Nozick, *Anarchy, State, and Utopia* (New York: Basic Books, 1974), p. 160.

51. On self-defeating theories generally see Derek Parfit, *Reasons and Persons* (Oxford: Oxford University Press, 1986).

52. The current debate in the United States was sparked largely by the extensive empirical studies of Charles Murray, *Losing Ground: American Social Policy, 1950–1980* (New York: Basic Books, 1984).

53. For a recent example, see the story of the attempts to encourage French people to help their less fortunate compatriots during a very cold winter, Charles Trueheart, "Can Winter Blast Melt Cold Parisian Hearts?" *Washington Post*, November 27, 1998, p. A39: "According to one recent study, the French citizen gives, on average, approximately 0.15 percent of his annual taxable income to nonprofit organizations. The figure in next-door Germany, according to the same study, is twice that. In the United States, it is eight times larger—about 1.2 percent of income." The issue is debated in David Schmidtz and Robert E. Goodin, *Social Welfare and Individual Responsibility* (Cambridge: Cambridge University Press, 1998). For a perspective from moral philosophy, see Tibor Machan, *Generosity: Virtue in Civil Society* (Washington, D.C.: Cato Institute, 1998). Similarly, state financial support for churches, such as those in Germany and Sweden, demonstrably undercuts church participation, in comparison with voluntary support for churches, such as those in the United States. See Laurence R. Iannacone, Roger Finke, and Rodney Stark, "Deregulating Religion: The Economics of Church and State," *Economic Inquiry* 35 (April 1997), pp. 350–64. For a history of the displacement of mutual aid by the welfare state, see David T. Beito, *From Mutual Aid to the Welfare State: Fraternal Societies and Social Services, 1890–1967* (Chapel Hill: University of North Carolina Press, 2000).

54. This problem was exemplified in a front-page article in the *Washington Post*, "5 D.C. Employees Charged: Only 10 of 400 New Rent Vouchers Issued since 1990 Didn't Involve Bribery, Probe Finds," by Cindy Loose, April 13, 1994, p. A1: "The city employees are accused of using their positions 'to prey upon the most vulnerable members in our community,' [U.S. Attorney Eric H. Holder, Jr.] said at a joint news conference of federal and city officials. 'Not only did they allegedly demand bribe money from those people least able to afford it, they also displaced from the housing list those who were rightfully entitled to government-subsidized housing and were playing by the rules,' Holder said."

55. Scalet and Schmidtz, "State, Civil Society, and Classical Liberalism," p. 29.

56. Quotation from an earlier version of their paper that was modified before publication.

57. Barber, *A Place for Us*, p. 62.

58. Thomas Jefferson, "The Kentucky Resolutions," in *The Portable Thomas Jefferson*, ed. Merrill D. Peterson (New York: Penguin Books, 1977), pp. 287–88.

59. Quotation from an earlier version of their paper that was modified before publication.

60. For a correction of communitarian mischaracterizations of liberal individualism, see Tom G. Palmer, "Myths of Individualism," *Cato Policy Report* 17, no. 5 (September/October 1996) (http://www.cato.org/pubs/policy—report/cpr-18n51.html), reprinted in this volume.

61. The problem of the fictive person who is a rights bearer, such as the church or the business corporation, has been addressed in a variety of ways in the history of jurisprudence. In general, classical liberals have seen such fictive persons as creatures of contract among rights-bearing individual persons. See Antony Black, "Society and the Individual from the Middle Ages to Rousseau: Philosophy, Jurisprudence, and Constitutional Theory," *History of Political Theory* 1, no. 2 (June 1980), pp. 145–66, and, for a contractual view of the business corporation, see Ronald Coase, *The Firm, the Market, and the Law* (Chicago: University of Chicago Press, 1988); Ronald Coase, "The Institutional Structure of Production," *American Economic Review* 82 (September 1992), and Robert Hessen, *In Defense of the Corporation* (Stanford, Calif.: Hoover Institution Press, 1979).

62. Thus, the recognition that there may be rape within marriage would not be construed by classical liberals as an assault on the family, but as a vindication of one of the inalienable rights of individuals who choose to marry.

63. This issue is carefully discussed in Andrew Vincent, "Can Groups Be Persons?" *Review of Metaphysics* 42, no. 4 (June 1989), pp. 687–714.

64. This is the approach of Will Kymlicka in *Multicultural Citizenship* (Oxford: Clarendon Press, 1995). Despite his insistence that the rights he defends are rights of individuals, Kymlicka rather consistently defers to groups as such, with such references as what "they wanted," "the historical preference of these groups," and so on. To determine the interests and therefore the rights of the individual members of the groups, he defers to the leaders (often self-appointed) of those groups; it is thus the group that determines the rights of individuals, and thus the groups that are the repository of the power to award rights.

65. That is a central theme of Henry Sumner Maine's *Ancient Law*, pp. 163–65. The retrograde motion from the Law of Contract to the Law of Persons in contemporary America is well described in Tom Bethell, *The Noblest Triumph: Property and Prosperity through the Ages* (New York: St. Martin's Press, 1998).

66. See Will Kymlicka, *Liberalism, Community, and Culture* (Oxford: Oxford University Press, 1989), p. 164: "Liberal values require both individual freedom of choice and a secure cultural context from which individuals can make their choices."

67. For an approach based on an examination of some common beliefs about group responsibility (e.g., collective responsibility) and state powers, see Vernon Van Dyke, "Collective Entities and Moral Rights: Problems in Liberal-Democratic Thought," in *Group Rights: Perspectives since 1900*, ed. Julia Stapleton (Bristol, UK: Thommes Press, 1995), pp. 180–200.

68. Will Kymlicka endorses only the former, namely, entitlements to benefits from the larger group, and opposes the group's right to restrict the activities of its own members ("Protecting people from changes in the character of their culture can't be viewed as protecting their ability to choose." *Liberalism, Community and Culture*, p. 167), but cannot help sliding toward the latter: "the viability of Indian communities depends on coercively restricting the mobility, residence, and political rights of both Indians and non-Indians" (p. 146). Vernon Van Dyke also endorses both: "Where a country or people is sovereign, the right to preserve a culture is a legal right; at least,

sovereign states are free to adopt laws designed to preserve a culture." "Collective Entities and Moral Rights," p. 186.

69. For some examples of such conflicts between ascriptive groups, see Donald L. Horowitz, *Ethnic Groups in Conflict* (Berkeley and Los Angeles: University of California Press, 1985), esp. chap. 5, "Group Entitlement and the Sources of Conflict," p. 185–228.

70. This is a central insight of Chandran Kukathas's critique of group rights: see "Are There Any Cultural Rights?" *Political Theory* 20, no. 1 (February 1992), pp. 105–39. See also Will Kymlicka, "The Rights of Minority Cultures," *Political Theory* 20, no. 1 (February 1992), pp. 140–46; and Chandran Kukathas, "Cultural Rights Again: A Rejoinder to Kymlicka," *Political Theory* 20, no. 4 (November 1992), pp. 674–80. See also the critique of Kymlicka's theory by Anthony de Jasay, "Liberty, Rights, and the Standing of Groups," chap. 11 in *Against Politics: On Government, Anarchy, and Order* (London: Routledge, 1997), esp. pp. 232–34. Jasay notes that Kymlicka turns liberalism on its head by presupposing in his theory of rights that "actions must be expressly permitted in order not to be taken for forbidden" (p. 232).

71. See Joseph Raz, *The Morality of Freedom* (Oxford: Oxford University Press), p. 166: "'X has a right' if and only if X can have rights, and, other things being equal, an aspect of X's well-being (his interest) is a sufficient reason for holding some other person(s) to be under a duty."

72. Ibid., p. 185.

73. Jeremy Waldron, "Rights in Conflict," in *Liberal Rights: Collected Papers, 1981–1991* (Cambridge: Cambridge University Press, 1993), p. 203. For an examination of the differences between the interest theory of rights and the more traditional liberal choice theory, as exemplified in legal cases, see John Hasnas, "From Cannibalism to Caesareans: Two Conceptions of Fundamental Rights," *Northwestern University Law Review* 89, no. 3 (Spring 1995), pp. 900–941.

74. Matthew H. Kramer, "Rights without Trimmings," in *A Debate Over Rights: Philosophical Enquiries*, ed. Matthew H. Kramer, N. E. Simmonds, and Hillel Steiner (Oxford: Clarendon Press, 1998), p. 19.

75. See also the similar treatment of rights in Stephen Holmes and Cass R. Sunstein, *The Cost of Rights: Why Liberty Depends on Taxes* (New York: W. W. Norton, 1999). According to Holmes and Sunstein, "an interest qualifies as a right when an effective legal system treats it as such by using collective resources to defend it" (p. 17). Their theory generates an extraordinary logical chaos, as I show in my review in the *Cato Journal* 19, no. 2 (Fall 1999) (http://www.cato.org/ pubs/journal/019n2/cj19n2.html).

76. James Madison, Alexander Hamilton, and John Jay, *The Federalist Papers*, ed. Isaac Kramnick (1788; reprint, New York: Penguin Books, 1987), no. 62, p. 368.

77. Josef Freiherrn von Eötvös, *Die Nationalitätenfrage*, trans. from the Hungarian to German by Dr. Max Falk (Pest, Hungary: Verlag von Moritz Rath, 1865), pp. 145–47. The liberal political economist Ludwig von Mises stated in 1919, following the catastrophe of the Great War, "Whoever wants peace among nations must seek to limit the state and its influence most strictly." *Nation, State, and Economy: Contributions to the Politics and History of Our Time* (New York: New York University Press, 1983), p. 77. (Actually, the text was originally written in German and translated into Hungarian.)

78. Wilhelm von Humboldt, *The Limits of State Action*, p. 36.

79. Herbert Spencer, *Social Statics* (1850; reprint, New York: Robert Schalkenbach Foundation, 1995).

80. See Eötvös's treatment of the relationship between what he called the "ruling ideas of the nineteenth century": freedom, equality, and nationality. As he observed, the three were in contradiction; therefore, if those ideas were to be realized, one among them had to be made the dominant one. Eötvös defended freedom as the idea to which the others would be made to conform. See his two-volume work *Der Einfluss der herrschenden Ideen des 19. Jahrhunderts auf den Staat*, trans. by the author from the original Hungarian (Leipzig, Germany: F. U. Brockhaus, 1854).

81. See Otto Bauer, *Die Nationalitätenfrage und Die Sozialdemokratie*, in Dr. Max Adler and Dr. Rudolf Hilferding, Herausgeber, *Marx Studien: Blätter zur Theorie und Politik der Wissenschaftlichen Sozialismus*, Zweiter Band (Wien, Austria: Verlag der Wiener Volksbuchhandlung, 1924); Karl Renner, *Das Selbstbestimmungsrecht der Nationen: In besonderer Anwendung auf Oesterreich* (Leipzig, Germany, and Wien, Austria: Franz Deuticke, 1918); and the descriptions in Robert A. Kann, *The Multinational Empire: Nationalism and National Reform in the Habsburg Monarchy, 1848–1918*, vol. 2, *Empire Reform*, esp. pp. 154–78.

82. Yael Tamir, *Liberal Nationalism* (Princeton, N.J.: Princeton University Press, 1993). Utilizing a quotation from Bruce Ackerman's *Social Justice in a Liberal State*, Tamir notes, "If liberal theory is unable to justify a situation in which 'noncitizens must depend upon the policy choices of citizens if they are to acquire rights on their own behalf,' it should advocate that barriers be pulled down and allow the market to control immigration" (p. 127). Only after a few paragraphs does it dawn on a classical liberal reader that this is not an invocation of a traditional liberal policy prescription, but a *reductio ad absurdum*.

83. Kymlicka, *Multicultural Citizenship*, p. 124.

84. Brian Barry, "The Quest for Consistency: A Sceptical View," in *Free Movement: Ethical Issues in the Transnational Migration of People and Money*, ed. Brian Barry and Robert E. Goodin (University Park: Pennsylvania State University Press, 1992), p. 284–85.

85. These are the words of Colonel Butler, who prosecuted emigrant agent R. A. "Peg Leg" Williams for violating Georgia's emigrant-agent law. In David E. Bernstein, "The Law and Economics of Post–Civil War Restrictions on Interstate Migration by African-Americans," *Texas Law Review* 76, no. 4 (March 1998), p. 809, pp. 781–847.

16. Classical Liberalism, Marxism, and the Conflict of Classes: The Classical Liberal Theory of Class Conflict

The history of all hitherto existing societies is the history of class struggle.
—Karl Marx[1]

The idea of class conflict has become virtually synonymous with Marxian political analysis. Indeed, it is widely believed that even to raise the topic is to indicate a sympathy for the Marxian program. Yet Marx did not originate this idea. He adopted it from others, adding to it his own innovations. As he stated in a letter to his German-American friend Joseph Weydemeyer:

> And now as to myself, no credit is due to me for discovering the existence of classes in modern society, nor yet the struggle between them. Long before me bourgeois historians had described the historical development of this struggle of the classes and bourgeois economists the economic anatomy of the classes. What I did that was new was to prove: 1) that the existence of classes is only bound up with particular historical phases in the development of production; 2) that the class struggle necessarily leads to the dictatorship of the proletariat; 3) that this dictatorship itself only constitutes the transition to the abolition of all classes and to a classless society.[2]

When Marx writes in this instance of "bourgeois" historians and economists he is referring to the classical liberal writers of the preceding decades, notably the French liberal writers associated with the publication *Le Censeur européen*. In another letter, Marx referred to historian Augustin Thierry, one of the editors of *Le Censeur européen*, as *"le père* of the 'class struggle' in French historiography."[3] Marx

---

Originally published as a working paper, George Mason University Institute for Humane Studies, July 1988.

borrowed a theory created by the fusion of a profound understanding of history and a powerful system of political economy and mired it in a mass of historical, political, and economic confusions.

At least four sources contribute to that confusion. First, by the time Marx began his study of French politics and history, the notion of the "bourgeoisie" as a class had been hopelessly confused; Saint-Simon and his disciples had needlessly complicated the model of classes elaborated by Thierry and his collaborators. Second, Marx misunderstood the writings of the so-called Ricardian Socialists, notably Thomas Hodgskin; Hodgskin's attacks on "capital" were aimed at what today would be called "feudalism" or "mercantilism" and not at the market economy. Third, Marx superimposes over the historical and economic account of classes elaborated by the French liberals (known at the time as "industrialists," or advocates of the system of "industrialism") the Hegelian dialectical system, with its opposition between man in his particular and in his universal aspects. And fourth, Marx takes the Ricardian system of economics—based on a labor theory of value—to its logical conclusion, a virtual *reductio ad absurdum* made all the more lamentable by the fact that the first volume of *Capital* appeared in 1867, just three years before the science of economics was revolutionized and placed on a secure foundation.

I shall present a picture of the origins of class theory and of the changes and variations it underwent at the hands of social theorists from the classical liberal *économistes* to the Saint-Simonians to Marx. An appendix will offer a brief critique of the Marxian approach to class conflict and exploitation.

Conquest, Class Theory, and the Liberal *Économistes*

Marxists often say of classical liberalism that it is "ahistorical" and "naive," while the scientific system of Marxism is rooted in history. It may be true that some variants of liberalism are ahistorical and naive, but it is certainly not true of the liberal tradition initiated by the French *idéologues* and *économistes*, from whose work Marx drew some of his inspiration. The success of Marxism in attracting scholarly adherents may account for the lack of attention and credit to those liberal thinkers whose work was informed by history. Indeed, as Larry Seidentop remarks of the contrast between liberalism and socialism, "the contrast has come to be made in a way that neglects the richness of liberal thought in the nineteenth century, and ignores the extent to which modes of argument and themes which are usually assigned to 'socialism' formed an important part of liberal thought in that period. Indeed, some of these modes of argument and themes were *introduced* by liberal thinkers, and only later adopted by socialist writers. To that extent, it is fair to say that the conventional contrast between the two traditions is particularly unfair to liberalism—excluding from it some of its own progeny."[4] Among that progeny were the theories of classes and class conflict.

The theory of classes is certainly not new. Ancient political scientists wrote of the divisions between the few and the many, rich and poor, slave and free. What was new was a grounding of class theory on a rich understanding of history and of historical development made possible by a new approach to historical writing based on original sources, on the one hand, and on an understanding of the forces of production made possible by the nascent science of political economy.

The French *économistes* of the early nineteenth century elaborated a historical and economic account of classes that distinguished between productive and predatory classes. In this they echoed the distinction between society and state that was drawn by the American revolutionary Thomas Paine, among others. Paine, in his revolutionary tract *Common Sense*, sought to remove the mantle of divinity from the European ruling classes: "[I]t is more than probable that, could we take off the dark covering of antiquity and trace them ['the present race of kings'] to their first rise, that we should find the first of them nothing better than the principal ruffian of some restless gang, whose savage manners of pre-eminence in subtilty obtained him the title of chief among plunderers and who, by increasing in power and extending his depredations, overawed the quiet and defenseless to purchase their safety by frequent contributions."[5] Of the origins of the English monarchy, Paine observed, "A French bastard landing with an armed banditti, and establishing himself King of England against the consent of the natives, is in plain terms a very paltry rascally original.—It certainly hath no divinity in it."[6]

The idea that conquest formed the foundation of political authority was also given prominence in French liberal thought because of the influence of Benjamin Constant's influential essay *De l'esprit de conquête et de l'usurpation dans leur rapports avec la civilization européene*

(1814), which distinguished between the spirit of commerce and the spirit of war. This distinction was to receive both historical grounding and a scientific system with the French *économistes*. Augustin Thierry, the historian and collaborator of Charles Comte and Charles Dunoyer on the leading liberal publication of the early nineteenth century in France, *Le Censeur européen*,[7] was a pioneer in the establishment of the conquest theory of the state on firm historical ground. Thierry wrote of his reading of David Hume's *History of England*, "In 1817, I contributed to the *Censeur européen*, the most serious, and at the same time most speculatively daring of all the liberal publications of that period. To a hatred of military despotism, a fruit of the reaction of the general spirit against the imperial government, I joined a profound aversion for revolutionary tyranny, and without a preference for any form of government whatever, I felt a certain disgust at English institutions, of which we then possessed only an odious and ridiculous imitation. One day when, in order to found this opinion on an historical examination, I had attentively read some chapters of Hume, I was struck with an idea which seemed to me a ray of light, and exclaimed as I closed the book, '*All this dates from a conquest; there is a conquest underneath it.*'"[8] In 1826 he published his *History of the Conquest of England by the Normans*.

Thierry's research focused to a large degree on the establishment of the English and French states, the former through his justly famous *History of the Conquest of England by the Normans* and the latter through his *Lettres sur l'Histoire de France* and the *Tales of the Merovingian Franks* (1840) and other works. The states of his day were the lasting legacy of the conquests of years before, in England of the Normans and in France of the Franks. Thierry set himself the task of writing the history of liberty, of chronicling the struggle of the oppressed and enslaved against their masters. In his *History of the Conquest of England by the Normans*, he recorded first the sufferings of the Celtic peoples under the rule of the barbarian Angles, Saxons, Jutes, and other invaders, then of the suffering of these groups under the assaults of the Danes, and finally of the cruelty of the fastening of Norman rule on the descendents of previous invaders, each invading group changing in turn from victor to vanquished. The history Thierry pioneered was to be a new history, a history that would tell the story of the growth of liberty, rather than of the crimes of the rulers, "the immemorable massacres which soil the annals of our nation."[9] As he wrote of the history of France in a review in *Le Censeur européen*,

> Who among us has not heard told of the misery of a class of men who, in the time of the barbarian invasions, conserved for humanity the arts and morality of industry? Outraged and despoiled each day by their conquerors and masters, they struggled on painfully, gaining little from their labor but the knowledge of doing good and of guarding for their children and for the world the seeds of civilization.
>
> These saviors of our arts were our fathers. We are the sons of these serfs, these tributaries, these townsmen whom the conquerors devoured at will. To their memory is attached the memories of virtue and glory. But, these memories shine palely, because history, which should transmit them, has been controlled by our fathers' enemies.[10]

The history of liberty was the history of the shaking off of the bonds of servitude, beginning with the establishment of the revolutionary communes of the eleventh and twelfth centuries, whose "first concern was to organize and to cement their unity with a solemn oath. These were associations of labor and liberty where each devoted himself to produce for society and to defend it. Thus were the communes born."[11] It was this movement that set the stage for the growth of the productive forces that were to change the world. While the feudal system of plunder and coercion grew and maintained itself, there grew alongside it—and in competition with it—a parallel system of liberty, production, and commerce. This change in the material productive forces of society was the driving power of the revolutions that were sweeping Europe.

While history had blurred and finally eliminated the distinctions of race and language that divided the predatory ruling classes from the oppressed and productive classes, the crucial distinction remained: through coercion some were able to plunder others who produced wealth through work and voluntary exchange.[12]

The distinction between production and society, on the one hand, and predation and the state, on the other, was given firm grounding in the science of economics being developed by Destutt de Tracy and Jean-Baptiste Say. Indeed, society was unambiguously identified with the market. As de Tracy wrote in his *Treatise on Political Economy*, "Society is purely and solely a continual series of exchanges."[13]

325

Exchange was paradigmatic for social intercourse, for "an exchange is a transaction in which the two contracting parties both gain. Whenever I make an exchange freely, and without constraint, it is because I desire the thing I receive more than that I give; and, on the contrary, he with whom I bargain desires what I offer more than that which he renders me."[14] As de Tracy remarks, "the true utility of society is to render possible amongst us a multitude of similar arrangements. It is this innumerable crowd of small particular advantages, unceasingly arising, which composes the general good, and which produces at length the wonders of perfected society."[15]

The world is divided between two great classes, the producers and the exploiters. As Charles Comte wrote in his essay "Of the Multiplication of Paupers, Officeholders, and Pensioners,"

> We have already said that there exist in the world only two great parties; that of those who prefer to live from the produce of their labor or of their property, and that of those who prefer to live on the labor or the property of others; the party of the farmers, manufacturers, merchants, and scientists, and the party of the courtiers, office holders, monks, permanent armies, pirates, and beggars.

"Since the origin of the world, these two parties have always been in a state of war."[16]

Charles Dunoyer, too, divided the means of accumulating wealth between pillage and production. As he wrote at the beginning of his essay "Of the System of the Equilibrium of European Powers," "The first means to satisfy their needs that men have perceived is to take; to rob has been man's first industry; this has also been the first object of human association, and history hardly knows of a society that was not at first formed for war and pillage. The ancient and best known peoples, the most civilized of modern nations, have been originally only savage hordes living from rapine."[17] Dunoyer elaborated a theory of history based on economics to explain the continuation of this system of exploitation; any group that might renounce war and pillage would merely open itself up as a target for the predation of others.[18] Thus, history and economics were joined in a sophisticated explanatory system.

The history of the human race was divided by these advocates of "industrialism" (i.e., of the system of industrial production rather than of coercive predation) into three stages: the stage of hunting, gathering, and robbing; the stage of war and exploitation; and the stage of production and cooperation.[19] Each stage was distinguished by the means of accumulating material wealth. In the first stage, material wealth was simply accumulated by means of appropriating the spontaneous products of nature or by taking what others had appropriated. In the second, wealth was accumulated by appropriating the *produce* of others, either through war, as in the case of the early Roman republic, or through exploitation of coerced labor, as in the manorial system of the feudal period. In the third and final stage, the new age into which European civilization was entering, wealth would be accumulated by production and voluntary exchange alone. In each case, "the means that the people are capable of employing in order to procure things necessary to their existence determine the form of their social organization and the choice of men who should direct them."[20] (This understanding of the relationship between "material base" and "superstructure" was later adopted in a more rigid form by Karl Marx.)

Thierry and his associates elaborated a theory of social and historical change that combined history with political economy. Stage did not succeed stage in an ever recurring cycle, nor in response to vague social "forces"; the interests of real human beings and the incentives they faced provided the motive force of historical change. As Thierry wrote, "Do you want to know accurately who has created an institution, who has conceived a social enterprise? Search among those who have truly had need of it; to them must belong the first thought, the will to act, and at least the greatest part in the execution."[21]

The French liberals associated with *Le Censeur européen* saw themselves in the transition phase between the second and third stages. The growth of productive forces begun with the establishment of the communes had outpaced feudalism and set the stage for a struggle between these two systems of social organization. As one historian characterized the liberals' view of this struggle, it was "a struggle between government and nations, between aristocrats and the industrious, between the non-productive and the productive elements within human society, in short, old Europe and new Europe. In this contest, according to the 'industrialists,' the former favored war, arbitrariness, and economic control while the latter wanted only peace, justice, and liberty."[22]

The parties in the war between the newly emerging industrial society of peace, freedom, and prosperity and the old order of war, exploitation, and poverty had come to blows with the French Revolution of 1789. The failure of this revolution provided a significant problem for the classical liberal historians and political economists. The Revolution had degenerated into the Terror, the Directory, and ultimately the Empire. Something had surely gone wrong. The group associated with *Le Censeur européen* explained the failure of the Revolution in two ways. First, along with many other defenders of the Revolution, they charged royalist plotting with diverting the Revolution from its true course, provoking the Terror.[23] Second, they pointed to the inappropriateness to the new social conditions of the ideas of the group that came to power.[24] In Comte's words, "in place of studying things, they had learned systems, and without ascertaining what was the state of civilization and what were the needs of their contemporaries, they made laws that were suitable only for a people of another age."[25] The ruling ideas of the age were atavistic remnants of the age of exploitation, inappropriate to the new age of production, exchange, and voluntarism. This cleft between ideas and social reality, so clearly pointed out by the French liberals, remains to this day a major factor in the growth of parasitic government.[26]

Henri Saint-Simon, however, saw things somewhat differently. Until 1817, in association with the classical liberal "industrialists" (Thierry was his secretary until they split over the priority given by Saint-Simon to order, by Thierry to liberty), Saint-Simon retained the historicist and deterministic approach of the "industrialists" but made it even more deterministic.[27] While Thierry, Comte, and Dunoyer blamed the failure of the productive classes in the French Revolution on the bad ideas of the revolutionists and accordingly set themselves the task of eliminating these atavistic remnants of feudalism that prevented the free society from replacing feudal society, Saint-Simon fell back on historicism and determinism to explain the degeneration of the Revolution of 1789. He posited another stage and another class in order to explain the failure of the "industrial class" to attain victory in its struggle with the parasitic class. As Shirley Gruner explains, around 1820, Saint-Simon "developed the idea that industrialism cannot come about without a period of transition, an intermediary system formed of a class derived from the old yet in some way independent of it, a kind of transitional aristocracy which provided the critical force to break up the old yet was itself unable to create the requirements of the new."[28] As Gruner remarks, "by a singularly unfortunate choice of words, this subclass of feudalism was termed the bourgeois class, the *bourgeoisie*, just at the time when Thierry was developing the notion that the *bourgeoisie* was, in fact, the mass of the nation—the industrials themselves. From now on, the *bourgeoisie* take on the alarming ability of shrinking to a vicious elite or expanding to the industrious masses, dependent on the views of the writer."[29]

The Marxian Confusion

This ambiguity of the term "bourgeoisie" led to so much confusion among later thinkers. In the hands of the later Saint-Simonists, the Fourierists, and Marx, the term bourgeoisie came to designate both an oppressive class of bureaucrats, soldiers, and privileged beneficiaries of state largesse and the class of merchants, bankers, and businessmen. The critical distinction between producers and non-producers founded in the union of history and political economy was lost in a tangled clot of terminological confusion and economic misunderstanding.

Marx manages to use both senses of the term "bourgeoisie" in his works. In the "Manifesto of the Communist Party," Marx writes, "The bourgeoisie, by the rapid improvement of all instruments of production, by the immensely facilitated means of communication, draws all, even the most barbarian, nations into civilization. The cheap prices of its commodities are the heavy artillery with which it batters down all Chinese walls, with which it forces the barbarians' intensely obstinate hatred of foreigners to capitulate."[30] Marx conjures up with these words a vision of an industrious class of producers, yet in his writings on the class struggles in France, Marx presents a completely different view of the "bourgeoisie." Writes Marx, "*The indebtedness of the state* was . . . in the *direct interest* of the bourgeoisie which ruled and legislated in parliament. The *state deficit* was, in fact, the actual object of its speculation and its main source of enrichment. At the end of each year a new deficit. After four or five more years a new loan. And every new loan gave the financial aristocracy a fresh opportunity to swindle the state, which was artificially kept hovering on the brink of bankruptcy and was forced to do business with the bankers on the most unfavourable terms."[31] "The July Monarchy," wrote Marx, "was nothing more than a joint-stock company for the exploitation of France's national wealth, whose dividends were divided among ministers, parliament, 240,000 voters and their adherents."[32]

In his pamphlet "The Eighteenth Brumaire of Louis Bonaparte," Marx wrote of the alienation of the state apparatus from civil society and of the aim of class struggle to gain access to this state:

> In France the executive has at its disposal an army of more than half a million individual offices and it therefore constantly maintains an immense mass of interests and livelihoods in a state of the most unconditional dependence; the state enmeshes, controls, regulates, supervises, and regiments civil society from the most all-embracing expressions of its life down to its most insignificant motions, from its most general modes of existence down to the private life of individuals. This parasitic body acquires, through the most extraordinary centralization, an omnipresence, an omniscience, an elasticity and an accelerated rapidity of movement which find their only appropriate complement in the real social body's helpless irresolution and its lack of a consistent formation. . . . [T]he *material interest* of the French bourgeoisie is most intimately imbricated precisely with the maintenance of that extensive and highly ramified state machine. It is that machine which provides its surplus population with jobs, and makes up through state salaries for what it cannot pocket in the form of profits, interest, rents, and fees. Its *political interest* equally compelled it daily to increase the repression, and therefore to increase the resources and the personnel of the state power.[33]

Thus, the bourgeoisie, as Marx is here using the term, is intimately connected with the state power and dependent on its predatory behavior for its income.

Further on he argues that the state takes on an existence of its own, altogether independent of the civil society over which it rules:

> This frightful parasitic body, which surrounds the body of French society like a caul and stops up all its pores, arose in the time of the absolute monarchy, with the decay of the feudal system, which it helped to accelerate. The seigniorial privileges of the landowners and towns were transformed into attributes of the state power, the feudal dignitaries became paid officials, and the variegated medieval pattern of conflicting plenary authorities became the regulated plan

of a state authority characterized by a centralization and division of labour reminiscent of a factory. . . . Every *common* interest was immediately detached from society, opposed to it as a higher, *general* interest, torn away from the self-activity of the individual members of society and made a subject for governmental activity, whether it was a bridge, a school-house, the communal property of a village community, or the railways, the national wealth and the national university of France. Finally, the parliamentary republic was compelled in its struggle against the revolution to strengthen by means of repressive measures the resources and centralization of governmental power. All political upheavals perfected this machine instead of smashing it. The parties that strove in turn for mastery regarded possession of this immense state edifice as the main booty for the victory.[34]

This conflict of classes looks much like that described by the French liberals, while the conflict in *Capital* is of an altogether different sort. The confusion is inherent in Marx's use of the term "bourgeoisie," for, as historian Ralph Raico remarks, "On the Continent . . . the term *bourgeoisie* has no . . . necessary connection with the market: it can just as easily mean the class of 'civil servants' and *rentiers* off the public debt as the class of businessmen in the process of social production."[35] Shirley Gruner makes it clear that "Marx felt he had got a grip on reality when he found the 'bourgeoisie' but in fact he had merely got hold of a very slippery term."[36] This slippery term is at the heart of Marx's class theory, resulting in a contradictory and incoherent theory.

Another source of the confusion comes from Marx's superimposition on to economic/political classes of the Hegelian distinction between man in his particular existence and man in his universal existence. By another unhappy coincidence, the term Hegel uses for civil society, in which man exists as particular, is "bürgerliche Gesellschaft," a term that is neatly translated into French as "société bourgeoise."[37] Thus, Marx was able to superimpose the Hegelian dialectical framework onto the conflict of classes founded on a material base, yielding a system of dialectical materialism.

Appendix: Confusions in the Marxian Theory of Exploitation

Yet another source of confusion in the Marxian attitude to class is located in his complementary theory of exploitation. This is in turn based on a virtual *reductio ad absurdum* of the Ricardian theory of wages and on a misreading of the English economic writer and political theorist Thomas Hodgskin, who had written extensively on the relations between "labor" and "capital." (This misreading of Hodgskin remains common today.) Each deserves at least a brief discussion before going on to a rehabilitation of the classical liberal theory of class and class conflict.

Thomas Hodgskin, the author of *Labor Defended against the Claims of Capital* (1825), *Popular Political Economy* (1827), and *The Natural and Artificial Right of Property Contrasted* (1832), among other works, is cited by Karl Marx a number of times in support of his exploitation thesis in *Capital*. Often called a "Ricardian socialist" by later writers, Hodgskin was in fact neither a Ricardian nor a socialist, as the terms are understood today.[38] He was instead more of a follower of the economic doctrines of Adam Smith and a defender of *laissez-faire*. To put the matter briefly, Hodgskin was interested only in the *justice* of the distribution of wealth and not in determining the quantitative relationships between wages, profits, interest, and rents. Working from the Smithian doctrine that wealth is produced by labor, Hodgskin criticized the landowners and "capitalists" whose wealth was originally acquired not through voluntary exchange of their products but through acts of conquest. Conquest was at the root of the European land system, for during the barbarian invasions

> all Europe was parcelled out by the German tribes, in what are now princely proportions. The followers of Alboin in Italy, of Theodoric in Spain, of Clovis in France, of Hengist in England, and subsequently of William the Conqueror, appropriated the land, not according to what quantity each man could dig by his hand, but rather according to the quantity his horse could gallop round. The appropriation of the land in such large portions was, for our subject the original sin. . . . The persons who thus appropriated the soil of Europe, did so by a right of conquest. They did not lay down the sword the instant they had overrun the land, they kept it drawn in their hand, and engraved with it laws for the conquered.[39]

Far from opposing property or the free market, Hodgskin opposed *feudalism* and its residue, mercantilism. Property titles founded on conquest were illegitimate. As Emilio Pacheco explains, for Hodgskin, "The payment of rent and profits, the cause of the labourer's misery, is only possible because the natural right of property on land has been overridden by the 'artificial' property that the law has enshrined."[40] Since labor produces all wealth, and workers must pay the hereditary owners of land and capital (originally acquired through conquest) fees for the use of the land, profits and rents simply represent deductions from the produce of labor. They are therefore exploitative.

To say this is certainly not to condemn the categories of profit and rent as they are understood in modern economics; rather, Hodgskin was condemning the system of feudalism, whereby producers had to pay the landed aristocracy and their allies for the use of their unjustly acquired land and other resources. Hodgskin offers as an alternative a system of *justice* in property titles—including land— that followed the argument of John Locke in his *Second Treatise of Government*.

Hodgskin's purpose was to address the justice of market relations, not to offer a "science of values" that would explain the relative proportions of wages, profit, and rent, in the manner of David Ricardo.[41]

To sum up, Marx misunderstood Hodgskin's comments on the claims of labor against capital as an attack on the market system (or "capitalism" in contemporary terms), while Hodgskin's true target was not the market at all, but feudalism and mercantilism.

The relationship of Ricardian economics to Marxian doctrines of exploitation is more complex. Marx is, unlike Hodgskin, directly interested in ascertaining the laws determining the relative proportions of wages, profit, and rent. Marx founded his theory of exchange on Aristotle's notion that exchange was based on equality, with the only factor common to all commodities being labor.[42] Real historical prices are therefore determined by the quantity of "congealed socially necessary labor time" required for the production of commodities. The prices of commodities will therefore be set by the amount of labor needed to reproduce them. The wages of labor, however, differ in a most important respect from the prices of other commodities, for labor is the *only* commodity that produces more than is necessary for its own reproduction. Marx follows Ricardo in postulating that the wages of labor will be driven down to the subsistence level—or, in Marx's terms, to the level required for the reproduction of labor power. (In Ricardo's account this driving down of wages is due to the increase in population and the consequent cultivation of ever less productive land, the two factors jointly diminishing the returns to labor.) Labor, then, produces more than its exchange value, the surplus being appropriated by the capitalist as profit.

This theory of exploitation allows Marx to combine his economic theory with both his theory of history and his theory of class conflict, for the vast accumulation of capital made possible by the rule of the bourgeoisie is none other than the surplus value accumulated by this class!

As Marx argues (echoing Thierry) in the "Manifesto of the Communist Party," "From the serfs of the Middle Ages sprang the chartered burghers of the earliest towns. From these burgesses the first elements of the bourgeoisie developed."[43] In the ensuing centuries this class "has accomplished wonders far surpassing Egyptian pyramids, Roman aqueducts, and Gothic cathedrals; it has conducted expeditions that put in the shade all former exoduses of nations and crusades."[44] Since seizing power and putting the feudal classes to flight, "The bourgeoisie, during its rule of scarce one hundred years, has created more massive and more colossal productive forces than have all preceding generations together. Subjection of nature's forces to man, machinery, application of chemistry to industry and agriculture, steam navigation, railways, electric telegraphs, clearing of whole continents for cultivation, canalization of rivers, whole populations conjured out of the ground—what earlier century had even a presentiment that such productive forces slumbered in the lap of social labor?"[45]

Thus, Marx brings together his theory of history, economics, and politics.

Unfortunately, the entire edifice is built on error and confusion. The political and historical confusions over the notion of the "bourgeoisie" and the evolution of classes have been dealt with above. What remains is to discuss briefly Marx's theory of exploitation, which not only rests on a theory of value that has been superseded, but also contains a fatal internal contradiction.

How sad it is that the first volume of *Capital* was to appear in 1867, only three years before William Stanley Jevons, Leon Walras, and above all Carl Menger put the science of economics on an entirely new footing. In 1870 these three thinkers simultaneously offered an answer to the value paradox of classical economics, to which school Marx is inextricably connected. In one version of this problem (known as the "water-diamond" paradox), this problem asks how an obviously valuable commodity such as water can command less in exchange than a diamond, which offers but little to the sustenance of human life. Classical economists had attempted to construct elaborate explanatory schemes based on labor. None was successful. (In Smith's *Wealth of Nations*, this is taken up in the famous deer-beaver model and then dropped in embarrassment to be replaced later in the text with references to "supply and demand.")

The "marginal revolution" of 1870 came from a realization that the question was improperly phrased. The key to solving the puzzle is determining what the relevant unit of choice is. Were one to be given a choice between all the water in the world and no diamonds and all the diamonds in the world and no water, almost nobody would choose diamonds. But we are never faced with such a choice. Rather, all choices are made "on the margin," that is, we face the choice of an additional unit of diamonds or an additional unit of water. Since water is available in most places in great supply, our more pressing needs for water are easily satisfied. And, since (for the purpose of understanding the essence of such an exchange) each unit of water is equivalent to every other unit, the value of a unit of water will be determined by the final use satisfied. That is to say, the value of water will be determined by the "marginal" unit. Diamonds, on the other hand, are in much shorter supply, and therefore there are fewer to satisfy our more pressing needs for diamonds, and, like water, their value will be determined by the marginal unit. Were diamonds as abundant as water, we would expect the value of each unit to fall to that of the marginal use, which might be that of paving stones or landfill. Without going on at greater detail into the determination of relative prices (also made possible by choice on the margin), we shall simply point out that this explanatory scheme offers a far better framework for understanding real historical prices than that offered by the classical economists, including Marx.

It is this problem of real historical prices that also proves fatal to Marx's system, not on the grounds that it has been supplanted by an economic theory of greater power, but because it suffers from an internal inconsistency.[46] Marx divided "capital" into two sorts. "Constant" capital denotes the means of production; it does not alter the amount of its value in its contribution to production and is therefore called "constant capital."[47] "Variable" capital, on the other hand, is capital that is converted into labor power, which, being the only source of value and producing more than it takes to reproduce, "reproduces the equivalent of its own value, and also produces an excess, a surplus-value, which may itself vary, may be more or less according to circumstances. This part of capital is constantly being transformed from a constant into a variable magnitude. I therefore call it the variable part of capital, or, shortly, *variable capital*."[48] The ratio between these two kinds of capital is known as the "organic composition" of capital.

The inconsistency lies in this: If profit arises only from investment in variable capital (for constant capital merely reproduces itself in the product, without a surplus), then we would naturally expect industries with varying ratios of constant to variable capital investments to yield varying rates of profit. But this is not observed to be the case. Indeed, the rate of return on capital investment tends to equalize over varying industries (*ceteris paribus*), as entrepreneurs shift capital from one use to another in response to discrepancies between expected rates of return, thus acting to equalize expected rates of return.

As Marx admits in the posthumously published third volume of *Capital*, according to the theory he set forth in the first volume,

> different lines of industry have different rates of profit, which correspond to differences in the organic composition of their capitals and, within indicated limits, also to their different periods of turnover; given the same time of turnover, the law (as a general tendency) that profits are related to one another as the magnitudes of the capitals, and that, consequently, capitals of equal magnitude yield equal profits in equal periods, applies only to capitals of the same organic composition, even with the same rate of surplus-value. These statements hold good on the assumption which has been the basis of all our analyses so far, namely that the commodities are sold at their values. There is no doubt, on the other hand, that aside from unessential, incidental and mutually compensating distinctions, differences in the average rate of

profit in the various branches of industry do not exist in reality, and could not exist without abolishing the entire system of capitalist production.[49]

Marx's solution to this problem is to deny his earlier contention, on which his entire system is based, "namely that the commodities are sold at their values"! I will abstain from presenting a critique of Marx's elaborate attempt to dodge this contradiction and merely note that—besides abandoning all pretence to a theory of the determination of the relative magnitudes of wages, labor, interest, and profit—his theory collapses into the triviality that all the labor in society is equal in value to all the labor in society.

Notes

1. Karl Marx, "Manifesto of the Communist Party," in David Fernbach, ed., *Karl Marx: Political Writings*, Vol. I, *The Revolutions of 1848* (New York: Vintage Books, 1974), p. 67.

2. Karl Marx, Letter of March 5, 1852, to Joseph Weydemeyer, in *Selected Works: Vol. I* (Moscow: 1951).

3. Karl Marx, Letter to Frederick Engels, July 27, 1854. In this letter Marx refers to Thierry's important work, *Essai sur l'histoire de la formation et des progrès du Tiers État* (1853; Geneva: Megariotis Reprints, 1974), in the introduction to which Thierry criticized those who see class conflict within the voluntary interactions of the free market.

4. Larry Seidentop, "Two Liberal Traditions," in Alan Ryan, ed., *The Idea of Freedom: Essays in Honour of Isaiah Berlin* (Oxford: Oxford University Press, 1979), p. 153.

5. Thomas Paine, *Common Sense* (New York: Penguin Books, 1976), p. 77. Paine was also quite explicit on the distinction between society and the state. In the opening lines of *Common Sense*, he paints the distinction with sure strokes:

> Some writers have so confounded society with government, as to leave little or no distinction between them; whereas they are not only different, but have different origins. Society is produced by our wants, and government by our wickedness; the former promotes our happiness positively by uniting our affections, the latter negatively by restraining our vices. The one encourages intercourse, the other creates distinctions. The first is a patron, the last a punisher.
>
> Society in every state is a blessing, but government even in its best state is but a necessary evil (ibid., p. 65).

6. Ibid., p. 78.

7. For discussion and background information on the social analysis of this group of thinkers, see Leonard P. Liggio, "Charles Dunoyer and French Classical Liberalism," *Journal of Libertarian Studies* 1, Summer 1977, and Mark Weinburg, "The Social Analysis of Three Early 19th Century French Liberals: Say, Comte, and Dunoyer," *Journal of Libertarian Studies* 2, Winter 1978.

8. Augustin Thierry, *The Historical Essays* (Philadelphia: Carey and Hart, 1845), p. vii. The disgust for English institutions Thierry expresses was a reaction to the idealization of "English liberty" by previous French writers and the realization that it was England that stood for illiberal reaction on the European continent. See the discussion of the change from the "Anglomania" of the French liberals to their "Anglophobia" by Ralph Raico, "Classical Liberal Exploitation Theory: A Comment on Professor Liggio's Paper," *Journal of Libertarian Studies* 1, Summer 1977, p. 181–182.

9. Augustin Thierry, Review of *Commentaire sur* l'Esprit des lois *de Montesquieu. Le Censeur européen* VII (1818). English translation by Mark Weinburg, "Theory of Classical Liberal *Industrielisme*," Occasional Paper no. 5 (New York: Center for Libertarian Studies, 1978).

10. Ibid.

11. Ibid. See also the discussion of the foundation of communes governed by oaths in Harold Berman, *Law and Revolution: The Formation of the Western Legal Tradition* (Cambridge, Mass.: Harvard University Press, 1983), esp. pp. 357–403.

12. Augustin Thierry, *History of the Conquest of England by the Normans* (New York: E. P. Dutton & Co., 1927), p. 3:

> The upper and lower classes which we now see struggling with each other for systems of ideas or of government are, in several countries, no other than the conquering nations and the enslaved nations of an earlier period. Thus the sword of conquest, while changing the face of Europe, and the distribution of its inhabitants into distinct nations, has left its original features to each nation created by the mixture of several races. The race of invaders, when it had ceased to be a distinct people, remained a privileged class. It formed a warlike nobility, which, to prevent its own extinction, recruited its ranks from the ambitious, the adventurous, and the turbulent, among the lower orders, and held dominion over the laborious and peaceable mass, until the termination of the military government resulting from the conquest. The invaded race, deprived of its property in the soil, of command, and of liberty—living, not by arms, but by labour—dwelling, not in castles, but in towns—formed another society, coexistent with the military society of the conquerors.

13. Antoine-Louis-Claude Destutt, comte de Tracy, *Treatise on Political Economy* (1817; New York: Augustus M. Kelley, 1970), p. 6.

14. Ibid., p. 8.

15. Ibid., p. 9. For a discussion of the influence of the political economy of Jean-Baptiste Say on Comte, Dunoyer, and Thierry, see Robert Warren Brown, *The Generation of 1820 during the Bourbon Restoration in France: A Biographical and Intellectual Portrait of the First Wave, 1814–1824* (Durham, N.C.: Duke University, unpublished Ph.D. dissertation, 1979), pp. 152–54.

16. Charles Comte, "De la multiplication des pauvres, des gens à place, et des gens à pensions," *Le Censeur européen* VII, 1818, p. 1.

17. Charles Dunoyer, "Du système de l'équilibre des puissances européenes," *Le Censeur européen* I, 1817.

18. Contemporary social scientists would describe this situation as a prisoner's dilemma.

19. Charles Comte, in his essay, "De l'organisation sociale considerée dans ses rapports avec les moyens de subsistance des peuples," *Le Censeur européen* II, 1817, identifies three means of satisfying human needs: the "spontaneous products of

nature," the "means by which he robs his fellows," and the "products of his industry." Cf. Robert Warren Brown, op. cit., pp. 157–162, 168–174.

20. Charles Comte, "De l'organisation sociale consideŕee dans ses rapports avec les moyens de subsistance des peuples," *Le Censeur européen* II, 1817, p. 5. A similar argument is advanced by Benjamin Constant. According to Shirley Gruner, Constant "explained the difference between the antique world and the modern world as being due to economic factors. Owing to the new method of production, the birth of commerce and industry, a new life had become possible so that without this development, the new life and the new man would be quite inconceivable, thereby erecting an effective barrier against any historical cyclicism." Shirley M. Gruner, *Economic Materialism and Social Moralism* (The Hague: Mouton, 1973), p. 91.

21. Augustin Thierry, "Sur l'Affranchissement des Communes," *Oeuvres Complètes*, Tome III (Paris: Fume et Ce., 1851), p. 492.

22. Robert Warren Brown, op. cit., p. 162.

23. See, however, the more recent work of the classical liberal economic historian Florin Aftalion, *L'Économie de la Révolution française* (Paris: Hachette, 1987) for a historical account of the inflationary policies of the Revolutionary government, which had assumed the debts of the monarchy, and of its decision to impose price controls. It was this chain of events that led to attacks on "speculators" and others and constituted much of the reign of Terror.

24. For a discussion of the response of the *Le Censeur européen* group to the failure of the Revolution, see Robert Warren Brown, op. cit., pp. 148–150. See also the discussion in Stanley Mellon, *The Political Uses of History: A Study of Historians in the French Restoration* (Stanford, Calif.: Stanford University Press, 1958). Mellon refers to Thierry as "perhaps the greatest French historian of the Restoration."

25. Charles Comte, "Considerations sur l'état présent," cited in Robert Warren Brown, op. cit., p. 149.

26. Not only did the ideas of parasitism survive, but so did the parasitic institutions themselves. See Arno J. Mayer, *The Persistence of the Old Regime: Europe to the Great War* (New York: Pantheon Books, 1981).

27. The relationship between Saint-Simon and Augustin Thierry, Charles Comte, and Charles Dunoyer is explored in Élie Halévy, "Saint-Simonian Economic Doctrine," in *The Era of Tyrannies: Essays on Socialism and War* (London: Allen Lane the Penguin Press, 1967). Of the break between this group and Saint-Simon, Halevy writes, "Thierry, who had led him to discover first political and then economic liberalism, was disturbed to see an authoritarian conception of social organization reappearing in his conversation. One day Saint-Simon declared, 'I cannot imagine association without government by someone.' Thierry answered, 'And I cannot imagine association without liberty.' Saint-Simon broke with Augustin Thierry, probably towards the end of July 1817. . ." (p. 27).

28. Shirley M. Gruner, op. cit., p. 116.

29. Ibid., p. 118.

30. Karl Marx, "Manifesto of the Communist Party," in David Fernbach, ed., *Karl Marx: The Revolutions of 1848: Political Writings, Volume I* (New York: Vintage Books, 1974), p. 71.

31. Karl Marx, "The Class Struggles in France: 1848 to 1850," in David Fernbach, ed., *Karl Marx: Surveys from Exile: Political Writings, Volume II* (New York: Vintage Books, 1974), p. 37.

32. Ibid., p. 38.

33. Karl Marx, "The Eighteenth Brumaire of Louis Bonaparte," in David Fernbach, ed., *Karl Marx: Surveys from Exile: Political Writings, Volume II*, op. cit., p. 186.

34. Ibid., p. 237–238.

35. Ralph Raico, "Classical Liberal Exploitation Theory: A Comment on Professor Liggio's Paper," op. cit., p. 179.

36. Shirley M. Gruner, op. cit., pp. 189–190.

37. Cf. Shirley M. Gruner, op. cit., p. 183: "By some strange chance of course, the German for civil society is bürgerliche Gesellschaft, the society of the burgher or 'bourgeois' although in fact neither Hegel nor Marx had any acquaintance with the French term 'bourgeoisie' as it developed in France, particularly after 1830 when it virtually became a mere term of abuse."

38. See the discussion of Hodgskin in Emilio J. Pacheco-Rodriguez, *Utility and Rights: The Science of Morals in Britain in the First Half of the Nineteenth Century* (Oxford: Oxford University, unpublished D.Phil. dissertation, 1986), esp. pp. 116–146.

39. Thomas Hodgskin, *The Natural and Artificial Right of Property Contrasted* (1832; Clifton, N.J.: Augustus M. Kelley, 1973), pp. 71–73.

40. Emilio Pacheco-Rodriguez, op. cit., p. 140.

41. Thomas Hodgskin, *Popular Political Economy* (1827; New York: Augustus M. Kelley, 1966), p. 43. Cf. Emilio Pacheco-Rodriguez, op. cit., p. 129: "The distinction between 'natural' and 'artificial' price does not explain how rents and profits are determined, but that should not be surprising since Hodgskin clearly stated he did not want to explain relative prices: political economy, he said, is not concerned with the question of values, an error made by the French and adopted by the English political economists."

42. Karl Marx, *Capital, Vol. I, A Critical Analysis of Capitalist Production* (1867; New York: International Publishers, 1967), p. 59: "Aristotle . . . clearly enunciates that the money-form of commodities is only the further development of the simple form of value—i.e., of the expression of the value of one commodity in some other commodity taken at random; for he says—5 beds = 1 house (*klinai pente anti oikias*) is not to be distinguished from 5 beds = so much money. (*klinai pente anti. . . hoson ai pente klinai*) He further sees that the value relation which gives rise to this expression makes it necessary that the house should qualitatively be made the equal of the bed, and that, without such an equalisation, these two clearly different things could not be compared with each other as commensurable quantities." Marx, of course, argues that the one thing common to both that makes the equality of exchange possible is labor, something Aristotle was unable to see because Greek society was founded on slavery, and that the equality of labor (p. 61) "cannot be deciphered, until the notion of human equality has already acquired the fixity of a popular prejudice." As with his reading of Hodgskin, Marx seems not to notice that Aristotle is offering an account of justice in exchange and not an account of the determinations of real historical exchanges. Aristotle's statements are based on his theory of justice (cf. *Nicomachean Ethics*, VI, iii on justice and equality), and they cannot be understood outside of that context. As James Bonar remarks in *Philosophy and Political Economy* (1893; New York: Humanities Press, 1967), p. 39, "When Aristotle gives us a theory of exchanges, under the head of Particular Justice (or justice in the narrow sense of the word as distinguished from justice in general), it is not an economic theory; and economic questions are touched very incidentally." Bonar uses the term "economic" in the same way that Hodgskin used the phrase "science of values."

43. Karl Marx, "Manifesto of the Communist Party," op. cit., p. 68.

44. Ibid., p. 70.

45. Ibid., p. 72.

46. The reader is referred for a detailed and complete treatment of this problem to Eugen von Böhm-Bawerk's work, *Karl Marx and the Close of His System* (1896; New York: Augustus M. Kelley, 1949). A better translation of Böhm-Bawerk's title would be, "On the Conclusion of the Marxian System." Böhm-Bawerk refers in his title to the publication of the third volume of *Capital*, which "concluded" the Marxian system. It should be noted that Böhm-Bawerk's criticism is altogether an internal critique, and does not rest in any way on the results of the "marginal revolution" in economic science that took place in 1870.

47. Karl Marx, *Capital, Vol. I*, op. cit., p. 209: "That part of capital then, which is represented by the means of production, by raw material, auxiliary material and the instruments of labor, does not, in the process of production, undergo any quantitative alteration of value. I therefore call it the constant part of capital, or, more shortly, constant capital."

48. Ibid., p. 209.

49. Karl Marx, *Capital, Vol. III, The Process of Capitalist Production as a Whole* (1894; New York: International Publishers, 1967), p. 153.

17. The Great Bequest

Limited government is one of the greatest accomplishments of humanity. It is imperfectly enjoyed by only a portion of the human race, and, where it is enjoyed, its tenure is ever precarious. The experience of the twentieth century is surely witness to the insecurity of constitutional government and to the need for both courage in achieving it and vigilance in maintaining it.

Advocates of limited government are not anti-government per se, as some people would charge. Rather, they are hostile to concentrations of coercive power and to the arbitrary use of power against right. With a deep appreciation for the lessons of history and the dangers of unconstrained government, they are for constitutional limitations: government should have the delegated authority and means to protect our rights, but not be so powerful as to destroy or negate them.

The American system was established to provide limited government. The independent existence of the United States was based on certain truths:

> that all Men are created equal, that they are endowed by their Creator with certain unalienable Rights, that among these are Life, Liberty, and the Pursuit of Happiness—That to secure these Rights, Governments are instituted among Men, deriving their just Powers from the Consent of the Governed, that whenever any Form of Government becomes destructive of these Ends, it is the Right of the People to alter or to abolish it, and to institute new Government, laying its Foundation on such Principles, and organizing its Powers in such Form, as to them shall seem most likely to effect their Safety and Happiness.

On this foundation the American Founders established a system of government based on delegated, enumerated, and thus limited powers.

Originally published in *The Freeman* 49, no. 3, March 1999.

The American Founders did not pluck those truths out of thin air, nor did they simply invent the principles of American government. They drew from their knowledge of thousands of years of human history, during which many peoples struggled for liberty and limited government. There were both defeats and victories along the way. The results were distilled in the founding documents of the American experiment in limited government: the Declaration of Independence, the Articles of Confederation, the state constitutions, and the Constitution of the United States.

Students of History

The American Founders were careful students of history. It was Thomas Jefferson, in his influential *A Summary View of the Rights of British America*, prepared in 1774, who noted that "history has informed us that bodies of men as well as individuals are susceptible of the spirit of tyranny." Another Founder, Patrick Henry, devoted great attention to the study of history. He summed up the importance of history thus: "I have but one lamp by which my feet are guided, and that is the lamp of experience. I know of no way of judging the future but by the past." History—the lamp of experience—is indispensable to understanding and defending the liberty of the individual under constitutionally limited, representative government.

Through the study of history the Americans learned about the division of power among judicial, legislative, and executive branches; about federalism; about checks and balances among divided powers; about redress and representation; and about the right of resistance, made effective by the legal right to bear arms, an ancient right of free persons. Liberty and limited government were not invented in 1776; they were reaffirmed and strengthened. The American Revolution set the stage for the benefits of liberty and limited government to be extended to all. As John Figgis, professor of modern history at Cambridge University, noted at the turn of the century:

> The sonorous phrases of the Declaration of Independence
> . . . are not an original discovery, they are the heirs of all the
> ages, the depository of the emotions and the thoughts of
> seventy generations of culture.

The roots of the history of limited government stretch far back, to the establishment of the principle of the higher law by the ancient

Hebrews and by the Greek philosophers. The story of the golden calf in the Book of Exodus and the investigations of nature by Aristotle both established—in very different ways—the principle of the higher law. Law is not merely an expression of will or power; it is based on transcendent principles. The legislator is as bound by law as is the subject or citizen; no one is above the law.

Many strands have been entwined to form the fabric of liberty:

- The struggle between church and state, which was put into high gear in the Latin West by Pope Gregory VII in the eleventh century under the motto, "freedom of the church." This movement, which created an institutional distinction between the church and the secular authorities, was the first major "privatization" of a previously state-owned industry (the church) and provided the foundation for such important institutions as the rule of law and legal accountability, federalism, and the independent and self-governing associations that make up civil society.
- The growth of civil society in the self-governing chartered towns of Europe, in which the guiding principle was "city air makes one free." The independent cities of Europe were the seedbeds of modern civil society—of the market economy, of personal liberty, and of the security of person and property.
- The fixing of limits on the powers of monarchs and executives through written constitutions. The Magna Carta of 1215 is the most memorable of those documents to inheritors of the Anglo-Saxon political tradition. It included the requirement that taxes could not be imposed without the consent of the "general council of the realm," which provided the origin of the English parliament, as well as other specific limitations on the king's power, including the stipulations that no one be imprisoned, outlawed, or exiled, or his estate seized, "except by the lawful judgment of his peers or the law of the land" and that "merchants shall have safe conduct in and out of England." This was the precursor of the Petition of Right of 1628, the Bill of Rights of 1689, the American Declaration of Independence, and the American Constitution and Bill of Rights.
-   Those various movements reinforced each other in a multitude of ways. The assertion of the freedom of the church and

even of its supremacy over the secular powers was bound up with the idea of the higher law by which all are judged—emperor, pope, and peasant alike. As legal scholar Henry Bracton, a judge during the reign of Henry III, noted of the royal authority, "The law makes him king. Let the king therefore give to the law what the law gives to him, dominion and power; for there is no king where will, and not law, bears rule." Were the king to consider himself above the law, it was the job of the king's council—the precursor of parliament—to rein him in: "if the king were without a bridle, that is, the law, they ought to put a bridle upon him." Not only was the nascent parliament above the king; the law was above the parliament, as Sir Edward Coke noted in the seventeenth century:

> [W]hen an act of Parliament is against common right and reason, or repugnant, or impossible to be performed, the common law will controul it, and adjudge such Act to be void.

Law Supreme

The supremacy of the law over the exercise of power is a hallmark of the Western legal tradition. The rule of law is not satisfied by merely formal or ceremonial exercises, such as the publication of edicts in barely understandable form, whether in the archaic "Law French" of the king's courts or the pages of the *Federal Register*; the laws must be understandable and actually capable of being followed.

There was also widespread recognition of the principle of reciprocity between the holders of power and the general populace. Rights were spelled out in contractual form in constitutions and charters. Those rights were not gifts from the powerful, which could be taken away on a whim, but something on which one could take a stand. Tied up in the notion of a chartered right was the ancillary right to defend that right, even to the point of resistance with force of arms. The higher law, reciprocity and mutuality of obligations, written charters of rights, the right to be consulted on policy and to grant or refuse one's consent, and the right of resistance in defense of those rights are the foundations of constitutionally limited government. They were won over many centuries at great sacrifice.

Just how precious this heritage is can be gleaned from comparing it with the history of Russia, where, until very recently, there was no reciprocity between rulers and ruled, no independent power able to challenge the rulers. The principality of Muscovy and its successors were despotic to a high degree, with no charters of liberty, no power higher than the Tsar (or his successor, the Communist Party), no limits on power—in effect, no law. As Harvard University historian Richard Pipes noted in his book *Russia under the Old Regime*, "There is no evidence in medieval Russia of mutual obligations binding prince and his servitor, and, therefore, also nothing resembling legal and moral 'rights' of subjects, and little need for law and courts." The immense difficulties in establishing the rule of law, a system of well-defined and legally secure property, and a market economy are testimony to the great and vital importance of building on a tradition of stable, constitutionally limited government. They also remind us how important it is for us to maintain our heritage of limited government and the rule of law.

Liberty Versus Power

The struggle for limited government was a struggle of liberty against power. The demands for religious liberty and the protection of property were fused in the heroic resistance of the Netherlands to the Empire of Spain in their great revolt. The Dutch became a shining example of what was possible when people were free: prosperity was possible without the guiding hand of the king and his bureaucrats; social harmony was possible without enforced religious conformity; law and government were possible without an unlimited and absolute sovereign. The Dutch inspired the English to rise up against the Stuart kings, who sought to fasten upon the English the absolutism that had made such headway on the Continent. The American Revolution was one link in a long chain of revolutions for liberty.

The story of the attempts to institute absolutism in the Netherlands and in England was well known by the American Founders, who were, after all, British colonists. One cannot understand the American attempt to institute limited representative government without understanding the history of England. What they were struggling against was the principle that the powers of the state are "plenary," that they fill up the whole space of power. King James I of England (then King James VI of Scotland) had written in 1598 that "the King is above the law, as both the author and giver of strength thereto."

In 1610 James made *A Speech to the Lords and Commons of the Parliament at White-Hall* in which he railed against the notions of popular consent and the rule of law and stated that "as to dispute what God may do is blasphemy . . . so it is sedition in subjects to dispute what a king may do in the height of his power."

In other words, there are no limits to power. Distinct echoes of that view are still heard today. For example, the solicitor general of the United States, Drew Days, arguing in the case of *United States v. Lopez* before the Supreme Court, was unable to identify a single act of Congress, other than those expressly prohibited by the Constitution, that would be impermissible under the Clinton administration's expansive view of the Commerce Clause. Solicitor Days contended that the powers of Congress are plenary, that is, unlimited, unless, perhaps, specifically prohibited.

That all-too-common view turns the notion of limited government on its head. Limited government means that government is limited both to the exercise of its delegated powers and in the means it can employ, which must be both "necessary and proper." The English Revolution of 1640, the Glorious Revolution of 1688, and the American Revolution of 1776 were fought precisely to combat unlimited government. What Americans need is not unlimited government, as Days proposes, but limited government under law, exercising delegated and enumerated powers. That is how the equal liberties of citizens are protected. As the philosopher John Locke, himself an active participant in the struggles for limited government in Britain and the primary inspiration of the American revolutionaries, argued in his *Second Treatise of Government*: "*the end of Law* is not to abolish or restrain, but *to preserve and enlarge Freedom*: For in all the states of created beings capable of Laws, where *there is no Law, there is no Freedom*. For *Liberty* is to be free from restraint and violence from others, which cannot be, where there is no Law."

Unprecedented Liberty

The American experiment in limited government generated a degree of liberty and prosperity that was virtually unimaginable only a few centuries before. That experiment revealed flaws, of course, none of which was more striking and repugnant than the toleration of slavery, or "man-stealing," as it was called by its libertarian opponents, for it deprived an individual of his property in his own person. That particular evil was eliminated by the Thirteenth Amendment to the Constitution, showing the self-correcting nature and basic resilience of the American constitutional system, which could survive such a cataclysm as the Civil War.

Other flaws, however, have been revealed or have surfaced since. Among them are the following:

- An erosion of the basic principles of federalism, as the federal government has consistently encroached on the authority of the states. Federal criminalization of acts that are already criminalized by the states, for example, usurps state authority (as well as circumventing—opinions of the Supreme Court notwithstanding—the prohibition of double jeopardy in the Fifth Amendment to the Constitution). An even more striking contemporary example of the overreach of federal law is the continued exercise of federal controls over marijuana use in states—California and Arizona—that have legalized the medical use of that drug. The Tenth Amendment is quite explicit on this point: "The powers not delegated to the United States by the Constitution, nor prohibited by it to the States, are reserved to the States respectively, or to the people."

- Violation of the separation of powers between the various branches of government. In article I, section 8, for example, the Constitution explicitly reserves the power to declare war to the Congress, a power that the Congress has allowed to be usurped by the executive branch and which it should retake to itself. Further, the Congress has illegally exceeded its authority by delegating its legislative powers to administrative agencies of the executive branch, such as the Food and Drug Administration and the Federal Trade Commission. In addition to violating the Constitution, that delegation has led to the erosion of the rule of law, as such administrative agencies have burdened the population with an unimaginably complex welter of edicts; the *Federal Register* runs to some 60,000 pages *per year*, representing a degree of minute regulation that is unreasonable and burdensome and that virtually guarantees that any citizen involved in a commercial transaction, for example, will run afoul of some part of it, no matter how well intentioned or scrupulous he may be. Such a situation is an invitation to the arbitrary exercise of power, rather than the application of law.

- Inattention to the important role of the federal judiciary as a check on arbitrary and unauthorized exercises of power. Especially since the threatened Court-packing "constitutional revolution of 1937," there has been too little attention by the federal judiciary—and by the Congress in ratifying judicial nominees—to fulfilling the role of the courts in enforcing constitutional restraints on both the federal and the state governments. For example, the Supreme Court has not consistently applied the prohibitions of the First Amendment to either commercial speech or political speech (the latter in the context of campaign finance), nor has the Court rectified the novel (and specious) distinction between personal liberties and economic liberties drawn by Justice Harlan F. Stone in *United States v. Carolene Products Co.* (1938).

- The failure to pass a constitutional amendment limiting members of the Senate to two terms and members of the House of Representatives to three terms. Just as the president is limited in the number of terms he can serve, so should be the other elected branch of government, to guarantee the rotation in office that the Founders believed essential to popular government.

Needed Corrective

Those flaws can, however, be corrected. What is needed is the courage to place the health of the constitutional order and the future of the American system above short-term political gain. The original American Founders were willing "to mutually pledge to each other our Lives, our Fortunes, and our sacred Honor." Nothing even remotely approaching that would be necessary for today's members of Congress to renew and restore the American system of constitutionally limited government.

The challenge facing Americans today in defending constitutionally limited government was succinctly stated by the English libertarian Herbert Spencer in 1884:

> The function of Liberalism in the past was that of putting a limit to the powers of kings. The function of true Liberalism in the future will be that of putting a limit to the powers of Parliaments.

Suggested Readings

Berman, Harold. 1983. *Law and Revolution: The Formation of the Western Legal Tradition.* Cambridge, Mass.: Harvard University Press.

Boaz, David. 1997. *Libertarianism: A Primer.* New York: Free Press.

Boaz, David, ed. 1997. *The Libertarian Reader: Classic and Contemporary Readings from Lao-tzu to Milton Friedman.* New York: Free Press.

Bramsted, E. K., and K. J. Melhuish, eds. 1978. *Western Liberalism: A History in Documents from Locke to Croce.* New York: Longman.

Brooks, David L., ed. 1993. *From Magna Carta to the Constitution: Documents in the Struggle for Liberty.* San Francisco: Fox & Wilkes.

Ely, James W., Jr. 1998. *The Guardian of Every Other Right: A Constitutional History of Property Rights.* New York: Oxford University Press.

Epstein, Richard A. 1985. *Takings: Private Property and the Right of Eminent Domain.* Cambridge, Mass.: Harvard University Press.

———. 1997. *Simple Rules for a Complex World.* Cambridge, Mass.: Harvard University Press.

Hamilton, Alexander, James Madison, and John Jay. 1961. *The Federalist Papers.* New York: Mentor.

Hayek, F. A. 1960. *The Constitution of Liberty.* Chicago: University of Chicago Press.

Higgs, Robert. 1987. *Crisis and Leviathan: Critical Episodes in the Growth of American Government.* New York: Oxford University Press.

Jefferson, Thomas. 1977. "A Summary View of the Rights of British North America." In *The Portable Jefferson.* New York: Penguin Books.

Locke, John. *Two Treatises of Government.* 1690 (1988). Cambridge: Cambridge University Press.

Sidney, Algernon. 1698 (1990). *Discourses Concerning Government.* Indianapolis: Liberty Fund.

Spencer, Herbert. 1994. *Political Writings.* Cambridge: Cambridge University Press.

Storing, Herbert, ed. 1985. *The Anti-Federalist.* Chicago: University of Chicago Press.

18. The Millennial Struggle for Liberty

The most important development of the past thousand years has been the growth of liberty, both because liberty is important in its own right and because it is what has made virtually all of the other achievements of humanity possible, as well, from science to art to material well-being.

For that reason, I would locate the first of the most significant moments of the past thousand years in March of 1075, when Pope Gregory VII issued the *Dictatus Papae*, in which he formally announced the independence of the Church from the state and the power of the Church to check the state. As Article 27 states, "The Pope may absolve subjects of unjust men from their fealty." The great historian Lord Acton wrote, "To that conflict of four hundred years we owe the rise of civil liberty . . . the aim of both contending parties was absolute authority. But although liberty was not the end for which they strove, it was the means by which the temporal and the spiritual power called the nations to their aid."

Second on my list would be the growth of European constitutionalism. This was a broadly European movement, but especially notable for the Anglo-American tradition is, of course, the issuance of the Magna Carta on June 19, 1215. The Magna Carta explicitly limited the royal power, established the principle of the consent of the governed and guaranteed rights of due process, freedom of trade, and more. These and other provisions later found their way into the U.S. Constitution.

Third would be the invention of movable type in Europe around 1436 or 1437 by Johann Gutenberg. This tremendous innovation broke the monopolies of the privileged few over knowledge. The printed book initiated an information sea change that is still going

Originally published in *Human Events*, December 31, 1999, as part of a group of essays on the greatest events of the past thousand years.

on; the worldwide Web is just the latest chapter in the freeing of information made possible by Gutenberg.

Fourth, in my view, is the rebirth of constitutionalism after its eclipse by absolutism and mercantilism. The struggle to place limits on government and at the same time to expand greatly the popular enjoyment of liberty took place dramatically in the 16th, 17th, and 18th centuries in the revolt of the Dutch against their Spanish over-lords, the revolts of the English against the Stuart kings and the revolt of the Americans against the British crown and Parliament. As the historian John Lothrop Motley wrote, "The rise of the Dutch Republic must ever be regarded as one of the leading events of modern times. . . . The maintenance of the right by the little provinces of Holland and Zealand in the 16th, by Holland and England united in the 17th, and by the United States of America in the 18th centuries forms but a single chapter in the great volume of human fate; for the so-called revolutions of Holland, England and America, are all links of one chain."

Or as John Figgis, professor of modern history at Cambridge University, noted at the turn of the century, "The sonorous phrases of the Declaration of Independence . . . are not an original discovery, they are the heirs of all the ages, the depository of the emotions and the thoughts of 70 generations of culture."

The fifth item on my list is the rise and fall of the totalitarian state. As the classical liberalism that inspired the American Revolution began to wane, various forms of collectivism—notably nationalism, racism, and socialism—rose to challenge liberty. The classical liberal journalist E. L. Godkin wrote in a chilling and depressing editorial on August 9, 1900, "Only a remnant, old men for the most part, still uphold the liberal doctrine, and when they are gone, it will have no champions." He predicted that the 20th century would be a century of war and statism: "The old fallacy of divine right has once more reasserted its power, and before it is again repudiated, there must be international struggles on a terrific scale."

Those struggles—against fascism, National Socialism and commu-nism—are now behind us. The struggle for liberty is not over, but, on the eve of the third millennium, the prospects are bright again.

19. Why Socialism Collapsed in Eastern Europe

Why 1990? Why has Eastern Europe's liberation happened in just the past year? Why not 10 years ago, or 25, if socialism was such a tremendous failure? Let me suggest several reasons.

Above all the other reasons is a sort of meta-reason, the Gorbachev factor. Gorbachev is no classical liberal; in fact, the origins of perestroika were immensely anti-liberal. Perestroika was an attempt to revive socialism, beginning with the law on unearned income, which was an attempt to smash the few elements of a free market there were in the Soviet Union, and a reduction of vodka production, which caused a massive sugar shortage as the Russians began making moonshine. But finally, it seems, Gorbachev and his advisers have figured out that you need market forces to make an economy work. They are now in the process of learning that you cannot have a market without property rights.

Gorbachev did not just decide to be a nice guy—to let Eastern Europe go and to allow people to speak freely. Instead, there was a realization that there was a very deep crisis in communism. In the case of Central and Eastern Europe, the empire was simply too expensive to maintain, and a kind of political decision was made—Moscow had to let those countries go. It could no longer afford to maintain the empire. Consequently, restraints were loosened and the communist leaders in Central Europe were told that they would get no further support from Soviet tanks and soldiers. The Czechs had a bit of good luck in that the major events of the Czechoslovakian revolution took place when Presidents Bush and Gorbachev were meeting in the Mediterranean; the story is that Gorbachev didn't

Originally a lecture that was published in *Cato Policy Report*, September/October 1990, drawing on several years of working in Central and Eastern Europe to promote libertarian ideas and policies.

want to have a bloodbath on his hands during his meeting with Bush, so the word was sent to Prague to lay off.

Several factors combined to force the Gorbachev leadership to let Eastern Europe go. The first was exhaustion of the capital stock. The capital accumulated over hundreds, indeed thousands, of years has been used up. Through the 1960s and the 1970s there was near unanimity among Western economists that the rate of growth in Soviet-style economies was not only positive but higher than in Western Europe or the United States. Clearly, a positive rate of growth, over a period of 40 years or so, should produce wealth, but it didn't. The mistake that was made, and pointed out by a few economists such as G. Warren Nutter, was to measure capital investment, the amount of inputs, not wealth creation. That was a big mistake. It led to what the Hungarian philosopher Michael Polanyi, a great critic of communism, called "conspicuous production"— production for the sake of production. Steel was produced to make a factory to make more steel to make more factories, but the whole process never produced the consumer goods. It did not translate into an increase in the standard of living. And, indeed, it was often politically motivated.

The industrial proletariat was to be the new universal class, which would subsume all other classes and resolve all previous conflicts among them, according to the Marxian system. So the communists had to create an industrial proletariat, even where there had been almost none. In Romania, for example, during the forced industrialization that followed the Second World War, almost all the horses were killed because, after all, in a modern society no one would need them anymore; everyone would have a tractor. Well, the tractors were never produced, so people began to breed horses in secret. Today horses are a common means of transportation in the countryside.

Instead of growing, the capital stock of socialist countries has been declining. They've been consuming it. Most of the textile mills in eastern Czechoslovakia were built before the First World War. They still operate with the original machinery. In East Germany, many of the buildings seem not to have been painted since 1945. In some cases, no one even painted over the old and faded Nazi slogans on the walls. In the Soviet Union, there are chemical factories built 110 years ago that are still producing the same chemicals in the same way. It is a general principle that under socialism no factory is ever closed.

The capital stock inherited from previous generations has been largely worn out, and there are real declines in the standards of living of many East European countries. Those declines would have taken place sooner had it not been for the enormous amount of Western capital that was pumped in by the International Monetary Fund, the World Bank, and other international lending institutions and used largely to finance current consumption.

A second factor that led to the revolutions of 1989 was the difficulty of controlling information. I mean not just political news but also the kind of information about how people live in other countries that you get from watching Western movies. The VCR and the Walkman have had a tremendous impact on life in socialist countries. Radio Free Europe was certainly important, especially in countries such as Romania that didn't have much access to VCRs, but Radio Free Europe could always be discounted as propaganda. In other countries, principally Poland and Hungary but also the Soviet Union, there was a massive influx of electronic devices. Initially, the state tried to control or outlaw them because it knew how subversive they could be. But their suppression was simply impossible.

Western movies show people a picture of Western life—a very funny and distorted picture, but still a view of Western clothes, homes, and the like. When we watch movies, that kind of information just washes over us, but to people of a different society, it can be very revealing. In Moscow last fall, for example, the Swedish movie *Fanny and Alexander* was showing, and a scene of a Christmas banquet had a big impact on viewers. There is a long table with wonderful food on it, and the camera begins at one end and very slowly, lovingly goes down the table, showing us turkeys, sauces, vegetables, and all sorts of fantastic things. At that point, the Soviet audiences stood up and applauded. Perhaps the silent heroes in the revolutions of 1989 were Sony and Mitsubishi and others who keep making more powerful and fantastic devices that convey more information in smaller packages at lower cost.

A third cause of the revolutions was virtual ecological collapse in many of the countries of Central and Eastern Europe. Many Western ecologists have argued for years that the causes of pollution are property rights and capitalism. That is an interesting hypothesis,

357

and it is subject to an empirical test. Let us find an economy with no private property and no capitalism. The theory says that there should be no pollution or, at least, less pollution. But in fact, where there are no private property rights or capital markets, pollution is a nightmare. Some places in the Soviet Union have infant mortality rates that are higher than the rate in Burkina Faso, the poorest nation in Africa. Silesia in Poland has one of the highest rates of birth defects in the world.

The ecological movement that has arisen in socialist states quite naturally is supported by people who want to defend their homes and their children against being poisoned. And that has had several effects. One is simply the growth of political movements, which in some cases have been very important. In Bulgaria, the first public demonstrations against the regime were called by Ecoglasnot, an ecological movement. A major realization of the movement is that not only does the ruling class not have the people's interests at heart, but also central planning is to blame for a lot of their problems. When the order comes from the Central Planning Bureau to produce so much cotton, the head of a collective farm will do anything to meet the dictated quota for this year. Next year can take care of itself. If the way to meet the quota this year is to pour herbicide on the earth or exhaust the soil, that is what he does. In economic terms, there is no residual claimant, no one who profits if the capital value of the resource is maximized. Among intellectuals and academics there is a growing discussion of the value of property rights in solving environmental problems.

The final cause of the revolutions was the virtual collapse of socialist ideology and of the legitimacy of the ruling class. Mere power is usually not enough to sustain a tyrannical regime; in most cases there also has to be, on the parts of both the ruled and the rulers, some sense that the ruling class has the right to rule—that it has moral legitimacy. In the Soviet Union, the rulers claimed to act on behalf of the proletariat. Of course, their primary motivation was power and privilege, but an important additional element was their own sense of legitimacy. The rulers thought that they were morally justified, that they were acting in the interests of the working class, so it was reasonable to ask the people for just a few more sacrifices. I don't think anyone really believes that anymore, but the people accepted the illusion for a very long time.

That illusion is gone for two reasons. One, according to Ibn Khal-dun, a historian of the Islamic world, it takes about two generations for fanatical ideas to lose their steam. It has been about that long since communism was imposed on most of Eastern and Central Europe; in the Soviet Union, it has been longer, but we have to take into account the shot in the arm that Soviet communism got from the Great Patriotic War against fascism. Two, it is typically the ruling class that travels outside the country, and the communist rulers have been to a large extent demoralized by the experience. Rich and powerful people travel to America or Germany and realize that their standard of living is lower than that of the average industrial worker in a Western country. So the ruling class has been more demoralized, in a sense, than the average person, who has never seen the West. The rulers still want to hold on to power, but they have lost the sense of their right to rule.

The socialist ideology promised equality, fraternity, and prosper-ity. Did it keep its promises? Did it deliver equality? The answer is no. Many people in the West will say, although they say it less often now, "Well, yes, of course they wait in lines in Poland or the Soviet Union, but they have a sense of solidarity; they are more equal; there is less income disparity." That's nonsense. If you compare the standard of living of the average citizen of East Germany, the richest of the fraternal nations of the socialist camp, with that of the party members who lived in Wandlitz, the neighborhood of the party elite, you find incredible disparities of income—but until recently they were kept secret. Similarly, if you look at the 22 palaces of the Ceausescu family in Romania, or the sports complexes in Bulgaria that were only for members of the Zhivkov family, or the dachas of the Soviet party elite, you find more inequality than in the market societies of the West.

The second promise of socialism was fraternity: Everyone would live together as one big, happy family. But in fact, the fight over a shrinking economic pie generates a lot more hostility than is found in a system with property rights and market exchange. Often after waiting in line for hours for a bar of soap, clothing, shoes, and so on, would-be consumers in Moscow get to the front of the line only to have the window closed on them and be told, "Go away; we have no more." Among the first things one sometimes hears is grumbling about the "goddamn Jews"—they are the ones who get all the goods—or the Armenians, or the Azerbaijanis, or whomever. Communism was supposed to subsume such malicious forms of nationalism, but it clearly failed.

And the third promise, prosperity? Socialism not only did not produce prosperity, it produced mass poverty.

So socialism is virtually gone as an ideology. Two other ideologies are emerging to replace it. First, nationalism, which takes two forms: Very broadly, there are malignant nationalism and benign nationalism. Malignant nationalism, or chauvinism, is the desire to impose your culture, your religion, your language on another group. And, unfortunately, we see a lot of that in the countries of Central and Eastern Europe. There is another kind of nationalism, however, that has been very important: the desire not to be ruled by foreigners, which is quite understandable and consistent with liberal principles. Overall, I found in Central Europe very little hatred of Russians per se. Central Europeans just want the Russians to go home and leave them alone.

The other ideology is liberalism, in many cases aligned with the benign form of nationalism and, indeed, in explicit opposition to chauvinism. The one name that you hear more than any other throughout Central and Eastern Europe is Friedrich Hayek. Underground, or samizdat, editions and rare English copies of *The Road to Serfdom* are widely read.

It should be no surprise that that influential and powerful book was written by a Central European, who spoke to his readers' condition most forcefully. Marx had failed. He had predicted something that didn't happen. Hayek predicted something that did: That the effort to implement socialism would lead to tyranny and serfdom. And he offered an alternative—liberty, a market economy, prosperity, and the rule of law.

Now, having gone through a kind of exercise in political economy, I'd like to mention a historical thesis that might explain some of the most recent occurrences. I'm borrowing this from a Hungarian scholar, Istvan Bibo, who propounded a thesis about the three parts of Europe: Western, East-Central, and Eastern. According to Bibo, East-Central Europe is more or less the region east of the Elbe. Western Europe is identified with Roman or common law and the emergence of civil society from "little circles of liberty"—associations, groups, neighborhoods, clubs, farms, markets, cities, and so on—from which political authority flowed upward in a limited way. Eastern Europe is identified with the Byzantine and Ottoman systems in which the state was at the top and enforced its will downward.

The big difference between Eastern and Western Europe is the relative separation of church and state in the West, where it came to be recognized that the empire had secular authority and the church spiritual authority. They were separate forms of authority that even had separate court systems. Under the Byzantine system, the emperor remained the head of the church, so such a separation never took place. Also, because of its feudal inheritance and German folk law, political authority in the West broke up much earlier than it did in the East.

The countries of Western Europe are fairly obvious—Britain, Germany, Switzerland, France, and so on. Eastern Europe can largely be identified by the sway of the Orthodox Church. Hungarian political scientist Laszlo Urban has pointed out that liberal parties have done well recently outside the areas long dominated by the Orthodox Church. Liberal parties have not done so well in Russia, Romania, Bulgaria, and Serbia. The division even cuts across a country in the case of Yugoslavia, where Catholic Slovenia and Croatia identify with the Roman West, but Serbia is Orthodox and less liberal. The mixed countries, or Central Europe, include Poland, Lithuania, to some extent Czechoslovakia, Hungary, and perhaps the Ukraine and Belorussia. Throughout their tempestuous history, those countries have been dominated or influenced by both the East and the West. Hungary was under Ottoman rule for quite a long time. Big pieces of Poland were once part of the Russian empire.

Thus there may be cultural factors that will make the transition to freedom easier for those countries than for the Eastern European countries. As Bibo points out, political developments that took place in Western Europe—liberation of the serfs and so on—usually hit East-Central Europe about 200 years later and took even longer to reach Eastern Europe. With our help and with the growth of technology, we could accelerate that process, but the liberals in those countries have a harder job.

One of the reasons that I am so excited about what is happening in Central and Eastern Europe is that I see a very real chance that in the next 10 to 20 years an intellectual and political culture that

361

is more liberal than the one we now have in Western Europe or North America will develop in those countries. I don't mean necessarily a more liberal system; we must remember that Central and Eastern Europe are starting from a different base. The seeds of liberal intellectual and political ideas that have been planted there may sprout; produce mighty trees; and, if we are lucky, drop seeds back into our societies to reinfuse us with the spirit of liberty.

20. The Origins of State and Government

Many people believe that the state is responsible for everything. According to Cass Sunstein, a professor of law at Harvard University and administrator of the Office of Information and Regulatory Affairs, "Government is 'implicated' in everything people own. . . . If rich people have a great deal of money, it is because the government furnishes a system in which they are entitled to have and keep that money."

That's the academic formulation of a concept that was restated recently in a popular form. "If you've been successful, you didn't get there on your own. . . . If you were successful, somebody along the line gave you some help. . . . Somebody helped to create this unbelievable American system that we have that allowed you to thrive. Somebody invested in roads and bridges. If you've got a business—you didn't build that. Somebody else made that happen." That was Sunstein's boss, President Obama.

Even a charitable interpretation of the president's remarks shows that he doesn't understand the concept of marginal contribution to output, for example, of the value added by one additional hour of labor. He doesn't understand how wealth is produced.

Sunstein and his colleagues reason that since they attribute all wealth to the state, the state is entitled to it, and those who may foolishly think of themselves as producers have no claim of their own over it.

What exactly is a state? The canonical definition was offered by Max Weber, who defined the state as "that human community which (successfully) lays claim to the monopoly of legitimate physical violence within a certain territory."

In fact, it cannot be the case that all wealth is attributable to the state.

This essay is extracted from a letter delivered at Cato University in Washington, D.C. in July 2012 and reprinted in *Cato's Letter*, Fall 2012.

Historically, the existence of a state apparatus required a pre-existing surplus to sustain it in the first place. The state, in other words, would not exist without wealth being produced before its emergence. Let's explore that a bit further.

Why do people have wealth? Charles Dunoyer, an early libertarian sociologist, explained that "there exist in the world only two great parties; that of those who prefer to live from the produce of their labor or of their property, and that of those who prefer to live on the labor or the property of others." Simply put, makers produce wealth while takers appropriate it.

In his important book *The State*, the sociologist Franz Oppenheimer distinguished between what he called the economic means and the political means of attaining wealth, that is, between "work and robbery." "The state," he concluded, "is an organization of the political means."

The economic means must precede the political means. However, not all kinds of work produce surpluses sufficient for sustaining a state. You don't find states among hunter-gatherers, for instance, because they don't generate enough of a surplus to sustain a predatory class. The same is true of primitive agriculturalist societies. What is needed is settled agriculture, which generates a surplus sufficient to attract the attention of predators and sustain them. Such societies are typically conquered by nomads—especially those with horses, who were able to overpower sedentary agriculturalists. We see that happening over and over again after nomadic people erupted out of Central Asia long ago.

There is a memory of that ancient conflict preserved in the Book of Genesis, which tells the fratricidal story of Cain and Abel. It is significant that "Abel was a keeper of sheep, but Cain was a tiller of the ground," an echo of the conflict between settled agriculturalists and nomadic herders.

State formation represents a transformation from "roving bandits" to "stationary bandits." As the economist Mancur Olson wrote, "If the leader of a roving bandit gang who finds only slim pickings is strong enough to take hold of a given territory and to keep other bandits out, he can monopolize crime in that area—he can become a stationary bandit." That is an important insight into the development of human political associations.

The state is, at its core, a predatory institution. Yet, in some ways, it also represents an advance, even for those being plundered. When the choice is between roving bandits—who rob, fight, burn what they can't take, and then come back the following year—and stationary bandits—who settle down and plunder little by little throughout the year—the choice is clear. Stationary bandits are less likely to kill and destroy as they loot you and they fend off rival bandits. That is a kind of progress—even from the perspective of those being plundered.

States emerged as organizations for extracting surpluses from those who produced wealth. In his book *The Art of Not Being Governed*, the anthropologist and political scientist James C. Scott of Yale University studied regions of the world that have never been successfully subdued by states. A central concept in his work is "the friction of power": power does not easily flow uphill. When waves of conquerors moved through an area, they subjugated the valleys, while those who escaped moved up into the less desirable highlands. Scott points out that those refugees developed social, legal, and religious institutions that make them very difficult to conquer. It's especially true of mountain people and of swamp people. (It's a shame various leaders did not read Scott's book before occupying Afghanistan and promoting "state building" there.)

What are the incentives of the rulers? Overly simplistic models posit that rulers seek to maximize wealth, or gross domestic product. Scott, however, argues that the ruler's incentive is not to maximize the GDP, but to maximize the "SAP," the state-accessible product, understood as that production that is easy to identify, monitor, enumerate, and confiscate through taxation: "The ruler . . . maximizes the state-accessible product, if necessary, at the expense of the overall wealth of the realm and its subjects."

Consider (a ruler might say, "take"), for instance, agriculture. Rulers in Asia suppressed the cultivation of roots and tubers, "which has been anathema to all state-makers, traditional or modern," in favor of paddy rice cultivation. That is rather puzzling. Why would rulers care so much about what crops are planted? The reason, Scott notes, is that you can't very effectively tax plants that grow under ground. Cultivators harvest them when they want; otherwise they remain in the ground. Paddy rice, on the other hand, has to be harvested at specific times by large concentrations of people, so it's easier for rulers both to monitor and tax the harvest and to draft the laborers into their armies. The incentives of rulers have systemic effects on many practices and permeate our societies.

State systems of social control—from military conscription to compulsory schooling—have thoroughly permeated our consciousness. Consider, for example, the passport. You cannot travel around the world today without a document issued by the state. In fact, you can no longer even travel around the United States without a state-issued document. Passports are very recent inventions. For thousands of years, people went where they wanted without permission from the state. On my office wall is an advertisement from an old German magazine that shows a couple in a train compartment facing a border official demanding, "Your passport, please!" It explains how wonderful passports are because they give you the freedom of the world.

That, of course, is absurd. Passports restrict your freedom. You are not allowed to travel without permission, but we have become so saturated with the ideology of the state—and have internalized it so deeply—that many see the passport as conferring freedom, rather than restricting it. I was once asked after a lecture whether I favored state-issued birth certificates. After a moment, I said I could see no compelling reason for it and since other institutions can do it, the answer was "no." The questioner pounced! "How would you know who you are?"

Even personal identity, it seems, is conferred by the state. Modern states also claim to be the sole source of law. But historically, states mainly replaced customary law with imposed law. There is a great deal of law all around us that is not a product of the state, for law is a byproduct of voluntary interaction. As the great jurist Bruno Leoni argued, "Individuals make the law insofar as they make successful claims." Private persons making contracts are making law.

In the 16th century, the influential thinker Jean Bodin focused on the idea of sovereignty, which he defined as "the most high, absolute, and perpetual power over the citizens and subjects in a commonwealth." He contrasted that "indivisible power" with another kind of social order, known as customary law, which he dismissed because, he said, "Custom acquires its force little by little and by the common consent of all, or most, over many years, while law appears suddenly, and gets its strength from one person who has the power of commanding all." In other words, Bodin recognized that custom creates social order, but *defined* law as requiring the hierarchical imposition of force, which in turn requires a sovereign—a power that is absolute, unconditioned, and therefore above the law.

That type of sovereignty is inherently contrary to the rule of law, as well as contrary to the principles of federal systems, such as that of the United States, in which power is divided among the different levels and branches of government. In constitutional regimes, the law, not absolute power, is held to be supreme.

The evolution of freedom has involved a long process of bringing power under law. The imposition of force has nonetheless left a powerful imprint on our minds. Alexander Rüstow, a prominent sociologist and a father of the postwar revival of liberty in Germany, meditated on the origins of the state in violence and predation and its lingering imprint: "All of us, without exception, carry this inherited poison within us, in the most varied and unexpected places and in the most diverse forms, often defying perception. All of us, collectively and individually, are accessories to this great sin of all time, this real original sin, a hereditary fault that can be excised and erased only with great difficulty and slowly, by an insight into pathology, by a will to recover, by the active remorse of all." It takes work to free our minds from our dependence on the state.

When meditating on what it means to live as free people we should never forget that the state doesn't grant to us our identities or our rights. The American Declaration of Independence states, "That to secure these rights, Governments have been instituted among men." We secure what is already ours. The state can add value when it helps us to do that, but rights and society are prior to the state. It's critical to remember that the next time someone says, "You didn't build that."

21. Bismarck's Legacy

Welfare states are sometimes referred to as "socialist," but they are distinguishable from socialist states. Socialism, as the term has been used for many decades, means at a minimum the attempt to plan the entire economy, known as "central planning," and more commonly it entails outright state ownership of the means of production; both entail the conscious attempt to use state planning to allocate capital and labor among competing uses. A socialist state will thus attempt to plan and direct the production of paper, vehicles, food, medicines, clothing, and other goods. Examples of attempts to create socialist states include the Soviet Union and its clients, Cuba and the People's Republic of China, before its partial turn toward allowing private ownership and markets. A welfare state, in contrast, need not entail state ownership of the means of production as a whole, although there may be significant state ownership in some industries, normally associated with certain services, such as education, medical care, recreation, and even housing, all of which are associated with "welfare."

A welfare state need not attempt to manage all productive activity, but it does undertake to be responsible for the welfare, or well-being, of the population. It is more extensive than a limited government that provides justice, defense against aggression, the rule of law, and perhaps a limited list of "public goods," as classical liberals propose. A classical liberal state limits itself to creating the peaceful conditions within which the people are free to secure their own well-being (welfare). Welfare states, in contrast, take responsibility for securing the welfare of the people, not only the conditions under which they seek their own well-being; accordingly, welfare states tend to dominate, or even to monopolize, provision of retirement security, medical care, education, and income security, and organize massive transfer payments, often justified in the name of transferring income

Originally published in *After the Welfare State*, edited by Tom G. Palmer. Ottawa, IL: Jameson Books, 2012.

from the "haves" to the "have nots," but typically shuffling—or churning—the great bulk of the transfer payments among the "haves."[1]

Welfare states do not transfer resources exclusively or even primarily to the poor. In many ways, welfare states victimize the poor for the benefit of those who are more capable of manipulating the system. (The same welfare states that deliver "food stamps" and other food subsidies to the poor also raise the price of the food they buy through agricultural subsidies, restrictions on less expensive imported food, and mandated minimum food prices, for example.) Welfare states achieve political stability by creating vast constituencies among all strata of society, from the wealthiest to the poorest. They are not primarily focused on "redistribution" of income downward, as a great deal of the redistribution of wealth goes in the opposite direction, from the poor to the rich. The great bulk of income redistribution in wealthier societies is churned among the middle classes, as money is taken out of one pocket and put into the other, minus the handling fees and inefficiencies generated by bureaucracies, political politicking, and cronyism.[2]

Origins of the Welfare State

The welfare state in its modern form originated in the late 19th century in Germany in the political maneuvering and "state building" of the German statesman Otto von Bismarck, the Iron Chancellor who defeated France and Austria militarily and unified the other German states into the "Second Reich" on the basis of "Iron and Blood."

Bismarck waged a lengthy political war on the free-trade classical liberals in Germany; they preferred peaceful means for the creation of a prosperous nation, as well as peace with Germany's neighbors, rather than war, colonization, and militarism. As a part of his state-building program in Central Europe, Bismarck pioneered the welfare state, which has since come to colonize much of the political space of the globe. Bismarck ushered in the German welfare state through a series of compulsory insurance schemes for accidents, health, disability, and old age, which he promoted and enacted in the 1880s. The militaristic Chancellor Bismarck called his measures "State Socialism," and stated in 1882 that "Many of the measures which we have adopted to the great blessing of the country are Socialistic, and the State will have to accustom itself to a little more Socialism yet."[3]

The historian A. J. P. Taylor explained that, "Bismarck wanted to make the workers feel more dependent on the state, and therefore on him."[4] It was, above all, a political stratagem to create a dependent population imbued with an ideology of national collectivism.

Bismarck confirmed that the purpose of his "State Socialism" was to generate the dependency, and thus loyalty, that a powerful Germany needed to dominate Europe:

> Whoever has a pension for his old age is far more content and far easier to handle than one who has no such prospect. Look at the difference between a private servant and a servant in the chancellery or at court; the latter will put up with much more, because he has a pension to look forward to.[5]
>
> I will consider it a great advantage when we have 700,000 small pensioners drawing their annuities from the state, especially if they belong to those classes who otherwise do not have so much to lose by an upheaval and erroneously believe they can actually gain much by it.[6]

Taylor concluded that "Social security has certainly made the masses less independent everywhere; yet even the most fanatic apostle of independence would hesitate to dismantle the system which Bismarck invented and which all other democratic countries have copied."[7] Indeed, the welfare state has made the masses "less independent everywhere," that is to say, more dependent everywhere. But we have now reached the point where we can, should, and must dare to dismantle "the system which Bismarck invented," for the welfare states of the world are fatally overextended.

It was the collapse in the 1930s of the over-extended welfare state of the Weimar Republic, widely known as the advanced welfare state in the world,[8] that ushered in dictatorship, war, and the most predatory and vicious welfare state the world has ever seen, the Third Reich. As the historian Götz Aly shows in *Hitler's Beneficiaries: Plunder, Racial War, and the Nazi Welfare State*, the National Socialist German Workers Party, also known as the Nazi Party,

> was propagating two age-old dreams of the German people: national and class unity. That was the key to the Nazis' popularity, from which they derived the power they needed

> to pursue their criminal aims. The ideal of the Volksstaat—
> a state of and for the people—was what we would now call
> a welfare state for Germans with the proper racial pedigree.
> In one of his central pronouncements, Hitler promised "the
> creation of a socially just state," a model society that would
> "continue to eradicate all [social] barriers."[9]

Aly goes on to say, "In a historically unprecedented fashion, they [the political leaders of the Third Reich] created the preconditions for the modern social welfare state."[10] The National Socialist welfare state, which instituted such an embracing system of patronage, dependence, and loyalty among the German population, was financed, as Aly documents in chilling detail, by means of stripping the Jews of their wealth (from their money, businesses, and homes down to their dental fillings, children's toys, and even their hair), confiscating the assets of enemies of the state, and looting the rest of Europe through requisitions and deliberate inflation of the currencies of occupied countries. It was also a pyramid scheme that required an ever-greater base of people paying into it to channel the loot upwards. Like all pyramid schemes, the Third Reich was doomed to fail.

The National Socialist welfare state was certainly the most destructive and vicious in world history, but it has closer connections to the less malignant welfare states we know today than many people realize. All welfare states begin by rejecting the classical liberal principles of limited government and individual freedom. They create systems of political control over the behavior of constituencies through deliberately induced dependence, typically justified through one doctrine or another of collective identity and collective purpose.

In the 18th and 19th centuries, classical liberalism eliminated slavery and serfdom, liberated the Jews and other religious minorities from second-class status, fought for religious freedom, and liberated commerce, entrepreneurship, and creativity, resulting in the most astonishing increase in living standards for the masses in human history. Such changes engendered a cultural and political backlash against liberalism and a yearning for an imagined past of harmony and solidarity, in which "selfish" motives were subsumed by communal love; liberalism's success triggered reactionary responses. Friedrich Engels, later collaborator with Karl Marx in forging one of the most influential critiques of liberalism, condemned liberalism precisely for promoting peace and the achievement of the common good through freedom of trade:

> You have brought about the fraternization of the peoples—but the fraternity is the fraternity of thieves. You have reduced the number of wars—to earn all the bigger profits in peace, to intensify to the utmost the enmity between individuals, the ignominious war of competition! When have you done anything "out of pure humanity," from consciousness of the futility of the opposition between the general and the individual interest? When have you been moral without being interested, without harboring at the back of your mind immoral, egoistical motives?
>
> By dissolving nationalities, the liberal economic system had done its best to universalize enmity, to transform mankind into a horde of ravenous beasts (for what else are competitors?) who devour one another just *because* each has identical interests with all the others.[11]

Moreover, Engels and others revived the old irrational hatred of charging interest on loans, an age-old resentment that combined anti-liberalism and anti-Semitism:

> The immorality of lending at interest, of receiving without working, merely for making a loan, though already implied in private property, is only too obvious, and has long ago been recognized for what it is by unprejudiced popular consciousness, which in such matters is usually right.[12]

The dynamism, the constant flux into which free markets placed economic and social relations, enraged elite critics who longed for stability, constancy, and moral certitude in economic relations:

> The perpetual fluctuation of prices, such as is created by the condition of competition completely deprives trade of its last vestige of morality. . . . Where is there any possibility remaining in this whirlpool of an exchange based on a moral foundation? In this continuous up-and-down, everyone *must* seek to hit upon the most favorable moment for purchase and sale; everyone must become a speculator—that is to say, must reap where he has not sown; must enrich himself at the expense of others, must calculate on the misfortune of others, or let chance win for him. . . . immorality's culminating point is the speculation on the Stock Exchange, where history,

and with it mankind, is demoted to a means of gratifying the avarice of the calculating or gambling speculator.[13]

Anti-liberalism and anti-Semitism went hand in hand. In his essay "On the Jewish Question," Karl Marx attacks freedom of enterprise for Judaizing the whole of Christian Europe, for, in effect, dissolving earlier forms of solidarity and turning the Christians of Europe into his own caricature of Jews.[14] It was a theme that was to be repeated over and over in the next century.

As classical liberalism continued to extend more freedom to more and more people, the reactionary backlash against it grew, reaching full flower toward the end of the 19th century and the start of the 20th in the anti-liberal doctrines of nationalism, imperialism, racism, and socialism. As Sheri Berman, herself a staunch defender of the welfare state (also known as "social democracy"), argues in her detailed history *The Primacy of Politics: Social Democracy and the Making of Europe's Twentieth Century*,

> The forward march of markets had caused immense unease in European societies. Critics bemoaned the glorification of self-interest and rampant individualism, the erosion of traditional values and communities, and the rise of social dislocation, atomization, and fragmentation that capitalism brought in its wake. As a result, the fin-de-siècle witnessed a surge in communitarian thought and nationalist movements that argued that only a revival of national communities could provide the sense of solidarity, belonging, and collective purpose that Europe's divided and disoriented societies so desperately needed.[15]

Marxist socialism was one political response, but while many intellectuals were attracted to it for its seemingly scientific claims about the inevitability the replacement of capitalism by communism, others abandoned it when those claims did not materialize and turned to other means of direct action to attack and eliminate liberal individualism. Thus, as Berman notes,

> Although obviously differing in critical ways, fascism, national socialism, and social democracy had important similarities that have not been fully appreciated. They all embraced the primacy of politics and touted their desire to use political power to reshape society and the economy. They all appealed to communal solidarity and the collective good.

374

> They all built modern, mass political organizations and presented themselves as "people's parties." And they both adopted a middle ground with regard to capitalism—neither hoping for its demise like Marxists nor worshipping it uncritically like many liberals, but seeking a "third way" based on the belief that the state could and should control markets without destroying them.[16]

The mass "people's parties" of Europe that paved the way for the welfare states of today have lost most of the exciting rhetoric that swept them to power. What has been left behind, however, are the unfunded liabilities attendant on grandiose promises of cradle-to-grave care, the debts and unfulfilled promises that pyramid schemes leave in their wake, and the social and economic turmoil of societies turned against themselves. (The elections of May 6, 2012, in Greece that were occasioned by the inability of that welfare state to fund itself brought to parliament the populist and extremist Coalition of the Radical Left Party and the openly fascist Golden Dawn Party, which should cause serious concern among supporters of liberal democracy who have any knowledge of 20th-century European history.)

The Welfare State Puts Down Roots in the United States

In the United States, the welfare state arrived in a somewhat different form, although with strong similarities to the anti-liberal movements in Europe. Policies promoting "transfers" of resources, often through granting special privileges of various kinds, became entrenched after the Supreme Court case of *Munn v. Illinois* (1877), which allowed state legislatures to control the prices and rates of railroads, grain storage facilities, and other businesses, meaning that those same legislatures now had enormous power to benefit some interests at the expense of others. Chief Justice Morrison Waite wrote in the majority opinion:

> Property does become clothed in the public interest when used in a public manner to make it a public consequence, and affect the community at large.[17]

Thus began a new phase in what has come to be known as "rent-seeking," seeking one's own profit at the expense of others through means of political action. Farmers sought benefits at the expense of railroads; railroads sought benefits at the expense of competitors; manufacturers sought benefits at the expense of consumers; and on and on and on. During the so-called Progressive Era, the transfer state bloomed on the American continent.

The economic collapse of the Great Depression followed the disastrous decisions of the Federal Reserve Board and the subsequent piling on of one bad policy after another, including the trade-destroying Smoot-Hawley Tariff, which set off a wave of protectionism that swept the world and led to a collapse of international trade. That experience led many to blame the severity and the duration of the Depression, not on destructively interventionist policies, but on *insufficiently* interventionist policies. During the 1932 presidential election, Republican President Herbert Hoover boasted about how he had increased interventionism to deal with the consequences of previous interventions:

> Two courses were open to us. We might have done nothing. That would have been utter ruin. Instead, we met the situation with proposals to private business and to the Congress of the most gigantic program of economic defense and counterattack ever evolved in the history of the Republic. We put that program in action.[18]

Hoover promised more of the same interventionism if he were to be elected. Franklin Roosevelt campaigned for president against the strongly interventionist Hoover administration. Roosevelt both promised to abolish the disastrous policy of alcohol prohibition (which was probably as important as anything else in securing his election), and thundered against Hoover's overspending:

> I accuse the present Administration of being the greatest spending Administration in peace times in all our history. It is an administration that has piled bureau on bureau, commission on commission, and has failed to anticipate the dire needs and the reduced earning power of the people. Bureaus and bureaucrats, commissions and commissioners have been retained at the expense of the taxpayer.[19]

Despite campaigning against the interventionist policies of Hoover, the new Roosevelt administration quickly moved to adopt, continue, and adapt the policies of the Hoover administration into what became known as the New Deal, an incoherent series of interventions into economic processes that prolonged the Depression into the longest in American history.[20]

Much of that program, inherited from Hoover and extended by Roosevelt, included actions to keep prices from adjusting downward (which was the normal response to the Federal Reserve's huge reduction in the money supply); those measures included destroying vast amounts of food and creating a system of harmful agricultural subsidies that are still a mainstay of the American welfare state, creating massive public works projects, which delayed economic adjustment and prolonged the Depression, and establishing the "Social Security" system of compulsory retirement taxes, modeled on the German system that hid half of the tax on labor by calling it an "employer's contribution." The establishment of mass entitlement programs (often promoted in the name of "the poor," but in fact embracing increasing segments of the population until they become universal) is what characterizes the modern welfare state, and the similarities of the American system with the developments in Europe are striking, indeed.[21]

Many Americans do not know that they live in a welfare state, because they have been taught to identify the term "welfare" exclusively with government programs oriented toward transferring income to the poor, without realizing that everyone pays taxes for Social Security, Medicare, and many other gigantic (and broke) entitlement programs that trap them all in the welfare state. Moreover, although black Americans are a minority of recipients of "means-tested" welfare programs, most Americans associate welfare almost exclusively with poverty and black Americans, primarily due to the introduction of the counter-productive "War on Poverty" and the "Great Society" programs launched in the 1960s by the U.S. government. The result was not quite what was promised, as the proliferation and expansion of programs targeted to the poor, and most significantly, to black Americans, resulted in social meltdown, the hollowing out of American cities, the withering of the voluntary organizations of civil society, the evisceration of the two-parent family, rising crime rates, and unprecedented levels of youth unemployment.

The sociologist Frances Fox Piven noted that the "War on Poverty" and the "Great Society" were rooted in the details of American partisan political struggle. In the 1950s, black voters were becoming increasingly important to the national electoral contest. Republican presidential candidate Dwight Eisenhower had received 21 percent of votes cast by black voters in 1952, and that percentage had risen to 39 percent in 1956. Richard Nixon received 32 percent of votes cast by black voters in 1960.[22] As Piven observed,

> By 1960 the Democrats felt that the black vote, especially in the cities, had become crucial in presidential elections. (The story of how Kennedy had captured Illinois by a mere 8,000 votes, the result of landslide majorities in the black South Side wards of Chicago, quickly became fixed in Democratic lore.) Yet blacks had not become integrated into urban political parties, nor were the agencies of city governments giving blacks a share of patronage, power, and services commensurate with their voting numbers. To remedy this imbalance, the Kennedy-Johnson administrations gradually evolved a two-pronged approach: First, they developed a series of novel programs directed to slums and ghettos, bypassing both state and local governments; second, they encouraged various tactics to pressure city agencies into giving more services to blacks.[23]

The key to the success of the strategy was to bypass levels of government that were dominated by groups who saw American black voters as threats to their patronage systems, notably state governments which, when run by Democrats, were often explicitly hostile to black voters (especially in the southern states then controlled by the Democratic Party), and northern urban governments, which were often run by coalitions of "white ethnic" (Polish, Italian, Slovak, etc.) Democrats, who were unwilling to share the spoils of patronage and political power with blacks. Thus, "The federal government had to take a unique initiative. It had to establish a direct relationship between the national government and the ghettos, a relationship in which both state and local governments were bypassed. . . . If the funds were channeled through local white ethnic political leaders, they would probably never reach the ghetto."[24]

Evidence for the strategic political nature of the "Great Society" was that the Republicans, when they took power, merely worked to shift the welfare benefits to their constituents. Sums of money that had been channeled directly into black neighborhoods were transformed into "block grants" to be administered by state governments (in most cases controlled either by white Democrats or by

Republicans) and new forms of patronage were created to suit their political agendas, for, as Piven noted, such moves "are not being made because Republican policy is based on a clearer formulation of the nature of our domestic problems, as [Daniel Patrick] Moynihan and other critics would have it, but simply because Republican proposals are designed to deal with different political imperatives."[25]

The "antipoverty programs" of the American welfare state not only secured a major voting bloc for one party (and thereby polarized American partisan politics along racial lines immensely), but also had enormous consequences for the economic well-being of millions of people. As I write this, black youth unemployment rates are roughly double those of Asian and white youth and 50 percent higher than among Hispanic youth.[26] Black youth unemployment rates had been comparable to, and often less than, white youth unemployment until the Great Society programs were initiated, when the numbers began to diverge.[27] The poverty rate in the United States, which had been falling steeply in the 1940s, 1950s, and even 1960s, stopped falling in the 1970s, when the Great Society programs were entrenched, and began to climb slightly, while labor force participation among young African American males dropped substantially.[28] Because of the visible failures of the "War on Poverty," many Americans, regardless of their race, associated "welfare" with programs targeted at inner city black populations. In fact, the money involved in programs targeted at the poor or at minorities comes to a fraction of the total controlled and allocated by the American welfare state.

Much of the money spent in the "War on Poverty" is, in any case, consumed by the bureaucracy itself. "With astonishing consistency," wrote Daniel Patrick Moynihan in 1973, "middle-class professionals—whatever their racial or ethnic backgrounds—when asked to devise ways of improving the condition of lower-class groups would come up with schemes of which the first effect would be to improve the condition of the middle-class professionals, and the second might or might not be that of improving the condition of the poor."[29] According to Richard A. Cloward and Frances Fox Piven, "The social-welfare bureaucracies were legislated in the name of the poor, but the poor were not their true clientele. The agencies were in fact oriented to other and far more powerful groups that could provide them with the legitimation and political support that public bureaucracies need for survival and expansion."[30]

379

The welfare state is not merely a collection of discrete and unconnected income transfer programs; it is a coherent *political strategy*, entailing harmful restrictions on the ability of the poor to improve their lot (to protect privileged groups from having to compete with them), coupled with income subsidies to partially compensate the poor for those grievous harms. The very politicians who portray themselves as friends of the poor when they distribute food subsidies to them, are the very same politicians who vote to keep food prices high by mandating floor prices for food; the same politicians who impose labor market entry restrictions through licensing and price unskilled workers out of the market through minimum wage laws offer income payments to those they forced out of employment through their policies. Walter Williams noted,

> The minimum wage law and other labor market restrictions do reduce employment opportunities and therefore the income of those forced out of the market. This fact suggests that, as a part of such union restrictive strategies, there must be a political strategy calling for various kinds of maintenance programs to provide income for those who are unemployed as a result of market closures: if the alternative to not working were starvation, it would present a socially volatile climate. Thus it is very probable that labor unions will lead the support for income subsidy programs (e.g., food stamps, welfare, Job Corps, Public Service Employment projects, and various kinds of make-work programs) which represent a redistribution of income from society at large to those who have restricted the labor market in the first place. They *disguise* the true effects of market entry restrictions caused by unions and other economic agents by casting a few crumbs to those denied jobs in order to keep them quiet, thereby creating a permanent welfare class.[31]

The welfare state was, is, and will continue to be at base a political strategy to control people, not to produce greater well-being ("welfare") for them, but to manipulate them as political constituencies, in a new version of the ancient relationship of "patrons" and "clients." The manipulation is not only of the poorer elements of the population, but of everyone.

The political scientist Edward Tufte, in *Political Control of the Economy*, showed how transfer payments, mainly among the middle classes, are systematically manipulated according to the rhythm set by election schedules, in ways that reinforce "electoral-economic cycles," that is, electorally synchronized booms and busts, as governments time transfer payments to maximize disposable income just before elections, which tends to reinforce voter support for the ruling party.

> The electoral-economic cycle breeds a lurching, stop-and-go economy the world over. Governments fool around with transfer payments, making an election-year prank out of the social security system and the payroll tax. There is a bias toward policies with immediate, highly visible benefits and deferred hidden costs—myopic policies for myopic voters. Special interests induce coalition-building politicians to impose small costs on the many to achieve large benefits for the few. The result is economic instability and inefficiency.[32]

The system of patronage and clientelism known as the welfare state has finally run up against something that ultimately can't be manipulated: *arithmetic.*

The total of government obligations, mainly for state pension, health, and other welfare state programs, has reached unsustainable levels. It's clearly evident on the streets of Athens, where crowds of "anti-government" rioters, composed almost entirely of government employees, have thrown petrol bombs onto other government employees, namely, the police. It's visible in the United States, where the last two administrations loaded on more debt than all previous governments in American history, not only to fund their global military presence and interventions, but even more to pay for uncapped liabilities in the forms of President Bush's "Medicare Prescription Drug, Improvement, and Modernization Act" and President Obama's "Patient Protection and Affordable Care Act" (also known as "Obamacare"). President Bush's folly alone added \$17–\$18 trillion to the budgetary imbalance.[33] The unfunded liabilities of President Obama's folly, if implemented, are harder to calculate, due to uncertainties about its implementation, but have been cautiously estimated at an additional \$17 trillion over a 75-year time horizon, based on calculations and methods of the Office of the Actuary at the Centers of Medicare and Medicaid Services.[34] In 2008, Dallas Federal Reserve President Richard Fisher described "the math of Medicare," the U.S. government's medical program, in stark terms:

> The program comes in three parts: Medicare Part A, which covers hospital stays; Medicare B, which covers doctor visits; and Medicare D, the drug benefit that went into effect just 29 months ago. The infinite-horizon present discounted value of the unfunded liability for Medicare A is $34.4 trillion. The unfunded liability of Medicare B is an additional $34 trillion. The shortfall for Medicare D adds another $17.2 trillion. The total? If you wanted to cover the unfunded liability of all three programs today, you would be stuck with an $85.6 trillion bill. That is more than six times as large as the bill for Social Security. It is more than six times the annual output of the entire US economy.[35]

Those obligations will be repudiated because there is not enough wealth to pay them. They may be repudiated through inflation, which means that the burden would fall disproportionately on the poor and the disadvantaged and at the cost of distortions and dislocations in the economies of the world; or they may be repudiated by simply not paying them; or they may be repudiated by "tweaking the rules" to disqualify groups or categories from receiving promised benefits. The official debts of the world's welfare states are already at enormous levels, but the budgetary imbalances, when they are calculated to include total unfunded liabilities—the promises to provide benefits in the future, for which there is no revenue available—dwarf those officially acknowledged debts. Debts will not be paid and promises will not be fulfilled. Increasingly, people—and most especially young people—need to start thinking about alternatives to the welfare state.

Before the Welfare State . . . and After

Politicians love to point to what happened after they instituted a policy. "Look!" they tell us: "Since the introduction of our law against injuries, injuries went down!" thus taking all the credit for any improvements after the implementation of the new law. To test their claims, it's a good idea to look at the trend *before* the law was passed. If it was also trending down, perhaps at an even steeper angle, it undercuts the credibility of the claim that the new law was responsible for the improvements afterwards.[36] Trend line analysis is a useful way of checking whether policies have improved conditions. What was going on before the policy was implemented? Maybe something else accounts for the improvements.

Apologists for the welfare state want us to believe that before the welfare state, there was no provision for those in need, no medical care, no education, no provision for old age, "no welfare." That is not the case. In fact, in many cases the welfare state simply took over institutions and arrangements that had been created by voluntary associations, and then proceeded to claim credit for them.

In the case of welfare institutions, prior to their displacement by the welfare state, there was a remarkable proliferation of voluntary institutions to help people to deal with the problems of life, from the need for medical care during times of misfortune to a friendly hand up when life had gotten one down. Historians have documented the remarkable story of the "friendly societies" that provided such "mutual aid" before the welfare state crushed them. Such societies provided social solidarity, insurance against misfortune, moral support, and much more, all on a voluntary basis. In the case of Britain, according to historian Simon Cordery,

> These collective-self-help organisations provided working people with the security of mutual insurance alongside opportunities for regular, ritual-based solidarity. They constituted the largest set of voluntary associations in Britain, reaching about six million members—equivalent to one-half of all adult males—by 1904.[37]

Too few people are aware that the friendly societies, which are documented in other chapters of this book, had more members than the far more extensively chronicled trade unions, far more support than the socialist movements that seized power in so many countries, and far superior systems of delivering social services and securing dignity for working people.[38]

Bismarck's State Socialist Imperial Germany used force to compel German workers to pay for "insurance," while more liberal Britain relied on voluntarism. As the historian E. P. Hennock observed,

> In Prussia, and subsequently the German Empire, insurance was compulsory for specified categories of the population. In England and Wales a Chief Registrar attempted rather unsuccessfully to monitor the action of a multitude of voluntary bodies. Yet in the 1870s voluntary insurance under the social and cultural conditions of England had penetrated the population more thoroughly than locally selective compulsion had done in Prussia. By the early 1890s, after compulsion

had been introduced across the [*German*] Empire, the voluntary system still penetrated English society at least as thoroughly. But once nationwide compulsion had been in force
long enough to generate political confidence in its operation,
its expansion accelerated and produced results well above
anything achieved by voluntary means. The advantage of
bureaucratically administered compulsion lay in procedures
that, politically acceptable, could be progressively imposed
on additional sections of the population.[39]

How valuable was any alleged increase in the velocity of extension
of coverage when it meant replacing self-government among working people with bureaucratic governance that eliminated or drastically attenuated competition among service providers?

Moreover, as Hennock dryly notes elsewhere, the Imperial German system was established on an unsustainable "pay-as-you-go"
basis from the beginning. Referring to the compulsory corporative
system known as "Berufsgenossenschaften" (Occupational Associations) to which workers were assigned and to which they were
required to pay for their insurance, Hennock notes, Bismarck "discovered that fully inclusive *Berufsgenossenschaften* would not need
to accumulate capital reserves to cover their future liabilities. Like
regular state institutions, they would be able to operate on a pay-
as-you-go principle, meeting their obligations each year by raising
the necessary contribution from their members in the year after.
Since liabilities would accumulate only gradually, this arrangement
reduced costs in the early years and made the proposed levels of
compensation feasible after all. Although this would be achieved
at the price of piling up problems in the future, it allowed any
consideration of state subsidies to be put off for the moment."[40]

In other words, politicians found that they could kick the can
down the road, because they did not have to deal with people who
were free to make their own choices, informed by prices and other
present indicators of future obligations and liabilities. Bismarck's
State Socialism replaced responsible concern for the future with
short-termism, with opportunism, through the pay-as-you-go system of deferring problems for future generations. It greatly weakened the voluntary associations that had been a mainstay of German
society before them and when exported to Britain and other countries
had the same effects there, as well. It was not the case that before

the welfare state there was nothing. There was something better, but it was killed off by the state.

Similarly, voluntarily provided educational services had already spread literacy before the state crowded them out and started to reverse the trend. The historian of education E. G. West observed that "When the government made its debut in education in 1833 mainly in the role of a subsidizer it was as if it jumped into the saddle of a horse that was already galloping."[41] As educational scholar James Tooley has documented repeatedly, states presently claim almost universally to provide pupils with education, but frequently one searches in vain for the education allegedly being provided on a "free and compulsory" basis. Where the state solution of "free and compulsory" education is failing, voluntary provision is working, even for the poorest of the poor, as Tooley has documented in his studies and in his book *The Beautiful Tree: A Personal Journal into How the World's Poorest Are Educating Themselves.*[42]

The voluntary institutions of civil society that provided social services, medical care, and education were deliberately targeted for destruction in some cases, and were merely made redundant in others. Voluntary associations of working people who were engaged in solving their own problems were a major impediment to various statist parties and causes. "The great majority of us have a strong and confirmed belief in the voluntary principle as opposed to state compulsion," intoned a writer in a 1909 edition of the *Oddfellows' Magazine.*[43] The friendly societies of Germany and Britain were targeted for destruction precisely because they fostered independence, rather than collectivism, among the masses of the population. The voluntary associations of civil society atrophied in the United States as the state asserted policies designed to create political constituencies and dependency. People everywhere became habituated to looking toward the state to solve their problems, rather than asking how they could work peacefully with others to improve their situations.

We can dismantle the welfare state and avoid the catastrophic effects of its collapse. If Greece is not a big enough warning, the fate of the Weimar Republic should concentrate our attention on the need to deal with the harm imposed on society by welfare states. We can avert catastrophe and we can replace the welfare state with institutions that are more just, more fair, more efficient, and more helpful to those who suffer in need.

The job of creating peaceful and orderly transitions from state-induced dependence, on the one hand, to freedom and independence, on the other; from perpetuated poverty to upward mobility; and from clientelism to active citizenship falls to the generation that is reaching adulthood today. Their elders have failed them. It is up to them to express in systematic and constructive involvement in public debate and policy formation their justified anger at the wastefulness, the irresponsibility, and the recklessness of their elders who thought that kicking the can down the road would make the problem disappear. We're down the road now, and this generation cannot kick the can any farther. It's the end of the road for the welfare state.

After the Welfare State

The welfare state is in crisis. The promises made in its name are a mixture of wishful thinking and outright lies. It emerged as a mechanism of power; it displaced, crowded out, and crushed voluntary and participatory institutions; it enervated and atomized societies and undercut personal responsibility; it substituted dependency and patronage for independence and rights. In usurping from citizens responsibility for their own welfare, it has turned them into clients, vassals, subjects, supplicants.

The ideology of the welfare state rests on a confusion between processes and outcomes. Welfare state advocates assert that they are aiming at noble outcomes, but pay little or no attention to the processes by which they are to be obtained. Even some self-professed liberals, who had worked to tear down the systems of power and subjugation that had oppressed men in the past, came to believe that beneficial outcomes could be legislated. Herbert Spencer called the emerging welfare-statist "social liberalism" of his day "the New Toryism," that is, the new conservatism, for they were adopting the methods of conservative, hierarchical systems of social control in the pursuit of what they thought of as liberal aims.

> The gaining of a popular good, being the external conspicuous trait common to Liberal measures in earlier days (then in each case gained by a relaxation of restraints), it has happened that popular good has come to be sought by Liberals, not as an end to be indirectly gained by relaxation of restraints, but as the end to be directly gained. And seeking to gain it directly, they have used methods intrinsically opposed to those originally used.[44]

Thus "social liberalism" came to diverge from authentic liberalism, now often known as "classical liberalism." The focus of reform became, not principles, rules, and institutions, but attempts to achieve outcomes directly through the use of coercive power. Outcomes are only very rarely subject to choice. Normally, we choose means (including rules and processes), not outcomes, in the hope that those means will yield the desired outcomes.[45] When policymakers forget that the means matter—in the case of human cooperation, that incentives matter, and that there are no magic wands to wave over the world to achieve outcomes directly, we can be sure that there will be terrible unintended consequences following on the policies they impose on us. The day is coming fast—and has arrived already in some countries—when the unintended consequences of welfare states have become unmistakable. It is time to end the magic show, to pull back the drapes and reveal that the wizards are just politicians and bureaucrats—normal human beings, like all the rest of us.

Those who believe in the moral worth, dignity, and rights of human beings should take their stand with the classical liberal Benjamin Constant:

> They [the holders of authority] are so ready to spare us all sort of troubles, except those of obeying and paying! They will say to us: what, in the end, is the aim of your efforts, the motive of your labours, the object of all your hopes? Is it not happiness? Well, leave this happiness to us and we shall give it to you. No, Sirs, we must not leave it to them. No matter how touching such a tender commitment may be, let us ask the authorities to keep within their limits. Let them confine themselves to being just. We shall assume the responsibility of being happy for ourselves.[46]

The welfare states we have known are failing. It is time to prepare for what comes after them. If intellectual and political leaders insist on more and more state intervention to solve the problems of previous state intervention, our societies will slide further into cronyism, populist authoritarianism, and the bitterness of yet more broken promises. What is needed is more freedom, more choice, more responsible behavior, and more attention to avoiding the gross unfairness of loading future taxpayers with liabilities to provide

387

benefits to present voters. Force is no substitute for liberty; neither does it produce security, nor happiness, nor prosperity, nor peace.

It is time to prepare for liberty, responsibility, and prosperity *after the welfare state.*

Notes

1. They have also generated a great deal of "morals legislation" to direct behavior toward what is considered virtuous by political elites. Those measures have included prohibiting prostitution, sterilizing the "morally degenerate," forbidding intoxicants (including alcohol, marijuana, opiates, etc.), outlawing interracial marriage, persecuting and criminalizing minority sexualities, banning behavior considered too risky to oneself, and generally suppressing substances and behaviors deemed incompatible with the welfare of the people. In recent years, as popular mores have changed, welfare states have sometimes changed with them, but the history of such "progressive" states is one of censoriousness and moralistic repression.

2. Daniel Shapiro makes the point that "government rationing generally favors the knowledgeable, connected, and well-motivated middle class." Daniel Shapiro, *Is the Welfare State Justified?* (Cambridge: Cambridge University Press, 2007), p. 149.

3. Quoted in Brink Lindsey, *Against the Dead Hand: The Uncertain Struggle for Global Capitalism* (New York: John Wiley & Sons, 2002), p. 33.

4. A. J. P. Taylor, *Bismarck: The Man and the Statesman* (1955; New York: Sutton Publishing, 2003), p. 204. Taylor points out that one element of Bismarck's plan was defeated in the Reichstag; he wanted an element of the "contribution" to be directly from the state budget. Instead, the Reichstag only imposed a contribution to be paid directly by the employee and another alleged to be paid "by the employer." As economists know, however, one hundred percent of the burden for both "shares" fell on the employee, because it came from money that otherwise would have been paid in wages; employers will pay the value of the work done, and not more, and tend to be indifferent to how much the employee receives in cash. Bismarck was pioneering the idea of a state formed by "corporative associations," which represented group interests, rather than representations of citizens with individual rights. As Taylor notes, "The idea carried further his emphasis on interest-groups instead of high principle. The phrase and the device were to be picked up again by the twentieth-century exponents of Fascism." (p. 204) The piling of additional taxes on labor in the form of "employer's shares" of social security contributions contributed to the collapse of the parliamentary government of the Weimar Republic, as Jürgen von Kruedener, "Die Überforderungen der Weimarer Republik als Sozialstaat," *Geschichte und Gesellschaft*, 11, no. 3 (1985), pp. 358-76, notes, for the collapse "was the consequence of the overstretched welfarism of the state, to which the wage and the wage burden contributed as a major cause." (p. 376)

5. Quoted in *A. J. P. Taylor, Bismarck: The Man and the Statesman*, p. 203.

6. Speech of May 18, 1889, quoted in David Kelley, *A Life of One's Own: Individual Rights and the Welfare State* (Washington, DC: Cato Institute, 1998), p. 39.

7. A. J. P. Taylor, *Bismarck: The Man and the Statesman*, p. 203. Taylor notes that Bismarck pioneered a wide range of welfare state schemes, and "At the end he talked of 'the right to work' and thought of insurance against unemployment—the final step to the welfare state of the twentieth century." (p. 204)

8. Jürgen von Kruedener, "Die Überforderungen der Weimarer Republik als Sozial-staat," shows the results of precisely what Bismarck had pioneered; the burden on workers of the so-called "employer's share" of "social security" payments rose dramatically during the Weimar Republic. Kruedener concludes, "The fateful pitfall, indeed the tragedy of this state, was that it was objectively overstretched as a welfare state." (p. 376)

9. Götz Aly, *Hitler's Beneficiaries: Plunder, Racial War, and the Nazi Welfare State* (New York: Henry Holt & Co., 2006), p. 13. Aly describes the plunder of the Jews of Germany, prior to the plundering of the rest of Europe: "By late 1937, civil servants in the Finance Ministry had pushed the state's credit limit as far as it could go. Forced to come up with ever more creative ways of refinancing the national debt, they turned their attention to property owned by German Jews, which was soon confiscated and added to the so-called *Volksvermögen*, or the collective assets of the German people. The ideologically charged concept of collective assets, which was by no means restricted to German society, implied the possibility of dispossessing those considered 'alien' (*Volksfremden*) or 'hostile' (*Volksfeinden*) to the ethnic mainstream." (p. 41) Forced labor, far from a subsidy to big private firms, was a redistribution from the enslaved Jews, Poles, Ukrainians, and others to the state as a whole. After calculating the taxes levied by the state on "wages" paid by firms to conscripted labor ("60 to 70 percent of the wages paid by those firms"), Aly concludes that it represented from 1941 to 1945 13 billion Reichsmarks (today about $150 billion): "The size of this figure belies the traditional historical assumption that it was companies that profited most from forced labor. Instead, the exploitation was perpetrated on a far grander scale, by the whole of society itself. The billions in state revenues from forced labor took a signifi-cant load off ordinary German taxpayers. And this was only one of the advantages that 'ethnic comrades' derived from their acceptance of a government campaign not only to wage war against others but to dispossess them of everything they had." (p. 162–63)

10. Ibid., p. 303.

11. Friedrich Engels, "Outlines of a Critique of Political Economy," in *The Young Hegelians: An Anthology*, ed. Lawrence S. Stepelevich (Amherst, NY: Humanity Books, 1999), p. 283.

12. Ibid., p. 289.

13. Ibid., p. 293.

14. See Jerry Z. Muller, "The Long Shadow of Usury: Capitalism and the Jews in Modern European Thought," in his *Capitalism and the Jews* (Princeton: Princeton University Press, 2010), pp. 15–71.

15. Sheri Berman, *The Primacy of Politics: Social Democracy and the Making of Europe's Twentieth Century* (Cambridge: Cambridge University Press, 2006), pp. 13–14.

16. Ibid., pp. 16–17.

17. 94 US 126 (1877), quoted in Douglass C. North, Terry L. Anderson, and Peter J. Hill, *Growth & Welfare in the American Past: A New Economic History* (Englewood Cliffs, N.J.: Prentice Hall, 1983), p. 146.

18. Herbert Hoover, "Address Accepting the Republican Presidential Nomination," August 11, 1932, www.presidency.ucsb.edu/ws/index.php?pid=23198&st=&s t1=#axzz1rUPyI5Ew. See also Murray N. Rothbard, "Herbert Hoover and the Myth of Laissez-Faire," in *A New History of Leviathan*, ed. Ronald Radosh and Murray N. Rothbard, (New York: E. P. Dutton & Co., 1972), pp. 111–145.

19. Franklin D. Roosevelt, "Campaign Address on Agriculture and Tariffs," *The Public Papers and Addresses of Franklin D. Roosevelt. Volume 1, The Genesis of the New Deal, 1928–1932* (New York: Random House, 1938), p. 742.

20. See Amity Shlaes, *The Forgotten Man: A New History of the Great Depression* (New York: Harper, 2007), Douglas A. Irwin, *Peddling Protectionism: Smoot-Hawley and the Great Depression* (Princeton: Princeton University Press, 2011), and Gene Smiley, *Rethinking the Great Depression* (Chicago: Ivan R. Dee, 2002).

21. For an examination of the similarities (combined with repeated statements of the clear differences, as well), see John A. Garraty, "The New Deal, National Socialism, and the Great Depression," *The American Historical Review*, vol. 78, no. 4 (October, 1973), pp. 907–944, and Wolfgang Schivelbusch, *Three New Deals: Reflections on Roosevelt's America, Mussolini's Italy, and Hitler's Germany, 1933–1939* (New York: Henry Holt & Co., 2006). Mussolini, in fact, in 1934 looked quite favorably on the New Deal: "The American experiment should be followed very closely. In the United States, Government intervention in business is direct; and sometimes it takes a preemptory form. The codes are nothing more than collective contracts to which the President compels both parties to submit. We must wait before passing judgment on that experiment." Benito Mussolini, "Speech in the Senate on the Bill Establishing the Corporations," 13th January 1934, in Benito Mussolini, *The Doctrine of Fascism* (Rome: Ardita, 1935; republished New York: Howard Fertig, 2006), p. 69.

22. From Hanes Walton, *Invisible Politics: Black Political Behavior* (Albany: State University of New York Press, 1985), p. 123.

23. Frances Fox Piven, "The Great Society as Political Strategy," in *The Politics of Turmoil: Poverty, Race, and the Urban Crisis*, Richard A. Cloward and Frances Fox Piven (New York: Vintage Books, 1975), pp. 271–2.

24. Ibid., pp. 276–77.

25. Ibid., p. 283.

26. http://bls.gov/news.release/youth.t01.htm.

27. Walter E. Williams, *Race and Economics: How Much Can Be Blamed on Discrimination?* (Stanford: Hoover Institution Press, 2011), pp. 41–43.

28. Charles Murray, *Losing Ground: American Social Policy, 1950–1980* (New York: Basic Books, 1984), introduction to 1994 10th anniversary edition, p. xviii.

29. Daniel P. Moynihan, *The Politics of a Guaranteed Income* (New York: Vintage Books, 1973), p. 54. Economist Walter E. Williams noted in 1980, "It turns out that if we tallied all federal, state, and local annual expenditures that are justified on the basis of fighting some aspect of poverty, we would find that over $250 billion dollars is spent on these programs. It turns out that if we were simply to give that money to the poor, each poor family of four would receive about $40,000 per year. They do not get that money. Most of it goes to non-poor people, bureaucrats, and professionals charged with caring for the poor. It is like feeding the sparrows through the horses." Walter E. Williams, "The Poor as First Victims of the Welfare State," *Imprimis*, vol. 9, no. 7 (July 1980), p. 6. Williams's book *The State Against Blacks* (New York: McGraw-Hill, 1982) presented a compelling and well-documented indictment of the entire system of interventionism as harmful to those allegedly being helped by the welfare state. Some of the data have been updated in his book *Race and Economics: How Much Can Be Blamed on Discrimination?*

30. Richard A. Cloward and Frances Fox Piven, *The Politics of Turmoil*, p. 4.

31. Walter E. Williams, *Black America and Organized Labor: A Fair Deal?* (Washington, D.C.: Lincoln Institute for Research and Education, 1980), p. 25.

32. Edward Tufte, *Political Control of the Economy* (Princeton: Princeton University Press, 1978), p. 143.

33. Cited in Testimony of Cato Institute Senior Fellow Jagadeesh Gokhale to the Committee on Homeland Security and Government Affairs, Subcommittee on Federal Financial Management, Government Information, and International Security, 109th Cong., 1st sess., September 22, 2005, www.hsgac.senate.gov/download/092205gok hale. See also Dallas Federal Reserve CEO Richard Fisher, "Storms on the Horizon: Remarks before the Commonwealth Club of California," www.dallasfed.org/news/speeches/fisher/2008/fs080528.cfm.

34. "President's Health 'Reform' Grows Unfunded Obligations By \$17 Trillion," http://budget.senate.gov/republican/public/index.cfm/2012/3/president-s-health-reform-grows-unfunded-obligations-by-17-trillion

35. Richard Fisher, "Storms on the Horizon."

36. The trendline test is explained in Charles Murray, *What It Means to Be a Libertarian: A Personal Interpretation* (New York: Broadway Books, 1997), pp. 47–56.

37. Simon Cordery, *British Friendly Societies, 1750–1914* (New York: Palgrave Macmillan, 2003), p. 1.

38. See David Beito, *From Mutual Aid to the Welfare State: Fraternal Societies and Social Services, 1890–1967* (Chapel Hill: University of North Carolina Press, 2000); David Green, *Working Class Patients and the Medical Establishment* (New York: St. Martin's Press, 1985); Nicolas Marques, "Le monopole de la sécurité sociale face à l'histoire des premières protections sociale," *Journal des Économistes et des Études Humaines*, vol. X, no. 2, Sept-Oct. 2000, www.euro92.com/acrob/marques%20mutuelles.pdf; David G. Green and Lawrence Cromwell, *Mutual Aid or Welfare State: Australia's Friendly Societies* (Sydney: Allen & Unwin, 1984); David Green, *Reinventing Civil Society: The Rediscovery of Welfare Without Politics* (London: Institute of Economic Affairs, 2000); Anton Howes, "Friendly Societies, the State and the Medical Profession in Great Britain 1900–1939," unpublished thesis, King's College, London, 2012.

39. E. P. Hennock, *The Origin of the Welfare State in England and Germany, 1850–1914* (Cambridge: Cambridge University Press, 2007), p. 176. Hennock seems not to understand (as many did not at the time) that the so-called "employer's contribution" came entirely from the worker's pay packet and did not represent a transfer from employers to employees, but merely a reduction in the employee's take-home pay.

40. Ibid., p. 92.

41. Quoted in James Bartholomew, *The Welfare State We're In* (London: Politico's, 2004), p. 153. Bartholomew's book admirably both shows how the welfare state has been credited for advances that were due to other causes and documents such negative effects of the welfare state as the deterioration of civility and the rise of dependency, criminality, and other pathologies of modern societies. West's books pioneered the study of education without the state. A short essay on the topic, "The Spread of Education Before Compulsion: Britain and America in the Nineteenth Century," can be found in *The Freeman*, vol. 46, issue 7 (July 1996), www.thefreemanonline.org/featured/the-spread-of-education-before-compulsion-britain-and-america-in-the-nineteenth-century/. For a survey of the issues, see James Tooley, *Education Without the State* (London: Institute of Economic Affairs, 1998), esp. chapter 3, "The Secret History of Education Without the State." www.iea.org.uk/sites/default/files/publi cations/files/upldbook56pdf.pdf.

42. James Tooley, *The Beautiful Tree: A Personal Journal into How the World's Poorest Are Educating Themselves* (Washington, D.C.: Cato Institute, 2009).

43. *Oddfellows' Magazine*, No. 414 (June 1909), cited in Simon Cordery, *British Friendly Societies, 1750–1914*, p. 155.

44. Herbert Spencer, "The New Toryism" [1884], in *Herbert Spencer, Political Writings*, ed. John Offer (Cambridge: Cambridge University Press, 1994), p. 69.

45. See also Mark Pennington, *Robust Political Economy: Classical Liberalism and the Future of Public Policy* (Cheltenham: Edward Elgar, 2011) for an expansion of the general point that processes, rather than outcomes, are the normal subject of political choice.

46. Benjamin Constant, "The Liberty of the Ancients Compared with that of the Moderns" [1819], in Benjamin Constant, *Political Writings*, ed. Biancamaria Fontana (Cambridge: Cambridge University Press, 1988), p. 326.

22. Democracy and Limited Government: The Unbreakable Partnership

Thank you for the kind invitation to address this distinguished audience on a topic of such significance.

This is my first visit to India, so I won't even pretend to try to inform you, who are much better informed on the matter than I, about the health or the sickness of democratic institutions, procedures, and outcomes in the world's largest democratic nation.

What I do hope to do is to stimulate some thought and discussion—and perhaps even some action—about certain structural features of democratic governance in general, to be followed—I hope—by a discussion of how those issues play out in India.

Let's start with a few clarifications, since democracy, like freedom and justice, is one of those "essentially contested concepts" of which the philosopher W. B. Gallie informed us. Indeed Gallie considered democracy to be "*the* appraisive political concept pat excellence." This is, the concept is wielded by different parties, schools, ideologies with quite different meanings. Alternatively, we could follow Ronald Dworkin's take on such debates by distinguishing between the "concept" of democracy and competing "conceptions" of democracy. Few people openly oppose democracy these days; but they do argue vociferously over its meaning.

The term is used in such confusing ways in much contemporary discourse that the contending parties simply talk past one another. Here are two significant ways in which the term is used:

1. The majority of the population (usually limited in some way by age or citizenship) make decisions about all those issues on which they wish to make decisions;

Presented in New Delhi, India, on June 13, 2009, as the 2009 Julian L. Simon Memorial Lecture of the Liberty Institute.

2. The substantive freedoms enjoyed by free and equal citizens, notably freedom of speech and assembly, but sometimes also including freedom of religion, freedom of exit, procedural rights to due process of law, and so on;

It is worth noting that the two are not obviously compatible. If a majority says that the minority has to shut up, or worship as the majority chooses, is that democratic? Many self-styled advocates of "democracy" insist that the majority can stop the speech of the minority. Indeed, the Chavez government of Venezuela has closed down opposition-oriented broadcasting stations in the name of democracy, for allegedly organizing a "gradual coup d'etat" by airing criticism of the government. Such criticism could eventually lead to a change of government, and, as such qualifies as a gradual coup and –in the name of democracy—must be suppressed.

On the other hand, insisting on various inviolable rights, such as freedom of speech, religion, and assembly, entails limits on the power of majorities, as well as of minorities to exercise collective choice.

Clearly a state needs both elements to qualify as a democracy. A system of individual rights with no body to protect them is a mere fantasy. Some system to determine *how* the rights will be protected is needed, and John Locke gave us arguments in his *Second Treatise of Government* as to why majorities are a good means to determine such policies. But a system of majoritarian democracy without free speech, for example, cannot determine what the majority opinion is and lapses into one or another form of oligarch cal or personal dictatorship.

One way to integrate those two conceptions into democratic thought is to focus on the concept of sustainable democracy. A political system that does not degenerate into dictatorship requires that there be democratic, or popular, input into governmental processes, and at the least that many officials of the government be replaceable by means of election. It also requires that the range of choices available to collective choice be limited, that is, that many issues be taken "off the table." We call those issues that are taken off the table "rights."

Sustainable democracies are those that are limited and that incorporate institutions that protect rights—both individual rights and rights of local autonomy. From being overridden by collective choice. That is sustainable democracy is liberal democracy.

I believe, and I think you should, too, that democracy without limited government is unsustainable. It is possible to have illiberal democracy, to be sure. But it is not a sustainable project.

The dangers of democratic government, of rule by the *demos*, have long been known. Democratic—or popular—government, without a suitable constitutional framework limiting power and hemming it in with a variety of checks and balances, undermines itself. Students of Roman history should be aware of the dangers of Marian-style democratic movements, which tend to focus power on one man or one party as the carrier of the will of the people, as the Roman popular politician Gaius Marius considered himself.

Unlimited democracies run the risk of "one man, one vote, one time," which is one of the worst legacies of some modern democratic thinking.

In 1819, Benjamin Constant, the great theorist of liberal constitutionalism, in a public address contrasted the exercise of "ancient liberty" with the exercise of "modern liberty." The latter, he said,

> "consisted I exercising collectively, but directly, several parts of the complete sovereignty; in deliberating, in the public square, over war and peace; in forming alliances with foreign governments; in voting laws, in pronouncing judgments; in examining the accounts, the acts, the stewardship of the magistrates; in calling them to appear in front of the assembled people, in accusing, condemning or absolving them. But if this is what the ancients called liberty, they admitted as compatible with this collective freedom the complete subjection of the individual to the authority of the community. You find among them almost none of the enjoyments which we have seen form part of the liberty of the moderns."

Constant warned that the Terror in France, and later the rise of the Napoleonic dictatorship and the Empire, originated in confusion regarding the nature of liberty of choice—collective or individual.

J.L. Talmon in his study of the French Revolutions, *The Origins of Totalitarian Democracy*, concluded that democracy is not an inherently liberal concept. FareedZakaria's fine book, *The Future of Freedom: Illiberal Democracy at Home and Abroad*, focused recent discussion on the dangers of illiberal democracy. Iran, which just yesterday held its presidential elections, is a fairly good example of such. Plausibly, you can change power through elections, although there are limits imposed on who can stand for office. The elections—for now, at least—even seem relatively clean. Iran is not a single party totalitarian state, but it is hardly a liberal society, hardly and example of modern liberty.

The dangers of unlimited democracy should be obvious to all who will but consult history. A desirable democracy—a democracy that is stable that can persist—requires limited government. Let me spell out a few reasons why:

First, a central element of a sustainable democracy is the existence of a loyal opposition. When one party replaces the other in control of parliament or congress, the party or group formerly in change of government shifts to become the loyal opposition. They don't take to the streets or blow up train stations because they lost the election. But such loyalty is impossible, or at least extremely unlikely, if the losers who form the opposition fear that by losing an election, they risk losing everything: their goods, their property, their rights, perhaps even their lives. You cannot have a loyal opposition without limitations on the power of the party that has won to punish those who lost. And without a loyal opposition, you cannot have a democracy. In the absence of limits on state power, no government can afford to relinquish power. That, by the way, is one of the problems facing the authentically popular government of Vladimir Putin in Russia; he knows that, having resurrected a police state, he can never afford to relinquish the levers of power, which means that he will never lose a free election, meaning, in turn that we should expect no free elections in Russia anytime soon.

Second, even reliable elections require independent authoritative bodies, not themselves subject to popular control, to determine the outcome of those elections. That includes independent electoral commissions and—to supervise them—some kind of independent judiciary, that is, a judiciary not easily subject to punishment or removal by the elected branches.

The literature on the necessity of the rule of law for sustainable economic development is quite well developed, but those insights are no less applicable to the sustainability of democracy.

Mancur Olson, the late political economist, very neatly pointed out:

> "[T]he conditions that are needed to have the individual rights needed for maximum economic development are exactly the same conditions that are needed to have a *lasting* democracy. Obviously, a democracy is not viable if individuals, including the leading rivals of the administration in power, lack the rights to free speech and to security for their property and contracts or if the rule of law is not followed even when it calls for the current administration to leave office. Thus the *same* court system, independent judiciary, and respect for law and individual rights that are needed for a lasting democracy, are also are required for security of property and contract rights."

That leads us to the third reason, which is that democratic governments, like all governments, face the problem of time-inconsistency in decision-making, that is, having made a commitment at one point, they find it difficult to fulfill it later, when—having already secured the advantages of making the commitment, they not longer find it in their interests to fulfill that commitment. It's easy to promise at time A to do something at time B, but when time B comes around, having already gotten the befit from the promise at time A, one may feel less inclined to fulfill the commitment. I promise to respect you in the morning is easy to say in the evening, in the throes of passion, but may be less easily carried out in the morning.

Institutional economists, such as Douglass North and Barry Weingast, have argued that solutions to those problems were key to long-term economic growth, by making it easier for them to make commitments that were advantageous to the rulers, as well as to the ruled, and then to stick to those commitments.

Limited government provides a vehicle for solving—or at least ameliorating—the problem of time-inconsistency.

Let me address two issues that are deeply implicated in the nature of sustainable democracy, resting on limited government, and then conclude with some thoughts on the strengths of democracy in India, and its roots in ancient Athens.

Weak Government, or Limited Government?

What does limited government—or a limited state—mean? Does it mean weak government, or a weak state? Should the goal of advocates of liberty and democracy seek to weaken the authority of the state? Not at all. Limited government should not be confused with

397

weak government. Our friend Benjamin Constant, who meditated long on such matters, distinguished between weak authority and circumscribed, or limited, authority. In his *Principles of Politics Applicable to All Governments* (385), he noted that

> "The circumscription of political authority, within its precise limits, does not tend to weaken that necessary authority. On the contrary, it gives it the only real strength it can have. The jurisdiction of authority must be scrupulously limited; but once that jurisdiction is fixed, it must be so organized as always to be capable of attain swiftly and completely all the purposes within its remit. Freedom gains everything from the government's being severely confined within the bounds of its legitimacy; but it gains nothing from government's being feeble within those bounds."

The opposite of overbearing government is not weak government or no government; it is limited government. Not all weak governments are friendly to liberty or even democracy; if they cannot protect life, liberty, and estate from violence, they are not protecting freedom or democracy. And for those who prefer anarchism, I remind them that not all anarchies are attractive; southern Somalia is without an effective state, as was Lebanon during much of its recent history. The worst situation may be to live in powerful and unlimited states, which crush individual freedom, local autonomy, and democracy. But weak, unlimited government—a situation in which the authority of the state knows no bounds, but within which it is unable to enforce the rules consistently or to provide a basic reliable framework for social cooperation—is also unacceptable. What is needed is not weak government, but limited government with authority to provide a limited range of services, such as protection of life, liberty, and legitimate legal claims of property, legal adjudication, and the perhaps a limited range of other collective goods.

Collective Goods and Collective Choice

That means a well defined range of goods subject to collective choice, to wit authentically collective goods. The trend for much of history has been to define collective goods as those goods provided through some form of collective choice, which means, for many choices, those imposed by some on others. Economists define collective goods, or public goods, as those characterized by two polar characteristics:

1. Non-rivalrous consumption, meaning that if one person or a group of persons consumes the good, it does not diminish the amount available for others to consume. When I eat a bite from an apple, there is less for others, but when I enjoy freedom of thought, it does not mean that others have less. (I should mention a subclass that will be shown to be relevant in a moment club goods, which are those goods such that the enjoyment by one person does not diminish the ability of others to enjoy it, up to some limit, such as watching a movie in a theater. If I open my eyes to watch it, it does not become dim for you, but if more than a certain number crowd into the theater, the ability to enjoy the show goes down for all.) The second characteristic is that

2. It is difficult, or perhaps at an extreme impossible, to exclude non-payers from the enjoyment of the good. If you enjoy the good of clean fresh air, it is hard to exclude others from enjoying that good. In many cases we do spend scarce resources to exclude others from enjoying the good, such as in the case of movie theaters, which have walls around them and ticket booths to exclude non-purchasers from enjoying the non-rivalrous spectacle.

Advocates of sustainable democracy should reject the single-minded focus on popular sovereignty that constitutes so much of the discourse of modern democracy and instead favor constitutional liberalism, which crucially includes a democratic component. To be successful as a democracy there must be clear limitations o the domain of public choice. It must be limited, or it will not be stable.

A constitutional framework for sustainable democracy must put certain questions and issues off the table. Decisions subject to collective choice must be those that are actually collective goods. The alternative approach, to define as collective goods all those subject to collective choice, is a recipe for conflict, for when those on whom such choices are imposed see them—not as collective goods, but as collective bads—they will rebel against them. Religion is an obvious example of that. Making religion subject to collective choice imposes on those who disagree with the majority what they see—not as merely under or over-provision of a collective good, but as a collective bad. And they are likely to respond to such imposed choice by resistance to the authority of the state, a process known in its more extreme phases as civil war or even genocide.

Social Foundations of Sustainable Democracy

Finally, I'd like to address the strength, if you will, of sustainable democracy. What social forces restrain power, thus preventing the conversion of democratic governance into undemocratic tyranny? One cannot rely simply on written provisions of a constitution, what James Madison referred to as "parchment barriers," if they do not have behind them existing social force to give them power.

Mere separation of powers isn't enough, especially when those powers are artificially delineated or subject to periodic revision by the center. For example, in California the two houses of the legislature—the Assembly and the Senate—are both based on apportionment by population, meaning that the same population is represented in both houses on the basis of the same principle, such that neither really checks the other. In contrast, the US Senate has limited the power of the House and the presidency, precisely because it represents the states, which are unchanging political entities with distinct interests. As the French political scientist Bertrand de Jouvenel concluded in his book *On Power* (p. 331–3),

> "Power cannot, therefore, be limited by the mere dismemberment of the *imperium* into constituent parts each with its distinct organ. For limitation of this kind to succeed, there must be in existence sectional interests in a sufficiently advanced state, conscious of their identity, and armed with strength to stop the encroachments of Power on their own spheres, together with a system of law which is independent enough to arbitrate their clashes and escape from being the instrument of the central command."

I was reminded of those principles when I read Pratap Bhanu Mehta's delightful and insightful book on Indian democracy, *The Burden of Democracy*. In it, he notes that

> "India has worked not because of 'unity in diversity,' the presence of a locus of identity beneath differences, as the state is fond of telling us. We have flourished rather because we are 'diverse in our unities,' each able to imagine the connection with other in his/her own way."

400

Mehta argues that "one of the reasons for the relative success of its [India's] democracy, and its hanging together as a nation, has been the profoundly cross-cutting character of cleavages within Indian society that has made collective action on a large scale, to overthrow the state, quite difficult to mount." I would add that the federal nature of the Indian political system, like the federal nature of the American political system, has been a great source of its durability, precisely because it establishes real sources of countervailing power, backed up by sectional interest, which can provide the power necessary to overcome majoritarian overstepping of constitutional limits.

I will conclude with some lessons from the first regime to be called "democratic," that of Athens following the reform of the constitution in 508/507 BCE by Cleisthenes, who orchestrated the overthrow of the tyranny of Hippias. The term he evidently used was not democracy, although that is the term used by Aristotle and others to describe his accomplishments, but *isonomia*, or equality before the law. The voting system was deliberately recast to make it harder to create monolithic ruling blocks and to check the power of the leading clans. The clans were themselves re-created to draw their sources from the various *demes*, which were in turn each drawn from a city region, a coastal region, and an inland region, to avoid the dominance of any one sectional interest in the management of the policy. But not only was power divided in such fashion, and put on a foundation of real interest, but a rule was established, the rule of *isegoria*, or equal freedom of speech, that deliberation on matters of collective choice required that people be able to speak frankly and that no one be punished for expressing his own opinion I a public debate.

So to return to the roots of democracy in Athens, we find not mere unlimited rule by the demos, or the multitude, but a complex system of checks and balances, based on cross-cutting and sectional loyalties and a strong limit on the power of the majority to dictate to minorities in the form of freedom of the right to freedom of speech.

In conclusion, sustainable democracy requires that the powers of the state be limited. Without limited powers, you cannot sustain a loyal opposition, or reliable peaceful transfers of power. Without limited powers and rights to freedom of speech and assembly, you cannot determine effectively in what ways majority preferences may be changing. Without limited powers, you cannot determine just who has won the election. Without limited powers, you cannot determine just who has won the election. Without limited powers, you cannot solve the problem of time-inconsistency. Without limited powers you risk turning choice of collective goods into imposition of collective bads on large numbers, resulting in internal strife. And without existing sectional various cross-cutting interests that can effectively assert themselves, mere parchment barriers are ineffective at restraining tyranny or sustaining democracy. The experience of Indian democracy testifies to the importance of all of those principles. The remarkable durability of democracy in India is testament, not only to the strength of Indian culture, but to the institutional foundations of that democracy, foremost among them its relatively limited character.

The roots of sustainable democracy were understood over 2,500 years ago. They have been demonstrated to today's public in this, the world's largest democracy. Why do so few people understand that to be sustainable, democratic politics must be limited?

PART III

PRACTICE

23. Madison and Multiculturalism: Group Representation, Group Rights, and Constitutionalism

There is no doubt that James Madison envisioned a republic that encompassed many different interests. At least three questions present themselves:

> 1) Did Madison envision a "multicultural" republic?
>
> 2) Are contemporary advocates of various forms of group rights or group representation, often presented under the banner of "multiculturalism," advancing the Madisonian project, or undermining it?
>
> 3) Are group-differentiated rights a necessary and proper element of a constitutional order ordained and established to "form a more perfect Union, establish Justice, insure domestic Tranquility, provide for the common defence, promote the general Welfare, and secure the Blessings of Liberty to ourselves and our Posterity"?

Madisonian Pluralism and the Common Good

Madison openly embraced a pluralistic constitutional order. Indeed, he believed such diversity was essential to maintain liberty. Madison's commitment to diversity in an extended republic directly contradicted the then widely held "small republic" theory forwarded by Montesquieu, who had famously declared,

> It is in the nature of a republic to have only a small territory; otherwise, it can scarcely continue to exist. In a large republic, there are large fortunes, and consequently little moderation in spirits: the depositories are too large to put in the hands of a citizen; interests become particularized; at first a man

Originally published in *James Madison and the Future of Limited Government*, edited by John Samples. Washington: Cato Institute, 2002.

> feels he can be happy, great, and glorious without his homeland; and soon, that he can be great only on the ruins of his homeland.
>
> In a large republic, the common good is sacrificed to a thousand considerations; it is subordinated to exceptions; it depends upon accidents. In a small one, the public good is better felt, better known, lies nearer to each citizen; abuses are less extensive there and consequently less protected.[1]

In contrast, Madison celebrated diversity and the extended republic. He believed that a wide diversity of what Montesquieu considered "particularized interests" supported, rather than threatened, liberty. In 1788 Madison declared, "Happily for the states, they enjoy the utmost freedom of religion. This freedom arises from that multiplicity of sects, which pervades America, and which is the best and only security for religious liberty in any society. For where there is such a variety of sects, there cannot be a majority of any one sect to oppress and persecute the rest."[2] Madison's remarks echo Voltaire, who wrote in his "Letter on the Presbyterians" that "if there were only one religion in England, there would be danger of tyranny; if there were two, they would cut each other's throats; but there are thirty, and they live happily together in peace."[3]

Madison's famous essay on the problem of faction, *Federalist* No. 10, is oft quoted but rarely carefully considered. Examine closely his definition of faction: "By a faction I understand a number of citizens, whether amounting to a majority or minority of the whole, who are united and actuated by some common impulse or passion, or of interest, adverse to the rights of other citizens, or to the permanent and aggregate interests of the community."[4] What is notable about that definition is that it presupposes:

- A) that interests are not the same as rights,
- B) that interests may be opposed to rights,
- C) that citizens may be motivated by passions, as well as by interests, and
- D) that there is a common good ("the permanent and aggregate interests of the community") to which particular interests or passions may be opposed.

Their critics often assert that classical liberals—among whom I count James Madison—believe that social and political life is merely a clash of particular interests, or even that there is no common good.[5]

But this is not what classical liberals (including modern libertarians) believe. They are liberals because they believe that liberty is, if not the overriding common good, then at least a central element of the common good. If there are permanent and aggregate interests of a community, they will be shared by all of the particular interests, and it is the business of government to secure that public good. As Madison remarked, "It is too early for politicians to presume on our forgetting that the public good, the real welfare of the great body of the people is the supreme object to be pursued; and that no form of government whatever, has any other value, than as it may be fitted for the attainment of this object."[6]

For classical liberals such as Madison at least one permanent and aggregate interest of the community *is* the securing of a regime of equal rights for all citizens. Indeed, Madison proposed in a speech before the House of Representatives:

> That there be prefixed to the Constitution a declaration, that all power is originally vested in, and consequently derived from, the people.
> That Government is instituted and ought to be exercised for the benefit of the people; which consists in the enjoyment of life and liberty, with the right of acquiring and using property, and generally of pursuing and obtaining happiness and safety.[7]

One might claim Madison as an advocate of a multicultural republic because he accepted a wide variety of commitments ("passions") and interests in the new republic. He is decidedly not a "multiculturalist" in the sense of endorsing group-specific rights or the rights of groups to special representation. As he noted in his essay on "Parties":

> In every political society, parties are unavoidable. A difference of interests, real or supposed, is the most natural and fruitful source of them. The great object should be to combat the evil: 1. By establishing a political equality among all.[8]

Madison noted that the existence of parties, based on different interests, did not warrant the creation of "artificial parties."

> From the expediency, in politics, of making natural parties, mutual checks on each other, to infer the propriety of creating artificial parties, in order to form them into mutual checks,

> is not less absurd than it would be in ethics, to say, that new
> vices ought to be promoted, where they would counteract
> each other, because this use may be made of existing vices.[9]

Madison envisioned a political system oriented toward the common good, not toward "conflicting rights" or group warfare. The common good consists of the maintenance of rules of conduct that are the same for all citizens.[10]

Madison's commitment to the common good, that is, a good common to all citizens, is reflected in one of the most misunderstood terms in the Constitution, the "general welfare." That term is found in the preamble, wherein are stated the reasons for which the Constitution has been ordained and established: "in order to form a more perfect Union, establish Justice, insure domestic Tranquility, provide for the common Defense, promote the general Welfare, and secure the Blessings of Liberty to ourselves and our Posterity." It is also found in the first clause of Article I, Section 8, which states that "The Congress shall have Power To lay and collect Taxes, Duties, Imposts and Excises, to pay the Debts and provide for the common Defense and general Welfare of the United States; but all Duties, Imposts and Excises shall be uniform throughout the United States." The Constitution does not authorize securing the welfare of some at the expense of others; securing the welfare that is common to *both* Peter and Paul is the purpose for which the Congress is granted its limited powers. Article I, Section 1 ("All legislative Powers herein granted shall be vested in a Congress of the United States") clearly implies that some powers are *not* "herein granted" and therefore cannot be legitimately exercised by the Congress.[11] The power to rob Peter to pay Paul, today referred to as "redistribution," is not a power granted to the Congress under the Constitution. The term general welfare, which is so often interpreted as a blanket grant of authority to the federal government to do anything and everything (at least, anything that is not explicitly prohibited in the Constitution), is regularly cited to justify thousands upon thousands of acts that promote the welfare of a few at the expense of others. But reflection upon the meaning of the term general welfare suggests that it is not merely *anyone's* "welfare" that is intended, but the welfare that is general, that is, common to all.

The Constitution was proposed and ratified "in order to" secure certain limited ends. It authorizes neither a regime of differentiated caste privileges nor an unlimited power of majorities to impose their preferences upon minorities. Madison made that clear when he proposed in his speech of June 6, 1787, to the federal convention that drafted the Constitution that the proposed Constitution would be superior to the Articles of Confederation in "providing more effectually for the security of private rights and the steady dispensation of Justice" and asked, "In all cases where a majority are united by a common interest or passion, the rights of the minority are in danger. What motives are to restrain them?"[12] After noting that conscience rarely has much effect on large numbers of men, and cataloguing various forms of oppression experienced by polities ancient and modern, he asks, "What has been the source of those unjust laws complained of among ourselves?" and responds, "Has it not been the real or supposed interest of the major number?"[13] He concludes that:

> The lesson we are to draw from the whole is that where a majority are united by a common sentiment, and have an opportunity, the rights of the minor party become insecure. In a Republican Gov[t] the majority if united have always an opportunity. The only remedy is to enlarge the sphere, and thereby divide the community into so great a number of interests and parties, that in the 1st place a majority will not be likely at the same moment to have a common interest separate from that of the whole or of the minority; and in the 2nd place, that in case they sh[d] have such an interest, they may not be apt to unite in the pursuit of it. It was incumbent on us then to try this remedy, and with that view to frame a republican system on such a scale & in such a form as will controul all the evils w[ch] have been experienced.[14]

In *Federalist* No. 10—itself largely an elaboration of his speech of June 6, 1787, before the Convention—Madison stated that "to secure the public good, and private rights against the danger of such a [majority] faction, and at the same time to preserve the spirit and the form of popular government, is then the great object to which our enquiries are directed."[15] Madison proposed, rather than democracy (the other form of "popular government"), a republic, "by which I mean a government in which the scheme of representation takes place," which differs from a democracy in "the delegation of the government . . . to a small number of citizens elected by the rest" and "the greater number of citizens, and greater sphere of country, over which [a republic] may be extended."[16]

The two solutions are, thus, first, to substitute representation for direct democracy in order to "refine and enlarge the public views, by passing them through the medium of a chosen body of citizens," and second, to increase the transaction costs necessary to assemble a majority faction animated by a common interest contrary to that of the whole.[17] A system of representation, as distinct from direct democracy, would encourage deliberation and protect the public good from great swings in public opinion ignited by passion. It would also weaken the advantages of potential demagogues, as Madison noted in *Federalist* No. 58:

> In all legislative assemblies, the greater the number composing them may be, the fewer will be the men who will in fact direct their proceedings. In the first place, the more numerous any assembly may be, of whatever characters composed, the greater is known to be the ascendancy of passion over reason. In the next place, the larger the number, the greater will be the proportion of members of limited information and of weak capacities. Now it is precisely on characters of this description that the eloquence and address of the few are known to act with all their force. . . . On the same principle the more multitudinous a representative assembly may be rendered, the more it will partake of the infirmities incident to collective meetings of the people.[18]

The qualifications and election procedures for the membership of the United States Senate set out in Article I, Section 3 of the Constitution exemplify Madison's republican principles: "Immediately after they shall be assembled in Consequence of the first Election, they shall be divided as equally as may be into three Classes. . . . so that one third may be chosen every second Year" and "No Person shall be a Senator who shall not have attained to the Age of thirty Years." Staggered elections insulate the Senate from the shifting passions of the electorate, and the age requirement seeks to limit the membership to a group more likely to have attained some wisdom, or at least to be less excited by the passions of the moment. The combination of the two is more likely to generate greater stability in the law, which is to say, a more consistent articulation and defense of the public good. As Madison noted in *Federalist* No. 62:

410

> The most deplorable effect of all [the effects of a mutable policy] is that diminution of attachment and reverence which steals into the heart of the people, towards a political system which betrays so many marks of infirmity, and disappoints so many of their flattering hopes. No government any more than an individual will long be respected, without being truly respectable, nor be truly respectable without possessing a certain portion of order and stability.[19]

Madison clearly stated the purpose of political representation:

> The aim of every political constitution is, or ought to be, first, to obtain for rulers men who possess most wisdom to discern, and most virtue to pursue the common good of the society; and in the next place, to take the most effectual precautions for keeping them virtuous, whilst they continue to hold their public trust. The elective mode of obtaining rulers is the characteristic policy of republican government. The means relied on in this form of government for preventing their degeneracy, are numerous and various. The most effectual one is such a limitation on the term of appointments, as will maintain a proper responsibility to the people.[20]

Madison focused attention upon the process of choosing representatives. Republican government relies on a democratic element ("the elective mode"), but it includes other elements, as well, such as the electoral college, apportionment of electors among the states, term limits, and the like.

Madison sought to create a stable system of government that can effectively promote the authentically common good and at the same time resist the natural tendency of human beings toward factional conflict. His political theory has little, if any, room for systems of group-specific or group-differentiated rights or representation. (There is an interesting exception, which is the rights of the politically organized Indian tribes, to which I will refer at the end of this essay.)

Multicultural Collectivism and Group Representation

Many political theorists now consider the idea of equality before the law to be old-fashioned or quaint. Others openly denounce it as a form of oppression. Some of those thinkers even claim the Madisonian mantle, by which they mean a concern for protecting the interests of minorities within a broadly democratic (or, in Madison's

411

term, popular) political framework. Those thinkers hope to protect minority interests not through guarantees of equal rights by a government of limited powers, but either by guaranteeing representation to groups as groups, or by erecting and continually adjusting a kaleidoscopic array of *unequal* group-specific rights, or by both.

Lani Guinier, an interesting and challenging defender of group representation, has set out an approach that she explicitly identifies with James Madison. She argues that Madison's concern with the protection of minorities from majority tyranny led him to embrace "the rule of shifting majorities, as the losers at one time or on one issue join with others and become part of the governing coalition at another time or on another issue." She calls "a majority that rules but does not dominate" a "Madisonian majority."[21] From the very beginning, however, Guinier mistakes what Madison means by representation, when she states that Madison objects to majority tyranny because "the majority may not represent all competing interests."[22] The majority, for Madison, does not represent interests; it *has* interests. Representatives deliberate about and attempt to secure the common interest and are answerable to those they represent. Guinier's misunderstanding of the role of representation sets the stage for a theory of political conflict in which the common good disappears as the goal of government. She claims that "including all sectors of society in government operation is consistent with Madison's vision" and offers as evidence *Federalist* No. 39, which she characterizes as "rejecting elitist plutocracy."[23]

Guinier does focus, however, on a problem with which a Madisonian should indeed be concerned: the permanent minority in a bipolar conflict. If there were a majority united by a common passion or interest that faced a minority that is both easily distinguished from the majority and incapable of becoming a majority, the minority would likely be systematically oppressed. In the case that Guinier considers, there are two major groups in America—blacks and whites—and one of them is an overwhelming majority. As such, it has been able to oppress the other systematically and brutally. Because of "the documented persistence of racial polarization . . . racism excludes minorities from ever becoming part of the governing coalition, meaning that the white majority will be permanent."[24]

Guinier's solution is what she calls, inspired by her young son's ideas about fairness, "the principle of taking turns."[25] She seeks not merely to secure the rights of black Americans to the suffrage, but also to obtain representation for blacks in the legislature by "authentically black" representatives. And she seeks not only representation of black voters by "authentically black" legislators, but also guarantees of particular legislative outcomes. She endorses the criterion of racial "authenticity," which for her "reflects the group consciousness, group history, and group perspective of a disadvantaged and stigmatized minority. Authenticity recognizes that black voters are a discrete 'social group' with a distinctive voice."[26] As such, representatives who are "descriptively black" but do not agree with the substantive policy agenda of Guinier either exhibit "false consciousness"[27] or are not authentically black. The "distinctive voice" of black America should be represented by authentically black representatives who represent authentic black policy preferences (which may or may not correspond to what the majority of descriptively black Americans say they prefer). Thus, "a theory of representation that derives its authority from the original civil rights' vision must address concerns of qualitative fairness involving equal recognition and just results. For those at the bottom, a system that gives everyone an equal chance of having their political preferences *physically represented* is inadequate. A fair system of political representation would provide mechanisms to ensure that disadvantaged and stigmatized minority groups also have a *fair chance* to have their policy preferences *satisfied*."[28]

Before considering Guinier's proposed means to ensure that minority groups have a fair chance to have their policy preferences satisfied, let's consider more carefully the issue of authenticity. In a discussion of authenticity that was cut from the version of her law review article that appeared in her book, Guinier states:

> Identifying "black representatives" raises several questions. For example, would descriptively black representatives who were also Republicans qualify as black representatives? More generally, is it the race of the representative that makes them part of the minority voting group? Although no one answer may suffice, the court should consider only a representative's status as the minority group's representative of choice. Therefore, only a representative sponsored by the black community and electorally accountable to it would count for purposes of a legislative bloc voting analysis.[29]

It is in this vein that opponents referred to Secretary of the Interior Gale Norton during the period of her confirmation hearings as "James Watt in a skirt," apparently on the grounds that an authentic woman could not hold the views that she held.[30] Similarly, Margaret Thatcher's enemies in Britain repeatedly referred to her as a "female impersonator." Thus, members of a group who disagree with a self-appointed leadership of that group are labeled "inauthentic" if they disagree with that self-appointed leadership. For example, Andrew Sullivan is an openly gay man who, on grounds of justice, opposes legislation interfering with contractual relations by banning private discrimination on the basis of sexual orientation. He is routinely pilloried by self-appointed gay politicians as "not really gay" and as a traitor to the authentic gay community.[31] An implication of such claims is that whites who agree with Lani Guinier would not be "authentically white," men who support feminism would not be "real men," and heterosexuals who favor gay marriage would not be "authentically heterosexual." If the latter are absurd, so are the former. Such claims that ideas are determined by race, gender, or sexual orientation are not far from the claims of polylogism made by the National Socialists (race or nationality) and Marxists (class) in the last century and are subject to criticism on the same logical grounds.[32]

In discussing legal solutions to cases raised by the Voting Rights Act, Guinier has proposed various forms of proportional representation to encourage group representation and the "fair chance" for the satisfaction of the authentic policy preferences of minorities. Although she is careful to hedge her proposals with various caveats, she prefers a form of proportional representation known as "cumulative voting," in which legislators are elected at-large (rather than in geographically separated districts) and voters are allocated a number of votes equal to the number of offices being chosen, which votes they can then cast in any manner they prefer, including casting all of them for one candidate. Similarly, she proposes cumulative voting as a method of legislation in order to avoid marginalization of minority legislators. In this manner, voters and legislators can reveal not only the existence of their preferences, but also the intensity of those preferences. If a proportional representation scheme succeeds in electing more "authentically black" legislators, but they fail to achieve effective "proportional interest representation," the minority legislators could be given a "minority veto":

> If modifying the exclusion threshold alone did not yield
> proportionate interest representation, winner-take-all major-
> ity rule by a permanent, hostile legislative majority could be
> modified. Where majority representatives refuse to bargain
> with representatives of the minority, simple majority rule
> votes would be replaced. "A minority veto" for legislation
> of vital importance to minority interests would respond to
> evidence of gross "deliberative gerrymanders."[33]

What is at stake is the guarantee that authentically black preferences be satisfied: "If it is true, as I have argued, that representatives
are equal only if existing distribution of power, resources, and prejudices do not play an 'authoritative' role in their deliberations, then
it is not clear that the remedial goal of equal political participation
in the form of a fair and equal distribution of preference satisfaction
is realistic, especially within a litigation context."[34]

Guinier does not directly propose that votes be differently weighted on the basis of race, but she does believe that black voters will
cast their votes as a bloc and thereby be represented as a group:
"As a discrete and insular minority, blacks may be able to take
maximum advantage of interest representation, in part because, as
a small group with group consciousness, they are better able to
organize collectively."[35]

Others have also endorsed replacing the dominant American form
of representation—geographically distinguished single-member districts that vote on a winner-take-all, first-past-the-post system—
with proportional representation as a means of representing racial
interests. Robert Richie and Steven Hill argue that proportional representation (PR) "provides better representation for racial minorities" and that "minorities would have greater opportunities to negotiate for influence because they could 'swing' among parties."[36]
Although they assert that "the case for PR is fundamentally nonparti-
san," they stake much of their case on their claim that "American
political progressives have a particularly urgent need to support PR
because of the growing problems created by a lack of a serious
electoral vehicle to the Democrats' left."[37]

Will Kymlicka generally endorses group representation as "not
inherently illiberal or undemocratic,"[38] but he does not try "to define
or defend any specific model of group representation," for he does
"not think it is possible to say much more at the general level."[39]

Among the alternatives he considers plausible are proportional representation as a means of securing group representation and guaranteeing seats for members of underrepresented or disadvantaged groups. In addition, Kymlicka and other writers endorse self government rights for indigenous national minorities, an issue that I will consider later. (I will deal at greater length with Kymlicka's endorsement of group-specific rights in the next section.)

Madison or Calhoun?

One of the most remarkable features of the case made for group representation by Guinier, Richie and Hill, Kymlicka, and others is not whom they cite, but whom they do not cite: John C. Calhoun. Rather than advancing Madison's project, they are advancing Calhoun's. The difference is significant, for Calhoun had effectively given up on the idea of a common good and replaced it with particular interests, each with the power to veto changes harmful to it. As Calhoun stated:

> If the whole community had the same interests, so that the interests of each and every portion would be so affected by the action of the government, that the laws which oppressed or impoverished one portion, would necessarily oppress and impoverish all others—or the reverse—then the right of suffrage, of itself, would be self-sufficient to counteract the tendency of the government to oppression and abuse of its powers; and, of course, would form, of itself, a perfect constitutional government.[40]

Calhoun explicitly rejected Madison's solution of an extended republic because "the more extensive and populous the country, the more diversified the condition and pursuits of its population, and the richer, more luxurious, and dissimilar the people, the more difficult it is to equalize the action of the government—and the more easy for one portion of the community to pervert its powers to oppress, and plunder the other."[41]

It may be obvious why Guinier would not cite a thinker who was one of America's most brilliant political theorists, but also a defender of slavery, the "peculiar institution" of the South. It is equally clear that Calhoun's work exercised a great influence on her.[42] In order to avoid systematic domination of one interest by another, Calhoun argued that interests themselves should be directly represented:

416

> There is ... but one mode in which this can be effected;
> and that is, by taking the sense of each interest or portion
> of the community, which may be unequally and injuriously
> affected by the action of the government, separately, through
> its own majority, or in some other way by which its voice
> may be fairly expressed; and to require the consent of each
> interest, either to put or to keep the government in action.
> This, too, can be accomplished only in one way—and that
> is, by such an organism of the government—and, if necessary
> for the purpose, of the community also—as will, by dividing
> and distributing the powers of government, give to each
> division or interest, through its appropriate organ, either a
> concurrent voice in making and executing the laws, or a veto
> on their execution.[43]

Thus, each interest should be guaranteed either a fair and equal distribution of preference satisfaction or a veto on the actions of the whole.

Calhoun, Guinier, Kymlicka, and other advocates of group representation have given up on the very idea of the common good, which is central to the Madisonian enterprise. Calhoun distinguished his approach precisely by eschewing the idea of a common interest:

> It results, from what has been said, that there are two
> different modes in which the sense of the community can
> be taken; one, simply by the right of suffrage, unaided; the
> other, by the right through a proper organism. Each collects
> the sense of the majority. But one regards numbers only, and
> considers the whole community as a unit, having but one
> common interest throughout; and collects the sense of the
> greater number of the whole, as that of the community. The
> other, on the contrary, regards interests as well as numbers—
> considering the community as made up of different and
> conflicting interests, as far as the action of the government
> is concerned; and takes the sense of each, through its majority
> or appropriate organ, and the united sense of all, in the sense
> of the entire community. The former of these I shall call the
> numerical, or absolute majority; and the later, the concurrent,
> or constitutional majority.[44]

Calhoun makes a strong case that even the normal functioning of a constitutionally limited government entails differential impacts, simply because of the value of the emoluments of office,[45] but slavery weighed heavier in his overall case. As Calhoun noted,

> We [the slave states] are already in a minority in the House
> of Representatives and the Electoral College; so that with
> the loss of the Senate, we shall be in a minority in every
> department of the Federal Government; and ever must con-
> tinue so, if the non-slaveholding States should carry into
> effect their scheme of appropriating to their exclusive use
> all the territories of the United States. But, fortunately, under
> our system of government, mere numbers are not the only
> element of power. There are others, which would give us
> ample means of defending ourselves against the threatened
> danger, if we should be true to ourselves.[46]

Proportional representation may have its advantages, but I believe that it would be unwise to implement it, at least in the forms pro-posed by Guinier and by Richie and Hill, mainly for the very reasons that its advocates give for proposing it: It would lead to a fracturing of the American polity and would undermine the common good. Proportional representation would substitute for the *general* welfare a constitutional vision of opposing interests engaged in a zero sum competition for limited resources. A greater dedication to the com-mon good, as instantiated by the Constitution, is far preferable to the Balkans-style politics that Guinier and other supporters of group representation envision. Proportional representation also has proce-dural disadvantages. It removes the search for consensus from the constituency to the legislature, with no obvious advantage to the republic as a whole. Tiny groups of extremists or single-issue zealots may find themselves in positions of exaggerated influence as swing votes. And governing coalitions and therefore policies may change dramatically, because of changing legislative coalitions, not changes in votes. Proportional representation has few advantages and several disadvantages. Since the United States is not in the midst of a political crisis, there is little reason to change what ain't (relative to the alternative) broke.

The advocates of group representation explicitly reject the Madi-sonian vision of the common good achieved through political repre-sentation of equal citizens in an extensive and pluralistic republic. Their vision is a war of all against all, not, to be sure, as the goal, but as the result. As the Lebanese Constitution rather innocently stated, "for the sake of justice and amity, the sects shall be equitably represented in public employment and in the composition of the ministry, provided such measures will not harm the general welfare of the state."[47] This commitment to "justice and amity" produced precisely the opposite, as Lebanon erupted into a veritable orgy of murder in 1975, when the Maronite Christians, who had been favored by the old constitutional order (based on the census of 1943), refused to cede power to the increasing portion of the population that followed Shiite Islam. A piece of paper may state that such representation is not to harm "the general welfare of the state," but once groups achieve representation, they are typically loathe to surrender it in the name of the common good or the general welfare.[48]

Multicultural Collectivism and Group Rights

Group consciousness has brought about not only calls for group representation, but also calls for group-specific (or group differentiated) legal and personal rights and entitlements. This essay cannot deal with all the arguments for these theories, but a few common elements can be identified. They include: 1) a rejection of the ideal of legal equality as itself a form of oppression; 2) demands for reparations for historical injustices; and 3) a new interpretation of freedom as requiring that legal equality of rights be abolished in favor of complex sets of rights that are differentiated by membership in ascriptive groups. I will provide a brief excursion through a rather extensive literature, along with a Madisonian-influenced commentary and critique, followed by a statement of what I take to be the most plausible Madisonian response.

Equality as a Form of Oppression

Catharine MacKinnon, law professor at the University of Chicago, has become a prominent advocate of the idea that equality itself is a form of oppression. Thus, in her *Toward a Feminist Theory of the State*, she states, "Taking the sexes 'as individuals,' meaning one at a time, as if they do not belong to genders, perfectly obscures these collective realities and substantive correlates of gender group status behind the mask of recognition of individual rights."[49]

Although it is not entirely clear what remedies would flow logically from MacKinnon's pronouncements, the incoherence of her approach is indicated by the following statement:

> Under sex equality law, to be human, in substance, means
> to be a man. To be a person, an abstract individual with

419

abstract rights, may be a bourgeois concept, but its content is male. The only way to assert a claim *as* a member of the socially unequal group women, as opposed to seeking to assert a claim as *against* membership in the group women, is to seek treatment on a sexually denigrated basis. Human rights, including "women's rights," have implicitly been limited to those rights that men have to lose. This may be in part why men persistently confuse procedural and abstract equality with substantive equality: for them, they are the same. Abstract equality has never included those rights that women as women most need and never have had. All this appears rational and neutral in law because social reality is constructed from the same point of view.[50]

She rejects what she calls "abstract equality" and asserts that such equality does not include "those rights that *women as women* most need." To consider "women as women" is precisely to consider them abstractly, that is, in abstraction from their other characteristics (age, race, size, education, etc.). To treat both Catharine and Dorine as women is precisely to abstract from the fact that one is white and the other black. Although MacKinnon tries to offer a general critique of abstract individualism as merely an ideological front for masculine privilege and the oppression of women, her generic arguments destroy her own case for women-specific rights. That extreme incoherence marks many attempts to show how the ideas of abstract rights, that is, rights that apply to unspecified persons, and equality before the law are in fact merely especially invidious forms of oppression.

Writing also from a self-described feminist perspective, Iris Marion Young argues for differentiated rights for men and for women, as well as for ethnic and other groups, on the general grounds that:

> where differences in capacities, culture, values, and behavioral styles exist among some groups, but some of these groups are privileged, strict adherence to a principle of equal treatment tends to perpetuate oppression or disadvantage. The inclusion and participation of everyone in social and political institutions therefore sometimes requires the articulation of special rights that attend to group differences in order to undermine oppression and disadvantage.[51]

More strongly, she claims that, "A general perspective does not exist which all persons can adopt and from which all experiences and perspectives can be understood and taken into account."[52]

420

In support of her strong claim that equality before the law is inherently oppressive, Young merely reports that "many" activists "struggling for the full inclusion and participation of all groups in this society's institutions and positions of power, reward, and satisfaction, argue that rights and rules that are universally formulated and thus blind to differences of race, culture, gender, age, or disability, perpetuate rather than undermine oppression."[53]

It is central to Young's case for assigning different rights to sexual genders (and to other ascriptive groups) that the very idea of a common good is a myth and that, in fact, it is impossible to "walk a mile in another's shoes" or to understand the claims that others may make. Thus:

> Instead of a universal citizenship in the sense of this generality, we need a group differentiated citizenship and a heterogeneous public. In a heterogeneous public, differences are publicly recognized and acknowledged as irreducible, by which I mean that persons from one perspective or history can never completely understand and adopt the point of view of those with other group-based perspectives and histories. Yet commitment to the need and desire to decide together the society's policies fosters communication across those differences.[54]

I do not believe that we should so readily accede to Young's claim that "persons from one perspective or history can never completely understand or adopt the point of view of those with other group-based perspectives and histories." If by "completely understand or adopt the point of view" she means actually become that other person, then her claim is correct but irrelevant. If to understand a play by Shakespeare I had to actually be Shakespeare (and be him at the very moment that he completed the play), then Young's words themselves would be incomprehensible to all but her. Similarly, if I had to have had the same experiences as another person to understand her claim of right, then acts of justice would be impossible.[55] That sets an erroneous standard of understanding, one that is as inappropriate for law and politics as it is for literature. To understand the claim for justice of another is not, in fact, impossible, just as it is not impossible to understand Young's writings; it is hardly absurd to seek to achieve an objective standpoint from which to judge claims of justice, as Young presumes.[56] Understanding a play, a foreign language, or a claim for justice may be difficult, but that is not the same as being impossible.[57] Furthermore, Madison and the other Founders understood quite well that one could not and should not expect citizens always to adopt the perspective of the common good; that would be a shaky foundation on which to build a republic. Madison in particular certainly understood that citizens are quite often motivated by both interests and passions that are contrary to the general interest. Madison's constitutional project assumed that the public would be, in Young's term, "heterogeneous." But the fact that citizens are diverse and that many or most of them fail to adopt the perspective of the common good entails neither that the system of rights and obligations secured by the Constitution cannot embody or secure the common good nor that we should abandon the idea of citizenship or republican virtue altogether. Some degree of republican virtue is required for a workable constitutional order, but Madison's defense of equal rights does not assume that all citizens will adopt a universal perspective or that citizenship requires that one "completely" understand or adopt the point of view of other citizens.

Young's position, like MacKinnon's, is fraught with problems of internal coherence, for if what she believes is true, how could she or those who join her in undermining the ideal of equality before the law know the histories or experiences of others and therefore be able to determine what their rights should be? After all, she does not assert that seekers of differentiated rights may unilaterally assert them against the rights, interests, or passions of others; indeed, she specifically denies it. Instead, they must emerge out of some kind of democratic process; they must be "publicly recognized." But if that democratic process presupposes differential rights to input, then the argument is circular, for it requires to be already established what it purports to produce.

In a way that brings to mind Oscar Wilde's complaint about socialism (too many committee meetings), Young writes, "All citizens should have access to neighborhood or district assemblies where they participate in discussion and decision making. In such a more participatory democratic scheme, members of oppressed groups would also have group assemblies, which would delegate group representatives."[58] But which groups are to get these special rights? Which groups "count"? According to Young, "These principles do not apply to any persons who do not identify with majority language or culture within a society, but only to sizeable linguistic or cultural minorities living in distinct though not necessarily segregated communities."[59] So size matters when it comes to determining fundamental rights. In abandoning the highly salient ideal of equal individual rights before the law, Young plunges into a morass of circular argumentation and self-contradiction.[60]

Reparations to Groups for Historical Injustices

The second form of group-specific rights that I will consider is, at least superficially, based on adherence to a liberal concern with rights and restitution. It is clearly differentiated from the view articulated by MacKinnon, Young, and many other advocates of group-differentiated rights. As Young notes of her approach, "The goal is not to give special compensation to the deviant until they achieve normality, but rather to denormalize the way institutions formulate their rules by revealing the plural circumstances and needs that exist, or ought to exist, within them."[61]

In contrast, demands for reparations rest on background claims for equal justice, on the claim that what has been taken unjustly should be restored.[62] Human history is filled with examples of injustices against groups of people, and when they can be corrected, there is certainly at least a good case that they should be. The suffering of Jews and Roma under the National Socialists, to take perhaps the most well-known example, has led to restitution and reparations of various kinds. Those whose property was expropriated under Communist rule have received compensation in some formerly Communist states. In the United States, surviving Japanese Americans who suffered loss of liberty and estate as a result of President Franklin D. Roosevelt's Executive Order 9066, issued on February 19, 1942,[63] received an official apology and payments of $20,000 each as a result of passage of the Civil Liberties Act of 1988, which President Ronald Reagan signed into law on August 10, 1988.[64]

As this essay is written, the primary claim in the United States for reparations from the U.S. government, or from all or some citizens of the United States, is the claim for reparations to black Americans.[65] Randall Robinson, founder and president of the TransAfrica Forum and author of *The Debt: What America Owes to Blacks*, argues that:

> there is much new fessing-up that white society must be induced to do here for the common good. First, it must

423

own up to slavery and acknowledge its debt to slavery's contemporary victims. It must, at long last, pay that debt in massive restitutions made to America's only involuntary members. It must help to rebuild the black esteem it destroyed, by democratizing access to a trove of histories, near and ancient, to which blacks contributed seminally and prominently. It must open wide a scholarly concourse to the African ancients to which its highly evolved culture owes much credit and gives none. It must rearrange the furniture of its national myths, monuments, lores, symbols, iconography, legends, and arts to reflect the contributions and sensibilities of all Americans. It must set afoot new values. It must purify memory. It must recast its lying face.[66]

Robinson offers a variety of arguments for reparations, but two are especially prominent. First, African Americans were robbed of the value of their labor, from which others benefited. The descendants of those who benefited are now richer than they would be otherwise, and the descendants of those who were robbed are poorer than they would be otherwise. Thus:

> Through keloids of suffering, through coarse veils of damaged self-belief, lost direction, misplaced compass, shit-faced resignation, racial transmutation, black people worked long, hard, killing days, years, centuries—and they were never *paid*. The value of their labor went into others' pockets—plantation owners, northern entrepreneurs, state treasuries, the United States government.[67]

This argument has considerable appeal to liberals (and I count authentic Madisonians as such) because it claims restitution for what was unjustly taken. Such a claim certainly could have provided justification for the confiscation of the estates of slave-holders and their distribution to freed slaves, as was proposed in the famous Special Field Order No. 15 issued by Major-General W. T. Sherman on January 16, 1865.[68] However, a substantial amount of time has passed between the enslavement and exploitation that Robinson so forcefully describes and the present. There are no living persons who were either slaves or slave-holders. That fact does not dispense with claims for reparations; those who inherited less because the wealth of their ancestors was stolen could, after all, be compensated by those who inherited more because their ancestors stole. This argument, however, is difficult to maintain after the passage of so long a time. The populations are today so mixed and the strands so intertwined that we cannot determine the justice of inherited endowments. For example, consider the heirs of the hundreds of thousands of soldiers who died in the war that eliminated slavery. What should those heirs receive in compensation for the loss of the lives and the livelihood of their ancestors, who might otherwise have left them wealth?[69]

In principle, reparations arguments are acceptable within a liberal theory of justice, but such reparations must be tied to the actual harm suffered by some and the existence of benefits that are unjustifiably held by others. If someone harms another, the victim should be made whole. If the one who committed the harm is dead, his or her heirs do not bear any criminal responsibility. If, however, they materially benefited from the harm and the wealth can be transferred to the heir of the harmed, who has a greater claim, then there is an argument for making the transfer. But if the heirs of the one who harms did not benefit, then taking anything from them is itself criminal. For example, transferring resources from "the Russians" to Tatars, as reparations for the harms imposed on Tatars by the Soviet state, would be unjust, for the overwhelming majority of Russians did not benefit from that state, but were also victimized by it. The average white American is not, in fact, a beneficiary of the criminal enslavement of others, past or present, and it would be an injustice to hold him or her responsible.[70]

The second commonly offered reason for reparations payments is that the culture of African Americans has been systematically harmed, and this harm translates into systematic disadvantage for African Americans, disadvantages that are imposed on them by whites and for which they deserve compensation. Thus, as Randall Robinson formulates the thesis:

> Culture is the matrix on which the fragile human animal draws to remain socially healthy.[71]
>
> Contemporary discrimination alone does not explain the persistence of these income gaps. Another culprit is a mutant form of the coarse and visible old discrimination. This sneaky and invisible culprit can be called conditioned expectation.[72]
>
> By now, after 380 years of unrelenting psychological abuse, the biggest part of our problem is inside us: in how we have

> come to see ourselves, in our damaged capacity to validate
> a course for ourselves without outside approval.[73]

For those reasons, Robinson supports the proposal made by Robert Westley that "a private trust be established for the benefit of all African Americans. The trust would be funded out of the general revenues of the United States" and would support programs designed to expand and improve the educational opportunities of African Americans and, notably, to fund political activities: "The broad civil rights advocacy necessitated by a persistent climate of American racism would be generously funded, as well as the political work of black organizations seeking, as Ron Walters has suggested, to 'own' the *politics* of the black community."[74]

Most advocates of reparations payments quickly dismiss the idea of individual compensation. As Darrell L. Pugh notes, "The fact that the reparations being suggested are prospective and primarily benefit nonvictims argues against the individual payment approach."[75] As with Robinson, Pugh (citing the authority of Boris I. Bittker, who wrote on the issue in the 1960s and 1970s) suggests instead that "creation of a national trust fund, administered by 'legitimate' representatives of the African American community with oversight by Congress, might be one answer."[76] The point is not to compensate individual harmed victims, but to rebuild a culture that has been damaged. (Note that the representatives must be "legitimate," a criterion that seems equivalent to the "authentic" criterion invoked by Lani Guinier.)

How long might such a group entitlement last? Will Kymlicka assumes that such race-differentiated entitlements would be remedial and time-limited: "A degree of short-term separateness and colour-consciousness is needed to achieve the long-term goal of an integrated and colour-blind society."[77] Others, however, make it clear that the debt owed by whites to blacks has no time limit. As Robinson argues, "The life and responsibilities of a society or nation are not circumscribed by the life spans of its mortal constituents. Social rights, wrongs, obligations, and responsibilities flow eternal."[78] Indeed, the debt can never be repaid until and unless the understanding of African history is changed:

> This then is the nub of it. America's contemporary racial
> problems cannot be solved, racism cannot be arrested,

426

achievement gaps cannot be fully closed until Americans—
all Americans—are repaired in their views of Africa's role
in history.[79]

Setting such a standard, and specifically one that relies on a highly
contested account of the history of Africa, indeed implies a perpetual
debt and, correspondingly, a perpetual entitlement of "legitimate"
representatives of the African American community to enrich those
they believe worthy at the expense of others.

The fact that Robinson even mentions the possibility of "punitive
damages"[80] indicates that he believes that "whites" as a group have
interests implacably opposed to those of "blacks" as a group. Otherwise, why even consider the possibility of *punishment* of whites as
a group?

In addition to enriching and empowering a class of authentic or
legitimate representatives (authentic or legitimate as determined by
whom?), the most serious consequences of the perpetual status of
the debt (dare I say dependency) is made clear by a moving description of a young girl who is struggling in school:

> The profound consequences constitute still another partic-
> ular in a long bill of them against the government of the
> United States and others who benefited from slavery. But
> this is why I have expended so much time here on the issue
> of reparations, for the very discussion engendered will help
> an embattled nine-year-old to know finally what happened
> to her, that she is blameless, that she has had something
> taken from her that has a far more than material value.[81]

Much more could be said both in favor of, and in criticism of,
reparations for the American descendants of enslaved Africans. But
current proposals would leave blacks perpetually in tutelage, second-class citizens lorded over by first-class overlords, all of whom
would be "authentic" and "legitimate" representatives of their community. It is certainly not a proposal for the protection of minority
interests of the sort that a Madisonian would envisage and bears
greater resemblance, instead, to the black Bantustans or "homelands"
established under the tribalism of Afrikaner apartheid. In such
homelands, the central state designated the ruling elites, funded
them, and charged them with supervising the development of their
communities.[82]

Empowering elites to administer (in perpetuity) resources to a dependent class distinguished by their race is incompatible with virtually any recognizably liberal vision of politics, Madisonian or otherwise. Reparations to individual victims from those who have benefited may be justified, but a case for that has not been established by Robinson's arguments.

There might even be a case for reparations of some sort as a means of securing the stability of a republican political and legal order that is more conducive to justice than the most likely alternative. Such an admission may, however, cut several ways, depending on which group would be most likely to undermine republican institutions absent special consideration. That is the upshot of Madison's speech on the slave trade clause of the Constitution before the Virginia Ratifying Convention:

> I should conceive this clause to be impolitic, if it were one of those things which could be excluded without encountering greater evils. The southern states would not have entered into the union of America, without the temporary permission of that trade. And if they were excluded from the union, the consequences might be dreadful to them and to us. We are not in a worse situation than before. That traffic is prohibited by our laws, and we may continue the prohibition. The union is not in a worse situation. Under the articles of confederation, it might be continued forever: But by this clause an end may be put to it after twenty years. There is therefore an amelioration of our circumstances.[83]

Such arguments from expediency are, however, premised on the existence of a clear danger to the continued existence of the republic itself. No such danger exists at the present time. Further, they could just as easily cut against reparations for the heirs of slaves as in favor; which way it would cut would depend on the bargaining powers of the different parties, rather than on any claims to justice.

Inequality of Rights as a Precondition of Freedom

Will Kymlicka has argued effectively for group-differentiated rights.[84] Such rights are necessary, he claims, to protect the viability of groups that provide communal ties, without which individuals could not enjoy the range of "meaningful choices" necessary to be able to enjoy freedom. Such ties might be eroded without such special rights, obligations, and correlative powers of enforcement.

In the case of North American Indians, Kymlicka claims that "the viability of Indian communities depends on coercively restricting the mobility, residence, and political rights of both Indians and non-Indians."[85] (It should be noted in passing that Kymlicka does consider the role of federalism in the U.S. constitutional system as a means of protecting minorities and finds it wanting. His account, however, is unfortunately full of factual errors.[86] More importantly, Kymlicka relies on an implicit baseline, in comparison to which American federalism allegedly worsens the positions of minorities: "Federalism may well serve to worsen the position of national minorities, as has occurred in the United States, Brazil, Australia, and other territorial federalisms."[87] Worsened in comparison to what? Perhaps the U.S.S.R., which did institutionalize explicitly national political units? Or worsened in comparison to a non-existent fantasy world?)

Kymlicka derives this right to cultural membership indirectly from the framework outlined by John Rawls in his *A Theory of Justice*. Kymlicka highlights Rawls's notion of "self-respect" as a precondition for the pursuit of any rational plan of life (hence as a "primary good") and then tries to determine the preconditions for self-respect. A cultural context within which choices can be made is such a precondition: "The decision about how to lead our lives must ultimately be ours alone, but this decision is always a matter of selecting what we believe to be most valuable from the various options available, selecting from a context of choice which provides us with different ways of life."[88] Thus, "Liberal values require both individual freedom of choice and a secure cultural context from which individuals can make their choices."[89] Furthermore, belonging replaces accomplishment as the focus of self-esteem: "national identity is particularly suited to serving as the 'primary foci of identification,' because it is based on belonging, not accomplishment."[90]

Kymlicka distinguishes between "internal restrictions" and "external protections": the former are restrictions placed by the group on its own members, and the latter are restrictions on the interaction of members of the wider society with members of the protected group or entitlements to benefits from the wider society.[91] He favors external protections and opposes internal restrictions. He opposes the latter on the ground that "protecting people from changes in the character of their culture can't be viewed as protecting their ability to choose."[92] But he cannot help but slide directly toward such paternalism and control on the members of minority groups: "The viability of Indian communities depends on coercively restricting the mobility, residence, and political rights of both Indians and non-Indians."[93]

Kymlicka believes that sets of group-differentiated rights pose no danger to social or political unity, since in the cases he considers the groups seek inclusion or integration: "Enabling integration may require some modification of the institutions of the dominant culture in the form of group-specific polyethnic rights, such as the right of Jews and Muslims to exemptions from Sunday closing legislation, or the right of Sikhs to exemptions to motorcycle helmet laws."[94] These examples could also be accommodated by a reformulation of the rule so that it would apply to all. Rather than propose exemptions, which means that some persons are empowered to decide who will be punished for infractions and who will not be punished, why not simply propose the abolition of compulsory shop closing laws and the elimination of compulsory helmet laws? It seems never to occur to Kymlicka that the state might have no business interfering in personal choice or voluntary transactions in this manner. If such foolish and paternalistic restrictions were removed for all, then no one would feel the exclusion that so concerns Kymlicka.

Moreover, compulsory shop closing laws in Europe and North America are usually defended as a requirement for the maintenance of the cultural and religious identity of the majority Christian community; some might argue that they are a precondition for the self-esteem of the members of that community. To be consistent, Kymlicka would have to argue that only non-Christians should be allowed to buy and sell on Sundays, whereas Christians should be forbidden by law from doing so. Perhaps special Christian police forces would enforce such group-specific restrictions. A more authentically liberal solution would be to propose the same rule—liberty—for all. That is true also of most of the other plausible examples that Kymlicka gives of means to avoid oppressing a minority, such as exemptions for the Amish from Social Security (which they erroneously believe is an actuarially sound insurance system) and compulsory education.[95]

Kymlicka's proposal for group-differentiated rights is flawed in other ways. Rights that are given and taken, and that have to be periodically revised by someone with power, are not rights at all.[96] Someone has to be in the position to grant, take away, or otherwise adjust Kymlickian differential rights, and that person or those persons will be, in effect, the real holders of the rights because they hold the powers to grant them or to take them away. Equality of rights for all has a salience that carefully tweaked inequalities do not. The latter require philosopher kings to create and administer them. Thus, the adoring newspaper headline about Will Kymlicka's worldwide crusade to eliminate equality before the law: "A Philosopher in Red Sneakers Gains Influence as a Global Guru."[97] But as Plato found during his disastrous mission to Syracuse, philosophers rarely get the final word on matters of political power. Establishing systems of unequal rights will probably foster intergroup conflict, not intergroup comity, and we have seen in the last century just how terrible such conflict can be. Stipulating that "such measures will not harm the general welfare of the state," as the Lebanese Constitution did, is about as effective as stipulating that socialism shall be imposed, provided that it works.

Further, the boundary between external protections and internal restrictions on which Kymlicka puts so much weight is less impermeable than he thinks. For example, a restriction on the rights of indigenous peoples to sell their land counts as an external protection, but it will certainly look to at least some members of the group as an internal restriction. Not only are outsiders restricted from contracting with them, but they are restricted from contracting with outsiders.[98] The unity of the community that emerges is likely to be manipulated by those with the power to control members of the group. And although this may in some cases (and in some sense) preserve a political community by restricting the rights of its members, it also ensures that opportunities for enrichment will be foregone, so that members of the community also share common poverty. Such poverty may bind a community together, but it is not usually so desirable for the non-elite members of the community who suffer from it. Such special rights are also often liabilities. For example, the inability to sell land means that one cannot get a mortgage on it. One has possession, but not capital.[99] Contrary to Kymlicka's assertions, the alleged protections for such groups have a poor historical record.

"Special rights" may also prove to be terribly disadvantageous in other ways. The special status of Jews in European history is instructive in this regard. In that case, R. I. Moore cogently points out:

> As so often in Jewish history special treatment was dangerous, and what began as a privilege later became the means of oppression. Protection of the Jews and jurisdiction over

> them became one of the rights which the counts usurped
> from the crown in the tenth century, and the feudatories
> from the counts in the eleventh.[100]

In the *Leges Edwardi Confessoris* it is stated that "All Jews wherever they are in the kingdom must be under the guardianship of the king; nor may any of them be subject to any baron without the licence of the king, because Jews and all their property are the king's."[101] The special status of many American Indian bands and nations as "domestic dependent nations"[102] also does not present an especially happy picture of how group-differentiated rights may actually work in practice.[103]

Although Kymlicka repeatedly insists that the group-differentiated rights he endorses are individual rights, he consistently refers to "the group" making choices about whether or how their culture will change. Thus, "While indigenous peoples do not want modernization forced upon them, they demand the right to decide for themselves what aspects of the outside world they will incorporate into their cultures."[104] Who are the "they" here? If he means the individual members, their rights to decide what aspects of the outside world they wish to accept would be respected in a regime of equal rights. It seems clear that Kymlicka means the group as a whole, or at least its political leaders, in which case majorities (as a matter of practice, this means oligarchic elites) have the right, and he cannot assert that such rights are individual, rather than collective, rights. In virtually every case, despite his persistent denials, Kymlicka gives to the elite members of groups (frequently people who are articulate, like himself, or people who are brutal, violent, and ruthless in eliminating opposition) the right to determine how the other members of the group will live, and if that is not an "internal restriction," it is not clear what would be.[105] As Charles Taylor notes of restrictive laws in Quebec, "Restrictions have been placed on Quebeckers by their government, in the name of their collective goal of survival."[106] Kymlicka's approach follows the general trend of declarations, conventions, and covenants governing indigenous people, most of which do not mention individual rights of the members of indigenous nations, such as the right to own land individually or freely in association with others, but consistently refer only to the right of "peoples" to "lands" and "territories." A philosophical defense of such restrictions is offered by Michael McDonald, who complains of "the distorting force of individual mobility rights" and asserts "such rights can intentionally or unintentionally lead to the destruction of worthwhile groups."[107] The approach is decidedly collectivist, rather than individualist. Thus, Article 17, Section 2 of the Convention Concerning Indigenous and Tribal Peoples in Independent Countries states, "The peoples concerned shall be consulted whenever consideration is being given to their capacity to alienate their lands or otherwise transmit their rights outside their own community."[108] Such "rights" are explicitly collective rights, founded on race or ethnicity, and not, *pace* Kymlicka, individual rights. They subject individuals to the rule of the collectivity to which they are assigned, which quite often means in practice subordination to the rule of parasitic and predatory elites who have attained preeminence or power within and therefore over their own national or ethnic group.

Kymlicka rests his case on the alleged unavoidability of the mixture of state and ethnicity: "The state cannot help but take an active role in the reproduction of cultures."[109] To avoid oppression and to guarantee each group the recognition its members need as a primary good necessary for the pursuit of rational plans of life, the state should interact with the members of each ethnic group differently. Thus, since "there is no way to have a complete 'separation of state and ethnicity,'" it follows that "the only question is how to ensure that these unavoidable forms of support for particular ethnic and national groups are provided fairly—that is, how to ensure that they do not privilege some groups and disadvantage others."[110] Further, he argues that "the most plausible reason" for not granting automatic citizenship to each and every human who might desire it is "to recognize and protect our membership in distinct cultures," and this, in turn, "is also a reason for allowing group-differentiated citizenship within a state."[111]

Such reasoning is compatible with nationalist or socialist thought but not with liberalism. The liberal approach recognizes the inevitability of conflicts over common goods among people with different ends and therefore limits the state to those things necessary to the maintenance of a civil society, to what is in fact a good common to all. That is the most plausible interpretation of the "necessary and proper" clause of the United States Constitution, a clause that is usually misinterpreted to mean "convenient and not clearly prohibited." If government schools inevitably impart some set of moral values (which, of course, includes the currently dominant null set promulgated in most government schools), we may consider alternatives to monopoly state schooling, rather than trying to fine-tune the curriculum so that each and every ethnic group will not feel excluded. The result of the latter has turned out to be (in the United States, at least) a curriculum remarkably devoid of moral and other content. Kymlicka never considers whether individuals may have a right to withdraw from coercive state-imposed systems; exemptions may be "granted" by the state, but they should always be understood to be gifts or dispensations made by those with the power and the right to grant or to deny them. They are not rights.[112]

Kymlicka and others start with the fixed point of national borders and restrictions on freedom of movement and trade, assuming that nothing could be less controversial than protectionism and controls on the movement of people. They treat the relatively recent invention of the passport and of controls on movement in European history as if they were an inheritance of the ages.[113] As Kymlicka writes of group-differentiated rights, "they are logically presupposed by existing liberal practice."[114] By this he means restricting rights to work, travel, own property, and the like to citizens. The statement is true only if we consider shooting people who try to sneak across the borders in search of opportunities to offer their services to willing employers to be part of "liberal practice." But Kymlicka does have a thin wedge to open the door to group-differentiated rights: Even if borders were open to trade and travel, one legal right at least would not be open to any and all who desired it. One right that should be reserved for citizens is the right to vote. That is an important limitation on the scope of a legal right, but voting is hardly a natural right like the right to own property or the right to choose one's profession; it is a procedural right that is useful as a means of protecting our fundamental rights, such as the right to freedom of religion or the right to choose one's profession or spouse. And it is a very, very, very thin wedge to use to create a general theory of group-restricted rights. "To recognize and protect our membership in distinct cultures" is hardly "the most plausible reason" for limiting the franchise to citizens and limiting citizenship to those who are a part of the civic culture of liberalism. Further, the idea that citizenship should be limited to members of distinct ethnic or cultural groups is hardly widely accepted as a part of liberalism. Kymlicka puts a great deal of weight on the alleged intuitive plausibility of his thesis, but his intuition is not shared by many other contemporary liberals.[115]

Unlike Madison and other classical liberals, Kymlicka is willing or even eager to jettison legal stability in favor of an ever changing kaleidoscope of rights and obligations. The very variety and flexibility of rights regimes that Kymlicka endorses—a plurality that requires wise supervisors, adjudicators, and assigners of rights to and among groups—has terrible consequences for the rule of law generally. Rather than being a condition of freedom, as Kymlicka asserts,[116] these regimes require subjection to the arbitrary will of others who are empowered to tweak, adjust, change, and rearrange rights as they see fit. Traditional liberalism defined that subjection as the very condition of tyranny, rather than of liberty.[117]

It seems that the one fixed point for Kymlicka is the existence of national state borders, protectionism, immigration controls, and armed border guards, not an especially promising point for an allegedly liberal theory of rights. Yet Kymlicka's own argument for group-differentiated rights can just as easily be used against him, by identifying groups with common identities and interests that transcend national state borders and whose claims or rights, therefore, to be protected, would require that those very borders be eliminated. One obvious example is the travel of nomadic peoples across state borders; examples include the Somali of the Ogaden; the Sami of Scandinavia, Finland, and Russia; and others. Other groups whose "identities" transcend national borders include religious groups and gay people. In the case of religion, Jeremy Waldron brings up the helpful example of a Catholic Breton who considers her religion, which is shared by people in many other national communities, as more important to her sense of self than her Celtic ethnicity: "That feature of her life—that as a Breton she shares a faith and a church with Irish, Italians, Poles, Brazilians, and Filipinos—may be much more important to her identity than anything which (say) a Tourist Board would use to highlight her cultural distinctiveness."[118] Barring her from freedom of travel, trade, and interaction with her fellow Catholics in the name of her Celtic ethnicity would likely be far more damaging to her than Kymlicka seems willing to admit. Taking border guards and protectionism as a given is to constrain the liberty that she would see as most instrumentally valuable to the fulfillment of her identity.

Another case overlooked by Kymlicka is that of gay people. As Carl Stychin points out, "If we accept the possibility of group based identity and rights," then the theories of multiculturalism and diversity advanced by Charles Taylor and Will Kymlicka "are going to be more complicated than we (and they) might first have considered."[119] Stychin's critique is not, however, based on a call for equal individual rights; he agrees fundamentally with thinkers such as Taylor and Kymlicka but carries their project to its own absurd conclusion. Stychin shows how a serious commitment to group-differentiated rights on Kymlickian foundations (self-esteem, recognition, etc.) ultimately destroys the very national borders that Kymlicka considered determined starting points. As Stychin argues, "lesbians and gays (and, for that matter, many others) are skeptical when they read Kymlicka's arguments about culture. For many of us, an important cultural reference point is queer culture, which seems more than capable of surviving (and thriving) in the current cultural conditions."[120] But he concludes from the fact that such identities and communities are transnational that "lesbian, gay, bisexual, and queer politics and culture can bring to a study of national identities a framework in which identity is self-consciously contingent and in process, characterized by reinvention and an ongoing questioning of borders and membership."[121] Stychin finds that prospect exciting, but one wonders whether people who have suffered through border changes in the past—those in Poland, for example—are likely to be as excited about an ongoing questioning of borders and membership. Stychin takes the multicultural project of Kymlicka and others seriously enough to bring it to its absurd conclusion: All the rules, all the time, are always open to "reinvention." As he says, "As nations struggle with their sense of self, they could do well to appropriate this excitement of reconstitution, which I would describe as a queering of the nation itself."[122] An authentically liberal perspective would simply recognize the equal individual rights of gay people, including the rights to travel and work where they wish, to marry, and so on, so that gay partners who are citizens of different countries would not be separated by odious border controls, residence permits, and work permits. Group-differentiated rights, when taken seriously, lead to both logical and legal instability. Equal individual rights, on the other hand, are stable, predictable, salient, and knowable by and to all and do not rest on such odious and immoral practices as terrorizing those who wish to cross state borders for peaceful purposes.

Madison's vision of "establishing a political equality among all"[123] provides a much more stable foundation from which to secure the common good than do any of the innumerable variety of systems of inequality proposed by multiculturalists. Madison envisioned a constitutional order encompassing a wide variety of factions living together under a regime of equal rights. He defended such a republican order in the name of liberty, for he did not think that liberty would be as secure in the small republic that Montesquieu and some of the anti-Federalists believed was the only secure repository of liberty.[124] For example, "Brutus," writing in opposition to adoption of the Constitution, argued that:

> History furnishes no example of a free republic, any thing like the extent of the United States. The Grecian republics were of small extent; so also was that of the Romans. Both of these, it is true, in process of time, extended their conquests over large territories of country; and the consequence was, that their governments were changed from that of free governments to those of the most tyrannical that ever existed in the world.[125]

> In a republic, the manners, sentiments, and interests of the people should be similar. If this be not the case, there will be a constant clashing of opinions; and the representatives of one part will be continually striving against those of the other. This will retard the operations of government, and prevent such conclusions as will promote the public good.[126]

Madison drew precisely the opposite conclusion:

> The lesson we are to draw from the whole is that where a majority are united by a common sentiment, and have an opportunity, the rights of the minor party become insecure. In a Republican Gov^t the majority if united have always an opportunity. The only remedy is to enlarge the sphere, and thereby divide the community into so great a number of interests and parties, that in the 1st place a majority will not be likely at the same moment to have a common interest separate from that of the whole or of the minority; and in the 2^d place, that in case they sh^d have such an interest, they may not be apt to unite in the pursuit of it. It was incumbent on us then to try this remedy, and with that view to frame

437

a republican system on such a scale & in such a form as will controul all the evils wch have been experienced.[127]

Kymlicka and others are trying to replicate within each extended or multicultural republic a set of little republics, each ethnically (relatively) homogeneous, and each, therefore, more likely to experience the tyranny by majorities over minorities. Madison sought to prevent such tyranny by expanding the scope of the American republic. The establishment of such little republics is likely to generate conflicts among those with group-differentiated rights about what the ultimate decisionmakers of the state are going to put into each Christmas stocking of rights.[128]

A fairly obvious example of the possible conflicts among groups that are made inevitable by such schemes of group-differentiated rights is presented by the conflict between feminist and multiculturalist approaches. Feminist theorist Susan Moller Okin has raised the problem of the treatment of women in cultural, ethnic, religious, or national groups whose traditions incorporate or rest upon the subordination of women.[129] In response, Will Kymlicka noted that

> Okin says she is concerned about the view that the members of a minority "are not sufficiently protected by the practice of ensuring the individual rights of their members," and minority group members are demanding "a group right not available to the rest of the population." But many feminists have made precisely the same argument about gender equality—i.e., that true equality will require rights for women that are not available to men, such as affirmative action, women-only classrooms, gender-specific prohibitions on pornography, gender-specific health programs, and the like. Others have made similar arguments about the need for group-specific rights and benefits for the disabled, or for gays and lesbians. All of these movements are challenging the traditional liberal assumption that equality requires identical treatment.[130]

The very fact of the limitless variety of group-differentiated rights may be the strongest argument for equal rights.

Madison and the Indians

There is one exception to the general argument for equal rights under the rule of law, and that is the status of the Native American nations, on whose behalf Madison devoted much effort and whose status is recognized in the Constitution of the United States of America. Thus, Article I, Section 8, Clause 3 of the Constitution vests in the Congress of the United States the power "To regulate Commerce with foreign Nations, and among the several States, and with the Indian Tribes." Article VI, Clause 2 further specifies that "This Constitution, and the Laws of the United States which shall be made in Pursuance thereof; and all Treaties made, or which shall be made, under the Authority of the United States, shall be the supreme Law of the Land; and the Judges in every State shall be bound thereby, any Thing in the Constitution or Laws of any State to the Contrary notwithstanding." This clearly means that all of the treaties with the Indian tribes that preceded the new Constitution of the United States were part of the "supreme Law of the Land," for it specifically refers to "all Treaties *made*, or which shall be made" (emphasis added). On the basis of the historical facts and the law of the land, Chief Justice Marshall declared in *Worcester v. Georgia*, "The Cherokee nation, then, is a distinct community, occupying its own territory, with boundaries accurately described, in which the laws of Georgia can have no force. . . ."[131] Thus, the new Constitution did not completely wipe out the preexisting political independence of the Indian tribes, although Marshall's denomination of them as "domestic dependent nations" in "a state of pupilage" to the U.S. government implied something less than independence. Whether Marshall's reading of the status of the Indian tribes is tenable, the U.S. government is obligated to respect all of the particular rights and obligations specified in the 367 ratified treaties between Indian tribes and the American government.[132] Adherence to all such treaties is justified not only by the preexisting status of the Indian tribes, but more importantly, by the fundamental legal obligation to fulfill the terms of the Constitution. Arguments about securing a higher kind of freedom by "recognizing" the special status of groups are irrelevant to adherence to the law of the land.

Special legal and political status for Indian tribes and bands is justified by the fact of their preexisting political status and the requirement that treaties already entered into be respected. To do otherwise would be to violate fundamental requirements of justice and to replace law with brute force and power. For the same reasons that new group-differentiated rights should not be conjured up by legislative fiat, legally binding treaties should not be unilaterally abrogated (unless the treaty itself provides for such abrogation).

The variety of regimes of group-differentiated rights that are presented as realizations of multiculturalism is too great to catalogue or to rebut in this essay.[133] The above remarks merely rebut some of the more prominent variants and should point the way to a general liberal defense of the idea of equality before the law.

Conclusion

The project that Madison and his colleagues (both those who supported and those who opposed the Constitution) launched has proven itself quite attractive in comparison to other existing regimes. Despite its many flaws and failings, it has secured more liberty and more prosperity for more people than any other regime in the history of humanity. I see no reason to replace a regime of equal individual rights, itself the result of heroic struggles familiar to students of American history, with any of the variety of mutually incompatible regimes of group-differentiated rights. Equality is unique; inequality is not. That fact alone should indicate to us that any proposed regime of unequal rights will be opposed by all the advocates of other competing regimes of unequal rights. Each group (or, more precisely, the elite self-appointed leaders of each group who expect to benefit) will struggle for maximum advantage, to the detriment of the common good.

In every case, advocates of unequal rights reject the common good, whether explicitly in theory or implicitly in practice. In place of Madison's attempt to protect "the rights of other citizens, or the permanent and aggregate interests of the community,"[134] advocates of group-differentiated rights have adopted Calhoun's vision of legal and political processes as "considering the community as made up of different and conflicting interests, as far as the action of government is concerned."[135] The common good is a central element of the classical liberal/libertarian tradition of thinking. The common good, at least under the normal circumstances of justice, is liberty and the rule of law. Advocates of group-differentiated rights reject both by subjecting citizens to those empowered to change the rules, reallocate rights, and create caste distinctions among them.

We may, then, answer the three questions with which I opened this essay:

1) Did Madison envision a "multicultural" republic?

Yes, if by multicultural we mean encompassing a wide variety of passions and interests. No, if by multicultural we mean regimes of group-differentiated rights.

2) Are contemporary advocates of various forms of group rights or group representation, often presented under the banner of "multiculturalism," advancing the Madisonian project, or undermining it?

Such thinkers are undermining Madison's project and advancing Calhoun's radically different vision of the Constitution.

3) Are group-differentiated rights a necessary and proper element of a constitutional order ordained and established to "form a more perfect Union, establish Justice, insure domestic Tranquility, provide for the common defence, promote the general Welfare, and secure the Blessings of Liberty to ourselves and our Posterity"?

Such group-differentiated rights are neither necessary to securing the goods listed in the preamble, nor proper, for they violate fundamental principles of republican government and the rule of law and are therefore not authorized under the Constitution.

Madison's vision of an extended republic as the framework for liberty remains inspiring. Millions of people, from virtually every nation, race, ethnicity, and religion still seek to become citizens of the United States of America. They seek to live in a nation in which "government is instituted and ought to be exercised for the benefit of the people."[136] For pursuit of the common good to be institutionally stable, it should not encompass too many goals. The more goods that are claimed to be common, the less likely that the entire bundle will, in fact, amount to the common good. That is why the Founders excluded supporting religion from the common good; not because they discounted the importance of religion, but because the variety of religions meant that no one religion could be considered the common good among practitioners of many religions. As Madison noted, the benefit of the people "consists in the enjoyment of life and liberty, with the right of acquiring and using property, and generally of pursuing and obtaining happiness and safety."[137] Accordingly the Constitution does not establish a particular religion; it prohibits the Congress from making any law "respecting an establishment of religion, or prohibiting the free exercise thereof." The common good—for Christians, Jews, Muslims, Buddhists, Hindus, atheists, and others—is liberty of religion. And the particular goods that people pursue are quite simply not the business of government. The Declaration of Independence asserts rights to "Life, Liberty, and the *Pursuit* of Happiness," just as Madison identifies the common good with "*pursuing* and obtaining happiness and safety" (emphasis added). Just as for religion, so for cultural goods and identity, education, preferences for material goods, and all the other means of pursuing happiness, government may secure our *right to pursue* those goods by providing for justice and defense but is not authorized to provide the goods themselves. That is the proper responsibility of the citizens themselves, acting in their capacities as private persons.

A legal order that can secure a framework within which a great variety of persons who are members of many different cultural, ethnic, religious, or national groups can pursue and obtain happiness and safety *is* the common good, and that legal order is undermined by attempts to use it to secure the concrete good of this or that group or to tweak it to fulfill the preferred arrangements of entitlements and obligations of this or that activist or philosopher. Americans should do as Madison's friend Thomas Jefferson urged them in his First Inaugural Address, "Let us then, with courage and confidence pursue our own federal and republican principles, our attachment to our union and representative government."[138]

Notes

1. Montesquieu, *The Spirit of the Laws*, trans. and ed. Anne M. Cohler, Basia Carolyn Miller, and Harold Samuel Stone (Cambridge: Cambridge University Press, 1989), Part I, Chapter 16, "Distinctive Properties of the Republic," p. 124.

2. James Madison, "Speech in the Virginia Ratifying Convention on Taxation, a Bill of Rights, and the Mississippi," in *James Madison: Writings*, ed. Jack N. Rakove (New York: Penguin Putnam, 1999), pp. 381–82. The context of Madison's remarks is that a bill of rights formally guaranteeing religious freedom is not necessary to the enjoyment of such liberty.

3. François-Marie Arouet Voltaire, *Candide and Philosophical Letters* (1734; New York: Random House, 1992), p. 141.

4. *The Federalist* No. 10 (James Madison).

5. See, for example, Amitai Etzioni, "The Responsive Community: A Communitarian Perspective," Presidential Address, American Sociological Association, August 20, 1995. *American Sociological Review*, February 1996, 1–11: "Most important for the point at hand is that libertarians actively oppose the notion of 'shared values' or the idea of 'the common good,'" (available at http://www.gwu.edu/~ccps/etzioni/A241.html). Further, Etzioni asserts in "Libertarian Follies," *The World & I*, May 1995, pp. 365–77, "Libertarians seem to fear that the recognition of the common good as a value that is co-equal with personal freedom will endanger the standing of that

liberty." For an attempt to set the record straight, and to articulate a classical liberal conception of the common good, see Tom G. Palmer, "Myths of Individualism," *Cato Policy Report* 18(5) (September/October 1996), reprinted in this volume. For a nuanced statement of the liberal idea of "self-interest," see "The Secret History of Self-Interest," in Stephen Holmes, *Passions and Constraint: On the Theory of Liberal Democracy* (Chicago: University of Chicago Press, 1995).

6. *The Federalist* No. 45 (James Madison).

7. James Madison, "Speech in the House of Representatives, June 8, 1789," in *The Mind of the Founder: Sources of the Political Thought of James Madison*, ed. Marvin Meyers (Hanover, N.H.: University Press of New England, 1981), p. 164.

8. Madison, "Parties," in *James Madison: Writings*, p. 504.

9. Ibid., p. 505.

10. Not only should the rules be common, but they must be stable if they are to be just and compatible with the order of a free society. Madison described the effects of a "mutable policy" starkly:

> It poisons the blessings of liberty itself. It will be of little avail to the people that the laws are made by men of their own choice, if the laws be so voluminous that they cannot be read, or so incoherent that they cannot be understood; if they be repealed or revised before they are promulgated, or undergo such incessant changes that no man who knows what the law is today can guess what it will be tomorrow. Law is defined to be a rule of action; but how can that be a rule, which is little known and less fixed?
>
> Another effect of public instability is the unreasonable advantage it gives to the sagacious, the enterprising, and the moneyed few, over the industrious and uninformed mass of the people. Every new regulation concerning commerce or revenue; or in any manner affecting the value of the different species of property, presents a new harvest to those who watch the change and can trace the consequences; a harvest reared not by themselves but by the toils and cares of the great body of their fellow citizens. This is a state of things in which it may be said with some truth that laws are made for the *few* not for the *many*.

The Federalist No. 62 (James Madison).

11. As Madison noted in opposing on the floor of Congress the establishment of a national bank, "No argument could be drawn from the terms 'common defence, and general welfare.' The power as to these general purposes, was limited to acts laying taxes for them; and the general purposes themselves were limited and explained by the particular enumeration subjoined. To understand these terms in any sense, that would justify the power in question, would give to Congress an unlimited power; would render nugatory the enumeration of particular powers; would supercede all the powers reserved to the state governments. These terms are copied from the articles of confederation; had it ever been pretended, that they were to be understood otherwise than as here explained?" James Madison, "Speech in Congress Opposing the National Bank," in *James Madison: Writings*, p. 483.

12. *Notes of Debates in the Federal Convention of 1787 Reported by James Madison*, ed. Gaillard Hunt and James Brown Scott (New York: W. W. Norton & Co., 1987), p. 76.

13. Ibid., p. 77. It is worth noting that just prior to these questions, Madison states, "We have seen the mere distinction of colour made in the most enlightened period of time, a ground of the most oppressive dominion ever exercised by man over man."

Madison, like many of the other Founders, was acutely aware of the injustice of slavery and saw it as one form of the oppression that their innovative approach to government was to eliminate. See also his "Memorandum on Colonizing Freed Slaves," in *James Madison: Writings*, pp. 472–73, in which he argued that incorporation of a freed black population into American society would be "rendered impossible by the prejudices of the Whites, prejudices which proceeding principally from the differences of colour must be considered as permanent and insuperable." He proposed colonization of Africa, for "an experiment for providing such an external establishment for the blacks might induce the humanity of Masters, and by degrees both the humanity and policy of the Governments, to forward the abolition of slavery in America."

14. Ibid., p. 77.

15. *The Federalist* No. 10 (James Madison).

16. Ibid.

17. Here Madison seemed not to consider the possibility of a tyranny of special interests that, having smaller transaction costs than the majority, can impose diffuse microburdens on the majority, the aggregate of which, when concentrated in the hands of a minority, provide a substantial incentive to organize factions against the common interest. This is the phenomenon of "diffused costs, concentrated benefits" with which students of rent-seeking in modern polities are so well acquainted. Second, such particular interests may engage in logrolling, in which legislators trade votes on issue A for votes on an unrelated issue B, to create legislative majorities that are systematically opposed to the common interest.

18. *The Federalist* No. 58 (James Madison).

19. *The Federalist* No. 62 (James Madison).

20. *The Federalist* No. 57 (James Madison).

21. Lani Guinier, *The Tyranny of the Majority* (New York: The Free Press, 1994), p. 4.

22. Ibid., p. 3.

23. Ibid., pp. 57, 216. A careful reading of *The Federalist* No. 39 did not reveal to me any connection of Madison's ideas to Guinier's statement that "all sectors of society" should be included in "government operation."

24. Ibid., p. 103.

25. Ibid., p. 5.

26. Ibid., p. 58.

27. Ibid., p. 227, footnote 154, and p. 245, footnote 42.

28. Ibid., p. 70.

29. Lani Guinier, "No Two Seats: The Elusive Quest for Political Equality," *Virginia Law Review* 77 (1991), p. 1514, footnote 299. Henry Louis Gates Jr. endorses *The Tyranny of the Majority* on the back cover of the book as "At last . . . the public hearing she was denied. . . . It doesn't matter where you think you stand; it's all here, to argue or agree with." Stephen L. Carter, in his foreword to the book, stated that "the debate, after all, was about her written record. It is high time, then, for the record to be available for all to view. Let readers make up their own minds, without the intercession of media experts and electronic sound bites." Apparently, Gates and Carter were deceived, for a number of the more startling claims that appeared in her law review articles did not make it into the book.

30. See, for example, Doug Kendall, "Gale Norton Is No James Watt; She's Even Worse," *Los Angeles Times*, January 9, 2001: "The more you learn about Norton, the more the label 'James Watt in a skirt' seems unfair to Watt."

444

31. See, for example, the remarks of gay writer Charles Kaiser, quoted in the *New York Times*: "I certainly think that Andrew's popularity, especially on the talk-show circuit has a lot to do with his own self-hatred, which makes him an especially attractive kind of homosexual to a certain kind of talk-show host. Which is the reason that his prominence is so infuriating to the rest of the community." "Conservative Gay Columnist Is under Fire," by Felicity Barringer, *New York Times*, August 6, 2001. The main topic of the essay is the firestorm of criticism attracted by Norah Vincent, a columnist for the *Village Voice* and the *Los Angeles Times* who is a lesbian and a libertarian, and therefore a prime target for collectivist gay writers. As one dissident editor at the *Village Voice*, Richard Goldstein, put it, "The liberal press needs to ask itself why they consistently promote the work of gay writers who attack other gay people." Note that the "other gay people" whom Norah Vincent and Andrew Sullivan have on occasion criticized are collectivists and statists, but their collectivism and statism are implicitly equated by Goldstein with their homosexuality, so anyone who criticizes them is criticizing "gay people," and not "collectivist statists." In Goldstein's view, it is an essential property of being homosexual that one favor state power over individual rights.

32. See, for example, Ludwig von Mises, *Human Action* (Chicago: Henry Regnery Company, 1966), pp. 75–91.

33. Lani Guinier, "The Triumph of Tokenism: The Voting Rights Act and the Theory of Black Electoral Success," *Michigan Law Review* 89 (1991), pp. 1140. This discussion, too, was deleted from the version of the essay that appeared in her book *The Tyranny of the Majority*.

34. Lani Guinier, *The Tyranny of the Majority*, p. 113.

35. Ibid., p. 254.

36. Robert Richie and Steven Hill, *Reflecting All of Us: The Case for Proportional Representation* (Boston: Beacon Press, 1999), pp. 14, 15.

37. Ibid., p. 18.

38. Will Kymlicka, *Multicultural Citizenship* (Oxford: Clarendon Press, 1995), p. 151.

39. Ibid., p. 150.

40. John C. Calhoun, *A Disquisition on Government*, in *Union and Liberty: The Political Philosophy of John C. Calhoun*, ed. Ross M. Lence (Indianapolis: Liberty Fund, 1992), p. 14.

41. Ibid., p. 15.

42. Guinier's discussion of what she calls a "Madisonian majority" (*The Tyranny of the Majority*, p. 4) is strikingly parallel to Calhoun's discussion of how "a minority might become the majority" (*A Disquisition on Government*, p. 20) and is rejected as a solution to the problem of majority domination for the same reasons, namely, that (for Guinier) blacks as a bloc facing another racial bloc cannot transform themselves into the majority and (for Calhoun) the minority bloc of slave states cannot transform itself into a majority bloc, at least given the demographic trends in the United States in Calhoun's time.

43. Calhoun, p. 21.

44. Ibid., pp. 23–24.

45. Ibid., pp. 16–19. Here Calhoun makes a powerful point that is fully consistent with a Madisonian approach; the more Madisonian solution, however, would seem to be to strive for strictly limited government and for strict economy in those functions best discharged by government, rather than to attempt to guarantee a system of

group representation that would, in any case, be more likely to generate collusion among groups represented to capture disproportionate shares of such emoluments.

46. John C. Calhoun, "Speech at the Meeting of the Citizens of Charleston" (March 9, 1847), in *Union and Liberty: The Political Philosophy of John C. Calhoun*, p. 526. In his *A Discourse on the Constitution and Government*, Calhoun presented an interpretation of the U.S. Constitution through his theory of the concurrent majority and asserted that the United States was "preeminently a government of the concurrent majority." In *Union and Liberty: The Political Philosophy of John C. Calhoun*, p. 121.

47. Lebanese Constitution, Article 95, cited in Enver M. Koury, *The Crisis in the Lebanese System: Confessionalism and Chaos* (Washington, D.C.: American Enterprise Institute, 1976), p. 5. Article 95 was added by the constitutional law of November 9, 1943. It effectively abrogated Article 7: "All the Lebanese are equal before the law. They enjoy equal civil and political rights and are equally subjected to public charges and duties, without any distinction whatsoever."

48. In the Lebanese case, the rough proportion between demography and political office was upset by an enormous demographic change; unsurprisingly, those who were favored by the old scheme did not want to give it up in favor of the new, and the result was a savage civil war that is still not fully over.

49. Catharine MacKinnon, *Toward a Feminist Theory of the State* (Cambridge, Mass.: Harvard University Press, 1989), p. 228.

50. Ibid., p. 229.

51. Iris Marion Young, "Polity and Group Difference: A Critique of the Ideal of Universal Citizenship," in *Feminism and Political Theory*, ed. Cass R. Sunstein (Chicago: University of Chicago Press, 1990), p. 118.

52. Ibid., p. 129.

53. Ibid., p. 134.

54. Ibid., p. 125. One might wonder why someone with Young's general philosophical presuppositions would favor "communication across those differences." Communication across difference presupposes something common, which seems to be what Young is rejecting.

55. These issues, in the context of the written word, are carefully explored by Roman Ingarden in *The Literary Work of Art: An Investigation on the Borderlines of Ontology, Logic, and Theory of Literature*, trans. George R. Grabowicz (Evanston, Ill.: Northwestern University Press, 1973). See also Roman Ingarden, *The Cognition of the Literary Work of Art*, trans. Ruth Ann Crowley and Kenneth R. Olson (Evanston, Ill.: Northwestern University Press, 1973) and *The Work of Music and the Problem of Its Identity*, trans. Adam Czerniawski (Berkeley, Calif.: University of California Press, 1986). Ingarden offers a powerful general critique of the sort of claim of incommensurability and incomprehensibility that Young makes.

56. On the issue of objectivity in general, see Thomas Nagel, *The View from Nowhere* (Oxford: Oxford University Press, 1986).

57. Note also that Young asserts the inability to "completely understand or adopt the point of view of those with other *group-based* perspectives and histories" (italics added), but certainly if this claim is true, it would be even more the case for communication among individual members of the same groups, for individual life histories among group members differ. Young has smuggled into the discussion a remarkable set of implausible ontological claims about groups and their relationships to both the individuals who comprise them and to other groups.

446

58. "Polity and Group Difference," p. 133. Nowhere does Young mention or consider the tremendous advantage in such meetings held by the articulate over the inarticulate. College professors, who live by the spoken and written word, are often quite eager to center the power over others in forums where—*mirabile dictu!*—it is they who have the greatest advantage; in this, they are no different from other minority factions and should be treated with the same suspicion as are all other special interest groups.

59. "Polity and Group Difference," p. 139–40.

60. The incipiently authoritarian nature of her case is indicated in her reference to the Nicaraguan state: "Reports of experiments with publicly institutionalized self-organization among women, indigenous peoples, workers, peasants, and students in contemporary Nicaragua offer an example closer to the conception I am advocating." Iris Marion Young, "Polity and Group Difference," p. 132. (The essay originally appeared in 1989; no mention is made of the war waged by the Sandinistas on the Mosquito Indians and other indigenous groups.)

61. Young, p. 140.

62. As Bartolomé de las Casas concluded his defense of the American Indians in 1550, "The Indians are our brothers, and Christ has given his life for them. Why, then, do we persecute them with such inhuman savagery when they do not deserve such treatment? The past, because it cannot be undone, must be attributed to our weakness, provided that what has been taken unjustly is restored." Bartolomé de las Casas, *In Defense of the Indians*, trans. Stafford Poole (DeKalb, Ill.: Northern Illinois University Press, 1992), p. 362.

63. See "Executive Order 9066: Authorizing the Secretary of War to Prescribe Military Areas," in *When Sorry Isn't Enough: The Controversy over Apologies and Reparations for Human Injustice*, ed. Roy L. Brooks (New York: New York University Press, 1999), pp. 169–70.

64. Civil Liberties Act of 1988, *U.S. Statutes at Large* 102 (1988), pp. 903. In addition, the act authorized the establishment of a special education fund.

65. For a representative statement on the issue, see the transcript of a TransAfrica Forum program at http://www.transafricaforum.org/reports/print/reparations_print.shtml.

66. Randall Robinson, *The Debt: What America Owes to Blacks* (New York: Penguin Putnam, Inc., 2000), pp. 107–8.

67. Ibid., p. 207.

68. See "Special Field Order No. 15," in *When Sorry Isn't Enough: The Controversy over Apologies and Reparations for Human Injustice*, pp. 365–66. The order does not specify the reasons for the settlement (beyond encouraging enlistment in the U.S. military) and merely refers to "The islands from Charleston south, the abandoned rice-fields along the rivers for thirty miles back from the sea, and the country bordering the St. John's River, Florida." This reflects its status as a document of war, rather than a postwar settlement of accounts or reparations.

69. For statements of some of the problems inherent in an attempt to make such endowment-based compensation, see John McWhorter, "Blood Money: Why I Don't Want Reparations for Slavery," and Deroy Murdock, "A Bean Counting Nightmare to Avoid," both in *American Enterprise*, July/August 2001.

70. Some of these points were made in a somewhat inflammatory manner by David Horowitz in newspaper advertisements in college papers. See http://www.frontpagemag.com/horowitzsnotepad/2001/hn01-03-01.htm for a list of Horowitz's ten

reasons to oppose reparations. I find numbers eight and nine on the list to provide very weak arguments against reparations, namely that transfer payments (welfare) to black Americans have already paid any putative debt and that the fact that American-born black people are richer than African-born black people indicates that they are better off than they would be if their ancestors had remained in Africa. The first is problematic because more white people have received transfer payments than have black people, and certainly many blacks have paid taxes to support nonworking whites, indicating that the system is hardly a just answer to the injustice of slavery. That the second is irrelevant is clear when we consider the following case: A Jewish family in Bratislava loses their liberty, their home, and their business when the National Socialists take power; the children survive the concentration camps and move to New York; they prosper in New York; after the fall of the Communist government in Slovakia, there is a debate about the homes and business establishments that were confiscated by the National Socialists and then by the Communists. Is it relevant to the proper allocation of the property that those who remained behind in the village, Jew and non-Jew alike, are poorer than those who later prospered in New York? The fact that someone did relatively well after suffering an injustice is a poor argument against compensation for the injustice.

71. Robinson, p. 218. For a meticulous statement of the principle of culture as a foundation for group-differentiated rights claims, see Will Kymlicka, *Liberalism, Community and Culture* (Oxford: Oxford University Press, 1989). Robinson notes that of other terrors visited on peoples, including the Jews, Cambodians under the Khmer Rouge, Native Americans, Rwandan Tutsis, and the peoples of the Belgian Congo under King Leopold II (the period of the so-called Free State), "All of these were unspeakably brutal human rights crimes that occurred over periods ranging from a few weeks to the span of an average lifetime. But in each of these cases, the cultures of those who were killed and persecuted survived the killing spasms" (p. 215).

72. Robinson, p. 62.

73. Ibid., p. 206.

74. Ibid., pp. 244, 245–46.

75. Darrell L. Pugh, "Collective Rehabilitation," in *When Sorry Isn't Enough*, p. 373.

76. Ibid., p. 373. As he notes on the same page, "The prospect of reparations to African Americans is an exciting one." If you hope to be on the board of a multi-billion-dollar fund with discretion to award funds, that would certainly be true.

77. Will Kymlicka, *Politics in the Vernacular: Nationalism, Multiculturalism, and Citizenship* (Oxford: Oxford University Press, 2001), p. 184.

78. Robinson, p. 230.

79. Ibid., p. 16.

80. Ibid., p. 209: "If one leaves aside the question of punitive damages to do a rough reckoning of what might be fair in basic compensation. . . ."

81. Ibid., pp. 239–40.

82. See Ralph Horwitz, *The Political Economy of South Africa* (New York: Frederick A. Praeger, 1967), esp. pp. 380–86.

83. James Madison, "Speech in the Virginia Ratifying Convention on the Slave Trade Clause," in *James Madison: Writings*, p. 39. It should be pointed out that Madison goes on to say that the compromise not only allows for abolition of the slave trade, but protects the interests of current owners of slaves. Madison argues, again, that the compromise represented an amelioration of the situation, and concluded, "Great as the evil is, a dismemberment of the union would be worse. If those states should

disunite from the other states, for not indulging them in the temporary continuance of this traffic, they might solicit and obtain aid from foreign powers." Ibid., p. 392.

84. Such proposals, although dressed up in new language, are hardly new. The idea of special national or confessional privileges has an ancient history, but it is largely *pre*-liberal, rather than liberal. That is to say, the recognition of rights, immunities, and privileges—or of liberties, with the emphasis on the plural—is a step to the recognition of the right to *liberty*, as a general right. But the liberal contribution lay in stepping from a mass of particular rights, privileges, and immunities for particular individuals and groups to an abstract principle of individual liberty for every individual person. One close observer described the results of differential rights based on religion in Europe thusly:

> For a confession to secure its position against the oppression by others and through establishment of the sphere of right of every individual to eliminate the occasion for frictions—that was the reason, whereby—as today the particular nationalities, so then the particular confessions—their demands were motivated. In catholic countries the Protestants were allotted particular territories; there were particular forts equipped, which were to serve as fortified places for the religion; the number of churches was determined by law; it was determined, how many individuals for a particular office from which confession were to be allowed to be candidates, what the determinate portion of the city council from these or those communities of belief should be;—and what was the result of all these rules and measures, where the solution of the religious question was sought in this way? What else, than endless frictions between the various confessions, the suppression of those who were in the minority on a particular territory, unbounded intolerance on the side of each of those, to which opportunity was offered, and as result of all of this, a century of continuous bloody struggle, which shook the most powerful states, created in one of the greatest nations of Europe a split that has not yet been filled [healed] and everywhere hindered the progress of civilization! In particular states the struggle was bloodier, in others it led to complete suppression of one confession, but everywhere, where this did not succeed and the reconciliation of the confessions was sought in the determination through law of the spheres of rights and the privileges of each, the result was the same, namely that *the citizens of each such country, split up by confessions, stood in hostility against each other and religious peace and harmony was the less achieved the more numerous and detailed were the laws created to achieve it.*

(Josef Freiherrn von Eötvös, *Die Nationalitätenfrage*, trans. from the Hungarian by Dr. Max Falk [Pest, Hungary: Verlag von Moritz Ráth, 1865], pp. 146–47.)

85. Kymlicka, *Liberalism, Community and Culture*, p. 146.

86. For example, he asserts that "because residents of Puerto Rico have special self-governing powers that exempt them from certain federal legislation, they have reduced representation in Washington. They help select presidential candidates in party primaries, but do not vote in presidential elections. And they have only one representative in Congress, a 'commissioner' who has a voice but no vote, except in committees." (*Politics in the Vernacular*, p. 108.) In fact, Puerto Rico has no congressional representation because it is not a state, not because it is exempt from federal legislation. And participation in presidential primaries is entirely a matter of the rules of political parties, not of constitutional law. Puerto Ricans are accorded U.S. citizenship, but

Puerto Rico is not a political unit of the United States of America. Kymlicka also makes no mention of the treatment of Indian tribes or Indian population in Article I, Section 2 ("Representatives and direct Taxes shall be apportioned among the several States which may be included within this Union, according to their respective Numbers . . . excluding Indians not taxed"; this provision was changed by the Fourteenth Amendment, but the exclusion of "Indians not taxed" was retained), Article I, Section 8 ("The Congress shall have Power . . . To regulate Commerce with foreign Nations, and among the several States, and with the Indian tribes"), and Article VI ("This Constitution, and the Laws of the United States which shall be made in Pursuance thereof; and all Treaties made, or which shall be made, under the Authority of the United States, shall be the supreme Law of the Land"; this clause includes under the "supreme Law of the Land" the treaty rights of Indians under treaties already made or to be made).

87. *Politics in the Vernacular*, p. 101.

88. Kymlicka, *Liberalism, Community and Culture*, p. 164.

89. Ibid., p. 169.

90. Kymlicka, *Multicultural Citizenship* (Oxford: Clarendon Press, 1995), p. 89.

91. See ibid., pp. 34–48.

92. Kymlicka, *Liberalism, Community and Culture*, p. 167.

93. Ibid., p. 146.

94. Kymlicka, *Multicultural Citizenship*, p. 97. (He also mentions military service and compulsory education of children on p. 177.)

95. Oddly enough, Kymlicka interprets the exemption from compulsory education for the Amish and other Christian sects as a form of an "internal restriction." He also regards the practice of shunning as putting "severe restrictions on the ability of group members to leave their group" (*Multicultural Citizenship*, pp. 41–42). It is true that a high cost is borne by those who wish to leave, in the form of the loss of family and friends, but to my knowledge there are no restrictions placed on exit. Indeed, the Amish, Mennonites, and others like them are very clear about the liberty of members to leave the group and embrace the wider world. The term "cost" and "restriction" should not be used interchangeably, as Kymlicka does, for a failure to make such distinctions would require us to say that not returning friendship to friends who betray us is to "restrict" their ability to leave our friendship, rather than to say that they would bear the cost of losing our friendship if they were to betray us. Such distinctions are needed if the variety of human relationships is to be properly understood and grasped.

96. I have dealt with this issue in a far more extensive and thoroughgoing manner in Tom G. Palmer, "Saving Rights Theory from Its Friends," reprinted in this volume.

97. *Wall Street Journal*, March 28, 2000, p. B1.

98. See Kymlicka, *Multicultural Citizenship*, p. 43.

99. See Hernando de Soto, *The Mystery of Capital* (New York: Basic Books, 2000), for an explanation of why the ability to alienate is so important to the development of capital and therefore of wealth.

100. R. I. Moore, *The Formation of a Persecuting Society* (Oxford: Basil Blackwell, 1987), p. 40.

101. Cited in ibid., p. 40.

102. They were so denominated by Chief Justice John Marshall, who stated that "Though the Indians are acknowledged to have an unquestionable, and, heretofore unquestioned, right to the lands they occupy, until that right shall be extinguished

by a voluntary cession to our government; yet it may well be doubted, whether those tribes which reside within the acknowledged boundaries of the United States can, with strict accuracy, be denominated foreign nations. They may, more correctly, perhaps, be denominated domestic dependent nations. They occupy a territory to which we assert a title independent of their will, which must take effect in point of possession, when their right of possession ceases. Meanwhile, they are in a state of pupilage; their relation to the United States resembles that of a ward to his guardian." 30 U.S. (5 Pet.) at 17. Cited in William C. Canby Jr., *American Indian Law* (St. Paul, Minn.: West Group, 1998), p. 15.

103. That is not to say that all of the problems or injustices faced by American Indians have been the result of such group-differentiated rights; the story is, at least, a very complicated one. But it should be kept in mind that merely asserting that such rights are intended to benefit the members of a group does not guarantee that they will have beneficial effects. The intention of the lawgiver is irrelevant to the outcome.

104. Kymlicka, *Multicultural Citizenship*, p. 104.

105. Charles Taylor has criticized Kymlicka for not fully understanding the demands implicit in the politics of difference: "Where Kymlicka's interesting argument fails to capture the actual demands made by the groups concerned—say Indian bands in Canada, or French-speaking Canadians—is with respect to their goal of survival. Kymlicka's reasoning is valid (perhaps) for *existing* people who find themselves trapped within a culture under pressure, and can flourish within it or not at all. But it doesn't justify measures designed to ensure survival through indefinite future generations. For the populations concerned, however, that is what is at stake." Charles Taylor, *Multiculturalism: Examining the Politics of Recognition* (Princeton, N.J.: Princeton University Press, 1994), p. 41.

106. Ibid., p. 53. Taylor himself, however, tries to have his liberal cake and eat it, too, by asserting "invariant defense of *certain* rights," exemplified by Taylor by the right of habeas corpus, but allowing that these can be distinguished from "the broad range of immunities and presumptions of uniform treatment that have sprung up in modern cultures of judicial review." Ibid., p. 61. His claims seem to be simply drawn from a philosophical hat. And, like Kymlicka, he is sometimes careless with alleged historical facts, such as that "the Americans were the first to write out and entrench a bill of rights" (p. 54), ignoring a remarkably rich history of bills of rights in European and transatlantic jurisprudence, from Magna Carta to the Golden Bull of Hungary to the English Bill of Rights to the various bills of rights of the American states.

107. Michael McDonald, "Reflections on Liberal Individualism," in *Human Rights in Cross-Cultural Perspectives: A Quest for Consensus*, ed. Abdullahi Ahmed An-Na'im (Philadelphia: University of Pennsylvania Press, 1992), p. 147. McDonald seems to rest his views on an implicit theory of the natural or "undistorted" development of groups in the absence of individual mobility rights.

108. International Labor Organization (ILO No. 169), 72 ILO Official Bull. 59, entered into force Sept. 5, 1991, available at http://www1.umn.edu/humanrts/instree/r1citp.htm. See also Section 17, "Traditional forms of ownership and cultural survival: Rights to land, territories and resources," of the Proposed American Declaration on the Rights of Indigenous Peoples (Approved by the Inter-American Commission on Human Rights on February 26, 1997, at its 1333rd session, 95th Regular Session), OEA/Ser/L/V/.II.95 Doc.6 (1997), available at http://www1.umn.edu/

humanrts/instree/indigenousdecl.html. Many other examples can be cited, some of which can be found at http://www.umn.edu/humanrts.

109. Kymlicka, *Politics in the Vernacular*, p. 50.

110. Kymlicka, *Multicultural Citizenship*, p. 115.

111. Ibid., p. 125.

112. Kymlicka refers to the "Amish and Mennonites who emigrated to the United States and Canada early in [the 20th] century, as well as the Hasidic Jews in New York. For various reasons, when these immigrant groups arrived, they were given exemptions from the usual requirements regarding integration, and were allowed to maintain certain internal restrictions" (*Multicultural Citizenship*, p. 170). The historical claim is an odd one; I am unaware of any collective negotiations by Jews in eastern Europe or Anabaptists in central Europe that resulted in their migration to North America on the condition that they were to be allowed to practice their religions. Further, to my knowledge, no one is forced to be Amish, Mennonite, or Hasidic, and the cost of exit is no greater than is the cost of exit from the Roman Catholic Church, which entails denial of the Beatific Vision, than which no worldly cost could be greater. When an acquaintance of mine had his name struck from the Book of Life by his own father, an Old Order Mennonite minister, on the grounds of the son's homosexuality, the loss of religious companionship and of family relations was enormously painful and certainly imposed a high cost on him. But that does not qualify as some kind of special dispensation "to maintain certain internal restrictions." It's a requirement of the First Amendment to the United States Constitution that the state not interfere with such processes, and the Constitution was not negotiated especially for the groups that Kymlicka mentions, but for all Americans.

113. See, in contrast, John Torpey, *The Invention of the Passport: Surveillance, Citizenship, and the State* (Cambridge: Cambridge University Press, 2000).

114. Kymlicka, *Multicultural Citizenship*, p. 124.

115. Maintaining liberty and justice is surely more important than recognizing one's membership in a distinct culture, a goal that can be achieved in a multitude of nonpolitical ways. It is not only classical liberals who are unlikely to embrace Kymlicka's view. The redistributionist "egalitarian liberal" Brian Barry subjects such views to withering criticism in his *Culture and Equality* (Cambridge, Mass.: Harvard University Press, 2001).

116. See especially *Multicultural Citizenship*, chap. 5, pp. 75–106.

117. In this Locke and Kant, although in many other ways offering different approaches to political morality and justice, were in agreement: "*the end of Law* is not to abolish or restrain, but *to preserve and enlarge Freedom*: For in all the States of created beings capable of Laws, *where there is no Law, there is no Freedom*. For *Liberty* is to be free from restraint and violence from others which cannot be, where there is no Law: But Freedom is not, as we are told, *A Liberty for every Man to do what he lists*: (For who could be free, when every other Man's Humour might domineer over him?) But a *Liberty* to dispose, and order, as he lists, his Person, Actions, Possessions, and his whole Property, within the Allowance of those Laws under which he is; and therein not to be subjected to the arbitrary Will of another, but freely follow his own." (John Locke, *Two Treatises of Government*, ed. Peter Laslett [Cambridge: Cambridge University Press, 1988], II, chap VI, §57, p. 306, italics in original); "Freedom (independence from the constraint of another's will), insofar as it is compatible with the freedom of everyone else in accordance with a universal law, is the one sole and

original right that belongs to every human being by virtue of his humanity." (Immanuel Kant, *The Metaphysical Elements of Justice*, trans. John Ladd [New York: Macmillan Publishing Co., 1985], pp. 43–44.)

118. Jeremy Waldron, "Multiculturalism and Mélange," in *Public Education in a Multicultural Society*, ed. Robert Fullinwider (Cambridge: Cambridge University Press, 1996), p. 100.

119. Carl F. Stychin, *A Nation by Rights: National Cultures, Sexual Identity Politics, and the Discourse of Rights* (Philadelphia: Temple University Press, 1998), p. 111.

120. Ibid., p. 110.

121. Ibid., p. 113.

122. Ibid., p. 114.

123. James Madison, "Parties," in *James Madison: Writings*, p. 504.

124. See Herbert J. Storing, *What the Anti-Federalists Were For* (Chicago: University of Chicago Press, 1981), esp. chap. 3, "The Small Republic," pp. 15–23.

125. Brutus, "To the Citizens of the State of New York, 18 October 1787," in Herbert J. Storing, *The Anti-Federalist: Writings by the Opponents of the Constitution* (Chicago: University of Chicago Press, 1985), p. 113.

126. Ibid.

127. *Notes of Debates in the Federal Convention of 1787 Reported by James Madison*, p. 77.

128. As Hillel Steiner notes of such schemes of unequal and incompatible rights claims, "such group rights are highly likely to generate claims incompatible with the rights of other groups, to say nothing of individuals' rights." *An Essay on Rights* (Oxford: Basil Blackwell, 1994), p. 165.

129. Susan Moller Okin with respondents, *Is Multiculturalism Bad for Women?* (Princeton, N.J.: Princeton University Press, 1999).

130. Will Kymlicka, "Liberal Complacencies," in *Is Multiculturalism Bad for Women?*, pp. 33–34.

131. 31 U.S. (6 Pet.) at 561 (cited in William C. Canby Jr., *American Indian Law*, pp. 16–17).

132. For a full list, see Francis Paul Prucha, *American Indian Treaties: The History of a Political Anomaly* (Berkeley: University of California Press, 1997), pp. 446–502. Prucha appends a list of six agreements that could plausibly be added to the list. William C. Canby Jr. notes that "in 1871, Congress passed a statute providing that no tribe thereafter was to be recognized as an independent nation with which the United States could make treaties. Existing treaties were not affected." *American Indian Law*, p. 18. Reservations created thereafter were created by statute, rather than by treaty. In reading for this essay, I was surprised to find that Indians born within the United States were made citizens only in 1924, by act of Congress (8 U.S.C.A. § 1401(b)).

133. A thorough survey is offered by Jacob Levy in his *The Multiculturalism of Fear* (Oxford: Oxford University Press, 2000).

134. *The Federalist* No. 10 (James Madison).

135. John C. Calhoun, *A Disquisition on Government*, in *Union and Liberty: The Political Philosophy of John C. Calhoun*, pp. 23–24.

136. Madison, "Speech in the House of Representatives, June 8, 1789."

137. Ibid.

138. Thomas Jefferson, First Inaugural Address (1801), in *Jefferson: Political Writings*, ed. Joyce Appleby (Cambridge: Cambridge University Press, 1999), p. 174.

24. Globalization and Culture: Homogeneity, Diversity, Identity, Liberty

Free trade is under attack. Advocates of free trade are accustomed to refuting the doctrine of the balance of trade and various fallacies about nations "competing" economically with each other.[1] They are less accustomed to responding to the "cultural" critiques of trade. Advocates of barriers to trade insist that free trade and globalization are destructive of culture. But does globalization produce cultural homogeneity and loss of diversity? Is cultural "authenticity" threatened by globalization? Is the planet in danger of being drowned in a vast soup of sameness? And should we fear a loss of personal identity as members of different cultures exchange ideas, products, and services? The cultural arguments against free trade, as we shall see, are hardly new. They are as fallacious as the economic arguments against free trade.

I. Definitions

It's usually helpful to start any discussion of globalization with a definition of the term. Like any term, we can stipulate whatever we want about the meaning of globalization, but not all stipulations are as good as all others. Most are merely attempts to win the debate before it starts. I offer a stipulation that I believe captures the core of what is being debated, rather than being a bit of propaganda one way or the other.

It's common for critics of globalization—who sometimes insist that they aren't enemies of globalization, but supporters of an "alternative globalization"—to use the term simply to mean human wickedness or greediness or the allegedly undesirable effects of increasing global trade; the undesirability is included as a part of the definition. Let's

Originally published by the Liberal Institute of the Friedrich Nauman Foundation, Berlin, 2004.

instead start with an operational definition and then ask whether the effects of globalization thus defined are desirable or undesirable. I use the term to refer to the diminution or elimination of state-enforced restrictions on voluntary exchange across borders and the increasingly integrated and complex global system of exchange and production that has emerged as a result of that diminution or elimination of state-enforced restrictions on voluntary trade across borders.

The core policy issue is whether borders should be used to stop transactions between people on different sides of them. Should American wheat farmers be allowed to buy cell phones from people in Finland? Should Ghanian weavers be allowed to sell the shirts and pants they make to German auto workers? Should Taiwanese investors be allowed to purchase assets from Kenyans? Should Mexican mechanics be allowed to repair cars in Ottawa or Chicago? Obviously, lists of that sort could go on indefinitely, but I think that it's clear enough what I'm getting at. If an exchange would be allowed if both parties were on one side of a border, should it be stopped if instead one party were on one side of that border, and the other party were on the other side?

Now let's turn to culture. The term is used in a multitude of ways, often in the course of the same essay or consideration. They include the cultivation of certain human capabilities; art (typically the term is reserved for "high" art; reaction against that reservation of the term has fueled much academic study of "popular culture"); and the concrete forms of life that people lead in common. In general the critics of globalization refer to the second and third uses of "culture" when making their critiques. My primary focus will be on the third use of the term, on what Peter Berger calls "its conventional social scientific sense: as the beliefs, values, and lifestyles of ordinary people in their everyday existence."[2]

Should we welcome and embrace, or fear and reject, the interaction and mixture of cultures, peoples, races, communities, and worldviews that global trade, commerce, and interconnectedness bring in their wake? In particular, is it true that globalization is leading to a homogenized global culture, one in which life in Brazil approaches being indistinguishable from life in Bavaria, or—more to the point— is it leading to a world in which every country looks like southern California?

456

II. Contrasting Approaches to Globalization

Globalization is hardly a new phenomenon. It's nearly as old as recorded history itself, and its advocacy is among the first coherently articulated political philosophies of the western world (at least). About the year 420 BCE the philosopher Democritus of Abdera wrote, "To a wise man, the whole earth is open; for the native land of a good soul is the whole earth."[3]

International trade has long been identified with civilization itself. In Book IX of the *Odyssey*, Homer depicts the Cyclopean race as savages precisely because they do not trade or have contact with others:

> For the Cyclops have no ships with crimson prows,
> No shipwrights there to build them good trim craft
> That could sail them out to foreign ports of call
> As most men risk the seas to trade with other men.[4]

Of course, such attitudes were not limited to the Greeks. The Song Emperor Gao Zong (1127–1162) explained in a defense of commerce that "Profits from maritime commerce are very great. If properly managed, they can amount to millions [of strings of coins]. Is this not better than taxing the people?"[5] The people of the Song capital, Hanzhou, had a famous saying: "vegetables from the east, water from the west, wood from the south, and rice from the north."[6]

To get a sense that the current debate over globalization and culture is hardly new, let's contrast several descriptions of globalization through commerce that were written, not in the 21st century, but in the 18th century. The English playwright and literary figure Joseph Addison published an account of his experiences with globalization in *The Spectator* in the year 1711. He described his frequent visits to the Royal Exchange in London:

> Factors [trading agents] in the Trading World are what Ambassadors are in the Politick World; they negotiate Affairs, conclude Treaties, and maintain a good Correspondence between those wealthy Societies of Men that are divided from one another by Seas and Oceans, or live in the different Extremities of a Continent. I have often been pleased to hear Disputes adjusted between an Inhabitant of Japan and an Alderman of London, or to see a Subject of the Great Mogul entering into a League with one of the Czar of Muscovy. I am infinitely delighted in mixing with these several

> Ministers of Commerce, as they are distinguished by their different Walks and different Languages: Sometimes I am jostled among a Body of Armenians: Sometimes I am lost in a Crowd of Jews; and sometimes in a Groupe of Dutchmen. I am a Dane, Swede, or Frenchman at different times, or rather fancy myself like the old Philosopher, who upon being asked what Countryman he was, replied, That he was a Citizen of the World.[7]

The second was written by a French literary figure and political campaigner named François-Marie Arouet, known to most of us as Voltaire, in his *Philosophical Letters*. In addition to popularizing and promoting the innovation of inoculation against smallpox (which is a pretty disgusting process when you think about it, but which saved many millions of lives), he described to his French audience the exciting, cosmopolitan, and comparatively tolerant and liberal world of England. Again, it was the stock exchange that caught his attention, as he related in his Sixth Letter:

> Go into the Exchange in London, that place more venerable than many a court, and you will see representatives of all the nations assembled there for the profit of mankind. There the Jew, the Mahometan, and the Christian deal with one another as if they were of the same religion, and reserve the name of infidel for those who go bankrupt. There the Presbyterian trusts the Anabaptist, and the Church of England man accepts the promise of the Quaker. On leaving these peaceable and free assemblies, some go to the synagogue, others in search of a drink; this man is on the way to be baptized in a great tub in the name of the Father, by the Son, to the Holy Ghost; that man is having the foreskin of his son cut off, and a Hebraic formula mumbled over the child that he himself can make nothing of; these others are going to their church to await the inspiration of God with their hats on; and all are satisfied.[8]

In his Tenth Letter, Voltaire remarked on the astonishing legal and social equality enjoyed by the English—something we would judge quite imperfect by the standards of our day, but which many at the time considered truly scandalous—and contrasted the commercial, open, dynamic English society he had observed with the greater deference to authority of his native France:

In France anybody who wants to can be a marquis; and whoever arrives in Paris from the remotest part of some province with money to spend and an ac or an ille at the end of his name, may indulge in such phrases as "a man of my sort," "a man of my rank and quality," and with sovereign eye look down upon a wholesaler. The merchant himself so often hears his profession spoken of disdainfully that he is fool enough to blush. Yet I don't know which is the more useful to a state, a well-powdered lord who knows precisely what time the king gets up in the morning and what time he goes to bed, and who gives himself airs of grandeur while playing the role of slave in a minister's antechamber, or a great merchant who enriches his country, sends orders from his office to Surat and to Cairo, and contributes to the well-being of the world.[9]

Addison and Voltaire celebrated the openness, the dynamism, the freedom, and the progress that they associated with globalization. More importantly, they celebrated what came to be known as the rights of man, or what we would today call human rights. They looked forward to the universal spread of the principles of liberty, toleration, and equal rights.

Not everyone appreciated the effects of commerce in the same way. Many were appalled by such social mobility, such chaos, such immoral mixing of classes, races, religions, and—horrors!—even the sexes. One especially influential critic of commercial globalization was the writer and man of affairs Justus Möser, a leading political and intellectual figure in the independent city of Osnabrück, which is situated not far from the Netherlands. Möser was not merely one of the most influential critics of globalization in the 18th century; his ideas were to influence all of the great enemies of globalization in years to come and are very much with us still. Unlike Addison and Voltaire, Möser condemned commerce, merchants, peddlers, and Jews. He campaigned against people who took goods to the countryside and corrupted the simple and "good morals" of the peasants by enticing them with new goods and previously unknown pleasures, in the process exposing them to new ideas and thereby undermining their culture, their accustomed way of life. As he wrote,

Our ancestors did not tolerate these rural shopkeepers; they were spare in dispensing market freedoms; they banned the Jews from our diocese; why this severity? Certainly in

459

> order that the rural inhabitants not be daily stimulated, tempted, led astray and deceived. They stuck to the practical rule: that which one does not see will not lead one astray.[10]

Commerce, he believed, undermines traditional morals, which he identified with good morals.

Möser was not, however, only concerned with morality within a political order, but with the effects of the spread of universal principles on the variety of political orders across the planet. In 1772 he bemoaned the spread of the idea of universal human rights, writing that ideas of universal and equal rights depart from the true plan of nature, which reveals its wealth through its multiplicity, and would clear the path to despotism, which seeks to coerce all according to a few rules and so loses the richness that comes with variety.[11]

When Möser wrote of variety, he was writing not of the variety of goods in the market, or even of the variety of experiences that people might have in open and commercial societies, but instead of the variety of political regimes and systems, most of which would of necessity be highly illiberal and based on political and legal inequality. After all, equality is unique, whereas there is an infinite range of possible forms and systems of inequality.

Möser and his modern followers suggest (or even insist) that freedom of trade and travel will cause the whole world to become homogeneous, bereft of variety, and thereby impoverished. As societies become more connected, the argument goes, they become more alike, and as they become more alike, the human experience of variety diminishes, and with it there is a net loss of something of value. Möser's criticism of trade and commerce has been revived and has become a significant form of attack for the anti-globalization movement. The only major difference is that the anti-globalizers now typically focus on rather large nation states (France, Germany, Brazil, Japan, Mexico) as the locus of what Möser called "multiplicity," rather than small regions or towns such as Osnabrück, which Möser sought to protect from being influenced by trade with such exotic places as Hamburg, Amsterdam, and Cöln.

III. Social Connectedness and Diversity

The authors of the report on "Alternatives to Economic Globalization" begin the chapter on "Diversity" with the following remarkable complaint.

> A few decades ago, it was still possible to leave home
> and go someplace where the architecture was different, the
> landscape was different, and the language, lifestyle, dress,
> and values were different.[12]

Echoing Justus Möser, they proclaim that diversity is key to the
vitality, resilience, and innovative capacity of any living system. So
too for human societies. The rich variety of the human experience
and potential is reflected in cultural diversity, which provides a sort
of gene pool to spur innovation toward ever higher levels of social,
intellectual, and spiritual accomplishment and creates a sense of
identity, community, and meaning.[13]

Is it true that global trade and commerce leads to a net loss of the
human experience of variety? The answer is: almost certainly not.
Once again, the debate is hardly new, but has been with us for many
years. The issue was addressed quite clearly by the sociologist Georg
Simmel, who studied processes of group formation and differentiation. Simmel observed that as groups expand in size and extent they
tend to become ever more differentiated internally. The greater the
number of interacting persons, the greater the number of available
social roles or niches and the greater the opportunities for individuation and diversity among persons. As groups become increasingly
differentiated internally, i.e., as the human experience of diversity
within groups grows, the diversity among groups will diminish.[14]
Thus, individualization and increasing diversity within the group
is likely to correspond to diminishing individualization and diversity
among groups.[15]

The economist Tyler Cowen recently described the relationship
between forms of variety in his *Creative Destruction: How Globalization
Is Changing the World's Cultures*:

> When one society trades a new artwork to another society,
> diversity within society goes up (consumers have greater
> choice), but diversity across the two societies goes down (the
> two societies become more alike). The question is not about
> more or less diversity per se, but rather what kind of diversity
> globalization will bring. Cross-cultural exchange tends to
> favor diversity within society, but to disfavor diversity
> across societies.[16]

If the existence of diversity is by itself valuable, then it would be
difficult to know whether we should favor or oppose the extension of

461

interconnectedness. There is a reason, however, for those concerned about human variety to favor greater interconnectedness. Mere diversity that is not experienced by anyone is by itself of no value to human life. The existence of diversity among isolated groups of humans with no experience of each others' diversity would be of no benefit to any of the members of those groups. For such diversity to be of value, someone or some group would have to experience the diversity. It may be true that "A few decades ago, it was still possible to leave home and go someplace where the architecture was different, the landscape was different, and the language, life-style, dress, and values were different,"[17] but that was generally only true of small numbers of mobile elites who represented a tiny percentage of world population. The vast majority of people, who lived within comparatively insular communities, did not enjoy any benefits from such diversity, because they did not experience it. Those living today, who experience the modern globalized world, experience more human variety and creativity than any previous generation of humanity.

If it is the experience of diversity that is valuable, then greater group interconnectedness and expansion of social groups generates more of the diversity that is desirable, since most experience of diversity is experience of diversity within social groups, not across them. Indeed, as more people experience diversity across groups, the less diverse those groups are likely to be among themselves, but the more diverse they will be within themselves, where most people actually have the opportunity to experience diversity. In general, globalization leads to more actually experienced diversity, not less. Tourists, diplomats, and those engaged in international commerce do directly experience diversity across cultures, but it is those very activities that constitute globalization and that lead to increased experience of diversity within societies. For such people to complain of the effects of globalization is a bit like those unreflective tourists who complain bitterly that places "X" or "Y" have been ruined by "too many tourists."

IV. Policies of Cultural Protectionism

Some people seek to ensure or protect cultural distinctiveness through coercive means, including the imposition of legal limits on imports of foreign films and books, special subsidies for local production of cultural products, restrictions on the use of foreign languages, restrictions on satellite dishes or interconnections, limits on the abilities of property owners to sell to foreigners, and other forms of social control. Indeed, exceptions to general principles of freedom of trade have been a part of international trade agreements since shortly after World War II. The General Agreement on Tariffs and Trade of 1947 included "Article IV," which covered "Special arrangements for cinema films" and validated screen quotas and domestic regulations on cinema. During the Uruguay Round that created the General Agreement on Trade in Services (GATS), cultural services were singled out for services negotiations. However, under GATS (in contrast to the General Agreement on Tariffs and Trade, GATT), exemptions may be sought from the Most Favored Nation (MFN) principle. The European Union has successfully exempted cultural industries from the GATS, allowing various European governments to impose domestic content restrictions on television broadcasting and film distribution.

Cultural protection via coercion takes many forms. The Canadian government taxes its citizens to subsidize the domestic film industry. The French government not only taxes its citizens to subsidize film making, but mandates that at least 40% of all films shown in France must be in the French language. The Iranian government restricts satellite dishes. The governments of Singapore, China, and Saudi Arabia restrict access to the Internet in the name of protecting their local cultures (not to mention their rulers' holds on power).

In defense of such restrictions and special exemptions from general free trade principles, François Mitterand argued that, "What is at stake is the cultural identity of all our nations. It is the right of all peoples to their own culture. It is the freedom to create and choose our own images. A society which abandons to others the way of showing itself, that is to the say the way of representing itself, is a society enslaved."[18]

Pascal Lamy, European Commissioner for Trade, insists that normal principles of free trade should not apply to cultural goods, for "Cultural products are special, in that, on the one hand, they can be bought, sold, imported and exported and, on the other, despite everything which points to their categorization as goods and services in merchandising, they still cannot be reduced to simple goods and services because of their values and creative content."[19] He explained that "According to the humanist theory of trade, this type of exchange must promote diversity, not limit it."[20]

To the extent that taxpayers in Country X are taxed to subsidize local film production, advocates of freedom of trade have no special complaint. (Taxpayers in those countries, of course, may have their own grounds of complaint.) But restrictions on the rights of consumers to purchase, view, read, or otherwise experience cultural products produced elsewhere are a different matter. They represent assertions of power by some over others, notably by well-connected elites over those who would willingly purchase or view films, surf Internet pages, or read books that the elites consider harmful to the fragile cultural identities of those who would be doing the purchasing, surfing, or reading. In no way should such assertions of power be represented as cases of "culture defending itself," for they are instead assertions by some persons of the right and power to determine for others what those others will see, hear, read, and think. The issue is whether some should be able to make choices for others and impose them by force. To think that such restrictions foster a greater sense of cultural freedom is an act of self-deception. As a Romanian student remarked to me recently at a conference at the University of Aix-en-Provence, "How does it make me freer or more secure in my culture to require that boring old movies be shown over and over and over on Romanian television, simply in order to meet a domestic production quota?"

François Mitterand was wrong when he stated that restrictions on trade in cultural goods represent "the freedom to create and choose our own images." They represent the power of political elites to use violence against others to override their freedom to create and choose their own images.

V. Identity and Cultural Authenticity

A common complaint against globalization is that it erodes cultural authenticity, or even that it dilutes the purity of a given culture. For example, the authors of the report on "Alternatives to Economic Globalization" claim that "Corporate logos replace authentic local cultures as the primary source of personal identity."[21]

Manfred Steger decries "McDonaldization" and asserts that "In the long run, the McDonaldization of the world amounts to the imposition of uniform standards that eclipse human creativity and dehumanize social relations."[22]

Maude Barlow of the "Council of Canadians" claims that, "Governments and people around the world are increasingly concerned about a global cultural homogenization dominated by the American and Western values and lifestyles carried through the massive U.S. entertainment-industrial complex."[23] Barlow argues in favor of an international "Convention on Cultural Diversity" that would "recognize the importance to all nations and peoples of maintaining cultural diversity." Notably, it would require, not lawyers for its interpretation, but "cultural experts" (although just who those people might be is never made clear):

> Challenges and disputes under the new charter would need to be judged by cultural experts, not trade bureaucrats. The instrument would have to be self-defining: what constitutes a matter of cultural significance to one nation may not be to another. These definitions must be allowed to change over time, because we cannot know today what form cultural expression will take in the future.[24]

Such claims rest on confusion about the nature of culture (the claims of purity and authenticity), on confusion about the nature of personal identity, and on a political theory that is both parasitic on liberal cosmopolitan theories of rights and justice (insistence on "free and informed consent" is frequent) and at the same time highly authoritarian and elitist ("cultural experts" get to decide what others will be allowed or required to produce or consume).

A. Cultural Purity/Authenticity

Let's begin with claims of cultural purity or authenticity. They rest on myth and fantasy. One would be hard pressed to find any culture anyplace on the globe that one could assert to be "pure," for each culture has been influenced by others. At a Cato Institute forum on Tyler Cowen's book *Creative Destruction*, Benjamin Barber, author of the anti-globalization book *Jihad vs. McWorld*, defended authenticity and gave as an example threats to "authentic Indian tea culture," which he sought to protect from the ravages of Coca-Colonization.[25] Of course, tea was not "native" to India, but had been introduced there from China by British merchants and cultivated for export. The search for "authenticity" is a pipe dream. There is no longer any culture that could be identified as "pure," i.e., that is not a mélange of bits and pieces contributed by or drawn from other cultures.[26]

Those who defend cultural authenticity typically find the borders of authentic culture to correspond to the territorial borders of nation states, which are hardly "authentic" expressions of culture. It is not simply the nation (i.e., the expression of a cultural nation) that built the state, after all, but rather more often the state that built the nation. As Charles Tilly notes,

> As direct rule expanded throughout Europe, the welfare, culture, and daily routines of ordinary Europeans came to depend as never before on which state they happened to reside in. Internally, states undertook to impose national languages, national educational systems, national military service, and much more. Externally, they began to control movement across frontiers, to use tariffs and customs as instruments of economic policy, and to treat foreigners as distinctive kinds of people deserving limited rights and close surveillance.[27]

Furthermore, it is hardly clear that the boundaries of nation states, which are where protectionist restrictions are normally enforced, are coincident with important common features of groups. As Robert Musil noted, "The German peasant stands closer to the French peasant than to the German city dweller, when it comes down to what really moves their souls."[28] Which is the more "authentic" identity: German, French, peasant, or city dweller?

Those who claim to protect authentic cultures from contact with or contamination by others are almost always acting on a set of ideas that emerged in Europe, even when they claim to be representing allegedly authentic African, Native American, Islamic, or other non-European cultures. The influence of European anti-liberal thinking (both red and brown) on Islamic radicalism, for example, makes a mockery of the idea that Osama bin Laden and others are merely acting to protect authentic Islamic purity from corrupting outside influences.[29] The very language of "authenticity" is, for most cultures, profoundly "inauthentic." The influence of the anti-liberal German philosopher Martin Heidegger's theory of authenticity (*Eigentlich-keit*) can be found throughout much of the literature on cultural authenticity.[30] Like Marxism and Fascism, which are often presented as "indigenous" expressions of local political culture, the fetish for authenticity is an import from Europe.

An example of the arrogance of the authenticity fetishists may be helpful. During a trip a few years ago to Guatemala, a Mayan-Guatemalan friend who teaches anthropology in Guatemala City took me on a very enlightening tour of the Mayan highlands. He related to me how academic visitors from abroad whom he takes on such trips bitterly complain that the Mayan women are increasingly less likely to wear their traditional—and I should add, both very beautiful and very laboriously hand-made—clothing than was the case in the past. Increasingly, they wear such clothes for special occasions, such as christenings, weddings, church, and the like. The reaction of the visitor is almost uniformly one of horror. The Mayan women, they say, are being robbed of their culture. They are the frontline victims of globalization.

My friend noted that he had never heard a visitor who made such a complaint actually bother to ask any Mayan women why they did not dress like their mothers or grandmothers. My friend, since he speaks various Mayan dialects and is, in addition, an authentic social scientist, does ask, and he says that the answers are invariably some version of the observation that traditional clothing is becoming "too expensive." Now what, we might ask, does it mean to say that a hand-made garment (almost invariably made by women) has become too expensive? It means that the labor of a Mayan woman is becoming more valuable. It means that she can spend many hard hours on a hand loom (often attached to a tree; I tried it, and it is astonishingly hard work) to make a skirt and wear it, or she could make such a skirt and sell it to a wealthy lady in Paris, New York, or Rome, and with the money she earns buy several outfits, as well as eyeglasses, or a radio, or medicine to combat dengue fever, or books for her children. She is not being robbed; she is becoming wealthier. And from her perspective, that doesn't seem to be such a bad thing, no matter how much far wealthier foreign visitors may complain about it.

Furthermore, we know that, as prosperity grows, traditional indigenous garments are often revived as a locus of creative design and innovation. The sari that some Indian women abandoned for western clothing is now back in demand among Indians, and with prosperity, it has become the height of fashion; the best designers work to call forth from the traditional sari ever more beautiful forms of itself.

B. Culture and Personal Identity

Cultural authenticity is closely tied to issues of personal identity, for if the identity of a person could only be constituted within a pure or authentic cultural context, and inauthentic, impure, or cross-cutting cultural loyalties threaten to dissolve such identity, each person might have an interest in protecting the purity or authenticity of that culture. Personal identity is understood as encased within a wider and inescapable collective identity. Thus, Victoria Tauli-Corpuz (rather presumptuously) claims, on behalf of "some three hundred million indigenous people on the earth," that "Ours is a collective identity with collective ownership of forests, waters, and lands. These are antithetical to individualism, private property, modernization, and global capitalism."[31]

Harvard professor Michael Sandel argues that cultural membership, and hence the primacy of the community, is a requirement for self-understanding and personal identity and that individualist approaches generally fail to deal adequately with the problem of personal identity, for

> to be capable of a more thoroughgoing reflection, we cannot be wholly unencumbered subjects of possession, individuated in advance and given prior to our ends, but must be subjects constituted in part by our central aspirations and attachments, always open, indeed vulnerable, to growth and transformation in the light of revised self-understandings. And in so far as our constitutive self-understandings comprehend a wider subject than the individual alone, whether a family or tribe or city or class or nation or people, to this extent they define a community in a constitutive sense.[32]

Thus, each of us has certain "constitutive self-understandings" without which we would simply have no fixed identity, and those self-understandings are so connected with the "family or tribe or city or class or nation or people" that what is really identified is not a numerically and materially individuated human person, but a collective person.

According to Sandel, an epistemological principle can be transformed into an ontological principle: "this notion of community [the constitutive conception] describes a framework of self-understandings that is distinguishable from and in some sense prior to the sentiments and dispositions of individuals within the framework."[33]

468

Because shared understandings are necessary for our self-understanding, i.e., because they are asserted to be an epistemic criterion for self-knowledge, it is asserted that those shared understandings are constitutive of our identity, and that therefore "the bounds of the self are no longer fixed, individuated in advance and given prior to experience."[34]

That move is unjustified, for "even if this were granted it would not follow from it that subjects of these relationships are anything other than distinct persons. To suppose otherwise is to infer fallaciously that epistemological considerations enter into the constitution of the object known."[35] That individuals share notions of justice, compassion, and self-understanding does not imply that the boundaries of those individuals melt into a vast fondue of communal understandings, for, as John Haldane points out, "Features can only be shared if they attach to bearers which at base are numerically diverse."[36]

Sandel is surely wrong to assert that people who participate in the "same" culture have, are, or constitute the same self. Indeed, it does not even follow that they share the same self-understandings. Modern societies encompass such a wealth of different self-understandings that it is meaningless to assert that that one's identity is uniquely determined by a monolithic culture.

And just as the identity of each necessarily cosmopolitan culture may be a shifting focus within overlapping influences, so the identity of the person may be a shifting focus within overlapping influences.[37] That is not to say that there are no ethnic or national characteristics, no commonalities among persons that distinguish them from others. There clearly are. But pointing that out is no refutation of cosmopolitanism or of a theory of identity consistent with cosmopolitanism. Indeed, it would be impossible to recognize the common nature of humanity in the absence of any identifiable differences; the "same" cannot be recognized without the "other," the "one" without the "many." Recognizing that we adopt beliefs and self-understandings that we believe to be true, useful, interesting, moral, amusing, and so on from other persons, other cultures, and other languages is not shameful; it is just a recognition of reality. The communitarian approach implicitly denies that one's identity might be constituted by universalist, individualist, cosmopolitan self-understandings. The devout Muslim or Christian, for example, may very well see her attachment to a universalist religious faith as constitutive of her identity in ways that her being American, Albanian, or Arab is not. Such identities are quite common—and therefore possible—and collectivist and communitarian theorists have offered little reason to believe that they are unhappier or poorer than are more localized identities. We can distinguish, then, among at least three different broad understandings of personal identity: 1) "thick" theories, which are associated with a wide variety of collectivists and communitarians, according to which the individual is constituted by all (or perhaps just by most, or by the most important) of the elements of a complex culture, with all of those elements considered as necessary and unchangeable conditions of identity; 2) "thin" theories, which are associated commonly with Immanuel Kant and his followers, according to which individual identity is associated with a purely formal characteristic of consciousness as such, such as the transcendental unity of apperception; and 3) "focal" theories, such as the "succession" theory of Aristotle and the "closest continuer" theory of Nozick, which are both "thinner" than the collectivist theories, for individual elements of identity may be added or subtracted without obliterating the identity of the person, and "thicker" than the formal or abstract theories, for each person is identified, individuated, and distinguished from others by reference to contingent characteristics. Focal theories recognize that personal identity can be a matter of both circumstance and choice. They capture better the way in which the elements of one's identity can change over time, without merely dissolving into unconnected and disparate parts. Unlike thick theories, they do not rule out the widely observed and acknowledged movement of persons from culture to culture, without loss of self. Unlike thin theories, they acknowledge that one's commitments are not simply phenomenal ornaments somehow stuck onto a merely noumenal transcendental object (or subject), which is posited as a kind of substrate—or pin cushion—that is itself devoid of characteristics. Unlike both thick and thin theories, focal theories of personal identity provide a plausible part of the metaphysical foundation for an increasingly globalized world of free persons.

A model of social interaction might be helpful. If we were to try to imagine collective identity geometrically, we would have a series of concentric circles, with the circle of "the culture" forming the outer circle. That outer circle would be rather like a hard shell, guaranteeing the discrete identity of the persons who find themselves within it. But such an image does not begin to describe even relatively small (by modern standards) social orders, which are increasingly sets of intersecting circles that connect via their intersections with circles that would be seen by holders of the "hard shell" approach as outside the culture entirely.[38] Georg Simmel, who was deeply interested in the processes of differentiation and individuation, characterized the relationship between identity and social affiliations as an "intersection of social circles" ("Die Kreuzung sozia21er Kreise"):

> The groups with which the individual is affiliated constitute a system of coordinates, as it were, such that each new group with which he becomes affiliated circumscribes him more exactly and more unambiguously. To belong to any one of these groups leaves the individual considerable leeway. But the larger number of groups to which an individual belongs, the more improbable it is that other persons will exhibit the same combination of group-affiliations, that these particular groups will "intersect" once again [in a second individual].[39]

The less a social circle to which a person belongs requires or entails membership in another, the more modern a set of relationships is. Thus,

> The modern pattern differs sharply from the concentric pattern of group-affiliations as far as a person's achievements are concerned. Today someone may belong, aside from his occupational position, to a scientific association, he may sit on a board of directors of a corporation and occupy an honorific position in the city government. Such a person will be more clearly determined sociologically, the less his participation in one group by itself enjoins upon him participation in another. He is determined sociologically in the sense that the groups "intersect" in his person by virtue of his affiliation with them.[40]

Moreover, implicit in the conception of culture involved in theories of collective identity is a static understanding of what constitutes a culture. But for a culture to qualify as a living culture, it must be capable of change. To insist that it not be influenced by other cultures, or that it be "protected" behind barriers to trade and other forms of external influence, is to condemn it to wither and die. It is also to impose on people an "identity," a vision of themselves, that they themselves do not share, as evidenced by the fact that their choices must be overridden by coercion in order to "protect" that vision. As Mario Vargas Llosa puts it, "Seeking to impose a cultural identity on a people is equivalent to locking them in a prison and denying them the most precious of liberties—that of choosing what, how, and who they want to be."[41]

Furthermore, the assumption that introduction of cultural novelties into an existing culture implies imposition of systems of meanings on the members of those cultures rests on an assumption that the members of those cultures are simply inert and incapable of creating new forms of meaning. As Joana Breidenbach and Ina Zukrigl ask, "What about the meaning that local people attach to globally distributed goods and ideas?"[42] As they point out, even the hated McDonalds restaurant has different meanings in different cultures.[43] Tyler Cowen shows in his book how materials from one cultural context have been appropriated for aesthetic or artistic purposes in others, from Trinidadian musicians appropriating steel barrels and creating their famous steel band music to trade blankets that were painstakingly unwoven by Navajo artists to be re-dyed and rewoven into works of great beauty.[44] By appropriating materials, ideas, and approaches from outside, carriers of cultural practices keep cultures alive. The alternative preferred by enemies of globalization is to "preserve" cultures through use of coercion, much as one "preserves" insects by pinning them to boards in exhibition cases.

C. Empowering Elites

The language of collective identity is frequently asserted in conjunction with appeals to "informed consent," a standard normally associated with liberal individualism. But the difference between "informed consent" under collectivism and liberalism is that the entity that is to be "informed" and to give "consent" is neither an individual human being, nor a voluntarily formed association of human beings, but a collective entity. Such approaches reveal a profound misunderstanding of how individuals and groups are related; they fall into the fallacy of misplaced concreteness. The error is in moving from the existence of a group to treating that group as if it were another individual person, just like the individuals that make up the group. Liberal individualism does not entail that there is no such "thing" as society or that we cannot speak meaningfully of groups. The fact that there are trees does not mean that we cannot speak of forests, after all. Just as a building is not a pile of bricks but the bricks and the relationships among them, society is not a person, with her own rights, but many individuals and the complex set of relationships among them. Society is neither merely a collection of individuals, nor some "bigger or better" thing separate from them. The group is not another person who can give informed consent to the introduction or adoption of new ideas in the same way that an individual can give informed consent to the administration of a new medical procedure.

The historian Parker T. Moon put the matter quite clearly in his study *Imperialism and World Politics*:

> Language often obscures truth. More than is ordinarily realized, our eyes are blinded to the facts of international relations by tricks of the tongue. When one uses the simple monosyllable "France" one thinks of France as a unit, an entity. When to avoid awkward repetition we use a personal pronoun in referring to a country—when for example we say "France sent her troops to conquer Tunis"—we impute not only unity but personality to the country. The very words conceal the facts and make international relations a glamorous drama in which personalized nations are the actors, and all too easily we forget the flesh-and-blood men and women who are the true actors. How different it would be if we had no such word as "France," and had to say instead—thirty-eight million men, women and children of very diversified interests and beliefs, inhabiting 218,000 square miles of territory! Then we should more accurately describe the Tunis expedition in some such way as this: "A few of these thirty-eight million persons sent thirty thousand others to conquer Tunis." This way of putting the fact immediately suggests a question, or rather a series of questions. Who are the "few"? Why did they send the thirty thousand to Tunis? And why did these obey?
>
> Empire-building is done not by "nations" but by men. The problem before us is to discover the men, the active, interested minorities in each nation, who are directly interested in imperialism, and then to analyze the reasons why the majorities pay the expenses and fight the wars necessitated by imperialist expansion.[45]

473

Treating the collective as a person who can give "informed consent" to the adoption of new technologies, ideas, or practices obscures, rather than illuminates, important political questions. Those questions, mostly centering around explanation and moral responsibility, simply cannot be asked within the confines of the group personification thesis. To propose group personification is to drape a cloak of mysticism around the actions of the real policy makers, who are flesh-and-blood individuals, not ghostly collectives.

The insistence on collective—rather than individual—consent means that it is invariably the case that some (whether a minority in power, a plurality in power, or a majority in power) will give consent for others. If cultural identity is a collective concept and if "the culture" has to maintain its authenticity if it is to provide the collective identity necessary for personal identity, then it follows that some person or persons has to determine what it is that's authentic about a culture, and what is not. Sometimes the group that insists on being empowered to decide what will be considered authentic is not even drawn from members of the culture in question. It is made up of outsiders, who seek to protect the culture from being spoiled by contact with the outside. Such are the anti-globalization activists from wealthy countries. They fail to appreciate the humanity of the poor. They see them, not as sources of cultural creativity, but as exotic pets. Their goal is to convert the poor nations of the world to zoos, in which "native peoples" can be displayed in their "authentic habitat." They do not see them as humans.

For such restrictions to be enforced, someone must be empowered to decide what is and what is not a part of the culture. In principle, it seems that virtually anything could be included in a "culture," understood as "the beliefs, values, and lifestyles of ordinary people in their everyday existence."[46] That includes everything from rice production (witness Japanese protection of the powerful and protected rice farmers, who enjoy disproportional representation in the Diet [both political and culinary] and who force Japanese consumers to pay high prices for domestically produced rice), to ownership of radio and television stations (witness U.S. restrictions on foreign ownership of broadcasting licenses), to coal mining (witness the impassioned pleas on behalf of "traditional" ways of life associated with coal mines that are no longer profitable to operate), and now even to information technology and computer programming (witness various complaints from formerly highly paid computer programs over outsourcing of coding to programmers in India). Who will be empowered to make such determinations, and how?

One solution is to rely on "cultural experts," but that assumes that we already know who is the proper, or authentic, interpreter of a culture. Another is to rely on local political power holders, who are frequently patriarchal, authoritarian, and quite intent on retaining the power they hold over other members of their culture. Of course, yet another approach is to rely on wealthy self-appointed activists from outside to serve as "cultural experts" and allow them to decide what the poor may or may not import, trade, adopt, or adapt.

The whole enterprise is more than faintly reminiscent of the time in Germany when "cultural experts" on authentic German culture were empowered to deny to Germans the enjoyment of "degenerate art." The cultural experts got to define Germanness, but millions of Germans who enjoyed (or would enjoy, had they had the chance) jazz and swing music, abstract art, and the like were denied the enjoyment of such experiences by those empowered to determine what was truly German and what was not and to protect German culture from pollution.[47]

VI. Trade, Change, and Freedom

None of the above defense of cultural freedom implies that nothing is lost when cultures change. The most extreme example of true loss is the loss of linguistic diversity, for as languages "die," i.e., when the last speakers of those languages stop speaking them, songs, poems, stories, and other forms of complex meaning are lost. Loss is not always, however, equivalent to net loss. The speakers of those languages may have abandoned them for a reason, viz. the net gain realized in switching from a language with a tiny number of speakers to a language with a large or growing number of speakers, such as Spanish, Kiswahili, Arabic, or Mandarin. (Contrary to popular imagination, English is not rapidly growing as a primary language; its main advantage is that it is a common second language, such that when people from Norway, Mexico, Iran, and Thailand meet, they are likely to speak English, rather than Norwegian, Yucatec Mayan, Farsi, or Thai.) For every chosen benefit, there is a cost, namely, what is given up in the act of choice, and that cost may sometimes be felt more acutely by those who don't reap the benefit, such as speakers of more widely spoken languages who might have benefited from the continued existence of small language groups as sources of cultural inspiration, without having themselves to bear the costs of being linguistically isolated. In any case, even loss of language, as great a loss as that is, need not entail complete extinction of a culture, as theological, artistic, familial, and many other elements of that culture may continue to be expressed and developed in other languages.

The extreme case of linguistic extinction is hardly the only—or even the dominant—experience of globalization. (And even in such extreme cases, it is more an experience of "regionalization" than of globalization, as there seems little likelihood of a global primary language emerging any time soon.) Even in the cases of relatively small language groups, however, globalization can often increase the cultural vitality of those groups, by increasing communication among otherwise isolated population clusters. As Tsering Gyaltsen, owner of an internet service that is connecting 13 remote mountain villages in Nepal, told a BBC reporter,

> We bring the web to distant places so they can project
> themselves, benefit from the exposure and maybe young
> people will stay at home and be proud of being Sherpas,
> rather than running to Kathmandu or America.[48]

Barun Mitra of India's Liberty Institute told me during a conference in Berlin that he was struck by seeing German-language editions of the Harry Potter books in German bookstores. The wealth of Germany (in his words, "a pretty small country") made possible a thriving German-language literary culture, whereas the relative poverty of India could not support editions of such books in indigenous Indian languages. Wealth makes it easier to support a culture. A remarkably striking example is the capacity of cosmopolitan and highly "globalized" Iceland, with a very small population, to support a flourishing cultural offering of Icelandic poetry (Reyjkavik is the only city where I have ever, in the course of an evening, been introduced to three people with the comment, "He's a poet"), novels, plays, cinema, music, and journalism.

Globalization has also led to the creation of communities of persons who are actively seeking to document, defend, and even revive dwindling cultures. As Kani Xulam states in a promotion for the group Cultural Survival, "We have made friends through the Internet in places that we could not have reached otherwise. I am talking about South Korea, New Zealand, South Africa, Costa Rica and many other places. We have an address, a face, and a message for the world."[49]

There is nothing implicit in the concept of culture that requires investing elites with the power to manage or protect "authentic culture" by using force to override the choices of the members of those cultures. Culture can exist and flourish without cultural dictatorship.

VII. Conclusion

Living cultures change. It is the very process of change that makes them themselves. Their sameness is not merely a matter of their difference from other cultures, but of their difference from themselves over time, just as a person who grows from childhood to adulthood remains the same person only by changing.[50] What too many observers from wealthy societies seem to identify as the essential cultural element of poorer societies is their poverty. I have observed the disappointment of visitors from wealthy cultures when colorful poor people dressed in brilliant clothes stop, pat themselves down, and take out cell phones in response to insistent ringing sounds. It's not authentic! It ruins the whole trip! Those people are being robbed of their culture! They're victims of global capitalism! The arrogance of those who want to keep the poor in their native environments, like lizards in a terrarium, is startling.

Although seeing a Dalit ("untouchable") or a Mayan highlander talking on a cell phone may ruin the visit of a wealthy poverty tourist, being able to use telephony to talk to their friends, family members, or business associates is often highly valued by the people who bought the cell phones and should not be seen as a threat to their identity. Globalization is making possible a culture of wealth and freedom for Dalits and Mayans, who can enjoy wealth and freedom without ceasing to be the people they are. Just as culture should not be identified with isolation or stasis, it should not be identified with poverty.

The right to trade is a fundamental human right. The "cultural" arguments on behalf of limiting trade to the boundaries of nation states are untenable. Trade protectionism perpetuates poverty, not culture. It should be resisted, not primarily in the name of economic efficiency, but in the name of culture, for living cultures flourish in freedom and prosperity.

Notes

1. For helpful discussions of various fallacies concerning international trade, see Paul Krugman, *Pop Internationalism* (Cambridge, Mass.: MIT Press, 1996) and the various essays on trade by Frédéric Bastiat.

2. Peter Berger, "Introduction: The Cultural Dynamics of Globalization," in *Many Globalizations: Cultural Diversity in the Contemporary World*, ed. by Peter L. Berger and Samuel P. Huntington (Oxford: Oxford University Press, 2002), p. 2. We could also distinguish between discrete forms of globalization, including the emergence of global business, professional, and academic cultures, the diffusion of pop culture, and the effects of globalization on the ways in which the majority of people live their lives.

3. In Kathleen Freeman, ed., *Ancilla to the Pre-Socratic Philosophers* (Cambridge, Mass.: Harvard University Press, 1971), fragment 247, p. 113.

4. Homer, *The Odyssey*, trans. by Robert Fagles (New York: Penguin, 1997), p. 215.

5. Quoted in Louise Levathes, *When China Ruled the Seas: The Treasure Fleet of the Dragon Throne, 1405–1433* (Oxford: Oxford University Press, 1994), p. 41.

6. Quoted in Louise Levathes, *When China Ruled the Seas: The Treasure Fleet of the Dragon Throne, 1405–1433*, p. 42.

7. Joseph Addison, *The Spectator*, Saturday, May 19, 1711, reprinted in Joseph Addison and Richard Steele, *Selected Essays from "The Tatler," "The Spectator," and "The Guardian,"* ed. by Daniel McDonald (Indianapolis: Bobbs-Merrill, 1973), p. 238.

8. Voltaire, "Letter Six, On the Presbyterians," in *Candide and Philosophical Letters*, ed. and trans. by Ernest Dilworth (New York: The Modern Library, 1992), p. 141.

9. Voltaire, "Letter Ten, On Commerce," in *Candide and Philosophical Letters*, op. cit., pp. 154–55. Of course, Voltaire is being quite clever here. It's not true that he doesn't "know which is more useful to a state," for he makes it quite clear which of the two is more useful and more deserving of praise: not the aristocrat clinging to the threads of a dying order, but the merchant, the trader, the entrepreneur, the agent of wealth production and progress. What is perhaps most remarkable is that he closes the letter with an invocation, not of the well-being of the merchant, but of how he "contributes to the well-being of the world."

10. Justus Möser, "Klage wider die Packenträger," in *Justus Mösers Sämtliche Werke* (Oldenburg/Berlin: Gerhard Stalling Verlag, 1943–1990), vol. 4, p. 188, cited in Jerry Z. Muller, *The Mind and the Market: Capitalism in Modern European Thought* (New York: Alfred A. Knopf, 2002), p. 97. See also the treatment in Jonathan B. Knudsen, *Justus Möser and the German Enlightenment* (Cambridge: Cambridge University Press, 1986), pp. 114–21.

11. Justus Möser, "Der jetzige Hang zu allgemeinen Gesetzen und Verordnungen ist der gemeinen Freiheit gefährlich," in *Justus Mösers Sämtliche Werke* (Oldenburg/Berlin: Gerhard Stalling Verlag, 1943–1990), vol. 5, p. 22, cited in Jerry Z. Muller, *The Mind and the Market: Capitalism in Modern European Thought*, p. 86.

12. *Alternatives to Economic Globalization [A Better World Is Possible]*, A Report of the International Forum on Globalization, drafting committee co-chaired by John Cavanagh and Jerry Mander (San Francisco: Berrett-Koehler Publishers, 2002), p. 64.

478

13. *Alternatives to Economic Globalization [A Better World Is Possible]*, A Report of the International Forum on Globalization, p. 65.

14. Georg Simmel, "Group Expansion and Development of Individuality," in *On Individuality and Social Forms*, ed. by Donald N. Levine (Chicago: University of Chicago Press, 1971), p. 252: "Different as its points of origin in M and N may have been, this process will inevitably produce a gradually increasing likeness between the two groups. After all, the number of fundamental human formations upon which a group can build is relatively limited, and it can only slowly be increased. The more of these formations that are present in a group—that is, the greater the dissimilarity of constituent elements in M and N respectively—the greater is the likelihood that an ever increasing number of structures will develop in one group that have equivalents in the other."

15. "The narrower the circle to which we commit ourselves, the less freedom of individuality we possess: however, this narrower circle is itself something individual, and it cuts itself off sharply from all other circles precisely because it is small." Georg Simmel, "Group Expansion and Development of Individuality," in *On Individuality and Social Forms*, p. 255

16. Tyler Cowen, *Creative Destruction: How Globalization Is Changing the World's Cultures* (Princeton, N.J.: Princeton University Press, 2002), p. 15. Cowen also identifies diversity over time as a kind of diversity to which protectors of "authentic" culture seem hostile. Critics of globalization tend to view cultural change as a pure loss, rather than as the emergence of new forms of human life that increase the store of possible human understandings and experiences.

17. *Alternatives to Economic Globalization [A Better World Is Possible]*, A Report of the International Forum on Globalization, p. 64.

18. François Mitterand, Speech given at Gdansk, Poland, September 21, 1993, cited in J. P. Singh, "Globalization, Cultural Identities, and Negotiations: The Evolution of European Preferences on Cultural Industry Negotiations," Paper submitted to the special issue of *The Information Society* on "Social Determinants of Public Policy in the Information Age."

19. Pascal Lamy, "The State of the GATS Negotiations," Speech before the 4th EBU Conference, Brussels, March 27, 2001, http://www.ebu.ch/news/press_archive/press_news_1301.html.

20. It's notable that so much attention has been directed toward the role of cinema and so little to the role of the written word and to music. Hollywood—itself substantially a creation of central European artists who fled from or were expelled by collectivist regimes that sought to insulate themselves from dangerous cultural influences—is presented as a homogenizing force. (The Indian film industry—Bollywood—and the Brazilian film industry, despite being tremendously popular around the world, are routinely ignored, mainly because most anti-globalization activists are profoundly Eurocentric.) Benjamin Barber insists that "Films are central to market ideology" and contrasts the sameness of "multiplex movie boxes" with the variety of "a Protestant church in a Swiss village, a mosque in Damascus, the cathedral at Rheims, a Buddhist temple in Bangkok." Barber finds the former less distinctive than the latter. (Benjamin Barber, *Jihad vs. McWorld: How Globalism and Tribalism Are Shaping the World* [New York: Ballantine Books, 1996], pp. 98–99.) Perhaps that has something to do with the difference between entertainment and worship; one suspects that worldwide variety among dental offices is also declining. (For a treatment of the case of the film industry, see chapter four of Tyler Cowen's *Creative Destruction: How*

Globalization Is Changing the World's Cultures.) Although most of the ire of the anti-globalization movement has been directed to the rise of films produced in the United States, almost no attention is paid by anti-globalization writers to the rise to international prominence of such authors as Naguib Mahfouz, Mario Vargas Llosa, V. S. Naipaul, or Yukio Mishima.

21. *Alternatives to Economic Globalization [A Better World Is Possible]*, A Report of the International Forum on Globalization, p. 71. See also "Culture Wars," *The Economist*, September 12, 1998, reprinted in *Globalization and the Challenges of a New Century*, ed. by Patrick O'Meara, Howard D. Mehlinger, and Matthew Krain (Bloomington: Indiana University Press, 2000), pp. 454–60.

22. Manfred B. Steger, *Globalization: A Very Short Introduction* (Oxford: Oxford University Press, 2003), p. 71.

23. Maude Barlow, "Cultural Diversity: The Right of Nations to Resist Cultural Homogenization," in *Alternatives to Economic Globalization [A Better World Is Possible]*, A Report of the International Forum on Globalization, p. 69.

24. Ibid., p. 71.

25. Available for viewing at http://www.cato.org/events/030304bf.html

26. As Jeremy Waldron asks, "What if there has been nothing but mélange all the way down? What if cultures have always been implicated with one another, through trade, war, curiosity, and other forms of inter-communal relation? What if the mingling of cultures is as immemorial as cultural roots themselves? What if purity and homogeneity have always been myths?" Jeremy Waldron, "Multiculturalism and Mélange," in *Public Education in a Multicultural Society*, ed. by Robert Fullinwider (Cambridge: Cambridge University Press, 1996), p. 107.

27. Charles Tilly, *Coercion, Capital, and European States, 990–1992* (Oxford: Blackwell, 1992), pp. 115–16.

28. "'Nation' as Ideal and as Reality," in Robert Musil, *Precision and Soul: Essays and Addresses*, ed. and trans. by Burton Pike and David S. Luft (Chicago: University of Chicago Press, 1990), p. 111. Musil continued,

> We—each nation for itself alone—understand one another very little, and fight or betray one another when we can. We can, to be sure, all be brought together under one hat when we plan to squash it on the head of another nation; then we are enraptured and have a shared mystical experience, but one may assume that the mystical in this experience resides in its being so rarely a reality for us. Once again: this is just as true for the others as it is for us Germans. But in our crises we Germans have the inestimable advantage that we can recognize the real connections more clearly than they, and we should construct our feeling for the fatherland on this truth, and not on the conceit that we are the people of Goethe and Schiller, or of Voltaire and Napoleon.

29. That issue is discussed in chapter three of Paul Berman's *Terror and Liberalism* (New York: W. W. Norton & Co., 2003). The radical anti-globalization writers Michael Hardt and Antonio Negri assert in their book *Empire* (Cambridge, Mass.: Harvard University Press, 2000) that radical Islamic "fundamentalism" (a misnomer, in any case) "might be better understood not as a premodern but as a postmodern project. The postmodernity of fundamentalism has to be recognized primarily in its refusal of modernity as a weapon of Euro-American hegemony and in this regard Islamic fundamentalism is indeed the paradigmatic case" (p. 149). *Empire* offers, among other things, a defense of terrorist attacks on commercial institutions, of wholesale murder,

and of totalitarian censorship; those themes are only thinly veiled by a style that is almost completely opaque and virtually unreadable. See, for examples, pp. 36–38 ("moral intervention," i.e., verbal criticism of murderous totalitarian regimes, is condemned, and the term "terrorist" dismissed as "a crude conceptual and terminological reduction that is rooted in a police mentality"), pp. 65–66 ("Don't we already possess 'arms' and 'money'? The kind of money that Machiavelli insists is necessary may in fact reside in the productivity of the multitude, the immediate actor of biopolitical production and reproduction. The kind of arms in question may be contained in the potential of the multitude to sabotage and destroy with its own productive force the parasitical order of postmodern command."), and pp. 154–56 ("Truth will not make us free, but taking control of the production of truth will. Mobility and hybridity are not liberatory, but taking control of the production of mobility and stasis, purities and mixtures is. The real truth commissions of Empire will be constituent assemblies of the multitude, social factories for the production of truth.").

30. Martin Heidegger, *Being and Time*, trans. by John Stambaugh (Albany: State University of New York, 1996), e.g., pp. 39–47.

31. Victoria Tauli-Corpuz, "Cultural Diversity: The Right of Indigenous Peoples to Remain Different and Diverse," in *Alternatives to Economic Globalization [A Better World Is Possible]*, A Report of the International Forum on Globalization, p. 65. Tauli-Corpuz and others like her offer no evidence that "indigenous peoples" are inherently collectivist or anti-thetical to individualism or property. The claim is pure assertion.

32. Michael Sandel, *Liberalism and the Limits of Justice* (Cambridge: Cambridge University Press, 1982), p. 172.

33. Michael Sandel, *Liberalism and the Limits of Justice*, p. 174.

34. Michael Sandel, *Liberalism and the Limits of Justice*, p. 183.

35. John J. Haldane, "Individuals and the Theory of Justice," *Ratio* 27, No. 2, December 1985, p. 195. This is an old debate, and its outlines can be traced quite clearly in the debate between the "Latin Averroists," notably Siger of Brabant, and St. Thomas Aquinas over whether there is one "intellective soul" for all of mankind. The Averroists argued that, for two individuals to know the same thing, they have to have the same form impressed by the agent intellect into the same material (or possible) intellect; to know the same form, they must share the same material intellect. It was reported by some in the thirteenth century that that thesis had radical implications for the moral responsibilities of the individual: If Peter was saved, then I will be saved too, as we share the same intellective soul, so I am free to engage in whatever sinful behavior I wish, in the knowledge that I will be saved nonetheless. Thomas Aquinas responded that the impressed intelligible species is not literally the very form of the thing raised to a higher level of intelligibility, but rather that by which we know the thing. See Siger of Brabant, "On the Intellective Soul," in *Medieval Philosophy: From St. Augustine to Nicholas of Cusa*, ed. by John F. Wippel and Allan B. Wolter, O.F.M. (London: Collier Macmillan Publishers, 1969) and Thomas Aquinas, *On the Unity of the Intellect against the Averroists* (Milwaukee: Marquette University Press, 1968).

36. John J. Haldane, "Individuals and the Theory of Justice," p. 196. A move essentially identical to Sandel's is made by Anna Elisabetta Galeotti in criticizing F. A. Hayek's liberal theory of isonomy and spontaneous order, which, she claims, presupposes a notion of "community/membership": "The simple quest for negative liberty, for impartiality, isonomy, rule of law, makes sense vis-à-vis a world of private individuals, each with his or her own identity aims, and life plans, conceived of as autonomous micro-spheres to be protected from disruptive influences. But, Hayek's

social theory holds that the single individual, in his or her isolation, without rules and ties acting as connections to context and environment, would lose his or her identity and common understanding; hence one's resulting liberty would be devoid of any significance. If in Hayek's social theory the need for community is recognized as crucial, is it then plausible in the political sphere to assume that individuals act as independent entities?" (Anna Elisabetta Galeotti, "Individualism, Social Rules, Tradition: The Case of Friedrich A. Hayek," *Political Theory* 15, No. 2 [May 1987], p. 178. See also the response by Eugene Heath, "How to Understand Liberalism as Gardening: Galeotti on Hayek," *Political Theory* 17, No. 1 [February 1989]). Charles Taylor connects this kind of claim directly with the question of political obligation by saying that the allegedly constitutive features of the autonomous self that have broken down the boundaries between selves generate a direct obligation to that greater self, and he ties this in with a view of the state ("political society") as the constitutive self to which we constituted selves owe our allegiance: "Now, it is possible that a society and culture propitious for freedom might arise from the spontaneous association of anarchist communes. But it seems much more likely from the historical record that we need rather some species of political society. And if this is so then we must acknowledge an obligation to belong to this kind of society in affirming freedom." (Charles Taylor, "Atomism," in *Philosophy and the Human Sciences: Philosophical Papers, Vol. II* [Cambridge: Cambridge University Press, 1985], p. 208.) It is noteworthy that Hayek would disagree on both counts, first that there is a wider constitutive community into which individuals must inevitably melt, and second that it is the attainment of unified states, rather than the "spontaneous association of anarchist communes" that is responsible for the conditions of our liberty, isonomy, and law. As Hayek remarks in *The Fatal Conceit* (Chicago: University of Chicago Press, 1988), "the revival of European civilisation" (and the attendant growth of order, law, and culture) "owes its origins and *raison d'être* to political anarchy" (p. 33), i.e., to the fragmentation of Europe into competing and overlapping political and legal jurisdictions with relatively low exit costs. Without a single overarching "constitutive community" or political society to which allegiance must be owed, the answer that would be given by Hayek (and by numerous legal, economic, and political historians) to Galeotti's opening question ("Can a political theory, in its conceptual framework, do away with any reference to a notion of community/membership?") would be, "Yes."

37. Cf. Aristotle, *Metaphysics* IV, ii. 24, "the unity is in some cases one of reference and in others one of succession." Aristotle, *Metaphysics*, trans. by Hugh Tredennick (Cambridge, Mass.: Harvard University Press, 1933), 1005a11, p. 157. The identity of the self may best be understood in terms of the "succession" of which Aristotle wrote, which has been explicated in the form of the "closest continuer" theory advanced by Robert Nozick in his criticism of the "property" theory: Elements of one's identity may be deleted or added, such that after a time no element remains from before, and yet the composite remains diachronically identical. See Robert Nozick, *Philosophical Explanations* (Cambridge, Mass.: Harvard University Press, 1981), pp. 29–114.

38. Otto von Gierke was a pioneer in describing the nature of modern association. As he noted, "No modern association of fellows encompasses the totality of a human being, even in economic terms: the aspect of their economic personality which forms part of the association is strictly defined." Otto von Gierke, *Community in Historical Perspective*, trans. by Mary Fischer, selected and ed. by Antony Black (Cambridge: Cambridge University Press, 1990), p. 208. The book is excerpted from Gierke's *Das Deutsche Genossenschaftsrecht*.

39. Georg Simmel, "The Web of Group Affiliations" (*Die Kreuzung sozialer Kreise*) in *"Conflict" and "The Web of Group Affiliations,"* trans. by Kurt H. Wolff and Reinhard Bendix (respectively) (New York: The Free Press, 1955), p. 140.

40. Georg Simmel, "The Web of Group Affiliations," p. 150. Mario Vargas Llosa amplified that point in his defense of global free trade: "The notion of 'cultural identity' is dangerous. From a social point of view, it represents merely a doubtful, artificial concept, but from a political perspective it threatens humanity's most precious achievement: freedom. I do not deny that people who speak the same language, face the same problems, and practice the same religions and customs have common characteristics. But that collective denomination can never fully define each one of them, and it only abolishes or relegates to a disdainful secondary plane the sum of unique attributes and traits that differentiates one member of the group from the others." Mario Vargas Llosa, "The Culture of Liberty," *Foreign Policy*, January/February 2001.

41. Mario Vargas Llosa, "The Culture of Liberty."

42. Joana Breidenbach and Ina Zukrigl, "The Dynamics of Cultural Globalization: The Myths of Cultural Globalization," http://www.inst.at/studies/collab/breidenb.htm.

43. One example that they give is the use of McDonalds in Beijing as a non-competitive alternative to giving lavish banquets, since the "menu is limited and the food standardized ... For people without a lot of money McDonalds has become the best alternative to host a meal."

Tomas Larsson takes up the many ways in which objects are appropriated and appreciated by different cultures involved in peaceful trade in his book *The Race to the Top: The Real Story of Globalization* (Washington, D.C.: Cato Institute, 2001), pp. 83–89.

44. Tyler Cowen, *Creative Destruction: How Globalization Is Changing the World's Cultures*, pp. 25–26, 43–46.

45. Parker T. Moon, *Imperialism and World Politics* (New York: The MacMillan Company, 1926), p. 58.

46. Peter Berger, "Introduction: The Cultural Dynamics of Globalization," in *Many Globalizations: Cultural Diversity in the Contemporary World*, p. 2.

47. For an inspiring treatment of the resistance of the resistance to such imposed authenticity, see Michael H. Kater, *Different Drummers: Jazz in the Culture of Nazi Germany* (New York: Oxford University Press, 1992).

48. Daniel Lak, "High Ambition for Himalayan Internet," BBC News, October 31, 2003, http://news.bbc.co.uk/1/hi/world/south_asia/3230069.stm.

49. Posted on http://www.culturalsurvival.org.

50. I am not suggesting a similar pattern of maturation among cultures.

25. Infrastructure: Public or Private?

Much public debate has recently been generated by claims that America's economic "infrastructure"—that is, mainly government-provided capital goods like roads, bridges, sewers, and water facilities—is crumbling. The passage in the last lame-duck Congress of new transportation taxes and increased government expenditures on transportation services was partially a result of this debate. Given the amount of public attention devoted to this issue, the time has certainly come to critically scrutinize the assumptions behind the arguments for state provision of public goods in general and the economic infrastructure in particular.

This analysis will focus primarily on the "public goods" arguments for state action. There are at least two other prominent arguments commonly wielded by proponents of state intervention, but I will mention them only in passing. The first is ethical in nature, and while often found in conjunction with the public goods argument, in fact contradicts it.[1] The state, some argue, should deliberately thwart the desires of consumers and alter the pattern of property ownership that arises in a voluntary market, usually justifying such action on the grounds of "equality." This argument has been cogently dissected by Harvard philosopher Robert Nozick, among others.[2] Another common argument advanced for government public-works projects is that they "create jobs" or act in a countercyclical manner, extricating the economy from depression. This argument has been thoroughly critiqued by economists from Frederic Bastiat to F. A. Hayek, and has been effectively rebutted by historical experience. Public-works expenditures are, if anything, procyclical in nature.[3]

Market Failure

Since at least the time of David Hume, many economists have argued that coercion is necessary to provide some economic goods

---

Originally published in *Cato Policy Report* 5, no. 5, May 1983, pp. 1–5, 11.

desired by consumers, since those goods cannot be provided on the market because of attributes of "publicness." Various approaches to the definition of public goods have been developed, but most share two related characteristics: jointness of supply (or consumption) and nonexcludability of nonpaying consumers.

Jointness of supply (also referred to as nonrivalrous consumption) means that one person's consumption of a good does not diminish another person's consumption of the same good. For example, if a signal is broadcast on the electromagnetic spectrum, its use by one receiver does not diminish the access of others to the same signal. Nonexcludability means that if one person consumes the good, it cannot feasibly be withheld from some other person(s). For example, if a lighthouse sends out a light beam, its services cannot be selectively withheld from nonpaying passers-by. Thus, each person has an incentive to "free-ride" off of the contributions toward the purchase of the good made by others. Under such conditions, consumers can be expected to under-reveal their "true" preferences for the good.

Proponents of state action then argue that, since the voluntary market process is incapable of producing such goods (at least in optimal quantities), state action becomes necessary. In the words of William Baumol, "[I]f we assume the role of government to be that of assisting the members of the community to attain their own aims with maximum efficiency, then . . . it becomes the task of government to override the decisions of the market. This is not because the government believes, on some peculiar ground, that the people are not competent to judge, but rather because the market fails to provide machinery for these decisions to be given effect."[4] Taxation and other forms of coercion then become necessary to ensure that all beneficiaries of the state's services pay for benefits received.

But this view of state action presents numerous problems. Any good can be alternately considered a private or a public good, depending upon the quantity supplied, the definition of the relevant marginal unit ("one corn chip" or "food"), and the simultaneous valuation of the same good by two or more persons (an attractive appearance, for example, can be considered a public good, because other parties benefit without paying for the costs of nice clothing, haircuts, etc.).[5] Further, any good can be produced at least one of two ways: One allows for exclusion of nonpurchasers and the other allows equal access to all.[6] In practice, there are no goods for which exclusion of nonpurchasers is impossible. As Tyler Cowen writes, "The costliness of exclusion is not an intrinsic function of the good, but rather it depends on how the good is supplied and at what levels it is produced or consumed."[7]

The cost of producing any service or good includes not only labor, capital, marketing, and other cost components, but also fencing (or exclusion) costs as well. Movie theaters, for example, invest in exclusion devices like ticket windows, ushers, and walls, all designed to exclude noncontributors from enjoyment of their service. The costs of exclusion are involved in the production of virtually every good imaginable. There is no compelling justification for singling out some goods and insisting that the state underwrite their exclusion costs simply because of a political decision to make the good available on a nonexclusive basis, which decision is itself the relevant factor in converting what could be a private good into a public good.

Further, the argument for state provision is framed in purely static, rather than dynamic, terms: *Given* a good, for which the marginal cost of making it available to one more person is zero (or less than the cost of exclusion), it is inefficient to expend resources to exclude nonpurchasers. But this begs the question. Since we do not live in a world where goods are a *given*, but have to be produced, the problem is how best to produce these goods. An argument for state *provision* that assumes the goods are already produced is no argument at all.

If a good can be considered either a private good or a public good, the distinction begins to break down. Few if any of the goods now provided by the state fall strictly within the standard definitions of public goods (most do not even approach jointness of supply), and it is often forgotten that the state also invests in exclusion devices to bar from enjoyment of goods those who refuse to pay the taxes that support them: The mechanism includes the Internal Revenue Service and the federal prison system. And it is by no means clear that this draconian system is superior to its noncoercive free-market alternatives.

Government Failure

The most serious flaw in the public-goods theory of state action lies in the standards of comparison and the divergence between the incentives necessary for efficient provision of goods and the incentives actually guiding political action. The voluntary market is held up to an impossibly exacting standard and found wanting (in theory, if not in practice); it is then asserted that the state "must" take action to provide an optimal supply of goods. With Alfred Marshall, we should ask proponents of this approach, "Do you mean government all wise, all just, all powerful; or government as it now is?" As economist William C. Mitchell notes, "The production and distribution of government services is guided not by profit possibilities, based on consumer preferences and production costs, but by the electoral aspirations of politicians and the budget-maximizing activities of bureaucrats."[8] If voluntary market mechanisms can be criticized for being insensitive to the preferences of consumers, the state must surely fare even worse in the comparison. The incentives faced by political decisionmakers are likely to generate consequences far more perverse than those faced by consumers and producers in free markets. These consequences have been well documented in the burgeoning literature of public choice (for example, uneconomical overproduction of some goods, elimination of possibilities for incremental choices, and upward redistribution of income).

Advocates of state action to provide public goods have failed to justify their claims; an examination of the incentives faced by political decisionmakers shows little resemblance to the incentives necessary to provide an optimal supply of public goods.

But if the case is shaky on theoretical grounds, it becomes even more so after examining case studies. For decades, economists opined that "even Adam Smith" supported state-run lighthouses, a clear case of market failure if ever there was one. The subject was rapidly dropped from textbooks after University of Chicago economist Ronald Coase published his investigations into the history of lighthouses in Great Britain. He showed that lighthouses were efficiently provided on the market (tolls were collected at ports and were considered a cost of safe-transit from one port to another), but were produced in inadequate supply after the state took over their production.[9] As economist Kenneth Goldin remarks, "Lighthouses are a favorite example of public goods, because most economists cannot imagine a method of exclusion. (All this proves is that economists are less imaginative than lighthouse keepers.)"[10] Other examples of disparities between the predictions of public-goods theorists and the behavior of entrepreneurs in the market abound.[11]

Goods with potential characteristics of publicness are regularly provided on the market voluntarily through clubhouse contracts, through mechanisms that internalize externalities (for instance, creation of a joint product), inclusion of public goods in the overhead costs of a firm, linkages of the sale and consumption of public with private goods, and other means.

Of course, it may be no accident that the claims made on behalf of state provision of public goods are not borne out in practice; as a consequence, perhaps the theory of government underlying such claims should be revised. Harvard economist Joseph P. Kalt suggests that we should view government "as a means whereby some free riders are able to force others to pay for their rides, rather than as a means whereby we all agree to coerce ourselves in order to overcome a free-rider effect that frustrates desires for public goods."[12] An insight into the real incentives motivating the recent infrastructure debate was provided by a striking advertisement that appeared in the *Washington Post* for a new newsletter: "*Infra$tructure* . . . is a new Washington 'buzzword' for: A. America's crumbling physical plant? $3 trillion is needed to repair highways, bridges, sewers, etc. B. Billions of federal reconstruction dollars? The 5¢ per gallon gasoline tax is only the beginning. C. *Your bible for infrastructure spending— where the money is going and how to get your share*—in a concise biweekly newsletter? ANSWER: All of the above. Subscribe today" (ellipses and emphasis in original). *Infra$tructure*, the ad informs us, is published by "Business Publishers, Inc., serving industry and government since 1963."

Roads and Infrastructure Repair

The public good that dominated public debate for several months recently, and which is likely to occupy a central place in the near future, is road and mass transit provision. Though the issue was imbedded in a more general "Chicken Little"–like panic over the nation's "crumbling infrastructure," light may be shed on the entire infrastructure debate by examining the case of transportation.

To begin with, the infrastructure is not in the alarming state the public was led to believe.[13] The changing age distribution of the interstate highway system has been the primary fact cited in support of claims that the system is crumbling; but older does not always mean worse. There is a no evidence to support the "universal collapse" thesis that garnered so many headlines in the recent debate. Road conditions vary widely from one locale to another, and the comprehensive Department of Transportation study on road conditions concluded that "the great majority of pavement in both urban and rural areas was in satisfactory or good condition."[14] The most recent federal report showed some decline, but pavement deterioration differed widely from state to state and was hardly of sufficient magnitude to be called a crisis.[15]

It is also unclear what is being purchased when roads are repaired. A recent Federal Highway Administration study makes clear the need for a significant reevaluation of current thinking about the importance of road conditions.[16] The study concluded that both accident rates and fuel consumption, two of the most important factors considered in road work cost-benefit analysis, are not influenced by pavement condition (for the range of conditions commonly encountered in the United States). Only nonfuel operating costs were seen to be so influenced. The assumptions underlying most cost-benefit analyses and informing public discussion for the past two decades may have been wrong.

Further, in the absence of markets, mechanisms for judging claims about repair or construction "needs" are insufficient at best. The needs presented to the public most commonly emanate from engineers or bureaucrats; the former often take little or no account of cost constraints (if a facility is not perfect, it is not good enough), while the latter's situation encourages budget-maximizing activity, including inflation of claims on the treasury. The hybridization of the two in government agencies is particularly likely to lead to extraordinary "needs" and uneconomic budget demands.

But perhaps most important, the problem is fundamentally one of management, and it is here that state action has shown itself to be most uneconomical and inefficient. A disproportionate amount of total funds allocated for public works has gone into new construction, due to federal matching-fund policies. The capital structure of public goods has been seriously distorted in favor of new construction and away from maintenance and repair, as state and local government jurisdictions allocate scarce funds in order to receive federal matching funds for new construction. This is true not only of roads and bridges, but also of sewage systems, water treatment and control, and other facilities.

This should not be surprising, given the political incentives in favor of new construction (with the possibilities of cost overruns, consultant's fees, facilities named after political figures, and the like) rather than maintenance of existing facilities. As has been commented, "Nobody ever held a ribbon-cutting ceremony over a filled pothole." The "Iron Triangle" system that dominates congressional action manifests itself in public-works programs as well as in defense, energy, agriculture, and other state-subsidized industries.[17]

In the case of transportation, use-inefficiencies and wealth transfers have been generated by the massive subsidization of interstate highways. While taxes are levied on fuel, tires, and other vehicle operating cost components, some users have managed to benefit at the expense of others. Most road damage is the result of heavy-vehicle operation, yet heavy vehicles bear little of the cost for road repair and maintenance. An Oregon Department of Transportation Cost Responsibility Study in 1980 showed that the per-mile cost responsibility of an 80,000-pound truck is roughly 16 times greater than that of an automobile.[18] Yet the 80,000-pound truck consumes only three-to-four times the fuel consumed by the average automobile over a comparable amount of travel (and hence only three-to-four times the fuel taxes).

Rational road pricing would most likely require differential fees based on vehicle weight, weight distribution (number of axles), and distance traveled.[19] But the imposition of damage-based weight-distance taxes, while encouraging more efficient road use, would not address the structural incentives for inefficient resource allocation that are unavoidable in state-managed enterprises. Demand would be affected, but not supply. The political incentives for wealth transfers would far outweigh any incentives for efficient management that weight-distance taxes might introduce.

"Even" Adam Smith was aware of the political incentives attending tax-financed roads: "A magnificent high road cannot be made through a desert country where there is little or no commerce, or merely because it happens to lead to the country villa of the intendant of the province, or to that of some great lord to whom the intendant finds it convenient to make his court. A great bridge cannot be thrown over a river at a place where nobody passes, or merely to embellish the view from the windows of a neighboring palace: things which sometimes happen, in countries where works of this kind are carried on by any revenue other than that which they themselves are capable of affording."[20]

Far more feasible than partial and one-sided fixes like weight-distance taxes is the introduction of a true market system, entailing freely transferable property rights. Under such a system, costs and risks would be borne privately rather than publicly, efficiency would be generated by a rational pricing system, and transportation decisions would no longer be held hostage to the aspirations of the "road gang" of politicians, bureaucrats, and construction-industry lobbyists. Roads, like other elements of the economic infrastructure, are neither nonrivalrous in consumption nor incapable of supporting exclusion devices for nonpurchasers.

The inefficiencies and distortions generated by state usurpation of the market can be eliminated by movements toward true markets. Proposals to introduce efficient production and maintenance of higher order public goods (infrastructure) via privatization are eminently practical. John Semmens, senior economist for the Arizona Department of Transportation, has a detailed plan for privatizing that state's highway system.[21] The plan would entail putting the state highway system on a non-tax-supported basis and then requiring divestiture to the market sector of all segments whose revenues from tolls failed to cover their costs of operation. Nonbureaucratic management, argues Semmens, is likely to turn "losers" into "winners" through entrepreneurial alertness to possibilities for cost-cutting innovation, marketing, and other opportunities for new combinations of factors of production.

Semmen's strategy for introduction of efficiency through real markets could be implemented on a more piecemeal basis as well. Much of the funding in the so-called repair bill passed by Congress is in fact intended for new construction of gaps in the interstate highway system. Construction of these gaps, amounting to 3.7% of the total 42,944-mile system, will cost the taxpayers some $40 billion under current cost estimates.[22] The construction should be opened to private enterprise, with the right to charge tolls and reap profits as the incentive. Some projects may not be undertaken (a likely example is New York's multibillion dollar Westway), but that will reflect an entrepreneurial estimate of costs and benefits, rather than pork-barrel decisions based on political incentives.

Voluntary market ownership and management of the infrastructure need not be limited to roads. Mass transit is a prime candidate for rapid privatization.[23] Other services—including water and sewage treatment, solid-waste collection and disposal, and fire protection—would also benefit from privatization.[24]

Present financing difficulties faced by federal, state, and local governments are already leading to moves away from general revenue tax financing to user fees and tolls.[25] The introduction of market pricing structures should be completed by allowing freely transferable property rights as well. Government has failed the public-goods test, and it is time to let the market succeed.

Notes

1. Lester Thurow, however, argues that certain kinds of income redistribution qualify as public goods. See "The Income Distribution as a Pure Public Good," *Quarterly Journal of Economics* (May 1971).

2. Robert Nozick, *Anarchy, State, and Utopia* (New York: Basic Books, 1974). Also see Richard B. McKenzie, "Taxation and Income Redistribution: An Unsympathetic Critique of Practice and Theory," *Cato Journal* 1 (Fall 1981), pp. 339–71.

3. Bruce Bartlett, executive director of the Joint Economic Committee, has demonstrated the procyclical nature of such programs. "Public Works Programs Don't Create Jobs," *Wall Street Journal*, November 30, 1982.

4. William J. Baumol, *Welfare Economics and the Theory of the State* (Cambridge, Mass.: Harvard University Press, 1969), p. 55. For alternative views, see Giovanni Montemartini, "The Fundamental Principles of a Pure Theory of Public Finance," in *Classics in the Theory of Public Finance*, ed. Richard A. Musgrave and Alan T. Peacock (New York: St. Martin's Press, 1967), and Joseph P. Kalt, "Public Goods and the Theory of Government," *Cato Journal* 1 (Fall 1981), pp. 565–84.

5. See Tyler Cowen, "Public Goods Definitions and Their Institutional Context," *Review of Social Economy* 43 (April 1985), pp. 53–63.

6. See Kenneth Goldin, "Equal Access vs. Selective Access: A Critique of Public Goods Theory," *Public Choice* (Spring 1977).

7. Tyler Cowen, "The Problem of Public Goods: A Preliminary Investigation," research paper (Menlo Park, Calif.: Institute for Humane Studies, 1981), p. 19.

8. William C. Mitchell, *The Anatomy of Public Failure: A Public Choice Perspective* (Los Angeles: International Institute for Economic Research, 1978), p. 5.

9. Ronald Coase, "The Lighthouse in Economics," *Journal of Law and Economics* (October 1974).

10. Goldin, "Equal Access vs. Selective Access," p. 62.

11. For a sampling, see Steven N. S. Cheung, "The Fable of the Bees: An Economic Investigation," *Journal of Law and Economics* (April 1973); Terry Anderson and P. J. Hill, "An American Experiment in Anarcho-Capitalism: The Not So Wild, Wild West," *Journal of Libertarian Studies* 3, no. 1; and William C. Wooldridge, *Uncle Sam, the Monopoly Man* (New Rochelle, N.Y.: Arlington House, 1970).

12. Kalt, "Public Goods," p. 573.

13. See Allan T. Demaree, "Infrastructure Chic: How to Judge the Jobs Bill," *Fortune*, December 13, 1982; and Tom G. Palmer, "The Infrastructure Scam," *Inquiry*, February 1983.

14. *The Status of the Nation's Highways: Conditions and Performance* (Washington, D.C.: Department of Transportation, 1977).

15. *The Status of the Nation's Highways: Conditions and Performance* (Washington, D.C.: Department of Transportation, 1981).

16. *Vehicle Operating Costs, Fuel Consumption, and Pavement Types and Condition Factors* (Washington, D.C.: Federal Highway Administration, March 1981).

17. See Gordon Adams, *The Iron Triangle: The Politics of Defense Contracting* (New York: Council on Economic Priorities, 1981).

18. L. Lee Lane, "The Case for Weight Distance Taxes," paper presented to the American Association of State Highway and Transportation Officials, November 22, 1982.

19. See Fred L. Smith, "Alternatives to Motor Fuel Taxation—Weight Mileage Taxes," paper presented at the North American Gasoline Tax Conference, September 15, 1982.

20. Adam Smith, *The Wealth of Nations*, ed. Edwin Cannan (New York: The Modem Library, 1937), p. 683.

21. John Semmens, *Investment Recovery Analysis: A Businessman's Approach to High-way Planning* (Phoenix, Ariz.: Department of Transportation), and Highways as Earning Assets, unofficial report.

22. *Economics of Completing the Interstate Highway System* (Woody Creek, Colo.: Skrotzki Associates, 1982).

23. See James B. Ramsey, *Selling the Subways in New York: Wild-Eyed Radicalism or the Only Feasible Solution?* (New York: C.V. Starr Center for Applied Economics, New York University, 1981).

24. See Robert Poole, *Cutting Back City Hall* (New York: University Books, 1979).

25. Rochelle L. Stanfield, "The Users May Have to Foot the Bill to Patch Crumbling Public Facilities," *National Journal*, November 27, 1982.

26. Future Schlock: Government Planning for Tomorrow

Bemoaning the fact that "sometimes when we try to glimpse into the future we get more confused than when we started," Senator Albert Gore Jr. (D.-Tenn.) has introduced legislation to establish a Federal Office of Prophecy. That's not what he would call it, of course; its official name would be the "Office of Critical Trends Analysis." Gore's crusade has been joined by a leading conservative, Representative Newt Gingrich (R.-Ga.), who is sponsoring an identical bill in the House.

As Gingrich presents the case for "National Foresight Capability," our chaotic political system lurches from one crisis to the next, with little ability to consider what awaits it around the next corner (or after the next election). He complains that too little thought is put into "how problems might have been avoided or turned into opportunities. We muddle through the political arena with short-term, 'cut and fit' policies and solutions." The solution is to hire bureaucrats who will work with a blue-ribbon advisory commission to study all sorts of "trends" (global, social, demographic, technological, political, economic, and environmental) and figure out what the next crisis will be.

Unfortunately for Messrs. Gore and Gingrich, this effort is doomed from the start and is likely to make government policy even more ineffective than it is now. As Mark Twain observed, "The art of prophecy is very difficult, especially with respect to the future."

Let's take the case of economic forecasting, where we seem to face well-defined and easily measurable variables, all subject to neat mathematical treatment. Yet economic forecasting has proved time and time again to be one of the most astounding failures of modern science. One study showed that gross national product predictions

Originally published in the *Wall Street Journal*, June 13, 1985.

based on economic forecasting models could have switched the signs from positive to negative or negative to positive and still have come closer to the truth. The reputation of forecasting has been so badly tarnished that no matter how eloquent its defenders may wax, they will never restore its original shine. The fact is that economic forecasting is to economic science as astrology is to astronomy.

But if the seemingly precise science of economic forecasting is meaningless, what are the chances that a bevy of GS-11 civil servants will have any luck predicting, in any way useful to public policy, future technologies or political developments? Both of these are based on the knowledge and ideas that will occupy the minds of the future. And, as the philosopher and historian of science Sir Karl Popper has demonstrated, it is incoherent to say that one can predict the knowledge or ideas one will have in the future, for then one would have them now, rather than in the future.

Indeed, who could have predicted the invention of the silicon chip or the tremendous role it plays in our lives today? No one could have predicted the effect the humble air conditioner would have on the political process (Congress now spends the entire year passing laws on top of one of the world's least inhabitable swamps) or on the growth of financial centers in the Southwest (few people would live in Houston absent air conditioning).

Who would have predicted video games (there wasn't even a demand for them before entrepreneurs created them) or laser disk personal medical insurance cards (800 pages of medical information on a wallet-sized card—the invention of an unpredictable 19-year-old student) or magnetic resonance scanning and kindred medical inventions (and their effect on the price of medical care)? The notion that a group of bureaucrats—among the professionally least imaginative creatures ever created—could have predicted any of these things is a colossal joke.

Examination of Eastern Bloc totalitarian states shows that even planned societies are thoroughly unpredictable. A free and dynamic society like ours is even more so. And National Foresight Capability may well be the camel's nose of central planning pushing into the tent of a free society. Gore raised the issue himself when he told his colleagues that his bill "would not be a method to invoke centralized planning into the federal government. I invite you to study the bill carefully. The word 'planning' never appears." And sure enough, it doesn't.

But there is little doubt that an Office of Critical Trends Analysis would be a potent instrument in any move toward central economic planning, mainly as a pseudoscientific justification for the power grab that such planning really is. And the creators of the concept have been fairly open about this, at least among themselves.

Don Lesh, executive director of the Global Tomorrow Coalition, a prime mover of National Foresight Capability, wrote in its internal newsletter in 1982, "in some circles, the very words 'government planning' are enough to set off sirens and alarms. To many, those words are synonymous with Big Brother, socialism, communism, authoritarianism, totalitarianism . . . choose your 'ism.' That's why we spend time searching for descriptive circumlocutions. . . . Right now, the term for that process is 'national foresight,' and that's not bad—especially if you can't say 'planning.'"

Russell Peterson, a former governor of Delaware and a supporter of national foresight, addressed the relationship of government planning to Big Brotherism and said in 1981: "In recognition of this unfortunate connotation often given to planning, we have substituted the term 'foresight capability.' It is a euphemism, to be sure, but one which seems necessary if the subject is to be discussed with objectivity. What we are talking about here, of course, is not a planned society, but rather the use of planning to meet society's needs." The distinction is so fine as to be no distinction at all, for it leaves unaddressed this question: What gets planned for whose needs as determined by whom?

Contrary to the perceptions of technocrats like Messrs. Lesh and Peterson, free societies incorporate more, not less, order and foresight than controlled societies. The spontaneous order of the market system, and of liberty in general, is far more abstract, complex, and farsighted than all the five-year plans or economic regulations ever devised. Government planning is, in fact, a disruption of the continuous process of plan coordination embodied in freely developed social institutions.

National Foresight Capability, as envisioned in an Office of Critical Trends Analysis, would be a major step toward greater government control over our economy and society. It would provide a smoke screen of pseudoscience to cover a major grab for power by the state.

27. Against Taxes

Hundreds of thousands of taxpayers will rush to file their 1981 income tax forms at the last minute tonight. In all the furor in Washington over how much to raise taxes, the taxpayers seem to have been left out of the discussion. The disbursement of tax funds— for El Salvador's junta, for the Department of Health and Human Services, for water projects and MX missiles—has come to dominate questions of tax policy, as politicians wrangle over how big the deficit will be and how much must be raised to meet expenditures. The collection of taxes has been ignored in the debate.

Suppose someone were to stop you at gunpoint and demand that you hand over half of your hard-earned income. Wouldn't you consider him a thief and consider yourself justified in resisting the robbery?

Now suppose that the thief is carrying a paper certifying him as an agent of the state. In addition, he claims that the robbery is being carried out for your own good. Is his act any different now?

While the Internal Revenue Service boasts of a "voluntary compliance" system of tax collection, the fact is that taxation is carried out at the point of a gun. If you choose not to pay—for whatever reason— armed men will seize you and forcibly take you to jail. If you resist, violence will be used against you. This is not "voluntary compliance." It is theft.

Of course, we are constantly reminded that there is a difference between the two cases, and the difference is that government exists to provide us with services, like police and fire protection and national defense, and that we have consented to allow ourselves to be taxed.

By contrast, you never consented to allow the "freelance" thief to take your money, nor does he do so in order to provide you with services like police and fire protection and national defense.

Originally published in the *New York Times*, April 15, 1982.

Most goods and services are provided on the market through voluntary and contractual agreement. Indeed, recent analyses and historical studies by free market economists—for example, Ronald Coase and David Friedman—have lent strong support to the view that all goods and services can be provided in this voluntary manner, from lighthouses to defense to fire protection. The free market provides such services in many communities, with no coercion of consumers.

The consent to be taxed turns out, upon closer examination, to be a less attractive notion than it might appear at first. The drapery of consent is wrapped around taxation in an attempt to make it appear no different from the voluntary purchase of, say, a clock radio. After all, the argument goes, if you vote for a policy (or a politician), you have agreed to bind yourself to that policy or to the policies of that politician. And if you voted against the policy or the politician? Why, then, you have participated in the very system by which such decisions are made, thereby agreeing to bind yourself to the result of the process. And if you had no opinion or did not vote? Then you have forfeited your right to complain, as you refused to exercise your option to influence the process. Thus, the individual has consented to be taxed, no matter how he or she acted.

This kind of "consent" surely is of a different kind from that found in voluntary agreements to purchase goods or services. One might conclude that it does not deserve the name "consent" at all.

If the facade of "consent" is stripped from taxation, government becomes merely an instrument for the advancement of powerful interests—at the expense of the public good.

As the English statesman Lord Bolingbroke (1678–1751) confessed in a letter to Sir William Windham: "I am afraid that we came to court in the same disposition that all parties have come; that the principal spring of our actions was to have the government of the State in our own hands; that our principal views were the conservation of this power, great employments to ourselves, and great opportunities of rewarding those who had helped to raise us, and of hurting those who stood in opposition to us."

True, those who make decisions for the American state are not members of a strictly hereditary class. The results, however, are little different. The few ("special interests") are subsidized by the many. It's not an accident, nor is it the result of some nefarious conspiracy.

It is the inevitable result of statism, of the systematic imposition of coercion.

One shouldn't be surprised that an institution whose members are devoted to, in Bolingbroke's terms, "great employments to ourselves," and which is founded on violence, engages in theft. Let's just use the right word.

28. Hothouse of Hate

If ignorance was the state of man in the Garden of Eden, then the much-hyped "Eden Project" in Cornwall is living up to its name. The Eden Project is a none too impressive botanical garden that advertises itself as an educational project and a "stage where science, art and technology blend to tell the story of our place in nature." Instead of what's promised, visitors get a farrago of false statistics, economic gibberish, and pseudo-science, all neatly contained in a second-rate terrarium.

The very first thing to greet visitors is a giant display of statistical ignorance drawn, I learned, from a bit of Internet spam that's been doing the rounds for years. Virtually none of what it claims is true, and some of it is downright hateful. According to the display, "If we could shrink the Earth to a village with a population of precisely 100 people, with all the existing human ratios remaining the same, there would be . . .", followed by a set of absurd claims dressed up as facts, such as "21 would be European" (try 12), "70 would be unable to read" (actually about 16, off by only 54), "89 would be heterosexual, 11 would be homosexual" (reliable studies indicate between 2 and 4 percent of males are homosexual), and so on.

Much more important, however, was the following: "Six people would possess 59 percent of the entire world's wealth and would be from the United States." Now that can't be true for several reasons, the first of which is that the United States has only about 4.6 percent of the world's population, not 6 percent. Second, not all Americans are rich and not all non-Americans are poor. Third, there are no reliable data available on shares of "the entire world's wealth." (As the World Bank puts it, "Unfortunately we don't have a standard way of defining wealth. Wealth requires an evaluation of all productive assets, which accumulate and depreciate over years.") Fourth, the data that we do have on gross national income by country indicates

Originally published in *The Spectator*, February 22, 2003.

that the United States produces a bit more than 31 percent—not 59 percent—of aggregate world income.

Two things are notable about those figures. First, gross national income represents the production of value, not control over natural resources. Americans are disproportionately wealthy compared with other countries because they are disproportionately productive. And they are so productive because their institutions—courts, markets, property registries, and so on—work relatively well. The production of value is not a zero or negative sum game; increasing productivity in one country does not decrease it elsewhere. In fact, the evidence is overwhelming that increasing productivity for one group tends to increase it among its trading partners, as it means greater opportunities for the division of labor, greater reliance on comparative advantage, and richer consumers of imports from trading partners. Even more striking, there is a negative correlation between natural resource endowment and average income; countries richly endowed with natural resources (think oil, gold, or diamonds) tend to have lower average incomes than less richly endowed countries, partly because parasitic thugs grab control of those resources and use the wealth to cement their dictatorial rule. The wealth of nations is produced by human ingenuity and voluntary co-operation. It is not determined to any substantial degree by natural endowments. Wealth is not something that just happens.

Second, similarly disproportionate statistics could have been brought up about France (0.97 percent of world population but 4.4 percent of world income), Sweden (0.14 percent of world population but 0.71 percent of world income) and, indeed, any of the other productive and prosperous countries of Europe or Asia. The display that greets visitors to the Eden Project implies that the people of the United States have somehow grabbed control of most of "the entire world's wealth," when the fact is that they produce nearly a third of the value produced worldwide annually.

What the Eden Project was putting on display is, quite simply, hate propaganda of the sort that has traditionally been manifested as anti-Semitism. It would be made more obvious if they had written instead a pseudo-fact like the following: "One person would possess 12 percent of the world's wealth and would be a Jew." In recent years American-baiting has become the favorite sport of small minds.

Interspersed throughout the rather poorly arranged botanical gardens were claims such as, "Around 90 percent of futures contracts are on paper and don't involve coffee at all." *Quelle surprise!* Futures contracts involve trades of future coffee: that is, coffee that hasn't been harvested yet. Even dumber, however, were claims that "Futures markets protect traders, but not small producers, from price changes." Being able to sell next year's crop at a guaranteed price today is of some benefit to a farmer, or he wouldn't do it. Futures contracts allow farmers to transfer their risk to people better placed or willing to handle it. Without such markets, prices would fluctuate far more, to the detriment of farmers.

When I was photographing the welcoming display of misinformation, a very friendly lady offered me a printed version of the text. I asked where the information had come from, and she said that "someone had seen it on the Internet" and so they'd put it up. Evidently no effort whatsoever was made to check the veracity of their claims. Even a quick check on an Internet search engine, such as Google, would have found that what was "seen on the Internet" was a hoax, a collection of urban myths even less credible than the stories of the alligators in the New York sewage system or the giant Peruvian rat that tourists thought was a dog. No doubt the "scientists" and "educators" at the Eden Project have also responded to all the email offers from the heirs of Mobutu Sese Seku or Jonas Savimbi that offer to share £25 million with them, on condition that they first wire £15,000 to an offshore account. It was, after all, "on the Internet."

Perhaps the Eden Project's primary claim to fame will be that it provided the backdrop to much of the action in the latest James Bond cinematic thriller, *Die Another Day*. At least the pseudo-scientific rubbish in the film was more entertaining than that in the Eden Project.

29. Census 2000: You May Already Be a Winner!

As soon as George W. Bush and Trent Lott cool off about the intrusive questions posed by Census 2000 ("Do you have difficulty dressing, bathing, learning, remembering, or concentrating ... "), somebody should introduce them to the real outrage of the decennial count: The U.S. Census Bureau is selling the 2000 count to the public in the ad-speak of Super Lotto. A full-page ad in the March 22 *Wall Street Journal*—part of the bureau's $111 million ad campaign— warns that "your community could miss out on its fair share" of $185 billion in government programs unless you complete the census form. In other words: *You can't win if you don't play!*

The lottery language is no accident. The reason the government sells the census as your ticket to getting goodies—rather than as your civic duty—is that distributing goodies is now all the government does.

Practically every Census 2000 pamphlet and advertisement includes a variation on the multibillion-dollar payout theme. The census "isn't just about numbers," says a video on the bureau's Web site. "It's about people ... and communities ... and services. By filling out our census form [sic] we tell our leaders who we are and what we need." The payout campaign has been translated into Hmong, Arabic, Chinese, Laotian, Japanese, Khmer, Korean, Polish, Russian, Tagalog, Thai, and Vietnamese, a peculiar civics lesson for the government to be teaching the newest Americans. The Super Lotto idea is reiterated as Reason No. 3 in the bureau flyer "Five BIG Reasons Why You Should Fill Out Your Census Form": "The numbers are used to help determine the distribution of hundreds of billions of dollars in federal and state funds. We're talking hospitals, highways, stadiums and school lunch programs."

Originally published in *Slate*, April 4, 2000.

Stadiums?!

Not making the "BIG" list is the original reason provided in Article 1, Section 2, of the Constitution: to provide for the apportionment of members of the House of Representatives.

The Census Bureau's propaganda campaign reaches all the way to the schools, where another $18 million is being spent teaching students to pester their parents into completing Census 2000. The bureau's "Census in Schools" Web site offers a raft of free propaganda to teachers: lesson plans for K–12 teachers, a series of "official school newsletters" about the census, fact sheets, Webcast info, adult literacy materials, and more. The lesson plan for Grades 3–4 urges teachers to ask the following questions and to steer the response to the "possible answers":

- What kinds of things does a place with a lot of young children need? *(Possible answers: schools, day care centers, playgrounds.)*
- How do government agencies know where these things are needed? *(Possible answer: they use census data.)*
- Besides promising billions to people who *do* fill out the form, the bureau is threatening hard times for those who *don't*. One Census Bureau public service announcement I heard on the radio warns, "Not filling it out is like inviting a reduction in government services."

That comes closer to the truth than the Super Lotto pitch. Indeed, the federal government allocates about $185 billion in programs and services based on population figures provided by the Census Bureau. The programs range from Medicaid to highway planning and construction to special education and adoption assistance. So, if you ignore the census and everybody else participates, your community will receive proportionately fewer federal dollars. But if everybody completes the form, the jackpot stays the same size and nobody will really come out ahead.

How did the simple business of counting noses for the purposes of representation become a mechanism for allocating government benefits? The first census in 1790 asked just six questions: the name of the head of the household, the number of free white males older than 16, the number of free white males younger than 16, the number of free white females, the number of other free persons, and the number of slaves. (Remember that before the Fourteenth Amendment slaves were counted as three-fifths of a person for purposes of apportioning representation, thus greatly inflating the congressional representation of the enfranchised populations of the slave states.) Later censuses added questions about occupations (for war-planning purposes) and agricultural and industrial production and the like.

The great expansion of the census accompanied the Progressive Era. "By the late nineteenth century," writes Margo J. Anderson in *The American Census: A Social History*, "the traditional role of the census as a mechanism to apportion political representation faded in importance. The statisticians began to think of apportionment as merely a necessary but relatively routine and unimportant footnote in the whole census effort." Reflecting the Progressive Era's mania for social engineering, "the census also became a full-fledged instrument to monitor the overall state of American society." As the New Deal and Great Society administrations increased the number of federal grant programs, the government began calling on the census to "distribute economic power," as Anderson puts it.

The Census 2000 ad campaign's "fair share" message hasn't been lost on some parts of the gay and lesbian community. The Policy Institute of the National Gay and Lesbian Task Force wants same-sex couples to check the "unmarried partners" box on the census. "All public policy flows from the U.S. Census," said an NGLTF spokeswoman. "If we are not counted, we lose out on federal funding for research, funding for community services and passage and implementation of laws that benefit our community." (NGLTF is considering asking the bureau to include sexual orientation questions in the 2010 census. Some homosexuals might not appreciate being asked. By answering truthfully about their sexual behavior, they confess to what is a felony in many states. By ignoring the questionnaire, they face a $100 fine and 60 days in jail. By lying, they could be punished with a $500 fine and one year in jail.)

The problem with the "fair share" PR campaign isn't that it's a lie. The problem is that it's the truth. The government has become a mechanism for distributing largess, and your census form is your ticket. Yes, the census is like a lottery—almost. The difference is that you get to decide whether to play the lottery.

30. The Egyptian Judiciary Blazing the Path to Democracy and Economic Development

The world is watching Egypt. It holds the key to the flourishing of the Arabs. For the Egyptian protesters are marching for one of the most precious elements of good government, of democracy, of freedom, and of prosperity: an independent judiciary.

The protesters understand quite clearly that an independent judiciary is necessary for free elections, to ensure that the law is followed, but it is more than that: an independent judiciary is the linchpin of a flourishing and free society and economy. Law must be predictable for it to provide social order. And it must be perceived to be fair to induce people to cooperate. It's widely understood that even a good person should not be a judge in his own case; it's even more important that the people who make the laws should not be the ones to judge how they are applied in particular cases, especially when their own interests are involved.

Impartial and independent judges are necessary for both democracy and free markets. The famous economist Mancur Olson, who devoted a lifetime to understanding how and why some societies flourish while others fail, identified the independence of the court system as the key, for "the same court system, independent judiciary, and respect for law and individual rights that are needed for a lasting democracy are also required for security of property and contract rights."

Democracy is not just the realization of some mystical "will of the majority," but a system that requires limits on behavior, such as respecting election results, respecting the rights of all to express their views freely, and respecting the rights of normal citizens. And

Originally published in Arabic in *Al Ghad*, May 2006, and distributed on the Arabic Forum of Freedom, www.Minbaralhurriyya.org.

all of those require an independent legal body that can limit the power of the legislative and the executive powers, especially in cases such as Egypt, where the executive holds almost all the reins of power in its hands.

Autocrats cannot be trusted to enforce the laws fairly or—just as importantly—to apply the laws to themselves, because there is no independent power to make them comply. Because of that, they cannot make credible commitments. As Olson pointed out in his last book, *Power and Prosperity*, a pure autocrat, an unlimited sovereign, has no incentive to respect his own promises: "the promise of an autocrat is not enforceable by an independent judiciary or any other independent source of power—by definition autocrats can overrule all other power sources. Due to this situation and the obvious possibility that a dictator could come to take a short-term view, the promises of an autocrat are never completely credible."

That leads to the problem that Nobel Prize winning economist Edward Prescott has named "time inconsistency," in which a ruler makes a commitment at time A, such as not to confiscate the property of people who invest in long-term development projects (for example, a factory), but finds at time B that he has no incentive to respect his earlier promise after the investment has been made. Since at time B the investment has already been made, the autocrat's incentive is to confiscate it. Because of that time inconsistency, no one can trust the autocrat, and no one makes the investment. Everyone suffers as a consequence.

So without an independent judiciary, the government's promises are not credible, and no one can trust the government not to go back on promises to respect rights. And when the judiciary is controlled by self-interested politicians, the promises of citizens when they make contracts among themselves are also rendered less credible, because the parties to a contract can't be sure that they'll get a fair hearing in the event of a dispute. Fair adjudication of disputes matters greatly for the success of an economy. It's long been known that the most successful economies are those that produce goods and services that require long-term planning, which in turn requires a great deal of trust and realistic expectations that long-term deals will be respected.

Egypt has not always been an autocracy. The country has a noble and proud tradition and a history of democracy, of parliamentary government, and of a well-trained and professional judiciary. That judiciary has been under attack for many years. And it has, to the credit of the Egyptian nation, fought back. In 1968 judges demanded greater safeguards of their independence, and over 100 were dismissed. And now a new generation of judges is protesting the silencing of some of their members for speaking out about corruption and election-rigging.

An independent judiciary is central to the reform process in any country, in any part of the world. There is not only no democracy without an independent judiciary; there is no impartial justice, and without impartial justice, there is no long-term investment and no economic development. In many ways, the future of Egypt and of all the Arab people is at stake in the struggle over judicial independence.

31. The "Crime" of Blogging in Egypt

By Raja M. Kamal and Tom G. Palmer

A former college student, Abdelkareem Nabil Soliman, is sitting in an Egyptian prison, awaiting sentencing tomorrow. His alleged "crime": expressing his opinions on a blog. His mistake: having the courage to do so under his own name.

Soliman, 22, was expelled from Al-Azhar University last spring for sharply criticizing the university's rigid curriculum and faulting religious extremism on his blog. He was ordered to appear before a public prosecutor on Nov. 7 on charges of "spreading information disruptive of public order," "incitement to hate Muslims" and "insulting the President." Soliman was detained pending an investigation, and the detention has been renewed four times. He has not had consistent access to lawyers or to his family.

Egyptian authorities have made a mistake in prosecuting Soliman. It is Egypt that will be hurt if he is convicted and sent to prison. That's why sincere friends of Egypt call on the government to drop the charges against him. It is the right thing to do, and it is the best thing for Egypt's standing in the modern world.

The case has gained attention in newspapers the world over and from human rights organizations such as Amnesty International. Informal networks of bloggers have spread the word, notably through http://www.freekareem.org. Last Thursday, bloggers and human rights activists around the globe gathered to call on Egyptian authorities to respect freedom of speech. We echo this call.

Soliman has criticized Egyptian authorities as failing to protect the rights of religious minorities and women. He has expressed his views about religious extremism in very strong terms. He is the first Egyptian blogger to be prosecuted for the content of his remarks. Remarkably, the legal complaint originated with the university that had expelled him; once, it was a great center of learning in the Arab

---

Originally published in *Washington Post*, February 21, 2007, with Raja M. Kamal.

world, but it has been reduced to informing on students for their dissent from orthodoxy.

One of us, Tom Palmer, met Soliman at a conference for bloggers in the Middle East last year. In person, Soliman seemed quiet and shy but very committed to championing women's rights and the rights of minorities.

Palmer kept in touch by Gmail chat. Despite occasional admonitions to be careful about what he posted online and to think about possible consequences of public dissent, Soliman said that he was not afraid to express his views.

Last October, Soliman instant-messaged that he had been ordered to attend an interview with prosecutors the next day. Friends at organizations such as Hands Across the Middle East Support Alliance and the Arabic Network for Human Rights Information quickly found Soliman a lawyer. Word spread when he had been detained, and protests were organized at Egyptian embassies. Soliman had no organized movement or group behind him, but his case came to be known around the world.

We find it shocking that a university would turn a student over to the authorities to be prosecuted for voicing his views. The future of learning and science is at risk when dissenting views are punished rather than debated. Jointly, we have contacted Egyptian authorities to ask that they correct a clear mistake and release Soliman.

Egypt is a signatory to the International Covenant on Civil and Political Rights, which guarantees the "freedom to seek, receive and impart information and ideas of all kinds, regardless of frontiers, either orally, in writing or in print, in the form of art, or through any other media." The exceptions allowed are narrowly drawn and require proof of "necessity" before restrictions can be imposed. The posting of opinions on a student's personal blog hardly qualifies as a threat to national security, to the reputation of the president or to public order.

Soliman is not a threat to Egypt, but this prosecution is.

Whether or not we agree with the opinions that Abdelkareem Nabil Soliman expressed is not the issue. What matters is a principle: People should be free to express their opinions without fear of being imprisoned or killed. Blogging should not be a crime.

516

32. Six Facts about Iraq

I've been to Iraq three times since the fall of Baghdad, and I expect to be back soon. I've learned a few things there that I probably wouldn't have learned had I not gone. Based on those lessons and the kind of information that's available to anyone who takes the time to read, here are six theses about the future of Iraq.

1. *Anyone who is certain about how things are going to turn out doesn't know what he's talking about.* The number of variables is simply too great to foresee the outcome, even in broad terms. The political and military conflicts take place along religious fault lines (Sunni, Shiite, secular); ethnic fault lines (Arab, Kurd, Turkmen); tribal fault lines (too numerous to mention); the fault lines of personal ambition (Moqtada al Sadr vs. Abdel Aziz al Hakim for leadership of the religious Shiite bloc, for example); and regional fault lines (with oil-poor western Iraq pitted against relatively oil-rich northern and southern Iraq). The international situation complicates matters further, with Turkey ready to intervene (with at least tacit Iranian and Syrian support) if the Kurdish autonomous area declares its independence, and with Iranian agents spreading walking-around money throughout the country, but especially among the Shia factions in the south.

Further, as the recent bombing of the Golden Mosque of Samarra shows, the role of contingency and accident is enormous. A gap in security that allows in a suicide bomber or the direction of a single mortar shell could completely change the direction of events. For example, were the Sunni insurgents or Shiite rivals able to assassinate Grand Ayatollah Ali al Sistani, it's impossible to predict the consequences, other than to say that they likely would be horrific, since al-Sistani has been a prominent voice for restraint among the Shiites.

In short, it's impossible to predict Iraq's future.

Originally published in *Reason*, June 2006, pp. 32–35.

517

2. *The war being fought in Iraq is unlike any other.* Parallels with Vietnam are of limited use for the simple reason that the Communists were seeking to kick out the Saigon government and replace it, not to create a firestorm that would engulf the region. For Al Qaeda in Iraq, it won't be over if the U.S. and allied forces withdraw or if the U.S.-backed government falls. In fact, many of those fighting the United States and the elected government don't want the United States to withdraw. They want to draw us in further, hoping, as Al Qaeda leader Ayman al-Zawahiri recently put it, to "make the West bleed for years." Nor is World War II a useful comparison: Once the Fascists and Nazis were beaten, they were beaten. They didn't go underground and wage a war of destruction; their ideology was effectively defeated with their armies.

The goal of at least a large faction among the insurgents is to create maximum chaos and maximum bloodshed. They account for a tiny fraction of the Iraqi population, and no one really knows what percentage of them are foreigners, but they are ruthless and determined. They will also be very difficult to defeat. No accommodation is possible with them. The existence of an armed faction that is dedicated to destruction per se makes the job of defeating the insurgency all the more difficult.

3. *Kurdistan is radically unlike the rest of Iraq.* When I drove around Suleimani, the major city in eastern Kurdistan, I saw new buildings with plenty of plate glass windows. That's a sign of a city that has little fear of suicide bombers or random gunfire. The feeling of relative freedom you get in Kurdish cities is remarkable. The security checkpoints around every city are efficient, and the security forces arrive promptly when they're called.

The Kurdish region presents an interesting case for political scientists, because it offers a chance to test the relative significance of intentions and of institutions. On the one hand, almost everyone seems intent on having a liberal, at least quasi-capitalist democracy. On the other hand, the Kurds have weak civil society institutions and a history of one-party rule; they suffer from the curse of oil (which has been shown time and time again to make the emergence of liberal democracy and free markets improbable, since efforts are devoted to dividing up resource rents rather than to productive activities); and they are surrounded by hostile or potentially hostile parties (a situation that tends to produce an atmosphere of groupthink).

Politics in Kurdistan is dominated by two parties, the Kurdistan Democratic Party (PDK) in the west and the Patriotic Union of Kurdistan (PUK) in the east. I got a sense of their influence when I went to one of the universities to give some lectures. I was told that no weapons could be taken in. This did not sit well with some of my friends, who demanded to know who had decided that. They were told, "It's been decided by the party." They didn't like that, either, and we kept our weapons. What was remarkable was that the answer wasn't "the dean decided it" or "the city council decided it" but "the party decided it." Still, the PDK and the PUK have agreed to allow offices of each party (and of other Iraqi parties) to exist throughout Kurdistan, and there is real debate in Kurdish political life and institutions. There are independent media outlets, and in the libraries of the universities one can find newspapers for every political party. The general direction is promising, but it's hard to overcome years of clan rule, which has been solidified by the organization of parties.

I am optimistic about Kurdistan, but the obstacles to a free society there are still enormous.

4. *The police are substantially unreliable, whereas the army may be the only authentically Iraqi institution in the country.* During a recent briefing with some senior Pentagon officers about the progress of the war in Iraq, I asked about the problem of the infiltration of many police forces by militias, most important among them Moqtada al Sadr's Mahdi Army, which has made inroads in the south. The response was that Sadr is now a part of the political landscape of Iraq and that he will have to be accommodated, as was shown by the renomination of Ibrahim Jafari for the post of prime minister by one vote, which was undoubtedly due to Sadr's influence.

More interesting has been the contrast in training and performance between the police forces and the army. The police forces have been largely ineffectual at stopping the insurgents and are, it seems, often controlled or intimidated by sectarian militias; even the security forces from the Ministry of the Interior are substantially controlled by sectarian forces, notably the Badr Brigades allied with Abdel Aziz al Hakim's Supreme Council for Islamic Revolution in Iraq party.

Meanwhile, the army increasingly has been taking on greater responsibility, accompanied by U.S. advisers, for combat operations in crucial areas of Iraq.

If the insurgents are defeated, it will probably be thanks to the Iraqi Army, not the local police or other security forces (at least outside of Kurdistan), which are perceived by many (often quite rightly) as enforcement arms of sectarian groups. That said, it should be emphasized that some units of the army are perceived as dominated by non-Sunnis and therefore hostile to Sunni interests; creating a nonsectarian national army is a daunting task in a country that has for so long been dominated by sectarian powers.

5. *It is hard for people in liberal democracies to understand the mentality of most Iraqis.* Iraqis live in a society that was long dominated by lies and propaganda. Rather than the clash of views in a free press, they are accustomed to relying on rumors. With the advent of a free press, that has changed somewhat, and people are less likely to believe everything they hear, but rational discourse is still in limited supply. Many Iraqis are convinced that foreign forces are there to steal their oil (which the world is "stealing" at more than $60 a barrel), that the country is wealthy and only requires a good leader to share that wealth (a refrain I heard from many and which I took great pains to explain was a deadly error; Iraq is not a rich society but a desperately poor one), and so on. Moreover, conspiracy theories are the most common form of political understanding. (That is a problem throughout the Middle East, but it is especially pronounced in Iraq.)

The neoconservative assumption that the default condition when you eliminate a dictatorship is liberal democracy has been shown to be false. It is not the default position of mankind but a rare achievement, one that is often won only at a high price.

Adopting the habit of listening to others, of testing claims against evidence, of comparing different sources of news and information, and the other elements of the Enlightenment mentality is proving very difficult. It is not impossible, but it is harder than many expected.

6. *If the United States were to withdraw tomorrow, the country would be plunged into a bloodbath. But if the United States does not make it clear that foreign forces will withdraw, it is unlikely that Iraqis will be able to unite to defeat the terrorists.* The prospect of an indefinite substantial military presence in Iraq will provide a ready scapegoat for all of

the country's problems (including the havoc wreaked by the insurgency). Only the credible prospect of a departure is likely to bring the parties to the table to create a relatively (and I stress relatively) liberal and stable regime for Iraq. And even that might not suffice. The country could break apart. That might not be the worst outcome, but the fighting to determine the borders of the resulting states could be fierce.

If the Bush administration is serious about defeating the insurgents, it has to realize that the Iraqis are better placed to do so and that they will have more incentive to do so if they know that the United States will be leaving.

There is a chance that things will turn out well in Iraq, or at least not badly. Whatever the outcome, libertarians should be eager to assist the Iraqis in creating a free society. That's why my Arab friends and I have established the Forum of Liberty (www.minbaralhurri yya.org) to bring the message of liberty to both Iraqis and the wider Arab world. I am working with Iraqi libertarians who are trying to do the best they can under very difficult circumstances to combat fanaticism, terrorism, and statism. It's a hard slog, but we have no choice.

33. Moscow's Pride and Prejudice

The debate over whether Moscow will witness a Gay Pride parade in May (2006) carries important implications for Russia's future.

How the Moscow authorities respond to the threats of violence issued by Talgat Tajuddin of Russia's Central Spiritual Governance for Muslims is important in its own right. According to Tajuddin, "The parade should not be allowed, and if they still come out into the streets, then they should be bashed."

Such threats have no place in a society governed by law. No one should be subjected to violence for holding hands in the street or walking peacefully in a parade. That much should be clear.

But the question of whether the parade should be allowed also raises a bigger question about whether Russia will be a leader in industry, technology, art, culture and science or will retreat to insularity and backwardness. It is a question of whether to be an open society or a closed one.

And how it is answered has implications that go far beyond whether someone likes or dislikes gay people.

Studies of American and Canadian cities have demonstrated quite effectively that the more open and welcoming a city or region is to peaceful diversity, the more economically productive, prosperous, and commercially and technologically advanced it is likely to be.

In a pioneering study of urban life in America published by the Urban Institute in 2001, Richard Florida of George Mason University and Gary Gates of the Urban Institute created a measure of homosexual presence in an urban population and then correlated it with the presence of high-tech industries and economic growth.

They concluded that "gays not only predict the concentration of high-tech industry, they are also a predictor of its growth. Five of the cities that rank in the top 10 for high-technology growth from 1990 to 1998 rank in the top 10 for the 'Gay Index.'"

Originally published in the *Washington Blade*, March 24, 2006.

They also found a strong correlation between the presence of artistic and creative people—writers, photographers, sculptors, actors—and high-tech industries. Of especially great importance to Russia, which faces a long-term demographic crisis, they discovered a robust correlation between the percentage who are foreign born and the success of high-tech industries.

It seems that it's not a case of the old cliché that "those people" are creative, but instead it turns out that places that exhibit lots of creativity are places that are open to creativity.

How does toleration of gay people figure into economic success? It is a good proxy of the openness and toleration of a society generally. And such openness and toleration is conducive to the flourishing of a society.

As Gary Gates put it during an Urban Institute conference on "The Demographics of Diversity," the presence of a gay population is important because, "They add to a social climate of tolerance toward diversity in cities, and that has specific positive economic outcomes for various regions and cities. The argument here is that a vibrant gay and lesbian community provides one of the strongest signals of diversity and tolerance, both within neighborhoods and cities."

It's rather obvious that welcoming talent is an essential condition for attracting it.

This is not a new issue. The relationship between toleration and prosperity has been known for a long time. The Netherlands emerged in Europe as a leader in commerce, the arts, technology and industry many years ago because of the greater degree of toleration it afforded minorities.

The decision about whether to allow a Gay Pride parade down Tverskaya Street in Moscow is not merely approval or disapproval of seeing gay people in public. It is much more a decision about Russia's future.

Thirteen years ago, Russia's democratically elected leaders made the right choice by decriminalizing homosexual love. In doing so, they advanced into the front ranks of modern, progressive, open societies.

The debate over whether to allow a Gay Pride parade in Moscow is a proxy for the much wider debate about whether Russia will choose to be counted among the nations known for creativity in technology, science, art, culture and wealth, or among those known for insularity, prejudice, poverty, and backwardness.

34. Challenges of Democratization

Introducing, consolidating, and maintaining democracy is not an easy task. Like all the good things in life, democracy faces many challenges. But they can all be overcome. Very importantly, we can learn from the experiences of others who have emerged from lawless dictatorship and tyranny to constitutional democracy.

1. The Challenge of Expectations

Expectations Too High

If expectations are unrealistically high and people expect that democracy will automatically deliver prosperity, health, education, and the other good things of life, they will become disappointed and support for democracy will drop. Democracy is not magic. Having a democracy does not guarantee instant wealth, health, or happiness. All that democracy can guarantee is the right to "the *pursuit* of happiness." It cannot guarantee the achievement of happiness, or even good fortune. Those must be earned by effort in a law-governed and just society in which the rewards to effort are protected by law and not confiscated by the injustice of the powerful.

Expectations Too Low

If expectations are too low, if people expect and accept unfair elections, illegal and unjust behavior by government officials, and violent exploitation by the police, then they will resign themselves to living with the outward form of democracy but without its substance. For democracy to be successful, citizens must expect as a matter of course that judges, governors, city councilors, mayors, members of parliament, presidents, ministers, and police officers will act in accordance with the law. In a corrupt and non-democratic state, the citizens are surprised when government officials act *legally*.

Speech delivered to members of the Iraqi National Assembly in the Assembly Hall, April 12, 2005, during a lecture visit to several cities in Iraq.

In a law-governed democratic state, the citizens are surprised when government officials act *illegally*.

Realistic expectations are a key element to consolidating democracy and making it stable. If people expect magical outcomes, they will be disappointed and will abandon democracy. On the other hand, if they do not expect just behavior from government officials and fair elections, they may not be disappointed, but they will certainly not long enjoy democracy.

2. The Challenge of Honor

It is important that honorable men and women come to understand that it is more honorable to accept a defeat in a fair election—in a law-governed democratic state—than to refuse to accept the outcome and to fight against it with weapons. In many societies emerging into democracy, it is difficult for people who have been opponents or who believe strongly in their causes to accept that the other side may fairly win an election. It may be hard to learn that there is more honor in accepting the results of a constitutional process than in challenging it by force. The status of the "loyal opposition" is an honorable one. The loyal opposition may someday become the government, and when that happens, the current government will show its commitment to honor by becoming the loyal opposition. What is dishonorable is rejecting the outcome of a fair election in a constitutional democratic state.

The honorableness of democracy is made easier to achieve when it is widely understood that to lose an election is not to lose everything, because a constitutional democracy protects the rights to life, liberty, and property and makes it possible for the honorable and loyal opposition of today to become the government in a future election.

3. The Challenge of Pluralism

Theories of democracy that are based on claims about the "will of the nation" are almost always doomed to failure. A nation may be made up of many individuals, families, tribes, religious communities, towns, regions, and ethnic groups. A nation is not like one person, who may have one decided opinion about something. A nation will contain within itself many opinions about many important matters, and not all of them will agree. If a democratic state tries to insist on uniformity in too many things, the nation will find itself divided against itself. There will be conflict, and that conflict may even become violent.

It is important that the issues to be decided by democratic processes be limited if democracy is to be harmonious and stable. In a stable constitutional democracy many issues are not decided by democratic elections, but are reserved to the free choices of individuals and groups, whose rights are protected by the constitution.

Constitutionally protected liberties are especially important in nations with "permanent minorities," such as small ethnic or religious groups. If they think that they can never become a majority capable of winning an election, *and* that their most basic rights will be taken away if they are in the minority, then they may be so alienated from the democratic process that they may resort to violence. Freedom of religion, freedom to choose to cover one's hair or not, freedom to speak one's language of choice, and freedom to assemble with others without fear of arrest or harassment: All those are protected in the Constitution of a democratic state and are not affected by the changing outcomes of majority decisions.

There is no one "will of the nation," but many different wills, views, interests, and opinions. One must beware of the politician who claims that there is a will of the nation and that he (or she) is its only legitimate voice. If it were ever meaningful to speak of the "will of the nation," it would only be in reference to the Constitution itself and not to any particular leader or to any particular decision on a matter of policy. The Constitution itself, including its protections of rights, is the measure of the unity of the nation.

4. The Challenge of Justice

Especially in pluralistic societies with strong ethnic, religious, familial, tribal, or linguistic variety, there is a danger that democracy may be perverted into an instrument of injustice. Some politicians may blame national problems on other groups, quite often minorities, and then demand that the state take their wealth and punish them. Opportunistic and unjust politicians may demand that the goods of some be redistributed to their own supporters. The state may be reduced to an instrument of plunder. In such a state, no one's life, liberty, or property will be safe; the group that wins today and plunders all the others may lose tomorrow and lose all that they had gained—and even more. Everyone loses in the long run.

By limiting the actions of the state to the provision of justice, and by not considering state policy as a means of rewarding political support and punishing opposition, a constitutional democratic state creates the conditions for prosperity for all.

By attempting to rob from some to give to others, a state merely creates universal poverty, except, of course, for those who manage to gain supreme power and who never lack for palaces and expensive cars. The defense of justice against aggression and violence must be the primary concern of the state. When the state itself becomes an instrument of aggression and violence, democracy itself is in danger.

35. The Tragedy of the Welfare State

The welfare state has something in common with fishing. If no one owns and is responsible for the fish in the lake, but does own all the fish he or she can catch and pull out of the lake, everyone tries to catch the most fish. Each reasons that "if I don't catch the fish, someone else will." Each of us may know that catching lots of fish now means that the lake will be fished out, but so long as others can catch whatever I don't catch, none of us have an incentive to limit our fishing and let the fish population replenish itself.[1] Fish are caught faster than they can breed; the waters are fished out; and in the end everyone is worse off.

Environmentalists, economists, and political scientists call that the "tragedy of the commons." It's a serious problem and is at the root of a great deal of the environmental crises facing the world today, from depleted ocean fisheries to air and water pollution and other problems. But it's not limited to environmental problems. The welfare state operates like a commons, too, and the tragedy is unfolding as you read this. In modern welfare states, everyone has an incentive to act like the irresponsible fishermen who fish out the lake, except that the resource we're plundering is each other. Each person seeks to get as much as he can from his neighbors, but at the same time his neighbors are trying to get as much as they can from him or her. The welfare state institutionalizes what the French economist Frédéric Bastiat called "reciprocal plunder."[2]

Because we can plunder each other, people reason, "if I don't get that government subsidy, someone else will," and each has an incentive to exploit the resource to exhaustion. They justify taking government funds on the grounds that they're "just getting back what they paid in taxes," even when some of them are getting a lot more than was ever taken from them. Everyone has an incentive to take. This tragedy has a dimension not present in the case of the

Originally published in *After the Welfare State*, edited by Tom G. Palmer. Ottawa, IL: Jameson Books, 2012.

depleted fisheries; because we're plundering each other, we not only spend resources to plunder our neighbors, but we also spend resources to avoid being plundered by those same neighbors, which makes us all worse off to that extent. Not only are we plundered, but we are increasingly being plundered beyond all sustainable levels. The result is exhaustion. It's where we're heading now with welfare states:

- Governments have promised so many benefits to so many constituencies, all at the expense of each other, that the systems are unsustainable, but none of the recipients want to give up their benefits. We might do so in exchange for lower taxes, but we don't even get that choice. Governments can borrow the money and put the taxes off until later, that is, until after the next election, when they'll promise even more, to be financed by more borrowing.

- The pensioner demands an increase in state pension payments and even argues that it's just payback for what was paid in. Those pensions are financed on a "PAYGO" ("Pay-As-You-Go") basis, meaning that the taxes taken from current workers are paid out to current recipients. Any surplus of taxes over expenditures is just "invested" in government bonds, that is, promises to pay out of future taxes. That's all the U.S. government's "Social Security Trust Fund" is: a big "IOU" "nestled in the bottom drawer of an unremarkable government file cabinet."[3] There really is no "Trust Fund." It's a gigantic scam. Today's young people are being forced to pay for their grandparents' retirement, their parents' retirement, and—if they have any money left over—they will have to finance their own. State pension schemes are indistinguishable in their structure from classic "pyramid schemes," also known as "Ponzi schemes" or "Chain Letters," which require that the base of people paying in increases indefinitely; when it stops growing, the pyramid collapses. Governments can postpone the inevitable by printing money or by borrowing money, but it's just that, a postponement, and with each postponement, the situation becomes worse. You can hear the rumblings of collapse now.

- The farmer demands a subsidy for his crops, which comes at the expense of taxpaying autoworkers; automobile firms and autoworkers demand "protection" from more affordable imports, as well as bailouts for failed firms. The trade restrictions raise the prices of vehicles for farmers and the bailouts for automobile firms raise the taxes paid by farmers. Autoworkers are plundered for the benefit of farmers, and farmers are plundered for the benefit of autoworkers. The cycle of reciprocal plunder goes round and round, with the vast majority of "winners" being losers after the cycle is completed. (Some, of course, who specialize in manipulating the political system and negotiating what Ayn Rand called the "aristocracy of pull,"[4] win much more than they lose. Politically connected Wall Street firms such as Goldman Sachs, mega agricultural firms such as Archer Daniels Midland, and others have profited handsomely from the aristocracy of pull.)

- We are boxed by tax systems into medical "insurance" systems (in the United States, payments for private insurance are tied to wages, while wage taxes finance "Medicare," and in Europe they are tied to taxes and in some cases to private insurers); this "third-party financing" affects the choices available to us. Since such pre-paid "insurance" typically pays for routine care, as well as catastrophic events (like injuries from car accidents, being diagnosed with cancer, or falling sick), we have to ask for permission from the insurer, whether private or state, before we get treatment. More often than not, "health insurance" is not really "insurance," although it's called that; it's pre-paid medical care, which creates incentives among consumers to overuse it, and incentives among insurance companies and governments to monitor consumers to determine whether we qualify for benefits. As consumers, we can't exercise the same choices as customers that we exercise with respect to other important goods, so we are forced to act like supplicants, rather than customers, and increasingly medical care is rationed by administrators, rather than purchased by customers.

Benefits to particular identifiable groups are concentrated and costs are diffused over vast numbers of taxpayers and consumers, giving beneficiaries incentives to grab for more, while the plundered have little incentive to defend their interests. Each one thinks himself or herself lucky when he or she gets a benefit, but doesn't stop to think of the cost of the benefits to everyone else; when everyone acts that way, the costs become enormous. The poor suffer the worst, because a trickle of benefits may seem like a boon to them, when their very poverty is both perpetuated by the welfare state and deepened by the hidden transfers from the powerless to the powerful caused by protectionism, licensing, and other restrictions on labor market freedom, and all the other privileges and special deals the powerful, the educated, the articulate, and the empowered create for themselves at the expense of the weak, the uneducated, the voiceless, and the disempowered.

Immigrants are systematically demonized as "here to get our welfare benefits." Rather than welcoming people to come and produce wealth, subjects of welfare states act to protect "their welfare benefits" by excluding would-be immigrants and demonizing them as locusts and looters.[5] Meanwhile, political elites loudly proclaim that they are helping poor people abroad by using money taken from taxpayers to fund a parasitic international "aid industry," dumping huge quantities of the agricultural surpluses that have been generated by welfare state policies (to subsidize farmers by guaranteeing floor prices for their products), and handing over loot to autocratic governments: in short, by internationalizing the welfare state. The entire process has been a disaster; it has undermined democratic accountability in developing nations, because the political leaders know that it is the foreign aid masters whose concerns must be addressed, not those of local citizens and taxpayers; it has fueled warlordism and civil war; and it has destroyed indigenous productive institutions.[6]

While citizen is set against citizen and citizen against immigrant in a vast system of mutual plunder (and defense against plunder), bureaucracies extend their control and both create and nurture the political constituencies that sustain them.

But mutual plunder is not the only salient characteristic of the modern welfare state. It has created one crisis after another, each an unintended consequence of foolish policies adopted for political reasons by politicians who don't have to bear the consequences of their policies. Two are gripping the world as I write this.

The Financial Crisis and the Welfare State

The financial crisis emerged at the intersection of human motivations and bad incentives. Those incentives were created by foolish policies, all of them traceable to the philosophy that it's government's purpose to control our behavior, to take from Peter to give to Paul, and to usurp responsibility for our lives.[7] The seeds of the current crisis were planted in 1994 when the U.S. administration announced a grandiose plan to raise home ownership rates in the United States from 64 percent to 70 percent of the population, through the "National Partnership in Homeownership," a partnership between the federal government and banks, home builders, financiers, realtors, and others with a special interest. As Gretchen Morgenson and Joshua Rosner document in *Reckless Endangerment: How Outsized Ambition, Greed, and Corruption Led to Economic Armageddon,* "The partnership would achieve its goals by 'making homeownership more affordable, expanding creative financing, simplifying the home buying process, reducing transaction costs, changing conventional methods of design and building less expensive houses, among other means.'"[8] That extension to the welfare state seemed to sound so reasonable to many. Why should people not own their own homes just because they haven't saved for a down payment? Or don't have good credit records? Or don't have jobs?

Why not make home ownership "more affordable" through "creative financing?" Government agencies, such as the Federal Housing Administration, and "government-sponsored enterprises," such as the Federal National Mortgage Association ("Fannie Mae"), were directed to convert renters into owners by lowering down-payment rates, drastically lowering lending standards among banks, increasing the amounts of money going into the home market by buying and "securitizing" more mortgages, and a host of other measures. It was a bipartisan effort at social engineering. The Federal Housing Administration under the Bush administration offered loan guarantees on mortgages with zero percent down payment rates. As Alphonso Jackson, acting secretary of the Department of Housing and Urban Development, gushed in 2004, "Offering FHA mortgages with no down payment will unlock the door to homeownership for hundreds of thousands of American families, particularly minorities." He added, "We do not anticipate any costs to taxpayers."[9]

The U.S. government deliberately and systematically undermined traditional banking standards and encouraged—in fact, demanded—increasingly risky lending. Risks that turned out well would generate private profits, and risks that turned out badly would fall on the taxpayers, for "a banker confronted with these new relaxed requirements could off-load any risky loans to the government-sponsored enterprises responsible for financing home mortgages for millions of Americans."[10] Private profits and socialized losses characterized the intersection of welfare statism and cronyism.

Home prices went up and up and up as more and more money was pumped into housing. It was like a party. Everyone was feeling richer, as the prices of their homes sky-rocketed. People took out "adjustable rate mortgages" to buy homes bigger than they were able to afford, because they expected to sell them before interest rates went up again. Credit was easy, and Americans took out second mortgages to finance vacations and boat purchases. More and more houses were built in anticipation of ever-rising prices. The result was a housing bubble of enormous magnitude. People bought houses to "flip" them and sell them to the next buyers. Meanwhile, government financial regulators worldwide rated as low-risk what were in fact high-risk loans, including both government debt (bonds) and mortgage-backed securities.[11] German banks bought Greek government debt and banks in the United States and all over the world bought mortgage-backed securities that they were led to believe were guaranteed by the U.S. government.

The interventionist policies of the U.S. government to make homeownership more affordable, expand "creative financing," and destroy sound banking practices were coupled with the arrogance of global government financial regulators who were sure that they knew the real magnitudes of the risks—and market participants risking their own funds did not. The result was that the global financial system was poisoned with risky loans, bad debts, and toxic assets, with disastrous results. Mortgage defaults rose as interest rates rose, and those "low-risk" mortgage-backed securities that institutions had been encouraged to buy turned out to be not so low risk, after all. Savings were wiped out, home owners found themselves unable to pay mortgages, financial institutions crashed and burned, and economic output fell. Numerous distortions of incentives caused by the entire system of intervention in both housing and financial markets are to blame, but without the policy of the American welfare state of "making housing more affordable" and "creative financing," the financial crisis would not have happened. The global financial train wreck was the outcome of one bad policy piled on another; it was a train wreck set in motion by the welfare state.[12]

The Debt Crisis and the Welfare State

While governments in the United States and some European countries were frantically pumping up a gigantic housing bubble, the explosion of spending on welfare state programs for retirement pensions, medical care, and many other programs has plunged the governments of the world into a debt crisis. Much attention has been focused on the huge increase in government debt, and it has indeed been staggering. At the same time, those numbers are small when compared to the accumulated mountains of unfunded liabilities, that is, promises that have been made to citizens and on which they are relying, for which there is no corresponding financing. If a private firm were to mislead the public and its principals about the magnitude of its obligations, as governments systematically do, the officers of the firm would be imprisoned for fraud. Governments manage to exempt themselves from sound accounting practices and deliberately and systematically mislead the public about the obligations they are loading onto the shoulders of future taxpayers. Governments find it easy to promise today to pay money in the future. But the future is arriving very fast.

Economists Jagadeesh Gokhale and Kent Smetters calculated (rather conservatively) in 2006 that the total federal budgetary imbalance for the U.S. government in 2012 would be about $80 *trillion.* The budgetary imbalance is defined as "the difference in present value between what the government is projected to spend under current law on all expenditure categories—entitlements, defense, roads, and everything else—and what it is projected to receive in taxes across all revenue accounts."[13] That was in 2006; Gokhale is currently updating the numbers, which he predicts will be higher. As Gokhale wrote, "Add the likely health-care cost increases associated with the new health-care law and this number is probably too optimistic, but we won't know until my project nears completion. For Europe, I estimate an overall imbalance of ¢53.1 trillion as of 2010. That is, 434 percent of the combined annual GDP of twenty-seven EU countries of ¢12.2 trillion. That is also an under-estimate because the projections are made only through 2050 (unlike the U.S. projections, which stretch into perpetuity)."[14]

That means that those promises cannot be fulfilled and will not be fulfilled. Taxes would have to rise to astronomical levels to fund even a fraction of the current promises. Governments are far more likely not only to default on their acknowledged debts (bonds held by creditors), but to repudiate the promises made to citizens for pensions, health care, and other benefits. They have been lying to their citizens for years about their finances, and the lies are made explicit when the promises are broken because they *cannot* be fulfilled, as we are seeing unfolding before our eyes in Greece. One way to repudiate their promises is to turn on the printing presses and pay them with piles of paper money, with more and more zeroes added to each note, which is to say, the currencies in which the promises are redeemed would be dramatically devalued. (Inflation is especially harmful as a means of dealing with debt, for it both distorts behavior and falls disproportionately on the poor and those unable to shield themselves from it.) The welfare states we know may be collapsing in slow motion in some countries, rapidly in others, but they are collapsing all the same and, as always, the burden will fall mostly on those lacking the political connections and the sophistication to avoid the consequences.

Many people indignantly respond to such facts by citing their intentions, in disregard of consequences. "Our aim is to help people; we did not deliberately aim to crash the world financial system by intervening into markets to make housing more affordable and lowering banking standards, nor did we intend to bankrupt our country!" they say. As the philosopher Daniel Shapiro quite aptly noted, "Institutions cannot be adequately characterized by their aims."[15] The best aims in the world, if combined with bad incentives via the wrong institutions, can generate terrible outcomes.[16] The intentions of advocates of the welfare state are irrelevant to the outcomes of their policies.[17] Most "political philosophy," as it is commonly practiced, is about comparing one intuition about right and wrong with another. That, frankly, is not very helpful to the task of creating institutions that work, that are sustainable, and that are just. For that we need much more than the mere comparison of intuitions; we need history, economics, sociology, and political science, not merely moral theory divorced from practice.

The Future is Imperiled, but Not Lost

The welfare states of today are directly responsible for the two great economic crises that are gripping the world: the global financial crisis that has turned economic growth rates negative in many countries and wiped out trillions of dollars of asset valuation, and the debt crisis that has rocked Europe and threatens to bring down some of the world's most powerful governments, currencies, and financial systems. Even the best of intentions can generate terrible consequences when implemented through perverse incentives and institutions.

The story is not all doom and gloom, however. We can get out from under the welfare state and its crushing debts, humiliating bureaucracies, and reciprocal plunder. It won't be easy and it will mean summoning the courage to stand up to special interests and manipulative politicians. But it can be done and it must be done. Those who have demonstrated in the streets against "budget cuts" (usually merely cuts in the rates of increase in spending) are demonstrating against arithmetic. You can't keep adding negative numbers to negative numbers and get a positive sum; the numbers don't add up. We need demonstrations in the streets on behalf of reason, of fiscal responsibility, of cutting back the state, of freeing and empowering people to decide their own futures. We need a rolling back of the state's powers so that it is limited to protecting our rights, not attempting to take care of us. We need clear-eyed decisionmaking about the capabilities of the state. We need an end to the welfare state.

Notes

1. "If land is not owned by anybody, although legal formalism may call it public property, it is used without any regard to the disadvantages resulting. Those who are in a position to appropriate to themselves the returns—lumber and game of the forests, fish of the water areas, and mineral deposits of the subsoil—do not bother about the later effects of their mode of exploitation. For them, erosion of the soil, depletion of the exhaustible resources and other impairments of the future utilization are external costs not entering into their calculation of input and output. They cut down trees without any regard for fresh shoots or reforestation. In hunting and fishing, they do not shrink from methods preventing the repopulation of the hunting and fishing grounds." Ludwig von Mises, *Human Action: A Treatise on Economics*, in 4 vols., ed. Bettina Bien Greaves (Indianapolis: Liberty Fund, 2007), vol. 2, chapter 6: *The Limits of Property Rights and the Problems of External Costs and External Economies.* Accessed from oll.libertyfund.org/title/1894/110599 on 2012-03-25.

2. Frédéric Bastiat, *Selected Essays on Political Economy*, trans. Seymour Cain, ed. George B. de Huszar, introduction by F. A. Hayek (Irvington-on-Hudson: Foundation for Economic Education, 1995), chapter 5: *The State* 1. Accessed from oll.liberty fund.org/title/956/35453 on 2012-04-02.

3. "Social Security trust fund sits in West Virginia file cabinet," *USA Today*, February 28, 2005, www.usatoday.com/news/washington/2005-02-28-trust-fund_x.htm.

4. Ayn Rand, *Atlas Shrugged* (New York: Signet, 1985), pp. 381–82.

5. Many of the claims about immigrants are factually incorrect, as immigrants in the United States, at least, typically pay more to the welfare state in taxes than they receive in benefits and in the past have contributed enormously to the economic dynamism and prosperity of the societies to which they emigrated by creating new businesses. The issues are canvassed in chapter 3 of Jason L. Riley, *Let Them In: The Case for Open Borders* (New York: Gotham Books, 2008), pp. 91–125.

6. The international reach of the welfare state has also had horrendous consequences, which are well documented in a number of studies, including Dambisa Moyo, *Dead Aid: Why Aid Is Not Working and How There Is Another Way for Africa* (London: Allen Lane, 2009); Graham Hancock, *Lords of Poverty: The Power, Prestige, and Corruption of the International Aid Business* (New York: Atlantic Monthly Press, 1989); and Michael Maren, *The Road to Hell: The Devastating Effects of Foreign Aid and International Charity* (New York: The Free Press, 1997), among many important works. A pioneering study of the effects of aid was P. T. Bauer's *Dissent on Development* (Cambridge, MA: Harvard University Press, 1976).

7. See the debate on the responsibility and state power in David Schmidtz and Robert E. Goodin, *Social Welfare and Individual Responsibility: For and Against* (Cambridge: Cambridge University Press, 1998).

8. Gretchen Morgenson and Joshua Rosner, *Reckless Endangerment: How Outsized Ambition, Greed, and Corruption Led to Economic Armageddon* (New York: Times Books, Henry Holt & Co., 2011), pp. 2–3.

9. Lew Sichelman, "Bush to Offer Zero Down FHA Loan," *Realty Times*, January 20, 2004, http://realtytimes.com/rtpages/20040120_zerodown.htm.

10. Gretchen Morgenson and Joshua Rosner, *Reckless Endangerment*, p. 38.

11. "Any mortgage that a GSE [Government Sponsored Enterprise] would securitize was, under the Basel rules [the global regulations adopted by governments], profitable for American banks to originate—and profitable for them to buy back as part of a security." Jeffrey Friedman, "A Crisis of Politics, Not Economics: Complexity, Ignorance, and Policy Failure," *Critical Review*, vol. 21, nos. 2–3 (2009), p. 144.

12. For more of the details on the combination of Federal Reserve policies to lower interest rates, government-backed "securitization" of mortgages, and international financial regulations that rated government debt and mortgage-backed security as "low risk," see Johan Norberg, *Financial Fiasco: How America's Infatuation with Home Ownership and Easy Money Created the Economic Crisis* (Washington, D.C.: Cato Institute, 2009). See also *Critical Review*, "Special Issue: Causes of the Crisis," ed. by Jeffrey Friedman, vol. 21, nos., 2–3 (2009), and Jeffrey Friedman and Wladimir Kraus, *Engineering the Financial Crisis: Systemic Risk and the Failure of Regulation* (Philadelphia: University of Pennsylvania Press, 2011).

13. Jagadeesh Gokhlae and Kent Smetters, "Do the Markets Care About the $2.4 Trillion U.S. Deficit?" *Financial Analysts Journal*, vol. 63, no. 3, 2007.

14. Personal communication with the author, March 26, 2012.

15. Daniel Shapiro, *Is the Welfare State Justified?* (Cambridge: Cambridge University Press, 2007), p. 5. Shapiro's book offers a fair-minded comparison of the justificatory claims made on behalf of welfare states with the evidence for their performance.

16. An example is the insistence of welfare state champion James P. Sterba that deliberate killing-by-starvation of productive citizens is appropriate to induce them to produce more so that the state can confiscate and redistribute the results of their productive efforts. Sterba argues that the right to welfare is a "negative right" that

is consistent with the freedom of all and proposes, on the basis of following his intuitions, to threaten to confiscate the "nonsurplus resources" of productive people, i.e., not only the surplus over what is necessary to survive, but the food needed for physical survival, as well, in order to induce the productive to produce more for the state to redistribute. This professor of philosophy believes that it is consistent with respecting the freedom of productive people to threaten them with deliberate starvation, for "our producer could respond by doing nothing. The poor [*in practice, of course, the state, allegedly acting on behalf of the poor—TGP*] could then appropriate the nonsurplus resources of the producer, and then, by not producing more, the producer would just waste away, because she is unwilling to be more productive." "Just waste away" is Sterba's euphemism for the catabolysis, edema, organ failure, and other symptoms of death by starvation. James P. Sterba, "Equality is compatible with and required by liberty," in Jan Narveson and James P. Sterba, *Are Liberty and Equality Compatible?: For and Against* (Cambridge: Cambridge University Press, 2010), p. 23. For chilling descriptions of how Sterba's proposal worked in practice, see Timothy Snyder, *Bloodlands: Europe Between Hitler and Stalin* (New York: Basic Books, 2010), and Frank Dikötter, *Mao's Great Famine: The History of Chinas Most Devastating Catastrophe, 1958–1962* (New York: Walker Publishing Co., 2010). Sweeping proposals based purely on intuitions about morality and justice that are untested against any knowledge of economics, sociology, or history generally lead to disaster and are, to say the least, morally irresponsible.

17. There is an abundant literature on the moral claims regarding the welfare state, mostly starting with intentions and ending with intentions. I address some of that literature in my essay "Saving Rights Theory from Its Friends," which originally appeared in *Individual Rights Reconsidered*, ed. Tibor Machan (Stanford: Hoover Institution Press, 2001). That version can be downloaded from http://tomgpal mer.com/wp-content/uploads/papers/palmer-individualrightsreconsidered-chap ter2.pdf. It was reprinted in Tom G. Palmer, *Realizing Freedom: Libertarian Theory, History, and Practice* (Washington, D.C.: Cato Institute, 2009), pp. 41–83.

36. Working for Liberty

After spending many years in the libertarian movement, I'm enormously pleased to know that it has grown so large and that it continues to attract so many bright young people. It warms my heart to see so many wonderful people at libertarian gatherings all over the world. I'd like to muse a bit about what motivates us to do what we do, and about the various shapes that our action has taken over the years.

In the early 1970s, I was active in organizations and even causes that are no longer around. In late 1971 I joined the Young Americans for Freedom, read some libertarian works, and joined YAF's remaining libertarian faction. I became a state officer. In 1974, I ran a statewide Republican youth campaign on behalf of H. L. "Bill" Richardson's Senate candidacy, then quit the conservative movement and never looked back. Of much greater significance for my life was the fact that I managed to meet some libertarians who were more visionary than others and—this is really the key—more effective and more linear in their thinking.

One of those people was Ed Crane, whom I met at a libertarian meeting in 1973 in southern California. Ed went on to found the Cato Institute. It was at a libertarian meeting at UCLA shortly after that, I think, that I met R. A. Childs, Jr., a truly brilliant libertarian writer, as well as the economists David Henderson and Harry Watson, and others whom I admired greatly. That year, I started my studies at the University of Southern California and had the honor of learning (if only a little and inadequately) from John Hospers, the philosophy professor who had been the 1972 presidential candidate of the then brand-new Libertarian Party. John served as campus adviser to our Campus Libertarian Society, which campaigned for

This speech was delivered to several hundred former Cato Institute research interns at the Cato Institute Intern Reunion in 2010. It was published in *Liberty*, November 10, 2010.

tax cuts, marijuana legalization, and elimination of the draft, much to the confusion of leftists and rightists who couldn't quite "get" us. During my time in high school and then my early entry (at 16) to USC, I met and became friends with such interesting people as the late Priscilla "P. K." Slocum, who was a pioneering libertarian bookseller and a wonderful libertarian mentor, Tibor Machan, Murray Rothbard, George H. Smith, Manuel Klausner, Wendy McElroy, and others, most of them still very much alive and still valued friends.

It was an exciting time. The world seemed ready to embrace our ideas. The state was clearly on its last legs. To characterize some enthusiastic libertarians of the day, Murray Rothbard, the economist and libertarian political theorist, deployed the term *Luftmensch* ("air person"), which could be translated as "someone who floats through life without connection to anything substantial." The label was appropriate for more than a few. There were some rather colorful people around.

In any event, I pursued my passion for liberty as a youthful organizer, making trouble for "the state," and driving all over California to visit high school and college campuses, trying to spread the ideas of liberty and hasten the collapse of the welfare-warfare regime. I helped set up libertarian clubs, worked for marijuana decriminalization, campaigned against the draft and militarism, organized antitax rallies, and so on. In 1975, after a stint writing copy for an advertising agency, I started working full-time as one of two employees of the Libertarian Party—Linda Webb was the other. Our base was the party's national office at 550 Kearney Street, San Francisco. We were a convenient two blocks away from the office of Ed Crane, who was then party chairman. I had an apartment on Larkin Street for which I paid $100 a month. When I opened the bed, there was literally no place to stand.

What was the cause of my enthusiasm for the libertarian movement? Books were a major inspiration. I had read Lane and Rand and Rothbard, Bastiat and Hazlitt, and Mises and Hayek (but did not appreciate Hayek at the time as much as I did later), and I wanted to change the world, to rid it of communism, fascism, socialism, and all other forms of oppression. (I also tried to read various conservative and socialist books, but found the disconnection from basic principles of economics—indeed, of the ideas of cause and effect—

too jarring.) In high school I had subscribed to *The Freeman*, from which I learned a great deal, and had also bought from its publisher, the Foundation for Economic Education, Mises' "Planned Chaos," "Human Action," and other works. I sent tons of money to Laissez Faire Books, Books for Libertarians, and Academic Associates—a book and audio recording review and sales service that Nathaniel Branden and others set up. I remember how impressed I was when I preordered George H. Smith's book "Atheism: The Case Against God" from Academic Associates; after my check was cashed, the firm went broke, but I got what I ordered and it came out of the individuals' own pockets. That devotion to paying their debts made an impression on me. Loathing for Richard Nixon was another inspiration. He was the great political presence in the late 1960s and early '70s in America, and you loved him or hated him. By 1973–74, more and more people seemed to hate him. He brilliantly combined so many things for a friend of liberty to hate: prosecution of a pointless and destructive war; wage and price controls; fiat money and inflation; illegal and arbitrary exercises of power. The collapse of the GOP seemed the perfect moment for the growth of a new party, a new political alignment, and a libertarian movement that would put an end to coercion, war, theft, censorship, and oppression. Well, we made a good start, I think. The world might be a lot worse if we hadn't made our best effort.

Knowing the interesting people of the libertarian movement was also important. I worked with Ed Crane on a number of projects, including the presidential campaigns of Roger MacBride in 1976 and of Ed Clark in 1980. In 1982, I was statewide campaign manager of the Dan Dougherty for Governor campaign in California. In 1975, I was on the Libertarian Party's platform committee and got to work with a lot of interesting people—including Rothbard; Walter Grinder, then teaching economics and later involved with the Institute for Humane Studies and other organizations; Williamson M. (Bill) Evers, now at the Hoover Institution; and Robert Nozick, whose 1974 book *Anarchy, State, and Utopia* would have a huge influence on academic understanding of libertarian thought—to craft what we considered a definitive statement of libertarianism. (Rothbard in his newsletter had backhandedly congratulated Bob for winning the National Book Award for his "quasi-libertarian inquiry into political philosophy, 'Anarchy, State, and Utopia.'" Bob autographed his copy for me with the question whether autographing an unread copy of a book would induce the reader to read it. It did.).

I recall defeating a proposal to include a denunciation of circumcision, on the ground that outlawing religious communities didn't sit well with libertarian thinking, regardless of what one might think of the practice. But most of the topics covered were major issues of public policy, such as nuclear weapons, foreign policy, taxes, and even environmental policy, by establishing property rights in fisheries and oyster beds, for example—leading to the quip that we were defending the virtues of shellfishness.

Those attempts to formulate and, more significantly, to apply libertarian thinking to concrete issues were later much expanded and improved in the outstanding "White Papers" and position papers issued in 1980 by the Ed Clark for President campaign. The documents were edited by a team that included a number of thinkers who were later involved at Cato and other organizations, people such as Crane, Childs, David Boaz, Sheldon Richman, Tyler Cowen, Joan Kennedy Taylor, and Earl Ravenal (memory fails to provide the complete list). The documents were significant steps forward for the libertarian movement. Articulating libertarian principles is important, but not really very valuable if you can't show how to apply them, or if you can't produce any kind of roadmap to their implementation.

I knew all the founders of Cato, which was established in 1977. Ed had gotten acquainted with some businessmen who were devoted to liberty. There was, for instance, a remarkable circle of libertarians in Wichita, including many involved with Coleman Lanterns, Love Box Company, and other firms, and they had put out some really radical antiwar libertarian publications in the 1960s. Notable among Ed's associates from the world of business was Charles Koch. Charles had been involved in libertarian activities for years. He was, and is, a passionate defender of liberty and foe of war, violence, and coercion. After his involvement with Cato, he has continued his support for liberty through the Institute for Humane Studies, the Mercatus Center, and other groups. Ed was fond of telling him, "Charles, with your money and your brains, you and I could go far."

Charles helped to launch Cato financially, with the idea that it would become independent of his funding. Ed realized that dream brilliantly, and created what I consider the single most important libertarian institution in the United States and quite probably the world. I was invited to work there in the summer of 1978, as one of the first three summer interns. We three, Ross Levatter, David Lips, and I, were known as the "Cato Clones." Our supposed clonishness caused some paranoia at the first Cato University Summer Seminar on Political Economy, held that summer. I remember one participant asking "Who are the Clones, and why are they here?"

I also recall sitting in the institute's fabulous conference room in San Francisco with Rothbard and others as we came up with the reading lists for the seminar—an absurd project that generated a gigantic stack of books and photocopied readings on everything from Earl Ravenal's writings on the contours of U.S. foreign policy, to Robert Carneiro's sociological theory of the formation of the state in the coastal valleys of Peru, to Ludwig von Mises' theory of the dynamics of interventionism, to a historian's description of the usurpation of the land rights of the mestizo population of New Mexico. All had to be included. None was too minor to be left out. The movement had to be informed . . . on everything! Stacked together, they were enough to fill a gigantic box for each participant. We've since learned how to be a bit more selective.

I later worked in Cato's academic affairs department, which was subsequently moved to the Institute for Humane Studies, then located in Menlo Park, California. (I ended up working at IHS in 1984, after it moved to George Mason University, and launched some adventures there.) After the MacBride for President campaign, I entered St. John's College in Annapolis, Maryland for an education. After tutorials and seminars and reading groups, I spent hours standing at the pay phone at the end of the hall of my dormitory, calling libertarian students and professors around the country on behalf of Cato's campus speakers bureau, study guides, and other programs. That was before Facebook. Before the internet. Before the mobile phone. Before the personal computer. Before the fax. Before the era when students could have phones in their rooms. Put like that, it seems like a long time ago, but it really wasn't. It was just a few years ago—but technology has changed the world so much, and with it, both the means the state uses to coerce us and the means we use to fight against it.

Just to give you an idea of how primitive the world was then, let me tell you a little more about how we communicated. When I worked for the Clark campaign in 1979 and 1980 as assistant director for communications, we had a "Mailgram machine." It was huge. In those days, to send out a press release or to reach people quickly, you sent them letters. You typed a letter directly onto a piece of paper, folded it, put it in an envelope, added a stamp, then gave it to a uniformed agent of the U.S. government. Eventually, it might arrive at the right address. With this machine, however, you could actually send a letter over the phone lines to a Western Union office in or near the city of the intended recipient, and Western Union would print it out, fold it, put it in an envelope, add a stamp, and give it to a uniformed agent of the U.S. government. That cut delivery time down, so it was worth the effort.

The Mailgram machine had a big black-and-white screen with a blinking white cursor, and you would type on it—very laboriously— every name and address of every recipient, along with the letter you wanted to send. The machine had no memory—at all. So if you bumped it or jiggled the power cord, it would "lose" all the information you had so painstakingly entered. Hours and hours of work. Gone. Never to be retrieved. If anyone went near the power cord, he was in mortal peril.

Here's another anecdote to tell you how far libertarian message work has come. Back in San Francisco, Cato had a really advanced IT department, as I suppose it would have been called, if the phrase had existed then. It had machines that allowed you to print out personalized letters, using either long paper tapes that had the letter content encoded in little holes punched in the paper that you would feed as a belt into a machine to control the sequence of keys striking the ribbon on the electric typewriter, or information that was encoded on magnetic cassette tapes of the kind used in Sony Walkman machines, which did the same thing. The manager worked two full-time jobs, of which this was one (he slept two or three hours a day).

One day when I was showing visitors around I introduced them and he told them, "Oh, it's a delight to work with Tom. He's one of our best content originators." This led me to consider the division of labor, and the role of pride in one's work, a bit more closely. He took pride in his work, without which mine would have been without effect, and he was generous to mine. Each colleague in the libertarian movement contributes to our common goals, whether as a writer, or building manager, or speaker, or data entry specialist, or accountant, or analyst, or editor, or receptionist, or petitioner, or conference organizer. And each should take pride in that contribution to our common goals.

Cato's San Francisco offices were cool and in one of the coolest cities in the world. I used to take the cable car to work, before they made it illegal to dangle by one hand on the post and swing out as the car quickly turned a corner. Working at Cato during the summer of 1978, I loved hanging out at the City Lights book store at night, reading anarchist beatnik poetry and having coffee at the Italian cafes in North Beach. Ed didn't hang out at City Lights, but he also loved San Francisco and, after moving Cato to D.C. in 1981, he remarked that satellite photos of the U.S. landmass clearly showed his fingernail marks as he was dragged eastward. The national media, the Congress, the administration, and the Supreme Court are based in Washington, and if you want to influence public discussion and opinion, to put libertarian reforms on the national policy agenda, and to influence the courts, it certainly helps to be where the media are and the three branches of government deliberate.

After that cool summer, I did a lot of other things in the movement; but all that time, wherever I was, I kept in touch with Cato. I wrote lots of book reviews and studies on many topics: public goods, infrastructure and private roads, public choice analysis and regulatory policy, U.S. foreign policy in El Salvador and Chad, and so on and so forth. I edited a few publications (*Dollars & Sense*, the monthly paper of the National Taxpayers Union, *Update*, a political newspaper on the libertarian movement, and some others) and wrote articles for various libertarian mags, as well as the *Washington Star*, the *Washington Post*, the *New York Times*, and the *Wall Street Journal*. I had some fun focusing attention on "industrial policy," indicative planning, and national foresight capability.

You see, Rep. Newt Gingrich had proposed creating a special government office tasked with predicting future technologies—a job that, I pointed out in a *Wall Street Journal* article, was absurd, since if you know what knowledge you will have in the future, you already have it now. Warren Buffett wrote to the *Journal* to denounce me. I also caused a stir, and made a tiny footnote in the history of public choice, when I toted up to a piece I published in the *Journal* the number of full-time professional pubic relations specialists employed by the federal government to lobby the public for more money for their agencies; I think I got to over 1,000, almost all of them disguised under other job titles. I explained in an essay in the *New York Times* that taxation is legalized theft and that the IRS's claim of "voluntary compliance" is an absurdity.

I worked as a reporter, a lobbyist, an editor of newsletters on politics, government, tax policies, and the libertarian movement, a troublemaker, a political researcher and organizer, an academic organizer for the Institute for Humane Studies, a smuggler of books, fax machines, and photocopiers into communist states, and a few other jobs I've forgotten. I started working with European libertarians in the early 1980s and traveled to Austria a few times to collaborate with libertarians there, after which I moved to Vienna to work with the now defunct Carl Menger Institut to find and help libertarians in communist states hasten the demise of those states and— very importantly—to promote institutions and attitudes conducive to the realization of freedom. IHS supported my initiative to move to Austria and start the "Eastern European Outreach Program," in conjunction with many other groups. When I worked in Austria, I helped Cato set up its first conference in the USSR, held in Moscow in 1990.

I helped to fund the translation into Russian of Mises' *Socialism*, Hayek's *The Fatal Conceit*, and many other books and essays by buying rubles from people leaving the USSR and giving them cash in the West. Instead of going by the absurd official rate (which was dangerous, in any case, as you had to show receipts for what you had spent your rubles on), I figured a better way. People leaving the USSR were allowed to take only a suitcase and 100 rubles with them, enough to buy a sandwich and a drink in Vienna. Some flights on Aeroflot from Moscow to Vienna would contain me and a lot of departing Jews. I remembered how Jews got their money out of the Third Reich—having foreign businessmen give them cash in the United States, or France, or England, and then having their relatives in Germany give them their Reichsmarks. So I made arrangements with a family of engineers (we had elaborate flow charts to show what money would go where) to deliver dollars to relatives in the United States, and their cousins would deliver their life savings of 30,000 rubles to me in Moscow. It worked.

I was in Prague during the collapse of the state and gave lectures at the universities when the students had expelled all of the professors. I assisted in the establishment of the still functioning Liberalni Institute in Prague. I had smuggled out a single typed copy (on carbon paper) of a Czech translation of Hayek's "The Road to Serfdom" and made 100 stapled copies in Vienna, which I then smuggled back in, along with a photocopier and 5,000 sheets of paper. It was a bit unnerving, as I was detained by the Czech police and arrested at the border train crossing. I flourished my official invitation (with a red stamp) from the Academy of Sciences of the Czech and Slovak Federal Socialist Republic and insisted on talking to the chief. He listened, realized he didn't want problems in case Comrade Bruzek was disappointed to discover that his invited guest speaker was detained, and told the soldiers to load my luggage on the train, all carefully camouflaged with layers of gifts for Czech friends, mainly toys and ladies' cosmetics, which were scarce in communist countries.

As they oofed and grunted, lifting the heavy suitcases, I was pretty sure they were asking in Czech, "What the hell is in this?" Luckily, they didn't find out. I learned the same lesson when taking photocopy machines into the USSR: never admit anything; produce official documents—even if outdated—that have red stamps on them; and talk the officials to death. They will finally realize that this guy might have friends, and they don't want to end up reassigned to the Tajik-Afghan border. When asked why I had two photocopy machines, I said that I always traveled with two, as I had to make lecture notes for the students, since I had an official invitation from the Academy of Sciences of the USSR and would give lectures at Moscow State University.

I was in Bucharest right after the Ceaucescus were executed, and helped Maria Valeanu organize the first libertarian seminars in Bucharest and in Transylvania. I was on one of the first flights to Tirana from Budapest when the Albanian regime collapsed, and became deathly ill from the decaying, slippery food that Albanians had to eat at that time. On that flight, I was befriended by the first Russian protocol officer to be sent to Tirana since the split between the USSR and Albania. He was very kind, gave me his card, and encouraged me to eat only in the Hotel Dajti, the "hard currency" hotel for foreigners. I asked why, and he said, "Well, I cannot really recommend the cuisine very highly, but under normal circumstances you can usually keep it down." I could not take his advice, but wished on a number of occasions that I had.

Speaking of dinners, after some lectures and seminars in Lublin, Poland, I invited the attendees to a dinner; we went to the poshest restaurant in town, at the Hotel Urania, which seemed primarily a state-run brothel for Arab clients to meet Polish women. I paid $5 to the cacophonous rock band to stop playing and go home, after which the various guests stood and introduced themselves. I recall a line of bearded professors who were identified by the dignified chairlady of the philosophy department in ways like this: "Professor X was in labor camp under the Nazis, then was free for a short time, and then was sent to labor camp under the communists, then was free, and was jailed again and was recently released, so we're pleased to have him with us this evening."

I spent a lot of time driving about Bulgaria in a tiny East German Trabi, with my knees under my chin. It ran out of gas on the way to the airport (there was a serious nationwide gas shortage), so I had to walk the rest of the way with my luggage. I had to be driven to the Tirana airport by the Minister of Light Industry, who later left the country, as there was no private transportation in the country and the public transportation had all broken down. I flew from Tirana to Bucharest on a little plane that had only a few big swivel seats; a chain-smoking Transylvania German lady from Hermannstadt (Sibiu in Romanian) was the only other passenger. We had two flight attendants with little 1960s flight attendant hats; instead of just talking to us about the flight, as they were only a few feet away, the attendant spoke into a microphone that issued in a malfunctioning little speaker that was dangling by wires from the ceiling. When we flew over Bucharest and I saw that it had electricity, which Tirana did not, it was like landing in Paris. That's how it was in those days.

One of my proudest accomplishments was arranging the publication of what was often the first non-Marxist economics textbook that some countries had seen since the communist takeovers, Paul Heyne's outstanding *The Economic Way of Thinking*, which I arranged to have translated and published in Czech, Russian, Hungarian, Romanian, and Albanian. I also arranged publication of books by Hayek, Mises, and Friedman into Russian, Estonian, Czech, Hungarian, and several other languages. (Arranging translation and publication of such works remains a project of mine; lately, I've focused on getting the works of Frédéric Bastiat into publication in numerous languages, including Swahili, Hindi, Bahasa, Arabic, Kurdish, Persian, Russian, Japanese, Nepali, Azerbaijani, and Vietnamese.)

Upon returning in 1995 to the United States from England, where I was working on my doctorate in politics at Oxford, I was offered a very cool job: coming to work full-time at the Cato Institute as Director of Special Projects. I could tell you all the projects I worked, on, but, of course, I'd have to kill you later. One project that it's permissible to reveal was the internship program, with which I have been very proudly involved ever since. The other was Cato University, which I also still direct. I got to work on expanding Cato's influence worldwide, in Russian, Chinese, Arabic, Persian, and other languages. After we libertarians failed to stop the juggernaut to war, and the United States invaded Iraq, I decided to see what could be done to promote liberty there and gave lectures and held seminars and meetings in Iraq a number of times, as well as in other countries in the region. I made friends with some remarkable people. At the beginning of last year, we moved those programs to the Atlas Economic Research Foundation, where they are flourishing. I'm Vice President for International Programs at Atlas and a Senior Fellow at Cato, and our programs at Atlas still work closely in partnership with Cato, but we've been able to expand them significantly at Atlas and to integrate them with the international network of classical liberal thinktanks and related organizations. It's very rewarding work.

I'm still on the road a lot. I just got back from Kabul, Mazar-e-Sharif, and Dushanbe, where I helped to launch two new libertarian thinktanks, Cato's granddaughters, in Afghanistan and Tajikistan. I met people in government, the media, and academia, and I gave lectures on individualism, civil society and pluralism, toleration, the political theories of limited government, property rights, externalities, economic development, the successes of the economic reforms in the Republic of Georgia, and how the Georgian libertarians helped to transform a nation from a disastrous failed state to a growing liberal democracy.

But I know that you do work like this, too. You make the case for liberty regularly with friends and family and coworkers. You know why you want to be free, and you know how to explain the benefits of liberty.

What is harder to explain is why we promote liberty for others, often at great cost to ourselves. We donate to causes and organizations. We work long hours. We rock boats. We're promoting a classic public good—even the paradigm case of a public good. Liberty is nonrivalrous in consumption: when you have more liberty, it doesn't mean that I have any less. And it's costly to exclude people from enjoying liberty: indeed, taking actions to exclude others is precisely the opposite of what a libertarian would do. But standard economic analysis tells us that public goods are underproduced, that no one has any incentive to produce them if everyone can freeride on the efforts of others. So why do we do it?

It's a harder question than it might appear. But here's a stab at answering it.

We—through our acts and our affiliations. Cato and Atlas sponsors whom I've met around the United States and the world typically identify themselves in this way: "I'm a member of the Cato Institute" or "I'm a member of the Atlas Economic Research Foundation." To speak precisely, those groups don't have dues-paying "memberships," but that's one of the ways in which people have constituted their identities. They're the kind of people who stand up for freedom, who stand up for peace, who stand up for the persecuted, who not only live and let live but also want to persuade other people to do so. It's not only good; it's right. And that act of standing up for liberty as right is a part of their identity. It's who they are.

Liberty is our cause. It is our passion. We will live free. And we will die free. Our cause is the cause of justice. Of truth. Of peace. Of life itself. I was introduced to the ideas of the Brazilian liberal abolitionist Joaquim Nabuco by former Cato intern and now Atlas colleague Diogo Costa. Nabuco dedicated his life to eradicating the evil of slavery from his country. Here is how he put the matter:

> Educate yourself, educate your children in love for the freedom of others, for only in this way will your own freedom not be a gratuitous gift from fate. You will be aware of its worth and have the courage to defend it.

PART IV

BOOKS AND IDEAS

37. The Literature of Liberty

This short guide is intended for those who wish to explore further the foundations, implications, and promise of libertarianism. In addition to works written from a libertarian perspective, or which have contributed to the development of libertarianism, I have included some contemporary and classic works that are critical of the libertarian approach, ranging from Plato's criticism of voluntary social organization to contemporary conservative, socialist, and social democratic criticisms. Libertarianism is central to virtually all of the currently exciting debates in ethical theory, political science, economics, history, and the other humane sciences, as well as to actual political struggles across the globe, and it is important to see it, not only as its proponents see it, but from the perspective of its critics as well.

Such a bibliographical guide could be organized in any number of ways (chronological/historical, thematic, by schools or countries), and each has its advantages. I have organized this guide so that the reader can first review broad introductions to the subject and then delve into more specific issues. Accordingly, I have organized the material into eight categories: (I) contemporary or relatively recent general works on libertarianism; (II) the history of civilization from a libertarian perspective; (III) imprescriptible individual rights; (IV) spontaneous order; (V) free markets and voluntary organization; (VI) justice and political organization; (VII) violence and the state; and (VIII) classical and contemporary works that are directly critical of libertarianism. The topic divisions are somewhat arbitrary, precisely because so many of the ideas considered here are mutually reinforcing and therefore likely to be found treated in the same book or essay.

I conclude with the critics of libertarianism in order to allow the reader the opportunity to see the issues from at least two perspectives, to think through some difficult problems, and to decide for

Originally published in *The Libertarian Reader*, edited by David Boaz. New York: The Free Press, 1997.

herself which arguments she finds most convincing. No one perspective is likely to have all the answers, or even to ask all of the interesting and important questions, and it is only through dialogue with other views—through criticism and hard thinking—that libertarianism is likely to grow and flourish and to make possible a better, freer, more peaceful, prosperous, and just world.

Readers trying to find an authoritative once-and-for-all answer to every question are likely to be disappointed, for not all the writers here discussed agree on all questions, and many of the most interesting works were written as criticisms of other libertarian or classical liberal writers. Broad agreement on the value and importance of imprescriptible rights to life, liberty, and property is the hallmark of the libertarian approach, but libertarianism remains a lively and exciting field for the thoughtful and creative, rather than merely a set of canonical answers. What is perhaps most remarkable about modern libertarianism is the way it illuminates the world, both morally and scientifically. The moral imperatives of peace and voluntary cooperation are brought together with a rich understanding of the spontaneous order made possible by such voluntary cooperation and of the ways in which coercive intervention can disorder the world and set in motion complex trains of unintended consequences.

This guide is, by necessity, somewhat eccentric—reflecting my own reading and the interests that have guided me over the years—and most definitely incomplete. I certainly anticipate objections from readers who will complain that works were excluded that were better, or more important, or "more libertarian" than works that were included. As excuse for the absence of important works, I can only plead the limitations of space. To the objection that works are included to which some may object, on the grounds that they are not "plumb line" libertarian texts, I respond with the words of the late Henry Hazlitt, formerly economics editor at the *New York Times*, a columnist for *Newsweek*, and the author of the extraordinarily influential book *Economics in One Lesson*, in his own bibliography of libertarianism, *The Free Man's Library* (Princeton, N.J.: Van Nostrand, 1956):

> In an effort to answer as many as possible of such objections in advance, I should like to say here that the inclusion of a book in this bibliography certainly does not imply that I myself subscribe to every doctrine or sentence in that book

> or that I think that every opinion it enunciates is an essential part of the libertarian or individualist tradition. What inclusion does imply is that in my judgment the book . . . makes on net balance a factual or theoretical contribution to the philosophy of individualism, and that at least some readers may derive from it a fuller understanding of that philosophy. (pp. 7–8)

Partly because this bibliography is so much smaller than Hazlitt's, which listed 550 books, I have employed more fine-grained selection criteria and have not included the many criticisms of totalitarianism that appeared in his 1956 listing, when the totalitarian state was a very present threat to liberty. The selection I have made, which is drawn entirely from material available in English, is far from comprehensive, but those who wish to read and study further will find that each book or essay invariably leads to others.

I. General Works on Libertarianism

One of the most prolific libertarian writers of this century was undoubtedly the late Murray N. Rothbard, whose writings ranged from his own area of academic expertise—economics—to political science, ethics, history, international affairs, and much more. In the 1970s he turned his attention to writing a "manifesto" of libertarianism, which appeared in two editions under the name *For a New Liberty: The Libertarian Manifesto* (2d ed.; New York: Macmillan, 1978). This book provides a good overview of the libertarian worldview, although the chapters on public policy issues and on the organized libertarian movement are by now somewhat dated.

Rothbard had published many articles and books in the 1950s and 1960s arguing against the legitimacy of the state (in American English, usually referred to as "government," although this implies the impossibility of "voluntary government," which Rothbard favored). The distinguished philosopher Robert Nozick found Rothbard's arguments a powerful case against the legitimacy of the state, and he was moved by Rothbard's challenge to write his tremendously successful and brilliant book defending the strictly limited state, *Anarchy, State, and Utopia* (New York: Basic Books, 1974). Although strictly speaking not a "general work on libertarianism," Nozick's book has come to enjoy canonical status among academics, who normally assign it to students as "the" libertarian book, with little appreciation of the broader tradition of libertarian thinking and scholarship within which Nozick's work took shape.

Nozick started his enterprise with the explicit assumption, stated in the first sentence of *Anarchy, State, and Utopia*, that "individuals have rights, and there are things no person or group may do to them (without violating those rights)," an assumption shared with Rothbard and other libertarians, and then he attempted to answer the question "How much room do individual rights leave for the state?" His response is that a very limited state, dedicated to protecting individual rights, is legitimate and consistent with individual rights. In the process of defending the (strictly) limited state, Nozick articulated many provocative ideas in this witty and dazzling book and offered a direct and strong criticism of John Rawls's then recently published and widely acclaimed defense of the redistributive welfare state, *A Theory of Justice* (Cambridge, Mass.: Harvard University Press, 1971). Largely because of his remarks on Rawls and the extraordinary power of his intellect, Nozick's book was taken quite seriously by academic philosophers and political theorists, many of whom had not read contemporary libertarian (or classical liberal) material and considered this to be the only articulation of libertarianism available. Since Nozick was writing to defend the limited state and did not justify his starting assumption that individuals have rights, this led some academics to dismiss libertarianism as "without foundations," in the words of the philosopher Thomas Nagel. When read in light of the explicit statement of the book's purpose, however, this criticism is misdirected, or should have been directed at some other book attempting to make another argument. (Other contemporary philosophers have taken up the task of justifying the strong claim that individuals have rights, and I will introduce a few of them shortly.)

A list of "general" works on libertarianism certainly must include the enormously popular essays of the best-selling novelist-philosopher Ayn Rand. Some of her better works, along with essays by three collaborators (psychologist Nathaniel Branden, historian Robert Hessen, and current Federal Reserve chairman Alan Greenspan), can be found in the collection *Capitalism: The Unknown Ideal* (New York: New American Library, 1966). Presented in vivid and dramatic language, the essays represent an attempted synthesis of Rand's political philosophy. Unlike most of her other books, which deal with

558

her theories of popular culture, art, personal morality, metaphysical truths, epistemology, and the many other issues to which Rand turned her formidable intellect, the essays in this volume are more narrowly political and libertarian. Rand was strongly influenced in developing her political philosophy by the American libertarian writers Isabel Paterson and Rose Wilder Lane, as well as the Austrian-school economist Ludwig von Mises. (It should be noted that Rand's dramatic style—so important to an artist—sometimes led to oversimplification, as in her characterization of "big business" as "America's persecuted minority"; her efforts to defend businesspeople from the kind of scapegoating directed at Jews in National Socialist Germany or at the "bourgeoisie" in her native Russia led her to downplay the efforts of many involved in "business" to get special favors from the state and to restrain the activities of their competitors. For such favor-seeking businesspeople she had only contempt.) One remarkable thing about Rand's approach that distinguished it from so much previous thinking is that she offered a distinctively *moral* defense of an economic system based on voluntary cooperation and exchange; it was not that people were not "good enough" for socialism, but that socialism was not good enough for people.

Two Austrian contributors to modern libertarian thought are Ludwig von Mises and F. A. Hayek, both articulate defenders of the older tradition of liberalism against the new threat of totalitarianism in the twentieth century. Mises published his positive political philosophy in his book *Liberalism* in German in 1927 (Kansas City, Mo.: Sheed, Andrews and McMeel, 1978). Hayek, who went on to win the Nobel Prize in economics in 1974, set forth his views on political matters in a number of books. Taken together, these books reveal a gradual evolution in his political thought. They include his extraordinarily influential book *The Road to Serfdom* (Chicago: University of Chicago Press, 1944), which undoubtedly represents one of the intellectual and political turning points of the century; *The Constitution of Liberty* (Chicago: University of Chicago Press, 1960); and his three-volume *Law, Legislation, and Liberty* (Chicago: University of Chicago Press, 1973, 1976, 1979). Another Nobel Prize-winning economist whose works have been enormously influential in the post–World War II libertarian movement is Milton Friedman, who, with his wife Rose Friedman, has written eloquently about the loss of freedom due to growing state power. Milton Friedman's *Capitalism and Freedom*

(Chicago: University of Chicago Press, 1962) was ground-breaking, and Milton and Rose Friedman's *Free to Choose* (New York: Harcourt Brace Jovanovich, 1980) introduced millions to libertarian ideas, especially through the television series associated with the book.

Political scientist Norman Barry's *On Classical Liberalism and Libertarianism* (New York: St. Martin's, 1987) presents a useful overview of libertarian thought, focusing mainly on twentieth-century writers. An attempt to place libertarianism on secure foundations and to defend it from various criticisms can be found in philosopher Jan Narveson's *The Libertarian Idea* (Philadelphia: Temple University Press, 1989). A rigorous attempt to place libertarianism (or thoroughgoing classical liberalism) on a foundation of well-formulated axioms is available in economist Anthony de Jasay's *Choice, Contract, Consent: A Restatement of Liberalism* (London: Institute of Economic Affairs, 1991). Law professor Richard Epstein has produced an outstanding defense of a broadly libertarian approach, including what he considers to be defensible but tightly delimited deviations from strict libertarianism, in his *Simple Rules for a Complex World* (Cambridge, Mass.: Harvard University Press, 1995).

There are several readers on libertarian thought, although most do not have the broad sweep or historical dimensions of *The Libertarian Reader*, David Boaz, ed. (New York: The Free Press, 1997). Among the best, mostly containing essays from the last few decades, are three that have been edited by the philosopher Tibor Machan, a Hungarian refugee from communism who was also influenced by Ayn Rand. These books are useful as sources of short essays on issues in ethics, history, economics, international relations, and public policy from a libertarian perspective. The collections edited by Machan are *The Libertarian Alternative* (Chicago: Nelson Hall, 1973); *The Libertarian Reader* (Lanham, Md.: Rowman & Littlefield, 1982); and, coedited with Douglas B. Rasmussen, *Liberty for the 21st Century* (Lanham, Md.: Rowman & Littlefield, 1995).

I cannot conclude this section without mentioning a little favorite of mine, *Liberty against Power: Essays by Roy A. Childs, Jr.*, Joan Kennedy Taylor, ed. (San Francisco: Fox & Wilkes, 1994), a collection of essays by the late libertarian scholar Roy A. Childs, Jr., which includes a selection of his scholarly articles, popular essays, journalistic pieces, speeches, and reviews. Childs, an autodidact and independent scholar who did not go to college, exercised an enormous influence on a generation of libertarian scholars, many of whom are now well-known professors, and kept up a vast and learned correspondence with distinguished academics, artists, musicians, businesspeople, journalists, and politicians. (He was one of the brightest and most dazzling personalities I have ever known and remains an inspiration to me and to many other libertarians.) The volume has a foreword by the famous libertarian psychiatrist Thomas Szasz.

Of course, as of this writing, the most up-to-date popular introductions to libertarian thought are *Libertarianism: A Primer* (New York: The Free Press, 1997), by David Boaz, executive vice president of the Cato Institute, and *What It Means to Be a Libertarian: A Personal Interpretation* (New York: Broadway Books, 1997), by the social scientist Charles Murray.

II. The History of Civilization from a Libertarian Perspective

One way of understanding the history of modern civilization is as a constant struggle between liberty and power. That was how it was understood by the historian John Emerich Edward Dalberg-Acton, known as Lord Acton. There are many available editions of his writings, as well as a number of fine biographies. Paradoxically, precisely because of his vast and unequaled learning (he read and annotated tens of thousands of books in his lifetime and was fluent in a mind-boggling number of languages), Acton never wrote a book. He fell prey to the mistake of allowing the best to be the enemy of good, as he always knew that there was more that could be learned before committing his views to print. Thus, his planned great history of liberty has been referred to as "the greatest history never written," but his collected essays and reviews run to many volumes. Especially noteworthy are his essays on "Nationality," "The History of Freedom in Antiquity," "The History of Freedom in Christianity," and his "Inaugural Lecture on the Study of History," all available in a recent edition edited by J. Rufus Fears, *Selected Writings of Lord Acton, Vol. I: Essays in the History of Liberty* (Indianapolis: Liberty Classics, 1985). It was Acton who summed up his study of thousands of years of history in the following now-famous terms: "Power tends to corrupt, absolute power corrupts absolutely."

A sweeping treatment of history as a struggle between liberty and power can be found in the work of the sociologist Alexander Rüstow, who opposed the National Socialists in Germany and then went into exile as Hitler destroyed the last remnants of continental European libertarianism. During his exile Rüstow strove to understand how the monstrosity of collectivism could emerge in a civilized country such as Germany, and the result was a massive work in social theory, which was abridged and edited by his son Dankwart Rüstow and published in English as *Freedom and Domination: A Historical Critique of Civilization* (Princeton, N.J.: Princeton University Press, 1980).

Another approach, resting on philosophical underpinnings quite different from those of either Acton or Rüstow (although he influenced both), can be found in the work of the nineteenth-century German legal historian Otto von Gierke, who distinguished between the principles of association (*Genossenschaft*) and domination or lordship (*Herrschaft*) and who saw both as operative in shaping modern social relations. A good selection from his work is available in *Community in Historical Perspective*, Antony Black, ed. (Cambridge: Cambridge University Press, 1990).

In all of the above accounts, society is distinguished from the state, which is the product of violence, conquest, and domination. Libertarians see such accomplishments as the rule of law, individual rights, toleration, and peace as victories won in a long struggle against power, and institutions such as representative government, the separation of powers, equality before the law, and independent courts as devices to bring the state itself—the organized system of plunder and domination—under law.

Just as there are histories of states (indeed so much of what most people think of as "history" is merely the chronicling of power, of kings and queens, courts and coups, wars and conquests), there are also histories of civil society, of the market, of property and law, of productive work and exchange, of voluntary cooperation. A good place to start is with the history of the revival of commercial civilization in Europe after the barbarian conquests found in the work of Henri Pirenne, notably his very readable and popular *Medieval Cities: Their Origins and the Growth of Trade* (1925; Princeton, N.J.: Princeton University Press, 1974). The birth and growth of commercial society are examined in many works. Two of the more outstanding are Robert S. Lopez, *The Commercial Revolution of the Middle Ages, 950–1350* (Cambridge: Cambridge University Press, 1976), and John Brewer and Roy Porter, eds., *Consumption and the World of Goods*

(London: Routledge, 1996). A sophisticated and very accessible treatment of the rise of "capitalism" can be found in Nathan Rosenberg and L. E. Birdzell, Jr., *How the West Grew Rich* (New York: Basic Books, 1986).

Similar accounts of the emergence of civil society, or the extended order of modern "capitalism," can be found in E. L. Jones, *The European Miracle* (Cambridge: Cambridge University Press, 1981), which locates the source of European economic and legal progress in the radical fragmentation of power on that continent, and Hayek's last book, *The Fatal Conceit: The Errors of Socialism* (Chicago: University of Chicago Press, 1988), which offers a sweeping account of the rise of liberal civilization. A primary feature of these accounts is the role played in the development of modern liberty by the fragmentation of power. Political fragmentation and commercial civilization (with movable forms of wealth, as Benjamin Constant emphasizes in his essay "The Liberty of the Ancients Compared with That of the Moderns," in Boaz, *The Libertarian Reader*) lower the individual's cost of exit from an oppressive political situation. Because people could escape from one political system to another, rulers and potential rulers had to compete among themselves to attract or maintain their base of taxpayers. Furthermore, in Europe, political power was rarely unitary in any one territory, but was usually at least shared (and disputed!) by the church and the secular authorities, unlike the situation in other areas of the world, where the king claimed either the title of head priest or of God it/him/herself, something unthinkable in the Judeo-Christian worldview. In Europe, because of this competition between church and state and among different kinds of secular authorities, liberty was able to grow up in the "jurisdictional cracks" between the different powers, and individuals were able to play powers off against one another, generally resulting in greater security of rights for the individual. A brilliant account of this history of "legal pluralism" and "jurisdictional cracks" is found in the legal historian Harold Berman's *Law and Revolution: The Formation of the Western Legal Tradition* (Cambridge, Mass.: Harvard University Press, 1983).

III. Imprescriptible Individual Rights

The source or justification of rights has always been a contentious issue among libertarian thinkers. Whether individuals have rights in virtue of their utility, their correspondence to the demands of pure reason, divine revelation, or for some other reason may indeed matter in debates over particular policy issues, but rather than seeing different kinds of justifications arriving at the same general conclusion as a problem, I prefer to see it as a kind of "fail-safe" mechanism: If many different nonexclusive arguments all converge on the same conclusion, we can be more sure of its truth than if only one of those arguments led us there and the others led to other conclusions.

In any case, in the history of political thought, "natural law" arguments and arguments from "utility," for example, were not generally seen as in opposition, for one comes to understand nature only indirectly, through experience, whether in the physical sciences or in the moral sciences, and the sign of a good institution is its good consequences, or utility. What is characteristic of the libertarian approach to rights and distinguishes it from others is that basic rights are held to be "imprescriptible," meaning that fundamental rights are not gifts or mere dispensations from power—whether king or parliament, commissar or congressman—but have moral force before and independently of particular political arrangements. Rights are what individuals bring to politics, not what they take out. When political society works properly, what individuals derive from politics is security for rights, but their previously justified rights are what they enter into political arrangements to secure. Imprescriptible rights are thus not subject to "prescription"; they are neither handed out by authoritative figures, as doctors hand out prescriptions for drugs, nor subject to being arbitrarily taken away without injustice.

A useful historical account of the origins of natural rights theories is found in Richard Tuck's *Natural Rights Theories: Their Origin and Development* (Cambridge: Cambridge University Press, 1979). (While Tuck's knowledge and scholarship are truly impressive, a useful supplement to his book can be found in an article by the Cornell University historian Brian Tierney, "Tuck on Rights: Some Medieval Problems," *History of Political Thought* 4[3], Winter 1983. Tuck himself extended his account in his essay "The 'Modern' Theory of Natural Law," in *The Languages of Political Theory in Early-Modern Europe*, Anthony Pagden, ed. [Cambridge: Cambridge University Press, 1987].) Another account by a distinguished philosopher, Fred D. Miller, Jr.'s, *Nature, Justice, and Rights in Aristotle's Politics* (Oxford:

Oxford University Press, 1995), argues that the roots of modern rights theory can be found in Aristotle, that "Locke's theory of 'the Law of Nature' is a direct descendant of Aristotle's theory of natural justice," and that in Aristotle's writings can be found a theory of "rights based on nature."

Especially important in the history of libertarianism are the contributions of the Spanish "School of Salamanca," whose members articulated so much of the foundation of the modern libertarian synthesis of spontaneous order and individual rights. The Argentine economist Alejandro Chafuen has written a good overview of this school in his *Christians for Freedom: Late-Scholastic Economics* (San Francisco: Ignatius Press, 1986).

Chafuen's focus is principally on the sophisticated understanding of the self-regulating free market that the Spanish Scholastics achieved, but this advance in social science was closely connected to the development of the idea of imprescriptible and universal rights of individuals in moral and legal philosophy, as well. (Markets are simply what emerge when people have secure rights, including the right to exchange.) Part of the interest in the issue of individual rights was occasioned by the treatment of the American Indians in the territories conquered by Spain, which raised deep questions regarding the rights of the indigenous peoples.

One writer whose defense of the rights of the Indians contributed greatly to the modern libertarian idea of imprescriptible individual rights is Francisco de Vitoria, whose "On the American Indians" (in Francisco de Vitoria, *Political Writings*, Anthony Pagden and Jeremy Lawrance, eds. [Cambridge: Cambridge University Press, 1991]) exercised a great influence on later rights theorists. Vitoria concluded that the Indians were not the "natural slaves" of which Aristotle had written and that "the barbarians undoubtedly possessed as true dominion, both public and private, as any Christians. That is to say, they could not be robbed of their property . . . on the grounds that they were not true masters (*veri domini*)."

Vitoria drew on the writings of one of the great lawyer-popes of the thirteenth century, Innocent IV, who had insisted that to deprive unbelievers ("infidels," including Jews and Muslims) of life, liberty, or property was unjust: "Lordship, possession, and jurisdiction can belong to infidels licitly and without sin, for these things are made not only for the faithful but for every rational creature as has been

565

said." (Innocent's arguments can be found in the outstanding collection edited by Brian Tierney, *The Crisis of Church and State, 1050–1300* [Toronto: University of Toronto Press, 1988], along with many other documents important to the development of libertarianism.)

Particularly active in the struggle to protect the rights of the Indians was Bartolomé de las Casas, who defended their rights in a famous debate with Juan Ginés de Sepúlveda in Valladolid in 1550 (Las Casas's arguments were later published as a book; see his *In Defense of the Indians* [c. 1552; DeKalb: Northern Illinois University Press, 1992]), and who wrote eloquently to alert European readers to the horrors visited on the native peoples by their conquerors (see his *The Devastation of the Indies: A Brief Account* [1552; Baltimore: The Johns Hopkins University Press, 1992]).

The proto-libertarians of the School of Salamanca succeeded in establishing a vigorous defense of the rights of every human being to life, liberty, and property, which is truly one of the great accomplishments of our civilization. Even if honored more in the breach than in the practice for many years, the principle of imprescriptible individual rights was established, and this principle spurred the later emancipation of slaves, the equalization of rights between men and women, and at least some degree of restraint in the treatment of the helpless, whose lot in earlier years was to be destroyed if they could not be enslaved.

What emerged from this tradition and from these debates was the idea that to be a moral agent was to be able to take responsibility for one's actions, referred to as "dominium," or self-mastery, which entailed that one had a *right* to fulfill one's responsibilities, essentially on the grounds that "ought implies can." This idea was expressed in English by the phrase "a property in one's person," an idea advanced by such figures as the English Leveller Richard Overton (see his essay "An Arrow against Tyrants," in Boaz, *The Libertarian Reader*) and the more widely known English physician, philosopher, and activist for liberty John Locke, several of whose works are also included in the Boaz volume. Locke brought together into an appealing synthesis ideas about property, consent, contract, and the origins and limits of legitimate government. Locke's influence on the modern world, as on modern libertarianism, is inestimable. It is, of course, especially obvious in the American Declaration of Independence, which articulated libertarian ideals for a worldwide audience. The book in which Locke brought together these important ideals is his *Two Treatises of Government*, the first of which is mainly a refutation of the arguments for absolutism of Sir Robert Filmer, while the second contains more of Locke's own arguments on behalf of individual liberty and limited government. The language remains remarkably readable, but it is advisable to obtain one of the annotated editions for footnotes explaining references that may be obscure to contemporary readers. (Locke's arguments are clearly restated, defended from criticism, and applied to new problems and issues—not always in ways entirely consistent with libertarian approaches—by A. John Simmons in *The Lockean Theory of Rights* [Princeton, N.J.: Princeton University Press, 1992].)

Contrary to the interpretation given to these developments by socialist historians (such as C. B. Macpherson, whose *The Political Theory of Possessive Individualism* [Oxford: Oxford University Press, 1962] has misled thousands upon thousands of university students), the idea of property was not a sneaky trick to justify the wealth of a nascent bourgeoisie, but was articulated first and foremost in defense of such groups as the defeated American Indians and persecuted religious dissenters. (The absurd interpretation of the idea of property in one's person as a kind of trick to justify "capitalist inequality" has been restated, on the basis of a mass of historical errors, by Attracta Ingram in her sustained screed against libertarianism, *A Political Theory of Rights* [Oxford: The Clarendon Press of Oxford University Press, 1994]. Being ignorant of the historical record, Ingram ultimately must rely on what she refers to as the "intuitive plausibility" [p. 75] of her misrepresentation of history as an argument against property in one's person.) The connection between the idea of property in one's person (sometimes referred to as "self-ownership") and freedom of conscience is nicely laid out by the philosopher/historian George H. Smith in his historical survey "Philosophies of Toleration" (in George H. Smith, *Atheism, Ayn Rand, and Other Heresies* [Buffalo, N.Y.: Prometheus Books, 1991]).

The history of the application of the idea of property to *alienable* objects (the more common use of the term "property" by contemporary writers) is traced and explained in the philosopher Stephen Buckle's very readable *Natural Law and the Theory of Property: Grotius to Hume* (Oxford: Oxford University Press, 1991). A recent updating of the theory is provided by Murray N. Rothbard in his book *The Ethics of Liberty* (Atlantic Highlands, N.J.: Humanities Press, 1982), which applies the theory to a variety of concrete problems.

The classical accounts of individual rights canvassed in the literature above tended to focus on the issue of responsibility for one's actions, or "dominium" (an issue to which F. A. Hayek returned in the chapter on "Responsibility and Freedom" in *The Constitution of Liberty* [Chicago: University of Chicago Press, 1960]). The idea has been restated in contemporary times in a somewhat more analytical way (focusing on the analysis of concepts or essences) by Ayn Rand and the philosophers she has inspired. Rand's own arguments, which are somewhat fragmentary (being found scattered over a variety of her essays), have been reconstructed by the philosopher Eric Mack in his essay "The Fundamental Moral Elements in Rand's Theory of Rights," in *The Philosophic Thought of Ayn Rand*, Douglas J. Den Uyl and Douglas B. Rasmussen, eds. (Chicago: University of Illinois Press, 1986). The idea that rights are a requirement of the life of a living reasoning entity, which is central to Rand's philosophy, is explored further in Tibor R. Machan's book *Individuals and Their Rights* (La Salle, Ill.: Open Court, 1989) and in Douglas B. Rasmussen and Douglas J. Den Uyl's *Liberty and Nature: An Aristotelian Defense of Liberal Order* (La Salle, Ill.: Open Court, 1991), both of which defend versions of "moral realism." Taking their cue from Aristotle's *Nicomachean Ethics*, Rasmussen and Den Uyl stress the importance of "self-direction" to human flourishing, a theme that also plays a role in the philosophically rather different account offered by the libertarian philosopher Loren E. Lomasky. In *Persons, Rights, and the Moral Community* (Oxford: Oxford University Press, 1987), Lomasky argues that human beings are "project pursuers," with the right to choose and pursue their own life projects.

Another illuminating approach to rights draws on the "transcendental" form of argument pioneered by Immanuel Kant, who (to simplify matters a bit) started with the accepted truths of arithmetic, Euclidean geometry, and Newtonian physics and then asked what would have to be true for these sciences to generate knowledge. Analogously, the libertarian bioethicist H. Tristram Engelhardt, Jr., has asked what would have to be true for the pluralistic extended order, or civil society, to exist; he presented a theory of two "tiers" of morality, the abstract rules of the free society, which provide a mere framework for social coexistence and cooperation, and the concrete customs, injunctions, and requirements of particular religious or philosophical or communal moralities, which provide the content of moral lives. This theory is set out in its general form and then applied to concrete problems and issues in biomedical ethics by Engelhardt in his book *The Foundations of Bioethics* (Oxford: Oxford University Press, 1986). (Interestingly, this transcendental argument has some affinity with the "hypothetical imperative" argument advanced by such thinkers as Samuel Pufendorf, who stressed "sociality" as the foundation of the rules of justice: If you wish to live with other humans in peace and harmony, then certain things are necessary, such as rights, rules of just conduct, and property. See Pufendorf's *On the Duty of Man and Citizen* [1673; Cambridge: Cambridge University Press, 1991] and Craig L. Carr, ed., *The Political Writings of Samuel Pufendorf* [Oxford: Oxford University Press, 1994].)

An account that begins with the nature of rights as such and derives consistent systems of justice is offered by the University of Manchester philosopher Hillel Steiner, who has emphasized the issue of "compossibility" as a necessary characteristic of genuine rights. A set of compossible rights includes only rights that can be exercised at the same time without entailing conflicts. The rights entailed by property in one's person fulfill that requirement, whereas various alleged "welfare rights," "national rights," and so forth do not. Steiner's principal work is *An Essay on Rights* (Oxford: Blackwell, 1994), which is a dazzling display of analytical rigor, leading to sometimes unexpected results, including a number from which libertarians would typically dissent. (Notably, Steiner endorses what has come to be known as a "Georgist" position on land and natural resources, after the nineteenth-century economist Henry George, according to which all have a right to an equal share of naturally occurring resources, rather than the Lockean position that all have an equal right to appropriate. As the reader can easily imagine, such an apparently slight difference in terms yields extraordinarily different conclusions.)

Another contemporary philosopher who has presented a strong defense of property in one's person (or "self-ownership") is Eric Mack, whose essays defending this approach include "Agent-Relativity of Value, Deontic Restraints, and Self-Ownership," in *Value, Welfare, and Morality*, R. G. Frey and Christopher W. Morris, eds.

(Cambridge: Cambridge University Press, 1993) and "Personal Integrity, Practical Recognition, and Rights," *The Monist* 76(1), January 1993. Mack applies the principle of property in one's person to the particular issue of whether profits from voluntary exchange are justified (in a somewhat technical discussion of the work of philosopher David Gauthier) in his essay "Rights to Natural Talents and Pure Profits: A Critique of Gauthier on Rights and Economic Rent," in *Profits and Morality*, Robin Cowan and Mario J. Rizzo, eds. (Chicago: University of Chicago Press, 1995). (The volume edited by Cowan and Rizzo also contains interesting discussions of the right to earn profits by the economist Israel Kirzner, who delineates the economic concept of profit and defends a "finders-keepers" rule of appropriation, and Jan Narveson, who defends market exchange and justly earned profits from a number of criticisms.)

Other accounts have stressed the general utility of rights. Notable in such accounts are those emphasizing the central role of rights in generating beneficial social cooperation. An interesting example of this kind of argument is found in the British economist Robert Sugden's essay "Labour, Property, and the Morality of Markets," in *The Market in History*, B. L. Anderson and A. J. H. Latham, eds. (London: Croom Helm, 1986). A similar approach is taken by the economist and law professor David Friedman in his essay "A Positive Account of Property Rights," in *Property Rights*, Ellen Frankel Paul, Fred D. Miller, Jr., and Jeffrey Paul, eds. (Cambridge: Cambridge University Press, 1994). Both Sugden and Friedman advance "self-ownership" as a salient, or prominent, solution to the problem of who gets to control the "most scarce" of all resources: you and your body.

It is sometimes objected that groups can have rights, too (or perhaps even that groups *are* the basic rights holders, and that individuals are the ones who *may* have rights, too, when the group decides to bestow them, meaning, of course, that they can be taken away again). This issue has again taken center stage in current discussions of such issues as "affirmative action," the rights of aboriginal tribes, and other concrete issues. A well-thought-out and nuanced treatment of the issue is offered by the political scientist Chandran Kukathas in his essay "Are There Any Cultural Rights?" *Political Theory* 20(1), February 1992. (The social democratic philosopher Will Kymlicka criticizes Kukathas in the same issue of *Political Theory*, and Kukathas responds in 20[4], November 1992.)

The extension of recognized imprescriptible rights is to a large extent the measure of civilization. One way of viewing the history of liberty is as the history of the recognition of rights among ever wider groups. The struggle for the rights of women is represented in the Boaz *Libertarian Reader*, notably by Mary Wollstonecraft and the Grimké sisters, but additional treatments of this important subject can be found in Wendy McElroy, ed., *Freedom, Feminism, and the State* (New York: Holmes and Meier, 1991). A defense of modern liberal society, focusing on the possibility of "role complexity" and emphasizing the liberation of women from imposed roles, is offered by Rose Laub Coser, *In Defense of Modernity: Role Complexity and Individual Autonomy* (Stanford, Calif.: Stanford University Press, 1991). A modern restatement of individualist feminism is Joan Kennedy Taylor, *Reclaiming the Mainstream: Individualist Feminism Rediscovered* (Buffalo, N.Y.: Prometheus Books, 1992).

It would not be appropriate to conclude a discussion of the literature of rights without pointing again to the important work of Robert Nozick mentioned in the first section, *Anarchy, State, and Utopia*. Many things could be said about this interesting and challenging book, but in this context Nozick's construal of individual rights as "side constraints" on acceptable behavior is especially noteworthy. Nozick argues against what he calls a "utilitarianism of rights," that is, the view that what we are all called morally to do is to minimize the amount of rights violation, even if we have to violate rights in the process. In response Nozick argued that the rights of others serve as constraints on our behavior and not as a quantity to be maximized. Rights are important moral signposts, for they guide us in what we ought to do or refrain from doing. Rights are action-guiding, and systems that require a God's-eye view (as so many of the "positive" welfare rights views do, with various conflicting rights being balanced against each other—and against other interests—by some all-powerful agency) hardly qualify as systems of rights at all.

IV. Spontaneous Order

Libertarianism as a *political* theory can perhaps best be understood as the synthesis of two mutually reinforcing theories, one "normative" (containing "ought" statements) and the other "positive" (containing "is" statements). The normative theory is a theory of individual rights; the positive theory is a theory of how order comes about. To

571

understand how these two themes are related, consider the following: If respect for individual rights were to be shown to lead not to order and prosperity, but to chaos, the destruction of civilization, and famine, few would uphold such alleged rights, and those who did would certainly be held the enemies of mankind. Those who can see order only when there is a conscious ordering mind—socialists, totalitarians, monarchical absolutists, and the like—fear just such consequences from individual rights. But if it can be shown that a multitude of individuals exercising a set of "compossible" rights (as described above, in the section on imprescriptible rights) generates not chaos, but order, cooperation, and the progressive advance of human well-being, then respect for the dignity and autonomy of the individual would be seen to be not only compatible with, but even a necessary precondition for, the achievement of social coordination, prosperity, and high civilization. Individual rights and spontaneous order are highly complementary elements of libertarianism.

The study of how order can emerge as an unintended consequence of the actions of many individuals is usually referred to as the study of "spontaneous order," and this field of study is one of the most important elements of the libertarian synthesis.

Thomas Paine recognized the immense attractiveness of this combination of order and rights. He defended natural and imprescriptible rights in *The Rights of Man, Part I* (1791), writing: "Natural rights are those which always appertain to man in right of his existence." This was combined in *The Rights of Man, Part II* (1792), with a most remarkable observation: "For upwards of two years from the commencement of the American war, and a longer period in several of the American states, there were no established forms of government. The old governments had been abolished, and the country was too much occupied in defense to employ its attention in establishing new governments; yet during this interval order and harmony were preserved as inviolate as in any country in Europe." (This section is excerpted in Boaz, *The Libertarian Reader*.) The advocates of royal power predicted chaos, disorder, disruption, and mass mayhem if one iota of the royal power were to be challenged, yet here the power of the state was not merely attenuated, but *completely* absent, and people continued to farm, to engage in manufacturing, to trade, to respect one another, and to live in "order and harmony." The question of how that could be has been a major topic of research for libertarian scholars and social scientists.

Paine was not, of course, the first to make the connection between social order and individual rights (the Spanish Scholastics had explored this territory long before), but as a forceful writer and popularizer he realized how attractive is a political theory based on the combination of a moral theory of imprescriptible rights and a social theory of spontaneous order. The intellectual history of the theory of spontaneous order is mapped out by the polymath economist F. A. Hayek in his essay "The Results of Human Action but Not of Human Design" in his *Studies in Philosophy, Politics, and Economics* (Chicago: University of Chicago Press, 1967), which traces the theme from ancient to modern times.

The observation of the self-regulating order of the free market was a most important impetus to the development of a classical liberal or libertarian system of political economy. As the English writer Charles Davenant noted in his 1695 pamphlet "A memorial concerning the coyn of England," price controls were ineffective, because "Nor can any law hinder B, C, & D from supplying their Wants [for in the] Naturall Course of Trade, Each Commodity will find its Price. . . . The supream power can do many things, but it cannot alter the Laws of Nature, of which the most originall is, That every man should preserve himself." Joyce Appleby comments on this passage, noting: "Economic writers had discovered the underlying regularity in free market activity. Where moralists had long urged that necessity knows no law, the economic analysts who pursued price back to demand had discovered a lawfulness in necessity, and in doing so they had come upon a possibility and a reality. The reality was that individuals making decisions about their own persons and property were the determiners of price in the market. The possibility was that the economic rationalism of market participants could supply the order to the economy formerly secured through authority" (Joyce Appleby, *Economic Thought and Ideology in Seventeenth-Century England* [Princeton, N.J.: Princeton University Press, 1978], pp. 187–88).

A seminal figure in the development of the idea of spontaneous order, often quoted and cited by Hayek, was the Scottish thinker Adam Ferguson. In his famous book of 1767, Ferguson pointed out that "nations stumble upon establishments, which are indeed the result of human action, but not the execution of any human design" (see Adam Ferguson, *An Essay on the History of Civil Society* [1767; Cambridge: Cambridge University Press, 1995]). A good overview of the contributions of the thinkers of the "Scottish Enlightenment" is found in Ronald Hamowy's brief work *The Scottish Enlightenment and the Theory of Spontaneous Order* (Carbondale: Southern Illinois University Press, 1987).

The study of spontaneous order has hardly been limited to economic phenomena. Michael Polanyi, a leading chemist, was moved to reject socialism and embrace free-market liberalism by his realization that the order of science was not, and could not be, "planned." When socialist intellectuals announced—as they were wont to do before the collapse of the socialist paradigm—that under "planned science" such-and-such would be discovered in year x, and another fact or theory or principle would be discovered in the next year, all in accordance with a rational plan for society, Polanyi realized that this sort of planning or social engineering was absurd, that one simply could not "plan" scientific progress. Scientific progress simply did not work that way, as Polanyi knew from personal experience. Polanyi applied his considerable intellect to understanding how order could emerge as an unintended consequence of human action, with special—but not exclusive—reference to the natural sciences, in the essays collected as *The Logic of Liberty* (Chicago: University of Chicago Press, 1951). Another classical liberal thinker and philosopher of science, Sir Karl Popper, has pointed out that the idea that one could predict one's future knowledge in the way the socialists insisted was philosophically incoherent: If one could predict one's future knowledge, then one would already know it, and the problem of discovery would simply be assumed away. (Popper criticized the idea of historical prediction in his brilliant book *The Poverty of Historicism* [Boston: Beacon Press, 1957]; his critique of collectivist philosophy appeared in *The Open Society and Its Enemies* [Princeton, N.J.: Princeton University Press, 1950], largely a criticism of Plato, Hegel, and Marx. Other essays on liberty and the open society appeared in *Conjectures and Refutations: The Growth of Scientific Knowledge* [New York: Harper and Row, 1968], notably the essays "Public Opinion and Liberal Principles" and "Utopia and Violence.") Arguments informed by an examination of the history of science have been employed by the journalist Jonathan Rauch against both "fundamentalist" and "politically correct" attempts to restrict freedom of expression in *Kindly Inquisitors: The New Attacks on Free Thought* (Chicago: University of Chicago Press, 1993).

The noted Italian jurist Bruno Leoni turned his attention to the subject of law itself—the very paradigm of order based on command, in the worldview of antilibertarians—as a system of spontaneous order. Some of his more important English-language lectures and essays are collected together as *Freedom and the Law* (3d ed.; Indianapolis: Liberty Press, 1991) (especially noteworthy is his essay "The Law as Individual Claim"). Much of the discipline that has come to be known as "law and economics" can be traced to the work of Leoni and other libertarian scholars (for example, the Nobel laureate Ronald Coase, whose work will be discussed later), and has focused on understanding how the legal institutions that shape the market, such as property and contract, have emerged over time, without being "planned" by anyone. The scientific literature that has appeared in recent decades is enormous, but a good basic overview is provided by the Icelandic economist Thráinn Eggertsson in his *Economic Behavior and Institutions* (Cambridge: Cambridge University Press, 1990) and by Oliver E. Williamson in his *The Economic Institutions of Capitalism* (New York: The Free Press, 1985).

There is also a vast literature that uses the mathematical and conceptual apparatus of "game theory," or the formal study of strategic interaction, to study the emergence of spontaneous order and cooperation. A particularly good introduction to these themes is found in the English economist Robert Sugden's *The Economics of Rights, Co-operation, and Welfare* (Oxford: Basil Blackwell, 1986), which also provides a good introduction for the nonspecialist to the techniques and theorems of game theory. (Sugden provides in a way a masterful updating of the work of David Hume on the emergence of spontaneous order.) A more mathematically challenging and technical approach is found in Michael Taylor's *The Possibility of Cooperation* (Cambridge: Cambridge University Press, 1987). A pathbreaking use of the theory of games, using computerized tournaments between programmed strategies to study how cooperation can emerge even under specified adverse conditions (known as a "prisoner's dilemma"), is found in the political scientist Robert Axelrod's *The Evolution of Cooperation* (New York: Basic Books, 1984).

The study of spontaneous order has been most systematically undertaken by economists, whose enterprise was placed on that track by Adam Smith, who used the metaphor of the "invisible hand" (already prominent in discussions of the subject) in his work *An Inquiry into the Nature and Causes of the Wealth of Nations* (1776) to describe how man "is led to promote an end which is no part of his intentions." Smith thereby set much of the scientific research agenda of economics for the next two centuries. A particularly noteworthy work that helped to place modern social sciences on a secure foundation and that emphasized the tracing of complex systems of order to the actions of individuals is the Austrian economist Carl Menger's *Problems of Economics and Sociology* (1883; Urbana: University of Illinois Press, 1963).

The idea of spontaneous order, even within the study of economic phenomena, is not limited to the study of the price system of the market economy but has been extended to the very institution of money, through which price ratios are expressed. Carl Menger, in *Principles of Economics* (1871; New York: New York University Press, 1981), showed how money emerges as an unintended byproduct of barter and thereby makes possible ever more complex forms of exchange. Institutions that provide complex monetary instruments, such as bank notes, also emerged as the unintended byproducts of acts of saving and lending. The history of "free banking," in which spontaneous monetary orders and complex systems of economic coordination are the results of voluntary interactions, is examined by economist Lawrence H. White in *Free Banking in Britain: Theory, Experience, and Debate, 1800–1845* (Cambridge: Cambridge University Press, 1984), and the economic analysis of free banking is undertaken by economist George A. Selgin in *The Theory of Free Banking: Money Supply Under Competitive Note Issue* (Totowa, N.J.: Rowman and Littlefield, 1988). (Both White and Selgin present evidence that free-banking systems offer greater stability, without economic cycles, than do systems of centralized state-controlled banking.) These studies of free banking are important not only because they offer the possibility of a society in which it is not necessary for the state to control the "commanding heights" of the economy, with all of the potential for abuse and malfeasance that that power represents, but also because they show that order can and does emerge precisely where it is so often assumed to be impossible.

The omnipresence and manifest importance of the price system of the market economy has offered a fertile field to economists interested in the study of spontaneous order (see Hayek's seminal essay "The Use of Knowledge in Society" in Boaz, *The Libertarian Reader*), and it is understandable therefore that the systematic study of spontaneous order should have reached a higher state of development in this field, but this should not blind us to the importance of spontaneous order in law, morality, and many other kinds of human interaction.

V. Free Markets and Voluntary Organization

It may help to examine the market system and its importance in libertarian thought by seeing it in light of the problem of spontaneous order discussed in the previous section. Socialists see markets and see disorder, chaos, and irrationality, and they insist that rationality simply demands that order be imposed on this anarchistic system by the state. Karl Marx himself complained of the "anarchy" of "capitalism," a complaint that would come to be characteristic of almost all criticisms of free-market economies. The remedy such critics offered, of course, was to replace markets with one form or another of state direction.

The issue of whether socialism could in fact create order, rather than chaos, was raised by Ludwig von Mises in his 1920 essay "Economic Calculation in the Socialist Commonwealth." That and other essays are available in F. A. Hayek, ed., *Collectivist Economic Planning: Critical Studies on the Possibilities of Socialism* (1935; Clifton, N.J.: Augustus M. Kelley Publishers, 1975). Mises argued in that essay and in his later work *Socialism: An Economic and Sociological Analysis* (1922; London: Jonathan Cape, 1936, 1951) that socialist planners would not be able to determine how to achieve the ends they set forth, for they would not know what was the least costly method of production in the absence of the prices (or exchange ratios) that are generated through exchanges of property rights in a market. "Socialism," he concluded, "is the abolition of rational economy." That challenge to socialism led naturally to greater interest in how markets solve the problems of economic calculation, an issue addressed by F. A. Hayek in "The Use of Knowledge in Society," presented in *The Libertarian Reader*, edited by David Boaz, and the integration of the understanding of the market economy into the general theme of spontaneous order that I have argued above is central to modern libertarianism. (Other good treatments of the socialist calculation problem include Don Lavoie's *Rivalry and Central Planning: The Socialist Calculation Debate Reconsidered* [Cambridge: Cambridge University Press, 1985] and his more popular and accessible *National Economic Planning: What Is Left?* [Cambridge, Mass.: Ballinger, 1985], as well as David Ramsay Steele's *From Marx to Mises* [La Salle, Ill.: Open Court, 1992], while the problem of how dispersed knowledge is made useful in complex social orders is examined in great detail by Thomas Sowell in *Knowledge and Decisions* [New York: Basic Books, 1980].)

A number of economics treatises have been written that offer the reader a thorough introduction to understanding the market economy, as have numerous outstanding economics textbooks. It would be impossible to do justice to them, or even barely to scratch the surface of the extant economics literature, but a few major works are especially noteworthy for those interested in exploring libertarian political economy. First is Ludwig von Mises, *Human Action: A Treatise on Economics* (New Haven, Conn.: Yale University Press, 1949, and many subsequent editions), which is far more than merely a treatise on economics. Mises offers a systematic view of the problems of social organization, from psychology to capital theory. Another work, written in a similarly classical treatise style and following in Mises's footsteps, is Murray N. Rothbard, *Man, Economy, and State* (Los Angeles: Nash, 1970), which most American readers will likely find less difficult than Mises's work, which was written originally in German and bears the marks of a distinguished continental scholar. Rothbard also wrote a sequel to his treatise, *Power and Market: Government and the Economy* (2d ed.; Kansas City, Mo.: Sheed Andrews and McMeel, 1977), which focused on the study of government intervention.

Perhaps the best book for someone entering into the study of economics for the very first time is Henry Hazlitt's wonderful short book, published in 1946, *Economics in One Lesson* (2d ed.; New Rochelle, N.Y: Arlington House, 1985), which updates and applies the insights of the great classical economists to issues of contemporary policy.

Markets are significant for the way in which they can overcome racism, tribalism, and irrational prejudice and can replace enmity and war with friendship and peace. As F. A. Hayek was fond of pointing out, the ancient Greek verb καταλλάσσω (*katalásso*) means to welcome into one's village, to reconcile, to change an enemy into a friend, or to exchange. As the historian Geoffrey Parker noted in his study of the Dutch rebellion against the taxing and religious policies of the Spanish king, there was "violent opposition" to his policies because "so many heretics came to Antwerp to trade that its prosperity would be ruined if a resident inquisition were introduced" (*The Dutch Revolt* [New York: Viking Penguin, 1988], p. 47).

Despite all of the language of "market takeovers" and "price wars," the market is a forum for voluntary persuasion, as Adam Smith emphasized in his *Lectures on Jurisprudence* when discussing the price system: "If we should enquire into the principle in the human mind on which this disposition of trucking [i.e., of trading] is founded, it is clearly on the naturall inclination every one has to persuade. The offering of a schilling, which to us appears to have so plain and simple a meaning, is in reality offering an argument to persuade one to do so and so as it is for his interest" (Adam Smith, *Lectures on Jurisprudence* [Indianapolis: Liberty Classics, 1982], p. 352).

It is often argued that markets are fine for many or even most purposes, but that they systematically fail and must be supplemented or overridden by coercive state power. This "market failure" approach argues that the state must either intervene to change the conditions of trade for the production and exchange of certain goods and services (usually referred to, somewhat misleadingly, as "regulation") or produce the goods and services itself (usually referred to as the production of "public goods").

A useful application of the insights gained from the socialist calculation debate to government's regulatory interventions into a fundamentally market economy is found in Israel Kirzner's essay "The Perils of Regulation," in his book *Discovery and the Capitalist Process* (Chicago: University of Chicago Press, 1985), which argues that coercive regulation by the state short-circuits the market's discovery processes. There is, in addition, an enormous volume of published empirical research on the issue of "government failure" and the harmful consequences for consumers of the edicts of governmental regulatory agencies. (A visit to the library to inspect such journals as the *Journal of Political Economy*, the *Journal of Law and Economics*, the *American Economic Review*, the *Cato Journal*, *Public Choice*, or any number of others would give the reader a taste of the literature available.) Some of the main themes derived from this vast array of studies of government failure and the free-market alternative are presented in a popular style in *Free to Choose* (New York: Harcourt Brace Jovanovich, 1980) by Milton and Rose Friedman, especially the chapters "Who Protects the Consumer?" and "Who Protects the Worker?"

The issue of public goods, which plays so large a role in the justification of governmental coercion, has also generated a huge literature, both critical of the state's ability to produce authentically "public" goods and revealing of how voluntary organization succeeds in producing public goods. In general, public goods are defined by reference to two characteristics: Once a public good is produced, it may be costly to exclude noncontributors from its enjoyment (exclusion costs), and the consumption of the good by one person does not diminish the consumption of the good by another (nonrivalrous consumption). The standard example of a public good that could not be produced on the market was for many years the lighthouse, which throws out its light beam to be seen by all, whether they have paid or not (one cannot exclude the nonpayers from seeing it), and sighting the beam does not necessarily mean that there is "less" of a beam for another to see (nonrivalrous consumption). This paradigm case was examined by Nobel laureate in economics Ronald Coase in a classic essay, "The Lighthouse in Economics" (*Journal of Law and Economics* 17[2], October 1974; reprinted in Coase, *The Firm, the Market, and the Law* [Chicago: University of Chicago Press, 1988]), which examined the actual history of how lighthouses were produced by private enterprise in England and concluded that "economists should not use the lighthouse as an example of a service which could only be provided by the government." Many similar examples, along with classic essays on the topic (including Paul Samuelson's seminal case for state provision of public goods), are collected by Tyler Cowen in *Public Goods and Market Failures: A Critical Examination* (New Brunswick, N.J.: Transaction Publishers, 1992), which is probably the best volume of essays on the subject.

Two other especially good treatments of the subject of public goods, tying in the economic aspect with ethical questions about fairness and justice, are Anthony de Jasay, *Social Contract, Free Ride: A Study of the Public Goods Problem* (Oxford: Oxford University Press, 1989) and David Schmidtz, *The Limits of Government: An Essay on the Public Goods Argument* (Boulder, Colo.: Westview Press, 1991).

One subclass of the public goods argument concerns the environment. "Environmental economics" has become especially relevant in recent years, as many policy debates have emerged regarding the proper role of government in this area. Ronald Coase, again, set much of the research agenda in this area with his essay "The Problem of Social Cost" (*Journal of Law and Economics* 3, October 1960; reprinted in *The Firm, the Market, and the Law*), in which he showed that the problem of "externalities" (smoke is normally considered a "negative externality," because it harms people who were not part of the decision to produce the smoke) could be understood in terms of a lack of property rights; most externality problems arise from government's failure clearly to define or to protect property rights. An outstanding and very readable primer on the economics of the environment, using a property rights approach, is *Free Market Environmentalism* (San Francisco: Pacific Research Institute, 1991) by Terry L. Anderson and Donald R. Leal.

An important objection that has been raised against markets is that they fail to generate a proper "distribution" of income: Markets are unfair, or generate politically unstable distributions of wealth, or are responsible for "the rich getting richer, and the poor getting poorer." There are many issues tied up in these claims, but two good libertarian analyses of the ethics of redistributionism, employing economic reasoning but abstracting from the practical issue of incentives to produce when the fruits of one's labor are taken away, are the French political scientist Bertrand de Jouvenel's brilliant essay *The Ethics of Redistribution* (1951; Indianapolis: Liberty Press, 1990) and the German economist Ludwig Lachmann's essay "The Market Economy and the Distribution of Wealth" in *Capital, Expectations, and the Market Process*, Walter E. Grinder, ed. (Kansas City, Mo.: Sheed Andrews and McMeel, 1977), in which Lachmann distinguished between "ownership" (or property), which is a legal concept, and "wealth," which is an economic concept. As we all know, wealth can change dramatically without any changes in ownership, as the value of one's property goes up and down due to the valuation of it by others and their estimation of how it will fit into their production plans. Thus, as Lachmann shows, "The market process is . . . a leveling process. In a market economy a process of redistribution of wealth is taking place all the time before which those outwardly similar processes which modern politicians are in the habit of instituting, pale into comparative insignificance."

581

Of course, attempts to alter the ever-changing pattern of wealth holdings by force, through taxation and other forms of coercive redistribution of property, can generate most unwelcome consequences, as the contemporary experience with the welfare state shows. A careful empirical study of the effects of redistribution on the poor in America was undertaken by the social scientist Charles Murray and published as his pathbreaking *Losing Ground: American Social Policy, 1930–1980* (New York: Basic Books, 1984), which pointed out the growth of dependency and the breakdown of family life and civil society brought about by the welfare state. Not only does the welfare state undercut institutions such as the family, but it also systematically displaces the many other institutions of civil society by which the poor are assisted and solidarity is fostered. The long-neglected history of "mutual aid" has recently received renewed attention, thanks partly to the careful historical research of the British historian and political scientist David Green, especially in his study of the voluntary provision of medical care in Britain, *Working Class Patients and the Medical Establishment: Self-Help in Britain from the Mid-Nineteenth Century to 1948* (New York: St. Martin's Press, 1985), which shows how the libertarian working people's organizations of earlier years fought against socialized medicine, and in his more recent study *Reinventing Civil Society: The Rediscovery of Welfare Without Politics* (London: Institute of Economic Affairs, 1993). The American scene has been studied by the historian David Beito, notably in his essay "Mutual Aid for Social Welfare: The Case of American Fraternal Societies," *Critical Review* 4, Fall 1990, and by Richard Cornuelle in his *Reclaiming the American Dream: The Role of Private Individuals and Voluntary Associations* (New Brunswick, N.J.: Transaction, 1993). As Cornuelle and others have pointed out, the free society is a society characterized by voluntary relations, of which market exchanges are only one category. A wide range of organizations are possible, and common, under freedom, including charities, self-help associations (such as Alcoholics Anonymous, an organization of recovering alcoholics who help each other to overcome their weaknesses), religious institutions, and much, much more. Just as socialism displaces profit-making firms from producing goods, so welfare statism displaces mutual aid organizations, families, churches, and fraternal organizations from producing solidarity, upward social mobility, and care for the least fortunate.

An especially important application of the understanding of markets is the maintenance of harmony and concord among people of different races, religious creeds, and nations. As markets are forums for persuasion, so they are opportunities for peaceful cooperation. A good introduction to the economic analysis of racial relations is the work of the economist and historian Thomas Sowell, *Markets and Minorities* (New York: Basic Books, 1982). The deleterious effects on minorities of state intervention in the market are examined in Walter Williams, *The State against Blacks* (New York: McGraw-Hill, 1982). And the history of "Jim Crow" laws, which forcibly separated African-Americans and whites and relegated African-Americans to "the back of the bus," is set forth by economic historian Jennifer Roback in a number of studies, including "Southern Labor Law in the Jim Crow Era: Exploitative or Competitive?" *University of Chicago Law Review* 51, Fall 1984, and "The Political Economy of Segregation: The Case of Segregated Streetcars," *Journal of Economic History* 46, December 1986. Law professor David Bernstein, in "Roots of the 'Underclass': The Decline of Laissez Faire Jurisprudence and the Rise of Racist Labor Legislation," *American University Law Review* 43, Fall 1993, and "Licensing Laws: A Historical Example of the Use of Government Regulatory Power against African-Americans," *San Diego Law Review* 31, Winter 1994, has examined facially neutral regulations that had the effect and sometimes the purpose of restricting economic opportunity for African-Americans. The more recent attempts to assist the victims of previous state interventions, often known as "affirmative action," are analyzed by civil-rights lawyer Clint Bolick in *The Affirmative Action Fraud* (Washington: Cato Institute, 1996).

Finally, it should be noted that although markets are not "perfect," neither is any other form of human interaction. Those who identify "market failure" by comparing the outcome of market interactions with some ideal outcome should do the same with government. Rather than comparing imperfect markets with perfect government, which is the normal approach of critics of the market, we should compare imperfect markets with imperfect government. In his witty book *Capitalism* (Oxford: Basil Blackwell, 1990), Arthur Seldon turns the tables on antilibertarians and compares imperfect governments with perfect markets, a clever move to show how unreasonable many proposals for substituting government coercion for market persuasion really are.

VI. Justice and Political Organization

It was claimed above that a belief in imprescriptible individual rights is a hallmark of libertarianism. Rights necessarily entail obligations on others. It is therefore a hallmark of libertarianism to maintain that all humans are under certain obligations. But what are those obligations? In general, we can say that the obligations are of a "negative" kind, that is, that one abstain from action harmful to the rights of others. Such obligations are universal, in the sense that they are binding on all moral agents, and "compossible," in the sense that they are all simultaneously possible of realization.

Of course, there are "positive" obligations, as well, such as the obligation to pay a dollar for the cup of coffee I drank this morning. This obligation is a particular one: I (and no one else) must pay the owner of the café (and no one else) an agreed-upon amount for the cup of coffee. John Locke and others in the libertarian tradition have insisted that all such particular obligations have to be based on consent. In contrast, nationalists, socialists, racists, and other sorts of collectivists typically insist that one has a multitude of particular obligations to which one did *not* consent, but to which one was born, as a member of a particular nation, class, or race. (Some of the better-articulated of these ideas are discussed in the last section, under the rubric of "communitarian" critics of libertarianism.)

Contract was a central element of Roman law, as the great Roman jurist Gaius noted in his famous *Institutes*: "We turn now to obligations. They divide first into two: all obligations arise from a contract or from a delict" (a delict is a violation of law or offense to another). The argument that government should be based on the principles of contract, which played so important a role in the American founding, as shown in the U.S. Declaration of Independence, has a long history. The noted historian Quentin Skinner has stated, in his *Foundations of Modern Political Thought: Volume Two, The Age of Reformation* (Cambridge: Cambridge University Press, 1978), "The idea that any legitimate polity must originate in an act of consent was of course a scholastic commonplace, one which the followers of Ockham no less than Aquinas had always emphasised" (p. 163). A typical example of the importance of consent, and of the retained right of the people to "alter or abolish" (in Thomas Jefferson's phrase) government when it overstepped its legitimate bounds was found in the ancient coronation ceremony of the kings of Aragon, in which the peers declared: "We who are as good as you, make you our king, on condition that you keep and observe our privileges and liberties; and if not, not."

This principle was carefully enunciated by the brilliant Whig writer Algernon Sidney, who was executed by the English king's forces (and was therefore referred to by Jefferson as "the Martyr Sidney"), when he identified himself in his *Discourses Concerning Government*, Thomas G. West, ed. (1698; Indianapolis: Liberty Classics, 1990) as, "I, who deny any power to be just that is not founded upon consent." John Locke insisted in his *Second Treatise of Government* that "no Government can have a right to obedience from a people who have not freely consented to it."

The argument that one has nonconsensual particular obligations to particular political organizations is subjected to withering criticism by A. John Simmons in *Moral Principles and Political Obligations* (Princeton, N.J.: Princeton University Press, 1979) and in his later updating of Locke's philosophy of government, *On the Edge of Anarchy: Locke, Consent, and the Limits of Society* (Princeton, N.J.: Princeton University Press, 1993).

Various attempts have been made to reconcile government—or institutions to protect individual rights—with consent, that is, to establish the legitimacy of government. It is certainly clear that most governments (or states, to use the more precise term) around the world did not originate in acts of consent on the part of the populations over which they rule. (Dictatorships, absolute monarchies, and the like are obvious examples.) To that extent, libertarians would certainly consider them illegitimate. Indeed, Lysander Spooner, in his famous essay "The Constitution of No Authority" (in *No Treason*, 1867–1807; http://www.lysanderspooner.org/notreason.htm#no6), and other radical libertarians argued that all existing states were illegitimate, and that no one was bound to obey them, except in so far as their commands coincided with one's natural and universally valid obligations to respect the rights of others.

Some libertarians have argued that profit-making business firms competing in free markets can provide defense from aggression more efficiently than monopoly states and without violating fundamental rights in the process. This is clearly at least partly true, as there are far more private law enforcement agents (security guards, bail bondsmen, and so on) in America than there are governmentally employed police, and rights violations by private security guards, while greater than zero, are a tiny fraction of rights violations by members of the police and other state enforcement agencies. It was this argument by Murray N. Rothbard, as articulated in books such as his *For a New Liberty: The Libertarian Manifesto* (2d ed.; New York: Macmillan, 1978), that inspired Robert Nozick to defend strictly limited monopoly government in his *Anarchy, State, and Utopia* (New York: Basic Books, 1974), which offers an ingenious argument for limited government that does not violate rights.

The argument of Rothbard, that protection from aggression can be considered a service to be provided on the market, has also been defended by law professor (and former prosecutor) Randy Barnett in a two-part essay, "Pursuing Justice in a Free Society: Part One— Power vs. Liberty; Part Two—Crime Prevention and the Legal Order," *Criminal Justice Ethics*, Summer/Fall 1985, Winter/Spring 1986. The economist Bruce Benson presents a useful history and economic analysis of voluntary provision of law in *The Enterprise of Law* (San Francisco: Pacific Research Institute, 1990). (Such approaches typically rest on the claim that restitution, or making the victim whole again, is preferable to punishment, or harming the perpetrator without making the victim whole again, and that the incentive to obtain restitution can drive a more efficient and humane legal system. Two scholarly and fascinating studies of how a stateless society with a restitution-based legal system functioned are found in William I. Miller's *Bloodtaking and Peacemaking: Feud, Law, and Society in Saga Iceland* [Chicago: University of Chicago Press, 1990] and Jesse Byock's *Medieval Iceland* [Berkeley: University of California Press, 1988].)

The model that Rothbard advocates is easily misunderstood, as it sometimes seems from his writings that law and justice are merely commodities to be purchased like hamburgers or lawn fertilizer on a free market. But since law and justice are what define markets, it seems rather odd, if not contradictory, to see them as the product of markets. This misunderstanding is easily corrected by examining contractual models of government, in which one does not "buy" particular commodities, but buys or agrees to sets of rules that are subsequently binding on one. Especially illuminating are those accounts that take as their starting point actually existing contractual governments, such as neighborhood associations, condominium

586

associations, and "proprietary communities." Economists Donald J. Boudreaux and Randall G. Holcombe provide a model of the contractual provision of public goods, including arbitration and security, in their essay "Government by Contract," *Public Finance Quarterly* 17(3), July 1989, and Fred Foldvary expands greatly on this approach in his outstanding work *Public Goods and Private Communities: The Market Provision of Social Services* (Aldershot, UK: Edward Elgar, 1994).

Other libertarians, citing the difficulties of obtaining the unanimity of consent that would be necessary to generate such legitimacy, have established unanimity as an ideal toward which one might aspire, even if it is never to be realized. Especially influential examples of this approach from the field of "public choice" or "constitutional economics" can be found in the work of James Buchanan and Gordon Tullock, notably *The Calculus of Consent* (Ann Arbor: University of Michigan, 1962), and in Buchanan's *The Limits of Liberty: Between Anarchy and Leviathan* (Chicago: University of Chicago Press, 1975). (A similar "second-best" approach to the legitimacy of government is found in Richard Epstein's *Simple Rules for a Complex World*.)

The theme of imprescriptible rights plays an important role in the legitimacy of government, for, as Thomas Jefferson insisted in the Declaration of Independence, some of our rights are *inalienable*. Even if we were to want to give these rights away to another person, we could not do so; it would be a violation of our very nature. "Voluntary slavery" is impossible, much as a spherical cube or a living corpse is impossible. Thus, a tyrannical government that attempted to destroy us or to take away all of our liberties would be ipso facto illegitimate; there are limits to the legitimate power of government, even when it has been constituted through initial acts of consent. The standard or canonical libertarian account of the origins and limitations of legitimate government is still to be found in John Locke's *Second Treatise of Government*, especially the chapters "Of the Beginning of Political Societies" and "Of the Dissolution of Government."

VII. Violence and the State

If it is the case that most states around the world are illegitimate, how did they come to have the unjust powers that they effectively claim? The historical answer is fairly clear, as Thomas Paine noted in *Common Sense* in dismissing the claims to legitimacy of the English monarchy: "No man in his senses can say that their claim under William the Conqueror is a very honourable one. A French bastard landing with an armed banditti, and establishing himself king of England against the consent of the natives, is in plain terms a very paltry rascally original.—It certainly hath no divinity in it." States originate in conquest and flourish through war.

If we consider the issue of the origins of states from the perspective of the different means to the accumulation of wealth (by no means the only way to consider the issue, but certainly a fruitful one), we may turn to a useful treatise by the German sociologist Franz Oppenheimer, *The State* (1914; New York: Free Life Editions, 1975). Oppenheimer noted that "there are two fundamentally opposed means whereby man, requiring sustenance, is impelled to obtain the necessary means for satisfying his desires. These are work and robbery, one's own labor and the forcible appropriation of the labor of others." The former he termed "the economic means" and the latter "the political means." "The state," he wrote, "is an organization of the political means." (The thesis that states originated in acts of conquest was woven through the history of civilization by Alexander Rüstow in his *Freedom and Domination: A Historical Critique of Civilization*, discussed earlier.)

The thesis that "war makes the state, and states make war" has been advanced by Charles Tilly (notably in his essay "War Making and State Making as Organized Crime," in *Bringing the State Back In*, Peter Evans, Dietrich Rueschemeyer, and Theda Skocpol, eds. [Cambridge: Cambridge University Press, 1985], and in his book *Coercion, Capital, and European States, AD 990–1992* [Oxford: Blackwell, 1992]) and presented in a more accessible form by political scientist Bruce D. Porter in his *War and the Rise of the State: The Military Foundations of Modern Politics* (New York: Free Press, 1994). (Another careful study of this theme by a distinguished historian is Otto Hintze, "Military Organization and the Organization of the State," in *The Historical Essays of Otto Hintze*, Felix Gilbert, ed. [Oxford: Oxford University Press, 1975].) A horrifying tabulation of how many people have been killed by states in the twentieth century is presented by political scientist R. J. Rummel in *Death by Government* (New Brunswick, N.J.: Transaction, 1994). *Excluding war dead*, he tabulates 169,202,000 people "murdered by government, including genocide, politicide, and mass murder" between 1900 and 1987.

Libertarians typically ask how one can expect an institution with such a bloody and savage record to accomplish all of the wondrous and humanitarian ends assigned to it by collectivists. This is no refutation of the collectivist arguments, of course, but it should at least raise questions about the appropriateness of the means chosen to the attainment of the ends. That the association of the state with war is not limited to the distant historical past is made evident by the experience of the twentieth century, when government power has grown by leaps and bounds through war. A good historical study of the growth of the American state and its association with war is found in the economic historian Robert Higgs's *Crisis and Leviathan: Critical Episodes in the Growth of American Government* (Oxford: Oxford University Press, 1987).

It is frequently assumed that the emergence of militarily organized territorial monopolies over violence (that is, states), extending their powers through conquest, is the only conceivable or even normal form of political organization. Counterexamples are presented by Hendrik Spruyt in *The Sovereign State and Its Competitors* (Princeton, N.J.: Princeton University Press, 1994), which examines other forms of political organization, often of a far more voluntary nature, such as the Hanseatic League of German merchants, and forms of nonterritorial organization, such as the Roman Church and the Holy Roman Empire.

Institutions that have seized and legitimized territorial monopolies have an advantage in their ability to "socialize" costs, that is, to spread costs over a "captive" population. By imposing relatively small costs on large numbers of people, great wealth can be accumulated and delivered to relatively small numbers of people. This process is sometimes referred to in the technical economics literature as "rent-seeking," and it is made possible by the different "transaction costs" faced by large and small groups. As Milton Friedman has observed, in every country where farmers form a large majority of the population, they are brutally oppressed and squeezed for the benefit of the much smaller urban population. But wherever farmers are in the minority, many of them manage to squeeze enormous sums of money from the much larger urban population, through governmentally guaranteed high prices, government purchases of surpluses at above market rates, acreage allotments, payments not to farm, and on and on. This seems a paradox, at least in democracies.

But it is easily understood when we realize that the costs of becoming informed and of organizing (identifying one another as having common interests, coming together, agreeing on ends, and so forth) can be very high for large groups, but disproportionately smaller for smaller groups. As the sociologist Gaetano Mosca noted in his classic study of group conflict,

> The dominion of an organized minority, obeying a single impulse, over the unorganized majority is inevitable. The power of any minority is irresistible as against each single individual in the majority, who stands alone before the totality of the organized minority. At the same time, the minority is organized for the very reason that it is a minority. A hundred men acting in concert, with a common understanding, will triumph over a thousand men who are not in accord and can therefore be dealt with one by one. Meanwhile it will be easier for the former to act in concert and have a mutual understanding simply because they are a hundred and not a thousand. It follows that the larger the political community, the smaller will the proportion of the governing minority to the governed majority be, and the more difficult it will be for the majority to organize for reaction against the minority (Gaetano Mosca, *The Ruling Class* [1896; New York: McGraw–Hill, 1939], p. 53).

The study of wealth transfers of this kind was of great interest to the members of the Italian school in fiscal theory, most of whom were libertarians, who raised the topic to the status of a science. Noteworthy among them was the social scientist Vilfredo Pareto (see Vilfredo Pareto, *Sociological Writings*, S. E. Finer, ed. [Totowa, N.J.: Rowman and Littlefield, 1976], especially pp. 114–20, 137–42, 162–64, 270, 276–78, 315, and 317–18 on what he termed "spoliation"). Pareto and his colleagues revealed the phenomenon of "rational ignorance" and its role in perpetuating the tyranny of special interests. As Pareto noted, "Very many economic matters are so complicated that few people have even a superficial understanding of them. Amongst the people who use sugar there is not one in a thousand who is aware of the appropriation of wealth that goes on under the system of production-subsidies." Pareto explained how the state can disperse costs over large groups and concentrate benefits among small groups through a simple story:

> Let us suppose that in a country of thirty million inhabitants it is proposed, under some pretext or other, to get each citizen to pay out one franc a year, and to distribute the total amount amongst thirty persons. Every one of the donors will give up one franc a year; every one of the beneficiaries will receive one million francs a year. The two groups will differ very greatly in their response to the situation. Those who hope to gain a million a year will know no rest by day or night. They will win newspapers over to their interest by financial inducements and drum up support from all quarters. A discreet hand will warm the palms of needy legislators, even of ministers [of government]. . . . In contrast, the individual who is threatened with losing one franc a year—even if he is fully aware of what is afoot—will not for so small a thing forgo a picnic in the country, or fall out with useful or congenial friends, or get on the wrong side of the mayor or *prefet*! In these circumstances the outcome is not in doubt: the spoliators will win hands down.

Other pioneers of the scientific study of government policy include Giovanni Montemartini (see his "The Fundamental Principles of a Pure Theory of Public Finance," in *Classics in the Theory of Public Finance*, Richard A. Musgrave and Alan T. Peacock, eds. [3d ed.; New York: St. Martin's Press, 1994]), Amilcare Puviani, Maffeo Pantaleoni, and the first president of the postwar Italian Republic, Luigi Einaudi. Nobel laureate in economics James Buchanan offers a study of the roots of public choice economics in the Italian school in his essay "'LaScienze delle Finanze': The Italian Tradition in Fiscal Theory," in *Fiscal Theory and Political Economy* (Chapel Hill: University of North Carolina Press, 1960).

Since, in complex societies that have progressed beyond simple lord/peasant arrangements of social differentiation, virtually every person is a member of some economic or social minority, each person faces a similar incentive to try to extract wealth from the many through special favors and subsidies. Thus, as Frédéric Bastiat observed, in modern times, "The state is the great fictitious entity by which everyone seeks to live at the expense of everyone else" (in his essay "The State," in *Selected Essays on Political Economy* [Irvington-on-Hudson, N.Y.: Foundation for Economic Education, 1968]). The coercive extraction of wealth is often referred to (rather unfortunately) in the economics literature as "rent-seeking," a term, according to James Buchanan, "designed to describe behavior in institutional settings where individual efforts to maximize value generate social waste rather than social surplus." The systematic study of this system of what Bastiat called "reciprocal plunder" and technical economists refer to as the "rent-seeking society" has generated a massive literature, which would be impossible to survey here. A good place to start, however, would be James M. Buchanan, Robert D. Tollison, and Gordon Tullock, eds., *Toward a Theory of a Rent-Seeking Society* (College Station: Texas A & M University Press, 1980).

What libertarians conclude from historical study and from economic and sociological analysis of the activity of the state is that, if the state cannot be replaced by other—voluntary—forms of organization, it must be carefully limited. Even if necessary, the state remains what Thomas Paine termed in *Common Sense* "a necessary evil," one that must always be watched over and guarded against. In the 1798 Kentucky Resolutions protesting the Alien and Sedition Acts, Thomas Jefferson maintained that "free government is founded in jealousy, not in confidence; it is jealousy and not confidence which prescribes limited constitutions, to bind down those whom we are obliged to trust with power." Domestically, the state must be restrained by the constitution and a vigilant population, and in foreign relations it must be held back from opportunities for conflict with foreign states. In his Farewell Address, George Washington counseled, "The great rule of conduct for us, in regard to foreign Nations is in extending our commercial relations to have with them as little *political* connection as possible." It is principally for this reason—the maintenance of peace and international harmony—that libertarians have favored freedom of trade, for in engaging in trade ties of amity and interest are established, and occasions for war avoided. As Washington maintained in the Farewell Address, "Harmony, liberal intercourse with all Nations, are recommended by policy, humanity and interest." (Most of Jefferson's essential writings can be found in Merrill D. Peterson, ed., *The Portable Jefferson* [New York: Viking Press, 1975]. A good collection of Washington's writings is W. B. Allen, ed., *George Washington: A Collection* [Indianapolis: Liberty Classics, 1988].)

VIII. Critics of Libertarianism

As long as people have yearned for a society of free and equal individuals, in which relations between people are determined by consent, rather than by coercion, there have been critics who have argued that such a system would be unworkable, chaotic, or immoral, that individuals would be alienated and deracinated, or that voluntary cooperation on a large scale is impossible because the interests of individuals are inherently conflicting and can only result in violence.

Perhaps the earliest, and probably the most influential and brilliantly presented, of such criticisms is to be found in *The Republic*, the dialogue written by the Greek philosopher Plato. Many of the ideas of the so-called Sophists (now largely a term of abuse, thanks to the brilliant polemics of Plato, their relentless critic) can be identified as protolibertarian, and as defenses of the emerging liberty, commerce, and toleration (relative to its predecessors and neighbors) of the Greek world. In Book II of *The Republic*, Adeimantus and Socrates discuss the emergence of markets, voluntary coordination, and what we would call civil society, and Adeimantus concludes that justice lies in "some need . . . men have of one another" (372a), a view that foreshadows David Hume and the thinkers of the Scottish Enlightenment. This line of thought is interrupted by Glaucon, who describes such a city as "a city of sows" (372d). Plato then has Socrates assert that the desire for luxury among such men will lead to conflict with their neighbors, for "the land, of course, which was sufficient for feeding the men who were then, will now be small although it was sufficient. . . . Then we must cut off a piece of our neighbors' land, if we are going to have sufficient for pasture and tillage, and they in turn from ours, if they let themselves go to the unlimited acquisition of money, overstepping the boundaries of the necessary . . . [and] after that won't we go to war as a consequence, Glaucon?"(372d–e). And with war will come the state and the end of the voluntary society.

This argument alleging an ultimate irreconcilability of human ends and aspirations also plays a role in the thinking of many critics of libertarianism—notably among collectivist racial and nationalist ideologies, according to which the interests of different races or nations are in irreconcilable conflict—and has proven a formidable opponent to libertarian views. A good statement of a libertarian response, showing the possibility of human cooperation when rules of just conduct are in place, can be found in *Human Action: A Treatise on Economics* (New Haven: Yale University Press, 1949, and many subsequent editions), by Ludwig von Mises, especially the treatment of what Mises called the "Ricardian law of association," which is something of an updated and more sophisticated defense of the principle that Adeimantus had proposed thousands of years earlier. As Mises notes:

> The fundamental facts that brought about cooperation, society, and civilization and transformed the animal man into a human being are the facts that work performed under the division of labor is more productive than isolated work and that man's reason is capable of recognizing this truth. But for these facts men would have forever remained deadly foes of one another, irreconcilable rivals in their endeavors to secure a portion of the scarce supply of means of sustenance provided by nature. Each would have been forced to view all other men as his enemies; his craving for the satisfaction of his own appetites would have brought him into an implacable conflict with all his neighbors. No sympathy could possibly develop under such a state of affairs.

The *locus classicus* of the claim that libertarianism leads to alienation and atomism is found in the writings of Karl Marx, another enormously influential critic of libertarianism, who argued in his essay "On the Jewish Question" that civil society, as libertarians understand it, is based on a "decomposition of man" such that man's "essence is no longer in community but in difference." Thus, to achieve man's true essence, we must insist not on individual rights, which merely separate one person from another, but instead on the primacy of the political community. (As the anthropologist Ernest Gellner pointed out in his *Conditions of Liberty: Civil Society and Its Rivals* [New York: Viking Penguin, 1994]), the experience of "real socialism" was that it led "not to a newly restored social man, but to something closer to total atomization than perhaps any previous society had known.") There is a great deal of literature that is critical of Marxism, but especially useful for its critique of the philosophy behind it (and not merely of the politics of Marxist states or of the impossibility of economic calculation without money prices) is the British philosopher H. B. Acton's work *The Illusion of the Epoch: Marxism-Leninism as a Philosophical Creed* (1955; London: Routledge & Kegan Paul, 1972). (See also his defense of the morality of market exchanges in *The Morals of Markets and Related Essays*, David Gordon and Jeremy Shearmur, eds. [Indianapolis: Liberty Press, 1993].)

An especially prominent line of criticism of libertarianism—related to that offered by Marx—is that libertarians have fundamentally misunderstood the nature of freedom. This issue was already canvassed by Benjamin Constant in "The Liberty of the Ancients Compared with That of the Moderns," in *The Libertarian Reader*, edited by David Boaz, but it has been revived by Charles Taylor (whose work is discussed below) and by others who have argued that "real freedom" is a matter of how much "self-control" (over one's passions, for example) one has, or how much one is able to participate in collective decisions, or how much power or wealth one has to attain one's ends, or some complex combination of these factors.

A recent defense—offered on the basis of a new stipulation of the meaning of freedom—of redistributive socialism, and of a "right" to be supported through the coerced taxation of others, even if one refuses to work, has been advanced by Philippe Van Parijs in his book *Real Freedom for All: What (If Anything) Can Justify Capitalism?* (Oxford: Oxford University Press, 1995), which argues for the right of the deliberately indolent to be supported by the coerced donations of others as a requirement of "real freedom." Merely "formal freedom" (of the sort defended by libertarians) allegedly consists in "security" and "self-ownership," but "real" freedom adds to the list "opportunity." Thus, two persons may be formally free to swim across a lake, but only the good swimmer is "really" free to do so, and it is this "real" freedom that really matters. A similar line of argument is found in Alan Haworth's *Anti-Libertarianism: Markets, Philosophy, and Myth* (London: Routledge, 1994), in which the author claims that what has come to be known as libertarianism is in fact "anti-libertarian," because it does not guarantee the enjoyment of "real" freedom, which evidently requires extensive coercion for its realization.

We can, of course, stipulate that we will use freedom to mean one thing, and not another, or that we will use freedom to mean power, or wealth, or good character, or whatever, but we already have perfectly good words for these things (power, wealth, and good character), and saying that "freedom" will be used to refer to one of those things offers us little help in examining difficult problems of justice. (A useful collection of essays on the nature of freedom, including a variety of views, is found in a volume edited by David Miller, *Liberty* [Oxford: Oxford University Press, 1991]; in the selection from F. A. Hayek's book *The Constitution of Liberty*, Hayek defends the traditional view that liberty refers to freedom from dependence on the arbitrary will of another human.)

A collection of essays critical of libertarianism on the grounds that both freedom *and* equality have been misunderstood by libertarians is Stephen Darwall, *Equal Freedom* (Ann Arbor: University of Michigan Press, 1995). Darwall points out that liberty and equality are sometimes seen as conflicting ideals, but that

> there are senses in which, on anyone's view, liberty and equality are not conflicting but interdependent and mutually reinforcing ideals. Central to libertarianism, for instance, is the doctrine that all persons have equal moral standing by virtue of holding identical natural rights not to be harmed in their "life, health, liberty, or possessions" (in Locke's phrase). Liberty, in the broad sense of freedom from these harms, is a value *among equals*; it is realized when everyone's rights are respected equally. In advancing an ideal of liberty, therefore, the libertarian simultaneously puts forward an ideal of equality. He interprets both as complementary aspects of a comprehensive conception of justice.

The essays in the book, by distinguished socialist and social democratic philosophers, "can all be read as critiques of libertarianism," that is, as showing that some alternative notion of freedom or equality is superior to the libertarian "complementary" conception. The arguments are varied and ingenious and each deserves its own response, but one general response offered by libertarians is unaddressed: When some have the power to "equalize" the possessions or conditions of all others, those with the power to do so will be elevated in power above the rest, who will no longer be equal to them. Equality of freedom, or equality before the law, may be incompatible with the existence of the power to impose equality of condition. This problem was eloquently stated by F. A. Hayek in *The Road to Serfdom* (Chicago: University of Chicago Press, 1944), especially in the chapters "Who, Whom?" and "Why the Worst Get on Top."

Another particularly ingenious line of criticism of libertarianism has been developed by the Oxford philosopher and Marxist theorist G. A. Cohen and presented in his book *Self-Ownership, Freedom, and Equality* (Cambridge: Cambridge University Press, 1995), which is largely a sustained critique of Robert Nozick. (Much of Cohen's argument is fairly technical and rests on contestable claims about the nature of rationality, bargaining theory, and other matters, so it is really for advanced readers who have already read Nozick, as well as John Locke and perhaps even some of the literature in the theory of bargaining and strategic interaction.) Cohen's arguments against libertarianism, along with many others, figure prominently in the treatments of libertarianism presented by the political theorist Will Kymlicka in his book *Contemporary Political Philosophy: An Introduction* (Oxford: Oxford University Press, 1990), Chapter 4, and by the socialist political scientist Attracta Ingram, in her book *A Political Theory of Rights* (Oxford: Oxford University Press, 1994), which sets new standards for personal invective and vituperation directed against libertarian theorists in an academic book.

Cohen seeks to undercut libertarianism by denying that property in one's person ("self-ownership") leads to a system of private property in alienable objects ("world ownership"). (Cohen rejects the idea of property in one's person, as well, but he is willing to assume it for the sake of argument.) In *Self-Ownership, Freedom, and Equality,* Cohen "entertained an alternative to Nozick's 'up for grabs' hypothesis about the external world, to wit, that it is jointly owned by everyone, with each having a veto over its prospective use. And I showed that final equality of condition is assured when the egalitarian hypothesis about ownership of external resources is conjoined with the thesis of self-ownership" (p. 14). In the process, however, Cohen makes several errors in bargaining theory (he assumes that there is a uniquely rational bargaining strategy with determinate results), and he confuses the various scenarios he describes. Of equal significance, however, is that a situation in which every resource in the world is "jointly owned by everyone, with each having a veto over its prospective use" is not justified by Cohen; it was considered and rejected as implausible several hundred years ago by John Locke, who noted in section 28 of his *Second Treatise of Government,* "If such a consent as that was necessary, Mankind had starved, notwithstanding the Plenty God had given him." The philosopher Jan Narveson responds to some of Cohen's arguments in *The Libertarian Idea* (Philadelphia: Temple University Press, 1988), as does David Gordon in his *Resurrecting Marx: The Analytical Marxists on Freedom, Exploitation, and Justice* (New Brunswick, N.J.: Transaction Books, 1990). See also my essay on "G. A. Cohen on Self-Ownership, Property, and Equality," reprinted in this volume.

Another set of arguments rejecting the claim that each person has a property in his person can be found in philosopher Richard Arneson's essays "Lockean Self-Ownership: Towards a Demolition" (*Political Studies* 39, 1991), which manages to assert both that "self-ownership is not nearly so determinate as competing conceptions" (a remarkably dubious and unsupported claim) and that "it is obvious that self-ownership conflicts with even the most minimal requirements of humanity" (also unsupported, but evidence that Arneson does not share a libertarian view of the possibility of spontaneous order), and "Property Rights in Persons" (*Social Philosophy and Policy* 9[1], 1992), in which he "bites the bullet" and argues that "the egalitarian should agree with Nozick that horizontal equity may require forced labor if there is to be redistribution to aid the needy" and that "forced labor can be a morally acceptable state policy." As Arneson notes,

> Judged by the criteria of enforcement of self-ownership, welfare-state liberalism and socialism appear to involve the moral equivalent of lord and serf relations. The response of the egalitarian welfarist is that elimination of feudalism is morally progressive, because feudalism's characteristic personal property relations dictate resource transfers from disadvantaged persons to already advantaged persons. The property rights in persons instituted by welfare-state liberalism and socialism, though superficially similar, are different in the morally crucial respect that (when rationally organized) they dictate resource transfers from better-off persons to worse-off persons.

Arneson's honesty is commendable, although he does not indicate what happens when "the property rights in persons instituted by welfare-state liberalism and socialism" are not "rationally organized," nor why we should ever expect such systems of power and violence to be systematically organized in the way he might prefer.

(This reflects the regular failure of antilibertarian thinkers to distinguish between intentions and consequences. This simple distinction is a hallmark of libertarian political economy, as of all truly scientific social science.)

The distinguished British academic Raymond Plant integrates libertarian thinkers into his treatment of current issues in political philosophy in his *Modern Political Thought* (Oxford: Blackwell, 1991), contrasting libertarian views with conservative and socialist ideologies in an interesting way. Norman P. Barry's *An Introduction to Modern Political Theory* (3d ed.; London: Macmillan, 1995) also places libertarian views in the context of modern political theory. (Both are more fair in their presentation of libertarian views, as well as of other views with which they may personally disagree, than most other introductory works in political theory.)

A work that is highly polemical in tone and intent, and which challenges the classical libertarian distinction between intentions and consequences, is Albert Hirschman's small tome *The Rhetoric of Reaction: Perversity, Futility, Jeopardy* (Cambridge, Mass.: Harvard University Press, 1991). (Hirschman's work is highly rhetorical itself, and conflates a variety of views—tarring them all with the same brush, so the work is not principally about libertarianism, but about the form of argument that "good consequences" do not always flow from "good intentions.") Perhaps the best "refutation" of this view is simply to point to the many insights that are gained by considering the unintended consequences of actions. The essay "What Is Seen and What Is Not Seen" by Frédéric Bastiat in *Selected Essays on Political Economy* (Irvington-on-Hudson, N.Y.: Foundation for Economic Education, 1968) is a good response to those who fail to distinguish between intentions and consequences.

The general theme of an alleged conflict between community and individual liberty has been articulated by the modern "communitarian" critics of liberalism. "Communitarianism" is a term rarely embraced by those to whom it is applied, but it is a useful way of grouping together a number of thinkers who, while they may in other respects be considered "leftist" or "rightist," generally reject moral individualism and insist on the primacy of community, which is almost always assumed without further argument to mean the state.

Charles Taylor, a prominent communitarian, has offered especially direct criticisms of libertarianism in his essays "Atomism" and "What's Wrong with Negative Liberty" (both available in his *Philosophy and the Human Sciences: Philosophical Papers* [Cambridge: Cambridge University Press, 1985], pp. 187–210 and 211–29). Among a number of criticisms, Taylor argues that freedom should be understood as a capacity, rather than as a relation to other people, and that a precondition for such a capacity is belonging to a certain kind of society that can foster this capacity, which claim he calls the "social thesis." Thus, "an assertion of the primacy of rights is impossible; for to assert the rights in question is to affirm the capacities, and granted the social thesis is true concerning these capacities, this commits us to an obligation to belong." And the obligation to belong entails the obligation to submit to the taxes, controls, and edicts of the state. The non sequiturs this essay contains are numerous, but perhaps most notable among them is the claim that submission to political society is necessary for the development of the capacity for choice. He does, however, leave a hole for an informed historical critique of the communitarian enterprise. (History is rarely a strong suit among communitarian critics of libertarianism, who usually substitute a priori musings for actual knowledge of historical events.) As Taylor admits, "Now, it is possible that a society and culture propitious for freedom might arise from the spontaneous association of anarchist communes. But it seems much more likely from the historical record that we need rather some species of political society." As medieval historians have pointed out many a time, it was *precisely* among the revolutionary ("anarchist," if you will) communes of Europe (more commonly known today as cities) that liberty and individualism flourished. (The work of Henri Pirenne on *Medieval Cities: Their Origins and the Growth of Trade* cited in Section II above is a good place to start, but many other works in European history tell the same story.) As the historian Antony Black noted in his *Guilds and Civil Society* (Ithaca, N.Y.: Cornell University Press, 1984), "*Commune* was used as a rallying cry by early towns in defense of their liberties" (p. 49), and "The crucial point about both guilds and communes was that here *individuation and association went hand in hand*. One achieved liberty by belonging to this kind of group" (p. 65). Liberty did not emerge in the great states and empires founded on conquest, but in the guilds, communes, and other associations founded on freely given consent.

One general theme in the communitarian criticism has been that individuals are "constituted" by their communities, rather than the other way around, and that among the factors that constitute a person are his or her obligations. Thus, rather than particular obligations being a matter of choice, we have—and are constituted as moral agents by—given obligations: obligations to a caste, clan, nation, or state. This view is eloquently set forth by the Harvard philosopher Michael Sandel in his *Liberalism and the Limits of Justice* (Cambridge: Cambridge University Press, 1982), which is largely a critique of two social democratic "liberals," John Rawls and Ronald Dworkin, showing the antiliberal collectivist foundations of their views and how they are incompatible with the elements of liberal individualism they espouse. Sandel also argues that because "shared understandings" are constitutive of what we are, and because these "comprehend a wider subject than the individual alone, whether a family or tribe or city or class or nation or people, to this extent they define a community in a constitutive sense." It is a short jump to the conclusion that individualism is fundamentally mistaken, and that "the bounds of the self are no longer fixed, individuated in advance and given prior to experience." This means that the "self" in question is not a numerically individuated biological person (Bill, or Mary, or Samuel, or Janet), but the "self" made up of all of them. This argument is refuted by the philosopher John J. Haldane ("Individuals and the Theory of Justice," *Ratio* 27 [2], December 1985), who argues straightforwardly that "features can only be shared if they attach to bearers which are at base numerically diverse." The "epistemological" route to collectivism (or wholism) that Sandel takes was already taken in the thirteenth century (by the "Latin Averroists," such as Siger of Brabant) and blocked by Thomas Aquinas, who articulated the case for moral and metaphysical individualism in his great defense of individualism, *On the Unity of the Intellect against the Averroists* (Milwaukee, Wis.: Marquette University Press, 1968). Thomas refuted essentially the same argument on behalf of the proposition that the human race had only one intellect, or one soul. Against this, Thomas argued that understandings or ideas can be shared by many people without our having to posit one intellect in which these ideas would be located, that the notion "is absurd and contrary to human life (for it would not be necessary to take counsel or make laws)," and therefore that "it follows that the intellect is united to us in such a way that it and we constitute what is truly one being."

601

Another communitarian argument has been advanced by the socialist and nationalist Oxford philosopher David Miller, who has effectively endorsed Hayek's contention that socialism and robust welfare states rest on a foundation of tribalism and anticosmopolitanism. Miller defends the propagation of national "myths" (akin to Plato's "noble lies") as the grounds for obligations to the socialist or redistributive state, notably in his book *On Nationality* (Oxford: Oxford University Press, 1995). As Miller notes, "The redistributive policies of the kind favoured by socialists are likely to demand a considerable degree of social solidarity if they are to win popular consent, and for that reason socialists should be more strongly committed than classical liberals to the nation-state as an institution that can make such solidarity politically effective." One fairly obvious libertarian response to this nationalist approach is simply to point to the horrors of twentieth-century nationalism and collectivism, but deeper philosophical responses are available, as well, which can offer an account for the bad consequences of nationalism. Notable among them is the book *Nationalism* (4th ed.; Oxford: Blackwell, 1993), by Elie Kedourie, which subjects the philosophy of nationalism to withering criticism. Another critic of nationalistic and socialist thinking was the Austrian economist Ludwig von Mises, who argued in his *Nation, State, and Economy* (1919; New York: New York University Press, 1983) that the existence of different nations and cultures provides an argument for *limiting* the state, rather than imposing nationalist uniformity to achieve socialist or welfare-statist goals: "Whoever wants peace among nations must seek to limit the state and its influence most strictly."

The general "communitarian" theme has been favored by "right-wing" critics of libertarianism, even if they rarely explicate their metaphysical wholism to the degree that "left-wing" communitarian critics often do. (Notably, libertarians typically reject the "left-right" dichotomy as offering, at the least, a nonexhaustive choice, and this is reflected in the criticisms of libertarianism by both self-identified "left" and "right.")

A particularly biting, polemical, and even personal attack on libertarianism was offered by a venerable figure of post–World War II American conservatism, Russell Kirk, in his essay "Libertarians: The Chirping Sectaries" (in George W. Carey, ed., *Freedom and Virtue: The Conservative/Libertarian Debate* [Lanham, Md.: University Press of America, 1984], which contains a number of essays on the issues dividing libertarians and conservatives). It has never been entirely clear just what the term "conservatism" means in American politics, so it should just be noted that Kirk's essay represents at least one conservative viewpoint that differs from the libertarian viewpoint in virtually every respect, from the significance of the individual to the roots of order to the nature of the state.

Kirk and other conservatives often quote Edmund Burke as an opponent of libertarian ideals, but Burke is in fact more complex, and a less forced reading would see him as advancing a particular version of the classical liberal or libertarian understanding of civil society and individual liberty. This deserves some explanation, for Burke has come to be associated in the public mind almost exclusively with one book, his *Reflections on the Revolution in France*, a book in which can be found many wise libertarian insights, as well as a very few truly absurd statements, the latter of which have come to color the appreciation of the book by later audiences. Among the absurd and even embarrassing statements is his description of the queen of France: "Surely never lighted on this orb, which she hardly seemed to touch, a more delightful vision. . . . Little did I dream that I should live to see such disasters fallen upon her in a nation of gallant men, in a nation of men of honour and of cavaliers. I thought ten thousand swords must have leaped from their scabbards to avenge even a look that threatened her with insult.—But the age of chivalry is gone.—That of sophisters, oeconomists, and calculators, has succeeded; and the glory of Europe is extinguished for ever."

This rhetorical excess is certainly an embarrassment to Burke's memory. But a few silly passages should not blind us to the brilliance of his critique of the events in France, from the confiscation of the church's property to finance the inherited debts of the state to the replacement of gold and silver by paper money.

Burke had defended the American Revolution, which he distinguished from the French by the Americans' defense of historically situated rights. The heart of Burke's criticism of the revolution in France is his objection to abstract rights, or rights justified in purely abstract terms, rather than to historically situated rights. In his defense of the English Revolution of 1688 in the *Reflections*, Burke wrote that "the Revolution was made to preserve our *antient* indisputable laws and liberties, and that *antient* constitution of government which is our only security for law and liberty." As he pointed out, the greatest English legal scholars "are industrious to prove the pedigree of our liberties." Rights that are merely abstractly formulated (such as the "rights of man") are, in this view, less likely to be stable and to secure liberty than are rights that have a "pedigree," that have emerged over time, enjoy the legitimacy of a tradition, and are understood to be the inheritance of a free people. One may certainly contest this claim, but it is consistent with, and has even proven a great contributor to, the growth of modern libertarianism. (A recent biography that shows Burke as a liberal is Conor Cruise O'Brien's *The Great Melody: A Thematic Biography of Edmund Burke* [Chicago: University of Chicago Press, 1992]. In addition, the purely conservative interpretation of Burke must deal with his 1756 work *A Vindication of Natural Society*, Frank N. Pagano, ed. [Indianapolis: Liberty Classics, 1982], which is either a stirring critique of the state or an extraordinarily subtle parody of antistatist thought, as conservative statists maintain.)

An influential conservative criticism of the libertarian idea that the state should limit itself to prohibiting well-defined harms to others and should not "legislate morality" is found in James Fitzjames Stephen's *Liberty, Equality, Fraternity* (1873; Indianapolis: Liberty Classics, 1993), which offers a defense of coercion as the foundation of religion and morality. This belief that, absent a coercive power to maintain morality, humans would simply run riot, and that the purpose of state power is to "make men moral," is also defended by the conservative Princeton philosopher Robert George in *Making Men Moral: Civil Liberties and Public Morality* (Oxford: Oxford University Press, 1993). In addition to the arguments offered by John Stuart Mill (see the selections from *On Liberty* in *The Libertarian Reader*, edited by David Boaz), a useful defense of libertarian views on morality can be found in the abolitionist and temperance advocate Lysander Spooner's 1875 essay "Vices Are Not Crimes" (in George H. Smith, ed., *The Lysander Spooner Reader* [San Francisco: Fox & Wilkes, 1992]. Further, the many empirical studies of the terrible consequences of attempts to impose morality on society (increases in violent crime due to the perverse incentives of black markets, diversion of scarce police resources from apprehending violent criminals, corruption of the police, and much, much more) offer strong reasons to oppose imposition of moral norms through force and coercion, rather than cultivating morality through the use of persuasion and example. (Good examples of such studies are David W.

Rasmussen and Bruce L. Benson's *The Economic Anatomy of a Drug War* [Lanham, Md.: Rowman and Littlefield, 1994], which shows how organized crime grows under prohibition and shows how and why the murder rate dropped for eleven consecutive years after the repeal of alcohol prohibition; Ronald Hamowy, ed., *Dealing with Drugs: Consequences of Government Control* [Cambridge, Mass.: Ballinger, 1987], which includes essays by scholars, prosecutors, and others arguing against prohibition of narcotics; Richard Posner's *Sex and Reason* [Cambridge, Mass.: Harvard University Press, 1992], in which a distinguished judge and law professor argues, largely on utilitarian grounds, that individual rights and self-ownership should be the rule; and Richard Epstein's *Bargaining with the State* [Princeton, N.J.: Princeton University Press, 1993], which examines the problems that arise from the power of the state selectively to distribute benefits and burdens, mandates and prohibitions.)

Conclusion

No short listing or essay can really do justice to the wealth of insights offered by libertarian thinkers. The test is not, however, how much they have written, but how much their ideas help us to understand the world and to guide us as we try to live lives of decency, justice, compassion, and humanity. Judged against that standard, I believe that libertarianism is superior to other theories or organized belief systems. But whether you agree with me will be for you to decide.

38. With Friends Like This

Review of *Wealth and Poverty*,
by George Gilder. New York: Basic Books, 1981,
318 pp.

The messiah of capitalism has come. Amid much fanfare and confetti, with paper hats and party favors, George Gilder has brought forth *Wealth and Poverty*, the only (to hear him tell it) moral defense of capitalism ever penned. Gilder's book, which has received all sorts of hosannas—from the *New York Times* to David Stockman ("promethean in its intellectual power and insight")—attempts a revolutionary breakthrough. Old Adam Smith and his successors, you see, defended the free market (which bears only a vague resemblance to Gilder's "capitalism") on the archaic Enlightenment grounds of reason, freedom, and individual rights; they tended to be skeptical of the aims of businessmen who would often rather pursue government grants of monopoly and privilege than face the rigors of free competition and laissez-faire. Now comes Gilder to stand Smith on his head. Capitalism is good, says Gilder, not because of any nonsense about freedom, but because *capitalists* are good. They are by nature "altruistic," admirably irrational, and in touch with the "underlying and transcendent order of the universe."

An important point should be noted at the outset. George Gilder is a nut. His theories are among the zaniest to be found in print—especially his theories about sex, which he keeps offering (here and in his other "major" work, *Sexual Suicide*) totally *ex cathedra*, without the slightest shred of supporting argument or evidence. As we shall see, he is profoundly antifeminist (indeed, antiwomen), and the terms in which he frames his repeated attacks on gay people give one the feeling that something very strange is going on. In *Sexual*

Originally published in *Inquiry*, April 27, 1981, pp. 24–26.

Suicide, for instance, he warns of the danger of encountering homosexuals lingering on street corners, "their genitalia pressed like vul-
tures against their jeans." Sexual metaphors are strewn throughout
his works: Some men, it seems, are in the humiliating position of
being habitually "cuckolded" by the state.

Capitalism has occasionally suffered in the past from screwball
defenders. It may not survive this one. That would be an added
pity, because what Gilder is advocating as capitalism is not a free
market economy, but a kind of *state capitalism,* the intermeshing of
state and economy. The state should be viewed, Gilder asserts, "not
as an external necessity, but as a factor of production. If the American
government could make itself more productive than the private
sector throughout the spectrum of needed economic activity, the
public would gladly surrender its earnings to the state." Of course,
some of us are not so enamored of the idea of making the government
more "productive"—Hiroshima, Vietnam, CIA plots, and all that—
and would prefer Will Rogers's sentiment: "Thank God we don't
get all the government we pay for."

In *Wealth and Poverty* Gilder gives an account of the origins of his
title subjects and a blueprint for attaining the former and eradicating
the latter. These goals boil down to two basic points: (1) decreasing
presently high marginal tax rates on income and (2) making poverty
as uncomfortable as possible by diminishing welfare benefits, especially to women. Most of the book consists of confused and often
garbled economic and sociological journalism, sometimes in support
of these two main proposals.

Gilder seeks to banish demand from economic thought altogether,
relegating it at best to the purely passive role of responding to
changes in supply. Even the classic formulations of intersecting
demand and supply curves are sneered at because "they seemingly
assert an equivalence between demand and supply." But the fact of
the matter is that "supply" is merely the flip side of "demand," and
a supply curve is merely a demand curve looked at from the other
side of the transaction. Whether we want to consider apples or
dollars as the "supply" depends on whether we are selling dollars
or apples. Gilder's uncomprehending embrace of the slogan "supply
creates its own demand" leads him off on a holy crusade against
demand per se, which he holds to be far less "potent" than supply.

His attack on demand is, of course, by way of bolstering his ardent
support for the latest fad on the right, supply-side economics. One

of the central concepts identifying supply-siders is the Laffer curve, named after economist Arthur Laffer of the University of Southern California; it is an old idea, however, to be found, for example, full-blown in Montesquieu's *The Spirit of the Laws* (1748). The notion is that there are two tax rates, 0 percent and 100 percent, which will produce zero tax revenue, and that there are other sets of points that will also produce identical revenues. Accordingly, tax rates may be so high as to produce a lesser revenue than some lower rate that would not penalize production as much.

This is incontestable. The real questions are: (1) Is there any evidence that we are above the tax rate that would maximize government revenue? (2) Why should we want to maximize government revenue anyway?

Gilder provides little evidence in support of the proposition that tax rates are presently above the long-run revenue maximization level; he is oblivious to the latter question, which to me is far more interesting. Fearless iconoclast and intellectual pioneer that he is, Gilder never asks why on earth we should seek to maximize the resources at the disposal of the successive cliques who happen to run the government of the United States.

With the Laffer curve, as elsewhere, Gilder latches on to a precise notion and uses it to explain nearly everything—even inflation. In his chapter on "The Inflationary State," he argues that high marginal tax rates cause inflation, but that, hey, inflation isn't so bad after all and may even be a sign that we are entering a new "post-industrial era." Throughout, Gilder shows no sign of understanding what money is or how it works. In particular, he manages to sidestep the crucial role that inflation plays in redistributing wealth from those who get the newly created money last to those who get it first. The last recipients, the ones who get the money only after prices have already been bid up, are generally the poor and disadvantaged. Gilder argues that inflation has benefited such groups, when in fact it is they who have been hurt the most.

This is only the first of many critical errors in Gilder's treatment of the poor and poverty. The poor, he claims, are really to blame for their plight. They don't work enough, they are oversexed, they don't have stable marriages, and they lack faith; that is, in his own terms, they are *too rational.* His argument is supposed to prove that the poor "choose leisure" because "they are paid to do so by welfare," and that female income, whether collected from the government or earned on the market, emasculates men as providers and thus destroys the family.

Having apparently OD'd on *Civilization and Its Discontents*, Gilder holds that all productive activity is merely the result of a sublimated (male) sex drive. "Civilized society," he writes,

> is dependent upon the submission of the short-term sexuality of young men to the extended maternal horizons of women. This is what happens in monogamous marriage; the man disciplines his sexuality and extends it into the future through the womb of a woman. The woman gives him access to his children, otherwise forever denied him; and he gives her the product of his labor, otherwise dissipated on temporary pleasures.

Love, of course, does not enter the picture.

Marriages break up among the poor, Gilder believes, because transfer payments and other forms of income are not dependent on, or else actively discourage, a continued male presence. The solution to this is to stop paying the poor to loaf and to make income dependent on the presence of a male. Women must be sent back to the kitchen where they will no longer threaten the shaky self-respect of men. Indeed, Gilder's fear of the harm women can do seems to know no bounds. In *Sexual Suicide* he even went so far as to argue that "the women's movement—particularly in its moderate manifestation—is the most important remaining organized enemy of black progress in America."

Only passing mention, at most, is ever made of all the obstacles placed in the path of the poor: licensing laws that restrict the opportunity to compete with established practitioners; minimum wage laws that prevent unskilled workers from even beginning a career in the job market; regulatory barriers to entry that discriminate in favor of largely white-dominated existing firms; and taxes that weigh more heavily on new and struggling firms, particularly those without access to government privileges and largesse. Made feverish by his own sociosexual theories, Gilder virtually ignores the institutional structure (except for welfare) that has victimized the poor.

In the case of welfare, of course, his argument contains a grain of truth. Welfare does diminish employment, not so much by rewarding unemployment as by penalizing income-producing work. As a welfare recipient earns additional income, his or her income from welfare is reduced. The effect is the same as that of Gilder's justly hated high marginal tax rates—only this time it's the poor who are involved. This granted, it should be noted that the analysis is hardly original with our author.

With only one exception, Gilder is at his most eloquent and incisive when quoting others. That exception is his critique of the static equilibrium analysis in neoclassical economic theory, which banishes the entrepreneur and profits from economic analysis, allowing little or no room for uncertainty or imperfect knowledge. Because of this, neoclassical theory is often powerless to explain the world we actually live in and sometimes leads to disastrous policy conclusions. Gilder points this out, with eloquence and force. But his alternative is no better.

Citing John Kenneth Galbraith, Gilder states that "as long as men are 'profoundly rational,' economic development will seem 'impossible' and it will not occur." Gilder holds all investment and entrepreneurship to be at base altruistic and irrational. It is this concept of the altruistic and irrational entrepreneur that forms the core of Gilder's analysis of wealth and poverty and is probably the main reason for the attention it has received. Investment is altruistic because you give things away: "Like gifts, capital investments are made without a predetermined return." Going into business is irrational, in Gilder's view, because of the high rate of failure among new business ventures. Given this, only irrationality and faith can explain the decisions of thousands of people who go into business anyway.

But this is not only a *non sequitur*; it is nonsense. Entrepreneurs seek out and exploit previously unseen opportunities, in an attempt to gain profits and better their situations. Merely because George Gilder would be discouraged by the business failures experienced by others does not mean that launching a business is irrational. This is egocentrism of the silliest sort.

It also contradicts his case for reducing high marginal tax rates. For if uncertainty is good, as Gilder explicitly maintains, then a reduction of high marginal tax rates would be bad, since such a rate reduction would restore exploitable cost-price differentials and therefore reduce the uncertainty of profiting from entrepreneurial activities. If uncertainty is a good in itself, why reduce it? This is a contradiction that by itself calls Gilder's whole confused effort into question.

Incidentally, those who are ready to receive Gilder as the prophet of capitalism might ponder the fact that he opposes socialism not because it can't plan, but because it *can*. One wonders what the critics of central planning—from Ludwig von Mises to Paul Craig Roberts—would make of Gilder's statement that under socialism, "rationality rules."

Toward the end of his book, Gilder goes into free fall, treating us to page after gushing page of high-sounding blather, a grab bag of half-baked ideas allegedly deriving from Karl Popper, Charles Peirce, and Carl Jung. Plus there is some cosmic collectivism to complete Gilder's assault on the mainstays of Enlightenment liberalism, e.g.:

> The human mind is not necessarily autonomous or limited to the individual brain. . . . As a person's mind merges with the living consciousness that is the ulterior stuff of the cosmos, he reaches new truths, glimpses new ideas—the projections of light into the unknown future—by which intellectual progress grows.

Limitations of space and a decent regard for the reader's sensibilities demand calling a halt at this point. That Gilder's book should be regarded as a new and dazzling defense of capitalism—that it should be thought to furnish us, in the words of the *Wall Street Journal's* reviewer, with "the key to a better world in the eighties and nineties"—is in one way understandable. With the manifest failure of modem liberalism, many are seeking a politics that will fill the vacuum. In many different parts of the world, and especially in our own country, there is a turning away from the state, often combined with a new readiness to entertain free market solutions. An ideology that would justify this change in opinion while firmly directing it toward a more clearly envisaged goal would be warmly welcomed. But Gilder's book does not provide such an ideology. Even if he believed in a consistent capitalism, it would be no great service to its cause to found the case for it on glib nonsense. The sooner Gilder is forgotten, the sooner friends of the market economy return to a defense based on reason, freedom, and individual rights, the better for capitalism and for the wholesomeness of the debate.

39. The Elitist as Egalitarian

Review of *The Pursuit of Inequality*,
by Philip Green. Pantheon Books, 1981, 306 pp.

As the libertarian movement grows, it is to be expected—and welcomed—that its growth will generate attacks and criticisms from the left and the right. In fulfillment of this expectation, academician Philip Green, chairman of the government department at Smith College in western Massachusetts, has come forth to do battle. Green, an outspoken "egalitarian," has previously attacked libertarianism in the pages of *The Nation* ("America Amok" and "In Defense of the State") and *democracy* ("Two Cheers for the State"). In *The Pursuit of INequality* he is at it again, attempting to refute not only libertarianism but other currently popular systems that oppose egalitarian statism.

The Pursuit of INequality is an important anti-liberal (in the classical liberal sense of that term) work that deserves close examination. For one thing, Green is a thoroughgoing and consistent egalitarian. He recognizes, as few leftist egalitarians do, that if we are to have "equality of outcomes," we cannot have "equality of opportunity." As Green points out, "The two aspects of liberal individualism that will be discussed—the principle of equal opportunity for individuals and the principle of limiting government interference with the 'free' market—might at first glance seem unrelated to each other; certainly many people who uphold the first of those principles would repudiate the second unqualifiedly. But in practical fact they are deeply related." Green at least has the courage to recognize this truth and to reject *both* market freedom and equality of opportunity.

Four chapters of his critique of "inegalitarianism" are devoted to a somewhat confused refutation of "sociobiology." While Green does

---

Originally published in *Libertarian Review*, September 1981, pp. 34–37.

occasionally score some solid hits, in the process he exhibits numerous flaws in his understanding (e.g., treating sociologist Steven Goldberg, author of *The Inevitability of Patriarchy*, as a "sociobiologist"). While I do not agree with the sociobiologists' genetic, sexual, and racial explanations and justifications of the existence of "inequality," I still found Green's attempted refutation of them unconvincing. As Green admits, he believes, "The crucial difference between explanations of social phenomena is not in their 'scientific validity' but in the purposes they serve." Since these arguments do not serve his purposes, Green opposes them. This is hardly a convincing starting point for a serious refutation.

It is libertarianism, however, which the author believes to be the most formidable opponent of his new egalitarian order. In the section titled "The New Individualism: The State, the Public, and Liberty," he focuses on the political theories of Milton Friedman and Robert Nozick, to the exclusion of such Austrian economists as F. A. Hayek and Murray Rothbard, seeming to deliberately sidestep any confrontation with the (to my mind) much more sweeping arguments for libertarianism, both from the classical liberal side and from that of more thoroughly anti-statist partisans.

Green presents himself as a mainstream modern liberal, but his basic analytical and sociological framework is Marxist. It is, however, a decadent pop-Marxism, without the virtue of Marx's understanding of social reality. Marx (along with Adam Smith, Carl Menger, Ludwig von Mises, F. A. Hayek, and Murray Rothbard, to name a few) understood social reality, as Thomas Sowell put it, "in terms of the mutually constraining complex of relationships whose results form a pattern not necessarily similar to the intentions of any of the individuals involved." That is, it takes more to explain society than the "intentional" goodness or wickedness of social actors. Green superficially employs a Marxist sociology of change, yet he simultaneously places the blame for injustice and inequality on the intentional behavior of discriminatory, racist, greedy, mean businesspeople, unfiltered by any matrix of incentives and disincentives, and thus reduces the Marxist system to a mere parody of social analysis.

He has apparently read Milton Friedman's *Capitalism and Freedom* and a book review of Robert Nozick's *Anarchy, State, and Utopia*. He makes some telling points against Friedman's "public goods" justification of the state. When it comes to Nozick, however, Green is on much shakier ground. Nozick's step-by-step justification of the minimal state is totally misstated by Green. Green states that Nozick is a social contract theorist, although Nozick himself writes in *Anarchy, State, and Utopia* that his view "differs from social compact views in its invisible-hand structure." Green has Nozick "postulating" the legitimacy of the minimal state, whereas Nozick attempts to *demonstrate* its legitimacy. Green reverses (to the detriment of the argument) the order of Locke's argument concerning the legitimacy of property, by listing it as property first in inanimate objects, then in one's own labor, although both Locke and Nozick have it the other way around. Green sidesteps the crucial Nozickian argument that, because one cannot avoid the assignment of rights to control objects that cannot be used by two or more different people at the same time and in the same respect, all political theories are property rights theories.

The distortions and misrepresentations of Green's argument could be catalogued forever, but the core of his anti-libertarian perspective is contained in his answer to the question he puts to the reader: "Is a 'free man' who owns large-scale means of production the same kind of 'free man' as one who does not, who owns nothing but his own body and its ability to do labor?"

To which he answers that "the owner of a mere body is 'free' to sell labor at its price, and get the returns on that sale from his or her employer. The latter sells *products*, the price of which includes the price of the employed labor *plus* profit. But whereas the employee can bargain with the employer about the rate of pay for labor, there is no bargaining about the disposition of profit: that belongs entirely to the employer; it is the 'property right' of ownership of productive property" (emphasis in original).

But this is self-contradictory. If profit is defined, as Green defines it, as the difference between the product of labor and its wage, and if wages are subject to negotiation, then profit *is* subject to negotiation. But Green's argument isn't just self-contradictory—it is in fact based on the fallacies of Marxist economics that have been explored again and again in economics, from Eugen von Böhm-Bawerk's famous refutation in his *Capital and Interest* and *Karl Marx and the Close of His System* to Israel Kirzner's recent brilliant analysis in *Competition and Entrepreneurship* and his most recent collection of essays, *Perception, Opportunity, and Profit*. The fallacious Marxist view holds that exchange is not "equal" when the transactors possess unequal resources; therefore the equality of opportunity offered by a liberal society is in reality inequality. Hence, Green's explicit opposition to the liberal or libertarian advocacy of equality of legal rights.

Green sketches a brief scenario that he believes typifies "capitalist society." A family lives

> in a house near a lake. . . . The members of the family all work at a nearby industrial plant. They contracted freely to work there, agreed quite cheerfully to the contractual terms of employment, and consider themselves free agents still. However, because of its ability to employ them and their fellow workers at average wages lower than the average revenue it earns from the workers' total contribution to the sale of the product they help make . . . the corporation is enabled to make a profit—to realize an investable surplus. With this investable surplus, which over time becomes immense, the company buys the neighbor's lakefront property for expansion purposes. It promptly closes down the family's access to the lake. Of course, the lake has a circumference, not all of which is taken over by the company; with some trouble, the family can still find a public beach. But then the company, which manufactures chemicals, begins to discharge their residues into the lake. . . . The family decides to take its freely earned wages and move. At this point, however, the company uses its surplus funds to contract with a road-building company to drive a giant highway from its expanded operation to the outside world—a sloping downhill road in which giant trailer trucks reach a double-clutched climax about ten feet from the family's front door. Their property has become worthless; they can no longer sell it at a price that will enable them to replace it with a similar abode. The company, of course, will buy it from them—for a song.
> . . . Without ever expecting to do so in the slightest, this family of workers have [sic] discovered the relationship between surplus value in the particular form of private profit outside their control, and alienation. . . .

It would indeed be shocking if Green's portrayal were an accurate picture of what the market was like. But it isn't. As an attempted portrait of the market economy in the real world, Green's horror story can perhaps best be described as plain silly. It conveniently leaves out all possible options and alternatives that the workers—

616

or for that matter, the corporation—might have in such a series of events. In a market system based on property rights, for example, the corporation would be legally accountable for the pollution of the lake. And once the highway was completed, it would make the worker's property more valuable as *commercial* property, whether the worker wanted to use it commercially or sell it. There is no mention of the possibility of collective action on the part of the workers at the factory, if in fact the employer's actions were damaging their interests, or of class action suits, if the other neighbors were not fellow employees. Equally unrealistic, and far worse in terms of a vision of humanity, is Green's elitism in portraying the family of workers as poor dumb saps, frozen in time and space, helpless against the omnipotent onslaught of the Corporate Monster.

From the point of view of economic analysis, Green's scenario is based on Marx's fallacious Labor Theory of Value, a theory refuted in the late nineteenth century by the "marginalist economists." The fallacies of this theory are worth discussing briefly here.

Green's analysis accepts Marx's belief that labor is the only possible unit of value and supposes that the only reason the corporation can make a profit, or "investable surplus," is that it pays the workers less than the value of their "total contribution" to the product, i.e., their labor. This in turn rests on the notion that the exchange of goods implies an equality of value between them (if 3 oranges are exchanged for 10 apples, then 3 oranges are equal in value to 10 apples). Marx tried to identify this equality by looking at various possible constituent elements of value, finally settling on labor. He concluded that commodities exchange in proportion to the amount of "crystallized labor time" contained in them; that is, the amount of labor necessary for their reproduction.

Since labor too is a commodity, it also contains "crystallized labor time," that is, the amount needed to produce the means of subsistence (food, shelter, clothing) required to reproduce it. But a laborer produces in a day more than the "equivalent labor" needed to support him or her at the subsistence level, which according to Marx determines his or her wages. This difference is called "surplus value" and is what constitutes profit. Hence the capitalist who employs labor reaps surplus value—profit—which would otherwise belong to the worker.

This theory fails totally to explain such phenomena as business losses, rising living standards, etc.—which gave rise to its refutation

617

by the marginalists, whose key point was that an exchange of goods is *never* based on equal valuations, for if valuations were truly equal, there would be no reason to exchange. Rather, voluntary exchange occurs because the parties to the exchange each place *unequal* valuations on the goods: I value your 3 oranges more highly than my 10 apples, and vice versa; the exchange is unequal for both parties; and the outcome is mutually beneficial.

Green never stops to analyze—or even to make explicit—the theories underlying his story of the family by the lake. Nor does he address the theories of the marginalist economists—he barely pauses to scoff at them, but in doing so he reveals that he does not even understand the economist's use of the word "marginal."

There are two further arguments that Green believes provide the *coup de grace* for libertarianism. The first is that consumers do not have "the faintest idea" of how to spend their incomes on the goods and services now provided by government agencies; "only trained people familiar with the specific problems and paid to devote time to them can do that," i.e., Green and his fellow would-be philosopher kings. This elitist argument is beneath contempt. If I cannot wisely run my life (or even choose others to advise me), why is Green more competent to do it for me? Does not the argument apply to him as well? How easily egalitarianism slides into elitism.

The second argument is that past statist interventions have had a powerful influence on present institutions, therefore justifying further interventions. It is regrettably true that previous injustices have had lasting effects, and to the extent that the victims of such injustices can be identified and compensated, libertarians favor strict and immediate restitution. That is, after all, the basic requirement and foundation of the system of justice underlying the free market. However, the results of many previous injustices cannot be so rectified (the criminal parties—or the victims—are dead, or the victimization did not result in any lasting theft of property with identifiable victims or their heirs). This decidedly does *not* justify further state action. By way of example, the past actions of states have had profound effect on the *ideas* widely held today. Had Socrates not been condemned to death by the Athenian jury, the world might be a far different place. Vagrancy laws and Green's beloved compulsory state "education" have done much to shape present values and attitudes toward work. Do these facts justify further censorship and crushing of dissent? or justify socialism? Quite the contrary. If anything, they should strengthen our resolve to do away with such injustices, not encourage us to heap on more of the same. Green's recitation of past state interventions merely provides us with powerful examples of how states inevitably use their power to exploit and oppress their subjects—as would Professor Green's egalitarian state.

We now come to what I consider to be the underlying purpose of the book. After studying the work, I found *The Pursuit of INequality* to be aptly named, though not for reasons the author might advance. It is appropriately named because, in the final analysis, inequality is precisely what Professor Green is pursuing.

Under the pretense of criticizing all those who oppose the imposition of egalitarian statism on society, Green argues that the opponents of egalitarianism are merely defending their "class interests." This is not only a questionable technique of argumentation (at least in isolation), it also neatly sidesteps the question of Green's *own* class interests. *The Pursuit of INequality* is first and foremost a polemic for the imposition of the rule of "intellectuals" such as Professor Green over the rest of us.

Why is this so? The answer is to be found in the characteristics that define intellectuals as a class. As Thomas Sowell argues in his brilliant *Knowledge and Decisions*, intellectuals are people who deal in the transmission of articulated knowledge. Knowledge comes in many forms. Prices in the market, for example, convey effective, but unarticulated, knowledge; one need not know the causes of a diminution or expansion of the supply of wheat, for example, for the price rise or fall to lead to a change in one's purchasing patterns. This is merely one example of the many kinds of unarticulated knowledge that come into play in the regular interactions of human beings. In another interesting work that supplements the point Sowell is making, Michael Polanyi's *The Tacit Dimension*, Polanyi discusses the implications of the fact that "we know more than we can say," that is, we know more than we can put into explicit language. Playing the piano, painting, sculpting, turning a lathe, all rest on kinds of knowledge that are "tacit" rather than explicit. But they are instances of knowledge, nonetheless.

Since intellectuals like Professor Green are interested both in the cognitive process and in the occupational process (job) of articulating and transmitting knowledge, they have unique class interests—interests vigorously advanced by Philip Green.

It is in a statist context that intellectuals can most fully advance these class interests, by attacking as "unjustified" and "irrational," all resort to cognitive processes other than those employed in their own occupation. Green criticizes entrepreneurs "whose own performances have never been explicitly judged by any 'objective' standard"; that is, they are not fully susceptible to the kind of cognitive process regularly employed by Professor Green's class. Professor Green merely seeks to establish and perpetuate a new ruling class, the intellectual class of which he is a member.

That this form of class rule is on the rise is incontestable, for intellectuals have in recent years come to tremendous power through the growth of a bureaucratic state that seeks, not merely the kind of forcible expropriation of resources that has characterized states since the first robber band began to systematically plunder its victims, but the subordination of all social decision making processes to its own power. Such "scientific" regulation of others requires the articulation of knowledge on a previously unprecedented scale. Notice, for example, the specifications for bus seat padding in Chris Hocker's article on "Transit as if People Mattered" in last month's (August 1981) *Libertarian Review*. The reams and reams of paper required by such a regulation can be the product only of the cognitive process of articulation, the stock-in-trade of the intellectual class.

That Professor Green is simply interested in his own class interests, or privileges, is nowhere more evident than in his claim that an egalitarian socialist state need not violate freedom. His notion of freedom, of course, is limited to the pursuit of the occupational interests of intellectuals—the freedom to engage in the articulation and transmission of certain kinds of knowledge. The freedom to work, trade, produce, love, and otherwise express one's values voluntarily is not to be protected; rather, such voluntary processes of choice are to be totally usurped by the scientific-rational-intellectual-egalitarian-bureaucratic state.

Green's egalitarian state would in fact prove to be more hierarchical than any previously witnessed. For in state-ruled societies, as Gaetano Mosca pointed out in his classic book *The Ruling Class*,

> [M]inorities rule majorities, rather than majorities minorities. . . . In reality the domain of an organized minority, obeying a single impulse, over the unorganized majority is inevitable. The power of any minority is irresistible as

against each single individual in the majority, who stands alone before the totality of the organized minority. At the same time, the minority is organized for the very reason that it is a minority. A hundred men acting uniformly in concert, with a common understanding, will triumph over a thousand men who are not in accord and can therefore be dealt with one by one. Meanwhile it will be easier for the former to act in concert and have a mutual understanding simply because they are a hundred and not a thousand. It follows that the larger a political community, the smaller will the proportion of the governing minority to the governed majority be, and the more difficult will it be for the majority to organize for reaction against the minority.

Green's elitism comes out clearly in his discussion of who will do the undesirable "dirty work" in an egalitarian community and who will hand out the assignments. The question of the "dirty work," says Green,

is a question that can seem daunting only to someone who is not an egalitarian in the first place. The logic of egalitarianism is that if any job has such an impact on those who do it as to become a degrading trap, then it cannot be a normal career line in an egalitarian society. The answer to the question, in other words, is either that no one will do such jobs (we will not have a society of equals until we have created machines that eliminate such work); or that everyone will share them out, or will do them in turn at different stages of life (e.g., *teen-agers by way of national service*); or that they will be done by *incorrigible criminals by way of punishment* (but a more humane punishment than being in prison), or by *the truly feeble-minded by way of "treatment" in the community*, or by *genuine drop-outs who don't want to do work that entails any responsibility at all.* [Emphasis added]

The last four alternatives, of course, are clearly the choices that will be implemented, being both non-utopian (machines, indeed!) and the path of least cost to the decisionmakers in the state apparatus (teenagers, for instance, have a lesser capability than their parents of fighting back; that is why they are always the first to be conscripted).

Lest we merely chalk this vision of a future Gulag up to an unfortunate dichotomy between a beautiful theory and the difficulties and exigencies of its practical implementation, it should be pointed out that Green is deliberately condemning all of society's "square pegs"—everyone who won't fit into Green's carefully prepared round holes—to chattel slavery. This is not merely an unfortunate and unintended result of Green's egalitarianism, it is the logical and intended means of its implementation. The poet whose poetry is not approved by the state, the entrepreneur driven to the black market, the "economic criminal" who saves a few grains of rice for his or her children, the "grumbler" unsatisfied with the job assigned to him or her by the state, the homosexual, the malcontent, and above all, the libertarian, must be forced at gunpoint to labor for the state (that is, for Green and Co.). This is the real meaning of Professor Green's humanitarianism; there is no humanity here, only the malodorous evil of coercion, exploitation, and naked class domination.

In short, Professor Green has presented us with a subtle attempt to rationalize the creation of a new hierarchical system of masters and slaves—with his class holding the whip—all in the name of humanity, justice, and equality. That he viewed libertarianism and the growing libertarian movement as the most significant obstacle in the path of the intellectuals' climb to class power (via the convenient political vehicle of egalitarian ideology) is a powerful testament to the emerging acceptance of libertarianism as the champion of freedom, progress, justice, and peace.

40. *The Dangers of Nationalism*

Review of *On Nationality*,
by David Miller, New York: Oxford University Press,
1995, 210 pp.

Even if nationalism itself is not on the rise, as some say, its study certainly is. One aspect that has received too little attention is the intimate relation between nationalism and forms of economic collectivism—especially socialism and welfare statism. This is no idle academic matter: the horrors wrought by the National Socialist German Workers' Party, popularly known as the Nazis, may be directly related to their fusion of two illiberal ideals, socialism and nationalism; and the ferocity of the current national conflicts in the Balkans and Eastern Europe may be traceable to the corrosive effects of socialist institutions on social order and the inclination toward peaceful cooperation.

A few classical liberals, such as the century's leading critic of socialism, Ludwig von Mises, have examined the connection between the two phenomena. As Mises (1983: 77) noted from Vienna in 1919, following the First World War and the fall of the multinational Austro-Hungarian dual monarchy: "Whoever wants peace among nations must seek to limit the state and its influence most strictly." When resources are owned or controlled by the state, rather than subject to several property and freely tradable on the market, then groups will come into conflict over how those resources will be deployed. Under systems of state ownership or control, one solution must be chosen for all, rather than letting individuals and groups choose for themselves, meaning that for some to win others must lose. When the conflict is between national groups that make claims on the full allegiance of their members, the conflict is especially dangerous, for the possibility of compromise or reciprocity is diminished. Nationalism tends to be jealous of cross-cutting interests—

Originally published in *Cato Journal* 16, no. 2, Fall 1996, pp. 276–80.

which allow individuals to win some even as they lose others. For one group to triumph, others must be suppressed, and, as Mises (ibid.: 56) observed, "Where only the choice is open either oneself to suppress or to be suppressed, one easily decides for the former." As game theorists would point out, in the "game" of socialism, suppression of other groups is the "dominant" strategy.

F. A. Hayek, whose classic work *The Road to Serfdom* (1944) was a shot across the bow of triumphal statism, connected socialism to primitive tribalism and a yearning for the solidarity and the morality of small groups, a yearning that, if extended much beyond the family, would prove incompatible with the requirements of the extended market order. The great novelist Robert Musil (1990 [1921]: 109), another Austrian critic of both nationalism and socialism, observed that socialism is "stuck in the ethics of fraternity." The morality appropriate for family members is, however, quite different from that appropriate for governing the relations of the countless strangers one encounters in an extended order.

Recently a distinguished socialist theorist, David Miller of Nuffield College, Oxford, has turned his attention to the issue of nationalism and statism and has arrived at an analysis similar to that of the classical liberals. Miller recognizes the same choices, but embraces nationalist collectivism rather than cosmopolitan individualism. Whereas Mises and Hayek rejected statism and embraced free markets in the name of pluralism and harmony among national (and other) groups, Miller seeks to bolster socialism (or his second best, welfare statism) by means of a revived nationalism. As Miller points out in his new book *On Nationality*, "the redistributive policies of the kind favoured by socialists are likely to demand a considerable degree of social solidarity if they are to win popular consent, and for that reason socialists should be more strongly committed than classical liberals to the nation-state as an institution that can make such solidarity politically effective" (p. 92).

Miller candidly admits that problems of conflict and instability associated with coercive redistribution "might be resolved by slimming down the obligations of citizenship—turning the state into something closer to a minimal state—or by making state and nation coincide more closely" (p. 72). Miller opts unequivocally for the latter, whereas classical liberals choose the former. In opting for redistributive statism over constitutionally limited government and free markets, Miller recognizes that his commitment to socialism or welfare statism obliges him to embrace nationalism, as well.

What is especially remarkable is that Miller dismisses with open contempt cosmopolitanism and the classical liberal prescription for group conflicts—"slimming down the obligations of citizenship," but ultimately falls back on classical liberal arguments to bolster his own socialist and nationalist position. Arguing against a world socialist state and obligations of international redistribution, Miller appeals to respect for the "autonomy of other nations," which "involves treating them as responsible for decisions they may make about resource use" (p. 108), without, apparently, noting that he is forced to adopt—in defense of national socialism—a core liberal argument against socialism per se, that private property makes rights and responsibility coordinate features of market resource allocation. The classical liberal alternative is only brought in as an element in a *reductio ad absurdum* argument: if we were to reject nationalism, then we would have to embrace free movements of individuals and free trade of goods, but that would be, Miller believes, absurd. Miller is reduced to arguing in a circle: we have national obligations that ground our obligations to the welfare state, and we have obligations to the welfare state that ground our national obligations.

Of perhaps the greatest significance in this interesting book is the way in which Miller applies the nationality principle to the defense of the contemporary national welfare state, a defense that sheds light on the rise of anti-immigrant violence in Europe as well as on the resentment of immigrants in the American welfare state, such as was revealed by California's Proposition 187 (denying welfare benefits to immigrants). Harvard philosopher John Rawls had offered an influential defense of redistribution in his *A Theory of Justice*, in which divergences from complete equality were to be allowed only if those very inequalities were "to the greatest benefit of the least advantaged" (Rawls 1971: 302). Inequalities not so justified are to be eliminated through redistributive policies. This argument has become in recent years a standard defense of the coercively redistributive state. But just *who* is considered to be the "least advantaged," whose disadvantage provides the benchmark, matters a great deal; is the least advantaged a Somali goatherder or a Mississippi sharecropper? Rawls never adequately answers what determines the boundaries drawn around the groups over which his redistributivist principles are to apply, so Miller seeks to complete the Rawlsian argument: it is nationality that provides the demarcation criterion. Since Miller believes that "nations are like teams" (p. 18), it makes sense that the benefits of teamwork be limited only to the members of the team. Miller ignores two problems with his comparison: first, teams are voluntary associations, the members of which choose to cooperate, whereas states are not; and second, so conceived, the various "teams" that are nation-states will necessarily be in competition, and, as we know, "teams" with the powers of states can compete through organized violence of a most horrifying sort.

If welfare benefits are to be limited to conationals, then the issue of controls on immigration and the free flow of peoples becomes especially important. Mises dealt with those issues quite prophetically in his 1919 study. He first pointed out that "internationalist" socialism could not avoid national conflicts without jettisoning democracy. But he went further and recognized earlier than others that

> the realization of socialism is also possible, however, otherwise than through a world state. We can imagine a series of independent socialist political systems—perhaps nationally unified states—existing side by side without there being a common management of world production. . . . In a socialism of that kind, national antagonisms will not only not be made milder in comparison with the situation in the liberal economic order but will be considerably sharpened. The migration problem would lose nothing of its capacity to create conflicts between peoples. The individual states would perhaps not completely shut themselves off from immigration, but they would not allow immigrants to acquire residence status and to acquire a full share of the fruits of national production. A kind of international migrant-worker system would arise [Mises 1983 (1919), p. 93].

That is a very accurate portrayal of the "guest worker" system of the contemporary welfare state in Mises' native Austria, as well as in other socialist and redistributionist systems. The "guest workers" are forced to pay social security taxes to finance the welfare state, but do not themselves qualify for benefits.

The canonical classical liberal rights to life, liberty, and property are universal, in the sense that they can, at least in principle, be enjoyed by *every* human being; in the term made popular by Manchester University philosopher Hillel Steiner (1994), they are "compossible." But "welfare rights" are of a different sort; they are particular, entitling this person to so much housing, medical care, or other benefits, and obligating that person to pay so much in taxes or forced labor. In practice, welfare rights stop at the border. On a theoretical level, socialists and welfare statists have a bit of a problem: how to justify as "human rights" claims that are not applicable to all humans, but only to those who share the accident of being members of a non-voluntary group. The only solution short of worldwide redistribution through a world state is to jettison cosmopolitanism entirely and to boldly retreat to the primitive tribalism that characterizes premodern societies.

In the process of abandoning cosmopolitanism and embracing nationalism, supporters of welfare statism and socialism put every civilized value and every liberal institution at risk. Miller claims that an "ethical particularist" such as himself can endorse "basic rights" (although he never says how or why they should) but goes on to note,

> The basic rights and the obligations that correspond to them are overlain by the special responsibilities that we have as members of these communities. Moreover, in each community there will be a specific understanding of the needs and interests of members which generate obligations on the part of other members. . . . Thus in one national community (the Republic of Ireland, for example) religious education may be regarded as a shared need which should properly be funded by the community as a whole, whereas in another (the United States for example) it may be seen as a private matter which should be left to each person to consider, and to provide for their children as they saw fit [p. 74].

In other words, whatever "basic rights" individuals may have (for which Miller gives no arguments), the state may still legitimately coerce religious dissenters to support the state religion. If the right to religious dissent is not a basic right, it is not clear what is.

In this book Miller does not seem to recognize just how dangerous to civilized values his appeal to nationalism is. He neatly sidesteps the dangers of nationalism by pointing out that "the aim of this book is by no means to offer a blanket defence of nationalism, but to discriminate between defensible and indefensible versions of the principle of nationality" (p. 40). Thus, the nationalism that Miller has in mind is by definition not an indefensible—or "bad"—nationalism. The late Ernest Gellner, also a keen student of nationalism, noted in his *Conditions of Liberty: Civil Society and Its Rivals* that enthusiasts for socialism tend to hide a normative element in their definition of socialism: "They do not use the term 'socialism' as a neutral term merely designating a specific set of social arrangements. Rather, they use it as a term whose primary constituent is the notion that it is *good*. They may not know precisely what it is, but they do know that it is good" (Gellner 1994: 151). Thus, if a putatively socialist regime generated some bad consequences, then it was not really socialist, after all.

David Miller has now applied a similar approach to nationalism; he favors good nationalism and opposes bad nationalism. That he does not seem to appreciate the dangers of the move he makes is evidenced by a remarkable characterization of the problem in his earlier essay on "The Ethical Significance of Nationality" that appeared in the journal *Ethics*; he cites as part of the reason for the distrust of nationalism among many thinkers "the 20th-century experience of rampant nationalism, an experience distasteful to liberals and the Left alike" (Miller 1988: 653). To describe the Holocaust, the slaughterhouse of the Balkans, or the Rape of Nanking as "distasteful" indicates how little even a fundamentally decent man such as David Miller seems to appreciate the dangers of nationalism.

References

Gellner, E. 1994. *Conditions of Liberty: Civil Society and Its Rivals.* New York: Viking Penguin.

Hayek, F. A. 1944. *The Road to Serfdom.* Chicago: University of Chicago Press.

Miller, D. 1988. "The Ethical Significance of Nationality." *Ethics* 98 (July), pp. 647–62.

von Mises, L. 1983 (1919). *Nation, State, and Economy: Contributions to the Politics and History of Our Time.* New York: New York University Press.

Musil, R. 1990. "'Nation' as Ideal and as Reality." In *Precision and Soul: Essays and Addresses.* Edited by B. Pike and D. S. Luft. Chicago: University of Chicago Press.

Rawls, J. 1971. *A Theory of Justice.* Cambridge, Mass.: Belknap Press.

Steiner, H. 1994. *An Essay on Rights.* Oxford: Blackwell Publishers.

41. Libertarianism in the Crosshairs

It's a sign of success when your ideas and proposals generate lots of detractors. Judged by that criterion, libertarianism is back in the mainstream of political debate, after being intellectually and institutionally eclipsed for much of the 20th century by various forms of statism and collectivism. And the Cato Institute, as a high-profile advocate of libertarian ideas, is a frequent target of those criticisms.

There are, of course, many hundreds of books published every year that make the positive case for expansive state power and are therefore implicitly critical of libertarianism. The core libertarian ideas of individual rights, of order emerging spontaneously from the enjoyment of rights, and of limited government to protect rights and allow order to emerge are rejected in favor of other conceptions of moral and legal relations, the sources of social order, and the role of government. What is striking is the number of recent works that explicitly engage libertarians, realizing that their arguments must be addressed—or denounced.

In the past few months, I've read a large stack of such books, nine of which I've selected to discuss in this short essay. Some of them are popular works, some are journalistic, and some are scholarly and academic. I'm going to start with the silly, to give the reader an idea of how strange academic criticism can be, and proceed to more serious work deserving of careful study and consideration.

Bad Enough to Make Grown Men (and Women) Cry

In *Cato's Tears and the Making of Anglo-American Emotion*, University of Michigan English professor Julie Ellison offers an investigation of "the cultural history of public emotion" (p. 2), a worthy project in the course of which she attacks libertarianism in an unconscious parody of academic literary criticism. The book's title refers to Cato the Younger's tears at the end of the Roman Republic, as depicted

---

Originally published in *Cato Policy Report*, July/August 2000, pp. 9–13.

in Joseph Addison's play *Cato*, which inspired the writers of "Cato's Letters," which inspired the American Founders and—two centuries later—the Cato Institute, which brings us to her chapter on "Liberal Guilt and Libertarianism." According to Ellison, "The Cato Institute represents a stoical opposition to liberal sensibility, an exhilarating adamancy that, as we know by now, is historically inseparable from sympathy" (p. 189). (Come again?) Libertarians oppose coercive wealth redistribution "both in itself" (a phrase that is not entirely clear) "and as a metaphor for the expenditure of feeling" (pp. 189–90).

In a critique of an essay of mine on individualism, Ellison congratulates me for understanding "that the individual is a social construct" (p. 190)—something I do not believe. The *concept* of the individual, like all concepts, is a social achievement, but "the individual" is not. She then rakes me over the politically correct coals: "Group identities such as those of race, ethnicity, and gender are erased through the machinery of libertarian 'abstraction' into judicial essences whose unequal social and economic histories are constitutionally irrelevant. Clearly it is not abstract thinking per se that I oppose, but the link here between masculinity, rationality operating in the service of the individual who wants to 'produce order,' and that individual's resentment of losing control to government that might 'command' him" (p. 190). The closest thing to an actual argument in Ellison's critique is an ad hominem argument commonly invoked by collectivist academics, the imputation of sinister motives to apologists for libertarianism ("multinational corporations" figure prominently) and the reduction of statements that could be judged on their logical rigor, historical accuracy, or plausibility to "deft psychological maneuvers" (p. 190).

From Comedy to Historical Tragedy

A more substantive but nearly as amusing critique of libertarianism is offered in *A Necessary Evil* by Garry Wills. Wills relies on guilt by association, lumping together a wide variety of people whose only common characteristic is a "distrust of government." For quite different (in fact, opposed) reasons, that list includes criminals and terrorists, as well as Henry David Thoreau, pious pacifists, and advocates of constitutionally limited government. Wills lumps them all together, but his main target is the last group, those who favor limited government, and accordingly the main thrust of the book is to rebut the claim that the American Founders sought to establish a government of strictly limited powers. Wills employs his keen insight to establish that the Constitution of the United States does not, in fact, check, balance, separate, or limit the powers of government. To assert that it does would be to "interpret the document in terms of concepts and words that are not in the document. Nowhere, for instance, does the Constitution mention checks, or balances, or separation of powers, or co-equal branches (or even branches) of government, or states' rights (or *any* rights in the original, unamended document)" (p. 57). That strikes me as a pretty weak argument. A document doesn't have to contain the word "document" to be one, and a constitution doesn't have to contain the words "separate," "check," or "balance," to do those things.

Philosophy is clearly not Wills's forte; maybe he does better as a historian. Unfortunately, he is so wedded to his belief that government is a "necessary good" (p. 317) that he twists himself (and the historical documents) into intellectual pretzels in his efforts to rebut the idea that the American constitutional order is one of delegated, enumerated, and therefore limited powers. Thus, to defend the supremacy of the federal government over the states, Wills insists that "the real point" (p. 105) of James Madison's switch to supporting a bill of rights (after Madison's earlier argument that enumerating and therefore limiting the *powers* of the federal government made an enumeration of *rights* redundant) was "to give the federal government power to forbid these incursions to *the states*" (p. 105). Whether Wills has revealed "the real point" of Madison's efforts or not, he does inadvertently show that Madison supported limits on the powers of *both* the federal government and the states, an unsurprising position for an advocate of limited government.

Wills glues together a number of historical claims with a theory of absolutism that is profoundly inconsistent with the general tradition within which the American Founders instituted their constitutional system. He argues that sovereignty is indivisible and absolute, hence not separated and checked: "The idea that sovereignty is indivisible is not vague or mystical, but practical and observable. There cannot be two powers to conclude the whole" (p. 67). Wills suggests, on the basis of such musings, that government cannot be limited by law, since government makes law, and government would then be limiting itself, just as King James argued in 1598: "[A]lthough a just

Prince will not take the life of any of his subjects without a clear law; yet the same laws whereby he taketh them, are made by himself, or his predecessors; and so the power flows always from himself. . . . the King is above the law, as both the author and giver thereto." That's the very philosophy so many Britons came to America to escape. Wills's enterprise is a case of political philosophy driving history; the Founders simply *must* have grasped the truth as Wills knows it.

Power, Power, Everywhere

Ellen Willis, a journalist now affiliated with New York University, offers a more interesting critique of libertarian ideas. In *Don't Think, Smile!*, Willis critically reviews David Boaz's *Libertarianism: A Primer* and Charles Murray's *What It Means to Be a Libertarian: A Personal Interpretation*. She takes the authors to task for what she calls their "resolutely pre-Freudian mentality," which asserts the rational character of human nature and therefore cannot "see morality for what it is—a structure of internalized coercion" (p. 187). Willis, in contrast, sees the world of human relationships as it really is: a system of coercion and power through and through. Thus, offering me a higher wage to induce me to work for you is a form of coercion, just as is threatening to kill me to induce me to work for you. In both cases you wield some power over me (carrots, sticks, whatever). Further, what seems like self-limitation through the achievement of moral virtue and self-restraint is merely another form of coercion. Willis does not oppose morality per se, but that is because she apparently does not oppose coercion per se: "This is not to say that all moral imperatives are oppressive, any more than all laws are: only that morals are no less socially imposed than laws, and should be no less subject to examination and criticism" (p. 187).

Although Willis takes leftist intellectuals to task for failing to grasp how the omnipotent states they support can crush freedom, she insists that any inequality between or among persons is a source of power, and power of any sort is incompatible with freedom. Thus, "[w]hile it's unlikely that social coercion—governmental or otherwise—will ever be entirely surpassed, my measure of a good society is the extent to which it functions by voluntary cooperation among people with equal social and political power" (p. 193). Much could be said in criticism of this perspective (and of the historical and economic beliefs in the background), but a central problem with Willis's approach was expressed by F. A. Hayek in *The Road to Serfdom* and George Orwell in *Animal Farm*: To eliminate such distinctions among persons as ability or wealth, someone must be empowered to do so, and that person or those persons will be unequal in political power to the rest of us, which means that one kind of inequality will merely have been substituted for another. And, given what we know of human motivation and history, such political power will soon be converted back into inequalities of wealth and status, thus compounding the inequality.

Big Government as Ally of the Little Guy

Like Willis, political scientist Benjamin Barber in *A Place for Us* tries to grapple with libertarian ideas, but he often relies on historical claims that seem implausible. Thus, he writes, "Big government has always been an ally of the little guy" (p. 5). I wonder, on what planet? Not the one whose history I have studied. Unlike big government, markets are "private, rapacious, and uncivil" (p. 5). According to Barber, "Libertarians think of civil society as a play space for private individuals and for the voluntary and contractual associations they choose to contract into, and treat it as little more than a condition for solitude" (p. 23). How is being in a voluntary association such as a church, a bowling league, or a Girl Scout troop "a condition for solitude"? Barber sets up a dichotomy between liberty and community and then seeks to take the best and avoid the worst of both, thus articulating a "strong democratic" approach that promises "a place for us between big government and commercial markets, where citizens can breathe freely" (p. 10). Barber is a good and decent man, but his work rests so much on a rather shaky grasp of economic principles (e.g., "People need wages to sustain the buying power upon which their consumption in a market society depends, but productivity does not necessarily need wage earners to sustain it" [p. 128]) and a similarly undefended (and odd) version of the history of the 20th century, indeed, of the past several millennia, that it does not engage directly the other perspectives he considers and rejects, including libertarianism and communitarianism.

Law as Porridge: The Goldilocks Thesis

Harvard law professor Lawrence Lessig, author of *Code and Other Laws of Cyberspace*, is sorely vexed by the prominent place of "cyberlibertarianism" in the world of high tech. "Cyberlibertarians" apparently fail to understand that "code is law" and that "[t]his code represents the greatest threat to liberal or libertarian ideals, as well as their greatest promise" (p. 6). The problem with "code" or "architecture" as it is now is that it is not subject to political determination: "[I]sn't it clear that government should do something to make this architecture consistent with important public values?" (p. 59). It turns out that sometimes rules of conduct (private property, freedom of contract, and all that) lead to *too much* privacy and sometimes to *too little* privacy, sometimes to *too much* accountability and sometimes to *too little* accountability, when in fact what we should want is *just the right amount* of privacy and accountability. And, of course, it's through politics that the Goldilocks option is discovered: "Politics is the process by which we *reason* about how things ought to be" (p. 59).

For Lessig, the problem of Goldilocks is solved by a literal deus ex machina: computers themselves. In a discussion of how political bodies could regulate Internet gambling, offshore banking, and the like, Lessig states: "Rules imposed by local jurisdictions could be made effective through their recognition by other jurisdictions. Servers, for example, would recognize that access is conditioned on the rules imposed by jurisdictions" (p. 57). According to Lessig, we can leave the actual determination of what's *just right* to . . . "servers."

In a very personal attack on a libertarian journalist in a chapter titled "What Declan [Declan McCullagh of *Wired Online*] Doesn't Get," Lessig insists: "We need to think collectively and sensibly about how this emerging reality will affect our lives. Do-nothingism is not an answer; something can and should be done. I've argued this, but not with much hope. So central are the Declans in our political culture today that I confess I cannot see a way around them. I have sketched small steps; they seem very small. I've described a different ideal; it seems quite alien. I've promised that something different could be done, but not by any institution of government that I know. I've spoken as if there could be hope. But Hope was just a television commercial" (p. 233). (The book came with no decoder ring to decipher it.)

More could be said about Lessig's call for collective reasoning, but I merely suggest that he reread the third book of David Hume's *Treatise on Human Nature*, where Hume explains the importance of stable rules of property: "The convention concerning the stability of possession is enter'd into, in order to cut off all occasions of discord and contention; and this end wou'd never be attain'd, were we allow'd to apply this rule differently in every particular case, according to every particular utility, which might be discover'd in such an application." We could title this "What Larry Doesn't Get."

How Libertarians (Especially Those at the Cato Institute) Dominate Everything

Paulina Borsook, in *Cyberselfish*, also laments the prominence of libertarianism among the high-tech set. Rather than a work on law, hers is a very personal (and highly abusive) attack on libertarians involved in the computer and software industries. (Libertarians are called or compared to nerds, sexual "nerverts," "neo-hippies," Christian fundamentalists and "neo-pagans," terrorists, pornographers, "ungrateful adolescent offspring of immigrants," and so on—a motley collection, indeed.) In a bow to substantive criticism, Borsook restates Lessig's main point: "The technolibertarian worldview likes to pretend that there are not social decisions embedded in code, to pretend that technology is neutral" (pp. 239–40). To support that assertion, Borsook points out that search engines don't always find what you're looking for. If you want to understand the world around us, set aside Milton Friedman and F. A. Hayek and turn to "Marx and his pal Engels," who had "relevant things to say about the spread of global capitalism (and much more accurate for the description of what is happening at the end of our own century than at the end of his)" (p. 44). Perhaps Borsook had in mind the theses of the immiseration of the masses and the inevitability of socialist revolution, but if she means only to highlight that Marx noted that the world was changing awfully fast, well, so did everyone else.

Borsook specializes in "color" paid-by-the-word journalism rather than accurate reporting: "Cato, with its menhir of a HQ smack in the middle of D.C., is among the sleekest and most fearsome of the right-wing, free-market, think-tank conquistadors. Hugely funded since the late 1960s and early 1970s [Note: Cato was founded in 1977 with a budget of $800,000], it has colonized political discourse in the United States" (p. 66). When done well, color journalism can be enlightening.

Another journalist incensed by libertarians is Trudy Lieberman, director of the Center for Consumer Health Choices at Consumers

Union. She devotes a chapter of her book *Slanting the Story*, which describes how terrible people with bad ideas "shape the news" and "dominate public policy debates," to the Cato Institute's "1993 assault on Head Start, one of the crown jewels of Lyndon Johnson's Great Society" (p. 99). That assault consisted of publishing one policy analysis by John Hood, "Caveat Emptor: The Head Start Scam." But even that is too much for Lieberman, for "Cato's analysis was an attempt to discredit Head Start by focusing on its weaknesses and offering the right wing's solutions for fixing them—in this case, eliminate the program" (p. 101). According to Lieberman, what saved Head Start from Cato's "assault" was that "the think tank soon turned its attention to Social Security" (p. 113). (A bit more research would have revealed to our crack journalist that Cato published its first book on the case for personalizing Social Security in 1980.) Lieberman portrays the Cato Institute as being like the dastardly Snidely Whiplash, cackling as he ties a damsel to the railway tracks, until his eye is caught by the chance to carry out an even more nefarious deed. The damsel (Head Start) may be saved for now. But beware! "Cato, by its own admission, is in for the long haul. This time destroying Head Start wasn't worth the effort. But who is to say that Cato won't try again when Head Start's sugar daddy [President Clinton] leaves office?" (p. 115). Indeed. And with all of that blatant media bias in favor of limited government, individual rights, free markets, and liberty on their side, who knows what the Cato Institute might accomplish?

A Serious Critique

I finish with one of my favorite books of the year, *The Myth of Liberal Individualism*, a truly thoughtful critique that grapples with libertarian ideas seriously. By thinking through his careful arguments, I learned a good deal from Colin Bird of the University of Virginia, who notes that "it is libertarian, not communitarian, ideas that have had a more direct impact on the politics of the Western countries over the past twenty-five years" but warns that "the secret of libertarianism's recent success lies precisely in its appeal to an alliance between liberalism and individualism, an alliance that even the critics of liberalism have so far been unwilling to question" (p. 19). For Bird, that alliance is "an unstable alliance of antagonistic principles and ideals" (p. 3) concocted by "cold war liberals" (Mises,

Popper, Hayek, and Berlin) to combat Nazi and Bolshevik total-itarianism.

According to such "cold war liberals," Bird claims, collectivism rests on an untenable belief in a kind of collective entity; but if you don't believe in collective entities, you're an individualist, and if you're an individualist, you have to be a liberal. Bird, however, attempts to deny the connection between liberalism and individual-ism (which merely reflects "the confusion of cold war rhetoric" [p. 25]); I don't believe that he succeeds, but in the process of trying he offers a very thoughtful exploration of what individualism means. Although his project involves "liberating us from these cold war assumptions about the priority of the individual over the collectiv-ity," the argument "is in no way intended as an apology for those regimes that have inflicted horrifying injustices on individuals in the name of a certain view of the common good" (p. 46). Here I believe that Bird has erred, for the fact that collectivist regimes *exterminated* millions of people (e.g., allegedly racial or class enemies) implies that their "view of the common good" did not refer to a *good common to all of the individuals.* It must instead have referred to the good of a collectivity that exists in some way independent of the individuals, who are dispensable, or to the good of a race, nation, or class whose good is opposed to that of "its" enemies. The Holo-caust and the Gulag resulted, not merely from an erroneous "view of the common good," but from an idea of the *Volk* or the proletariat as collective entities that necessarily excluded Jews, liberals, capital-ists, rival collectivists, and others as implacable enemies and that considered even constituent individuals as purely dispensable means to its own ends. (It should also be noted that the arguments connecting individualism and liberty were formulated long before the Cold War, although Bird seems unaware of this.)

Bird considers liberal individualism a "myth" because "there may be no way for a set of public principles to remain neutral about how one ought (not) to act towards oneself *and* for them to embody a claim about the moral inviolability of individuals strong enough to underwrite the ideal of inviolable libertarian rights" (p. 183). That is to say, if you articulate reasons why individuals should be respected, then you cannot consistently argue that those reasons should not be used to override the choices of individuals; if the value of auton-omy is the reason we should respect rights, then using your rights to undermine your own autonomy (by becoming intoxicated, for example) is not an allowable use of your rights. On the other hand, if rights are primary and to be respected, then we should violate rights whenever their violation would result in a net diminution of rights violations. I did not find Bird's argument persuasive, for more reasons than I could develop here (wait for my longer review elsewhere), but I found his arguments far more challenging and well crafted than others I have read recently.

Conclusion

A movement that calls forth lively criticisms is a movement that is alive and well. The more critiques, the better off libertarians are, especially if they take note of the critiques and learn from them. Who knows, we may be wrong, and a commitment to truth should keep us open to that possibility.

References

Barber, Benjamin R. 1998. *A Place for Us: How to Make Society Civil and Democracy Strong.* New York: Hill and Wang.

Bird, Colin. 1999. *The Myth of Liberal Individualism.* Cambridge: Cambridge University Press.

Borsook, Paulina. 2000. *Cyberselfish: A Critical Romp through the Terribly Libertarian Culture of High-Tech.* New York: Public Affairs.

Ellison, Julie. 1999. *Cato's Tears and the Making of Anglo-American Emotion.* Chicago: University of Chicago Press.

Holmes, Stephen, and Cass R. Sunstein. 1999. *The Cost of Rights: Why Liberty Rests on Taxation.* New York: W. W. Norton.

Lessig, Lawrence. 1999. *Code and Other Laws of Cyberspace.* New York: Basic Books.

Lieberman, Trudy. 2000. *Slanting the Story: The Forces That Shape the News.* New York: New Press.

Willis, Ellen. 1999. *Don't Think, Smile! Notes on a Decade of Denial.* Boston: Beacon Press.

Wills, Garry. 1999. *A Necessary Evil: A History of American Distrust of Government.* New York: Simon and Schuster.

42. John Locke Lite: The Strange Philosophy of a "Left Libertarian"

Review of *Libertarianism without Inequality*,
by Michael Otsuka, Oxford: Oxford University Press,
2003, 180 pp.

People fight about love and lucre. They also fight about labels. A little tussle is under way right now among academic political theorists over the label *libertarian*.

Advocates of massive redistribution who seek to make every property title subject to expropriation have decided they want to be known as "libertarians." Since it's hard to appropriate a label outright, they're willing to share it: They have taken to calling themselves "left libertarians," to distinguish themselves from "right libertarians." One of them, Philippe van Parijs, uses the term "real libertarianism," because he feels real liberty is about doing whatever you want to do, which means you have a right to be comfortably supported by others, even if you are able-bodied but refuse to produce anything and instead spend all your time surfing and hanging out.

The central goal of these "left libertarians" is to show that one can maintain a core commitment to what John Locke termed "property in one's person"—and thus can call oneself a libertarian—and yet support a state that is empowered to redistribute property on an ongoing basis in accordance with some formula of fairness or justice.

The latest attempt to capture the *libertarian* label for a radically egalitarian redistributive state is Michael Otsuka's *Libertarianism without Inequality*, a collection of essays that try to reconcile individual freedom, egalitarian redistribution, and consensual government. (The middle section, which seems to have been added to pad out an otherwise very thin book, attempts to defend some rather implausible claims about criminal justice and the right to self-defense. Since they're not particularly relevant to the issue of "left libertarianism,"

Originally published in *Reason*, January 2005, pp. 56–59.

639

I'll set them aside.) The work is an attempt to say something interesting by exploring the author's hunches and intuitions. It fails.

Otsuka, a reader in philosophy at University College London, was a student of the analytical Marxist philosopher G. A. Cohen, who holds forth at Oxford University and to whom Otsuka dedicates the book as his "teacher, mentor, comrade, friend." Cohen gained some fame for a series of attacks on Robert Nozick's defense of free market capitalism—collected in his book *Self-Ownership, Freedom, and Inequality*—that simultaneously demonstrated Cohen's flair for bizarre examples and his weak grasp of economics and bargaining theory.

Otsuka attempts to show that the radically egalitarian redistribution he favors is intuitively plausible if you share his intuitions (which many people will not); that he is entitled to call himself a Lockean after he has reformulated Locke's ideas sufficiently that they have "been fully cleansed of the regressive ideological commitments of Locke's (and more recent) times"; and that as a "Lockean" he is committed to fully consensual government, so long as a nonconsensual super-government is around to make sure that nothing bad happens.

Otsuka complains that "even many of Locke's more moderate or left-leaning interpreters have not yet provided a sufficiently egalitarian reconstruction of his political philosophy." In other words, Locke wouldn't agree with Otsuka, but once Otsuka has "cleansed" Locke's ideas and made them "sufficiently egalitarian," Otsuka can call himself a Lockean.

Otsuka seeks to reconcile libertarian self-ownership with what he calls a "welfarist specification of the egalitarian proviso." That proviso requires that all the unowned stuff in the world be so divided that each person (take a deep breath) "would be able (by producing, consuming, or trading) to better herself to the same degree as you, where 'betterment' is to be measured in terms of welfare understood as the 'satisfaction of the self-interested preferences that the individual would have after ideal deliberation while thinking clearly with full pertinent information regarding those preferences.'"

Able-bodied persons would get only a little, while the disabled would get more, and those with very expensive tastes and little ability would get the most, since they would need the most to satisfy their preferences. (Of course, somebody would have to measure all those abilities and work out how each person's ideal deliberation would proceed, but solving such problems for every human being should be a pretty easy task for any reasonably qualified college professor.)

This scheme is Otsuka's response to Locke's proviso governing the appropriation of unowned resources. In his *Second Treatise of Civil Government*, Locke said an appropriator would have to ensure there was "enough, and as good left" to meet the objection that appropriation might be "any prejudice to any other Man." In *Anarchy, State, and Utopia*, Robert Nozick adopts a formulation similar to Locke's, specifying that you may acquire previously unowned resources "if and only if you make nobody worse off than she would have been in a state of nature in which no land is privately held." Otsuka asserts that the alternative proviso he proposes is "convincing" and "fair," although he offers no reason that anyone else should find it either convincing or fair. He seems unaware of Locke's arguments for *why* appropriation of unowned resources meets Locke's proviso.

According to Locke, "he who appropriates land to himself by his labour, does not lessen but increase the common stock of mankind. For the provisions serving to the support of humane life, produced by one acre of enclosed and cultivated land, are (to speak much within compasse) ten times more, than those, which are yielded by an acre of Land, of an equal richnesse, lyeing waste in common. And therefor he, that incloses Land and has a greater plenty of the conveniencys of life from ten acres, than he could have from an hundred left to Nature, may truly be said, to give ninety acres to Mankind."

The only way to satisfy Locke's proviso is to create exclusive property rights, for the simple reason that people produce more when they can reap the rewards, which ensures that there is more for all and thus that appropriation is not harmful to others. Both Locke and Nozick rely on the historical evidence that property is more conducive to wealth production, which makes everyone better off. It seems never to have occurred to Otsuka that there was a reason they wrote what they wrote; it's just a matter of being intuitive, plausible, fair, etc. Why bother with history, evidence, or reasons when you can consult your intuitions and leave it at that?

The result of Otsuka's appeal to his own intuitions is an assignment of property that would have to be changed every time its value

641

changed (which happens constantly in a dynamic market) and every time the population of the world changed (which happens many times a minute). Also, no property could be inherited, as that would be unfair. Otsuka, like other "left libertarians," fails to distinguish between wealth and value, which are economic concepts, and property, which is a legal concept. Legal institutions can reassign property titles, but if property is constantly, chaotically, and unpredictably reassigned, it's not "property" at all; it has no legal security.

If the way we know about changes in wealth and value is through changes in prices, and prices are generated by exchange of secure property titles, then eliminating the security of property would mean there would be no way to know how wealth or value had changed. The "solution" to the problem of maintaining the kind of equality Otsuka seeks would entail eliminating the very means by which the solution could be reached. The entire enterprise is not merely impractical; it is self-defeating.

Libertarianism without Inequality is a good example of the dead end so much contemporary political philosophy has reached. Rather than being informed by history, jurisprudence, economics, psychology, sociology, anthropology, or even a close knowledge of classic texts, it posits outlandish examples as the central tests of all theories. Thus Otsuka explains "self-ownership" and the right to the fruits of our labor by asking us "to imagine a highly artificial 'society' of two strangers, each of whom will freeze to death unless clothed. Unfortunately, the only source of material for clothing is human hair, which can be woven into clothing. One of the two is hirsute and capable of weaving, whereas the other is bald and incapable of weaving." Otsuka concludes that to force the hairy one to weave his own hair into (presumably rather uncomfortable) garments for the bald one merely to achieve an egalitarian outcome would be a violation of the hairy one's rights. That kind of philosophizing provides little or no useful guidance in the world in which we live.

After affirming that full libertarianism is achieved when you can sell your body hair to other people but the state (or someone) assigns you your property in everything else and adjusts your shares on what, for consistency's sake, would have to be at least a minute-by-minute basis, Otsuka goes on to show that the kind of government he has in mind would be radically voluntary. It would be like Nozick, man! Only better!

Otsuka spills a lot of pixels discussing such staples of the theory of political legitimacy as the difference between express consent and tacit consent and whether residence constitutes consent. His approach reads like a parody of libertarianism, according to which people might give their "consent" to live in radically unequal, feudal, slavish conditions, meaning that libertarianism (as Otsuka understands it) would lead to truly disturbing forms of oppression. But that would be cool, as far as Otsuka is concerned, because they would be *chosen*.

Otsuka brings up exit rights only to dismiss them as uninteresting. He never tries to apply the theory of consent to interesting real-world examples, such as condominium associations, gated communities, and religious cloisters that have rules governing pet size, loud music, religious observances, and so forth. (I consented to governance by my condo association when I bought my condo. People who like large pets would not have consented and so wouldn't live in my condo building. But no one can put me to death if I play my music too loudly or invite my boyfriend over for the night.) None of that for Otsuka. Instead, in Otsuka's world, people would freely choose to be governed by feudal lords with powers of life and death over them.

After a tedious and unhelpful treatment of consent, Otsuka gives the game away. Remember that all that free choice has to be fair to everyone else, so your property would be constantly readjusted to reflect the claims of others, as demanded by Otsuka's proviso. That means there would have to be constant readjustment of property claims among people subject to different governments. There would also have to be some adjudication of conflicts among the governments. Otsuka therefore imagines "a fluid confederation of political societies and monities [a monity is 'a political society of one'] that is regulated by an interpolitical governing body." He explains:

> It would be necessary for this governing body to possess limited powers which encompass the overseeing of the drawing of the boundaries that demarcate these societies and monities and the settling of disputes that might arise among these parties. While the legitimate authority of the governments of the various societies would be based upon consent, the legitimate authority of this governing body would not necessarily be so based. Given the disorder and chaos which would ensue in the absence of such a governing body, all

individuals would legitimately be subject to its authority—
even those who do not consent to it. Hence, the ideal of
political societies as voluntary associations would need to
be underpinned by involuntary governance at the interpolitical level.

In other words, Otsuka "solves" the problems his theory of political legitimacy throws up by positing a nonconsensual government
that would rule over the consensual ones. That body would exercise
power legitimately because without it there would be "disorder and
chaos." But legitimacy is supposed to be a solution to the problem
of who has the authority to exercise power, a problem that Otsuka
simply waves away in a footnote.

In that note, Otsuka concedes that, "given this interpolitical governing body, what I have just called the 'governments' of what
I have just called '[political] societies' would not retain complete
monopolies on the powers to legislate and punish. Therefore, given
my definitions at the beginning of this chapter, we do not, strictly
speaking, have 'governments' and 'political societies' here." Still, he
says, "they are close enough to be called that."

Libertarianism without Inequality is kind of like a serious book, but
not really close enough to be called that.

43. Liberal Flagship Turns 70, Burning the Midnight Oil

Not many people subscribe to *The New Republic*—97,000 at last count—but the magazine is the envy of publishers elsewhere for its dedicated and influential readership. And the writers who have used *TNR* as a springboard to national prominence are an honor roll of American journalism, from Walter Lippmann in 1914 to Morton Kondracke and Michael Kinsley today. *TNR*, the venerable old man of establishment liberalism, celebrated 70 years of reporting, commenting, and agenda-setting Tuesday night at an extravagant anniversary party at the National Portrait Gallery. The attendees from the political world ran the gamut from Henry Kissinger to Jerry Brown, while other celebrities included such people as Mr. and Mrs. Vidal Sassoon and world-renowned cellist Yo-Yo Ma.

The tributes took place over a three-hour period. The last encomium to "The Magazine," as both readers and writers insist on referring to it, was by its editor in chief and publisher, Martin Peretz. "Washington is a town where if other people don't arrange a testimonial for you or your institution, you can always arrange one for yourself," he said as midnight neared.

The political-intellectual-media glitterati turned out in high style to celebrate their own magazine, at a time when the magazine itself is having second thoughts about the direction of the liberal movement it has nurtured for seven decades. The lead editorial in the 70th anniversary issue asserts, to no one's surprise, that, "American liberalism is in crisis" because liberals "have hardly begun to figure out a coherent response, first, to the unhappy social facts; and second, to the vast defection of voters from the liberal dispensation in public policy." *TNR* calls for some hard thinking and "commits itself to this effort of understanding and reappraisal." In translation, the

---

Originally published in the *Wall Street Journal*, November 29, 1984.

welfare state has failed, its main accomplishments the creation of a dependent underclass of welfare recipients, a massive and self-perpetuating bureaucracy and a staggering financial burden, while the middle class, recognizing the failure of the liberal agenda, has revolted against the crushing burden it has imposed.

One sign of this process of rethinking may be the impending departure from the magazine of editor Hendrik Hertzberg, a former speech writer in the Carter White House. Mr. Hertzberg has complained of the magazine's departures from established liberal doctrine.

A change of personnel may not be enough, for, as *TNR*'s official historian, David Seideman, said during the reception: "The magazine's inability to understand the attraction of Reagan to the voters shows the gulf between the magazine and the public." Despite the call for "new ideas" and "reappraisal" in a "time of crisis," liberals still don't understand why the voters have so overwhelmingly repudiated the liberals' policies. There is clearly an awareness that it wasn't just Walter Mondale who precipitated the crisis. As Eugene McCarthy, former Democratic senator and presidential candidate, said during the reception, "Walter Mondale didn't lead the Democrats to defeat, he just escorted them."

A second term in the political wilderness, no longer able to play the role of court intellectual, ever at the king's ear, may allow *TNR* to stray ever further into new heresies. Certainly, during the heady days of Camelot, when John F. Kennedy was in office, *TNR* editors indeed had the president's ear. But the president had theirs, too. For example, in 1961 Kennedy was able to call then-editor Gilbert Harrison and kill a potentially embarrassing story about the Bay of Pigs invasion. As Mr. Seideman says, "It's hard to imagine Ronald Reagan being able to do that." Life at the apex of political power is a corrupting thing, and it may be to the long-term benefit of liberals that they no longer enjoy it.

But if any group can lead liberalism out of the political wilderness, it is probably those who edit and write for *The New Republic*, if only because of the openness to diversity and well-reasoned challenges to liberal orthodoxy that its editors have shown. That banquet toaster Lane Kirkland of the AFL–CIO, representing the last bastion of the New Deal, chided *TNR* for its "occasional spells of wanderlust," and "our occasional stings at your hand" may signal *TNR*'s willingness to jettison the selfish politics of subsidies for all and interest-group pandering that has passed for liberal domestic policy in recent decades. But the magazine's endorsement of one "new idea" that's been gathering dust since Mussolini ran the trains on time, namely industrial policy, shows how far it still is from grasping the roots of liberalism's failure.

Good intentions and beneficial consequences are not always the same thing. That is the lesson that American liberals have to learn and are now learning the hard way. Libertarian philosopher Robert Nozick of Harvard University, whose presence was itself a sign of the intellectual openness that *TNR* has encouraged, said: "Liberalism had good intentions and its policies didn't work. I am waiting with great interest to see how this process of rethinking will turn out." Aren't we all.

44. Life on the Edge

Review of *The Art of Not Being Governed: An Anarchist History of Upland Southeast Asia*,
by James C. Scott, New Haven, CT: Yale University Press, 442 pp.

In the dominant narrative of civilization's march, cultured people are ruled by centralized law-giving institutions (city-states, kingdoms, empires, and now nation-states), usually centered in relatively flat lowlands and sustained by grain agriculture. By contrast, according to this view, people who live in the mountains, in swamps, or in "remote" jungles are rude, primitive, and backward, relying on nomadism, slash-and-burn agriculture, and hunting and gathering. They live not in cities or nations but in bands, clans, and tribes. The way they live is the way everyone used to live before some of us became civilized; they are windows onto our past, living museums of prehistoric life.

How lucky we are not to be backward. How fortunate we are to be ruled by wise kings and far-sighted legislators, by shepherds who protect us from barbarian wolves. Surely, as Oliver Wendell Holmes instructed us, "Taxes are the price we pay for civilization." Those who evade taxes are evading civilization and all that it entails.

Now along comes James C. Scott to show how absurd that narrative is. In his dazzling, enlightening, and enjoyable new book, *The Art of Not Being Governed*, the Yale anthropologist and political scientist boldly challenges the age-old story of "rude barbarians mesmerized by the peace and prosperity made possible by the king's peace and justice."

To begin with, people who live in relatively "ungovernable" peripheries do not really live like people before states existed. They live alongside state-governed populations, in constant contact with

---

Originally published in *Reason*, June 2010.

their cousins who live under state control. The inhabitants of such peripheries, Scott shows, are overwhelmingly refugees or descendants of refugees from states' predatory behavior: slavery, war, and taxation. Their ways of life have made it more difficult for states to control them.

Their agricultural products are not harvested all at once, so it is harder to tax them. Their kinship systems decentralize power through networks of families. Their residence on difficult terrain, such as hills and swamps, makes them less accessible to slave raiders, tax collectors, or press gangs (or draft boards, "revenuers," or drug agents). Their ways of life are adaptations to living near, and attempting to escape from, predation and violence. Those adaptations have made them harder to rule.

Once you understand Scott's point, you can't see such people the same way again. They are not a museum of ancient life. They are a display of what people will go through to escape being enslaved, robbed, and pressed into war. Their agriculture, social structures, religions, and other features, Scott writes, are "better seen on a long view as adaptations designed to evade both state capture and state formation. They are, in other words, political adaptations of nonstate peoples to a world of states that are, at once, attractive and threatening."

As Scott notes at the outset, the "standard civilizational narrative" leaves out "two capital facts. First . . . it appears that much, if not most, of the population of the early states was unfree; they were subjects under duress. The second fact, most inconvenient for the standard narrative of civilization, is that it was very common for state subjects to run away. Living within the state meant, virtually by definition, taxes, conscription, corvée labor, and, for most, a condition of servitude; these conditions were at the core of the state's strategic and military advantages. When these burdens became overwhelming, subjects moved with alacrity to the periphery or to another state."

Political and military history, with its palace coups, religious conflict and persecution, wars, looting, rapine, and subjugation, produced not only victors but vanquished, some of whom escaped into regions inaccessible to their pursuers. Each successive wave of refugees carried new languages, religions, and other cultural accoutrements with them. Thus, "Much of the periphery of states became a zone of refuge or 'shatter zone,' where the human shards of state formation and rivalry accumulated willy nilly, creating regions of bewildering ethnic and linguistic complexity. State expansion and collapse often had a ratchet effect as well, with fleeing subjects driving other peoples ahead of them seeking safety and new territory." Even the tribal systems of such peoples are, to a significant extent, the creations of the states they are fleeing, who foster them as means of "institutional linkage and control."

Scott focuses his attention on the region of upland Southeast Asia he calls "Zomia" (from a term for "highlander" in the Tibeto-Burman languages). "Much of the Southeast Asian massif is, in effect, a shatter zone," he writes. Similar "shatter zones" can be found in the mountains of the Caucasus (the ethnic, linguistic, and religious complexity of the region is staggering, with at least 13 languages spoken in Georgia alone), in the Balkans, in highland West Africa, in highland South America, in the Mekong Delta, in the Don River Basin, and elsewhere—even in Appalachia and the Great Dismal Swamp along the Virginia/North Carolina border.

For millennia, rulers have attempted to eliminate such zones of refuge, sometimes through relatively benign methods, such as road building in highland areas, and sometimes with brutal methods, such as forced relocation, "ethnic cleansing," or habitat destruction. An example of the latter would be Saddam Hussein's destruction of the Tigris-Euphrates marshlands, an effort to bring the Marsh Arabs under control following their unsuccessful 1991 uprisings against him.

Scott illustrates the case in great detail, drawing on his remarkable knowledge of Southeast Asia. The early public choice theorist Amilcare Puviani asked what tax collection systems would minimize taxpayer resistance to taxation, a question that led him to the study of "fiscal illusion." Scott focuses our attention on the geography of predation, asking what conditions "would be most favorable to the state and its ruler" and "what arrangements are most likely to guarantee the ruler a substantial and reliable surplus of manpower and grain at least cost."

From the perspective of the rulers, but perhaps not of the ruled, wet rice cultivation seems ideal. It requires large concentrations of manpower (i.e., taxpayers and soldiers) and produces a crop that is relatively easy to appropriate and that can be stored to support

651

armies in the field in ways that yams, vegetables, and other food-stuffs cannot. Scott finds a close relationship between states and agriculture, one that helps explain the rise and fall of the region's various kingdoms, empires, and other state formations.

In addition to discussing the appropriation of agricultural sur-pluses to sustain the ruling houses and their wars, Scott focuses attention on the appropriation of population itself, noting that "most powerful kingdoms constantly sought to replenish and enlarge their manpower base by forcibly resettling war captives by the tens of thousands and by buying and/or kidnapping slaves." Successful rulers were preoccupied with keeping subjugated people under the state's thumb; as Scott notes, the Great Wall of China was built not merely to keep barbarian raiders out but to keep Chinese peasants in.

Having a large supply of manpower was "the only means by which wealth could be securely held." To keep subjects from escap-ing, various states established means of tattooing, branding, and otherwise designating the human population as chattel. In *Freedom and Domination*, his great libertarian work of sociology, Alexander Rüstow notes that some early rulers, typically nomadic pastoralists who had conquered farmers, insisted that their subjects approach them on all fours, with tufts of grass in their mouths, to underscore their chattel status.

Scott observes that rulers are less interested in the gross domestic product than in the "State-Accessible Product," which "had to be easy to identify, monitor, and enumerate (in short, assessable), as well as being close enough geographically." He documents various campaigns to discourage forms of agriculture that are hard to appro-priate, such as "shifting" or "slash-and-burn" cultivation, even when the value to the agriculturalists of such crops was greater than that of the ruler-preferred methods. Scott notes that the government "maximizes the state-accessible product, if necessary, at the expense of the overall wealth of the realm and its subjects." What's best for the ruler is not always best for the ruled.

Topography plays an important role as well, with state power tending to be greatest where the "friction of distance" is least. "Politi-cal control sweeps readily across a flat terrain," Scott writes. "Once it confronts the friction of distance, abrupt changes in altitude, rug-gedness of terrain, and the political obstacle of population dispersion and mixed cultivation, it runs out of political breath."

Understanding the nature of such zones where political control "runs out of breath" is not merely of interest to historians and social scientists. It's central to understanding many things about the modern world, including the difficulties that NATO and its allied forces face in Afghanistan, the problems with other nation-building campaigns around the globe, the nature and costs of resistance to predatory state power, and the evolutionary relationship between tax systems and economic structures—that is, between systems of theft and structures of production. In effect, Scott gives us a libertarian geography.

Scott draws on the insights of Pierre Clastres, whose 1974 book *Society Against the State* undermined the narrative of the progressive transition from archaic society to state-governed civilizations by showing how a variety of Native American tribes developed systems to keep the state at bay. Such groups did not merely "fail to develop a state"; they *succeeded* in keeping one from developing. The insight is important, but Scott follows Clastres in making questionable claims about the conjunction of the state, private property, and material inequality.

"Why would private property spring up in a type of society in which it is unknown because it is rejected?" Clastres asked. He suggested that the state preceded property, rather than the other way around. Scott is well known for advancing a "moral economy" thesis, formulated in his 1976 book *The Moral Economy of the Peasant: Rebellion and Subsistence in Southeast Asia*, in which peasants live by a "safety-first maxim" that "embodies a relative preference for subsistence security over high average incomes" and thus tend to resist the creation of property rights, fixed-rents (rather than sharecropping), and production for the market. In *The Art of Not Being Governed*, Scott writes: "Permanent padi-field cultivation also leads to systems of landed property and inheritance and the social class distinctions they foster. Inequalities *per se* do not distinguish the valleys from the hills. Status differences and inequalities abound in the hills, but in contrast to inequality in the padi state, they are not underwritten by inherited inequalities of property enforced, if need be, by the coercive power of a rudimentary state." Further, "Just as fixed, inheritable property in land facilitates permanent class formation, a common property frontier equalizes access to subsistence resources and permits the frequent fission of villages and lineages that seems central to the maintenance of egalitarianism."

653

Maybe. But inequality can take many forms, from the exclusive privilege of chiefs to multiple wives, as described by Clastres, to the use of common property to perpetuate material inequality, as described by Scott's critic Samuel Popkin in his 1979 study of the history of rural Vietnam, *The Rational Peasant: The Political Economy of Rural Society in Vietnam.* According to Popkin, access to communal lands in rural areas, rather than being a source of egalitarian redistribution, was more likely to be manipulated by the rich and powerful to shift the burdens of taxation to the poor. "The procedures for paying national taxes, the system for allocating communal lands, and the methods for financing village projects were regressive," Popkin wrote. "Some communal lands were reserved for widows, orphans, and the aged without children. For 'regular' families, however, communal lands were distributed not according to need, but ascriptively, on the basis of rank within the village." Scott rejects Popkin's characterizations of his views, but the debate between the "moral economy" perspective and the "political economy" perspective is both complex and ongoing. Despite its many insights, *The Art of Not Being Governed* offers no more evidence to resolve the issue.

But whether or not Scott is on the right side of the argument, *The Art of Not Being Governed* is chock-a-block with fascinating observations. For example, he shows a new way to understand the dispersal of ethnic groups: horizontally. Merely looking down on a two-dimensional ethnographic map shows what appear to be random scatterings, but by looking at the topography horizontally, Scott notes a pattern: The same altitude tends to harbor the same (or closely related) ethnic groups. "Thus, for example, the Hmong have tended to settle at very high altitudes (between one thousand and eighteen hundred meters) and to plant maize, opium, and millet that will thrive at that elevation," he writes. "If from a high-altitude balloon or on a map they appear to be a random scattering of small blotches, this is because they have occupied the mountaintops and left the midslopes and intervening valleys to other groups." Moreover, Scott's thesis about the close connection between state formation and the promotion of certain kinds of agriculture offers an occasion to think about how vulnerable new forms of wealth creation are to state control and, for those who favor escape from the state, how to promote the kinds of wealth that help people evade predation.

The Art of Not Being Governed also provides a healthy antidote to the ahistorical and naive views of the "communitarians," who posit static traditional communities as the framework for personal identity. As Scott demonstrates, "traditional identities" more often than not are hybrid, porous, plural, and fluid. The idea of an unchanging way of life going back millennia is, in general, bunk. Subordination to states is not necessary to identity, as stateless peoples show, and "tribal" or ethnic identities are neither as unchanging nor as inescapable as communitarians think. Fluid identities are features of freedom, whether in modern liberal society or in peripheral "zones of refuge" from state predation.

Scott is clearly sympathetic to the Zomians, but he doesn't romanticize the lives of people who reside outside the reach of state power. Sometimes the escape from predation has preserved other forms of oppression that shock modern liberal sensibilities. Some hill peoples who escaped slavery, for example, supplemented their incomes by organizing slave raids of their own.

Scott concludes his book on a sober note. As states extend their sovereign power from one internationally recognized border to another and intrude into every space, he writes, "the world I have sought to describe and understand here is fast disappearing. For virtually all my readers it will seem a very far cry from the world they inhabit. In the contemporary world, the future of our freedom lies in the daunting task of taming Leviathan, not evading it."

I think that Scott is essentially correct, but I wonder whether evading Leviathan is part of the process of taming it. The history of freedom in Europe is to a substantial degree the history of lowering costs of exit, as the Australian historian E. L. Jones shows in his 1981 book *The European Miracle*. We may simply need to follow Scott's example and think more creatively about the ways in which wealth is produced and exchanged and the means by which predatory state behavior can be evaded.

If you wish to have your comfortable preconceptions about the history of humanity shaken and to see things anew, *The Art of Not Being Governed* is for you. The lives of people on the periphery have often been hard, but less so than the slavery they were escaping. Although the search for freedom does not always yield optimal results, understanding its history is essential to understanding the future of freedom.

45. Are Markets Immoral?

Review of *What Money Can't Buy: The Moral Limits of Markets*, by Michael J. Sandel, New York: Farrar, Straus and Giroux, 256 pp.

Michael Sandel knows something about money. After all, the Harvard political philosopher exchanges his ideas for money—a lot of money, in fact. Now Sandel has written a book about what things should not be for sale.

Sandel's basic warning goes like this: Markets-by which he means the use of prices expressed in money-lead inevitably to commodification, which "corrupts" and "crowds out" the moral norms that should otherwise guide our interactions. In *What Money Can't Buy: The Moral Limits of Markets*, Sandel looks upon other people's purchases and frowns. Important things in life—tickets to rock concerts, private medical consultations, access to shorter airline check-in lines—are being exchanged for money, he reports. "The reach of markets, and market-oriented thinking, into aspects of life traditionally governed by nonmarket norms is one of the most significant developments of our time," he writes, necessitating "a public debate about what it means to keep markets in their place."

Although Sandel is fuzzy on the specifics, he wants an enlightened debate to determine whether other people should be allowed to use prices when they cooperate or allocate scarce goods. "Democracy does not require perfect equality, but it does require that citizens share in a common life," he writes. "And so, in the end, the question of markets is really a question about how we want to live together." Let's see where that takes us.

What Sandel offers as a moral/philosophical analysis of this alleged problem amounts to little more than an exploration of his own moral intuitions, unencumbered by critical self-scrutiny. Thus,

---

Originally published in *Reason*, October 2012.

657

"Treating religious rituals, or natural wonders, as marketable commodities is a failure of respect. Turning sacred goods into instruments of profit values them in the wrong way." This flat assertion
may come as news to much of organized religion.

Synagogues regularly sell seats for the Days of Awe, or High Holy
Days, which helps finance religious activities. One of my great aunts,
a conservative French Catholic, sent me cards when I was a boy that
said she had given money to an order of nuns to pray for me. Sikhs
pay for scholars to read from their holy book. The candles one lights
in Catholic cathedrals when saying a prayer are priced (not given
away free); guests at traditional Polish weddings pin paper money
on the dress of the bride in exchange for a dance. Do these practices
show a lack of respect for religion and the sacrament of marriage?
Should the collective "we" (Sandel uses the term a great deal in all
of his books) prohibit the use of money to allocate synagogue seats,
prayers, holy readings, candles, and dances with the bride? Or
should those decisions be made by members of the respective synagogues, churches, and temples?

Sandel never once in his book entertains the idea that maybe we
should let people sort such matters out for themselves, without
having the decision made for them by "us." Instead, his own tastes
are presented as suitable for everyone else. There's a serious danger
with such intuitive collectivism: It disguises restatements of one's
own unacknowledged and unexamined prejudices as a philosophical investigation and then imposes them on everyone else.

For Sandel, not deciding collectively on "competing conceptions
of the good life" does not leave such questions undecided. Instead, "It
simply means that markets will decide them for us." This statement
is both ominous and incoherent. "Markets" are not some kind of
omnipotent, singular, malevolent intelligence. When people
exchange goods and services we use the term market. When the
exchanges take place through the medium of money, the exchange
ratios of goods against money are called prices. Sandel confuses
prices with markets and then suggests that the question of whether
something should be exchanged on markets will be "decided" by
markets, which is a singular bit of confusion.

Sandel at least recognizes that a common alternative to pricing is
waiting in line. But bizarrely, he seems rather fond of queues. He
devotes a chapter to "Jumping the Queue," with subsections on

"Markets Versus Queues" and "The Ethic of the Queue," and quotes approvingly a writer who moans that "gone are the days when the theme-park queue was the great equalizer, where every vacationing family waited its turn in democratic fashion." Sandel claims there are two arguments favoring prices over queues: "a libertarian argument. . .that people should be free to buy and sell whatever they please, as long as they don't violate anyone's rights," and a utilitarian economic argument. He then proceeds to ignore the libertarian argument while misunderstanding the economic.

Sandel acknowledges that "as markets allocate goods based on the ability and willingness to pay, queues allocate goods based on the ability and willingness to wait." Moreover, "there is no reason to assume that the willingness to pay for a good is a better measure of its value to a person than the willingness to wait."

Sandel thinks he has scored a fatal blow against the economic case for markets here, but what he doesn't get is that the price mechanism provides a decentralized system of signals and incentives that help us to better coordinate our behavior. Consider that a longer queue without prices sends no signal to producers to make more of the product for which people are queuing. Using prices, rather than queues, has the advantage of disseminating information about supply and demand. Sandel sees no coordinating advantages to price allocation and bemoans "the tendency of markets to displace queues and other nonmarket ways of allocating goods." He describes substitution of prices for queues as "places that markets have invaded."

Sandel is right that the use of prices can have disadvantages, which is the core insight of Ronald Coase's theory of the firm. If market pricing is so great, why are there firms? Because using the price system has costs. Firms, teams, and organizations are islands of nonprice allocation and coordination in a wider sea of price allocation. Price coordination co-exists with nonprice coordination. The issue is not which system will award scarce goods to those who value them the most but which will coordinate behavior better in which situations. Sometimes it's queues and sometimes it's prices, and sometimes it's both. (I'm in a Starbucks now, and the system here is first come, first served, probably because it would be too costly to have an auction on who gets served first. Still, the coffee is exchanged for money.)

Bakers of communion wafers generally sell them to churches for money. The churches provide them as part of a sacrament for which the faithful queue. Whether to use prices or queues and at which point is really none of Sandel's business.

Sandel is not only rhapsodic about queues but again invokes the collective we when he states: "Of course, markets and queues are not the only ways of allocating things. Some goods we distribute by merit, others by need, still others by lottery or chance." He's not just pro-queue but rather strongly against prices, which seem to him somehow dirty ("corrosive") as a coordinating mechanism. Never addressed is whether some of "us" should be allowed to work out for ourselves our own solutions, without having one imposed on all.

Sandel explains that some things "can't be bought," e.g., friendship. Aristotle may beg to differ; the Greek philosopher discussed "friendship for advantage" in Book 8 of the Nicomachean Ethics, declaring them one kind of friendship, though not the highest. Still, we may insult friends when we reward a favor with money; sometimes "the monetary exchange spoils the good being bought." That sounds right to me, if not all that original or deep.

Still, Sandel doesn't seem to have thought very hard about these things. His research skills have discovered that there is "a company in China" that you can pay to write an apology, and that at ThePerfect Toast.com you can purchase a prefab wedding toast. "Apologies and wedding toasts are goods that can, in a sense, be bought," he writes. "But buying and selling them changes their character and diminishes their value." Perhaps. But so what? Drug store companies have been selling syrupy Hallmark cards for decades. I don't use them. Like Sandel, I speak and write for a living. Unlike Sandel, I understand that not everyone else does.

Among the many items Sandel believes are "degraded" when exchanged for money are human kidneys. Of course, allowing people to offer money for voluntarily donated kidneys may save lives (or "ease the gap between supply and demand," as Sandel delicately puts it), but it "taints" the goods exchanged. Making it illegal to exchange kidneys for money may be costing thousands of people their lives, but, hey, it satisfies our—which is to say, Professor Sandel's—desire to avoid tackiness.

In a book full of praise for the moral virtues of nonmonetary exchanges, there is only one concession to the advantages of markets:

"As the cold war ended, markets and market thinking enjoyed unrivaled prestige, understandably so," Sandel graciously concedes. "No other mechanism for organizing the production and distribution of goods had proved as successful at generating affluence and prosperity."

It's something, but it ain't much. In contrast, nonmarket norms, such as queuing, subsistence hunting, need, chance, and honor (mostly unaccompanied by any specific mechanisms of allocation), are consistently praised as "higher." That's a remarkably obtuse approach. There is a long tradition of thinkers, from Montesquieu and Voltaire to Milton Friedman and Deirdre McCloskey, that has focused attention on the moral virtues of markets, not merely their ability to produce wealth.

Sandel is surrounded by market exchanges that enhance his life, but all he can see is corruption, corrosion, and degradation. Never is the price system praised for displacing an inferior moral norm. It seems that whatever form of interaction is displaced by a price system must be better, higher, nobler. Au contraire! Markets punish and eventually push out tribalism, confessionalism, racism, cronyism, and many other traditions. And good riddance.

It's not as if this point has never been made. "Commerce is a cure for the most destructive prejudices; for it is almost a general rule, that wherever we find agreeable manners, there commerce flourishes," Montesquieu wrote in 1748, "and that wherever there is commerce, there we meet with agreeable manners." Sandel never acknowledges that intellectual tradition.

As Milton Friedman (who Sandel dismisses without engaging) once noted, "no one who buys bread knows whether the wheat from which it is made was grown by a Communist or a Republican, by a constitutionalist or a Fascist, or, for that matter, by a Negro or a white. This illustrates how an impersonal market separates economic activities from political views and protects men from being discriminated against in their economic activities for reasons that are irrelevant to their productivity-whether these reasons are associated with their views or their color."

Prices, contra Sandel, "corrode" many nonmarket norms that we are better off without. Markets promote color blindness, punctuality, mutual respect, the "double thank you" of voluntary exchanges, and peace. Somehow those virtues don't make it into Sandel's musings on the moral limits of markets.

What Money Can't Buy will titillate with its examples of odd things some people buy and sell. But it fails to provide moral guidance to how we should behave (other than not fooling ourselves by thinking we can buy true friendship), and it gives even less insight into the roles that prices and markets play in our lives.

Index

About the Author

Tom G. Palmer is a senior fellow at the Cato Institute, where he directs the Cato University educational program, and executive vice president for international programs at the Atlas Network, where he supervises libertarian programs in 14 languages and works with a global network of over 400 research institutes and think tanks. Before joining Cato and Atlas, he was an H. B. Earhart Fellow at Hertford College, Oxford University, and a vice president of the Institute for Humane Studies at George Mason University.

He has been active since the 1970s in researching, articulating, and promoting libertarian ideas. In the 1980s and 1990s, he smuggled books, photocopiers, and fax machines into Soviet Bloc countries. He frequently lectures in the Americas, Europe, Africa, Asia, and the Middle East on political science, public choice, civil society, economic policy, and the moral, legal, and historical foundations of individual rights and limited government. He has helped to organize libertarian organizations and programs all over the world, from Afghanistan to Brazil to Kenya to Iceland to Malaysia and many other countries, and he travels hundreds of thousands of miles per year spreading the ideas of liberty. He is sometimes referred to as the "Johnny Appleseed" of libertarianism.

Palmer has edited a number of publications, including *Humane Studies Review* and *Dollars & Sense,* and has published reviews and articles on politics, morality, and public affairs in journals such as the *Harvard Journal of Law and Public Policy, Ethics, Critical Review, Constitutional Political Economy, Slate, Wall Street Journal, New York Times, Die Welt, Caixing, Al Hayat, Washington Post,* and *The Spectator of London.* He has also contributed scholarly articles for books from a number of academic publishers.

He has served on the boards of directors of a number of organizations, including the Foundation for Economic Education, the Oxford

University Civil Liberties Society, and the Committee against Registration and the Draft.

Palmer received his B.A. in liberal arts from St. John's College, his M.A. in philosophy from The Catholic University of America, and his doctorate in politics from Oxford University. He is editor of and contributor to *The Morality of Capitalism* (2011), *After the Welfare State* (2012), *Why Liberty* (2013), and *On Peace* (forthcoming 2014).

Cato Institute

Founded in 1977, the Cato Institute is a public policy research foundation dedicated to broadening the parameters of policy debate to allow consideration of more options that are consistent with the principles of limited government, individual liberty, and peace. To that end, the Institute strives to achieve greater involvement of the intelligent, concerned lay public in questions of policy and the proper role of government.

The Institute is named for Cato's Letters, libertarian pamphlets that were widely read in the American Colonies in the early 18th century and played a major role in laying the philosophical foundation for the American Revolution.

Despite the achievement of the nation's Founders, today virtually no aspect of life is free from government encroachment. A pervasive intolerance for individual rights is shown by government's arbitrary intrusions into private economic transactions and its disregard for civil liberties. And while freedom around the globe has notably increased in the past several decades, many countries have moved in the opposite direction, and most governments still do not respect or safeguard the wide range of civil and economic liberties.

To address those issues, the Cato Institute undertakes an extensive publications program on the complete spectrum of policy issues. Books, monographs, and shorter studies are commissioned to examine the federal budget, Social Security, regulation, military spending, international trade, and myriad other issues. Major policy conferences are held throughout the year, from which papers are published thrice yearly in the Cato Journal. The Institute also publishes the quarterly magazine Regulation.

In order to maintain its independence, the Cato Institute accepts no government funding. Contributions are received from foundations, corporations, and individuals, and other revenue is generated from the sale of publications. The Institute is a nonprofit, tax-exempt, educational foundation under Section 501(c)3 of the Internal Revenue Code.

CATO INSTITUTE
1000 Massachusetts Ave., N.W.
Washington, D.C. 20001
www.cato.org